Sport & Tourism

The last decade has seen a significant growth in the quantity of published research in the fields related to sport and tourism. *Sport & Tourism: A Reader* from Routledge offers the field's first comprehensive review.

Articles selected for the Reader cover a broad range of contemporary research in the field of sports tourism, including diverse areas such as the economic analysis of sports events, leveraging strategies, sub-cultures and identity, adventure tourism and policy and marketing.

Sport & Tourism: A Reader is in four Parts, each opening with a substantial new introduction by the Editor. Throughout the text the key themes and new conceptual thinking defining sports tourism are set out.

In four Parts, the Reader examines:

1   Sport & Tourism research approaches
2   Understanding the sports tourist
3   Impacts of Sport & Tourism
4   Policy and management considerations for Sport & Tourism.

Mike Weed is Professor of Sport in Society and Director of Research in the Department of Sport Science, Tourism and Leisure at Canterbury Christ Church University, UK. He is the Editor of the *Journal of Sport & Tourism*.

For my Nan,
Dorothy Grace Rollings
(1912–2007)

Sport & Tourism:
A Reader

Edited by

Mike Weed

 Routledge
Taylor & Francis Group

LONDON AND NEW YORK

First published 2008
by Routledge
2 Park Square, Milton Park, Abingdon, Oxon OX14 4RN

Simultaneously published in the USA and Canada
by Routledge
270 Madison Avenue, New York, NY 10016

Routledge is an imprint of the Taylor & Francis Group, an informa business

Typeset in Perpetua and Bell Gothic by
Florence Production Ltd, Stoodleigh, Devon
Printed and bound in Great Britain by
TJ International, Padstow, Cornwall

British Library Cataloguing in Publication Data
A catalogue record for this book is available from the British Library

Library of Congress Cataloging in Publication Data
Sport & tourism: a reader/edited by Mike Weed.
    p.cm.
    Sports and tourism. I. Weed, Mike. II. Title: Sport and tourism.
    G155.A1S626 2007
    338.4'791–dc22   2007017395

ISBN10: 0–415–42687–1 (hbk)
ISBN10: 0–415–42688–X (pbk)
ISBN10: 0–203–93768–6 (ebk)

ISBN13: 978–0–415–42687–9 (hbk)
ISBN13: 978–0–415–42688–6 (pbk)
ISBN13: 978–0–203–93768–6 (ebk)

Contents

Acknowledgements

I would like to thank Jonathan Manley at Taylor & Francis journals, in discussion with whom the idea for this Reader emerged. Also thanks to the books team at Routledge, Samantha Grant, Ygraine Cadlock and Kate Manson, for supporting me in the completion of this project.

I am also grateful to my colleagues at Canterbury Christ Church University, particularly my Head of Department, Dr Chris Bull, for their support in allowing me the space to work on this and a range of other research projects.

Finally, I would like to thank my wife, Sonja, for everything!

Publication acknowledgements

The editor would like to thank the following for permission to reprint their material:

Beedie, P. (2003) Mountain Guiding and Adventure Tourism: Reflections on the Choreography of the Experience. *Leisure Studies*, 22(2), pp. 144–67 (Taylor & Francis Ltd, www.tandf.co.uk/journals), reprinted by permission of the publisher.

Chalip, L. & Leyns, A. (2002) Local Business Leveraging of a Sport Event: Managing an Event for Economic Benefit. *Journal of Sport Management*, 16(2), pp. 132–58 (Human Kinetics Inc.), reprinted by permission of the publisher.

Costa, C. & Chalip, L. (2005) Adventure Sport Tourism in Rural Revitalisation: An Ethnographic Evaluation. *European Sport Management Quarterly*, 5(3), pp. 259–81 (Taylor & Francis Ltd, www.tandf.co.uk/journals), reprinted by permission of the publisher.

Downward, P. (2005) Critical (Realist) Reflection on Policy and Management Research in Sport, Tourism and Sports Tourism. *European Sport Management quarterly*, 5(3), pp. 305–22 (Taylor & Francis Ltd, www:tandf.co.uk/journals), reprinted by permission of the publisher.

Fairley, S. (2003) In Search of Relived Social Experience: Group-Based Nostalgia Sport Tourism. *Journal of Sport Management*, 17(3), pp. 284–304 (Human Kinetics Inc.), reprinted by permission of the publisher.

Fredline, E. (2005) Host and Guest Relations and Sport Tourism. *Sport in Society*, 8(2), pp. 263–79 (Taylor & Francis Ltd, www.tandfco.uk/journals), reprinted by permission of the publisher.

Gibson, H. (2001) Sport Tourism at a Crossroad? Considerations for the Future. Keynote address to the Leisure Studies Association Annual Conference, *Journeys in Leisure*, Luton, July, reprinted by permission of the author.

Gibson, H. & Pennington-Gray, L. (2005) Insights from Role Theory: Understanding Golf Tourism. *European Sport Management Quarterly*, 5(4), pp. 443–68 (Taylor & Francis Ltd, www.tandf.co.uk/journals), reprinted by permission of the publisher.

Gibson, H., Willming, C. & Holdnak, A. (2003) Small-Scale Event Sport Tourism: Fans as Tourists. *Tourism Management*, 24(2), pp. 181–90 (Elsevier), reprinted by permission of the publisher.

Green, B.C. (2001) Leveraging Subculture and Identity to Promote Sport Events. *Sport Management Review*, 4(1), pp. 1–19, reprinted by permission of the author.

Green, B.C., Costa, C. & Fitzgerald, M. (2003) Marketing the Host City: Analysing Exposure Generated by a Sport Event. *International Journal of Sport Marketing & Sponsorship*, December/January, pp. 335–53 (International Marketing Reports), reprinted by permission of the publisher.

Hautbois, C. & Durand, C. (2004) Public Strategies for Local Development: The Effectiveness of an Outdoor Activities Model. *Managing Leisure*, 9(4), pp. 212–26 (Taylor & Francis Ltd, www.tandf.co.uk/journals), reprinted by permission of the publisher.

Higham, J. & Hinch, T. (2002) Tourism, Sport and Seasons: The Challenges and Potential of Overcoming Seasonality in the Sport and Tourism Sectors. *Tourism Management*, 23(2), pp. 175–85 (Elsevier), reprinted by permission of the publisher.

Higham, J. & Hinch, T. (2006) Sport and Tourism Research: A Geographic Approach. *Journal of Sport & Tourism*, 11(1), pp. 31–49 (Taylor & Francis Ltd, www.tandf.co.uk/journals), reprinted by permission of the publisher.

Hinch, T. & Higham, J. (2001) Sport Tourism: A Framework for Research. *International Journal of Tourism Research*, 3(1), pp. 45–58 (John Wiley & Sons, Ltd), reprinted by permission of the publisher.

Hinch, T. & Higham, J. (2005) Sport, Tourism and Authenticity. *European Sport Management Quarterly*, 5(3), pp. 245–58 (Taylor & Francis Ltd, www.tandf.co.uk/journals), reprinted by permission of the publisher.

Hudson, I. (2001) The Use and Misuse of Economic Impact Analysis. *Journal of Sport & Social Issues*, 25(1), pp. 20–39, copyright by Sage Publications Inc. Reprinted by Permission of Sage Publications Inc.

Hudson, S., Ritchie, B. & Timur, S. (2004) Measuring Destination Competitiveness: An Empirical Study of Canadian Ski Resorts. *Tourism and Hospitality Planning and Development*, 1(1), pp. 79–94 (Taylor & Francis Ltd, www.tandfco.uk/journals), reprinted by permission of the publisher.

Kane, M. & Zink, R. (2004) Package Adventure Tours: Markers in Serious Leisure Careers. *Leisure Studies*, 23(4), pp. 329–45 (Taylor & Francis Ltd, www.tandf.co.uk/journals), reprinted by permission of the publisher.

Kasmati, E. (2003) Economic Aspects and the Summer Olympics: A Review of Related Research. *International Journal of Tourism Research*, 5(6). pp. 433–44 (John Wiley & Sons, Ltd), reprinted by permission of the publisher.

Petrick, J. & Backman, S. (2002) An Examination of the Determinants of Golf Travelers' Satisfaction. *Journal of Travel Research*, 40(3), pp. 252–58, copyright by Sage Publications Inc. Reprinted by permission of Sage Publications Inc.

Preuss, H. (2005) The Economic Impact of Visitors at Major Multi-Sport Events. *European Sport Management Quarterly*, 5(3), pp. 283–303 (Taylor & Francis Ltd, www.tandf.co.uk/journals), reprinted by permission of the publisher.

Sung, H. (2004) Classification of Adventure Travelers: Behavior, Decision Making and Target Markets. *Journal of Travel Research*, 42(4), pp. 343–56, copyright by Sage Publications Inc. Reprinted by permission of Sage Publications Inc.

Vaske, J., Carothers, P., Donnelly, M. & Baird, B. (2000) Recreation Conflict Among Skiers and Snowboarders. *Leisure Sciences*, 22(4), pp. 297–313 (Taylor & Francis Ltd, www.tandf.co.uk/journals), reprinted by permission of the publisher.

Weber, K. (2001) Outdoor Adventure Tourism: A Review of Research Approaches. *Annals of Tourism Research*, 28(2), pp. 360–77 (Elsevier), reprinted by permission of the publisher.

Weed, M. (2001) Towards a Model of Cross-Sectoral Policy Development in Leisure: The Case of Sport and Tourism. *Leisure Studies*, 20(2), pp. 125–41 (Taylor & Francis Ltd, www.tandf.co.uk/journals), reprinted by permission of the publisher.

Weed, M. (2003) Why the Two Won't Tango! Explaining the Lack of Integrated Policies for Sport and Tourism in the UK. *Journal of Sport Management*, 17(3), pp. 258–83 (Human Kinetics Inc.), reprinted by permission of the publisher.

Weed, M. (2005) Sports Tourism Theory and Method: Concepts, Issues & Epistemologies. *European Sport Management Quarterly*, 5(3), pp. 229–42 (Taylor & Francis Ltd, www.tandf.co.uk/journals), reprinted by permission of the publisher.

Weed, M. (2006) Sports Tourism Research 2000–2004: A Systematic Review of Knowledge and a Meta-Evaluation of Methods. *Journal of Sport & Tourism*, 11(1), pp. 5–30 (Taylor & Francis Ltd, www.tandf.co.uk/journals), reprinted by permission of the publisher.

Williams, P. & Fidgeon, P. (2000) Addressing Participation Constraint: A Case Study of Potential Skiers. *Tourism Management*, 21(4), pp. 379–93 (Elsevier), reprinted by permission of the publisher.

General introduction

■   Mike Weed

TRAVEL RELATING TO SPORTING ACTIVITY has clearly taken place for thousands of years. Authors across the last thirty-five years have traced the earliest documented example of this type of tourism to the ancient Olympic Games dating from 776 BC (Baker, 1982; Davies, 1997; Finley and Pleket, 1976; Standeven and De Knop, 1999; Van Dalen and Bennett, 1971; Weed and Bull, 2004). However, despite this long history, and what appears to be an academic interest stretching back thirty-five years, the study of the relationship between sport and tourism is still in a relatively early stage of development.

One of the earliest writings on the relationship between sport and tourism appears to have been a paper entitled, 'Sport and Tourism' written by Don Anthony for the Central Council of Physical Recreation in the UK in 1966, which simply reviewed the role sport might play in holiday tourism. Some authors have argued (e.g. De Knop, 1990) that it was during the following decade, the 1970s, that academic interest in sport and tourism began to develop seriously, pointing to conference papers (e.g. Schreiber, 1976) and the odd report by tourist organisations (e.g. Baker and Gordon, 1976) to evidence this. However, it is perhaps Sue Glyptis' study of sport and tourism in five European countries, published in 1982, that marked the start of a sustained academic spotlight being turned on to the area. In that publication, Glyptis pointed to a problem that endures in relation to sport and tourism today, namely that:

> [Despite] . . . a linkage between sport and tourism in the minds of participants, commercial providers and local authorities, [there remains] a lack of conscious integration – or even resistance to it, by policy-makers, planners and public providers at national level.
>
> (Glyptis, 1982: 63)

Nine years later Glyptis reached a similar but more wide-ranging conclusion:

> Sport and tourism tend to be treated by academic and practitioner alike as separate spheres of activity. Each has its own journals, academic departments, learned societies and government agencies. At an institutional level, integration of the two is rare. Yet in terms of popular participation and some aspects of practice, they are inextricably linked; and, in principle, there are sound reasons for those links to strengthen.
>
> (Glyptis, 1991: 165)

A further seven years on, Heather Gibson (1998: 45) took up Glyptis' concerns:

> the field suffers from a lack of integration in the realms of policy, research and education. At policy level, there needs to be better co-ordination among agencies responsible for sport and those responsible for tourism. At a research level, more multidisciplinary research is needed, particularly research which builds upon existing knowledge bases in both sport and tourism. In the realm of education, territorial contests between departments claiming tourism expertise and those claiming sport expertise need to be overcome.

The reason for presenting these relatively lengthy quotations alongside each other is to highlight some of the enduring problems that the study of sport and tourism has faced. In fact, the central issue, that of lack of integration, seems to have been exacerbated over this sixteen-year period. Initial concerns highlight policy, later concerns highlight policy and academic structures, and the latest concerns focus on problems with the research base. These concerns perhaps originate from the nature of the body of publications at the time. In a review in 1999, I noted that there appeared to be two identifiable strands of literature relating to sport and tourism[1] (Weed, 1999). The first of these, and at the time by far the largest strand, focused on advocacy, simply attempting to identify a link between sport and tourism, and to establish it as a legitimate field – one worthy of consideration by both academies and providers. Initially such advocacy work comprised speculative reviews, as befits early work in a field of study, for example: 'Some Thoughts on the Influence of Sport Tourism' (De Knop, 1987), 'Sport and Tourism in the Modern World' (Redmond, 1988). However somewhat frustratingly, as the comments of Glyptis and Gibson indicate, many authors continued in this vein into the late 1990s. Yet there was some indication of a body of work, the second strand I identified in 1999, that was attempting to quantify the links between sport and tourism, thus providing evidence of the volume and value of different types of sports tourist. Much of Jackson and Reeves' work at this time was centred on the theme of 'Evidencing the sport–tourism relationship', and explicitly sought to move away from the speculative forms of advocacy that seemed to pervade much work in the field (see, for example, Jackson and Reeves, 1996, 1998).

However, despite a move away from speculative advocacy towards a more empirical approach, there was an early indication in Gibson's (1998) comments of a further concern that still remains today, namely the lack of a theoretical or conceptual base for research in sport and tourism. This was further highlighted at an international conference in 2002 when a keynote speaker in a plenary session was asked about what theoretical perspectives and concepts underpinned the study of sport and tourism. While the speaker was able to point to one or two areas in which theory was prominent, this question highlighted a weakness in the body of knowledge relating to sport and tourism at that time. Furthermore, the perception of much of the audience, who were not researchers in sport and tourism, that the area lacked theoretical rigour was undoubtedly grounded in the speculative advocacy work that had been so pervasive in the 1980s and 1990s – a point Chris Bull and I made in 2004:

> The large amount of unconnected small-scale sports tourism case studies, and the continued pre-occupation with advocacy work, have meant that there is a perception among academics in sport, tourism and leisure studies that sports tourism research is not theoretically informed.
>
> (Weed and Bull, 2004: 205)

It was as a result of these concerns that I agreed to be Guest Editor of a special issue of *European Sport Management Quarterly* on 'Sports Tourism Theory and Method', which was published in 2005 (vol. 5, no. 3). This special issue was conceived specifically to address the perception that research in sport and tourism was not theoretically informed, and aimed to showcase the use of theory in the area by leading authors in the field. This is highlighted in the call for papers for the special issue, which was written in 2004:

> indicative of sports tourism's status as a relatively youthful field of study, many papers and articles have sought simply to establish the link between the two areas rather than advance the theoretical approaches that might underpin its study. This has led to suggestions from some quarters that sports tourism should not be given specific attention as a distinctive field of study.

The suggestion that sports tourism was not a legitimate field of study underpinned the conference question mentioned above, and has also been discussed by Gammon and Kurtzman (2002: v) who noted:

> those writing and researching in the area have been accused of clumsily diluting two already established disciplines in order to profit from professional precedence and thus committing the indefensible crime of academic triviality.

Yet, just as more public concerns about the study of sports tourism were beginning to surface, there was a small but emerging body of work (since the year 2000 approximately) responding to the call for greater theorisation on the subject. In introducing a volume of such work in 2005 (a special issue of *Sport in Society* on Sport Tourism: Concepts and Theories'), Gibson (2005: 134) suggested that researchers should be 'linking their work to theories in the well-established parent disciplines such as sociology, social psychology, geography and anthropology'. This has resulted in a clear and explicit use of such theories beginning to emerge in the study of sport and tourism (e.g. Higham and Hinch, 2006; Harris, 2006). Of course, the use of theoretical perspectives from parent disciplines requires that researchers read around such disciplines, rather than limiting their reading to their own subject area. All too often, sport psychologists, for example, will read only work that appears in journals such as *Psychology of Sport and Exercise* and *Journal of Sport & Exercise Psychology*. Such an approach limits knowledge to the second-hand appreciation of the application of psychological theory to a particular subject, rather than ensuring that knowledge is grounded in the debates that are underpinning theory development in the broader discipline. The use of this example is not to single out sport psychologists – similar accusations might be made about a range of other areas of study that apply disciplines to a particular subject area sport sociologists, tourism management scholars and, of course, those studying the relationship between sport and tourism). The need, therefore, is for researchers to return to disciplinary texts to ensure their work is theoretically and conceptually robust.

The special issue of *European Sport Management Quarterly* (*ESMQ*) on 'Sports Tourism Theory and Method' provided the initial impetus for the development of this Reader. The five papers in the *ESMQ* special issue covered the broad areas of Research Approaches (Weed), Understanding the Sports Tourist (Hinch and Higham and Costa and Chalip), Impacts (Preuss) and Policy and Management Considerations (Downward). In addition, a further paper by Gibson, which was received too late for inclusion in the special issue and appeared in the subsequent issue (*ESMQ*, vol. 5, no. 4), also fell under the Understanding the Sports Tourist area. These four themes, therefore, provide the structure for this Reader, with one or more of the *ESMQ* special issue papers being the 'lead' article(s) in each Part.

At the time that the *ESMQ* special issue was published (September 2005), I was involved in discussions surrounding the future of the *Journal of Sport Tourism* (*JST*). This journal, which had been published online for seven years before being launched in hard copy in 2003, was owned by the Sport Tourism International Council (STIC). As befits a publication for such an organisation, the *JST* attempted to serve a trade/professional audience as well as the academic community. However, although this dual role was laudable, in practice it proved difficult to fulfil, with the result that the content of *JST* sometimes disappointed the academic community, and this, albeit inadvertently, perhaps contributed to some of the negative perceptions of research in sport and tourism. To address these concerns, the ownership of the journal was transferred from STIC to Taylor & Francis in 2006 (thus releasing it from its obligations to its trade/professional audience), and the journal was relaunched, repositioned and renamed as the *Journal of Sport & Tourism* (*JS&T*), with a new editorial team as well as new aims and scope emphasising its new academic direction:

> the standard for publication in the Journal of Sport & Tourism is that manuscripts must make a clear contribution substantively, theoretically, or methodologically to the body of knowledge relating to the relationship between sport and tourism.

At the start of 2006 I had just completed a five-year systematic review and meta evaluation of research in sport and tourism that identified eighty papers in twenty-four peer-reviewed journals in the sport, tourism and leisure subject area between 2000 and

2004 inclusive. The results of this systematic review and meta-evaluation were published in the first issue of *JS&T* (vol. 11, no. 1) and are also included in this Reader (Chapter 6). While the discussions in that paper provide a useful contemporaneous overview of the body of research in sport and tourism in the first five years of the millennium, the eighty papers returned in the search also provided an excellent resource from which to select papers for inclusion in this Reader. Consequently, of the thirty papers included, six are from the work prepared for the *ESMQ* special issue on 'Sports Tourism Theory and Method', one is a conference keynote address, twenty have been selected from the systematic review, and a further three have been selected from papers published since that systematic review. All except one of the papers are from peer reviewed journals, and all have been published since 2000.

The intention in compiling this Reader has been to present the highest quality contemporary peer-reviewed research into the relationship between sport and tourism. The thirty chapters contained within cover a range of sub-areas of sport and tourism (e.g. adventure tourism, sport events, ski tourism) and the differing perspectives of a range of authors. In addition, it bridges not only research into the relationship between sport and tourism, but also work from areas *relevant* to the study of the relationship between sport and tourism (e.g. sports economics and recreation conflict).

Any field (or sub-field) of academic study requires various markers to establish its legitimacy and, as the discussions above suggest, such markers have not necessarily been readily identifiable in the study of sport and tourism to date. Gartner suggested in 1996 that the study of sport and tourism would establish its own 'cadre' of researchers, and the presence of the work of many familiar names from the sub-field in this Reader might be taken as evidence that such a cadre of researchers has now emerged. The existence of a quality peer-reviewed academic journal in the sub-field might be another marker of legitimacy, and as such the relaunch of the *Journal of Sport & Tourism* as such a publication in 2006 is an important milestone. Furthermore, the recognition of the sub-field by established journals in sport (e.g. *Journal of Sport Management, European Sport Management Quarterly, Sport in Society*) and tourism (e.g. *Journal of Vacation Marketing, Current Issues in Tourism, Tourism Review International*), each of which have published special issues on sport and tourism in recent years, is a further marker. Finally, the publication of a Reader such as this, in which it is possible to present thirty of the best peer-reviewed papers in the area from the previous six years, is a clear indication that the study of sport and tourism may now be considered to be a legitimate academic sub-field.

NOTE

1   A further, third, strand focusing on policy was also identified, but this was a very small proportion of the overall work in the area at the time.

REFERENCES

Baker, W.J. (1982) *Sports in the Western World*. Totowa, NJ: Rowman & Littlefield.

Baker, M.J. and Gordon, A.W. (1976) *Market for Winter Sports Facilities in Scotland*. Edinburgh: Scottish Tourist Board.

Davies, N. (1997) *Europe: A History*. London: Pimlico.

De Knop, P. (1987) 'Some Thoughts on the Influence of Sport Tourism' in *Proceedings of the International Seminar and Workshop on Outdoor Education, Recreation and Sport Tourism*, Wingate Institute for Physical Education and Sport, Netanya, Israel, pp. 38–45.

De Knop, P. (1990) 'Sport for All and Active Tourism', *Journal of the World Leisure and Recreation Association*, Fall: 30–6.

Finley, M.I. and Pleket, H.W. (1976) *The Olympic Games*. Edinburgh: R & R Clark.

Gammon, S. and Kurtzman, J. (2002) Editors' Introduction, in S. Gammon and J. Kurtzman (eds), *Sport Tourism: Principles and Practice*. Eastbourne: LSA.

Gartner, W. (1996) *Tourism Development: Principles, Processes and Policies*. New York: Van Nostrand Reinhold.

Gibson, H.J. (1998) 'Sport Tourism: A Critical Analysis of Research', *Sport Management Review*, 1 (1): 45–76.

Gibson, H.J. (2005) 'Sport Tourism: Concepts and Theories. An Introduction', *Sport in Society*, 8 (2): 133–41.

Glyptis, S.A. (1982) *Sport and Tourism in Western Europe*. London: British Travel Education Trust.

Glyptis, S.A. (1991) 'Sport and Tourism', in C.P. Cooper (ed.), *Progress in Tourism, Recreation and Hospitality Management* (Vol. 3). London: Belhaven Press.

Harris, J. (2006) 'The Science of Research in Sport and Tourism: Some Reflections upon the Promise of the Sociological Imagination', *Journal of Sport & Tourism*, 11 (2): 152–71.

Higham, J. and Hinch, T. (2006) 'Sport and Tourism Research: A Geographic Approach', *Journal of Sport & Tourism*, 11 (1): 31–50.

Jackson, G.A.M. and Reeves, M.R. (1996) 'Conceptualising the Sport–Tourism Interrelationship: A Case Study Approach', Paper to the LSA/VVA Conference, Wageningen, September.

Jackson, G.A.M. and Reeves, M.R. (1998) 'Evidencing the Sport–Tourism Interrelationship: A Case Study of Elite British Athletes', in M.F. Collins and I. Cooper (eds), *Leisure Management: Issues and Applications*. London: CABL.

Redmond, C. (1988) 'Points of Increasing Contact: Sport and Tourism in the Modern World', Paper presented at the Second International Conference, Leisure, Labour and Lifestyles: International Comparisons, Brighton, UK.

Schreiber, R. (1976) 'Sports Interest: A Travel Definition', *The Travel Research Association 7th Annual Conference Proceedings*. Boca Raton, FL: TRA.

Standeven, J. and De Knop, P. (1999) *Sport Tourism*. Champaign, IL: Human Kinetics.

Van Dalen, D.B. and Bennett, B. (1971) *A World History of Physical Education*, Englewood Cliffs, NJ: Prentice Hall.

Weed, M. (1999) 'More Than Sports Tourism: An Introduction to the Sport–Tourism Link', in M. Scarrot (ed.), *Proceedings of the Sport and Recreation Information Group Seminar, Exploring Sports Tourism*. Sheffield: SPRIG.

Weed, M. and Bull, C.J. (2004) *Sports Tourism: Participants, Policy and Providers*. Oxford: Elsevier.

PART ONE

Sport & Tourism
research approaches

EDITOR'S INTRODUCTION

AS NOTED IN THE GENERAL INTRODUCTION, the structure and impetus
for this Reader was provided by the special issue of *European Sport Management
Quarterly* published in 2005 on 'Sports Tourism Theory and Method'. In my Editorial
Introduction to the special issue (the first chapter in this Part), I drew on an analogy
used by Bernard Forscher in 1963 to highlight what he saw as a significant problem in
the construction of social science knowledge. Forscher was concerned that too many
studies ('bricks') were being randomly produced, thus contributing to haphazard piles of
research that did little to build coherent bodies of knowledge ('edifices'). This analogy
has been used by a number of authors (e.g. Biddle, 2006; Weed, 2005) to discuss the
nature and potential of research synthesis approaches in various disciplines in sport. In
presenting a number of chapters that have, in one form or another, conducted syntheses
or reviews of research in sport and tourism since 2000, this Part plays a useful introductory
role in assessing the development of the body of knowledge in sport and tourism and the
range of research approaches that have been used or suggested. As a collection, the
chapters in this Part, spanning the years 2001 to 2006, demonstrate how research in
sport and tourism has developed and progressed in recent years, while individually, the
chapters each present a different perspective on the development of the subject.

The General Introduction to this Reader mentioned a number of reviews conducted
before 2000, with two in particular (Gibson, 1998; Weed, 1999) providing a useful
benchmark for the state of the field immediately prior to 2000. Also worthy of mention
is an international review of the literature on sport and tourism commissioned by the
Great Britain Sports Council in 1992. This review, conducted by Guy Jackson and Sue
Glyptis, considered material largely related to *impacts*: the impact of sport in developing

tourism, of tourism in developing sport, and the positive/negative economic/non-economic impacts of sports tourism. Jackson and Glyptis' (1992) review was constrained by the limited number of works at that time that focused explicitly on sports tourism: 'much of importance had to be extracted from more general studies, and those dealing with the sport or tourism sectors separately' (1992: 14). Fortunately, this is no longer the case, although, as mentioned in the General Introduction, there are many useful works currently available that are *relevant* to the study of the relationship between sport and tourism, rather than being directly concerned with the relationship between sport and tourism.

A note on the Jackson and Glyptis (1992) report is useful here, as a comparison between this report and the chapters included in this Part highlights the way in which the field has developed. First, my systematic review of the field in the five years from 2000 to 2004 inclusive (see Chapter 6) returned eighty articles in refereed journals that focused on the relationship between sport and tourism, and this did not include the numerous chapters, books and conference papers also published in that period. As such, the volume of published work on sport and tourism has increased since the Jackson and Glyptis (1992) review but, more importantly, the volume of work meeting the quality standards of peer-reviewed journals has also increased. Second, the nature of the work included in this Part indicates a broadening of the field beyond the study of impacts, although impacts research still comprises a significant corpus of the work.

As such, research on behaviours, policy and provision also feature prominently in the reviews featured in this Part, as do commentaries on the way in which research in the field might develop in the future. In this respect, it might be expected that chapters featuring suggestions for the future development of the field would feature in a final or concluding part. However, as noted earlier, this material provides a useful context within which to understand the rest of the papers in the Reader. It is intended that this Part should outline the development of the field of sports tourism to date, establish the current 'state of play' and provide a range of visions for the development of the field in the future. This 'map' of past and present, and of potential routes in the future, therefore, provides a point of reference for the chapters in the remaining parts of this Reader on behaviours (Part Two), impacts (Part Three), provision and policy (Part Four), and how these papers are located within the overall body of knowledge relating to the study of sport and tourism.

The Editorial from the 2005 special issue of *European Sport Management Quarterly* (vol. 5, no. 3), entitled *Sports Tourism Theory and Method: Concepts, Issues and Epistemologies* is the 'lead' chapter in this Part and is written by myself, **Mike Weed**. In this paper I was concerned to highlight some of the problems that the study of sport and tourism faced, and which the special issue of *ESMQ* had been conceived to address. As an editorial introduction, this contains both personal views on the development of the field and some comments on contemporary debates. In particular, this chapter outlines my preference for a 'conceptualisation' of the area of sport and tourism (rather than a definition), and explains how Chris Bull and I came to develop our conceptualisation of the field as being derived from 'the unique interaction of activity, people and place' (Weed and Bull, 2004: 7). The chapter also explains how this conceptualisation leads to my preference for the term 'sports tourism', rather than the more commonly used 'sport tourism', to refer to the genre. Also included in the chapter are discussions about the need for a greater focus on explanations rather than descriptions in the research on sport and tourism, and for a more explicit and careful consideration of the application of the research methods from which knowledge about sport and tourism is derived.

Gibson's (1998) 'critical analysis of research' in sport and tourism has already been highlighted as a useful benchmark for the state of the field immediately prior to the period covered by this Reader. In fact, in a keynote address to the Leisure Studies Association conference in 2001, **Heather Gibson** updated this review in a presentation entitled *Sport Tourism at a Crossroad? Considerations for the Future*, and this updated view, the second chapter in this Part, provides the earliest overview of the field presented here. This chapter, in contrast to my arguments in the previous paper, presents the case for the use of the term 'sport tourism', and suggests a definition that subdivides the area into 'three distinct behavioural sets':

> Leisure-based travel that takes individuals temporarily outside of their home communities to participate in physical activities, to watch physical activities, or to venerate attractions associated with physical activities.
>
> (Gibson, 1998: 49)

Gibson addressed the way in which the link between sport and tourism is considered by policy-makers, by researchers, and by those responsible for curriculum development. Her conclusions, in 2001, were that the clearest need was to bring together the bodies of knowledge relating to sport and to tourism in order to develop a body of knowledge relating to sport *and* tourism that would be conceptually grounded, thus sowing the seeds for critiques of the field – critiques that both Gibson and others have presented in more recent years (see Chapters 1, 5 and 6 in this Part).

One of the papers cited by Gibson in her 2001 review was an article published in the same year by **Tom Hinch** and **James Higham** entitled, *Sport Tourism: A Framework for Research*. This is the third chapter presented in this Part. Gibson suggested that the framework presented by Hinch and Higham 'proffers a promising avenue for future research'. In fact, as my *ESMQ* editorial (Chapter 1) notes:

> There have been a number of publications that have sought to define and classify the area, but it is only really the framework presented by Hinch and Higham (2001) and my own analysis with Chris Bull (Weed & Bull, 2004) that have offered any conceptualisation of the area ... [I]n the absence of any other contributions to this fundamental aspect of debate within sports tourism, these two propositions are clear points of reference for future research in the field.

Hinch and Higham derive their framework for research in sport and tourism from the activity, spatial and temporal dimensions of the area. Sport is positioned as the activity dimension, while the temporal and spatial dimensions are derived from tourism. Nine illustrative rather than exhaustive themes are described, which combine via the three dimensions to suggest twenty-seven potential areas of investigation within sports tourism, thus providing a clear manifesto for future work.

The fourth chapter in this Part focuses on outdoor adventure tourism, an area that might be viewed as part of, or as overlapping with, the study of sport and tourism, depending on how the two areas are delineated. Also written in 2001, **Karin Weber**'s paper, *Outdoor Adventure Tourism: A Review of Research Approaches* argues for a greater focus on adventure experiences in the study of outdoor adventure tourism. Weber suggests that adventure tourism has traditionally been seen as an extension of adventure recreation and, consequently, the tourism element has been overlooked. As such, there are clear corollaries here with the study of sport and tourism that has also struggled, as Gibson notes (Chapter 2), to genuinely bring two bodies of knowledge together. In analyses of adventure tourism, Weber suggests that risk has been too narrowly conceived as physical risk, whereas psychological and social risk can be equally important in the adventure experience. In fact, Weber believes that adventure tourism can be conceptualised as being as much about the quest for insight and knowledge as the desire for elements of physical risk. Furthermore, Weber advocates a greater focus on interpretive qualitative methodologies in understanding adventure experiences, a theme that is discussed in the final two papers in this Part.

James Higham and **Tom Hinch** present, five years on from their earlier chapter in this Part, a further potential programme for research in *Sport and Tourism Research: A Geographic Approach*, which is the penultimate chapter in this Part. This chapter responds to the call for a greater focus on building 'edifices of knowledge' in my *ESMQ* Editorial (Chapter 1) through developing further the geographical perspectives on sport and tourism that, at least in part, underpinned their earlier paper (Chapter 3). Higham and Hinch use the concepts of space, place and environment as the theoretical foundations for this paper, which prompts research questions that could contribute to the development of a body of knowledge for sport and tourism. Hinch and Higham note that a geographic approach is but one of a number of approaches that could be applied to the study of sport and tourism, and invite scholars from other disciplines, for example, sociology and anthropology, to contribute to discussions surrounding the development of the field.

The final chapter in this Part is the second by myself **Mike Weed**, entitled *Sports Tourism Research 2000–2004: A Systematic Review of Knowledge and a Meta-Evaluation of Methods*. In this chapter, I provide an overview of the peer-reviewed research in sport and tourism included in the systematic review, not on the basis of personal judgement, but on clear and replicable criteria outlined in the chapter itself. The chapter not only identifies trends in the substantive issues addressed by contemporary research in sport and tourism, but also highlights some limitations of the methods and epistemologies employed. Higham and Hinch, in the earlier chapter (Chapter 5) comment on my discussion in the *ESMQ* Editorial relating to the predominance of empirical research employing quantitative research design. I made these comments in 2005 based on a preliminary version of the systematic review and meta-evaluation presented in this paper, which shows that over 70 per cent of primary peer-reviewed research in the period in question used a positivist research design. The chapter notes that the problem here is not with positivist approaches, but with the dominance of such approaches and their use on the basis of convention rather than their suitability in answering research questions.

The chapters in this Part have been selected to give deliberately varying views – some of which are complementary, some of which are not – on approaches to research in sport and tourism in the past and present, and potential avenues and approaches for the future. The discussions in each of these chapters are fundamental to the future development of the field, and I hope they provide a useful context for the remainder of the Reader.

REFERENCES

Biddle, S.J.H. (2006) 'Research Synthesis in Sport and Exercise Psychology: Chaos in the Brickyard Revisited', *European Journal of Sport Science*, 6 (2): 97–102.

Gibson, H.J. (1998) 'Sport Tourism: A Critical Analysis of Research', *Sport Management Review*, 1 (1): 45–76.

Hinch, T.D. and Higham, J.E.S. (2001) 'Sport Tourism: A Framework for Research', *International Journal of Tourism Research*, 3 (1): 45–58.

Jackson, G.A.M. and Glyptis, S.A. (1992) 'Sport and Tourism: A Review of the Literature', Report to the Sports Council, Recreation Management Group, Loughborough University, Loughborough: unpublished.

Weed, M. (1999) 'More Than Sports Tourism: An Introduction to the Sport–Tourism Link', in M. Scarrot (ed.), *Proceedings of the Sport and Recreation Information Group Seminar, Exploring Sports Tourism*. Sheffield: SPRIG.

Weed, M. (2005) 'Research Synthesis in Sport Management: Dealing with Chaos in the Brickyard', *European Sport Management Quarterly*, 5 (1): 77–90.

Weed, M. and Bull, C.J. (2004) *Sports Tourism: Participants, Policy and Providers*. Oxford: Elsevier.

Chapter 1

Mike Weed

SPORTS TOURISM THEORY AND METHOD—CONCEPTS, ISSUES AND EPISTEMOLOGIES

I N 2005 I WROTE A PIECE in ESMQ on approaches to research synthesis in sport management (Weed, 2005). This piece was subtitled "Chaos in the brickyard". The analogy from which this subtitle was taken was drawn by Bernard Forscher in 1963 who, commenting on the development of social science knowledge, expressed concern about what he saw as the "random" and often excessive production of studies (bricks) that were thrown on to the pile of research without any consideration as to how bodies of knowledge ("edifices") could be constructed. Forscher's analogy was constructed thus:

> It became difficult to find a suitable plot for construction of an edifice because the ground was covered with loose bricks. It became difficult to complete a useful edifice because, as soon as the foundations were discernable, they were buried under an avalanche of random bricks. And, saddest of all, sometimes no effort was made even to maintain the distinction between a pile of bricks and a true edifice.
>
> (Forscher, 1963, p. 35)

This analogy seems particularly appropriate to describe the development of research in the "field" of sports tourism. Following what can perhaps be identified as a groundbreaking study in 1982 by Sue Glyptis, which investigated the links between sport and tourism in five European countries and compared them with the UK situation, there was an initially sporadic and subsequently burgeoning publication of material relevant to sports tourism. Some landmark publications, such as Jackson and Glyptis' report to the Sports Council of Great Britain in 1992 and Standeven and De Knop's first full text dedicated to the area in 1999, have appeared alongside a progressively increasing number of refereed journal articles and overviews of the area. However, 23 years after Glyptis' European study, and almost 40 years after the publication of what appears to have been one of the first overviews of the field (Anthony, 1966), it is still somewhat difficult to identify a coherent edifice of knowledge in the field, although there are plenty of bricks!

The concern with the production of bricks rather than the building of edifices is something that has been the subject of contemporary comment in *Tourism Management*, with Stephen Page commenting in a recent opinion piece on tourism research (2005, p. 664):

> So often one reads some of these papers and asks why have they been written? Do they add anything meaningful to knowledge? In some cases not very much. . . . I would venture to suggest if only 25% of the current tourism outputs were produced, our knowledge base in the subject would not be adversely affected. It might be improved as we are able to assimilate more of what is good rather than having to wade through more mediocre and seemingly mundane research findings.

In a similar vein, Chris Ryan, also writing in *Tourism Management* (2005, p. 662), comments:

> The multiplicity of journals has meant that it has been relatively easy for researchers to gain publications of technically skilled quantitative based pieces . . . which actually offer little in terms of new conceptualisation or are able to articulate any significant addition to the literature.

Drawing on the comments of Forscher, Page, and Ryan it is possible to paint a picture of what appears to be the "state of play" in sports tourism research. After more than 20 years of serious research attention, the "foundations" for sports tourism research have surely become "discernable". In this context, the foundations to which I refer are what I have previously identified as advocacy work (Weed, 1999; Weed & Bull, 2004), that which attempts to establish that there is a link between sport and tourism, and to establish it as a legitimate field worthy of consideration by both academics and providers. Each of the "landmark" publications mentioned earlier (Glyptis, 1982; Jackson & Glyptis, 1992; Standeven & De Knop, 1999) has formed part of this foundational literature. However, again drawing on Forscher's (1963, p. 35) analogy, "as soon as the foundations were discernable, they were buried under an avalanche of random bricks". Such random bricks, as noted by Gibson (1998, 2002), are often duplications of the already solid foundations, and so we are left asking (cf., Page, 2005) "do they add anything meaningful to knowledge?". That there are significant links between sport and tourism, and the broad nature of such links and their impacts, has already been established by a considerable range of published material. There is little need for further foundational work, but the "body" of sports tourism publications is peppered with economic (and other) impact studies which, while internally valid and technically competent in their own right, add little to the body of knowledge and do little to shape future research directions. Here we are faced with the problem identified by Ryan (2005), the publication of an increasing number "of technically skilled quantitative based pieces . . . which actually offer little in terms of new conceptualisation".

Evidence for this view of the sports tourism area is provided by a preliminary four-year (2000–2003) systematic review and meta-evaluation of sports tourism knowledge and methods (Weed, 2004) (a full five-year review is currently being completed).[1] This review covered 53 refereed articles in hard copy journals in the broad sport, tourism and leisure fields. There was a clear year-on-year growth, with only five articles published in 2000, compared to the publication of 22 articles in 2003. Unsurprisingly, the most studied topic was event sports tourism (42% of articles), with outdoor and adventure sports tourism coming a distant second (17%). In terms of the phenomena investigated, the largest single area of investigation was experiences, perceptions and profiles (35%) with other work taking place on impacts (32%), provision, management and marketing (21%), policy (6%), and definitions, classification and conceptualisation (6%). However, typically the work on experiences was descriptive, with findings tending to show that many participants enjoy the sports tourism experience, and that many would like to repeat the experience at some point in the future. What this research does not investigate is *why* the experience is enjoyable and *why* participants would like to repeat the experience. The reason for this is perhaps revealed by the analysis of method, with 87% of empirical sports tourism research employing a positivist quantitative research design, and 50% presenting descriptive results that were devoid of any theoretical discussion (Weed, 2004). The overall picture, therefore, was that sports tourism as an area of study lacks methodological diversity, rarely tends to answer "why" questions, and in around half of cases, does not employ any clear theoretical perspective to underpin what is largely descriptive research, This reinforces the picture painted above, of a field where the number of bricks is increasing, but where there is little attempt to assemble any coherent edifice of knowledge.

It would seem clear, therefore, that a change in direction is needed, and some guidance on such a change might lie in the comments of Chris Ryan relating to the need for "new conceptualisation". In fact, I would argue that there has never been any real debate about how sports tourism is conceptualised. There have been a number of publications that have sought to define and classify the area, but it is only really the framework for research presented by Hinch & Higham (2001) and my own analysis with Chris Bull (Weed & Bull, 2004) that have offered any conceptualisation of the area. Such conceptualisations are vital as they can underpin the development of a coherent programme of research and consequent body of knowledge in the area. Drawing again on the brickyard analogy, conceptualisations are the architect's plans that allow piles of bricks to be built into edifices of knowledge. A clear concept of sports tourism contributes to an understanding of the range of issues that are central to the development of the area. To date, the area has been dominated by the largely routine assessment of events, often to the detriment of other significant forms of sports tourism. Furthermore, research methods, and the assumptions underpinning such methods, are drawn from assumptions about the ontological character of the phenomenon being researched. As such, a clear conceptualisation of sports tourism can ensure that robust and appropriate methods are used to

---

1 At the time this paper was written, the full five-year (2000–4) systematic review and meta-evaluation (Weed, 2006, featured later in this Reader) was not completed, as such, the statistics quoted here refer to the period 2000–3 and consequently differ from those quoted in Weed (2006). As Weed notes: 'The addition of further articles from 2004 has increased the number of articles embedding discussions within a clear theoretical framework from 'around half' to 62%.' As such, there are signs that more recently conducted sports tourism research is paying heed to previous criticism.

investigate relevant aspects of the phenomenon. Consequently, the remainder of this paper will examine in more detail the problems outlined above, under the headings of "Concepts", "Issues" and "Epistemologies".

Concepts

As mentioned above, there has been a proliferation of definitions of sports tourism, but few attempts at conceptualising the area. Typical of many such definitions is that offered by Standeven and De Knop that "sport tourism" comprises:

> All forms of active and passive involvement in sporting activity, participated in casually or in an organised way for noncommercial or business/commercial reasons, that necessitate travel away from home and work locality.
> (Standeven & De Knop, 1999, p. 12)

Such a definition, while allowing an inclusive approach to the study of sports tourism, does little more than combine widely-accepted definitions of sport (cf., Council of Europe, 1992) and tourism (cf., British Tourist Authority, 1981). As such, it is really no definition at all as it doesn't add anything to an understanding of the area that couldn't be established from definitions of sport and of tourism as it simply identifies tourism activity involving sport. In fact, such a definition would seem to cast doubt on whether sports tourism is a serious subject for study, or whether it is merely a convenient descriptive term with little explanatory value. Other authors (see Gammon & Robinson, 1997/2003; Sofield, 2003; Robinson & Gammon, 2004) have attempted to separate out "sports tourists" (for whom sport is the primary purpose of the trip) and "tourism sportists" (sic) (for whom tourism is the primary purpose), and to further classify these categories into "hard" and "soft" participants. However, the flaw in such work is that it is dependent on defining tourism activity in terms of sport, or sport activity in terms of tourism, and as such inevitably establishes a subordinate role for either tourism or sport in an understanding of the area. This is something that Pigeassou, Bui-Xuan, and Gleyse (1998/2003) explicitly argue for, claiming that there is a need to establish an "epistemological rupture" (p. 30) that "divides the phenomena and prevents any confusion between sport, tourism and sports tourism", and that this is only possible through such subordination, without which "sports tourism would not exist and the activities described or observed would be confused with tourism phenomena" (p. 30). However, as has been argued elsewhere (Weed & Bull, 2004; Downward 2005), sports tourism is a synergistic phenomenon that is more than the simple combination of sport and tourism. As such, it requires an understanding of both sport and tourism (cf., Standeven & De Knop's definition, above), but it needs to be conceptualised in a way that is not dependent on definitions of sport and of tourism, and which allows its synergistic elements to be understood. Inevitably, sports tourism will be "confused" with both sport and tourism, particularly by participants who are familiar with the concepts of sport and of tourism, but less likely to be familiar with the idea of sports tourism. This is not a problem, definitional boundaries are always fuzzy, and there is no clear need to establish such boundaries between sport, tourism and sports tourism. There is, however, a need to establish a clear conceptual understanding of the sports tourism phenomenon. One way in which this can be done is to examine the features of both sport and tourism and establish an understanding of sports tourism derived from those features.

Sport can be seen as involving some form of activity (kayaking, cycling, etc.), be it formal or informal, competitive or recreational, or actively or vicariously/passively participated in. Furthermore, sport also involves other people, as competitors and/or co-participants. For vicarious/passive participants, the people element is likely to be both other vicarious/passive participants (i.e., other spectators) and the active participants (i.e., competitors). Similarly, active competitors and co-participants may experience other people as active and/or vicarious/passive participants. Even activities that are sometimes participated in alone (e.g., mountaineering, running) are likely to involve other people because participants may reference their participation in terms of the subculture of the activity and thus experience a feeling of "communitas" (Turner, 1974). Similarly, tourism involves other people, either as co-travellers and/or as hosts. Even solitary tourism entails passing through areas that have been constructed by other people or other communities, and it is rare for a tourist to complete a trip without encountering other travellers. Tourism also involves visiting places outside of the tourist's usual environment. There is, of course, a travel element, but this is either an instrumental factor in arriving at an "unusual" place, or the travel takes place in or through "unusual" places. Considering the interaction of these features of sport and tourism, it is possible to arrive at Weed & Bull's (2004, p. 37) conceptualisation of sports tourism as "arising from the unique interaction of activity, people and place". Notice here that the focus is on the "interaction" of activity, people and place, thus emphasising the synergistic nature of the phenomenon and moving it away from a dependence on either sport or tourism as the primary defining factor. Thinking about sports tourism in this way establishes the phenomenon as *related to but more than the sum of* sport and tourism, and thus establishes sports tourism as something that cannot be understood as simply a tourism market niche or a subset of sports management.

This conceptualisation has implications for terminology. Deriving from definitions of sports tourism that are dependent on definitions of sport and tourism, the term "sport tourism" (rather than "sports tourism") has achieved common currency. This is usually on the basis that "sport" refers to the social institution of sport, while "sports" refers to a collection of activities that have come to be defined as such. However, given the discussions above and the conceptualisation of sports tourism as derived from the unique interaction of activity, people and place, a reliance on the social institution of sport to delimit the area of sports tourism is somewhat contradictory. Furthermore, the concept of sport can in many cases be a misnomer in that it implies coherence where none exists and detracts from the heterogeneous nature of sporting activities. As the conceptualisation outlined here assumes that one of the unique aspects of sports tourism is that the interaction of people and places with the activities in question expands rather than limits heterogeneity, it is argued that the term "sports tourism" should be used, along with the focus on diverse and heterogeneous activities that this implies.

In my analysis with Chris Bull (Weed & Bull, 2004, p. 37) we also explicitly locate sports tourism as a "social, economic and cultural phenomenon". This is important as all too often sports tourism's social and cultural aspects are overlooked in favour of an economic analysis. However, economic aspects are derived from social and cultural interactions. As such, our analysis of "stakeholders" in sports tourism begins with an analysis of participants. This is because policy, provision and impacts are all derived from participation, and it is to the detriment of the subject area as a whole that there is, as yet, only a very limited understanding of sports tourism participation. As mentioned earlier, and also as argued by Gibson (2004), there is a need to move beyond an understanding of the "what" of sports tourism participation to understand the "why". A more detailed understanding of participation can obviously lead to a clearer understanding of the impacts derived from such participation and can further inform policy and provision decisions. As such, I would argue that the greatest need in sports tourism research is the development of a greater understanding of sports tourism participation experiences underpinned by a clear conceptualisation of the ontological nature of sports tourism.

Hinch and Higham (2001, 2005) conceptualise sport as a tourism attraction understood through the lens of Leiper's (1990) attraction framework. While, on the surface, this conceptualisation appears to subordinate sport to tourism, they make it clear that "the complexity of sport when combined with the complexity of tourism leads to countless diverse variations of the sport tourism phenomenon" (Hinch and Higham, 2005, p. 247) and that sports tourism is an heterogeneous rather than an homogenous phenomenon. Moreover, their discussions focus on the nature of sports tourism attractions and they cite Nauright (1996) in support of their view that "in many cases, sporting events and people's reactions to them are the clearest public manifestations of culture and collective identities in a given society" (Hinch and Higham, 2005, p. 247). Here the experience of the sports tourist is derived not only from the enjoyment of the sports event but also from the participation in a manifestation of local culture. This experience is derived from a synergistic interaction of activity, people and place, and the primacy of either the sport or the tourism element (if, indeed, such elements can be separated out) cannot be established.

Hinch and Higham's focus on authenticity features a discussion of the nature of authentic experiences, and that rather than seeking objective authenticity, many tourists seek enjoyable and meaningful experiences, or the entry into an "authentic state of being". As such, their analysis, utilising Wang's (1999) concepts of objective, symbolic and existential authenticity, has great potential to contribute to an understanding of sports tourism experiences and to shape the nature of future research in this neglected area of the field.

Issues

The above discussions contextualise the study of sports tourism within Weed & Bull's (2004, p. 37) conceptualisation that "Sports tourism is a social, economic and cultural phenomenon arising from the unique interaction of activity, people and place".

To a certain extent, this conceptualisation suggests some of the issues that might be considered by the sports tourism research enterprise. Firstly, that social, economic and cultural aspects of the phenomenon should be considered; secondly, that aspects of activities, people and places might be investigated; and, thirdly, and most importantly, that the interaction of activity, people and place should be researched. This, of course, is largely a research programme for understanding sports tourism participation experiences, but it is also a programme that can underpin the construction of policy responses, the nature of provision, and the understanding and management of impacts, all of which are derived from participation (see Weed & Bull, 2004, pp. 204–206, for a more detailed discussion of future research needs based on this conceptualisation).

As mentioned earlier, Hinch & Higham (2001) have also offered a potential programme for sports tourism research that is derived from their conceptualisation of the activity, spatial and temporal dimensions of sports tourism. This positions sport as the activity dimension, while the temporal and spatial dimensions are derived from tourism. Unlike the Weed & Bull (2004) conceptualisation, the institutional features of sport are invoked as delimiting sports tourism, and as such there is less of a focus on the area as derived from experiences. However, Hinch & Higham (2001) describe nine illustrative rather than exhaustive themes that combine via the three dimensions to suggest 27 potential areas of investigation within sports tourism.

Both Hinch & Higham (2001) and Weed & Bull (2004) have produced clearly conceptualised and coherent analyses that present clear recommendations for future research. There are perhaps two differences between them. Firstly, Hinch and Higham's conceptualisation, seeing sport as a tourist attraction, is based more in tourism studies, whereas Weed and Bull place considerable importance on not giving primacy to sport or tourism in conceptualising the area. Secondly, there is a difference in emphasis: Weed and Bull place greater emphasis on the area as derived from participation experiences, whilst Hinch and Higham's analysis perhaps focuses more (although not exclusively) on supply-side issues. Regardless of such differences, and in the absence of any other contributions to this fundamental aspect of debate within sports tourism, these two propositions are clear points of reference for future research in the field.

The preliminary four-year systematic review of published peer-reviewed work in sports tourism briefly referred to above (Weed, 2004) shows that in terms of topic areas, sports tourism is dominated by studies of events, with a secondary focus on adventurous outdoor activities, and that the two most investigated phenomena are experiences, perceptions and profiles (but, dominated by descriptive work) and impacts. While the field would benefit from a broader focus, a larger problem is the nature of these publications.

The experiences, perceptions and profiles category comprised a broad range of work that focussed on sports tourism participants. The vast majority of this work was descriptive, whilst a significant proportion involved only basic data reporting and did not draw on theoretical perspectives or concepts to underpin the empirical work. Furthermore, work which did claim to investigate experiences focussed on the basic nature of the experience as positive or negative, and whether the experience would encourage participants to take part again (Weed, 2004). While it is useful to know that many sports tourists are enjoying positive experiences, this does not really help broaden our understanding of participants, policy or providers. What is required is an understanding of which aspects of experiences are positive and why, thus broadening our understanding of participation. This further informs an understanding of how and why impacts are generated and how they might be managed and what policy initiatives might be developed. The area would also benefit from a focus on the role various aspects of the sports tourism experience play in initial trip decision making and planning, and on decisions to repeat such trips, thus feeding into the development of policy and planning in the public sector and provision and practice in the private sector. Such work has the potential to make a substantial contribution to sports tourism knowledge.

A clear example of such work is Costa and Chalip's (2005) paper, "Sport tourism in rural revitalization—an ethnographic evaluation", which collects in-depth information on the nature of participation in paragliding in a Portuguese village. This, in itself, would be a useful and interesting study. However, this information is then employed to suggest that the popular perception of the positive impacts of paragliding on this village is flawed, and that specific leveraging strategies need to be employed by local policymakers and providers to maximise, or even generate, a positive impact. The concept of leveraging is one which Chalip, with various colleagues (see Chalip, 2004; Chalip & Green, 2001; Chalip & Leyns, 2003), has employed in the past largely in relation to sports events. The suggestion in such work has been that instead of using an assessment of potential impacts to inform decisions about whether to host a particular event, policy-makers and providers should assess the extent to which there is the potential to employ a range of leveraging strategies to maximise and extend such impacts. Costa and Chalip's (2005) paper is an attempt to extend the concept of leveraging strategies to ongoing provision, and their paper not only extends our understanding of the potential application of leveraging approaches, but also offers practical suggestions to inform policy, provision and practice in this Portuguese village.

Costa and Chalip (2005) reinforce the point made by Hinch and Higham (2005) that sports tourism is a heterogeneous area. As such, their paper provides a template for further *action research* of this nature, which has a local rather than a global focus. Again, it is perhaps useful to consider aspects of the interaction of activity, people and place. Costa and Chalip (2005) show that the social and cultural aspects of this interaction result in a weak economic impact on the village concerned, as the place is only really experienced from the sky. The subcultural nature of paragliding means that participants would rather create their own "place" for socialising and eating in the evening, rather than interact with the local villagers who put up a great deal of cultural resistance to change, regardless of the extent to which it would maximise the economic impact of the paragliders on the village. Costa and Chalip's contribution here is to show that leveraging strategies need to be based on a detailed knowledge of the local interaction of activity, people and place, otherwise false perceptions of the nature of impacts can become common currency. As such, they have clearly demonstrated the way in which research on participants can be the key to developing an understanding of provision and policy.

A key lesson from Costa and Chalip's (2005) paper, therefore, is the need for an understanding of the nature of impacts and how and why they are generated. This is something that is generally missing from much of the impacts research included in the systematic review of sports tourism knowledge (Weed, 2004). Generally, impacts research tends to be a straightforward "end result" assessment, rather than an assessment of the processes that generate such impacts. This has particularly been the case in relation to event impact assessments, with which the field of sports tourism research is swamped. In fact, had the systematic review been extended to "grey" literature, particularly conference papers and presentations, the proportion of event impact assessments would have significantly increased. Many such assessments are derived from consultancy reports which, while often "technically skilled quantitative pieces" (Ryan, 2005) that are interesting for the event hosts and sponsors, do little to add to our knowledge or theoretical understanding of the area. In fact, as Crompton (1995) and Hudson (2001) have both noted in the past, in many cases the assumptions underlying such studies can be, at best, misguided and can make comparisons between such studies virtually useless without conducting further detailed meta-analytical manipulations. Hudson's (2001) meta-analysis in particular, identified a range of "methodological" flaws in economic impact assessments of professional sports teams in the US. which included, *inter alia*, failure to differentiate between additional and displaced spending, failure to allow for time switchers, and inconsistent consideration of geographical boundaries. Inconsistent and poorly conducted impact studies are something that the field of sports tourism has been blighted with for some time now, and Holger Preuss's (2005) paper, "The economic impact of visitors at major multi-sport events", attempts to address some of these issues.

Preuss (2005) discusses the economic impact of "event affected" people and like the paper by Costa and Chalip (2005), demonstrates how an understanding of impacts needs to be clearly informed by an understanding of the nature of sports tourism participants. Preuss's paper identifies 10 groups of event affected people, with a further discussion of some further sub groups. In the words of one of the anonymous reviewers, it "is the most elaborate and sophisticated model yet to appear in the literature". Preuss' analysis demonstrates that the economic impact of an event not only requires an analysis of the behaviours of sports tourists, but also an analysis of the behaviours of local residents and tourists who would have otherwise have visited the area were it not for the presence of the event. Even this description is a major simplification of Preuss' ground-breaking analysis, which now undoubtedly sets the standard for meaningful economic evaluations of major events. As such, aside from the significant methodological standard that Preuss (2005) sets, a further major contribution of this paper will hopefully be to "clear the brickyard" (cf., Forscher, 1963) of less robust papers in this area which may now be seen as inadequate.

Epistemologies

The lack of any explicit consideration of epistemology is a deficiency that the area of sports tourism shares with much research in the broader sport and tourism fields. Notwithstanding the recent advent of a "methods and practice" section in the journal *Current Issues in Tourism*, a special issue of *Journal of Sport Management* on innovative methodology, and the hosting of the first *International Conference on Qualitative Research in Sport and Exercise* in Liverpool in 2004 (with the second conference to follow in 2006), methodological and epistemological considerations tend to be glossed over in many refereed journal articles. This can take the form of the unquestioning application of quantitative techniques without any consideration of the epistemological or ontological grounds for doing so, or a very vague description of the type of qualitative method used which leaves the reader with no means of assessing its epistemological appropriateness.

There are perhaps two epistemological concerns that might be raised in relation to sports tourism research. The first is that few papers discuss the epistemological assumptions that underpin the methods used, and thus often methods are employed on the basis of convention rather than the extent to which they generate appropriate or legitimate knowledge. The second is derived from a "meta-evaluation" of methods used across the field as a whole that demonstrates a lack of epistemological diversity, with 87% of empirical sports tourism research between 2000 and 2003 using quantitative methods with (implicit) positivist assumptions (Weed, 2004). These findings are consistent across a range of disciplines, with psychological, sociological, economic and management perspectives on sports tourism all falling within this positivist hegemony. As such, the two concerns are related, in that the positivist dominance in the area encourages individual researchers to apply positivist methods on the basis of convention rather than epistemological considerations. I would argue that this has resulted in the dominance of descriptive research on participant profiles, particularly as 50% of empirical research contained no discernable theoretical discussion, rather than research that seeks to understand the nature of sports tourism experiences. Clearly such research, as the Costa and Chalip paper in this collection demonstrates, needs to draw on more interpretivist epistemologies. Such epistemologies can focus on individuals and their experiences of sports tourism as derived from the interaction of activity, people and place. This can be aided by a focus on disciplines (psychology, sociology, economics, etc.) rather than subjects (sport, tourism, leisure, etc) and further reinforces the need for a conceptualisation of sports tourism that is not derived from definitions of sport and of tourism.

This theme is picked up by Paul Downward (2005), in putting forward some "Critical (realist) reflections on policy and management research in sport, tourism and sports tourism". Whilst Downward actually focuses more on ontological than epistemological concerns. His discussion has clear epistemological implications for the study of sports tourism and he, too, describes sports tourism as "clearly a synergistic phenomenon that benefits from a focus on disciplines rather than subject areas". Downward further argues that methods should be linked to disciplines rather than subjects:

> any specific conceptual view upon the research methods employed to generate insights within the sport, tourism and sports tourism literatures must be predicated upon that which emanates from the originating disciplinary theory or research approach.
>
> (Downward, 2005, p. 304)

Downward's critical realist view argues that reality is a structured and open system in which the real, the actual and the empirical domains are organically related. The implications of this for sports tourism researchers are that empirical observations can be manifestations of reality, but that they are inevitably partial manifestations. As such, Downward argues that explanations of phenomena require "ontic depth", that is, they must move beyond the level of events towards an understanding of the processes that produce them. An understanding of such processes is inevitably derived from theoretical perspectives that contribute to a conceptual understanding of the ontological character of the sports tourism phenomenon. Downward (2005) argues that such conceptual understandings can allow researchers to move towards analyses that are genuinely interdisciplinary, as opposed to multidisciplinary analyses with ontological clashes.

There will inevitably be researchers who disagree with Downward's (2005) critical realist view of the nature of policy and management research in sport, tourism and sports tourism, However, undoubtedly his paper is the first real attempt to address ontological and epistemological issues in sports tourism research. In the absence of any other contributions to this debate, either within methodology sections of substantive papers or as full contributions on the nature of methodology, Downward's piece at present remains unchallenged. If the value of Downward's analysis is measured, if nothing else, by its potential to force other researchers to face up to these issues within their own work, then his paper will make a substantial contribution to future sports tourism research.

These discussions take this paper full circle to the observations made in the opening pages. Namely, that sports tourism needs to be clearly conceptualised if research is to be underpinned by an understanding of its ontological nature, that sports tourism research needs to be theoretically informed and methodologically robust, and that there is a need to move beyond events (the *what*) to develop an understanding of the processes that produce them (the *why*). This is not the only place in which such observations are made, Recent (Gibson, 2004; Weed & Bull, 2004) and future publications have made and will make similar observations because despite the increasing number of sports tourism "bricks" being produced, there still remains no coherent "edifice" of sports tourism knowledge. Therefore, invoking for the final time Bernard Forscher's (1963) brickyard analogy, the recent development of knowledge in sports tourism has been afflicted by the difficulty in "completing a useful edifice because . . . the foundations were . . . buried under an avalanche of random bricks" (p. 35). This paper has sought to emphasise the clear need for conceptual, theoretical and methodological foundations for sports tourism research. The challenge now is for others to focus on edifice construction rather than brick production.

References

Anthony, D. (1966). *Sport and tourism*. London: CCPR/ICSPE Bureau for Public Relations.

British Tourist Authority (1981). *Tourism in the UK – the broad perspective*. London: BTA.

Chalip, L. (2004). Beyond impact: A general model for sport event leverage. In B.W. Ritchie and D. Adair (eds), *Sport tourism: Interrelationships, impacts and issues* (pp. 226–252). Clevedon: Channel View Publications.

Chalip, L. and Green, B.C. (2001). Leveraging large sports events for tourism: lessons learned from the Sydney Olympics. *Supplemental proceedings of the Travel and Tourism Research Association Thirty-Second Annual Conference*. Boise, ID: TTRA.

Chalip, L. and Leyns, A. (2003). Local business leveraging of a sport event: Managing an event for economic benefit. *Journal of Sport Management*, 16: 133–159.

Council of Europe (1992). *European sports charter*. Strasbourg: Council of Europe.

Crompton, J.L. (1995). Economic impact analysis of sports facilities and events: Eleven sources of misapplication. *Journal of Sport Management*, 9 (1): 14–35.

Forscher, B.K. (1963). Chaos in the brickyard. *Science*, 142: 35.

Gammon, S. and Robinson, T. (1997/2003). Sport and tourism: A conceptual framework. *Journal of Sport Tourism*, 8 (1): 21–26.

Gibson, H.J. (1998). Sport tourism: A critical analysis of research. *Sport Management Review*, 1 (1): 45–76.

Gibson, H.J. (2002). Sport tourism at a crossroad? Considerations for the future. In S. Gammon and J. Kurtzman (eds), *Sport tourism: Principles and practice*. Eastbourne: LSA.

Gibson, H.J. (2004). Moving beyond the "what is and who" of sport tourism to understanding "why". *Journal of Sport Tourism*, 9 (3): 247–265.

Glyptis, S.A. (1982). *Sport and tourism in Western Europe*. London: British Travel Education Trust.

Hardin, S.E. (2005). Book review: *"Sports tourism: Participants, policy and providers"*, by Mike Weed and Chris Bull. *Journal of Travel Research*, 43 (3): 320–321.

Higham, J.E.S. (ed.) (2005). *Sport tourism destinations: Issues, opportunities and analysis*. Oxford: Elsevier.

Hinch, T.D. and Higham, J.E.S. (2004). *Sport tourism development*. Clevedon: Channel View Publications.

Hinch, T.D. and Higham, J.E.S. (2001). Sport tourism: A framework for research. *International Journal of Tourism Research*, 3 (1): 45–58.

Hudson, I. (2001). The use and misuse of economic impact analysis. *Journal of Sport & Social Issues*, 25 (1): 20–39.

Jackson, G.A.M. and Glyptis, S.A. (1992). Sport and tourism: A review of the literature. Unpublished report to the Sports Council, Recreation Management Group, Loughborough University.

Kulczycki, C. (2005). Book review: "*Sport tourism development*" by Thomas Hinch and James Higham. *Journal of Travel Research*, 43 (3): 319–320.

Leiper, N. (1990). Tourist attraction systems. *Annals of Tourism Research*, 17 (2): 367–384.

Nauright, J. (1996). "A besieged tribe"? Nostalgia, white cultural identity and the role of rugby in a changing South Africa. *International Review for the Sociology of Sport*, 31 (1): 69–89.

Page, S. (2005). Academic ranking exercises: Do they achieve anything meaningful? A personal view. *Tourism Management*, 26 (5): 663–666.

Pigeassou, C., Bui-Xuan, G. and Gleyse, J. (1998/2003). Epistemological issues on sport tourism: Challenges for a new scientific field. *Journal of Sport Tourism*, 8 (1): 27–34.

Robinson, T. and Gammon, S. (2004). A question of primary and secondary motives: Revisiting and applying the sport tourism framework. *Journal of Sport Tourism*, 9 (3): 221–233.

Ryan, C. (2005). The ranking and rating of academics and journals in tourism research. *Tourism Management*, 26 (5): 257–662.

Sofield, T.H.B. (2003). Sports tourism: From binary division to quadripartite construct. *Journal of Sport Tourism*, 8 (3): 144–166.

Standeven, J. and De Knop, P. (1999). *Sport tourism*. Champaign, IL: Human Kinetics.

Turner, V. (1974). *Dramas, fields and metaphors*. New York: Cornell University Press.

Wang, N. (1999). Rethinking authenticity in tourism experience. *Annals of Tourism Research*, 26 (2): 349–370.

Weed, M. (1999). More than sports holidays: An overview of the sport-tourism link. In M. Scarrot (ed.), *Proceedings of the Sport and Recreation Information Group Seminar, Exploring Sports Tourism*. Sheffield: SPRIG.

Weed, M. (2004). *Sports tourism research 2000–2003: A systematic review of knowledge and a meta-evaluation of method*. Paper presented at the Twelfth European Association of Sport Management Congress, Ghent, Belgium, September.

Weed, M. (2005). Research synthesis in sport management: Dealing with "chaos in the brickyard". *European Sport Management Quarterly*, 5 (1).

Weed, M. and Bull, C.J. (2004). *Sports tourism: Participants, policy and providers*. London: Elsevier.

Chapter 2

Heather J. Gibson

SPORT TOURISM AT A CROSSROAD?
Considerations for the future

Introduction

SINCE MID TO LATE 1990S, academic attention has turned increasingly to the interconnections between sport and tourism and the term sport tourism has been adopted to describe sport related travel. In the last years of the 1990s, several special issues of journals were devoted to sport tourism (*Journal of Vacation Marketing*, 1998, vol. 4, no. I; *Tourism Recreation Research*, Vol. 22, no. 1 1997; *Visions in Leisure and Business*, 1999, vol. 18, spring), indeed the online *Journal of Sport Tourism* is completely devoted to the topic. The first specialist textbook was published in 1999 (Standeven and De Knop, 1999) and various conferences adopted a sport tourism theme (e.g., TEAMS, Travel, Events and Management in Sports held annually in the US since 1997; Illinois Sport Tourism Conference, mid 1990s). It would be misleading to claim that sport tourism is a new phenomenon. As scholars of sport tourism are the first to acknowledge, people have been traveling to watch or pursue sport for centuries (Delpy, 1998; Gibson, 1998 a and b). However, sport tourism has increasingly gained attention as a topic of research and academic discussion, particularly since the mid 1990s.

This paper is based on the plenary address I gave at the 2001 LSA Conference, The purpose of this address was to review the progress that had been made in sport tourism research, policy and curricula since 1998 when I conducted a comprehensive review of literature in sport tourism that was subsequently published in *Sport Management Review* (Gibson, 1998a). At the end of this review, I concluded the following:

> there is a lack of integration in three domains: (1) policy development and implementation . . . (2) in academe, a lack of interdisciplinary research . . . (3) in the education of future sport tourism professionals.
>
> (Gibson, 1998a: p. 65)

I was certainly not the first scholar to come to this conclusion, Glyptis (1982) concluded in her review of sport tourism in five Western European countries that there was resistance to links between policy makers, planners and public providers and almost a decade later she concluded that "[s]port and tourism tend to be treated by academic and practitioner alike as separate spheres of activity" (Glyptis, 1991: p. 165). De Knop (1990) arrived at the same conclusion in a review of active sport tourism in Europe. And, I am certainly not the last to arrive at this conclusion (Foley and Reid, 1998; Standeven and De Knop, 1999; Weed and Bull, 1997; Weed, 1999). Nonetheless, particularly in the last three years when sport tourism seems to have grown rapidly in published articles, chapters and books, course offerings, government, non-government organizations (NGO), and industry attention, it is useful to revisit my earlier conclusion and ask: What progress has been made? Where do we go next? And to address the wider question: Is sport tourism at a crossroads?

In addressing these questions I will take each of three topics in turn: 1) Policy development and implementation; 2) Research and scholarship; and 3) Curricular considerations.

Policy development and implementation

Around the world there appear to be mixed results in developing and implementing integrated sport tourism policies. In the United States there has been a growing awareness of the importance of sport related travel in recent years. In 1999 the Travel Industry Association of America (TIA), one of the leading agencies tracking travel related trends in the US, conducted a study on sport tourism and found that more than 75 million American adults (two fifths of the population) attended a sports event while on vacation (TIA 1999). At the state and local levels, since 1986, thirteen sports commissions have been established whose mission is to attract sports events to their communities. Some of these sports commissions are independent, nonprofit organizations, some are a division of local convention and visitors bureaus and others are a government agency at the city, county or state level. The National Association of Sports Commissions (NASC) started with fifteen members in 1992 and currently has more than 280 members, less than 10 years later. The NASC was formed by a group of individuals who had the foresight to realize the potential that sport tourism held for their communities and the need to collaborate if this potential was to be achieved. Despite the growing awareness of the importance of sport related travel in the US, there is still a lack of overall coordination and cooperation as is characteristic of the nature of the tourism industry in the US as a whole. On a state by state basis, some states have explicit policies and bodies to ensure the promotion of sport tourism, for example, the Florida Sports Foundation is contracted by the Office of Tourism, Trade and Economic Development to promote sport and Florida as a sports venue. But even with such organizations, individual communities actively compete against one another to host events. Since 1997, Walt Disney World (WDW) in Orlando, Florida has also entered the sport tourism arena opening its Disney's Wide World of Sports. This venue contains world-class facilities for hosting a range of sports events from baseball and beach volleyball to basketball and gymnastics. The intent of WDW however, still remains the promotion of their core product, the theme parks, and athletes and spectators are actively encouraged to visit the parks during their stay.

In fact, theme park tickets are packaged with tournament fees and on-site hotel accommodation. Thus, with regards to the US there is a growing awareness of the potential benefits of sport tourism for communities, however, this awareness has not been accompanied by an integrated policy or even cooperation among agencies in some eases. The focus of this growing awareness has also been overwhelmingly on event sport tourism with some attention on a regional basis to golf and skiing as active sport tourism pursuits, however, the recognition of active sport tourism as an important segment of sport tourism remains limited.

Reviewing the situation in South Africa, Swart (1998) observed that the South Africans, encouraged by the success of hosting of the 1995 Rugby World Cup, embarked on a policy of attracting more international events. A government white paper on tourism in 1996 identified sport tourism as one of the ways of developing the tourism industry. Subsequently in 1997, the South Africa Sports Tourism (SAST), a government initiative was launched. This initiative identified sport tourism as having a strategic role to play in achieving the aims of the Reconstruction and Development Program in the post-apartheid era. However, in common with similar initiatives around the world, Swart suggests that the SAST campaign has concentrated primarily on attracting the mega events, which tend to be resource intensive and may not deliver the promised economic and tourism related benefits (Burgan and Mules, 1992; Hall and Hodges, 1996; Roche, 1994). She writes that subsequently there has been little coordination across sport and tourism agencies, little forward planning by tourism agencies, and a lack of financial assistance to aid community level development of sport tourism events.

In the UK, Glyptis' (1991) assessment of the links between sport and tourism agencies seems not to have changed significantly over the last decade. Foley and Reid's (1998) examination of the popularity of activity holidays in Scotland concluded that there is a need for greater linkages between operators and governing bodies of sports. In fact, Foley and Reid found that individual agencies are so keen to promote their own particular services that there is not only a lack of coordinated policy and practice, but there are also conflicting goals among the agencies. Weed and Bull (1996; 1997) have written several papers examining the lack of coordination among English government agencies responsible for sport and tourism despite the mutual advantages of linking sport and tourism (Weed, 1999). Indeed, Weed (2001) portrays a bleaker picture in recent years whereby the English Tourist Board (ETB) has been successively marginalized by ministerial policies to the extent that there no longer exists a primary agency for tourism with which sports agencies can liaise to promote sport tourism. Moreover, the English Sports Council in contrast has not been marginalized in the same way as the ETB and is in position to exclude tourism interests and promote its own agenda unilaterally. The one bright point on the horizon might be the Sports Tourism Initiative launched by the British Tourism Authority in January 2000, The aim of this initiative is to market British sport as a tourist attraction to overseas visitors with the long-term goal of making sport "one of Britain's key tourist attractions" (www.visitbritain.com/sport).

Thus, in looking at the situations in the US, South Africa and the UK, the conclusion I made in 1998 regarding a lack of integrated practice and policy among sport and tourism agencies seems to describe the situation in 2001. Despite a growing awareness of the prominence of sport related tourism, agencies and governments around the world have not heeded the advice of sport tourism scholars from the 1980s (Glyptis, 1982) and the early 1990s (De Knop, 1990; Glyptis, 1991; Standeven and Tomlinson, 1994). In fact,

Standeven and Tomlinson's recommendations that there is a need for 'balanced development' with local community provision developed alongside facilities for tourists and coordinated provision and policy should be heeded. This seems particularly relevant in light of an example from the legacy of the Sydney 2000 Olympic Games whereby it was too expensive for the Australian swimming association to hold their national championships at the Olympic aquatics center and they had to find an alternative facility (Chalip, 2001).

Nonetheless, despite the bleak views we are left with in terms of a lack of coordination and cooperation at the level of policy and implementation, such a situation provides scholars in this area with much to study. For example, Beresford (1999), in addressing some of the key issues in developing and marketing sport tourism in the Yorkshire region points to several potential research opportunities including exploring ways in which an integrated promotion of sport tourism should include other sectors of tourism such as heritage, culture and the arts. Weed and Bull (1997) developed a Policy Area Matrix for Sport Tourism and recommended empirical verification of these conceptual suppositions. Marwick (2000), in a study of golf course development in Malta examined the different discourses among the various stakeholders involved and recommended that future research needs to address both the local and wider political economies to effectively understand such developments and their full practical and policy implications. Thus, the area of policy and implementation in sport tourism is wide open in terms of both practice and scholarship and it seems that little has changed in terms of the conclusions I made regarding this area in 1998.

Research and scholarship

Despite the growing maturity of research and scholarship in sport tourism, there are still inconsistencies evident in definitions and terminology. Should we use the term sport tourism or sports tourism, and does it make a difference? In the realm of sport studies which encompasses among others, such fields as sport sociology, sport psychology and sport management, it has generally been agreed over the years that the term sports (with the 's') refers to individual or a collection of sporting activities and as such tends to down play the wider social significance of engaging in sport. Alternatively, the term sport (without the 's') refers to the wider social institution of sport which encompasses not only sporting activities, but recognizes that sport has social significance in terms of politics, the economy, nationalism, health, education, socialization, perpetuating patterns of inequality, and so forth. Thus, in line with scholars in sport studies I would recommend using the term sport tourism to encompass a wider analysis of sport as a social institution rather than the micro view of individual sports (see Parkhouse, 1991: p. 4). By adopting the macro term sport, we can more readily address such questions as "what makes sport tourism unique from other forms of tourism?" The answer to this is sport. Sport, as any introductory text in sport sociology will explain is a major social institution in most countries of the world with a role to play in the global economy, international relations, patriotism, entertainment, and now travel (e.g. Coakley, 1990).

In my 1998 article I devoted several pages to examining the various definitions of sport, tourism and sport tourism that have been used over the years (Gibson, 1998a: pp. 46–49). I recommended the use of the following definition of sport tourism:

> Leisure-based travel that takes individuals temporarily outside of their home communities to participate in physical activities, to watch physical activities, or to venerate attractions associated with physical activities.
>
> (Gibson, 1998a: p. 49)

This conceptualization of sport tourism as three distinct behavioral sets: a) travel to take part; b) travel to watch; and c) travel to venerate, worship or celebrate sport have guided my work in the area. My three categories of sport tourism stand in contrast to other scholars who tend to distinguish two types of sport tourism participating and watching (e.g., Hall, 1992; Hinch and Higham, 2001; Standeven and De Knop, 1999). As such, I think this debate provides ample opportunities for discussion and empirical verification, however, I would like to suggest that future studies in these areas are guided by theoretical paradigms, some of which already exist and have yet to be investigated fully. For example, Hall (1992) identified two categories of sport tourism: a) travel to participate and b) travel to observe. Underlying these categories he suggested the use of a two dimensional framework within which to examine these behaviors: a) level of activity (less active to more active), and b) motivation (level of competition: non competitive to competitive). In discussing sport tourists who travel to participate, he recommended the use of Stebbins' (1979; 1992) model of serious leisure to understand the levels of participation. I would also suggest that the model of serious leisure provides us with insights regarding sport tourists who watch as well (Gibson et al., 2001; Jones, 2000). With regards to the motivational construct, Hall recommended drawing upon classic work in tourism studies such as push and pull factors (Dann, 1977; Crompton, 1979) to understand the motives underpinning the behaviors of sport tourists, Similarly, Standeven and De Knop (1999) proffered a multidimensional model of sport tourism distinguishing sport as a cultural experience of physical activity and tourism as a cultural experience of place. They draw upon Heywood and Kew's (Haywood, 1994) model of sport and suggest that sport tourists not only differ in terms of active or passive participation, but also in the degree to which the sport or the tourist experience dominates their travels.

Hinch and Higham (2001: p. 47) critiqued Standeven and De Knop's definition of sport tourism suggesting "it tends to treat each sport as a homogenous entity even though many internal variations may exist within a sport". Indeed, they argued that a problem with existing definitions of sport tourism in general is that they do not adequately delineate the term sport. Drawing upon Loy's (1968) and McPherson et al.'s (1989) classic definitions of sport, they conceptualize sport tourism around the spatial, temporal and activity components of tourism and combine these with the rule-based nature of sport, the idea of a continuum of competition related to physical prowess, and the ludic qualities of sport. In advocating the use of their definition of sport tourism, Hinch and Higham suggested that it is possible examine various patterns of participation in sport by tourists including competitive and recreational, nature-based and indoor. They propose further that Leiper's (1990) attractions framework may serve to guide future research in sport tourism and I agree that this proffers a promising avenue for future research. Indeed, I commend Hinch and Higham for their thought provoking discussion and like them I would suggest that the challenge is now to conduct future studies guided by these theoretical suppositions. It is this theme that I would like to explore now as we take a look at trends in research and scholarship in sport tourism over the past three years.

Active sport tourism

De Knop's (1987; 1990) seminal work in active sport tourism identified three types of activity holiday: a) the pure sport holiday, b) the incidental sport holiday, and c) the private sporting holiday. Much of the early work investigating active sport tourism which largely followed De Knop's work (Glyptis, 1982; 1991; Glyptis and Jackson, 1993; Redmond, 1990; 1991) tended to adopt a European perspective in terms of research subject and audience. The notable exceptions to this trend were Nogowa, Yamaguchi and Hagi's (1996) work in Japan and my work with Yiannakis, and later Attic, in the US (Gibson and Yiannakis, 1992; 1994; Gibson, Attic, and Yiannakis, 1998). Since, 1998, Gilbert and Hudson (2000), Hudson (2000) and Williams and Fidgeon (2000) have published work looking at skiing, largely from a constraints framework (Crawford, Jackson and Godbey, 1991); Pitts (1999) examined the experiences of gay and lesbian sport tourists at the Gay Games; Ritchie (1998) investigated bicycle tourism in New Zealand using a performance-importance analysis to identify issues of concern for planning and management; and Bentley, Paige and Laird (2000) examined the risks associated with participating in adventure tourism activities in New Zealand. Thus, in geographical terms the focus of active sport tourism as a topic of research has expanded, however, there is still much that remains to be done. As Beresford (1999) and Standeven and De Knop (1999) caution us, we still need to remember that while the numbers of tourists engaging in active sport tourism are increasing, this is still a minority of the traveling population, ranging somewhere between 10 and 20–30 percent. However, for people who participate in active sport tourism, such vacations may be a meaningful part of their lives (Gibson *et al.*, 1998; Green and Chalip, 1998a; Nogowa *et al.*, 1996). Moreover, we also need to be cognizant of the environmental impacts of participation in sports such as golf (Pleumarom, 1992) and skiing (Hudson, 1995; Buckley, Pickering, and Warnken, 2000).

In terms of making recommendations for future research into active sport tourism, I would argue that we need to move beyond profiling the active sport tourist into explanations of participation or non-participation. In doing this we need to integrate concepts from the wider fields of leisure, tourism and sport studies to help us address and understand the influences of, for example, gender (leisure studies, sport sociology and tourism studies); disability (disability studies, therapeutic recreation, and sociology of sport); social class (leisure studies, sport sociology and tourism studies), race (leisure studies and sport sociology) and life course (leisure studies, sport sociology and tourism studies). We also need to understand the motivation and meaning of participation for active sport tourists and the role it plays in their, overall lives (leisure studies and tourism studies). There is also a need to ground future studies in conceptual models that have been used previously in sport tourism work. For example, Bull and Weed (1999) used Glyptis' (1982) typology of five markets for sport vacations (sports training; activity holidays; up market sports holidays; sport opportunities on general holidays; and spectator events) to examine sport tourism development in Malta. They recommended that future work needs to investigate, among other topics, commitment levels among sport tourists. One way to do this might be as Hall (1992) suggested using Stebbins' (1979; 1992) model of serious leisure to gain insights about active sport tourists. Another approach which Richards (1996) used to examine British skiers was Gratton's (1990) concept of skilled consumption. Similarly, a model which has been used extensively by US researchers in outdoor recreation has been Bryan's (1977; 1979) concept of recreational specialization.

As mentioned previously, an approach adopted to understand patterns of participation and non participation in skiing has been to use Crawford, Jackson and Godbey's (1991) hierarchical model of constraints. Williams and Lattey (1994) and more recently Gilbert and Hudson (2000) and Hudson (2000) found that women perceived skiing as dangerous and required too much athleticism, whereas, men were more concerned about crowding and lack of snow. Similarly, Williams and Fidgeon (2000) found that the image of non-skiers of the sport was pain, injury, risk and cost. They recommended future studies draw upon concepts from both sport and tourism to understand skiers and non-skiers behaviors' further. I would also caution future work using the constraints model to be aware of the critiques of this paradigm (e.g. Henderson, 1991; Samdahl and Jekubovich, 1997; Shaw, 1994) about the gendered nature of the constraints model and the fact that socio-structural influences may be more powerful than intra, inter and structural constraints (Shaw, Bonen, and McCabe, 1991) in explaining behavior.

Event sport tourism

The overwhelming attention in sport tourism research over the past three years continues to be on event based sport tourism, especially on hallmark events such as the Olympic Games or in the US on professional sports, despite the fact that studies have found that hosting such sports events have mixed results for a community (Brown, 2000, 2001; Horne, 2000; Ritchie, 1999). In the US, studies have shown that as many as 70 percent of spectators come from the immediate metropolitan area (Crompton, 1995; Stevens and Wootton, 1997) leading to questions as to whether professional sports actually constitute sport tourism despite the rhetoric of the franchise owners and politicians who maintain that building new stadia and hosting a team will result in economic development for the region (Stevens and Wootton, 1997). In terms of the economic impact of event sport tourism, the debates in the literature continue as to how best to measure it (Gratton, Dobson, and Shibli, 2000). Recent work by members of the Cooperative Research Centre for Sustainable Tourism in Australia (CRC) in regards to their multi-year project investigating various aspects of the 2000 Sydney Olympics suggests that rather than emphasizing economic impact that a cost-benefit analysis is more appropriate (Chalip and Green, 2001), Moreover, some of the preliminary lessons learned from the Olympics have been not to focus on the impacts of an event, but to use strategic leveraging with the aim of maximizing the effects. Some of the other work to come out of the CRC research projects, thus far, have increased our understanding of the role that volunteers play in enabling communities to host both mega or small scale sport tourism events (Green and Chalip, 1998b) Academic attention has also been focused over the last three years on a number of other impending events such as the America's Cup in New Zealand (Obrams and Brons, 1999).

Work adopting a critical analysis of event sport tourism has also continued, Hiller (1998) advocated the use of a linkage model which necessitates a longitudinal approach to conduct a comprehensive assessment of hallmark events, with a particular focus on issues of displacement in the surrounding communities. Similarly, Olds (1998) focused on community level action in three Canadian cities, Vancouver, Calgary and Toronto, when faced with the potential impacts on housing of hosting a mega event in their city. Indeed, in line with earlier work (Hall and Hodges, 1996; Whitson and McIntosh, 1993) there is still a need to critically examine what Roche (1994; p. 1) called "short-term events with long-term consequences" adopting a sociological analysis to examine the production, politics and planning of hallmark events. Indeed, Hall (1993) suggested that "the question of why and for who are these events held" should be a central question for a critical analysis of event sport tourism. Indeed, the overemphasis on hallmark events and questions as to who benefits from such events has led a growing call to focus on small-scale event sport tourism (Higham, 1999). Investigations into small scale sport tourism are few and far between, yet past research points to the psychic income for the community hosting such an event (Garnham, 1996), the benefits to the participants of such events (Green and Chalip, 1998 a), and the visibility of the city or town (Ritchie, 1999; Weed, 1999), as well of course the economic benefits. Consistent with my recommendations for future research in active sport tourism, I will reemphasize the need to ground future work in theoretical paradigms which help the researcher explain the phenomenon under investigation as well as link their particular study to the wider body of knowledge in not only sport tourism, but leisure, tourism and sport studies.

Nostalgia sport tourism

At the 1988 LSA conference, Gerry Redmond spoke of a type of sport tourism which involves visiting sports halls of fame or taking sports themed vacations on cruise ships or playing alongside top sport stars at fantasy camps. Over the years, Redmond remains one of the few scholars to investigate the sport tourism associated with sports museums (Lewis and Redmond, 1974; Redmond, 1973). He writes of the "the ultimate *raison d'être* for a sports hail of fame, like the ancient Greek statuary, is the glorification of sporting heritage" (Redmond, 1973: p. 42). The motivations of worship and heritage which appear to underlie this form of sport tourism led me to use the term nostalgia sport tourism to describe it (Gibson, 1998 a and b). In subsequent readings I came across a special issue of the *Sociology of Sport Journal* (1991; vol. 8, no. 3) devoted to exploring the topic of nostalgia in sport including an article by Eldon Snyder in which he explored nostalgia and sports halls of fame (Snyder, 1991) which confirms somewhat my original conceptualization of this type of sport tourism as characterized by nostalgia.

At present, nostalgia sport tourism has been a relatively underdeveloped area of study. Gammon (2001) explored the relationship between sport tourism and nostalgia with particular reference to the sports fantasy camp. Grounding his analysis in the broader discussion of nostalgia in postmodern life (Davis, 1979; Fowler, 1992) and tourism (Dann, 1994), Gammon suggested, "fantasy camps provide both the opportunity to relive the past and the propensity to rewrite it" (Gammon, 2001: p. 6). This paper raises many potential research avenues such as why have fantasy sports camps become so popular in the last decades of the twentieth century? What motivates the attendees of such camps? Does nostalgia play a major role in their motivations? What wider social conditions have encouraged the pervasiveness of nostalgia in our everyday lives?

In teaching about nostalgia sport tourism I have drawn upon two works in particular which may suggest ways forward for future research in this area. Like, Gammon, I think that studies of nostalgia and heritage tourism (Dann, 1994) may hold potential for us in furthering our understanding of nostalgia sport tourism. Dann writes: "[t]oday a great deal of time and energy is dedicated to looking backwards, toward capturing a past which, in many ways is considered superior to the chaotic present and the dreaded future" (Dann, 1994: p. 55). It seems that the past has become more highly valued than the present or the future, in fact Urry (1990: p. 107) writes of a postmodern museum culture in which almost anything can be regarded as an object of curiosity. I also draw upon John Bales' book *Sports Geography* particularly his ideas about mystique, place identity and place attachment.

Bale (1988: p. 120) writes that some sports facilities "can develop overtime, a sufficient mystique to become tourist attractions in their own right" With tours of former and future Olympic stadia and other top sports arenas around the world such as Yankee Stadium in New York and Wembley Stadium in London (before it was rebuilt) have been popular tourist attractions for years and perhaps some of Bales' thoughts about the mystique that accompanies these "shrines" might develop our understanding of this type of sport tourism. Bale also writes of two other concepts which might also be of use to us in understanding nostalgia sport tourism: a) place attachment and sport: "sport has become perhaps the main medium of collective identification in an era when bonding is more frequently the result of achievement" (Bale, 1988: p. 14); and b) place pride which is often generated by success in sport resulting in psychic income for the community and frequently characterized by a "masculine celebration of community" (Bale, 1988: p. 18). Some of the tours shaped around football teams such as Manchester United would fit under this category, coupled with understanding the collective identity of fans who frequently spend a lot of their time and money traveling to support their teams (Gibson, *et al.*, 2001; Jones, 2000). Indeed, in my work on American college football fans, many of them describe their journeys to the games as pilgrimages and they use the term Mecca to describe the town and the stadium. I have always thought that Turner's (1969) conceptualization of ritual process and liminoid space, used in wider tourism studies (e.g. Gottlieb, 1982; Graburn, 1983; Lett, 1983; Wagner, 1977) might provide some insights into sport tourism of this sort, or as MacCannell (1976) has done, apply a Durkheimian analysis to tourism behavior and examine the pilgrimage-like aspects of nostalgia sport tourism.

Understanding the meanings and motivations associated with this sort of tourism is an area of study that holds much potential for unique work in the area of nostalgia sport tourism. However, as with all of my recommendations regarding future research in sport tourism, it is important to ground such work in theoretical models which can help scholars interpret their findings and also link their work to the wider body of knowledge in leisure, sport and tourism studies. As I have noted in my discussion on nostalgia sport tourism, John Bale's work in sport geography and the work in nostalgia and heritage in the wider study of tourism (Dann, 1994; Davis, 1979; Fowler, 1992) may be useful starting points.

Education and curricular considerations

In fall 1999, Swart (2000) surveyed academics via electronic list serves about the existence of sport tourism curricula at their institutions. Twenty-eight academics responded from around the world including the UK, USA, Belgium, Australia, South Korea and Canada. She found that 84 sport tourism courses were being offered. Seventy-eight percent of the respondents reported that sport tourism was taught within existing course modules.

Forty percent reported that their institutions offered specialist degrees in sport tourism. Swart found that a range of departments within institutions offering sport tourism content included departments of physical education, tourism, hospitality, sport management, and recreation. However, her overall conclusion mirrors my analysis from 1998: "[i]t is recommended that in order provide students with this opportunity [sport tourism], the relevant academic departments within institutions should consider joint initiatives" (Swart, 2000). It appears that while there has been some improvement since 1998 in terms of more courses being offered (Swart found that most sport tourism courses were instituted between 1996 and 1999), more specialist texts were published and there was more awareness among academics in related fields (sport, tourism, recreation etc.), there was still work to be done, especially in terms of collaboration across departments and cross listing of course (module) offerings to avoid unnecessary repetition within institutions. Unfortunately, some of the lack of cooperation may be systemic. In the highly competitive environment of higher education, enrollment of students, research funding, and even the number of publications attributed to individual faculty may increasingly preclude interdisciplinary work. The result of this however, will only serve to retard the growth of sport tourism as an area of study and a subject for degree specialization around the world.

Conclusion

So the question raised at the start of this paper, is sport tourism at a crossroads needs to be a readdressed. Gartner (1996: p. 317) prophesized that "sport tourism will probably develop its own cadre of researchers . . ." This appears to be true. There are researchers, especially since the last years of the 1990s, who have specialized in the area. As I discussed earlier, it is crucial that we standardize terminology and develop a conceptual base as the body of knowledge pertaining to sport tourism evolves. As Williams and Fidgeon (2001: p. 379) observe, "traditionally the two literatures viz sport and tourism have tended to be quite distinct. Each has claimed its own ideas, concepts and abstract theories." If we are at a crossroads, the time has come now to bring the two bodies of knowledge together as they have much to offer future work in the area. In 1997, Pigeassou argued "[s]port tourism finds itself in a constitutional phase of its true identity – the absence of globalized information of sports tourism is an obstacle in the analysis of this phenomenon and its delimitation" (Pigeassou, 1997: p. 29). I would argue that four years later, this situation is still somewhat true, but it is improving, although there are still critics who do not understand that sport tourism is more than and distinct from event management (Gammon and Robinson, 1997). Although, we are still hampered by our access to non-English language research and publications as work is being conducted in a range of countries including France, Germany and Japan. Unfortunately, if such works are not accessible in English, they tend to go unnoticed by English speaking scholars. Nonetheless, I would argue that there is no excuse among the English-speaking scholars not to adopt a global perspective in their work. I still see traces of the bias that I wrote about in 1998, whereby sport tourism scholars and practitioners in the US have a tendency to concentrate on event sport tourism, while a European focus on sport tourism has been on the active form, although this is changing. There is also a need to start looking at the effects of globalization on sport tourism. In the wider fields of sport sociology (Maguire, 1994), leisure studies (Gratton and Kokolakadis, 1997), sport management (Silk and Amis, 2000), and tourism studies (Richards, 2001) globalization has become increasingly a research focus and holds promise for work in sport tourism.

Thus, in summary I would suggest that sport tourism is at a crossroads, and now is the time to adopt two general strategies as we move forward into the next phase of practice, research and education in the area. I recommend that we still focus on cooperation at all levels in policy and practice, research and scholarship, and education and curricula decisions. I would also suggest, in line with the theme, which has been running through this paper, that we need to build a body of knowledge, which is conceptually grounded. A starting point would be to draw upon existing frameworks in leisure, sport and tourism studies as well as other pertinent disciplines. We need to be aware of the growing number of sport tourism scholars and take heed of their work by conducting comprehensive literature reviews. One way of helping us to complete this charge would be to use the key word sport tourism in our abstracts or key word identifiers so that locating new work is easier. Another way forward, is to ensure that the sport tourism scholar community has the opportunity to come together at conferences thereby raising awareness not only of each other, but among other academics in the field who may not have been cognizant of what sport tourism is and who is working in the area. The stage has been set for the next phase in the education, practice and understanding of sport tourism. It will be interesting to see which directions are taken.

References

Bale, J. (1988) *Sports Geography*, E & FN Spon, London.

Bentley, T., Page, S. and Laird, I. (2000) Safety in New Zealand's adventure tourism industry: The client accident experience of adventure tourism operators. *Journal of Travel Medicine*, 7 (5), 239–245.

Beresford, S. (1999) The sport–tourism link in the Yorkshire region, in *Proceedings of a SPRIG seminar exploring sports tourism* (edited by M. Scarrot), University of Sheffield, April 15, pp. 29–37.

British Tourism Authority Sports Tourism Initiative. www.visitbritain.com/sport accessed September 12, 2001.

Brown, G. (2000) Emerging issues in Olympic sponsorship: implications for host cities. *Sport Management Review*, 3 (7), 1–92.

Brown, G. (2001) Sydney 2000: An invitation to the world. *Olympic Review*, 27 (37), 15–29.

Bryan, H. (1977) Leisure value systems and recreational specialization: The case of trout fishermen. *Journal of Leisure Research*, 9, 174–187.

Bryan, H. (1979) *Conflict in the great outdoors: Toward understanding and managing for diverse sportsmen preferences*, Birmingham Publishing Company, Birmingham, AL.

Bull, C. and Weed, M. (1999) Niche markets and small island tourism: The development of sports tourism in Malta. *Managing Leisure*, 4 (3), 142–155.

Buckley, R., Pickering, C. and Warnken, J. (2000) Environmental management for Alpine tourism and resorts in Australia, in *Tourism and Development in Mountain Regions* (edited by P. Godde, M. Price and F. Zimmermann), CAB International, Wallingford, pp. 27–45.

Burgan, B. and Mules, T. (1992) Economic impact of sporting events. *Annals of Tourism Research*, 19, 700–710.

Chalip, L. (2001) *Leveraging the Sydney Olympics to optimize tourism benefits*. Paper presented at the International Conference on the Economic Impact of Sports, Athens, Greece, February 2001.

Chalip, L. and Green, B.C. (2001) Leveraging large sports events for tourism: Lessons learned from the Sydney Olympics. Supplemental proceedings of the Travel and Tourism Research Association 32nd Annual Conference, Fort Myers, FL, June 10–13, 2001.

Coakley, 3. (1990) *Sport in society: Issues and controversies*, Times Mirror/Mosby, Boston.

Crawford, D., Jackson, E. and Godbey, G. (1991) A hierarchical model of leisure constraints. *Leisure Sciences*, 13, 309–320.

Crompton, J. (1979) Motivations for pleasure vacation. *Annals of Tourism Research*, 6, 408–424.

Crompton, J. (1995) Economic impact analysis of sports facilities and events: Eleven sources of misapplication. *Journal of Sport Management*, 9, 14–35.

Dann, G. (1977). Anomie, ego-enhancement and tourism. *Annals of Tourism Research*, 4, 184–194.

Dann, G. (1994) Tourism: The nostalgia industry of the future, in *Global Tourism: The Next Decade* (edited by W. Theobold), Butterworth-Heinemann, Oxford, pp. 56–67.

Davis, F. (1979) *Yearning for Yesterday. A Sociology of Nostalgia*, Free Press, New York.

De Knop, P. (1987) Some thoughts on the influence of sport tourism, in *Proceedings of The international seminar and Workshop on outdoor education, recreation and sport tourism*, Wingate Institute for Physical Education and Sport, Netanya, Israel, pp. 38–45.

De Knop, P. (1990) Sport for all and active tourism. *World Leisure and Recreation*, 32, 30–36.

Delpy, L. (1998) An overview of sport tourism: Building towards a dimensional framework. *Journal of Vacation Marketing*, 4, 23–38.

Foley, M. and Reid, G. (1998) Activities, holidays and activity holidays in Scotland, in *Tourism and visitor attractions: Leisure, culture and commerce* (edited by N. Ravenscroft, D. Phillips, and M. Bennett), vol. 61, LSA Publications, Eastbourne, pp. 61–73.

Fowler, P. (1992) *The Past in contemporary society: Then and now*, Routledge, London.

Gammon, S. and Robinson, T. (1997) Sport and tourism: A conceptual framework. *Journal of Sports Tourism*, 4 (3), 824.

Gammon, S. (2001) *Fantasy, nostalgia and the pursuit of what never was – but what should have been*. Paper presented at the Leisure Studies Association Conference Journeys in Leisure: Current and Future Alliances, University of Luton, July 17–19.

Garnham, B. (1996) Ranfurly Shield Rugby: An investigation into the impacts of a sporting event on a provincial city, the case of New Plymouth, Taranaki, New Zealand. *Festival Management and Event Tourism*, 4, 145–149.

Gartner, W. (1996) *Tourism development: Principles, processes and policies*, Van Nostrand Reinhold, New York.

Gibson, H. (1998a) Sport tourism: A critical analysis of research. *Sport Management Review*, 1, 45–76.

Gibson, H. (1998b) Active sport tourism: Who participates? *Leisure Studies*, 17 (2), 155–170.

Gibson, H. (1997) *Sport tourism for all?* Presented at the Leisure Studies Association Conference, Roehampton Institute, London, UK, September 9–11.

Gibson, H. and Yiannakis, A. (1992) *Some correlates of the sport lover (tourist): A life course perspective*. Presented at the North American Society for the Sociology of Sport Conference, Toledo, OH, November 4–7, 1992.

Gibson, H. and Yiannakis, A. (1994) *Some characteristics of sport tourists: A life span perspective*. Paper presented at the North American Society for the Sociology of Sport Conference, Savannah, GA, November 12, 1994.

Gibson, H., Attle, S. and Yiannakis, A. (1998). Segmenting the sport tourist market: A life-span perspective. *Journal of Vacation Marketing*, 4, 52–64.

Gibson, H., Holdnak, A., Willming, C., King, M., Patterson, T. and Copp, C. (2001) *"We're Gators . . . not just a Gator fan:" Serious leisure, social identity, and University of Florida football*. Paper presented at the National Recreation and Parks Association Congress, Denver, CO, October 3–6.

Gilbert, D. and Hudson, S. (2000) Tourism demand constraints on skiing participation. *Annals of Tourism Research*, 27 (4), 906–925.

Glyptis, S. (1982) *Sport and tourism in Western Europe*, British Travel Educational Trust, London.

Glyptis, S. (1991) Sport and tourism, in *Progress in Tourism, Recreation and Hospitality Management*, Vol. 3 (edited by C. Cooper), Belhaven Press, London, pp. 165–183.

Glyptis, S. and Jackson, G. (1993) *Sport and tourism – Mutual benefits and future prospects*. Paper presented at Leisure in Different Worlds, the Third International Conference of the Leisure Studies Association, Loughborough University, UK, July 14–18.

Gottlieb, A. (1982) American's vacations. *Annals of Tourism Research*, 9, 164–187.

Graburn, N.H.H. (1983) The anthropology of tourism. *Annals of Tourism Research*, 10 (1), 9–33.

Gratton, C., (1990) *Consumer behavior in tourism: A psycho-economic approach*. Paper presented at the Tourism Research into the 1990s Conference, Durham, UK, December, 1990.

Gratton, C., Dobson, N. and Shibli, S. (2000) The economic importance of major sports events: A case study of six events. *Managing Leisure*, 5 (1) 17–28.

Gratton, C. and Kokolakadis, T. (1997) The leisure revolution. *Leisure Management*, 17 (6), 36–39.

Green, B. and Chalip, L. (1998a) Sport tourism as the celebration of subculture. *Annals of Tourism Research*, 25, 275–292.

Green, C., and Chalip, L. (1998b). Sport volunteers: Research agenda and application. *Sport Marketing Quarterly*, 7 (2), 14–23.

Hall, C. (1992) Adventure, sport and health tourism in *Special Interest Tourism* (edited by B. Weiler and C.M. Hall), Belhaven Press, London, pp. 141–158.

Hall, C. (1993) The politics of leisure: An analysis of spectacles and mega-events, in *Leisure and Tourism: Social and Environmental Changes* (edited by A.J. Veal, P. Johnson, and G. Cushman), World Leisure and Recreation Association, University Technology, Sydney, pp. 620–629.

Hall, C. and Hodges, J. (1996) The party's great, but what about the hangover? The housing and social impacts of mega-events with special reference to the 2000 Sydney Olympics. *Festival Management and Event Tourism*, 4, 13–20.

Haywood, L. (1994) Community sports and physical recreation, in *Community Leisure and Recreation* (edited by C. Haywood), Butterworth-Heinemann, Oxford, pp. 111–143.

Henderson, K. (1991) The contribution of feminism to an understanding of leisure constraints. *Journal of Leisure Research*, 23, 363–377.

Hinch, T. and Higham, J. (2001) Sport tourism: A framework for research. *International Journal of Tourism Research*, 3, 45–58.

Higham, J. (1999) Commentary – sport as an avenue of tourism development: An analysis of the positive and negative impacts of sport tourism. *Current Issues in Tourism*, 2 (1), 82–90.

Hiller, H. (1998) Assessing the impact of mega-events: A linkage model. *Current Issues in Tourism*, 1 (1), 47–57.

Horne, W. (2000) Municipal economic development via hallmark tourist events. *Journal of Tourism Studies*, 11 (1), 30–35.

Hudson, S. (1995) *The 'greening' of ski resorts: A necessity for sustainable tourism, or a marketing opportunity for skiing comminutes.* Paper presented at the Leisure, Sport and Education – the Interfaces Annual Conference for the Leisure Studies Association, September 12–14.

Hudson, S. (2000) The segmentation of potential tourists: Constraint differences between men and women. *Journal of Travel Research*, 38 (4), 363–369.

Jackson, G. and Reeves, M. (1996) *Conceptualizing the sports-tourism relationship: A case study approach.* Paper presented at the LSA/VVS 1996 Conference, Accelerating Leisure? Leisure, Time and Space in a Transitory Society, Wageningen, Netherlands, September 14, 1996.

Jones, I. (2000) A model of serious leisure identification: the case of football fandom. *Leisure Studies*, 19, 283–298.

Leiper, N. (1990) Tourist attraction systems. *Annals of Tourism Research*, 17 (2), 367–384.

Lett, J. (1983) Ludic and liminoid aspects of charter yacht tourism in the Caribbean. *Annals of Tourism Research*, 10, 35–56.

Loy, J. (1968) The nature of sport: A definitional effort. *Quest*, 10, 1–15.

Lewis, G. and Redmond, G. (1974) *Sporting heritage: A guide to halls of Fame, special collections, and museums in the US and Canada*, A.S. Barnes, New York.

MacCannell, D. (1976) *The tourist: A new theory of the leisure class*, Schocken Books, New York.

Maguire, J. (1994) Sport, identity politics, and globalization: Diminishing contrasts and increasing varieties. *Sociology of Sport Journal*, 11 (4), 398–427.

Marwick, M. (2000) Golf tourism development, stakeholders, differing discourses and alternative agendas: The case of Malta. *Tourism Management*, 21, 515–524.

McFee, G. (1988) *The Olympic games as tourist event: An American in Athens, 1896.* Paper presented at the Leisure Studies Association Second International Conference, Leisure, Labour and Lifestyles: International Comparisons, Brighton, UK.

McPherson, B., Curtis, J., and Loy, J. (1989) *The social significance of sport*, Human Kinetics, Champaign, IL.

Nogawa, H., Yamguchi, Y., and Hagi, Y. (1996) An empirical research study on Japanese sport tourism in sport-for-all events: Case studies of a single-night event and a multiple-night event. *Journal of Travel Research*, 35, 46–54.

Obrams, M., and Brons, A. (1999) Potential impacts of a major sport/tourism event: The America's Cup 2000, Auckland, New Zealand. *Visions in Leisure and Business*, 18 (1), 14–28.

Olds, K. (1998) Urban mega-events, evictions and housing rights: The Canadian case. *Current Issues in Tourism*, 1 (1), 246.

Parkhouse, B. (1991) *The management of sport: Its foundation and application.* Mosby Year Books, Boston.

Pigeasson, C. (1997) Sport and tourism: The emergence of sport into the offer of tourism. Between passion and reason. An overview of the French situation and perspectives. *Journal of Sports Tourism*, 4, 20–36.

Pitts, B. (1999) Sports tourism and niche markets: Identification and analysis of the growing lesbian and gay sports tourism industry. *Journal of Vacation Marketing*, 5 (1), 31–50.

Pleumarom, A. (1992) Course and effect: Golf tourism in Thailand. *The Ecologist*, 22, 104–110.

Redmond, G. (1973) A plethora of shrines: Sport in the museum and hail of fame. *Quest*, 19, 41–48.

Redmond, G. (1988) *Points of increasing contact: Sport and tourism in the modern world.* Paper presented at the Second International Conference, Leisure, Labour, and Lifestyles: International Comparisons, Brighton, UK.

Redmond, G. (1991) Changing styles of sports tourism: Industry/consumer interactions in Canada, the USA and Europe, in *The tourism industry: An international analysis* (edited by M. Sinclair and M. Stabler), CAB International, Wallingford, pp. 107–120.

Richards, G. (1996). Skilled consumption and UK ski holidays. *Tourism Management*, 17, 25–34.

Richards, G. (2001) *Cultural attractions and European tourism*, CAB International, Publishing, Wallingford.

Ritchie, B. (1998) Bicycle tourism in the South Island of New Zealand: Planning and management issues. *Tourism Management*, 19 (6), 567–582.

Ritchie, J.R.B. (1999) Lessons learned, lessons learning: Insights from the Calgary and Salt Lake City Olympic Winter Games. *Visions in Leisure and Business*, 18 (1), 4–13.

Roche, M. (1994) Mega-events and urban policy. *Annals of Tourism Research*, 21, 1–19.

Samdahl, D. and Jekubovich, N. (1997) A critique of leisure constraints: Comparative analyses and understandings. *Journal of Leisure Research*, 29 (4), 430–452.

Shaw, S. (1994) Gender, leisure, and constraint: Towards a framework for the analysis of women's leisure. *Journal of Leisure Research*, 26, 8–22.

Shaw, S., Bonen, A. and McCabe, J. (1991) Do more constraints mean less leisure? Examining the relationship between constraints and participation. *Journal of Leisure Research*, 23, 286–300.

Silk, M. (2001) *Bangsa Malaysia: Global spectacle, mediated sport and the refurbishment of local identities*. Paper presented at the Leisure Studies Association Conference, Journeys in Leisure: Current and Future Alliances, University of Luton, July 17–19.

Silk, M. and Amis, J. (2000) Institutional pressures and the production of televised sport. *Journal of Sport Management*, 14 (4), 267–292.

Snyder, E. (1991) Sociology of nostalgia: Sports halls of fame and museums in America. *Sociology of Sport Journal*, 8 (3), 228–238.

Standeven, J. and Tomlinson, A. (1994) *Sport and tourism in South East England*, South East Council for Sport and Recreation, London.

Standeven, J. and De Knop, P. (1999) *Sport tourism*, Human Kinetics, Champaign, IL.

Stebbins, R. (1979) *Amateurs. On the margin between work and leisure*, Sage, Beverly Hills, CA.

Stebbins, R. (1992) *Amateurs, professionals, and serious leisure*, McGill Queen's University Press, Montreal.

Stevens, T. and Wootton, G. (1997) Sports stadia and arena: Realising their full potential. *Tourism Recreation Research*, 22 (2), 49–56.

Swart, K. (1998) Visions for South Africa sport tourism. *Visions in Leisure and Business*, 12 (2): 4–12.

Swart, K. (2000) An assessment of sport tourism curriculum offerings at academic institutions. *Journal of Sports Tourism*, 6 (1).

Travel Industry Association of America (TIA) (1999) *Profile of travelers who attend sports events*.

Turner, V. (1969) *The ritual process*, Aldine, Chicago, IL.

Urry, J. (1990) *The tourist gaze*, Sage, London.

Wagner, U. (1977) Out of time and place – Mass tourism and charter trips. *Ethnos*, 42, 38–52.

Weed, M. (1999) More than sports holidays: An overview of the sport tourism link, in *Proceedings of a SPRIG seminar exploring sports tourism* (edited by M. Scarrot), University of Sheffield, April 15, pp. 6–28.

Weed, M. (2001) Toward a model of cross-sectorial policy development in leisure: The case of sport and tourism. *Leisure Studies*, 20 (2), 125–142.

Weed, M. and Bull, C. (1996) *The search for a sport tourism policy network*. Paper presented at Free Time and Quality of Life for the 21st Century, World Congress of the World Leisure and Recreation Association, Cardiff, Wales, UK, July 15–19.

Weed, M. and Bull, C. (1997) Integrating sport and tourism: A review of regional policies in England. *Progress in Tourism and Hospitality Research*, 3, 129–148.

Whitson, D. and Macintosh, D. (1993). Becoming a world-class city: Hallmark events and sport franchises in the growth strategies of western Canadian cities. *Sociology of Sport Journal*, 10, 221–240.

Williams, P. and Lattey, C. (1994) Skiing constraints for women. *Journal of Travel Research*, 32, 21–25.

Williams, P. and Fidgeon, P. (2000) Addressing participation constraint: A case study of potential skiers. *Tourism Management*, 21, 379–393.

Chapter 3

Tom Hinch and James Higham

SPORT TOURISM
A framework for research

Introduction

O NE HAS ONLY TO LOOK at the scoreboard at most team sporting competitions to see reference to the fundamental tourism concepts of the hosts and visitors. The prominent position of these concepts within sport implies a travel dynamic that has until recently been largely ignored by scholars in both tourism and sport. Yet the affinity between sport and tourism has not been ignored by the travelling public nor by the vibrant industry that has emerged in response to this demand.

Until the 1990s, sport tended to be treated as a general or even accidental context for tourism research rather than as a central focus. For example, research associated with hallmark events such as the Olympic Games has added significantly to our understanding of the impacts of mega events but it has provided much less insight into the features that distinguish the nature of sport-based events from other types of events. A similar criticism can be made related to other areas of related research, such as outdoor recreation and health-based tourism. The purpose of this paper is therefore to conceptualize sport tourism by positioning sport as a central attraction within the activity dimension of tourism and then considering its relationship with the spatial and temporal dimensions of tourism.

Despite the benefits of an explicit focus on sport tourism, it should be appreciated that the conceptual boundaries that are articulated or implied in this article are in fact permeable and dynamic. The paper is not an attempt to position sport tourism as an isolated field of research but rather to capture the synergies associated with the treatment of spoil tourism within the broader realms of sport and tourism. It is meant to add to an emerging literature and to provide a unique perspective for productive research in this area. The paper therefore has been organized into three sections including: (i) clarification of the conceptual domain of sport tourism, (ii) articulation of the distinguishing features of sport as a tourist attraction based on Leiper's (1990) systems model of attractions, and (iii) the presentation of a research framework for the continued examination of sport-focused tourism.

The domain of sport tourism

As befits an emerging area of scholarly study, sport-tourism researchers have dedicated a substantial amount of their energy toward clarifying the conceptual foundations of this field. This section of the paper will review the key contributions of these individuals and will build on the foundation that they provided by considering the independent concepts of sport and tourism prior to focusing on their confluence. Like most social science concepts, there are no universally excepted definitions of sport or tourism that would make this exercise easy. Each concept is rather amorphous and a variety of definitions have been developed to address a broad range of needs. Despite the lack of definitional consensus, there are commonalities associated with each concept that help to clarify their relationship.

Current lines of inquiry

Although this subfield is still in its infancy, a number of important publications exist that explicitly focus on sport tourism. It is not the intent of the authors to duplicate these efforts but rather to focus on those aspects of the literature that are particularly, relevant to understanding the conceptual base of sport tourism.

Especially noteworthy advances in the study of sport tourism have included the proceedings of a 1987 conference on Outdoor Education, Recreation and Sport (Garmise, 1987), the establishment of an electronic journal titled the *Journal of Sport Tourism* in 1993, and seminal articles in other tourism journals such as *Progress in Tourism and Hospitality Research* (Glyptis, 1991; Weed and Bull, 1997a, b). The major contribution of these publications was to highlight the significance of sport to tourism and to legitimate it as an important focus for academic study.

A good example of this body of work was provided by Glyptis (1991), who drew attention to the fact that sport and tourism are 'treated by academics and practitioners alike as separate spheres of activity' (Glyptis, 1991: 165). She went on to identify the close behavioural relationship between sport and tourism participants but argued that this relationship was not reflected in journal publications, academic departments, learned societies or government agencies. Glyptis (1991) presented a compelling case for the integration of the two in terms of government policy, strategic planning, the development of facilities and services, urban planning and promotion.

This contribution stimulated further in-depth studies of sport tourism, although such studies remained the exception rather than the rule throughout the early 1990s. The most notable attempts to rectify this situation were undertaken by Kurtzman and Zauhar (1995) and later by Gammon and Robinson (1997), who developed early models of sport tourism.

Although these contributions provided valuable insights into the dynamic nature of sport tourism, they failed to harness the potential synergies of the field in a comprehensive manner. As a consequence, directions for future lines of inquiry are notably rare. The clearest call for a systematic approach to this subfield came from Kurtzman and Zauhar

(1995), who presented an agency report on the Sport Tourism International Council (STIC) in *Annals of Tourism Research* identifying the emergence of sport as a 'touristic endeavour' in the 1980s and 1990s. Since that point, special issues of *Tourism Recreation Research*. (Stevens and van den Broek, 1997) and *Vacation Marketing* (Delpy, 1997) have been devoted to the topic and have clearly attempted to be more systematic and integrative in their approach.

Gibson's (1998) comprehensive review of publications in this area highlights the connections between what on the surface is a very disparate literature. Not only does she provide a critical analysis of existing literature in this area, she articulates the need for better coordination among agencies at a political level, more multidisciplinary research approaches, and more cooperation between tourism and sport-centred units in academic settings. Further advances in this direction can be seen in the work of Standeven and De Knop (1999) and De Knop (1998). A series of frameworks are presented in their publications that highlight the interdependent relationship between sports and tourism, beginning with the basic premise that not only does sport influence tourism but that tourism influences sport. They then build on this starting point with a classification matrix based on key touristic and sport characteristics. The major contribution of this classification system is that sport tourism is recognised as offering 'a two-dimensional experience of physical activity tied to a particular setting' (Standeven and De Knop, 1999: 63). Furthermore, each of these dimensions is articulated in terms of its key components, thereby allowing a more in-depth analysis of the concept of sport tourism than has been generally been the case to date. A limitation, of their typology is that it tends to treat each sport as a homogeneous entity even though many internal variations may exist within a sport. Faulkner *et al.* (1998) avoid this limitation by classifying sports tourism in terms of motivational, behavioural and competitive dimensions. Each of these dimensions is presented as a continuum and individual sports are illustrated as fitting into a range rather than being represented as a single point on each continuum.

These attempts to articulate the relationships between the unique characteristics of tourism and the unique characteristics of sport are the key to scholarly advances in this field. By clarifying these relationships, more probing research questions can be asked and the findings of individual studies can be placed within the broader contexts of the field as a whole. In doing so, the potential synergies of the field are more likely to be captured.

The domain of tourism

Tourism definitions can be classified into those associated with the popular usage of the term (e.g. W.H. Smith/Collins, 1988), those used to facilitate statistical measurement (e.g. WTO, 1981), and those used to articulate its conceptual domain (e.g. Murphy, 1986). Although the last of these has the most direct relevance for this paper, all of the definitions tend to share key dimensions. The most prevalent of these is a spatial dimension. Tourism involves the 'travel of non-residents' (Murphy, 1985: 9). To be considered a tourist, individuals must leave and then eventually return to their home. Although the travel of an individual does not constitute tourism in and of itself, it is one of the necessary conditions. A variety of qualifiers have been placed on this dimension including a range of minimum travel distances, but the fundamental concept of travel is universal.

The second most common dimension involves the temporal characteristics associated with tourism. Central to this dimension is the requirement that the trip be characterized by a 'temporary stay away from home of at least one night' (Leiper, 1981: 74). Definitions developed for statistical purposes often distinguish between excursionists who visit a destination for less than 24 h and tourists who visit a destination for 24 h or more (WTO, 1981). Often, however, the term visitor is used to refer to both groups.

A third common dimension of tourism definitions concerns the purpose or the activities engaged in during travel and it is within this dimension that many subfields of tourism find their genesis (e.g. eco-tourism, urban tourism and heritage tourism). Of the three dimensions, this is perhaps the one characterized by the broadest range of views. For example, dictionary interpretations of tourists tend to focus on leisure pursuits as the primary travel activity (W.H. Smith/Collins, 1988), whereas definitions developed for statistical and academic purposes tend to include business activities as well (Murphy, 1985). Specific reference is made to sport in the tourism definition of the World Tourism Organisation (1981), which lists it as a subset of leisure activities.

The domain of sport

Defining sport has proven equally as difficult, but as in the case of tourism, common dimensions have emerged. The popular perception of sport is best reflected by the adage that sport is what is written about on the sport pages of daily newspapers (Bale, 1989). A typical dictionary definition of sport describes it as 'an individual or group activity pursued for exercise or pleasure, often taking a competitive form' (W.H. Smith/Collins, 1988).

Definitions arising from the realm of the sociology of sport are particularly insightful when combined with the concept of tourism. One of the most influential definitions of sport to emerge within this area is that of Loy et al. (1978), i.e. the game occurrence approach. From this perspective, sport is conceptualized as a subset of games, which in turn is a subset of play. Sport is described in terms of institutionalized games that require physical prowess. In a similar fashion McPherson et al. (1989: 15) have defined sport as 'a structured, goal-oriented, competitive, contest based, ludic physical activity'.

Sport is structured in the sense that sports are governed by rules that relate to space and time. These rules may be manifest in a variety of ways, including the dimensions of the playing area and the duration and pacing of the game or contest. They also tend to be more specific in formal variations of a sport, especially as the level of competition increases. In informal variations of a sport these rules are often very general.

Sport is also defined as being goal-oriented, competitive and contest-based. All three characteristics are closely related. Sport is goal-oriented in the sense that sporting situations usually involve an objective for achievement in relation to ability, competence, effort, degree of difficulty, mastery or performance. In most instances this goal orientation is extended to some degree of competition. At one extreme this competition is expressed in terms of winning or losing combatants. Alternatively, competition can be interpreted much less rigidly in terms of competing against individual standards, inanimate objects or the natural forces of nature. In the context of sport tourism, the latter interpretation of competition offers a much more inclusive concept that covers recreational sports, such as those commonly associated with outdoor pursuits It is also inclusive of the 'sport for all' concept of participation (e.g. Nogawa et al., 1996). Essentially, competition is probably best conceptualized as a continuum that ranges from recreational to elite both between and within sports. Closely associated with competition is the contest-based nature of sport in which outcomes are determined by a combination of physical prowess, game strategy and, to a lesser degree, chance. Physical prowess consists of physical speed, stamina, strength, accuracy and coordination and when viewed in these terms, across the whole competition continuum, it is one of the most consistent criterion used to define sport.

The final aspect of sport that is highlighted in the definition is its ludic nature, a term which is derived from the Latin word *ludus*, meaning play or game. Sport is, therefore, rooted in, although not exclusive to play and games. This derivation carries with it the ideas of 'uncertainty of outcome' and 'sanctioned display'. Uncertain outcomes create excitement and are consistent with the concept of play. Sanctioned display allows for the demonstration of physical prowess and broadens the realm of sport involvement to spectatorship as well as direct athletic participation.

The confluence of sport and tourism

Clearly the concepts of tourism and sport are related and overlap. Sport is an important activity within tourism and tourism is a fundamental characteristic of sport. The specific confluence of the two concepts varies as to the perspectives of those dealing with the topic and the definitions that they adopt. Attempts to articulate the domain of sport tourism have also resulted in a proliferation of definitions (Table 3.1). These definitions tend to be written along the same lines as those presented for tourism in that they often include activity, spatial and temporal dimensions. Sport is generally positioned as the primary travel activity, although Gammon and Robinson (1997) make a distinction between sport tourists and tourism sports. The latter recognizes sport as a secondary activity while travelling. Most definitions include spectators as well as athletes and recreational as well as elite competition. They also tend to include explicit requirements for travel away from the home environment along with an implicit, if not explicit, temporal dimension that suggests that the trip is temporary and that the traveller will return home within a designated time. The temporal dimension is usually inclusive of day visitors as well as those that stay overnight. Somewhat surprisingly, the major limitation of existing definitions is that the concept of sport is rather vague. In an attempt to capture the strengths and address the stated limitations of these definitions in this paper, sport tourism is defined as: *sport-based travel away from the home environment for a limited time, where sport is characterized by unique rule sets, competition related to physical prowess, and a playful nature.*

This definition parallels the underlying structure of most tourism definitions in terms of their spatial, temporal and activity dimensions with the difference being that the activity dimension is specified as sport. Sport is recognized as a significant travel activity whether it is a primary or secondary feature of the trip. It is seen to be an important factor in many decisions to travel, to often feature prominently in the travel experience, and to often be an important consideration in the visitor's assessment of the travel experience.

Sport tourism is further clarified by drawing on the previous discussion of the domain of sport. First, each sport has its own set of rules that provide characteristic spatial and temporal structures. Second, competition related to physical prowess is a consolidation of what McPherson *et al.* (1989) described as the goal-orientation, competition and contest-based aspects of sport. It is used here in a broad sense to indicate a continuum of competition

Table 3.1 Selected definitions related to sport tourism

Dimension	Definition and source
Sport tourism	— Travel for non-commercial reasons to participate or observe sporting activities away front the home range (Hall, 1992a: 194)
	— An expression of a pattern of behaviour of people during certain periods of leisure time — such as vacation time, which is done partly in specially attractive natural settings and partly in artificial sports and physical recreation facilities in the outdoors (Ruskin, 1987: 26)
	— Holidays involving sporting, activity either as a spectator or participant (Weed and Bull, 1997b: 5)
	— Leisure-based travel that takes individuals temporarily outside of their home communities to participate in physical activities, to watch physical activities or to venerate attractions associated with physical activity (Gibson, 1998: 49)
	— All forms of active and passive involvement in sporting activity, participated in casually or in an organized way for noncommercial or business/commercial reasons, that necessitate travel away from home and work locality (Standeven and De Knop, 1999: 12)
Sport tourist	— A temporary visitor staying at least 24 h in the event area and whose primare purpose is to participate in a sports event with the area being a secondary attraction (Nogawa *et al.*, 1996: 46)
	— Individuals and/or groups of people who actively or passively participate in competitive or recreational sport, while travelling to and/or staying in places outside their usual environment (sport as the primary motivation of travel) (Gammon and Robinson, 1997)
Tourism sport	— Persons travelling to and/or staying in places outside their usual environment and participating in, actively or passively, a competitive or recreational sport as a secondary activity (Gammon and Robinson, 1997)

inclusive of what is often thought of as recreational sport or 'sport for all'. Finally, sport is characterized by its playful nature. This element includes the notions of uncertainty of outcome and sanctioned display. In more competitive versions of sport, one of the basic objectives is that the competitors should be evenly matched, thereby making the outcome uncertain. If, on the other hand, the outcome is predetermined as in 'all-star wrestling', the game or contest is a form of spectacle rather than sport and therefore falls outside of this definition. Sanctioned display is, however, distinct from spectacle. It is characteristic of sport in as much as sport is not limited to acts of physical prowess but is also inclusive of the demonstration or display of these acts. Many different types of sports involvement are therefore possible for sports tourists.

To a large extent, it is these three characteristics that make sport tourism such an interesting area for research. The systematic exploration of the relationship between these characteristics of sport and the characteristics of the spatial and temporal dimensions of tourism has the potential to provide significant insight into this phenomenon. Prior to this discussion, however, it is necessary to consider the merit of sport as a central attraction of tourism.

Sport as a tourist attraction

A review of the early academic literature that spans the discipline of both sport and tourism confirms a disparate approach to this topic. Before the 1990s, insights to sport tourism were mainly provided through research in related domains. As the academic study of sport tourism has progressed, sport began to receive much more targeted attention as reflected in the assortment of sport tourism typologies that have recently emerged. Despite increasing focus on the basic nature of sport within a tourism system, there has been very little explicit discussion of the fit of sport within current theories on tourist attactions.

Related domains

Hall (1992a, b) not only identified sport as a major special interest of tourism, he also articulated three related tourism domains including hallmark events, outdoor recreation (adventure tourism) and tourism associated with health and fitness (Figure 3.1). Of these three related domains, the area of *hallmark events* is probably the most direct link to sport as epitomized by national championship competitions, such as American football's Super-bowl and international sport mega-events such as the Olympic Games. The profile and

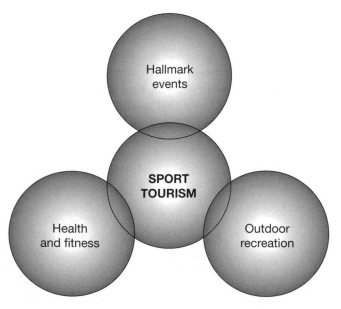

Figure 3.1 Related contextual domain

scale of these sport events attracts the attention of both tourists and tourism researchers. This attention is reflected in the prominence of sport based articles published in the journal of *Festival Management and Event Tourism*. However, Ritchie's (1984) classification of hallmark events identifies sport as just one of seven event categories, although it is arguably one of the most significant of these categories (Getz, 1997; Ryan *et al.*, 1997). Although providing significant insight into sport tourism, publications in this area seldom highlight the distinguishing features of sporting events relative to other types of events.

Outdoor recreation represents a second related area that is inextricably linked to sport tourism. The essence of this contextual domain lies in recreational activities that occur within natural settings, many of which are commonly classified as sports, such as canoeing, skiing and surfing. One of the most dynamic components of outdoor recreation is adventure tourism. Hall (1992a) identifies adventure tourism as a rapidly growing segment of the special interest tourism market. As in the case of hallmark events and sport tourism, there is a clear overlap between outdoor recreation and sport tourism both conceptually and in terms of research activity. However, these domains are not synonymous. A substantial amount of sport activity occurs outside the the realm of the natural environment, whereas conversely, many tourism activities that occur in natural settings are inconsistent with the definition of sport used in this paper (e.g. camping, and picnicking).

Health and fitness activities provide a third related domain of relevance to sport tourism The essence of this domain is presented from both historical and contemporary perspectives. The former is illustrated most commonly by the tourist activity associated with the therapeutic spas of Eastern and Mediterranean Europe in Roman times (Hall, 1992a). In a contemporary context, travel to partake in therapeutic spas continues but it has broadened to resorts focusing on activities such as tennis and golf (Redmond, 1991; Spivack, 1998). Although the realm of health and fitness can be defined in very ubiquitous terms, it generally has been treated much more narrowly in the literature. In particular, character-istics such as the nature of the rule structure of sports have not been a dominant feature in the literature on health and fitness.

Although research in all three of these areas has contributed to the understanding of sport tourism, the essence of sport extends beyond the collective parameters of these related domains. The defining characteristics of sport are not the central interest of research in hallmark events, outdoor recreation or health tourism.

Emerging typologies

A noticeable shift in the source of insights into sport tourism has occurred over the past decade but especially in the past five years. Manifestations of this new source include the development of a series of sport tourism typologies. Redmond (1991) presented one of the first typologies of sports tourism featuring categories associated with resorts and vacations, sports museums, multisports festivals and sports facilities in national parks. Increasingly sophisticated versions of this typology followed, including that of the Sport Tourism International Council (STIC), which identified five categories including: (i) attractions such as heritage sport facilities, (ii) resorts with a sports focus, (iii) cruises that centre around sport celebrity themes, (iv) sport tours such as playing several golf courses at a particular destination, and (v) major sporting events (STIC Research Unit, 1995; Kurtzman and Zauhar, 1997). An interesting variation of this pattern was presented by Gammon and Robinson (1996) with their distinction between sport tourism and tourism sport on the basis of contrasting trip motivations. One of the most recent typologies was published by Standeven and De Knop (1999) in which the complexity of sport tourism is recognized through additional distinctions, such as, holiday versus non-holiday, passive (spectatorship) versus active (athletic participation), organized versus independent, high versus low motivations, and single versus multiple sport holidays.

Leiper's attraction framework

A logical extension of the development of these typologies is the examination of sport as an attraction within the tourism destination system. This examination is facilitated by using Leiper's (1990) systems perspective, which builds on the earlier work of MacCannell (1976) and Gunn (1988). Under this approach, a tourist attraction is defined as 'a system comprising three elements: a tourist or human element, a nucleus or central element, and a marker or informative element. A tourist attraction comes into existence when the three elements are connected' (Leiper, 1990: 371).

The first component of Leiper's (1990) attraction system is the *human element*. Like other types of tourists, sport tourists seek to satisfy a variety of needs and wants in their search for leisure away from home. Two characteristics of these sport tourists are particularly noteworthy in the context of the destinations and typologies just reviewed. The first of these involves the inconsistency between the understanding of visitors from a sport and from a tourism perspective. For example, from a tourism perspective, spec- tators at an international sporting occasion who reside outside of the host city would normally be classified as tourists in that city. From a sport perspective, however, these spectators view their national team as their 'home team'. At a psychological level, these spectators feel at 'home' even though they may have travelled a substantial distance to attend the game.

A second distinguishing aspect of sport tourists in terms of the human element of attraction systems is that they can be categorized into several groups: e.g. spectators and players. One of the more interesting aspects of this division is the inverse relationship that may exist between the size of each group, ranging from elite through to recreational sporting events. For example, at World Cup Football matches there are only a handful of players who may arguably be referred to as tourists during their visits to foreign countries. In contrast, when defined from a tourism perspective, a high proportion of spectators attending one of these matches may be classified as tourists. The opposite situation is likely to occur at the recreational levels of football competitions in that the number of tourists is much greater in terms of the participating athletes relative to spectators. By recognizing competition as a continuum, the differences between types of involvement (e.g. spectator versus athlete) can be explored for elite versus recreational versions of the sport. These are just two unique characteristics of sports tourists that can be addressed under the human element of attraction systems. They illustrate the types of research questions that can be articulated by using attraction frameworks to examine sport tourism.

The second major element of Leiper's (1990) tourist attraction system is the *nucleus* or any feature of a place that a traveller wishes to experience. This is the site where the tourist experience is ultimately produced and consumed. It is the site where the tourism resource is commodified. Individual sports and more particularly, individual sporting events, become unique attractions based on their defining characteristics.

Unique rules and institutional sporting structures have evolved over time, often reflecting and sometimes influencing the country's culture. Sport therefore can act as a powerful symbol of a destination's culture (e.g., ice hockey in Canada, Nordic skiing in Norway). In contrast, trends such as the globalization of sport may erode the distinction between places in terms of the culture of sport Each sport is characterized by its own types of physical competition and playful nature. One of the most significant implications of these characteristics is that sport competition outcomes are uncertain. This inherent uncertainty means that sporting attractions tend to be authentic and renewable. Although value-added entertainment such as pre-game concerts have been coupled with sporting events at the elite levels of competition, the core product remains the excitement of the sport itself, the question of what the optimum balance is between the game and the added entertainments is likely to become increasingly important in the future.

Leiper (1990) also raised the idea of a nuclear mix and hierarchy of attractions. A nuclear mix refers to the combination of nuclei that a tourist wishes to experience, and the hierarchy suggests that some of these nuclei are more important in influencing visitor decisions than others. This aspect of the attraction is very similar to the categories of sport tourism typologies associated with multiple sport trips and levels of motivations (Standeven and De Knop, 1999; Gammon and Robinson, 1996). For many sport tourists a specific sporting event may function as the primary attraction in a destination, but the cluster of other nuclei found in the surrounding area may be needed to finalize the decision to travel. Alternatively, sports can also serve as an important albeit secondary nuclei. Appreciating the place of sport within a destination's attraction mix and hierarchy is likely to have significant management implications.

Markers are items of information about any phenomenon that is a potential nuclear element in a tourist attraction (Leiper, 1990). They may be divided into markers that are detached from the nucleus or those that are contiguous. In each case the markers may either consciously or unconsciously function as part of the attraction system. Examples of conscious generating markers featuring sport are common. Typically, they take the form of advertisements showing visitors involved in destination-specific sport activities and events. Perhaps even more pervasive are the unconscious detached markers. At the forefront of these are televised broadcasts of elite sport competitions and advertisements featuring sports products in recognizable destinations. Although sport broadcasts may result in come spectators choosing to watch the game from the comfort of their home rather than in person, in a broader sense, television viewers have the location marked for them as a tourist attraction, which may influence future travel decisions. Chalip *et al.*'s (1998) paper on sources of interest in travel to the Olympic Games lends itself well to this framework, although markers were not specifically mentioned in the paper. However, reference to the influence of Olympic narratives, symbols and genres essentially addresses issues that emerge in the context of detached markers within the tourist attraction system. Contiguous markers include on-site signage that labels the attraction. Other on-site markers include game programmes, team mascot, and even the products of commercial sponsors of the subject sports.

Leiper's (1990) tourist attraction system does provide insight into the relationship between sport and tourism. Although space limitations have not allowed an in-depth examination of the characteristics of individual sports, the theory-based attraction system enables a more methodical examination of this topic than has occurred to date The insights gained by using this type of framework can be used to identify important research questions that should be pursued. Yet even though the attraction system framework allows for a greater focus on sport within tourism, it does not directly address the spatial and temporal dimensions.

Frameworks for research

A new framework is required to not only capture the synergies of existing contributions to the subject but to identify future directions for research. Attractions do not function in isolation of the tourism system as a whole. By retaining a focus on sport as an attraction, it is possible to return to the original definitions of sport tourism and develop a guiding frame work for research that can systematically explore the relationships between sport, space and time.

Figure 3.2 provides a graphic representation of the sport tourism research framework proposed in this paper. Sport is positioned as the central focus and attraction. In a sense, sport becomes the first among equals in relation to the other two dimensions. It therefore will be addressed first in this discussion. Three research themes are presented within each dimension. These themes are meant to be illustrative rather than definitive. Researchers with different backgrounds and interests are encouraged to identify additional themes as well as to project their own perspectives within each theme.

Sport dimension

The sport dimension gives this framework a unique focus on sport as an attraction. Each sport theme reflects the elements that emerged from the earlier discussion of the domain

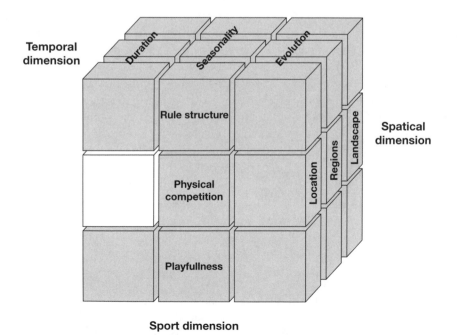

Figure 3.2 Framework for sport tourism research

of sport. Under the first theme, individual sports are characterized by their own rule structure, which dictates their spatial and temporal characteristics at the attraction level. A variety of research questions therefore can be pursued that have direct bearing on the management and design of sport attractions. For example, what are the implications of rule changes on the essence of the sport's attraction? Will the changes have an impact on the propensity of spectators to travel to the sporting event?

Competition forms a second theme within the sport dimension. A variety of issues exist in this area that have received little attention to date. One example is whether the level or type of competition associated with a particular sport, influences the nature of the travel experience. Using skiing as a case in point, how important is the nature of competition as a determinant of the visitor's perception of the destination? For example, do highly competitive skiers develop similar perceptions of a ski destination in comparison to less competitive skiers? Alternatively, sport performance may be a more significant factor in terms of its influences on the sense of place that a competitive skier develops for a particular ski destination in that the athlete's view of the destination may be more positive the better that he or she performed while at that destination.

The playful nature of sport represents the last major thematic area represented within the sport dimension of the research framework. It encompasses a broad range of potential lines of inquiry, including but not limited to the uncertainty of sport outcomes, sanctioned display, and the utility and seriousness of sport. One of the most intriguing characteristics of sport tourism in this regard is the relationship between the uncertainty of sport outcomes and the concept of authenticity as it has been discussed within the field of tourism. Given trends toward the positioning of professional sport as part of the entertainment industry and in extreme cases, as spectacle, the competitive advantages related to the authenticity of sport needs to be studied carefully.

The sanctioned display aspect of this theme also suggests a number of research possibilities that converge around the type of involvement that sport tourists may have with sport. At a very basic level, the distinction between athletes and spectators as sport tourists needs further attention. However, this distinction represents only two of many types of sport involvement (Kenyon, 1969), including that of coaches, management and officials. A broad range of research questions can be raised about the socio-demographic characteristics, travel behaviours and impacts of each of these groups of sport tourists.

An additional line of inquiry under this theme is whether the nature of the travel experience varies between amateur and professional sport tourists. Perhaps a prerequisite question is whether professional athletes should even be considered tourists given that they are remunerated for their travel. Similarly, the whole issue of commodification of sport poses some interesting questions that have been raised in the context of other types of tourism.

Spatial dimension

For illustrative purposes, the spatial themes that have been highlighted include location, region and landscape (Figure 3.2). There appears to be considerable potential to build on the work of Bale (1989), with his focus on the geography of sport, and the work of Pearce (1987), whose focus is the geography of tourism. These authors base their discussions on similar spatial theories but they hold contrasting perspectives. In terms of location themes, basic geographical theories, such as central place theory and distance decay theory, offer much potential for gaining an understanding of practical issues, such as where to locate sport facilities and the determination of threshold levels of players and/or spectators needed to sustain a given sport, team or facility. Such insights would be of direct relevance to both private and public sector investors in sport facilities and programmes.

Regional studies represent a second major thematic area within the spatial dimension. The myriad of significant research questions that could be raised within this theme include those relating to the influence of a sport, team, or an individual athlete on the image of a destination. One aspect of region that needs further attention is scale. Although sport tourism has been examined in the context of the host sites of international and national sporting events, little published literature exists on sport tourism associated with smaller scale events within the region. This lack of attention may be due to the lower profile of sport in these regions, even though it is possible that the cumulative impact of these sporting activities is of equal or more significance than that associated with international and national events.

The third theme identified within the spatial dimension of the framework concerns landscape, both in terms of the dependency of particular sports on the presence of certain physical resources and, conversely, the impact of sport on tourism landscapes. In terms of resource dependency, a basic distinction exists between sports that are highly dependent on the presence of specific natural resource features and those that function independently of them. The spatial distribution of these two types of sports is therefore likely to be quite distinct. At the same time, sports appear to have significant impacts on a tourism landscape in terms of its cultural and physical dimensions. In many cases the differences between international sportscapes are decreasing owing to the application of facility design standards by international sport governing bodies. This trend raises Bale's (1989) spectre of uniform 'sportscapes', which are divorced from the very place in which they are situated. Alienation from place introduces fundamental issues about the propensity of sports fans to travel to a generic sportscape, especially if the game or contest can be experienced through television.

Temporal dimension

Temporal themes make up the final dimension of the framework (Figure 3.2) and trip duration (day visitors as well as those who stay one or more nights) is the first theme to be highlighted in this group. This trip characteristic not only serves as a basic element of most definitions of tourism but holds significance in terms of such diverse issues as the extent of the economic impact associated with a visit and the nature of the relationship formed between hosts and guests. For example, in a Japanese study of participants in crosscountry skiing and walking special events, it was found that participants were likely to leave the hosting community soon after their sporting activity was finished rather than extending their trip for post-competition tours (Nogawa *et al.*, 1996). The authors of this study did, however, speculate that this behaviour was due to external factors rather than an inherent characteristics of these particular sport tourists.

Tourism seasonality represents a second temporal theme that merits further attention. The vast majority of tourism destinations are characterized by significant fluctuations in tourism activity throughout the year that have been attributed to a variety of natural and institutional factors (Allcock, 1989; Butler, 1994; Snepenger *et al.*, 1990). This fluctuation is typically viewed as a problem by tourism operators who must address the challenge of meeting ongoing expenses in the face of fluctuating flows of revenue. Sports are also characterized by seasonal patterns such as those manifest in the placement of various sports into the Summer or the Winter Olympic Games. Trends in professionalization, globalization and technology have all acted as modifying factors for the seasonality of sport and much work is needed to assess the impact and management potential of these changes for tourism.

Finally, the third temporal theme in the framework condemns the pattern of development or the evolution of tourism products and destinations over time. This evolution has particular significance in the context of the current research trends in sustainable tourism and the need to consider process as well as form in tourism studies. Butler's (1980) idea of a life cycle associated with tourism destinations complements Bale's (1989) discussion of the evolution of various types of sport. Changes in either sphere of activity will have implications in the other. By understanding the changes likely to occur in one sphere, stakeholders will be better able to understand the probable impacts in the other sphere and perhaps be in a position to manage these impacts.

Synergistic benefits

Although there is utility in examining each theme in isolation, a higher level of insight can be achieved if these themes are examined in conjunction with themes from each of the other dimensions. The thematic dimensions of sport can be used to anchor research in this area and may even suggest testable hypotheses about the relationship between sport characteristics as independent variables relative to spatial and temporal characteristics as dependent variables. This potential is illustrated graphically in Figure 3.2, which can be viewed as a cube made up of multiple component blocks. Each of these component blocks represents a unique combination of themes from each dimension and therefore, a unique set of relationships between variables.

The highlighted block represents just one of twenty-seven unique combinations of themes that can be examined. It should, however, be appreciated that the value of exploring the specific relationships found in each block of the cube is not uniform. Some of these relationships will be of more interest and utility than others. In Figure 3.2, one possible investigation would be to explore the impact of performance (competition) relative to the length of stay and the willingness of sport tourists to travel. Specific measures of these variables would have to be identified and hypotheses about the likely impact of performance on length of stay distance travelled could be tested. Alternatively, the impacts of different types of recreational versus elite competition could be studied. This type of information would be useful in the development of management strategies for sport and tourism. The point is that a variety of possible research questions could be asked depending on which variables are chosen within these themes Once these variables have been selected, the framework suggests the key relationships that can be investigated. Interchanging themes creates new directions for sport tourism research. Rather than posing research questions in one dimension, this framework enables researchers to systematically consider the relationships between themes across either two or three basic dimensions.

Conclusion

This article conceptualizes sport tourism in the context of its activity, its spatial and its temporal dimensions. Sport tourism is defined as *sport-based travel away from the home environment for a limited time, where sport is characterized by unique rule sets, competition related to physical prowess, and a playful nature*. Sport was then examined as a tourist attraction using Leiper's (1990) systems model and the paper concludes with a proposed framework for research in this area.

In terms of the definition of sport tourism, the major contribution of this paper is to anchor a sociological approach to sport within a generalized three-dimensional definition of tourism. Sport is positioned as the activity dimension thereby highlighting its relationship to tourism's spatial and temporal dimensions. One of the key differences of this definition relative to most existing ones is that the distinguishing characteristics of sport are explicitly stated in terms of sport's institutional rule structure, competitive continuum and basis in play. Sport is seen as being more than physical activity. Furthermore, competition is seen as a defining characteristic of sport and is presented as a continuum ranging from recreational to elite. The inclusion of this continuum is one of the strengths of this definition, as it allows for comparisons between different levels of competition in lens of specified spatial and temporal variables For example, under this definition it is possible to address questions such as 'what are the spatial and temporal implications of a resort's decision to focus on elite versus recreational skiers?'

By considering sport within an attraction system framework, this paper has presented an alternative perspective to the typologies that have been presented to date. Although these typologies have identified specific groupings of travel products and have made explicit and implicit reference to attractions, much of this has been done with no conscious linkage to existing attraction theory. Anchoring this discussion within an attraction system framework has allowed some of the more distinct features of sport to be highlighted in a systematic fashion. One example of this is the advantages that sport presents as an attraction in terms of fulfilling tourists search for authenticity. Although this issue was not discussed in detail, the use of an attraction system framework enables the identification of these types of important issues.

The last section of the paper presents and explains a research framework for sport tourism that addresses the criticisms of the existing literature raised by Gibson (1998). More specifically, it is developed as an attempt to help the authors make sense of a broad-based literature and to identify future research avenues in this area. It extends the two-dimensional framework offered by Standeven and De Knop (1999) to three dimensions based on the underlying structure of many broadly accepted definitions of tourism. Each dimension is then subdivided into selected themes. The next logical step in this process is to breakdown the themes into specific variables. The relationship between these variables can then be hypothesized and tested in a systematic fashion.

The framework is intended to be flexible so that other researchers can find some utility in it, whether they are managers looking for practical solutions to real problems, graduate students just initiating a research programme in this area or established scholars in the field. All of these researchers are encouraged to substitute their own themes into this framework or to make further modifications as they see fit. What is most important is that research recognizes not only the breadth of sport tourism but that it is also characterized by an increasing depth of analysis. Furthermore, depth and breadth must be linked. The framework presented in this paper represents an instrument that can be used to address this challenge.

References

Allcock, J.B. 1989. Seasonality. In *Tourism Marketing and Management Handbook*, Witt, S.F., Moutinho, L. (eds). Prentice Hall: Englewood Cliffs; 387–392.

Bale, J. 1989. *Sports Geography*. E & FN Spon: London.

Butler, R.W. 1980. The concept of the tourist area cycle of evolution, implications for the management of resources. *Canadian Geographer* 24 (1): 5–12.

Butler, R.V. 1994. Seasonality in tourism: issues and problems. In *Tourism: The State of the Art*, Seaton, A.V. (ed.). Wiley: Chichester; 332–339.

Chalip, L.B., Green, B.C., Vander Velden, L. 1998. Sources of interest in travel to the Olympic Games. *Journal of Vacation Marketing* 4: 7–22.

De Knop, P. 1998. Sport tourism, a state of the art. *European Journal for Sport Management* 5 (2): 5–20.

Delpy, L. 1998. An overview of sport tourism: building towards a dimensional framework. *Journal of Vacation Marketing* 4: 23–38.

Falkner, B., Tideswell, C., Weston, A.M. 1998. Leveraging tourism benefits from the Sydney 2000 Olympics. Paper presented at the Fourth Annual Conference of the Sport Management Association of Australia and New Zealand, 26–28 November, Gold Coast International, Gold Coast, Australia.

Gammon, S., Robinson, T. 1997. Sport and tourism: a conceptual framework. *Journal of Sport Tourism* 4: 3, 8–24. www.free-press.com/journals/jst/vol14no3/jst.15.html.

Garmise, M. (ed.). 1987. *Proceedings of the International Seminar and Workshop on Outdoor Education, Recreation and Sport Tourism*. Gill Publishing: Netanya, Israel.

Getz, D. 1997. Trends and issues in sport event tourism. *Tourism Recreation Research* 22 (2): 61–62.

Gibson, H.J. 1998. Sport tourism, a critical analysis of research. *Sport Management Review* 1: 43–76.

Glyptis, S.A. 1991. Sport and tourism. In *Progress in Tourism, Recreation and Hospitality Management*, Cooper, C. (ed.). Belhaven: London, 3; 165–183.

Gunn, C. 1988. *Vacationscape: Designing Tourist Regions*, 2nd edn. Van Nostrand Reinhold: New York.

Hall, C.M. 1992a. Adventure, sport and health tourism. In *Special Interest Tourism*, Weiler B., Hall, C.M. Belhaven Press: London; 141–158.

Hall, C.M. 1992b. *Hallmark Tourist Events: Impacts: Management and Planning*. Belhaven Press: London.

Kenyon, G. 1969. Sport involvement: a conceptual go and some consequences thereof. In *Aspects of Contemporary Sport Sociology*, Kenyon, G. (ed.). Athletic Institute: Chicago; 77–100.

Kurtzman, J., Zauhar, J. 1995. Tourism Sport International Council. *Annals of Tourism Research* 22 (3): 707–708.

Kurtzman, J., Zauhar, J. 1997. Wave in time: the sports tourism phenomena. *Journal of Sport Tourism* 4 (2): 5–20. www.mch.co.uk/journals/jst/ archive/vol 14no2/welcome.html (28 May 1998).

Leiper, N. 1981. Towards a cohesive curriculum in tourism the case for a distinct discipline. *Annals of Tourism Research* 8 (1): 69–74.

Leiper, N. 1990. Tourist attraction systems. *Annals of Tourism Research* 17 (2): 367–384.

Loy, J.W., McPherson, B.D., Kenyon, G. 1978. *Sport and Social Systems*. Addison Wesley: Reading, MA.

MacCannell, D. 1976. *The Tourist: New Theory of the Leisure Class*. Schoken: New York.

McPherson, B.D., Curtis, J.E., Loy, J.W. 1989. *The Social Significance of Sport*. Human Kinetics: Champaign, IL.

Murphy, P. 1985. *Tourism: A Community Approach*. Methuen: New York and London.

Nogawa, H., Yamaguchi, Y., Hagi, Y. 1996. An empirical research study on Japanese sport tourism in sport-for-all events, case studies of a single-night event and a multiple-night event. *Journal of Travel Research* 35 (2): 46–54.

Pearce, D.C. 1987. *Tourism Today: A Geographical Analysis*. Longman Scientific and Technical: Harlow.

Redmond, G. 1991. Changing styles of sports tourism industry/consumer interactions in Canada, the USA and Europe. In *The Tourism Industry: An International Analysis*, Sinclair M.T., Stabler, M.J. (eds). CAB International: Wallingford; 107–120.

Ritchie, J.R.B. 1984. Assessing the impact of hallmark events: conceptual and research issues. *Journal of Travel Research* 13 (1): 2–11.

Ruskin, H. 1987. Selected view on socio-economic aspects of outdoor recreation, outdoor education and sport tourism. In *Proceedings of the International Seminar and Workshop on Outdoor Education, Recreation and Sport Tourism*, Garmise, M. (ed.). Emmanuel Gill Publishing: Natanya, Israel.

Ryan, C., Smee, A., Murphy, S. 1996. Creating a data base of events in New Zealand: early results. *Festival Management and Event Tourism* 4 (3/4): 151–156.

Snepenger, D., Houser, B., Snepenger, H. 1990. Seasonality of demand. *Annals of Tourism Research* 17: 628–630.

Spivack, S.E. 1998. Health spa development in the US: a burgeoning component of sport tourism. *Journal of Vacation Marketing* 4: 65–77.

Standeven, J., De Knop, P. 1999. *Sport Tourism*. Human Kinetics: Champaign, IL.

Stevens, T., van den Broek, M. 1997. Sport and tourism – natural partners in strategies for tourism development. *Tourism Recreation Research* 22 (2): 1–3.

STIC Research Unit. 1995. Sports tourism categories revisited. *Journal of Sport Tourism* 2 (3): 9–11.

Weed, M., Bull, C.J. 1997a. Integrating sport and tourism, a review of regional policies in England. *Progress in Tourism and Hospitality Research* 3: 129–148.

Weed, M., Bull, C.J. 1997b. Influences on sport-tourism relations in Britain: the effects of government policy. *Tourism Recreation Research* 22 (2): 5–12.

W.H. Smith/Collins. 1988. *English Dictionary*. William Collins Sons & Co: Glasgow.

WTO. 1981. *Technical Handbook on the Collection and Presentation of Domestic and International Tourism Statistics*. World Tourism Organization: Madrid.

Chapter 4

Karin Weber

OUTDOOR ADVENTURE TOURISM
A review of research approaches

Introduction

DEFINITIONS OF ADVENTURE TOURISM have traditionally centered on adventure recreation (Hall and Weiler 1992; Sung, Morrison and O'Leary 1997). Such experiences are characterized by the interplay of competence and risk (Martin and Priest 1986). Recently, Walle (1997) offered an expansion and redefinition of adventure tourism by proposing the insight model as its basis. He argues that it is the quest for insight and knowledge (rather than risk) that underlies adventure tourism. Common to these definitions is that it is researchers who have determined what constitutes it with research taking place within these set parameters. The question, however, is whether such a relatively narrow focus of research is sufficient to gain a comprehensive understanding of adventure tourism.

This paper proposes an alternative, yet complementary, approach. It argues that individuals' subjective experience and perception of adventure need also to be considered for a more complete understanding. In developing this argument, the paper first reviews the current literature on the subject, especially Walle's (1997) proposal to replace the prevalent "risk theory" as the foundation of adventure tourism – a proposition that requires critical assessment. The literature review suggests that at present adventure tourism is essentially viewed as an extension of adventure/outdoor recreation; the contribution of the tourism aspect is generally ignored.

To address this shortcoming, the paper discusses the overland tourist. This turns from the traditional focus on the destination region to that of the transit route and necessitates a review of some previously forwarded propositions. Most importantly, however, the paper shifts focus to differences in individuals' perceptions, resulting from differences in personality and previous tourism experience, to open up further research. The proposed change in research focus to individuals' perception has implications for both the management and marketing of adventure tourism.

Outdoor adventure tourism

When assessing adventure tourism it is necessary to also refer to adventure recreation, as the latter is at the heart of the former as it is currently defined. The vast majority of studies accept adventure recreation as its integral part (Christiansen 1990; Hall 1989; Johnston 1992). Adventure recreation has its origin in traditional outdoor recreation. While both types involve activities and specific skills in outdoor settings, they differ, according to Ewert, in the "deliberate seeking of risk and uncertainty of outcome" (1989: 8) associated with adventure recreation. To him, risk takes on a central role as satisfaction with the experience, and a desire to participate may decrease if risk is absent. In this context, risk is most commonly equated to the physical risk of serious injury or death. This notion characterizes an adventure recreation experience as does the construct of perceived competence (Martin and Priest 1986; Priest 1992), or more accurately the interplay between them (Ewert and Hollenhorst 1989; Martin and Priest 1986).

Walle sought to expand the notion of adventure by arguing that one can distinguish between two types: risk taking adventure and that which is pursued to gain knowledge and insight. While this expansion to incorporate insight seeking is useful, several comments in regard to his argument are in order. He refers to Maslow's (1954) hierarchy of needs to point out contradictions between this and the prevalent risk theory of adventure, to open his argument for the need for the alternative insight theory. It is, however, important to note that Maslow's theory itself has been questioned on several grounds. Cooper, Fletcher, Gilbert and Wanhill, for example, note that:

> While a great deal of tourism demand theory has been built upon Maslow's approach, it is not clear from his work why he selected five basic needs; why they are ranked as they are; how he could justify his model when he never carried out clinical observation or experiment; and why he never tried to expand the original set of motives.
>
> (1993: 21)

When discussing Maslow's theory, Walle implies that lower level needs have to be fully satisfied before individuals attempt to fulfill needs at higher levels of the hierarchy. However, it has been shown that individuals move on to focus on the fulfillment of the latter once the former are satisfied to a degree acceptable to them (Mills 1985). In the context of adventure tourism it would mean that individuals, by not fully addressing their safety needs, do accept a certain element of risk and danger in order to satisfy higher level needs through adventurous pursuits. But such a situation is not indicative of Walle's claim that adventurers willingly abandon safety in order to fulfill themselves at a higher level. In fact, research has shown that they are very much concerned with safety, reflected in the meticulous preparation of their equipment, the careful examination of environmental conditions, or in a commercial setting in the selection of experienced operators (Celsi, Rose and Leigh 1993; Ewert 1994; Hall and McArthur 1994).

Walle continues by stating that according to the conventional risk theory, the adventurer seeks risk for its, own sake and because of the emotional rewards provided by experiencing it. Consequently, "adventure involves pursuing risk as an end in itself" (1997: 269). While such an interpretation contrasts rather nicely with his alternative "insight seeking" theory, it is somewhat inaccurate. Numerous studies have shown that risk is not pursued as an end in itself (Ewert 1985, 1993, 1994). In fact, risk often plays a negligible role. Ewert and Hollenhorst note that "although adventure recreators seek out increasingly difficult and challenging opportunities, they paradoxically do not necessarily seek higher levels of risk" (1994: 188). However, what they do seek is to match their skills and competence with the situational risk. In summary, an adventure recreation experience is a "search for competence with a valuation of risk and danger" (1989: 127). Therefore, learning and gaining insight are not possible side effects of risk/adventure recreation as argued by Walle, they are integral parts. This is particularly pronounced for adventure recreationists at a higher level of engagement (Celsi Rose and Leigh 1993; Ewert 1994).

Therefore, gaining insight is a motive for both the traditional adventure recreationist and the insight seeker. Yet, what is likely to vary is the level of risk accepted by the individual. Walle asserts that certain activities such as fly fishing and bird watching constitute adventure activities since participants seek insight and knowledge. He goes further to imply that ecotourism at large, by virtue of participants gaining insight, can be regarded as adventure tourism. While most ecotourism activities do not involve great actual risk for participants, some of these activities, for example bird watching, may not pose any risk at all to an individual, neither actual nor perceived. Thus, at this point it becomes necessary to ask "what is the original meaning of adventure?" If risk – physical, psychological, or social – is completely absent and a person only gains insight and knowledge, can these experiences still be regarded as adventure?

The Oxford English Dictionary (Brown 1993: 31) defines adventure as "a chance of danger or loss; risk, jeopardy; a hazardous enterprise or performance." Clearly, it has in the English language acquired a connotation of risk and uncertainty. Suggesting that "insight seeking" could replace "risk" to refer to adventure appears to be in clear contrast to its historic meaning. It seems more appropriate that both risk and insight seeking have to be present, in varying degrees, for an adventure to take place.

In accord to this line of thinking, gaining insight as one motive for and a result of adventure has been pointed to in earlier writings. Quinn (1990) notes that the human desire or drive to experience what is hidden and unknown initiates adventure. Similarly, Dufrene states: "We are attracted by a deep forest or lake because it gives the impression that there is some truth to discover, some secret to abduct from the heart of the object. It is the eternal seduction of the hidden" (1973: 398). The reward for those who seek adventure lies in the discovery and unveiling of the hidden and unknown.

Therefore, adventure is quite obviously linked with exploration. Yet the focus of the latter has changed over the centuries. Originally adventure was associated with the exploration of foreign, faraway places to search for new land, wealth, and scientific advances. Examples include the voyage of Pytheas (*c.* 330 BC) to the ultima Thule (ultimate land) – the Arctic Circle, Pizarro's journey to Peru (1526), and Cook's expedition to Tahiti (1768–71). In the latter part of the 19th century, however, resulting from a new appreciation of the wilderness and the emerging need for adventure

> the reason for adventuring shifted from the necessary by-product of searching for scientific knowledge [land and wealth] to reasons related to an individual's own personal desires. Adventure became a legitimate quest for its own sake, or an end in itself rather than a means to an end.
>
> (Ewert 1989: 26)

Mountains were climbed and wild rivers navigated, purely for the experience and to determine one's strengths and abilities. It is debatable whether adventure was only a by-product of travel in earlier times, as claimed by Ewert, rather than also a primary motive. However, until the end of the 19th century, outdoor adventure recreation did not have the widespread acceptance it would gain in the following decades. All this bears on the question of how adventure recreation relates to adventure tourism. As mentioned earlier, the former has long been accepted as the integral part of the latter. Hall and Weiler's definition of adventure tourism represents one of the most frequently cited definitions on the subject:

> A broad spectrum of outdoor touristic activities, often commercialized and involving an interaction with the natural environment away from the participant's home range and containing elements of risk; in which the outcome is influenced by the participant, setting, and management of the touristic experience.
>
> (1992: 143)

Later definitions by Johnston (1992) and Sung, Morrison and O'Leary (1997) essentially rest on the same premise. In contrast, Walle (1997) incorporates certain outdoor activities other than the traditional recreation ones into the confines of adventure tourism. Nevertheless, there is a commonality among these to date rather few definitions/concep-tualizations. They all view adventure tourism essentially as an extension of adventure/ outdoor recreation; the introduction of the tourism element merely serves to transfer the place at which the outdoor/adventure recreation activity takes place from the participant's home base to the destination.

As already noted, adventure has historically been associated with the exploration of foreign, faraway lands. Yet, the current conceptualization of adventure tourism captures only one aspect of adventure (specific recreation activities), while ignoring the contribution of the tourism aspect to reach distant localities. In order to highlight the contribution of the tourism aspect, it is useful to put the phenomenon of adventure tourism in the context of the tourism system.

Tourism's contribution to adventure

Leiper (1979, 1995) proposes the conceptualization of tourism as a system comprising five distinct elements: the tourist(s), a generating region, a transit route, a destination region, and the tourism industry (Figure 4.1). The various environments (sociocultural, physical, technological, and political) surround the system. Of particular interest to the discussion are its geographical elements, namely the tourist generating market, the transit route, and the destination region. As mentioned earlier, conceptualizing adventure tourism as an extension of adventure/outdoor recreation confines the role of tourism to transfer-ring the place at which adventure/outdoor recreation activities take place from the generating market to the destination region. Therefore, the focus is on the activities that take place at the destination. As such it completely ignores the role of the transit route. Yet, the latter is of particular importance to adventure tourism, as it is this element which can be the most important aspect for the traditional adventure tourist.

Figure 4.1 Tourism system

Source: Leiper (1995: 25).

The Asian Overland Route, originally used for regional trade, has been described by many people as the classic overland trip of modern times. In the late 60s and 70s, thousands of young people from Western countries embarked on their journey. Tourists often commencing the trip in Europe, crossed Turkey, Iran, Afghanistan, Pakistan, and India to reach their final destination, Nepal. In doing so they mainly used local modes of transport, ranging from buses to boats to camels or horses. But while reaching Nepal was the aim of the trip, the journey itself was for most people more important than the final destination.

Zurick (1995) provides an account of his travels along the Asian Overland Route in the mid-70s. He recalls his first encounter with Istanbul – a city that provided to overland tourists an initial taste of the mysterious Orient and a parting from the world known to them. Passing through Erzurum in Eastern Turkey meant, according to Zurick, that "[even though] there were no violent civil wars [in the area at the time], the threat of robbers was constant in a place where murder was commonplace and theft even more so." Crossing Afghanistan, he found himself "traversing an uneasy landscape of feudal wars, unfettered nomads . . . and a vast, generally inhospitable terrain, a landscape that bakes in the summer sun and freezes under winter's snow". A popular stop enroute, Kabul and its main thoroughfare in particular harbored "a volatile mix of Western and Afghan drug and gem smugglers, Pakistani gunrunners, convicts, spies and international pleasure seekers". Following the descent of the Khyber Pass, overland tourists were exposed to Pakistan, a "spicy land, full of humidity, haggard beggars, and cow dung, reverence and bustling markets," simply in the way enroute to India. Yet India, "pointing in new directions rather than confirming the Orient as a singular place," disappointed many overland tourists who subsequently moved on to Kathmnandu, the final destination on the Asian Overland Route (Zurick 1995: 62, 63, 66, 69, 73).

Two important observations can be made from the above account of overland travel. First, the traditional prerequisites for adventure – risk and uncertainty – are present. It is also apparent that the quest to gain insight features prominently. Yet, at the same time, the absence of specific adventure/outdoor recreation activities, as outlined in Table 4.1, is noticeable. The physical movement through a variety of hostile environments rather than the participation in a specific activity poses risks and dangers to the overland tourist. These risks and dangers introduce the element of uncertainty about the outcome of the journey.

Second, it is evident that most of the countries on the Asian Overland Route are, in spatial terms, situated on the periphery rather than being core countries (Pearce 1979). This also applies to other important adventure travel circuits, for example the "Gringo Trail" in Latin America or the "Salt Road" in Africa. Tourist flows linking generating regions in developed countries with Third World nations have been noted for various

Table 4.1 Adventure recreation pursuits[a]

Backpacking	Kayaking	Rogaining
Bicycling	Orienteering	Sailing
Diving	Mountaineering	Snowshoeing
Hanggliding	Rafting	Spelunking
Ballooning	Rappelling	Trekking
Hiking	Rock climbing	Sky diving

a Ewert (1987: 5); Hall and Weiler (1992: 144).

types of tourism. However, for overland travel the flow of tourists from core countries (in Europe and North America) both to and through a variety of peripheral countries is of particular importance.

Zurick (1992) proposes a spatial hierarchy model specific to adventure tourism. He notes that in most instances individuals proceed from the generating region through an intervening gateway, located in the semiperiphery, to a national gateway in the periphery destination. Their flow is further channeled through regional gateways to the actual adventure region, both of which extend into the frontier of the peripheral destination. To be applicable in the present context, Zurick's model would have to take into account the overland movement from the adventure region to further regional, even national gateways, and from there to other adventure regions. This cycle may be repeated several times, depending on the particulars of the overland trip.

By extending the perspective on adventure tourism beyond specific adventure/outdoor recreation activities, another viable market segment can be identified: the overland tourist. The physical movement along the transit route constitutes the key adventure element. Zurick's journey along the Asian Overland Route falls into this category, representing independent (non-commercial) overland adventure tourism. Still today there are many people who embark on such trips independently, traveling, for instance, on the South American Circuit without the assistance of a tour operator. However, there are now also numerous commercial overland operators. For example, Encounter Overland, a British operator, offers an "Africa A–Z" expedition. The expedition from London to Cape Town undertaken with a special four-wheel drive expedition truck, travels through Morocco, Mali, Niger, Zambia, Malawi, and Namibia, to name just a few countries. The experiences of traveling along the 27,500 kilometer route are the focus of the journey and of greater importance than the final destination, Cape Town, itself.

Adventure recreation is not an integral part of commercial overland travel; at most it is optional to tour participants and then usually of low actual risk. Consequently, skills required to participate would be minimal to moderate and optional, given the commercial setting. For independent overland trips where some adventure recreation activities such as backpacking or hiking may be means of alternative transport, skills would be essential. However, given the nature of overland travel, skills pertaining to a specific adventure recreation activity are generally less important than skills required to deal with distinct and sometimes hostile sociocultural or political environments. The setting (non-commercial vs. commercial) determines who provides skills to deal with these environments and who controls the risk.

Reviewing Zurick's (1995) account of his journey, it becomes apparent that motivations beyond those traditionally identified for adventure tourism – gaining and assessing skills and competence in a natural setting posing some risk – are important to overland tourists. The desire to travel through peripheral destinations, often rich in cultural traditions, suggests a strong motivation. The difference between overland tours and "cultural tours" lies in the acceptance of actual risk and danger as part of the experience due to the regions traveled through and the usually extended time frame for the former. Furthermore, encountering the culture would only be part of the total experience. The desire to encounter various distinct, often remote physical environments, without necessarily engaging in any adventure recreation, appears also important.

Of relevance here is Cohen's work (1972, 1973) on the various tourist types. The non-institutionalized form of tourism (drifting), the effect of *Vermassung* (loss of individuality), and its consequent institutionalization are of particular interest, Cohen's "drifter" is characterized by not adhering to a fixed itinerary or timetable, not having well-defined goals of travel, and by the desire to be immersed almost fully into the host culture by adopting the hosts' way of life. This original drifter corresponds closely with the early independent overland tourist. However, already in the 70s Cohen (1973) notes the effects of *Vermassung* with the formation of fixed drifter itineraries and a system of tourism facilities and services catering specifically for this segment. Accompanying this institutionalization was a certain loss of drifters' interest in and involvement with the local people, and a growing orientation towards other drifters. He concludes that even though the element of adventure is still present in commercial overland trips, the spontaneous individualism of the original form of drifting is gone.

Several parallels can be drawn to Walle's work. But there are also important differences. First, both the overland adventure tourist and his insight seeker have motives beyond those traditionally associated with adventure tourism. They both seek to gain knowledge and insight more than matching their skills and competence with situational risk. However, in contrast to Walle who focuses mainly on gaining insight into wilderness settings, it is argued here that gaining insight into the cultural environment is also important to the adventure tourist. Insight is also sought by the overland tourist through encounters along the transit route rather than merely adventurous activities at the destination. Furthermore, there are also some similarities in the practical context. Walle notes that at times "forward thinking practitioners have seemingly outdistanced both scholars and the profession in general" (1997: 278). He points to the fact that ecotourism emerged in the industry before scholars focused on it. Similarly, numerous, particularly British, adventure tour operators have serviced overland tourists for more than 20 years, either exclusively (Dragoman) or in conjunction with the adventure recreation segment (Exodus, Encounter Overland).

Management and marketing propositions

Several propositions applied to the whole spectrum of adventure tourism have to be reviewed once the overland tourist is brought into the discussion. Darst and Armstrong (1980) note that competition among individuals and groups is minimal, while competition between people and their environment is the norm. This relates mainly to adventure recreation. In these instances participants are foremost concerned with mastering the challenges posed by the physical environment. Hall and Weiler (1992) add that under these circumstances group considerations take on a secondary role. However, competition and conflict among individuals in groups is almost always evident in commercial overland travel. Due to the extended period of travel in a group (commercial overland tours can last up to 40 weeks), conflict and competition among individuals, exacerbated by travel through a variety of challenging environments, can be anything but minimal.

Hall and Weiler (1992) claim that in adventure tourism the environmental setting takes on a subordinate role. They argue that the setting provides only the backdrop for the activity with the latter being what attracts the individual. This proposition is certainly valid when the focus of the trip is on engaging in adventure recreation. Overland tourists, however, are more attracted by the environmental setting than by a specific activity. They seek remote environments, possessing natural beauty and rich cultural traditions, with adventure recreation activities being at best of secondary importance.

It is evident that the motivations of adventure tourists who foremost seek to gain knowledge about the external environment, and those who are more concerned with the discovery of their own strengths and capabilities differ significantly. Therefore, it is necessary to clearly differentiate between these market segments since marketing strategies devised to appeal to one segment are unlikely to address the needs of the other. Walle also notes the need for individually tailored marketing strategies for different segments of the market, concluding that his "insight seeker," equated by him with the ecotourist, represents an under-served market. It is open to debate whether ecotourism indeed represents an under-served segment at present. However, what is questionable is his claim that 'this form of tourism . . . has been successful precisely because it goes beyond theories and strategies that assume that adventure is merely risk seeking" (1997: 278). Insight seekers/ecotourists are a viable and legitimate segment. However, it is doubtful that they necessarily had to be assigned to the adventure market in order to be adequately served by the industry in terms of product formulation and promotional strategies. Since the presence of risk and challenge has been shown a prerequisite for adventure, some but not all forms of ecotourism fall under the adventure tourism realm.

This paper has so far identified several distinct segments: the traditional adventure recreationist, the ecotourist seeking insight but also accepting and being exposed to risk, and the overland tourist. Dividing the market is of course crucial from a marketing point of view in order to define target populations and develop appropriate marketing mix strategies to meet their needs. The question, however, becomes whether with such preconceived notions of what constitutes adventure tourism, practitioners and scholars really do gauge the full size of the market. After all, the discussion has so far centered on what they consider as adventure tourism. However, this conception may disagree with what individuals themselves regard as adventure experiences.

A starting point for this discussion of individuals' view of adventure is the realization that a "psychological movement" or process accompanies the adventure tourist's geographical movement from the generating region via the transit route to the destination region and back. Turner (1969) views societies as products of the ongoing dialectic between structure and antistructure. Structure refers to the institutionalized set of political and economic positions, offices, roles, and statuses that constitute social organizations, whereas antistructure points to experiences beyond the confines of society. While Turner, in his subsequent writings (1972, 1973) focuses on pilgrims, his work has relevance in the present discussion. According to Turner, once individuals are out of the structural context of society, they go through a three-stage ritual process: a spatial and social separation, liminality, and reintegration. This process can also be observed with adventure tourists. They, by traveling to destinations peripheral to their home environment, have removed themselves both physically and symbolically from their normal structured world and their social group. The separation stage is followed by the entry into the state of antistructure where "communitas" can be experienced.

The formation of communitas has been particularly recognized in the context of adventure recreation activities, mostly in conjunction with the "flow" experience (Csikszentmihalyi 1975). As shown in Figure 4.2, two dimensions – skills and challenges – characterize any activity. If the latter posed by an activity are greater than a person's skills, anxiety is a likely outcome. Conversely, a person experiences boredom if his/her skills are greater than the challenges inherent in the activity. Only when a person's skills match the challenge posed by the activity, does flow occur. The "flow experience," a transcendent state, has been described as a phenomenological state where self, self-awareness, behavior, and context form a unitized singular experience (Csikszentmihalyi 1975). The literature asserts that flow is attained when the situational risk (mainly physical) matches the participant's competence for the specific activity. Or alternatively, it has been described as exercising "control over the relationship between the individual's abilities and the demands of the context" (Celsi *et al.* 1993: 12) in connection with skydivers, and Ewert (1994) notes this in his study of climbers. This common experience of flow is said to create a bond, or "communitas" among participants, with Turner (1972) describing communitas as "a shared flow."

The establishment of communitas and shared experience assuming transcendental character is also conceivable in contexts other than adventure recreation. As discussed earlier, overland travel, as along the Asian Overland Route, can bring people in contact with unique cultures, sacred places, and what Horne (1992) defined as the cultural genes bank of places. Encounters with these aspects of the external environment can challenge individuals' abilities, less in a physical than in a psychological or intellectual sense. Previously

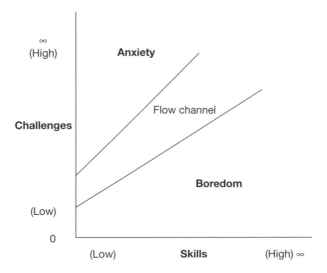

Figure 4.2 Flow concept

Source: Csikszentmihalyi (1990: 74).

held views of oneself and one's world may be challenged, reviewed, and revised, Horne (1992) refers to such experiences as "discovery" – a sense of excitement and wonder when experiencing something that will make the world seem much wider. These "discoveries" can vary in intensity, even resulting in profound changes in perception. Following such experiences of "flow" and "discovery" in the state of liminality is the process of reintegration whereby adventure tourists, upon returning home, usually acquire new roles and a higher status in their ordinary social group as a result of their travels.

Perceptions of challenge and risk

As is apparent from the above discussion, the individual is at the center of the movement in both geographical and psychological terms. Yet, to date individual differences in perception of challenges and risks resulting from variations in people's personality and previous travel experience have not entered the discussion on adventure tourism. In this respect individuals vary in their approaches and strategies to situations posing challenges and risks (Knowles 1976) and in their perceptions of what constitutes them. These perceptions are partly a result of assessing one's specific skills. They are, however, also a matter of how one is predisposed to regard situations of challenge and risk in general.

Berlyne (1960) suggests that every individual has a preferred or "optimum stimulation level" (OSL) and is motivated to increase or decrease novelty, a construct closely related to arousal/sensation seeking (Lee and Crompton 1992), and complexity if the environmental stimulation is below or above the optimum. A high OSL is indicative of sensation seekers while sensation avoiders are characterized by a low OSL (Zuckerman 1979). The former have received much attention in the literature to date (Ewert 1994; Schuett 1993). However, despite the work of Wahlers and Etzel (1985) who discussed the influence of lifestyle stimulation, people with a low OSL were generally not perceived as likely to engage in activities like mountaineering or skydiving, or to join an overland trip through Central Africa. To them even a comparatively tame ecotourism venture was said not to appeal and their typical choice of vacation was more likely to be a cultural tour of Rome or a beach holiday on the Canary Islands.

While such vacations may not be thought of as adventure holidays from a marketing point of view, for individuals characterized by a low OSL, they may have all the elements of an adventure. The risks and challenges may not be so much of a physical nature as they are psychological and social in these instances, yet skills are equally required from these tourists to confront challenging situations during the trip. Such situations may or may not be relatively easy to handle for the individuals in the home environment, yet the separation and transgression into tourism are likely to accentuate them, giving them a more challenging character. Under such circumstances individuals may even experience flow.

Previous travel experience is a further aspect that is likely to affect an individual's perception of a holiday as an adventure. Pearce and Caltabiano (1983) proposed the concept of a travel career ladder. While it has been further developed (Pearce and Moscardo 1985; Pearce 1988), adopted (Kim 1997), and critiqued (Ryan 1998), the essential premise of the concept based on Maslow's need hierarchy is as follows: Tourists are initially more concerned with fulfilling physiological and safety needs. With greater experience they increasingly seek to satisfy higher level needs such as relationship, self-esteem, and self-actualization. Adventure tourism has so far been mostly related to an individual's pursuit of peak experiences, attempting to address a need for self-actualization. According to the travel career ladder, this would generally refer to more experienced tourists. However, it is conceivable that a first-time tourist, attempting to satisfy mainly lower level needs, perceives the above-mentioned cultural tour to Rome as more challenging and risky, and requisite of many more skills, than, for instance, an experienced, high altitude trekker would perceive his 50th trip to the Himalayas.

To potentially substantiate such a viewpoint, and consequently, incorporate the subjective adventure experience of an. individual into the conceptualization of adventure tourism it would he necessary to approach and investigate the subject not only from the currently prevalent etic but also more from an emic perspective. These two concepts were first introduced by Pike (1954) who derived them from the linguistic terms "phonetic" and "phonemic," to be used in a more general context than linguistics. Pike was a proponent of the emic approach, regarding etic analysis merely as a means of access to emics. The discussion on the two perspectives took on momentum when Harris, an anthropologist, published *The Nature of Cultural Things* (1964) in which he strongly advocated the etic approach. He viewed it as important in itself, independent of emics. Over the years proponents of both methods have begun to acknowledge the value of the other and the necessity to employ both to further advance knowledge. A full discussion of the on-going and complex debate appears elsewhere (Headland, Pike and Harris 1990), so a brief summary of the two perspectives will suffice.

Etics involves the study of behavior from outside a particular system. It requires scholars to utilize logical and empirical analysis, adopting strict scientific methods to study the phenomenon under investigation. According to Harris,

> Etic statements depend upon the phenomenal distinctions judged appropriate by the community of scientific observers. Etic statements cannot be falsified if they do not conform to the actor's notion of what is significant, real, meaningful, or appropriate.
>
> (1968: 575)

In contrast, emics is concerned with studying behavior from inside a system. The premise of the emic approach is the adoption of the subject's viewpoint by the researcher. A variety of methods are utilized to gain such insights, including interviews, participant observation, or observation. Qualitative approaches are employed to derive values, meanings, etc., from subjects on which an emic perspective can be developed. Gottlieb (1982) first introduced the emic approach into tourism research. In the context of authenticity, she notes:

> this [emic] perspective . . . proceeds from the premise that what the vacationer experiences is real, valid and fulfilling, no matter how "superficial" it may seem to the social scientist . . . it assumes that the vacationers' own feelings and views about vacations are "authentic," whether or not the observer judges them to match the host culture.
>
> (1982: 167)

In the study of adventure tourism, researchers have established that the notions of risk and challenge are paramount. As argued earlier, this is in agreement with the meaning adventure has acquired throughout history. However, it is researchers who have evaluated peoples' recreation/tourism experiences and categorized them to be either adventurous or non-adventurous. Thereby they have come to focus their attention on certain segments of the market, mostly specific forms of outdoor recreation. But does that mean that only these market segments, be they outdoor adventure recreation, overland travel, and certain forms of ecotourism, can be regarded as adventure tourism? Or could it be that by assessing individuals' perceptions of their vacations, adventure experiences may fall into market segments that so far have been perceived by both scholars and practitioners as anything but adventure tourism?

Conclusion

This article has reviewed the existing literature on adventure tourism, proposing that the prevalent focus on researchers' and marketers' understanding of it is too narrow to gauge the full size and potential of this market. Underlying this proposition is the recognition that individuals' subjective experience of adventure and their self-perception may not be consistent with researchers' and practitioners' classifications. This has several implications for the research, management, and marketing of adventure tourism.

In terms of research, the approach to the subject from an emic perspective, utilizing qualitative research methods is essential. It will be useful to establish exactly how factors such as personality characteristics and previous travel experience affect an individual's perception of adventure and what other factors are of importance in this context. The use of this research approach itself is, however, not enough. With it has to come the realization that the type of setting and the type of risk associated with adventure tourism are not necessarily confined to the ones researchers currently focus on.

The spatial context may not only be tied to wilderness outdoor settings, which in the past have been focal due to the ready presence of physical risk. Yet, this may be equally, in some instances more, present in some large cities, for instance, than it is in certain outdoor settings. In fact, it could even be argued that adventure tourism does not have to be associated with any specific type of setting but is rather a function of a person's exposure to the unknown that poses risk and challenge. Therefore, it is important to conduct this type of research also in nontraditional settings.

It is equally important to avoid a preoccupation with situations posing physical risk only. Risk is a multidimensional construct (Brooker 1983; Cheron and Ritchie 1982; Jacoby and Kaplan 1972). Yet, risk dimensions other than the physical one have only been briefly mentioned in the literature without being further investigated. The recognition and research of the psychological and social risk dimensions in particular may, however, have important implications for the management of the experience. At present, adventure operators do make allowances that deal mainly with the physical risk, but the management of adventure may equally require a focus on specific skills and tools that assist participants to deal with these other types of risk. Given the subjective experience of adventure, further research may reveal that the provision of such coping mechanisms is perhaps equally important to those addressing the physical risk, even in environments that many experienced tourists would consider safe. It may be these measures, reflective of the intimate understanding of the customer, that offer a competitive advantage for a specific operator in an increasingly competitive marketplace. Consequently, these alternative types of risk should be afforded the same prominence in the research as physical risk to understand their impact on the individual and his/her perception of adventure, and to utilize this knowledge both in the management and the marketing of adventure tourism.

The expansion of the types of settings and risks to be considered obviously introduces difficulties in deriving at an exact definition of adventure tourism. Yet, it has perhaps more fluid boundaries than a single definition could capture. These boundaries, challenging the exclusivity of only certain market segments being associated with this type of tourism, may also open up new opportunities for marketers. Market segmentation using psychographics in combination with the currently used segmentation approaches would appear critical in this context, as it may result in the identification of "marginal" adventure tourists. These individuals may currently choose products other than those offered by adventure tourism operators. However, they may be turned into potential customers by targeting them with appropriate promotional messages and media. Expending some marketing effort on select people in these previously untapped markets may increase adventure operators' customer base without the need for substantial marketing expenses. Promotional messages alone, reflecting an intimate understanding of the subjective nature of adventure experiences, may be sufficient to turn these potential customers into actual ones. In other instances, adjustments to the actual products being offered may be required to better meet their needs. These adjustments, of course, would have to be of a rather subtle nature so as not to alienate operators' core markets. Consequently, it is not suggested that these product modifications should be foremost in terms of destination/activity coverage, but perhaps more in the management of these adventure experiences, as outlined above.

As suggested here, the proposed change in research focus on the subjective adventure experience may both have theoretical implications and prove profitable to practitioners. Therefore, it should be of interest to researchers and practitioners alike to engage in more research to further explore the adventure tourism phenomenon along the lines suggested in this paper.

Acknowledgements

Valuable comments on earlier versions of the paper by Wesley Roehl, the late Martin Oppermann, and Christopher White are gratefully acknowledged.

References

Berlyne, D.E. (1960) *Conflict, Arousal and Curiosity*. New York: McGraw Hill.
Brooker, G. (1983) 'An Assessment of an Expanded Measure of Perceived Risk', in *Advances in Consumer Research* 11, T.C. Kinnear, ed., pp. 439–441. Provo UT: Association of Consumer Research.
Brown, L., ed. (1993) *The New Shorter Oxford English Dictionary*, Vol. 1, Oxford: Clarendon Press.
Celsi, R.L., R.L. Rose, and T.W. Leigh (1993) 'An Exploration of High-Risk Leisure Consumption through Skydiving', *Journal of Consumer Research* 20(1): 1–23.
Cheron, E.J., and J.R.B. Ritchie (1982) 'Leisure Activities and Perceived Risk', *Journal of Leisure Research* 14: 139–154.

Christiansen, D.R. (1990) 'Adventure Tourism', in *Adventure Education*, J.C. Miles and S. Priest, eds, pp. 433–441. State College PA: Venture.

Cohen, E. (1972) 'Toward a Sociology of International Tourism', *Social Research* 39(1): 164–182.

—— (1973) 'Nomads from Affluence: Notes on the Phenomenon of Drifter-Tourism', *International Journal of Comparative Sociology* 14(1/2): 89–103.

Cooper, C., J. Fletcher, D. Gilbert, and S. Wanhill (1993) *Tourism, Principles, and Practice*, London: Pitman.

Csikszentmihalyi, M. (1975) *Beyond Boredom and Anxiety*, San Francisco CA: Jossey-Bass.

—— (1990) *Flow: The Psychology of Optimal Experience*, New York: Harper & Row.

Darst, P.W., and G.P. Armstrong (1980) *Outdoor Adventure Activities for School and Recreation Programs*, New York: Macmillan.

Dufrene, M. (1973) *The Phenomenology of Aesthetic Experience*, Evanston IL: Northwestern University Press.

Ewert, A. (1985) 'Why People Climb: The Relationship of Participant Motives and Experience Level to Mountaineering', *Journal of Leisure Research* 17: 241–250.

—— (1987) 'Recreation in the Outdoor Setting: A Focus on Adventure-Based Recreational Experiences', *Leisure Information Quarterly* 14: 5–7.

—— (1989) *Outdoor Adventure Pursuits: Foundations, Models and Theorie,*. Columbus OH: Publishing Horizons.

—— (1993) 'Differences in the Level of Motive Importance Based on Trip Outcome, Experience Level and Group Type', *Journal of Leisure Research* 25: 335–349.

—— (1994) 'Playing the Edge: Motivation and Risk Taking in a High-Altitude Wildernesslike Environment', *Environment and Behavior* 26: 3–24.

—— and S. Hollenhorst (1989) 'Testing the Adventure Model: Empirical Support for a Model of Risk Recreation Participation', *Journal of Leisure Research* 21: 124–139.

—— and —— (1994) 'Individual and Setting Attributes of the Adventure Recreation Experience', *Leisure Sciences* 16: 177–191.

Gottlieb, A. (1982) 'Americans' Vacations', *Annals of Tourism Research* 9: 165–187.

Hall, C.M. (1989) 'Special Interest Travel: A Prime Force in the Expansion of Tourism?', in *Geography in Action*, R. Welch, ed., pp. 81–89. Dunedin: Department of Geography, University of Otago.

—— and B. Weiler, eds (1992) *Special Interest Tourism*, London: Belhaven.

—— and S. McArthur (1994) 'Commercial Whitewater Rafting in Australia', in *New Viewpoints in Australian Outdoor Recreation Research and Planning*, D. Mercer, ed., pp. 109–118. Melbourne: Hepper Marriott & Associates.

Harris, M. (1964) *The Nature of Cultural Things*, New York: Random House.

—— (1968) *The Rise of Anthropological Theory*, New York: Thomas Y. Crowell.

Headland, T.N., K.L. Pike, and M. Harris, eds (1990) *Emics and Etics. The Insider/Outsider Debate*, Newbury Park CA: Sage.

Horne, D. (1992) *The Intelligent Tourist*, Sydney: Margaret Gee.

Jacoby, J., and L.B. Kaplan (1972) 'The Components of Perceived Risk', in *Proceedings 3rd Annual Conference*, M. Venkatesan, ed., pp. 382–393. Chicago IL: Association for Consumer Research.

Johnston, M.E. (1992) 'Facing the Challenges in the Mountains of New Zealand', in *Special Interest Tourism*, C.M. Hall and B. Weiler, eds, pp. 159–169. London: Belhaven.

Kim, E.Y.J. (1997) 'Korean Outbound Tourism. Pre-Visit Expectations of Australia', *Journal of Travel and Tourism Marketing* 6(1): 11–19.

Knowles, E.S. (1976) 'Searching for Motivations in Risk-Taking and Gambling', in *Gambling and Society*, W.R. Eadington, ed., pp. 295–322. Springfield IL: Charles & Thomas.

Lee, T.H., and J. Crompton (1992) 'Measuring Novelty Seeking in Tourism', *Annals of Tourism Research* 19: 732–751.

Leiper, N. (1979) 'A Framework of Tourism', *Annals of Tourism Research* 6: 390–407.

—— (1995) *Tourism Management*, Melbourne: RMIT Press.

Martin, P., and S. Priest (1986) 'Understanding the Adventure Experience', *Adventure Education* 3(1): 18–21.

Maslow, A. (1954) *Motivation and Personality*, New York: Harper.

Mills, A.S. (1985) 'Participation Motivations for Outdoor Recreation: A Test of Maslow's Theory', *Journal of Leisure Research* 17: 184–199.

Pearce, D.G. (1979) 'Towards a Geography of Tourism', *Annals of Tourism Research* 6: 245–272.

Pearce, P.L. (1988) *The Ulysses Factor: Evaluating Visitors in Tourist Settings*, New York: Springer.

—— and M.L. Caltabiano (1983) 'Inferring Travel Motivations from Travelers' Experiences', *Journal of Travel Research* 22(1): 16–20.

—— and G. Moscardo (1985) 'Travelers' Career Levels and Authenticity', *Australian Journal of Psychology* 37(2): 157–174.

Pike, K.L. (1954) *Language in Relation to a Unified Theory of the Structure of Human Behavior*, Glendale CA: Summer Institute of Linguistics.

Priest, S. (1992) 'Factor Exploration and Confirmation for the Dimensions of an Adventure Experience', *Journal of Leisure Research* 24: 127–139.

Quinn, B. (1990) 'The Essence of Adventure', in *Adventure Education*, J.C. Miles and S. Priest, eds, pp. 145–148. State College PA: Venture Publishing.

Ryan, C. (1998) 'The Travel Career Ladder. An Appraisal', *Annals of Tourism Research* 25: 936–957.

Schuett, M. (1993) 'Refining Measures of Adventure Recreation Involvement', *Leisure Sciences* 15: 205–216.

Sung, H., A.M. Morrison, and J.T. O'Leary (1997) 'Definition of Adventure Travel: Conceptual Framework for Empirical Application from the Providers' Perspective', *Asia Pacific Journal of Tourism Research* 1(2): 47–67.

Turner, V. (1969) *The Ritual Process*, Chicago IL: Aldine.

—— (1972) 'Passages, Margins, and Poverty: Religious Communitas', *Worship* 46 (July): 390–412.

—— (1973) 'The Center Out There: Pilgrim's Goal', *History of Religion* 12: 191–230.

Wahlers, R.G., and M.J. Etzel (1985) 'Vacation Preference as a Manifestation of Optimum Stimulation and Lifestyle Experience', *Journal of Leisure Research* 17: 283–295.

Walle, A.H. (1997) 'Pursuing Risk or Insight: Marketing Adventures', *Annals of Tourism Research* 24: 265–282.

Zuckerman, M. (1979) *Sensation Seeking: Beyond the Optimal Level of Arousal*, Hillsdale NJ: Erlbaum.

Zurick, D.N. (1992) 'Adventure Travel and Sustainable Tourism in the Peripheral Economy of Nepal', *Annals of the Association of American Geographers* 82: 608–628.

—— (1995) *Errant Journeys: Adventure Travel in a Modern Age*, Austin TX: University of Texas Press.

Chapter 5

James Higham and Tom Hinch

SPORT AND TOURISM RESEARCH
A geographic approach

Introduction

WEED'S (2005A) EDITORIAL for *European Sports Management Quarterly* provides a review of research serving the study of sport and tourism that is both timely and critical. He adopts Forscher's (1963) analogy of 'chaos in the brickyard' to highlight a considerable obstacle to the development of social science knowledge. In doing so he describes the tendency, common in the field of sport and tourism, to produce 'pieces' of research (i.e. bricks) en masse, with little or no attempt to integrate the outcomes of research into coherent bodies or 'edifices' of knowledge. Thus papers and article are produced (like piles of bricks) that are neither informed by, nor in turn inform, social science knowledge. While the field of sport and tourism has been addressed by scholars for upward of 20 years (see Glyptis, 1989; Weed & Bull, 2004), the bodies of knowledge serving the field – including concepts and theories – remain worryingly obscure (Gibson, 2006).

Additionally, Weed's editorial highlights the 'lack of any explicit consideration of epistemology (as) a deficiency that the area of sports tourism shares with much research in the broader sport and tourism fields' (2005a, p. 238). Data from his meta-analysis of sport tourism publications highlights the predominance of empirical research employing quantitative research design. Typical of much research in the field are simple self-completed questionnaires generating individual pieces of descriptive research. While survey research of this nature may be appropriate in some instances, Weed (2005a) rightly highlights the concern that a preponderance of such research, which lacks wider theoretical discussion, does little to serve the scholarly development of the field.

This article offers a response to Weed's critical appraisal of research that addresses the field of sport and tourism (Weed, 2005a; Weed, 2005b). It acknowledges the validity of his criticism and attempts to initiate a discourse that may enhance the relevance and scholarly value of research programmes serving this field. It aims to highlight research directions (research questions and approaches) that arise from a geographical perspective of sport and tourism. The concepts of space, place, and environment are used as the theoretical foundation for this paper. These concepts are defined and explained and then discussed in terms of the study of sport and tourism in the context of geography as a social science. By adopting these theoretical concepts, and questions arising from them (one of many varied approaches to investigating the field), researchers will serve the study of sport and tourism in a way that is informed by, and in turn informs, existing or developing edifices of knowledge.

Geographical perspectives on the confluence of sport and tourism

Geography offers a multitude of perspectives that can be used to help conceptualise the field of sport and tourism. One useful geographic categorisation is space, place, and environment (Hall & Page, 1999). Under this framework, space refers to specific locations, be they local, regional, national, or supranational, and explores the interrelationships linking sport tourism generating areas and destinations (Mitchell & Murphy, 1991; Boniface & Cooper, 1994). The basic concepts and themes relating to sport tourism and space have their roots in economic geography. These concepts are drawn from the study of sports geography and the spatial analysis of sports (Rooney, 1988; Bale, 1989, 1993). The concept of space also relates to the travel patterns associated with sport tourism markets. Thus, space relates to the ways in which sports may influence the spatial travel patterns and itineraries of tourists, whether sport functions as a primary, secondary, or tertiary travel motivation (Hinch & Higham, 2004).

Place refers to space that is infused with meaning (Lew, 2001). The sports played in any region or country influence the meanings that are associated with that area in terms that are often examined by cultural geographers (Rooney & Pillsbury, 1992). It has been argued that sport infuses tourism destinations with one of the most authentic types of attractions (Hinch & Higham, 2005). The link between culture and sport takes many forms, from the juxtaposition of cultural performances against sport events through to the central role that sport plays as a manifestation of contemporary culture. The concept of place, as addressed by geographers, raises important questions about the field of sport and tourism (Hinch & Higham, 2004). These relate to the use of sport to promote tourism destinations in a variety of markets, and the significant challenges associated with the commodification and corporatisation of culture (e.g. see Jackson & Andrews, 1999; Jackson et al., 2001; Hinch & Higham, 2005).

Environment relates to the natural and built resources that are used to support activities, as well as the impacts that various activities have on these resources (Lew, 2001; Hall & Page, 1999). Standeven and De Knop (1999) explore the geography of natural and built resources relating to sport and tourism. They highlight the common resource base for sport and tourism facilities and infrastructure. However, quite different issues are associated with natural resources and built facilities in sport tourism (Hinch & Higham, 2004). Many outdoor sports tend to be dependent on specific landscape and/or climatic conditions while other types of sport are more transportable and feature standard facilities that can be built in locations designed to maximise market access (Bale, 1989). Thus, the geographical concepts of space, place, and environment provide an established organisational heuristic that serves as the structure for the following discussions.

Space

Space and place are concepts that are central to the geography of sport (Bale, 1989) and the geography of tourism (Pearce, 1987; Lew, 2001). Unlike recreation and play, sport tends to be characterised by defined spatial delineations, such as the length of a marathon course or the spatial parameters of a football field (Bale, 1989). Spatial boundaries in sport may be written into rules and codes of regulations. 'In many cases sport involves the dominance of territory or the mastery of distance; spatial infractions are punished and spatial progress is often a major objective' (Bale, 1989, p. 12). Tourism is also characterised by a spatial component (Cooper et al., 1993). To be considered a tourist, individuals must leave and then eventually return to their home. Travel is one of the necessary conditions of tourism, and it is for this reason that the spatial implications of tourism are important (Mitchell & Murphy, 1991).

The spatial analysis of sport tourism involves the study of the locations in which sports occur and the movement of tourists to these locations (Hinch & Higham, 2004). Such an analysis finds its theoretical foundation in the geography of sport (Bale, 1989, 1993; Rooney, 1988), which introduces concepts such as central place theory, distance decay, and location hierarchies for consideration in the study of sport tourism. This analysis also draws on the geography of tourism, which considers the 'spatial expression of tourism as a physical activity, focusing on both tourist-generating and tourist-receiving areas as well as the links between' (Boniface & Cooper, 1994).

From this starting point it is clear that the spatial concept of distance decay applies to both sport and tourism. For example, in the case of sport, a discernable pattern exists in terms of the home or away status of a sports contest and the probability of winning. Not only is winning away less probable than at home, but 'the probability of winning forms a clear gradient according to distance from home' (Bale, 1989, p. 31). In the context of sport tourism, sports that take place in central locations are advantaged by proximity to markets (Pearce, 1989). The distance decay model postulates that tourist flows decrease with distance from the origin (Boniface & Cooper, 1994). In theory, therefore, the power of attraction that a sport may exert upon the travel decision process diminishes as distance increases due to increasing travel costs and declining knowledge of distant locations (Mitchell & Murphy, 1991).

In reality, the distance decay function is moderated by a range of factors (Miossec, 1977), such as political, cultural, and climatic characteristics, which may act as barriers or facilitators to travel (Cooper et al., 1993; Mitchell & Murphy, 1991). Travel flows may be mediated by a number of interrelated variables (Boniface & Cooper, 1994). Zonal travel patterns can be 'modified by the hierarchy of resort destinations, the spatial advantages offered by major transport routes and locations with outstanding or unique reputations' (Mitchell & Murphy, 1991, p. 63). Furthermore, Urry (1990) addresses the desire to extend the 'tourist gaze' to more exotic and distant places, which may run counter to distance decay travel patterns. The distance decay function of sport tourism may also be mediated by such things as the quality of the opposition and the importance of the competition or, in terms of non-competitive sports, the accessibility, availability, and cost of engaging in chosen sports activities at a destination. Factors that may intervene to distort the distance decay function of sport tourism are not well understood, and merit academic attention. While quantitative methods have most commonly been adopted to investigate the demographic and motivational profiles of visitors to tourism destinations, the potential for qualitative methods to provide more advanced, critical, and analytical insights into the travel patterns and experiences of those engaged in sport-related tourism is also considerable.

Clearly, sport tourism takes place within a complex milieu of spatial parameters. Different sports are reliant to differing degrees on the availability and quality of natural and/or built resources. While some sports are rigidly anchored to specific and non-transportable natural resources, others are relatively free of resource constraints and may be located where proximity to concentrations of population offers the greatest competitive advantage. Distance-time-cost thresholds also shape the spatial travel patterns of sport tourists. However, sport tourism market range and travel flows are influenced by a range of factors that are not well understood. This ensures that a variety of questions emerge from discussion of the spatial elements of sport and tourism (Hinch & Higham, 2004).

Sport centres and location hierarchies

Modern sports exist in a continual state of change (Keller, 2001). The dynamics of change are often driven by economic processes that bear upon the structure of competitive sports (e.g., the development of new league competitions), the location of sport facilities, and the rise and fall of sports destinations (Butler, 2005). Bale (1989, p. 77) refers to 'the growth and decline in importance of different sport locations' which parallels Butler's (1980) tourist area lifecycle theory. These dynamics have implications for the scale of the player and spectator catchment areas. In professional sport, player catchment limitations are commonly alleviated through external recruitment, player transfers and draft schemes. The spectator catchment, and the propensity for residents and non-residents in different regions to attend live sport, is a separate issue that is of particular relevance to sports marketing managers. Indeed, at the elite level of professional sports such as football both player catchments and spectator markets have been internationalised through processes of globalisation.

Sports attractions, then, exist within a hierarchical organisational structure in a similar fashion to other tourist attractions (Leiper, 1990). The hierarchy reflects the fact that some sports centres primarily draw upon a local catchment, while others situated higher in the sports hierarchy draw upon regional, national, or international catchments. Bale (1989, p. 79) explains that sports facilities situated in central locations are located 'as close to potential users as possible in order to maximise pleasure from the sport experience and to minimise travel, and hence cost'. This characteristic has been complicated in recent years, as new factors have emerged that influence the status of sports locations. These factors include facility sharing, changing access to infrastructure and travel nodes, proximity to tourism and service developments, and prominence within media markets (Stevens, 2001). Tourism destinations may compete to ascend the sport location hierarchy. Some have used sports generally in this respect. Dubai is currently advancing its goal of being the world's first dedicated 'sports city'. Others use specific sports such as surfing (Hawaii) to position themselves as destinations of prominence.

The attractiveness of sport locations may draw upon the uniqueness of different sports regions (Rooney & Pillsbury, 1992). Sport tourism location requires the presence of sports facilities and resources as well as tourism infrastructure and services (Standeven & De Knop, 1999). 'To the visitor the amenities appear to be related to each other; the whole is more attractive than each separate amenity' (Dietvorst, 1995, p. 165).

Alternatively, resources such as streetscapes and scenery can be used for sporting purposes (e.g. Monaco Grand Prix). Nonetheless, sport tourism centres have the capacity to accommodate significant inward travel flows at a destination. National and/or international transport nodes, an established accommodation sector, tourist attractions to complement the sport industry, and a well-developed service sector including tourism information services contribute to its functionality.

Thus, a number of questions need to be addressed to advance an understanding of sport centres and location hierarchies. What are the forces driving demand for sports? What are the means by which destinations can ascend the sport location hierarchy? How may sport and tourism resources be developed in a manner that is of mutual benefit?

Sport tourism market range

The market range of a sports resource or a sports team varies according to a wide range of factors. These include standard of facilities, costs of use, and ease of access. In professional sports, market range may be influenced by style of play, team image, public promotion, and the success of the team, which influence the status of a team as a tourist attraction (Hinch & Higham, 2001). 'Hallmark teams' are those that 'regularly attract large spectator crowds (and) have now become synonymous with tourism place promotion as well as short break leisure tourism packages' (Stevens, 2001, p. 61). Bale (1993) notes that football clubs such as Liverpool, Arsenal, and Manchester United receive high levels of media attention. This has helped to build a support base throughout England, Europe and, particularly in the case of Manchester United, all over the world. The implications for tourist market range are significant. Manchester United premier league games played at Old Trafford regularly attract between 4,000 and 6,000 international tourists to the Greater Manchester area (Stevens, 2001). Similarly, 46% of all spectators that attend Baltimore Orioles (USA) baseball matches at the Camden Yards stadium are sport excursionists and sport tourists, approximately 11,000 of whom remain in Baltimore for at least one night. Questions relating to the prominence of sports teams in media markets and the status of such teams as tourist attractions currently remain largely unanswered.

Extending market range beyond the geographical boundaries that a team actually represents may be achieved nationally or internationally through match attendance, as well as merchandise sales or supporters' club memberships (Hinch & Higham, 2004). The continued success of a team influences its market range, but enduring success is very rare (Gilson et al., 2000). This factor alone cannot explain the sustained and extended fan bases that some teams enjoy. Individual star players and the aura, glamour, and heritage associated with teams and the venues at which they compete contribute to the enduring allure of some sports teams. The same factors influence the propensity of visitors to engage in nostalgia sport tourism (Fairley & Gammon, 2006). The atmosphere of the home stadium, colour and parochialism of the home fans, and public presentation of prominent team players may also bear upon the supporter catchments that are generated by sports teams (Bale, 1989). Thus, questions may be raised that consider the strategies that destination managers may use to extend sport market range, and the effectiveness of those strategies. How can sports managers endeavour to develop hallmark team status, and how can this be used to foster tourism? How can sports managers generate prominence in media markets and how can such efforts be leveraged for tourism?

Sport, space, and the visitor experience

The time-distance-cost thresholds of tourism are such that the increasing investment of discretionary time and income on travel will bear upon most aspects of the visitor experience. For instance, the further sports tourists travel, the more likely it is that they will spend some time at the destination engaging in tourist activities (Nogawa et al., 1996; Gibson, 2002a, b). It is also noteworthy that the area that a sports team represents may in fact require 'home' supporters to travel considerable distances to support their team. National teams may attract 'home' supporters from throughout the country that it represents, many of whom travel as domestic tourists. Indeed expatriates may also return to their country of origin to support or compete in sports (Hinch & Higham, 2004). This raises intriguing questions relating to social identity and sport-related tourism (Jones & Green, 2006). Thus the spatial area that a team or club actually represents may vary considerably from the spatial extent of the team supporter and player catchments. This raises the prospect of spectators travelling as domestic or international tourists, without feeling that they are leaving 'home', or indeed feeling that they are going 'home' (Gibson, 2002a, b). Similarly, in international competition teams may be supported by expatriates who feel a strong sense of support for teams representing countries/regions where they have lived in the past. This phenomenon opens questions concerning professional sport, the migration of elite athletes, and implications for tourism and tourist experiences. These scenarios raise interesting questions about sense of personal identity, representation, and multiple sport fandoms in an increasingly mobile world (Bale & Maguire, 1994). Each may have interesting implications for travel mobilities and visitor experiences at tourist destinations (Hall & Williams, 2002).

Visitor experiences and expenditure patterns are of particular interest to sport, tourism, and service industries. Studies of the economic impacts of sport tourism are commonplace in North America and elsewhere (Preuss, 2005). Insights exist into 'both the costs and benefits to a community of attracting a professional sports outfit and the economic impact of an existing sports franchise on the city in which it is located' (Bale, 1993, p. 77). The expenditures that may be associated with the location of a sports club or franchise in an urban area may include club expenditures, or those associated with the production of the sport, and expenditures generated by local and non-local spectators. It is noteworthy that the spending patterns of different sport spectator catchments may be quite unique, with variation between local and non-local visitor expenditure patterns particularly evident (Gibson et al., 2002b). However, relatively little research has been published on this aspect of sport tourism, in contrast to the prevalence of economic impact studies (Mules & Dwyer, 2006).

Sport tourism in the core-periphery

Quite different forces act upon sport tourism development in core and peripheral locations. Bale (1989) summarises the theory underpinning the development of sports facilities in central locations. He notes that sports facilities are centrally located to provide sports outlets within their market areas. Low-order sports locations provide sporting facilities that are used by smaller catchment areas; the threshold population needed for the viability of a lower-order place is smaller. Higher order locations, which command larger population thresholds, are fewer in number and are more widely spaced. However, these theoretical discussions have not been well tested as they apply to sport tourism. This is increasingly the case in a world where places compete passionately with each other for economic advantage, particularly in terms of expanding upon limited local markets by exploiting enhanced business, media, competitor, and tourist (e.g. spectator) mobilities (Kotler *et al.*, 1993; Hall, 1998).

Conversely, Christaller (1963, p. 95) states that tourism is 'a branch of the economy that avoids central places and the agglomerations of industry. Tourism is drawn to the periphery . . . (where) one may find, easier than anywhere, the chance of recreation and sport'. Sport tourism in peripheral locations is typically resource dependent and, therefore, determined by the physical nature of the landscape rather than proximity to market areas (Hinch & Higham, 2004). Sport tourism market zones, travel patterns, and tourist experiences in peripheral locations stand in contrast to those associated with sports that take place in central locations.

Sports space theory applied to peripheral areas suggests that the natural resource base, rather than market access, determine the locations where sport tourism takes place (Bale, 1989). A ski resort, for example, is dependent on the requisite elevation, terrain, and snow conditions, among other things, to allow participants to engage in their sport in favourable conditions (Hudson, 1999). This is especially the case for niche sport tourism markets where specific sport motivations requiring unique environmental attributes often apply. As Bourdeau *et al.* (2002, p. 23) observe, 'the location of sites and itineraries thus depend on diverse natural conditions which do not readily lend themselves to the satisfaction of geographic (accessibility), demographic or economic needs'. The resource require-ments of sports may be moderated through, for example, snow making technology in the case of alpine winter sports. Resources such as artificial ski slopes can be constructed at considerable expense in central locations, with immediate access provided for con-centrations of population. Notwithstanding these points, the resource requirements of sport tourism in peripheral areas remain the fundamental characteristic of the locations in which they take place (Hudson, 2004).

The inescapable circumstances of sport tourism in peripheral areas provide sport and tourism managers with unique challenges in terms of commercial development (Christaller, 1963; Bourdeau *et al.*, 2002). Remoteness and terrain may limit access while reliance on weather conditions and climatic uncertainty may compromise the viability of sports or render them impossible. The consequences include seasonal use variations, low-intensity use due to institutional factors, high mobility of visitors between alternative sites, and self-sufficiency on the part of many users in terms of service requirements (Bourdeau *et al.*, 2002). However, these sorts of weaknesses and threats can also be viewed as potential strengths and opportunities – especially in the context of 'extreme' sports. Researchers may seek to address how peripheral sport tourism destinations can seek to create competitive advantages by exploiting favourable or unique natural resources. This may require, among other things, a comprehensive understanding of demand and regional travel flows, and how these can be modified and/or exploited.

Place

Standeven and De Knop (1999, p. 58) treat sport and tourism as cultural experiences – 'sport as a cultural experience of physical activity; tourism as a cultural experience of place'. They go on to argue that the nature of sport tourism is therefore 'about an experience of physical activity tied to an experience of place'. Tuan (1974) describes place as space that has been infused with meaning. Initially, place scholars argued that the concept of sense of place was most applicable in the home environment, where individuals are in a position to develop deep attachments to place (Relph, 1976). In contrast, tourists were seen as one of the least likely groups to develop this connection due to the superficiality of their experience of destinations. Relph (1976) argued that the 'disneyfication' of landscapes to meet the needs of tourists served to undermine the likelihood that they would connect to place. This characterisation of tourism as a superficial activity ran counter to the views of tourism scholars like MacCannell (1976), who argued that tourists are involved in a serious search for meaning and authenticity. If one adopts MacCannell's view, it seems probable that tourists are interested, or at least are potentially interested, in connecting to the places that they visit.

Geographers continue to study the concept of place with an appreciation that globalisation has changed the way we relate to place (Lew, 2001). In recognition of these changes Williams and Kalternborn (1999, p. 215) note:

> With circulation and movement more the rule than the exception an important geographic dimension of leisure practices is to understand how people in differing cultural contexts use leisure and travel to establish identity, give meaning to their lives, and connect with place.

Increasingly, scholars are recognising that the concept of place is very relevant to tourism and leisure. Crouch's (2000, p. 64) views on the importance of place in a leisure and tourism context represent an important development in the progressively more abstract ways that geographers view place. He describes tourism places as

> a physical image that can be rendered metaphorical as the content of brochures, 'landscape' as a foil for what people might imagine they do . . . In this way it may be that place is understood to be a cultural text that people read and recognize directed by the particular intentions of a producer or promoter.

Culture and the agency of producers and consumers of places play central roles in this perspective.

In contrast to space, place cannot be objectively measured (Hinch & Higham, 2004). It is a subjective concept that is constantly being constructed and reconstructed, negotiated and renegotiated (Hinch & Higham, 2005). As such it is likely that alternative research approaches are necessary to address aspects of sport and tourism that relate to the concept of place. Qualitative approaches, including content analysis coupled with semiotics, may be adopted to provide unique insights into the study of sport and tourism places. Content analysis provides an unobtrusive measure for systemically classifying material and making references leading to deductive and/or inductive interpretations, while semiotic analysis is understood as 'subversive reading' of sign content and underlying meaning (Dann, 2005). The analysis of sport tourism promotional material, personal accounts, and media articles are just a few examples of the types of studies that could provide insights into place (e.g. see Pigeassou, 1997) that are unlikely to be achieved through more standard research approaches.

The negotiation of place is one of the ways that individuals and groups, including sport tourists, develop their identities. Differences in place identity serve as the basis for place marketing and may in turn be influenced by the efforts of place marketers. In the context of sport tourism, this construction of place has a direct bearing on the experience of sport tourists and the experience of the hosts. It is therefore central to the conceptualisation of this field of research and merits further attention if sport and tourism scholarship is to be advanced in a meaningful way from a geographic perspective.

Increased understanding of the way that sport tourism is involved in the construction and reconstruction of places

Standeven and De Knop (1999, p. 58) argue that sport tourism is 'an experience of physical activity tied to an experience of place', but the nature of these ties has yet to be explored in depth. A variety of relevant research questions can be articulated in this area that contribute to edifice building rather than resulting in a random pile of bricks. At the foundation level, basic questions need to be addressed related to the way that sport tourists and managers relate to places and whether they have agency in the construction of place meaning. Variations across general categories of event, active, and nostalgia types of sport tourism should be explored as well as possible differences between different sports. Once the foundations are in place, the framing of the edifice will be built by addressing the why and the so what questions. For example, if research demonstrates that sport tourists and sport tourism managers do have agency in the construction of places then the processes and implications of this agency need to be articulated.

Sport tourism researchers do not have to start from 'scratch' to build this edifice of knowledge. The work of leisure and tourism geographers found in the collections of *Leisure/Tourism Geographies* (Crouch, 1999) and *A Companion to Tourism* (Lew et al., 2004) provide excellent starting points. Each of these publications provides useful conceptualisations of the nature of place meaning and the processes associated with it. Crang (2004, p. 82) provides one such theoretical link in a discussion on the cultural geographies of tourism, in which he comments on the relationship between physical activity and the meaning that people attach to places. The 'beach' is highlighted as a place where there is a particularly strong link between physicality and place, but he goes on to suggest that the physicality of walking holidays and a range of sports and adventure tourist activities may also have direct bearings on the way that place is experienced. More specifically he states that (p. 82):

> the mode of perceiving the landscape and our bodily relationship may well change, as where we think of a shift from the physical exertion of slowly climbing a peak to the stomach-churning thrill of hurtling from a bridge on a bungee line – from an appreciation of the individual and sublime nature we have an accelerated body and an inverted sublime or a body pitted against the rocks and rapids in whitewater rafting.

The concept of authenticity is also relevant to the way that sports tourists view place. Wang's (1999) concept of existential authenticity, focused on the experience of the individual, provides intriguing insight into the authenticity of sport tourism. In addition to using a variety of sport tourism examples, such as mountaineering and adventure tourism, to illustrate his argument, Wang highlights intra-personal and interpersonal dimensions of existential authenticity. In the former, bodily feelings such as health, vigour, and movement are seen as contributing toward authenticity, while in the latter, touristic communitas, which have parallels in terms of sport subcultures, and fandoms were seen as positive factors. Hinch and Higham (2005) used Wang's conceptualisation of authenticity to highlight the unique advantages that sport tourism activities have related to authenticity and a similar argument could be used to explore the way that sport tourists relate to the places that they visit.

Bale's work (e.g. 1999) provides a rich pool of theoretical perspectives from which to address the question of whether sport tourism managers have agency in terms of the construction of places. His concept of 'sportscapes', in which 'one place increasingly – and often necessarily – becomes much the same as any other', suggests a process leading to 'placelessness'. This result is accelerated by sport managers trying to ensure uniform conditions for competition. In contrast, however, Bale has also argued that the hard scientific metaphors of sport places as 'assembly lines for production' could possibly be replaced with a more feminine metaphor of 'parks and gardens'. Using this metaphor, Tuan's concept of the 'playful dominance' of place is highlighted, as is the idea of liminality, which helps erode place boundaries between the players and the spectators thereby facilitating a park-like place rather than a sportscape.

What is the nature of the interaction between activity, people, and place in the context of sport tourism?

Weed and Bull (2004, p. 37) conceptualise the sports tourism phenomenon as 'a social, economic and cultural phenomenon arising from the unique intersection of activity, people and place'. From a geographic perspective this intersection between activity, people, and place is germane. It begs further questions of the nature of this relationship. While this relationship has not been systematically addressed in the sport tourism literature, it has surfaced periodically. In their study of women football players from across the United States who were participating in an annual tournament in Florida, Green and Chalip (1998) noted that the real attraction for the football players was the opportunity 'to celebrate their subculture with others from distant places, rather than the site itself ...' (p. 275). In addition, it is noteworthy that people themselves can have 'place-making qualities'. The creation of sporting place through the congregation of football fans to watch sport in public spaces on a temporary screen (e.g. during the 2006 FIFA World Cup in Germany) is one example of this. If this emphasis on the 'people' dimension of the activity-people-place tripartite is common, then valuable insight into the conceptualisation of sport tourism will be achieved.

In addition to the body of literature in geography that focuses on place, there are other sources of conceptual and theoretical framework that can serve as a foundation for this line of research. For example, Williams (1988) introduces the idea that there are three primary modes of experience in outdoor recreation: activities, companions, and settings. He recognises that the setting might be the primary part of the experience for some while serving only as a backdrop for others. Place attachment is postulated as being stronger for individuals with a setting focus than for individuals focusing on activities.

The lessons learned in this outdoor recreation context may have direct relevance to conceptualisations of sport tourism. Again, the consideration of variations across event, active, and nostalgia sport tourism types is needed as is the consideration of variations across sports. It also seems likely that the degree of competition inherent in an experience may influence the mode of experience. Knowing the patterns of the relationships between activity, people, and place will 'in and of itself' help to conceptualise the field, but understanding why these relationships exist should be the goal of this type of research.

How do sport tourists vary in terms of place attachment, place identity, and place dependence?

Three variants of place that have relevance to sport tourism are place attachment, place identity, and place dependence. Each of these variants has the potential for clarifying the nature of place in the context of sport tourism. Place attachment is a positive affective bond between an individual and a specific place (Shumaker & Taylor, 1983). Positive bonds can be formed with a place even if one is not rooted to the place through actual residence. To a considerable extent, pursuing greater insight into the nature of this attachment is an extension of the previous call to develop an understanding of the relationship between activity, people, and place. Weak place attachment, as in the case of the female football players in Green and Chalip's (1998) article, implies little commitment to a specific destination. In contrast, high levels of attachment not only suggest commitment but also that a visitor may actively protect a particular setting. Place attachment is itself a function of place identity and place dependence.

Place identity involves the 'dimensions of the self that define the individual's personal identity in relation to the physical environment' (Proshansky, 1978, p. 155). This connection between place and identity is a common theme among geographers (Williams & Kalternborn, 1999). It has relevance in terms of an individual's identity as well as a group identity. Members of subcultural sport groups may identify strongly with particular sites that are associated with their sport. Similarly, whole groups, even nations, may identify with certain sport places, for example, Swiss nationals and alpine ski resorts.

Place dependence is a form of attachment that is based on the potential of a certain place to satisfy specific needs or goals (Williams et al., 1992, p. 13). In contrast to place identity, an individual may gain no real sense of identity from a place but may depend upon it to participate in a certain activity. Place dependence includes the consideration of accessibility, the availability of alternative sites, and the level of importance that an individual attaches to the activity or people components associated with at a particular site. Research that examines the relative balance between these dimensions of place will help conceptualise sport tourism experiences. At a practical level, answers to research questions in this realm will aid in the management of sport tourism impacts.

As a greater understanding of the way sport tourists and managers develop connections to place emerge, additional questions can be asked. Examples of these questions include: do place meanings vary between locals and visiting sport tourists? Do place meanings vary between different types of sport tourists? Do place meanings vary by the degree of competitiveness of active sport tourists? Why do these differences exist and what are the implications?

Environment

The extent to which tourists find a destination to be attractive is strongly influenced by the physical environment, including landscapes and climate (Krippendorf, 1986; Boniface & Cooper, 1994; Burton, 1995). Many sports are closely tied to the physical geography of a destination. Priestley (1995, p. 210) observes that single integrated golf resorts 'have mushroomed in the hotter climates where traditional sun, sand and sea tourism could or does exist'. The sport tourism development potential of a destination is also determined by cultural influences on the landscape. Tourism development at a destination requires, in most cases, constructed resources, including sport facilities and tourism infrastructure (Maier & Weber, 1993). Sports may require facilities that are purpose built, such as stadia, marinas, sports arenas, and gymnasia (Bale, 1989). Alternatively, sports may make temporary use of buildings or infrastructures that are developed primarily for purposes other than sport. Roads, central parks, and urban tourism icons (e.g. New York's Central Park and the Sydney Opera House) may figure prominently as locations or backdrops to sporting scenes.

The potential for sport tourism development at a destination is determined in part by the existence of requisite sport and tourism resources and infrastructures. A sport tourism resource inventory would include natural environments, constructed sports facilities, tourism transport, and infrastructure, as well as political and economic resources and cultural/perceptual aspects (Bull, 2005). Considerable opportunity exists for sport and tourism resources to be developed in a coordinated fashion that maximises the mutual benefits of multiple stakeholders. Event sport tourism, for example, offers the potential for the inner city resource base for sport, recreation, entertainment, retail, and service to be transformed in a planned and coordinated manner (Hinch & Higham, 2004). However, many questions regarding policy, planning, and development in this field remain unanswered (Weed & Bull, 2004, Weed, 2006). In order to address unanswered questions, quantitative and qualitative approaches in combination may contribute to a critical understanding of policy initiatives, planning directions, and the effectiveness and consequences of development programmes in the field of sport and tourism.

Landscape and sportscape

It has been noted that 'the search for regional diversity in the landscape has remained an important motive for travellers, despite the standardisation and homogenisation of the tourism industry' (Mitchell & Murphy, 1991, p. 61). The term sportscape is used in the geography of sport to describe the highly impacted (e.g. golf courses), modified (e.g. ski slopes), and technologised (e.g. corporate suites, closed circuit television) sports environment (Bale, 1994). Thus, sportscape describes an evolutionary tendency to transform landscapes into confined and homogenised sporting environments. The modern stadium, for example, has evolved through phases that have been influenced by the formalisation of sports rules and the imposition of spatial limits in sport, which allowed the development of facilities for spectators to observe games at close proximity (Bale, 1989). More recently technological developments, such as video screens, virtual advertising, floodlighting, and retractable enclosures, have been imposed on the modern stadium (Edwards, 2003).

This course of development may significantly alter the overall sporting experience, from the viewpoint of both competitors and spectators. Relph (1985, p. 23) notes that landscapes can 'take on the very character of human existence. They can be full of life, deathly dull, exhilarating, sad, joyful or pleasant'. Bale (1989) proposes that the same applies to the landscapes of sport. One implication of creeping standardisation may be erosion of 'the cultural mosaic that encourages tourism' (Williams & Shaw, 1988, p. 7). This raises important questions as to how unique stadium design, contiguous markers, distinctive elements of the destination, and the natural elements that differentiate destinations can be considered in relation to the development of sports resources and the sustainable management of sports and tourism environments.

The reproducibility of sports

Sport tourism environments may be classified in various ways. One approach draws on the distinction between those that can be reproduced, or transported, and those that are non-reproducible (Boniface & Cooper, 1994). Resorts, theme parks, and stadia are readily reproduced and can be developed in a variety of locations. In contrast, natural landscapes and cultural heritage are generally non-reproducible (Hinch & Higham, 2004). Sports resources may also vary on the basis of their transportability. Nature-based sports such as downhill skiing and rock climbing tend to be dependent on certain types of landscapes or specific landscape features. Green sports are those that are dependent on the integration of a physical activity with specific environmental attributes (Bale, 1989). Sports such as surfing, cross country skiing, windsurfing, sailing, mountain climbing, and orienteering are built around specific features of the natural environment as sources of pleasure, challenge, competition, or mastery. The experiential value of these sports is largely dependent upon the mood of the landscapes where they are performed. These landscapes are inherently non-transportable (Christaller, 1963; Hinch & Higham, 2004).

In contrast, other sports are more readily transported. Indoor arenas have transformed sports such as ice hockey in terms of spatial and temporal distribution (Higham & Hinch, 2002). Spatially these sports have spread from high to low latitudes and temporally from winter sports to year-round activities (Higham, 2006). Outdoor winter sports such as ski jumping may also be transported from peripheral to central locations in the high latitudes to capture the advantage of proximity to markets. The Holmenkollen (Oslo, Norway) and Calgary (Canada) 1988 Olympic ski jumps are examples of constructed ski jump facilities that have been developed adjacent to central locations. Many sports, such as competitive swimming, diving, squash, and racket ball, are performed in indoor sports centres and are highly transportable.

Applications of technology to the modern stadium demonstrate the height of sport transportability (Bale, 1989). The reproducibility of the sportscape facilitates the transportation of sports and sport experiences. Viewed another way, sports facilities may be built, permanently or temporarily, at locations designed to maximise market access (Hinch & Higham, 2004). Such developments offer the potential to enhance the status of sports, such as snowboarding and beach volleyball, through increased public awareness and spectatorship. However, the transportability of sports also presents the threat of the displacement of a sporting activity from its location of origin. The importance of retaining and enhancing idiosyncrasies, elements of uniqueness, and heritage values associated with sports locations is an important strategy to mitigate this threat (Bale, 1989, p. 171).

Research in this area is required to address how uniqueness can be protected and enhanced in an environment that is both increasingly competitive and mobile.

The environmental compatibility of sports

The compatibility of sports, as applied to the field of sport tourism, exists within several interesting variations. At one level the compatibility relates to the extent to which sports may comfortably coexist alongside each other. Sports can be viewed as compatible (able to use the same space at the same time), partially compatible (take place in the same area but at different times), and incompatible (must be zoned into exclusive spaces) (Hinch & Higham, 2004). The extent to which sports are compatible varies considerably based on specialisation, equipment, safety, and level of competition (Bale, 1989). Competitive or elite levels of sport often require specialised and sometimes exclusive use of facilities.

The notion of compatibility may be extended to consider the appropriate balance between user specialisation and multiple use in the design of sports facilities. The scale and design of sports resources bears heavily on long-term utility. This applies not only to sports people, but also to spectator comfort and optimum spectator experiences. The development of generalised or multiple-use sports resources can cause unacceptable compromises to the sport experiences of both participants and spectators. Stadia with running tracks, for example, typically are characterised by non-optimal viewing for a high proportion of spectators (Bale, 1989).

A variation of compatibility relates to how sports complement each other in terms of destination development and the fostering of desired destination imagery (Chalip, 2005). Destination managers are most likely to develop interests in sports that complement the brand or enhance the imagery associated with their destination. Thus, a range of questions relate to this aspect of sport tourism. How can destinations most effectively develop multiple-use facilities, particularly those that cater for sports at various levels of competition? What are the relative merits of specialised or multiple-use sport facility developments? To what extent are sports compatible in both spatial (e.g. dimensions of the playing surface, parking, and spectator capacities) and temporal (e.g. daily/week use patterns, sport seasonality) terms? How compatible are new or emerging sports with existing destination brands?

Conclusion

The concepts of space, place, and environment provide an organisational heuristic that gives useful guidance to scholars who adopt a geographical approach to the study of sport and tourism. In adopting these concepts, an attempt is made here to highlight a number of research directions with which researchers may seek to engage. Other disciplines within the social sciences, such as sociology and anthropology, also offer distinct perspectives that may influence particular research directions and add considerable value to the work of social scientists engaged in the study of sport and tourism. In addressing particular research directions in the social sciences, it is critical that scholars adopt appropriate research methods. Given the complexity and depth of the concepts of space, place, and environment, researchers who apply innovative but rigorous methods in a sport and tourism context will make important contributions to better understanding this field of scholarship.

While this article explores geographical perspectives on the study of sport and tourism, its underlying argument, in response to Weed (2005a), is that research in the field of sport and tourism should be informed by, and in turn inform, existing disciplinary concepts and theories if it is to contribute to building edifices of knowledge (Weed, 2005a; Gibson, 2006). By using clear and coherent research foundations, such as those articulated in this article, researchers addressing the field of sport and tourism will be in a good position to address Weed's call to advance from descriptive to analytical and explanatory contributions to their field.

References

Bale, J. (1989) *Sports geography*, London: E & FN Spon.

Bale, J. (1993) *Sport, space and the city*, London: Routledge.

Bale, J. (1994) *Landscapes of modern sport*, Leicester: Leicester University Press.

Bale, J. (1999) 'Parks and gardens: Metaphors for the modern places of sport', in D. Crouch (ed.), *Leisure/tourism geographies*, London: Routledge, pp. 46–58.

Bale, J. & Maguire, J. (eds) (1994) *The global sports arena: Athletic talent migration in an independent world*, London: Frank Cass.

Boniface, B.G. & Cooper, C. (1994) *The geography of travel and tourism* (2nd edn), Oxford: Butterworth-Heinemann.

Bourdeau, P., Corneloup, J. & Mao, P. (2002) 'Adventure sports and tourism in the French mountains: Dynamics of change and challenges for sustainable development', *Current Issues in Tourism* 5(1): 22–32.

Bull, C. (2005) 'Sport tourism destination resource analysis', in J.E.S. Higham (ed.), *Sport tourism destinations: Issues, opportunities and analysis*, Oxford: Elsevier Butterworth-Heinemann, pp. 25–38.

Burton, R. (1995) *Travel geography* (2nd edn), London: Pitman Publishing.

Butler, R.W. (1980) 'The concept of the tourist area lifecycle of evolution: Implications for the management of resources', *Canadian Geographer* 24(1): 5–12.

Butler, R.W. (2005) 'The influence of sport on destination development: The case of golf at St. Andrews, Scotland', in J.E.S. Higham (ed.), *Sport tourism destinations: Issues, opportunities and analysis*, Oxford: Elsevier Butterworth-Heinemann, pp. 274–282.

Chalip, L. (2005) 'Marketing, media and place promotion', in J.E.S. Higham (ed.), *Sport tourism destinations: Issues, opportunities and analysis*, Oxford: Elsevier Butterworth-Heinemann, pp. 162–176.

Christaller, W. (1963) 'Some considerations of tourism location in Europe: The peripheral regions underdeveloped countries – recreation areas', *Papers, Regional Science Association* 12: 95–105.

Cooper, C., Fletcher, J., Gilbert, D. & Wanhill, S. (1993) *Tourism: principles and practice*, Harlow: Longman Group Limited.

Crang, M. (2004) 'Cultural geographies of tourism', in A.S. Lew, C.M. Hall & A.M. Williams (eds), *A companion to tourism*, Oxford: Blackwell Publishing, pp. 74–82.

Crouch, D. (ed.) (1999) *Leisure/tourism geographies: Practices and geographical knowledge*, London: Routledge.

Crouch, D. (2000) 'Places around us: Embodied lay geographies in leisure and tourism', *Leisure Studies* 19(2): 63–76.

Dann, G.M.S. (2005) 'Content/semiotic analysis: Applications for tourism research', in J. Aramberri & R. Butler (eds), *Tourism development: Issues for a vulnerable industry*, Clevedon: Channel View Publications, pp. 27–43.

Dietvorst, A.G.J. (1995) 'Tourist behaviour and the importance of time-space analysis', in G.J. Ashworth & A.G.J. Dietvorst (eds), *Tourism and spatial transformations: Implications for policy and planning*, Wallingford, UK: CAB International.

Edwards, K. (2003) 'Partners from the ground up', *Australian Leisure Management* 41: 14–17.

Fairley, S. & Gammon, S. (2006) 'Something lived, something learned: Nostalgia's expanding role in sport tourism', in H. Gibson (ed.), *Sport tourism: Concepts and theories*, Oxon: Routledge, pp. 50–65.

Forscher, B.K. (1963) 'Chaos in the brickyard', *Science* 142: 35.

Gibson, H. (ed.) (2006) *Sport tourism: Concepts and theories*, Oxon: Routledge.

Gibson, H., Willming, C. & Holdnak, A. (2002a) 'Small-scale event sport tourism: Fans as tourists', *Tourism Management* 24(2): 181–190.

Gibson, H., Willming, C. & Holdnak, A. (2002b) 'We're Gators, not just a Gator fan: Serious leisure, social identity and University of Florida football', *Journal of Leisure Research* 14(4): 397–425.

Gilson, C., Pratt, M., Roberts, K. & Weymes, E. (2000) *Peak performance: Business lessons from the world's top sports organizations*, Hammersmith: Harper Collins Business.

Glyptis, S.A. (1989) 'Leisure and patterns of time use'. Paper presented at the Leisure Studies Association Annual Conference, Bournemouth, England, 24–26 April 1987, Eastbourne: Leisure Studies Association.

Green, B.C. & Chalip, L. (1998) 'Sport tourism as a celebration of subculture', *Annals of Tourism Research* 25(2): 275–291.

Hall, C.M. (1998) 'Imaging, tourism and sports event fever: The Sydney Olympics and the need for a social charter for mega-events', in C. Gratton & I.P. Henry (eds), *Sport in the city: The role of sport in economic and social regeneration*, London: Routledge, pp. 166–183.

Hall, C.M. & Page, S.J. (1999) *Geography of tourism and recreation: Environment, place, and space*, London: Routledge.

Hall, C.M. & Williams, A.M. (eds) (2002) *Tourism and migration: New relationships between production and consumption*, Dordrecht: Kluwer Academic Publishers.

Higham, J.E.S. (2006) 'Sport tourism as an attraction for managing seasonality', in H. Gibson (ed.), *Sport tourism: Concepts and theories*, Oxon: Routledge, pp. 106–130.

Higham, J.E.S. & Hinch, T.D. (2002) 'Sport, tourism and seasons: The challenges and potential of overcoming seasonality in the sport and tourism sectors', *Tourism Management* 23: 175–185.

Hinch, T.D. & Higham, J.E.S. (2001) 'Sport tourism: A framework for research, *The International Journal of Tourism Research* 3(1): 45–58.

Hinch, T.D. & Higham, J.E.S. (2004) *Sport tourism development*, Clevedon: Channel View Publications.

Hinch, T.D. & Higham, J. (2005) 'Sport, tourism and authenticity', *European Sport Management Quarterly* 5(3): 243–256.

Hudson, S. (1999) *Snow business: A study of the international ski industry*, London: Cassell.

Hudson, S. (2004) 'Travel flows and spatial distribution in the ski industry', Case study in T.D. Hinch & J.E.S. Higham, *Sport tourism development*, Clevedon: Channel View Publications, pp. 95–98.

Jackson, S.J. & Andrews, D.L. (1999) 'Between and beyond the global and local: American popular sporting culture in New Zealand', in A. Yiannakis & M. Melnik (eds), *Sport sociology: Contemporary themes* (5th edn), Champaign, IL: Human Kinetics, pp. 467–474.

Jackson, S.J., Batty, R. & Scherer, J. (2001) 'Transnational sport marketing at the global/local nexus: The Adidasification of the New Zealand All Blacks', *International Journal of Sports Marketing & Sponsorship* 3(2): 185–201.

Jones, I. & Green, C. (2006) 'Serious leisure, social identity and sport tourism', in H. Gibson (ed.), *Sport tourism: Concepts and theories*, Oxon: Routledge, pp. 32–49.

Keller, P. (2001) 'Sport and tourism: Introductory report'. Paper presented at the World Conference on Sport and Tourism, Barcelona, Spain, 22–23 February 2001, Madrid: World Tourism Organization.

Kotler, P., Haider, D.H. & Rein, I. (1993) *Marketing places: Attracting investment, industry, and tourism to cities, states and nations*, New York: The Free Press.

Krippendorf, J. (1986) *The holidaymakers: Understanding the impact of leisure and travel*, London: Heinemann.

Leiper, N. (1990) 'Tourist attraction systems', *Annals of Tourism Research* 17(3): 367–384.

Lew, A.A. (2001) 'Tourism and geography space', *Tourism Geographies* 3(1): 1.

Lew, A.A., Hall, C.M. & Williams, A.M. (eds) (2004) *A companion to tourism*, Oxford: Blackwell.

MacCannell, D. (1976) *The tourists: New theory of the leisure class*, New York: Schoken.

Maier, J. & Weber, W. (1993) 'Sport tourism in local and regional planning', *Tourism Recreation Research* 18(2): 33–43.

Miossec, J.M. (1977) L'image touristique comme introduction ý la géographie du tourisme, *Annales de géographie* 86: 473.

Mitchell, L.S. & Murphy, P.E. (1991) 'Geography and tourism', *Annals of Tourism Research* 18(1): 57–70.

Mules, T. & Dwyer, L. (2006) 'Public sector support for sport tourism events: The role of cost-benefit analysis', in H. Gibson (ed.), *Sport tourism: Concepts and theories*, Oxon: Routledge, pp. 206–223.

Nogawa, H., Yamaguchi, Y. & Hagi, Y. (1996) 'An empirical research study on Japanese sport tourism in sport-for-all events: Case studies of a single-night event and a multiple-night event', *Journal of Travel Research* 35(2): 46–54.

Pearce, D.G. (1987) *Tourism today: A geographical analysis*, Harlow: Longman Scientific and Technical.

Pearce, D.G. (1989) *Tourism development* (2nd edn), Harlow: Longman Scientific and Technical.

Pigeassou, C. (1997) 'Sport and tourism: The emergence of sport into the offer of tourism', *Journal of Sport Tourism* 4(2): 20–38.

Preuss, H. (2005) 'The economic impact of visitors at major multi-sport events', *European Sport Management Quarterly* 5(3): 281–302.

Priestley, G.K. (1995) 'Sports tourism: The case of golf', in G.J. Ashworth & A.G.J. Dietvorst (eds), *Tourism and spatial transformations: Implications for policy and planning*, Wallingford, UK: CAB International, pp. 205–223.

Proshanky, H.M. (1978) 'The city and self-identity', *Environment and Behaviour* 10: 147–169.

Relph, E. (1976) *Place and placelessness*, London: Pion Limited.

Relph, E. (1985) 'Geographical experiences and being-in-the-world: The phenomenological origins of geography', in D. Seamon & R. Mugerauer (eds), *Dwelling, place and environment*, Dordrecht: Nijhoff, pp. 15–38.

Rooney, J.F. (1988) 'Mega sports events as tourist attractions: A geographical analysis'. Paper presented at Tourism Research: Expanding the Boundaries, Travel and Tourism Research Association, 19th Annual Conference, Montreal, Quebec.

Rooney, J.F. & Pillsbury, R. (1992) 'Sports regions of America', *American Demographics* 14(10): 1–10.

Shumaker, S.A. & Taylor, R.B. (1983) 'Toward a clarification of people-place relationships: A model of attachment to place', in N.R. Feimer & E.S. Geller (eds), *Environmental psychology: directions and perspectives*, New York: Praeger, pp. 219–25.

Standeven, J. & De Knop, P. (1999) *Sport tourism*, Champaign, IL: Human Kinetics.

Stevens, T. (2001) 'Stadia and tourism related facilities, *Travel and Tourism Analyst* 2: 59–73.

Tuan, Y. (1974) *Topophilia: A study of environmental perception, attitudes, and values*, Englewood Cliffs, NJ: Prentice Hall.

Urry, J. (1990) *The tourist gaze*, London: Sage.

Wang, N. (1999) 'Rethinking authenticity in tourism experience', *Annals of Tourism Research* 26(2): 349–370.

Weed, M. (2005a) 'Sports tourism theory and method – Concepts, issues and epistemologies', *European Sport Management Quarterly* 5(3): 229–243.

Weed, M. (2005b) 'Research synthesis in sport management: Dealing with "chaos in the brickyard"', *European Sport Management Quarterly* 5(1): 77–90.

Weed, M. (2006) 'A grounded theory of the policy process for sport and tourism', in H. Gibson (ed.), *Sport Tourism: Concepts and theories*, Oxon: Routledge, pp. 224–245.

Weed, M. & Bull, C. (2004) *Sports tourism: Participants, policy and providers*, Oxford: Elsevier.

Williams, A.M. & Shaw, G. (eds) (1988) *Tourism and economic development: Western European Experiences*, London: Belhaven.

Williams, D.R. (1988) 'Measuring perceived similarity among outdoor recreation activities: A comparison of visual and verbal stimulus presentations', *Leisure Sciences* 10: 153–166.

Williams, D.R. & Kalternborn, B.P. (1999) 'Leisure places and modernity: The use and meaning of recreation cottages in Norway and the USA', in D. Crouch (ed.), *Leisure/tourism geographies*, London: Routledge, pp. 214–229.

Williams, D.R., Patterson, M.E., Roggenbuck, J.W. & Watson, A.E. (1992) 'Beyond the commodity metaphor: Examining emotional and symbolic attachment to place, *Leisure Sciences* 14: 29–46.

Chapter 6

Mike Weed

SPORTS TOURISM RESEARCH

2000–2004

A systematic review of knowledge and a meta-evaluation of methods

Introduction

L IKE MANY OTHER AREAS of academic study, sports tourism has spawned a number of works that in one way or another can be seen as 'reviews' or 'overviews'. Perhaps the first of these was the position paper produced by Don Anthony for the Central Council of Physical Recreation in the UK in 1966. However, since 1990, such reviews have appeared more regularly, with notable examples being those by De Knop (1990), Jackson and Glyptis (1992), Standeven and Tomlinson (1994), Gibson (1998), Weed (1999), Gibson (2002), Jackson and Weed (2003), Gibson (2003), and Weed (2005a). These reviews take a range of forms: some have been commissioned by sport or tourism agencies (e.g. Jackson and Glyptis, 1992; Standeven and Tomlinson, 1994); some have been published as journal papers (e.g. De Knop, 1990; Gibson, 1998); some are introductory chapters for student text books (e.g. Gibson, 2003; Weed, 2005a); and some are strategic overviews derived from invited conference keynotes (e.g. Weed, 1999; Gibson, 2002). However, in the vast majority of cases these works are subjective overviews based on the author's own judgements about the area. Furthermore, they are rarely evaluative in that they make no judgements about the works reviewed.

While the various types of reviews outlined above each have different audiences, they are all essentially 'narrative literature reviews' (Neuman, 2002) that offer a 'tour' of research in the area selected by the author. They do not present, nor do they aspire to, a comprehensive coverage of the area, and they make no distinction between different types of works (e.g. refereed journal article, book chapter, conference paper). As introductions to sport tourism research they are very useful, but as evaluation of research in the area they may often be lacking.

Systematic review and meta-evaluation

Systematic review and meta-evaluation are both forms of what is increasingly becoming known as research synthesis (see Weed, 2005b, for a review of a range of synthesis approaches). Systematic review as a method of synthesis is widespread in the fields of medicine (Cook *et al.*, 1997), psychology (Biddle *et al.*, 2003), and policy (Pawson 2002) and is used in these fields to ensure that treatment, interventions, and initiatives are based on the 'best evidence (Davies *et al.*, 1999). However, it can also be used to assess the nature and extent of knowledge in an area (e.g. Weed *et al.*, 2005). Systematic reviews differ from traditional narrative reviews in that they provide objective, replicable, systematic, and comprehensive coverage of a defined area. Klassen *et al.* (1998, p. 701) define the systematic review as follows:

> A systematic review is a review in which there is a comprehensive search for relevant studies on a specific topic, and those identified are then appraised and synthesised according to a pre-determined explicit method.

The key to systematic review is that the criteria for the inclusion or exclusion of studies in the review is explicit from the outset, and while others may not agree with the inclusions, the criteria for such inclusions, and thus the scope of the review, are clearly delimited.

Meta-evaluation initially emerged in the policy studies area and, simply put, was developed as the evaluation of evaluation(s). There is some disagreement in the literature as to whether meta-evaluation refers to the evaluation of a single study (e.g. Finn *et al.*, 1997), or to the evaluation of a number of studies (e.g. Scott-Little *et al.*, 2002). However, given that the prefix 'meta' literally means 'beyond' or 'across' and that its other uses – e.g. meta-analysis and meta-interpretation – refer to synthesis methods, the use of the term meta-evaluation is here taken to mean the evaluation of a number of studies. A further clarification is also perhaps needed in relation to the idea of meta-evaluation being entirely concerned with evaluating evaluation studies. Woodside and Sakai (2001) note that meta-evaluation report on the validity and usefulness of the methods that studies employ, while Scot-Little *et al.* (2002) present a 'meta-evaluation of methodologies'. Furthermore, Finn *et al.* (1997) describe the important role of meta-evaluation in assessing the extent to which, regardless of the internal consistency and validity of a study, the methodology and methods used result in findings that have any broader utility in the area as a whole. Therefore, the use of the meta-evaluation approach here will be to focus on an evaluation of methodologies and methods used and on the utility of research findings.

This paper uses the systematic review procedure to identify articles relating to sports tourism that appear in refereed journals in the broad sport, leisure, and tourism area in the five-year period from the start of 2000 to the end of 2004 (see methods discussion below for an explanation of the search strategy and aims). It examines the range of substantive topics (e.g. events, outdoor and adventurous activities, etc.) and the range of area (e.g. experiences, impacts, etc.) covered in these articles, thus establishing a picture of current knowledge and issues in the area. It subsequently conducts a meta-evaluation of methods, examining both the application of methods to topics and areas and the extent of methodological diversity in the area. As part of the meta-evaluation procedure, the paper also examines the extent to which a coherent body of sports tourism knowledge is developing.[1] In conclusion, the development of future sports tourism research is discussed.

Methods

The complementary methods of systematic review and meta-evaluation commence with the systematic review search strategy and criteria. The search aims to be comprehensive within clearly defined boundaries, and as such should be objective and replicable. The objectives for the search were:

- to search all English-language hard copy refereed journals in the sport, leisure, and tourism area;
- to retrieve all refereed journal articles in the sports tourism area published in such journals between 2000 and 2004 inclusive.

In respect of the first objective, the research was limited to journals in sport, leisure, and tourism because it is these publications that are most regularly read by those conducting sports tourism research. Consequently, articles published in such journals both shape the perception of the extent of the sports tourism area and shape the direction of future research. While this strategy may mean that articles in, for example, mainstream management journals may be overlooked, such articles contribute less to the development of sports tourism knowledge because they are less widely read by sports tourism researchers. The search was limited to hard copy refereed journals as these are widely recognised as being the 'gold standard' of published research quality, whilst the restriction to English-language research was made on the grounds of practicality. The second search objective limits the search to the five years since 2000. This is long enough to build a full picture of the range of research being carried out, but recent enough for the articles review to retain contemporary currency.

While the systematic review search is intended to be replicable as with any research there is an element of researcher judgement that affects the outcome. In this case that judgement relates to the definition of what is included as an 'article in the sports tourism area'. In order to avoid an extended discussion of the scope or definition of the area, the first criteria for inclusion was the definition of the work as sports tourism research by the author of the article. As such, if the title, keyword, abstract, or text of the article referred to the research as relating to sports tourism, then it was included in the review. However, this alone was not a wide enough criteria. Therefore, articles that were not 'self-identified' as sports tourism research were assessed according to the extent to which the topic they covered fell into any of the five types of sports tourism identified by Weed and Bull (2004): sports training, sports events, luxury sports tourism, sports participation tourism, and tourism with sports content. This, however, proved to be too broad a criteria (particularly in relation to sports events). Consequently, any articles covering topics that fell into Weed and Bull's (2004) categorisation were further assessed to ensure that they included a consideration of a travel element (including day trips) and some form of 'sport' activity (as either an active participant or a spectator) as defined by the European Sports Charter Council (Council of Europe, 1992):

> Sport means all forms of physical activity which, through casual or organisation participation, aims at improving physical fitness and mental well being, forming social relationships, or obtaining results in competition at all levels.
>
> (in Sports Council, 1994: 4)

Consequently, the inclusion criteria were all English-language articles in refereed journals in the broad sport, leisure, and tourism area that were either:

1   self-identified as sports tourism research; or
2   covered topics that fell into one of Weed and Bull's (2004) five types of sports tourism AND included a consideration of a travel element and a sport activity.

Because the objective of the review was to comprehensively cover the area, the inclusion criteria for the search aimed to be as comprehensive and inclusive as possible. However, undoubtedly researcher judgement may have affected the range of inclusions. It is perhaps useful to give an example of one excluded article to illustrate the boundaries of the review. A paper by Jones and Stokes (2003), entitled 'The Commonwealth Games and urban regeneration: an investigation into training initiatives and partnerships and their effects on disadvantaged groups in East Manchester', in *Managing Leisure*, was excluded on the basis that it did not include a consideration of a travel element. While it might be argued that this paper considers some of the impacts of sports tourism, the link was felt to be too tenuous as the main role of the paper was to consider the detail of training initiatives and partnerships that were not related to sports tourism.

Having established the inclusion criteria for the search, the initial strategy involved electronic searches of Sports Discus, TOUR CD, and CABI Abstracts as well as manual searches of known journals in the sport, leisure, and tourism area.[2] The search of Sports Discus used 'tourism' as a keyword, while the search of TOUR CD used 'sport' as a keyword. The CABI Abstracts search used 'sports tourism' and 'sport tourism' both hyphenated and un-hyphenated. Further manual searches took place of any further sport, leisure, or tourism journals that were identified by the electronic searches, and this was followed by a snowball search of any further journals identified from the reference lists of the articles retrieved in the previous searches. In total this led to a search of 38 journals (plus the former *Journal of Sport Tourism* – see note in Systematic Review Results section for details of the status of *Journal of Sport Tourism* in the review), which are listed in Table 6.1. Table 6.1 shows the numbers of articles returned from the search, which will be discussed in more detail in the results section. A systematic review usually includes some exclusion criteria that relate to research quality. However, such criteria were not used in this review for two reasons: first, limiting the research to refereed journal articles implies some form of quality control; and, second, part of the role of the meta-evaluation procedure is to assess the quality of the research.

As noted earlier, meta-evaluation seeks to focus on an evaluation of methodologies and methods used and on the utility of research findings. In discussing the nature of evaluation and its implications for meta-evaluation, Apthorpe and Gasper (1982) identify two interrelated dimensions of evaluation: an immanent/transcendent dimension and an essentialist/instrumentalist dimension. An immanent evaluation will evaluate research on the basis of whether it achieves its own stated goals, whereas a transcendent evaluation will evaluate research according to externally established criteria. Similarly, an

Table 6.1 Systematic review search returns

Journal name	2000	2001	2002	2003	2004	Total
Current Issues in Tourism	—	—	6[a]	—	1	7
Leisure Science	2	1	—	—	4	7
Journal of Sport Management	—	—	1	5[b]	1	7
Journal of Travel Research	1	1	2	1	2	7
Annals of Tourism Research	—	1	—	2	1	5
International Journal of Tourism Research	1	2	—	1	1	5
Journal of Leisure Research	1	—	1	2	1	5
Tourism Management	1	1	1	1	2	5
Tourism Analysis	1[RN]	—	1	1	1	4
Event Management	—	1	2	—	—	3
Journal of Travel and Tourism Marketing	1	—	1	1	—	3
Leisure Studies	—	1	—	1	1	3
Tourism and Hospitality Planning and Development (est 2004)	—	—	—	—	3	3
World Leisure Journal	—	—	1	1	1	3
Annals of Leisure Research	—	1	1	—	—	2
International Journal of Sports Marketing and Sponsorship	—	—	1	1	—	2
Managing Leisure	—	—	—	—	2	2
International Review for the Sociology of Sport	—	—	—	—	1	1
Society and Leisure	—	—	1	—	—	1
Sport Management Review	—	1	—	—	—	1
Sport Marketing Quarterly	—	—	—	1	—	1
Tourism, Culture and Communication	-	1	-	-		1
Tourism Recreation Research	—	—	—	—	1[RN]	1
Tourism Review International (formerly *Pacific Tourism Review*)	—	—	—	—	1	1
European Sports Management Quarterly	—	—	—	—	—	0
Leisure/Loisir (formerly *Journal of Applied Recreation Research*)	—	—	—	—	—	0
Journal of Parks and Recreation Administration	—	—	—	—	—	0
Journal of Sport and Social Issues	—	—	—	—	—	0
Journal of Sports Economics	—	—	—	—	—	0
Journal of Sustainable Tourism	—	—	—	—	—	0
Journal of Tourism Studies	—	—	—	—	—	0
Journal of Vacation Marketing	—	—	—	—	—	0
Sociology of Sport Journal	—	—	—	—	—	0
Sport in Society (formerly *Culture, Sport & Society*)	—	—	—	—	—	0
Sport, Education and Society	—	—	—	—	—	0
Tourism Economics	—	—	—	—	—	0
Tourism Geographies	—	—	—	—	—	0
Tourist Studies	—	—	—	—	—	0
Total	8	10	20	18	24	80
Journal of Sport Tourism (launched in hard copy in 2003)	—	—	—	13+1[RN]	18	32

Notes:
(a) includes 5 articles in a sports tourism special edition.
(h) these 5 articles formed a special edition on sports tourism.
RN = Research Note

instrumentalist approach will consider how far research contributes towards the achievement of a more general end, whilst an essentialist approach focuses on the means and will be more concerned with the way the research has been conducted. Each of these approaches has its value, and Apthorpe and Gasper (1982) argue that they can be rationalised into two types of evaluation. First, an immanent-essentialist evaluation examines the internal consistency, validity, and quality of a piece of research as an independent study. While this paper is not uninterested in this type of evaluation, such an evaluation of the internal quality of the articles included in this review should have been largely covered by the peer-review process. The second type of evaluation is a transcendent-instrumentalist evaluation, which is more concerned with evaluating the research according to external criteria rather than its internal consistency and conduct. As such, a transcendent-instrumentalist evaluation is interested in the significance of research questions, the appropriateness of methodologies and methods used in answering such questions, and the contribution research makes to the body of knowledge in the area. It is this second type of evaluation that forms the basis of the meta-evaluation in this paper, as this is not often considered in the immanent-essentialist evaluation of studies in the peer-review process.

Of course, the reason that the peer-review process does not conduct a transcendent-instrumentalist evaluation is because such an evaluation is concerned with the relationship of studies to each other and the contribution that a group of studies as a whole can make to the development of an area. While it is possible for studies to satisfy all the criteria of an immanent-essentialist evaluation, through replication, parochialism, or naivety studies may be found lacking in a transcendent-instrumentalist meta-evaluation. This problem was highlighted over 40 years ago by Bernard Forscher (1963), who expressed concern about what he saw as the 'random' and often excessive production of studies (bricks) that were thrown on to the pile of research without any consideration as to how bodies of knowledge ('edifices') could be constructed. Forscher's piece was entitled 'Chaos in the brickyard':

> It became difficult to find a suitable plot for construction of an edifice because the ground was covered with loose bricks. It became difficult to complete a useful edifice because, as soon as the foundations were discernable, they were buried under an avalanche of random bricks. And, saddest of all, sometimes no effort was made even to maintain the distinction between a pile of bricks and a true edifice.
>
> (p. 35)

As such, the purpose of this paper is to 'map out' research in sports tourism through a systematic review of articles (identifying the bricks), and then to conduct a meta-evaluation of the extent to which the articles identified can be said to form a true edifice of knowledge rather than a random pile of bricks.

Systematic review results

This section outlines the largely descriptive results of the systematic review which maps out the nature and extent of knowledge in the area of sports tourism since 2000. The later discussion section is concerned largely with the meta-evaluation.

Table 6.1 outlines the main results of the systematic review search. The initial electronic keyword searches resulted in a vast number of obviously irrelevant returns. For example, a search for 'tourism' in Sports Discus returned articles on exercise physiology that had been conducted in a 'Department of Sport Science, *Tourism* and Leisure'. Once these obviously irrelevant returns had been filtered out, the electronic searches produced 112 articles, of which 54 were excluded through the application of the criteria outlined in the methods section, resulting in 58 articles from the electronic searches. The manual searches of known journals returned 15 articles that satisfied the inclusion criteria, whilst the subsequent snowball search produced a further 7 articles. Therefore, in total, 80 articles were included in the review. The search was limited to quarterly publications, hence articles in annual publications such as *Olympika – the International Journal of Olympic Studies* were not included. In addition, historical articles, although initially included in a preliminary four-year (2000–2003) version of this review (Weed, 2004), were excluded as they were only marginally relevant to a review of contemporary knowledge.

All articles published in the former incarnation of this journal, *Journal of Sport Tourism*, have been excluded and some comment is required on the reasons for this. *Journal of Sport Tourism* was launched as a hard copy journal in 2003 (having previously operated. as an online journal for seven years), and thus only fulfilled the inclusion criteria for the last two years of the review. During these two years, two issues of the journal consisted of reprints of articles from its online days, whilst many of the articles in other issues were shorter papers that were targeted at the journal's trade/professional audience rather than the academic community.[3] To include such articles in the review would skew the overall picture of sports tourism research because articles targeted at the trade/professional community are not expected to discuss relevant academic theory. As the inclusion criteria for the review did not include a quality dimension (because the role of the meta-evaluation is to assess the quality of research in the area as a whole), it was not possible to screen articles from the former *Journal of Sport Tourism* on quality criteria. Consequently, in order to secure the integrity of the systematic review as relating to peer-reviewed academic knowledge in the area, the contents of *Journal of Sport Tourism* were excluded *en bloc* (although the number of articles published has been noted at the foot of Table 6.1).

The 80 articles included in the review are listed at the end of this paper. Table 6.1 shows that there is a general growth trend, from eight articles published in 2000 to 24 articles published in 2004. During the five-year period, two journals published special issues on sports tourism *Journal of Sport Management*, 17(3), and *Current Issues in Tourism*, 5(1) with a further growth indicator, although outside of the review period, being the publication of two further special issues in 2005 – *European Sport Management Quarterly*, 5(3), and *Sport in Society*, 8(2).

The articles included in the review represent the work of 65 different first authors, which on one hand is an encouragingly large number in relation to the total number of articles. However, on the other hand, this may mean that some academics are 'dabbling' in the area and have little commitment to the overall development of a body of knowledge. There were only 12 authors with more than one first-author publication in the area, and of this group it is possible to identify four authors – Laurence Chalip, Mike Weed, James Higham and Tom Hinch (who invariably write as a team), and Christine Green – who have been involved with three or more of the publications in the review and have a record of publications in the sports tourism area outside of the review period. Furthermore, each of these authors has aligned themselves with the sports tourism area and three of them have other (non peer-reviewed) sports tourism publications during the review period. Chalip has lead-authored two journal articles, been a co-author on another two, and authored two book chapters (Chalip, 2001; 2004) in the period of the review, whilst Weed has published three single-authored journal articles, lead-authored a book (Weed & Bull, 2004), and authored/co-authored two book chapters (Weed, 2002; Jackson & Weed, 2003). Higham and Hinch have a similar profile to Weed, having co-authored three journal articles, published a book (Hinch & Higham, 2004), and co-authored a book chapter (Higham & Hinch, 2002). Finally, Green has single/first-authored two refereed journal articles and co-authored another one. In addition to these authors, James Petrick (three first-authored journal articles), Gerard Kyle (three first-authored journal articles), and Jerry Vaske (two first-authored and one co-authored journal articles) have each also contributed more than two articles to the area. However, unlike the four authors identified above, these authors do not see themselves as sports tourism academics and have not concerned themselves with any broader comment on the area as a whole, although their work does fall within the sports tourism area as delimited in this review.

Table 6.2 shows both the sports tourism activities and the topics that the articles in the review covered. Not surprisingly, the largest sports tourism activity covered by the articles was sports events tourism (40% of articles), with outdoor and adventure sports tourism coming a relatively close second (29% of articles), whilst skiing and winter sports (15%), golf (4%), sport fishing (4%), and generic articles covering the area as a whole (8%) made up the remainder of the papers. The most featured topic in the articles was the behaviours, profiles, and motivations of sports tourists (38%), although as later discussions will show, much of this work is fairly basic, providing profiles of, rather than explanations for, sports tourists' behaviours. Impacts (25%) also featured strongly as a research topic, as did provision (24%), whilst the remainder of the articles covered policy (8%) and conceptualisation and classification (6%). Taking topics and activities together, unsurprisingly event impacts (23%) is the most researched combination, with the behaviours, profiles, and motivations of outdoor and adventure sports tourists (20%) and event provision (11%) being the only other combinations featuring in more than 10% of articles.

It is perhaps worth noting that the authors of many of the articles discussing outdoor and adventure sports tourism rarely identify the work as falling within the sports tourism area, whereas authors working on events and skiing/winter sports often do. This affects the extent to which keyword searching for 'sport(s) (-)tourism' will return such work. In fact, many outdoor/adventure sports tourism articles are 'self-identified' as falling

Table 6.2 Sports tourism activities and topics covered in the review

	Events	Outdoor/ adventure activities	Skiing/ winter sports	Golf	Fishing	Generic	Totals
Behaviours	6	16	5	3			30
Impacts	18		1		1		20
Provision	9	2	5		2	1	19
Policy		2	1			3	6
Concepts/classification		3				2	5
Totals	32	23	12	3	3	6	80

within an 'adventure tourism' area, which might be seen as overlapping with sports tourism. While debates about the boundaries between these areas, and indeed between sports tourism and events tourism, have taken place elsewhere, it is not the intention of this paper to rehearse these here. However, it is important to note the influence that the research community with which the research is identified may have on the paradigmatic and methodological underpinnings of the work, and this is something that is addressed in the meta-evaluation discussions that follow.

Meta-evaluation discussion

As noted earlier, the main concern of meta-evaluation is with a transcendent-instrumentalist evaluation of the research and research area in question. As such, meta-evaluation addresses the significance of research questions, the appropriateness of methodologies and methods used in answering such questions, and the contribution that research makes to the body of knowledge in the area. Consequently, the first task of this meta-evaluation is to identify the approaches used by the 80 studies under consideration.

Table 6.3 summarises the basic features of the 80 studies, whilst Tables 6.4, 6.5, and 6.6 break down these features by research topic and area. Table 6.3 shows that 54 studies (68%) collected primary data, nine studies (11%) conducted a secondary analysis, whilst 17 studies (21%) did not use any data. Given the emphasis on sports events, and more specifically event impacts across the studies as a whole, it is perhaps surprising that there are not more secondary analyses (although more than half of the secondary studies (5) did focus on event impacts). This may be indicative of a tendency to focus on specific case studies of particular events, especially if studies are funded by event hosts or policy makers, at the expense of cumulatively using event impact research to build a knowledge base about the range of impacts of events more generally. While the former is obviously of use to the event host, the latter would better serve the needs of the area (and of event hosts in general) as a whole.

An example serves to illustrate this point. One of the event impact studies, which was funded by a local policy agency, neither locates the study within the broader context

Table 6.3 Basic features of the studies included in the review

Primary studies (54)		Secondary studies (9)		Studies not using data (17)	
Theoretical	35	Theoretical	4	Theoretical	11
Quasi-theoretical	14	Quasi-theoretical	1	Quasi-theoretical	1
Descriptive	5	Descriptive	4	Descriptive	5
Quantitative data	36	Quantitative data	6		
Mixed data	3	Mixed data	1		
Qualitative data	15	Previous studies	2		
Interviews	9			Model development	5
Media analysis	3			Theoretical/philosophical	5
Ethnography	3			Descriptive commentary	4
				Methodological	3
Positivist	39	Positivist	6		
Interpretivist	15	Interpretivist	3		

Table 6.4 Features of articles using primary data included in the review

		Positivist			Interpretivist			
		Theoretical	Quasi-theoretical	Descriptive	Theoretical	Quasi-theoretical	Descriptive	
Events	Behaviours	2	1	1	2	1	–	(7)
	Impacts	2	2	1	1	–	–	(6)
	Provision	4	1	–	1	–	–	(6)
	TOTALS	(8)	(4)	(2)	(4)	(1)	(0)	(19)
Outdoor and Adventurous Activities	Behaviours	7	(14) 2	1	5	(5) –	–	(15)
	Policy	–	1	–	1	–	–	(2)
	Concept/Classification	–	1	–	1	–	–	(1)
	TOTALS	(7)	(3)	(1)	(7)	(0)	(0)	(18)
Skiing	Behaviours	3	(11) 2	–	–	(7) –	–	(5)
	Impacts	1	–	–	–	–	–	(1)
	Provision	–	2	–	–	–	–	(2)
	TOTALS	(4)	(4)	(0)	(0)	(0)	(0)	(8)
Golf	Behaviours	2	(8) 1	–	–	(0) –	–	(3)
	TOTALS		(3)			(0)		(3)
Fishing	Impacts	–	(3) –	1	–	(0) –	–	(1)
	Provision	1	–	1	–	–	–	(2)
	TOTALS	(1)	(0)	(2)	(0)	(0)	(0)	(3)
Generic	Provision	–	(3) –	–	1	(0) –	–	(1)
	Policy	–	–	–	2	–	–	(2)
	TOTALS	(0)	(0)	(0)	(3)	(0)	(0)	(3)
Total		22	(0) 12	5	14	(3) 1	0	54
			39			15		

Table 6.5 Features of articles using secondary data included in the review

		Positivist			Interpretivist		
		Theoretical	Quasi-theoretical	Descriptive	Theoretical	Quasi-theoretical	Descriptive
Events	Impacts	1	–	3	1	–	(5)
	Provision	–	–	–	1	–	(1)
	TOTALS	(1)	(0)	(3)	(2)	(0)	(6)
Outdoor and adventurous activities	Provision	–	1 (4)	–	–	(2)	(1)
	TOTALS						
Skiing	Provision	1	– (1)	1	–	–	(2)
	TOTALS	(2)			(0)	(0)	(2)
Totals		**2**	**1**	**4**	**2**	**0 (0)**	**0**
		7			**2**		**9**

Table 6.6 Features of articles not using data included in the review

		Theoretical			Quasi-theoretical	Descriptive	
		Methodological discussion	Theoretical/philosophical discussion	Model development	Model development	Descriptive commentary	
Events	Impacts	3	1	–	–	3	(7)
	Provision	–	–	–	–	1	(1)
	TOTALS	(3)	(1)	(0)	(0)	(4)	(8)
Outdoor and adventurous activities	Behaviours	–	1	–	–	–	(1)
	Provision	–	–	–	–	1	(1)
	Concept/classification	–	2	–	–	–	(2)
	TOTALS	(0)	(3)	(0)	(0)	(1)	(4)
Skiing	Provision	–	–	1	–	–	(1)
	Policy	–	–	1	–	–	(1)
	TOTALS	(0)	(0)	(2)	(0)	(0)	(2)
Generic	Policy	–	–	1	–	–	(1)
	Concept/classification	–	–	1	1	–	(2)
	TOTALS	(0)	(0)	(2)	(1)	(0)	(3)
Totals		**3**	**4**	**4**	**1**	**5**	**17**

of other event impact studies nor discusses the implications of the findings for further event impact research. This is evidenced by only 70 words in the introduction referring to 'other research' on events and a conclusion of 540 words making no mention of any implications other than those for the future hosting of the particular event in question. While this study may have passed muster under a peer-review immanent-essentialist evaluation, in that it fulfils its own goals and is internally consistent in its methodology and methods, it is found lacking under a transcendent-instrumentalist meta-evaluation because its research question (the impacts of a particular event in isolation) and the contribution it makes to the body of knowledge are of very little significance. While such studies are clearly of value to the agencies that fund them, unless their findings are located within the broader body of knowledge, and implications for, or the contribution to, this body of knowledge is identified, they contribute very little. This is something that has been noted by Stephen Page (2005, p. 664) in recent correspondence in *Tourism Management*:

> So often one reads some of these papers as asks why have they been written? Do they add anything meaningful to knowledge? . . . I would venture to suggest if only 25% of the current Tourism outputs were produced, our knowledge base in the subject would not be adversely affected. It might be improved as we are able to assimilate more of what is good rather than having to wade through more mediocre and seemingly mundane research findings.

In further contributing to this debate, Chris Ryan (2005, p. 662) links the problem to research methods:

> The multiplicity of journals has meant that it has been relatively easy for researchers to gain publications of technically skilled quantitative based pieces . . . which actually offer little in terms of new conceptualisation or are able to articulate any significant addition to the literature.

This is something that is borne out by this meta-evaluation. Each of the studies was evaluated according to the extent to which it was underpinned by relevant theory. Somewhat shockingly, less than two-thirds of studies (62%) had a clearly articulated theoretical basis, with 18% being entirely atheoretical and descriptive. However, an interesting finding was the existence of a number of studies (16 studies, 20%) that were 'quasi-theoretical' in nature. Such studies discussed relevant theory as context in an introduction or literature review, but made no attempt to apply such theory to the results or to discuss theoretical or conceptual implications or developments in their discussions or conclusions. What is also interesting is that of these 16 quasitheoretical studies, the overwhelming majority (13 studies, 81%) used a positivist epistemology to analyse quantitative data, thus reinforcing Ryan's point about the failings of many 'technically skilled quantitative based pieces'.[4] Again, such studies, whilst meeting the standards of the immanent-essentialist peer review, are found to be lacking in the broader transcendent-instrumentalist perspective of meta-evaluation.

Of course, it would be wrong to equate positivist and/or quantitative research[5] with a quasi-theoretical or descriptive approach, a point made by Higham and Hinch in this issue. The systematic review returned many high-quality positivist and/or quantitative studies in which the method is clearly appropriate in answering the research question and which make a clear contribution to the area. However, the review returns do highlight a positivist hegemony within sports tourism research, with 45 of 63 primary and secondary studies (71%) employing a positivist approach. While this may be no different to many other research areas, it does highlight a lack of heterogeneity in the way in which sports tourism issues are researched. The implications of this are perhaps clearest in relation to research on behaviours, where 22 of the 30 studies (73%) are underpinned by a positivist epistemology. Such behavioural research is important to the development of knowledge in the sports tourism area as a whole, as emphasised by Weed (2005c, p. 234):

> policy, provision and impacts are all derived from participation, and it is to the detriment of the subject area as a whole that there is, as yet, only a very limited understanding of sports tourism participation.

However, if 30 of 80 studies in this systematic review (38%) cover issues relating to behaviours, profiles, and motivations, why is the understanding of sports tourism participation 'very limited'? The answer is that, as Gibson (2004) notes, the majority of research on sports tourists' behaviours tends to focus on the 'what' of behaviours (i.e., providing profiles and description) rather than attempting to understand the 'why Gibson (2004), along with Downward (2005) and Weed (2005c), calls on sports tourism researchers to move beyond the level of a basic understanding of what sports tourists do, to try to understand and explain why they do it, if a more detailed explanation of participation is important in understanding the impacts derived from such participation and in informing policy and provision decisions then, as noted by Downward (2005, p. 315), 'explanations require "ontic depth", that is moving beyond the level of events towards an understanding of the processes that produce them'.

Returning to the issue of epistemology and methods, 36% of the empirical articles on behaviours underpinned by a positivist epistemology were either descriptive or quasi-theoretical, whereas only one of the articles underpinned by interpretive epistemology was quasi-theoretical and no articles were purely descriptive. The intention here is not to demonise positivist methods, which can provide very useful perspectives on sports tourism behaviours, but to encourage a greater use of interpretivist approaches, which can often provide a deeper understanding of the processes that produce behaviours, rather than providing broader profiles of such behaviours. As such, the call is for researchers to break away from the positivist hegemony highlighted above and, as was implied in the quote from Chris Ryan earlier, to think about the transcendent-instrumentalist contribution of their work to the body of knowledge, rather than simply producing 'technically skilled quantitative based pieces . . . which actually offer little in terms of new conceptualisation'. It has also been argued that the positivist hegemony in sports tourism can be self-perpetuating, 'in that the positivist dominance in the area encourages individual researchers to apply positivist methods on the basis of convention rather than epistemological concerns' (Weed, 2005c, p. 239).

Whether this is or is not the case, this meta-evaluation clearly shows that sports tourism research lacks methodological diversity, with 71% of primary and secondary research articles utilising a positivist approach. Such homogeneity in relation to methodology cannot be healthy for the development of the subject area, particularly given its potential breadth and depth in terms of both subject-derived knowledge (e.g. perspectives from sport, tourism, leisure, physical education, etc.) and disciplinary approaches (e.g. perspectives from psychology, sociology, economics, geography, etc.). Given the potential range of subject areas and disciplinary perspectives that can inform the study of sports tourism, it is particularly important that research is clearly located within the broader body (and in some cases, bodies) of knowledge. It is simply not good enough that more than a third of the studies in this systematic review and meta-interpretation were not embedded within a clear theoretical framework. Perhaps the most extreme example of this was an article on provision within the outdoor and adventurous activities area that utilised only five references, three of which were by the author(s) themselves. While this may be appropriate for a conference paper, it is not good enough in a refereed journal article, where greater links to the broader area of study should be a requirement, not least because it avoids futile repetition of previous research, something that the area of sports tourism has also suffered from in the past (Gibson, 2002).

A final note in this meta-evaluation discussion section on the influence of the research community within which research is conducted is illuminating. As noted at the end of the systematic review results section, many authors of research in the outdoor and adventurous activities area do not identify their work as falling within the sports tourism area. In fact, much of this work is 'self-identified' as falling within an 'adventure tourism' research area, and an analysis of the primary empirical articles in this review falling within the outdoor and adventurous activities area suggests a slightly different picture to the overall picture of sports tourism research discussed above. First, there is less of a bias (although there still is a bias) towards research using positivist methods, with 38% of empirical papers employing an interpretivist approach (compared with 29% across the sports tourism area as a whole). Second, only 22% of articles are descriptive or quasi-theoretical (compared to 38% in sports tourism as a whole). The outdoor and adventurous activities area is dominated by research on behaviours (83%), with only 20% of this research being descriptive or quasi-theoretical. Again, this compares favourably with research on sports tourism behaviours as a whole, where 26% of primary empirical research is descriptive or quasi-theoretical. Furthermore, if research on outdoor and adventurous activities behaviours is removed from the overall sports tourism behaviours research category, 40% of 'the rest' of empirical sports tourism behaviour research is descriptive or quasi-theoretical. The reasons for these differences can be little other than the subject of speculation, however, it is perhaps likely that the direction of an area is shaped by the way research in that area is currently conducted. Whilst there is clearly a positivist hegemony within sports tourism research, it may be that there is more of a 'norm' of theoretical discussion in adventure tourism research.

Although discussions of adventure tourism and sports tourism clearly take place at the level of 'sub field' there are corollaries here with Kuhn's (1962) concept of 'normal science', where research in an area (he was talking at the much broader level of science as a whole) is conducted according to the conventions of what is considered to be 'normal science', Kuhn's (1962) seminal text was called *The structure of scientific revolutions* and remains a much quoted, and still hotly contested, text in the philosophy of research today. The title of the text represents Kulns's view that 'normal science' will remain the norm until a critical mass of alternative research conducted according to a more insightful approach is achieved. Until this point, any 'dissenting voices' from the practice of 'normal science' will be seen as anomalous, or small adaptations will be made – Kuhn calls this 'stretching normal science' – to accommodate such dissenting voices.

In a recent keynote presentation, McFee (2006) claimed that there is no such thing as 'normal science' in the social sciences because there are a multiplicity of competing and complementary paradigms, none of which are dominant or hegemonic. McFee sees this as being a healthy state of affairs which brings a range of alternative perspectives to bear on the issues that the social sciences face. Drawing on McFee's view, the intention here is not to initiate a 'scientific revolution' that will replace the dominant positivist approach in sports tourism research with a different dominant approach. Rather, the aim is to encourage the sports tourism research enterprise to become epistemologically and methodologically heterogeneous and diverse, as befits a multidisciplinary research area that draws on a range of subject areas for synergistic insights (Weed, 2005c).

Concluding comments

In discussing the results of the preliminary four-year systematic review and meta-evaluation (2000–2003), the following conclusions regarding sports tourism research in this period were drawn:

> The overall picture, therefore, was that sports tourism as an area of study lacks methodological diversity, rarely tends to answer 'why' questions, and in around half of cases, does not employ any clear theoretical perspective to underpin what is largely descriptive research.
>
> (Weed, 2005c, p. 231)

The full five-year review reported here covers an additional year (2000–2004) and the signs are that the situation is improving, because the addition of further articles from 2004 has increased the number of articles embedding discussions within a clear theoretical framework from 'around half' to 62%. However, the lack of methodological diversity remains, and there is still a lack of research answering 'why' questions.

A further conclusion from the preliminary four-year review relates to the brickyard metaphor introduced earlier: 'the picture painted [is] of a field where the number of bricks is increasing, but where there is little attempt to assemble any coherent edifice of knowledge' (Weed, 2005c, p. 231). Sports tourism is a wide-ranging and diverse area in which, as already noted, researchers can draw both on previous research in range of subjects and on perspectives from a range of disciplines. Weed and Bull (2004, p. 37) take a wide-ranging and inclusive view of the area, conceptualising it as 'a social, economic and cultural phenomenon arising from the unique interaction of activity, people and place'. This conceptualisation embraces a whole range of professional and amateur, competitive and non-competitive, social, recreational, and informal activities, as well as leisure, business, and day-trip tourism. Furthermore, this journal also takes such a wide-ranging view of sports tourism as an area of study. The point has been made in the past (Weed & Bull, 2004, p. xv) that sports tourism is far from an homogenous phenomenon, and that the interaction of people and place with the activities in question expands the heterogeneity of the area. As such, building edifices of knowledge in such a heterogeneous area is no simple task. Therefore, while there are identifiable 'volumes of bricks' in relation to particular sports tourism activities (e.g. events and outdoor and adventurous activities), this is not necessarily any indication that such bricks have been assembled into a coherent edifice. Consequently, the same conclusions that were reached in the preliminary four-year review still apply here. In attempting to provide suggestions for how edifices of knowledge might be more effectively built in the future it may be useful to consider the aims of the meta-evaluation process applied in this paper.

Meta-evaluation focuses on the methodologies and methods used in a research area and on the utility of research findings. Drawing on the work of Apthorpe and Gasper (1982), this can be understood as a transcendent-instrumentalist evaluation, which assesses research according to the extent to which it addresses significant research questions, uses appropriate methodologies and methods, and contributes to the body of knowledge in the area. In encouraging sports tourism researchers to contribute to the edifice of sports tourism knowledge, rather than producing random bricks, this paper suggests that authors pay attention to the transcendent-instrumentalist dimension of their research. In practice this means locating their empirical work within the current body (or bodies) of knowledge in the area, building on, rather than repeating, previous research, and paying attention to methodological and epistemological concerns in constructing their research, rather than simply applying methods on the basis of current practice and convention. The ambition of this paper is that it might encourage researchers to contribute to the construction of an edifice of sports tourism knowledge that is epistemologically and methodologically diverse, and theoretically and conceptually robust. In short, that a replication of this systematic review and meta-evaluation in five years' time will be able to report on the construction of edifices rather than the production of bricks.

Notes

1   It should be noted that it is not the role of meta-evaluation to identify and comment on the quality of individual studies but to identify trends and directions in an area as a whole.

2   The nature of the electronic searches is such that initial screening is on the basis of titles, keywords, and, where available on databases, abstracts. The manual searches are initially on the basis of titles, with further investigation of abstracts and subsequently main texts taking place if the title indicates that the article may potentially meet the inclusion criteria. The volume of potential articles to be searched renders this the only practical strategy, and it is recognised as a weakness in the systematic review method (Davies *et al.*, 1999) that this may mean that a very small minority of potentially includable articles may be overlooked.

3   See Weed (2006) for a discussion of the tensions that the former *Journal of Sport Tourism* experienced in attempting to serve both trade/professional and academic communities.

4   It is worth noting here that these studies do not indicate any inherent problem with research underpinned by a positivist epistemology, rather they are simply examples of poorly conducted positivist research where the emphasis has been on the technical application of the method rather than on its epistemological appropriateness (see later discussions on the basis for the application of methods).

5   While the vast majority of articles in this review underpinned by positivist epistemologies have employed quantitative methods, there is no implication that a positivist epistemology necessarily implies quantitative methods nor that quantitative methods are necessarily underpinned by a positivist epistemology.

References

Anthony, D. (1966). *Sport and tourism*. London: CCPR/ICSPE Bureau for Public Relations.

Apthorpe, R., & Gasper, D. (1982). Policy evaluation and meta-evaluation: the case of rural cooperatives, *World Development*, *10*(8), 651–668.

Biddle, S.J.H., Wang, C.K J., Kavussanu, M., & Spray, C.M. (2003). Correlates of achievement goal orientations in physical activity: A systematic review of research. *European Journal of Sport Science*, *3*(5). Retrieved from http://www.humankinetics.coni/ejss.

Chalip, L. (2001). Sport and tourism: Capitalising on the linkage. In D. Kluka & G. Schilling (Eds), *The business of sport*, pp. 77–88. Oxford: Meyer & Meyer.

Chalip, L. (2004). Beyond impact: A general model for sport event leverage. In B.W. Ritchie & D. Adair (Eds), *Sport tourism: Interrelationships, impacts and issues*, pp. 226–252. Clevedon: Channel View Publications.

Cook, D.J., Mulrow, C.D., & Haynes, R.B. (1997). Systematic reviews: synthesis of best evidence for clinical decisions. *Annals of Internal Medicine*, *126*(5), 376–380.

Davies, H.T.O., Nutley, S.M., & Smith, P.C. (1999). Editorial: What works? The role of evidence in public sector policy and practice. *Public Money and Management*, *19*(1), 3–5.

De Knop, P. (1990). Sport for all and active tourism. *Journal of the World Leisure and Recreation Association*, Fall, 30–36.

Downward, P. (2005). Critical (realist) reflection on policy and management research in sport, tourism and sports tourism. *European Sport Management Quarterly*, *5*(3), 303–320.

Finn, C.E., Stevens, F.I., Stufflebeam, D.L., & Walberg, H. (1997). The New York City public schools integrated learning systems project: Evaluation and meta-evaluation. *International Journal of Educational Research*, *27*(2), 159–174.

Forscher, B.K. (1963). Chaos in the brickyard. *Science*, *142*, 35.

Gibson, H.J. (1998). Sport tourism: a critical analysis of research. *Sport Management Review*, *1*(1), 45–76.

Gibson, H.J. (2002). Sport tourism at a crossroad? Considerations for the future. In S. Gammon & J. Kurtzman (Eds), *Sport tourism: Principles and practice*, pp. 123–40. Eastbourne: Leisure Studies Association.

Gibson, H.J. (2003). Sport tourism. In J. Parks & J. Quarterman (Eds), *Contemporary sport management*. Champaign, IL: Human Kinetics.

Gibson, H.J. (2004). Moving beyond the 'what is and who' of sport tourism to understanding 'why'. *Journal of Sport Tourism*, *9*(3), 247–265.

Higham, J.E.S., & Hinch, T.D. (2002). Sport and tourism development: avenues of tourism development associated with a regional sport franchise at an urban tourism destination. In S. Gammon & J. Kurtzman (Eds), *Sport tourism: Principles and practice*, pp. 19–34. Eastbourne: Leisure Studies Association.

Hinch, T.D., & Higham, J.E.S. (2004). *Sport tourism development*. Clevedon: Channel View Publications.

Jackson, G.A.M., & Glyptis, S.A. (1992). Sport and tourism: A review of the literature. Unpublished report to the Sports Council, Loughborough: Recreation Management Group, Loughborough University.

Jackson, G.A.M., & Weed, M. (2003). The sport-tourism interrelationship. In B. Houlihan (Ed.), *Sport in society: A student introduction*, pp. 235–251. London: Sage.

Jones, M., & Stokes, T. (2003). The Commonwealth Games and urban regeneration: an investigation into training initiatives and partnerships and their effects on disadvantaged groups in East Manchester. *Managing Leisure*, *8*(4), 198–211.

Kiassen, T.P., Jahad, A.R., & Moher, D. (1998). Guides for reading and interpreting systematic reviews. *Archives of Pediatric Adolescent Medicine*, 152, 700–704.

Kuhn, T.S. (1962). *The structure of scientific revolutions*. Chicago: University of Chicago Press.

McFee, G. (2006). Paradigms and possibilities. Invited paper to the 11th Congress of the European College of Sport Sciences, Lausanne, Switzerland, July.

Neuman, W.L. (2002). *Social research methods: Qualitative and quantitative approaches* (5th edn). Boston: Allyn & Bacon.

Page, S. (2005). Academic ranking exercises: do they achieve anything meaningful? *Tourism Management*, 26(5), 663–666.

Pawson, R. (2002). *Does Megan's Law work? A theory-driven systematic review* (Working Paper 8). London: ESRC UK Centre for Evidence Based Policy and Practice.

Ryan, C. (2005). The ranking and rating of academics ad journals in tourism research. *Tourism Management*, 26(5), 657–662.

Scott-Little, C., Hamann, M., & Jurs, S. (2002). Evaluations of after-school programs: a meta-evaluation of methodologies and narrative synthesis of findings. *American Journal of Evaluation*, 23(4), 387–419.

Sports Council (1994). *Sport in the Nineties – New Horizons*. London: Sports Council.

Standeven, J., & Tomlinson, A. (1994). *Sport and tourism in South East England*. London: South East Council for Sport and Recreation.

Weed, M. (1999). More than sports holidays: an overview of the sport-tourism link. In Scarrot, M. (Ed.), *Proceedings of the sport and recreation information group seminar, Exploring sports tourism*, pp. 3–15. Sheffield: SPRIG.

Weed, M. (2002). Football hooligans as undesirable sports tourists: some meta-analytical speculations. In S. Gammon & J. Kurtzman (Eds), *Sport tourism: Principles and practice*, pp. 35–52. Eastbourne: Leisure Studies Association.

Weed, M. (2004). Sports tourism research 2000–2003: a systematic review of knowledge and a meta-evaluation of method. Paper to the 12th European Association of Sport Management Congress, Ghent, Belgium, September.

Weed, M. (2005a). Sports tourism. In J. Beech & S. Chadwick (Eds), *The business of sport management*, pp. 305–322. Harlow: Financial Times Prentice Hall.

Weed, M. (2005b). Research synthesis in sport management: dealing with 'chaos in the brickyard'. *European Sport Management Quarterly*, 5(1), 77–90.

Weed, M. (2005c). Sports tourism theory and method: concepts, issues and epistemologies. *European Sport Management Quarterly*, 5(3), 229–242.

Weed, M. (2006). Editorial: Introducing the Journal of Sport & Tourism. *Journal of Sport & Tourism*, 11(1), 1–4.

Weed, M., & Bull, C.J. (2004). *Sports tourism: Participants, policy and providers*. Oxford: Elsevier.

Weed, M., Robinson, L., Downward, P., Green, M., Henry, I., Houlihan, B., & Argent, F. (2005). Academic review of the role of voluntary sport clubs. Unpublished report to Sport England. Loughborough: Institute of Sport & Leisure Policy.

Woodside, A.G., & Sakai, M.Y. (2001). Meta-evaluations of performance audits of government tourism marketing programs. *Journal of Travel Research*, 39, 369–379.

Appendix: articles included in the systematic review

Andersson, T.D., Rustad, A., & Solberg, H.A. (2004). Local residents' monetary evaluation of sports events. *Managing Leisure*, 9(3), 145–158.

Barker, M., Page, S.J., & Meyer, D. (2002). Evaluating the impact of the 2000 America's Cup on Auckland, New Zealand. *Event Management*, 7(2), 79–92.

Barker, M., Page, S.J., & Meyer, D. (2003). Urban visitor perceptions of safety during a special event. *Journal of Travel Research*, *41*(4), 355–361.

Beedie, P. (2003). Mountain guiding and adventure tourism: reflections on the choreography of the experience. *Leisure Studies*, *22*(2), 147–167.

Beedie, P., & Hudson, S. (2003). Emergence of mountain-based adventure tourism. *Annals of Tourism Research*, *30*(3), 625–643.

Bourdeau, P., Corneloup, J., & Mao, P. (2002). Adventure sports and tourism in the French mountains: dynamics of change and challenges for sustainable development. *Current Issues in Tourism*, *5*(1), 22–32.

Bricker, K.S., & Kerstetter, D.L. (2000). Level of specialization and place attachment: an exploratory study of whitewater recreationists. *Leisure Sciences*, *22*(4), 233–257.

Burton, R. (2003). Olympic Games host city marketing: an exploration of expectations and outcomes. *Sport Marketing Quarterly*, *12*(1), 37–47.

Carothers, P., Vaske, J.J., & Donnelly, M.P, (2001). Social values versus interpersonal conflict among hikers and mountain bikers. *Leisure Sciences*, *23*(1), 47–61.

Cegielski, M., & Mules, T. (2002). Aspects of residents' perceptions of the GMC 400 – Canberra's V8 supercar race. *Current Issues in Tourism*, *5*(1), 54–70.

Chalip, L., & Leyns, A. (2002). Local business leveraging of a sport event: managing an event for economic benefit. *Journal of Sport Management*, *16*(2), 132–158.

Chalip, L., Green, B.C., & Hill, B. (2003). Effects of sport event media on destination image and intention to visit. *Journal of Sport Management*, *17*(3), 214–234.

Cloke, P., & Perkins, H.C. (2002). Commodification and adventure in New Zealand tourism. *Current Issues in Tourism*, *5*(6), 521–549.

Coble, T.G., Selin, SW., Erickson, B.B. (2003). Hiking alone: understanding fear, negotiation strategies and leisure experience. *Journal of Leisure Research*, *35*(1), 1–22.

Cornelissen, S. (2004). Sport mega-events in Africa: processes, impacts and prospects. *Tourism and Hospitality Planning and Development*, *1*(1), 39–55.

Crompton, J. (2004). Beyond economic impact: an alternative rationale for the public subsidy of major league sports facilities. *Journal of Sport Management*, *18*(1), 40–58.

Daniels, M.J. (2004). Beyond input-output analysis: using occupation-based modeling to estimate wages generated by a sport tourism event. *Journal of Travel Research*, *43*(1), 75–82.

Daniels, M.J., Norman, W.C., Henry, M.S. (2004). Estimating income effects of a sport tourism event. *Annals of Tourism Research*, *31*(1), 180–199.

Dermody, M.B., Taylor, S.L., & Lomanno, M.V. (2003). The impact of NFL games on lodging industry revenue. *Journal of Travel and Tourism Marketing*, *14*(1), 21–36.

Dionigi, R.A. (2001). Participant experiences in a special sporting event: the case of the United Games in Bathurst, Australia. *Annals of Leisure Research*, *4*(1), 17–37.

Fairley, S. (2003). In search of relived social experience: group based nostalgia sport tourism. *Journal of Sport Management*, *17*(3), 284–304.

Faulkner, B., Chalip, L., Brown, G., Jago, L., March, R., & Woodside, A. (2001). Monitoring the tourism impacts of the Sydney 2000 Olympics. *Event Management*, *6*(4), 231–246.

Flagestad, A., & Hope, C.A. (2001). Strategic success in winter sports destinations: a sustainable value creation perspective. *Tourism Management*, *22*(5), 445–461.

Fluker, M.R., & Turner, L.W. (2000). Needs, motivations and expectations of a commercial whitewater rafting experience. *Journal of Travel Research*, *38*(4), 380–389.

Gandhi-Arora, R., & Shaw, R.N. (2002). Visitor loyalty in sport tourism: an empirical investigation. *Current Issues in Tourism*, *5*(1), 45–53.

Gard-MeGehee, N., Yoon, Y., & Cardenas, D. (2003). Involvement and travel for recreational runners in North Carolina. *Journal of Sport Management*, *17*(3), 305–324.

Gibson, H.J., Willming, C., & Holdnak, A. (2003). Small-scale event sport tourism: fans as tourists. *Tourism Management*, *24*(2), 181–190.

Green, B.C. (2001). Leveraging subculture and identity to promote sport events. *Sport Management Review*, *4*(1), 1–19.

Green, B.C., Costa, C., & Fitzgerald, M. (2003). Marketing the host city: analyzing exposure generated by a sport event. *International Journal of Sports Marketing and Sponsorship*, December/January.

Grecnaway, R. (2002). Measuring the significance of multi-use outdoor recreation resources: a comparative analysis of three sites in New Zealand. *Annals of Leisure Research*, *5*(1), 65–79.

Gyimothy, S., & Mykletun, R.J. (2004). Play in adventure tourism: the case of arctic trekking. *Annals of Tourism Research*, *31*(4). 855–878.

Hautbois, C., & Durand, C. (2004). Public strategies for local development: the effectiveness of an outdoor activities model. *Managing Leisure*, *9*(4), 212–226.

Higham, J.E.S., & Hinch, T.D. (2002). Tourism, sport and seasons: the challenges and potential of overcoming seasonality in the sport and tourism sectors. *Tourism Management*, *23*(2), 175–185.

Higham, J.E.S., & Hinch, T.D. (2003). Sport, space and time: effects of the Otago Highlanders franchise on tourism. *Journal of Sport Management*, *17*(3), 235–257.

Hinch, T.D., & Higham, J.E.S. (2001). Sport tourism: a framework for research. *International Journal of Tourism Research*, *3*(1), 45–58.

Home, J.D., & Manzenreiter, W. (2004). Accounting for mega-events: forecast and actual impacts of the 2002 Football World Cup finals on the host countries Japan/Korea. *International Review for the Sociology of Sport*, *39*(2), 187–203.

Hudson, S., Ritchie, B., & Timur, S. (2004). Measuring destination competitiveness: an empirical study of Canadian ski resorts. *Tourism and Hospitality Planning and Development*, *1*(1), 79–94.

Jones, C. (2001). Mega-events and host region impacts: determining the true worth of the 1999 Rugby World Cup. *International Journal of Tourism Research*, *3*(3), 241–251.

Kasimati, E. (2003). Economic; aspects and the Summer Olympics: a review of related research. *International Journal of Tourism Research*, *5*(6), 433–444.

Kane, M.J., & Zink, R. (2004). Package adventure tours: markers in serious leisure careers. *Leisure Studies*, *23*(4), 329–345.

Kim, M. (2004). A critical research model of sports tourism studies. *World Leisure Journal*, 3/2004, 58–64.

Kim, N., & Chalip, L. (2004). Why travel to the FIFA World Cup? Effects of motives, background, interest and constraints. *Tourism Management*, *25*(6), 695–707.

Kyle, G., Bricker, K., Graefe, A., & Wickham, T. (2004). An examination of recreationists' relationships with activities and settings. *Leisure Sciences*, *26*(2), 123–142.

Kyle, G., Graefe, A., Manning, R., & Bacon, J. (2003). An examination of the relationship between leisure activity involvement and place attachment among hikers along the Appalachian Trail. *Journal of Leisure Research*, *35*(3), 249–273.

Kyle, G., Graefe, A., Manning, R., & Bacon, J. (2004). Predictors of behavioural loyalty among hikers along the Appalachian Trail. *Leisure Sciences*, *26*(1), 99–118.

Little, D.E. (2002). Women and adventure recreation: reconstructing leisure constraints and adventure experiences to negotiate continuing participation. *Journal of Leisure Research*, *34*(2), 157–177.

Madden, J.R. (2002). The economic consequences of the Sydney Olympics: the CREA/Arthur Andersen study. *Current Issues in Tourism*, 5(1), 7–21.

Melian-Gonzalez, A., & Garcia-Falcon, J.M. (2003). Competitive potential of tourism in destinations. *Annals of Tourism Research*, 30(3), 720–740.

Mihalik, B.J. (2000). Research note – host population perceptions of the 1996 Atlanta Olympics: support, benefits and liabilities. *Tourism Analysis*, 5(1), 49–53.

Miler, L.M., Herrmann, M., Giraud, K., Skogen-Baker, M., & Hiser, R.F. (2003). Research note – international sport fishing: the case of the German angler in Alaska. *Tourism Analysis*, 8(1), 89–94.

Needham, M.D., Rollins, R.B., & Wood, C.J.B. (2004). Site specific encounters, norms and crowding of summer visitors at alpine ski areas. *International Journal of Tourism Research*, 6(6), 421–437.

Patterson, I. (2002). Baby boomers and adventure tourism: the importance of marketing the leisure experience. *World Leisure Journal*, 2/2002, 4–10.

Pennington-Gray, L., & Holdnack, A. (2002). Out of the stands and into the community: using sports events to promote a destination. *Event Management*, 7(3), 177–186.

Perdue, R.R. (2004). Stakeholder analysis in Colorado ski resort communities, *Tourism Analysis*, 8(2), 233–236.

Petrick, J.F., & Backman, S.J. (2002). An examination of the determinants of golf travelers' satisfaction. *Journal of Travel Research*, 40(3), 252–258.

Petrick, J.F., & Backman, S.J. (2002). An examination of the construct of perceived value for the prediction of golf travelers' intentions to revisit. *Journal of Travel Research*, 41(1), 38–45.

Petrick, J.F., & Backman, S.J. (2002). An examination of golf travelers' satisfaction, perceived value, loyalty and intentions to revisit. *Tourism Analysis*, 6(3/4), 223–237.

Riddingion, G.E. (2002). Learning and ability to pay: developing a model to forecast ski tourism. *Journal of Travel and Tourism Marketing*, 13(1/2), 111–126.

Ritchie, B., Mosedale, L., & King, J. (2002). Profiling sport tourists: the case of Super 12 rugby union in the Australian Capital Territory, Australia. *Current Issues in Tourism*, 5(1), 33–44.

Siderelis, C., & Attarian, A. (2004). Trip response modeling of rock climbers' reactions to proposed regulations. *Journal of Leisure Research*, 36(1), 73–88.

Siderelis, C., Moore, R., & Lee, J.-H. (2000). Incorporating users' perceptions of site quality in a recreation travel cost model. *Journal of Leisure Research*, 32(4), 406–414.

Sugerman, D. (2002). The relationship of age to motivation and skill development level in outdoor adventure programs for older adults. *Loisir et Societe/Society and Leisure*, 25(2), 351–376.

Sung, H.H. (2004). Classification of adventure travelers: behavior, decision making, and target markets. *Journal of Travel Research*, 42(4), 343–356.

Sung, H.Y., Morrison, A.M., & O'Leary, J.T. (2000). Segmenting the adventure travel market by activities: from the North American industry providers' perspective. *Journal of Travel and Tourism Marketing*, 9(4), 1–20.

Thapa, B., & Graefe, A.R. (2003). Level of skill and its relationship to recreation conflict and tolerance among adult skiers and snowboarders. *World Leisure Journal*, 2003/1, 13–25.

Tuppen, J. (2000). The restructuring of winter sports resorts in the French Alps: problems, processes and policies. *International Journal of Tourism Research*, 2(5), 327–344.

Twynam, G.D., & Johnston, M. (2004). Changes in host community reactions to a special sporting event. *Current Issues in Tourism*, 7(3), 242–261.

Tyrrell, T.J., Williams, P.W., & Johnston, R.J. (2004). Research note – estimating sport tourism visitor volumes: the case of Vancouver's 2010 Olympic Games. *Tourism Recreation Research*, *29*(1), 75–81.

Upneja, A., Shafer, E.L., Seo, W., & Yoon, J. (2001). Economic benefits of sport fishing and angler wildlife watching in Pennsylvania. *Journal of Travel Research*, *40*(1), 68–78.

Vaske, J.L Carothers, P., Donnelly, M.P., & Baird, B. (2000). Recreation conflict among skiers and snowboarders. *Leisure Sciences*, *22*(4), 297–313.

Vaske, J.J., Dyar, R., & Timmons, N. (2004). Skill level and recreation conflict among skiers and snowboarders. *Leisure Sciences*, *26*(2), 215–225.

Vitterso, J., Chipeniuk, R., Skar, M., & Vistad, O.I. (2004). Recreational conflict is affective: the case of cross-country skiers and snowmobiles. *Leisure Sciences*, *26*(3), 227–243.

Vrana, V., Zafiropoulos, C., & Paschaloudis, D. (2004). Measuring the provision of information services in tourist hotel web sites: the case of Athens-Olympic City 2004. *Tourism and Hospitality Planning and Development*, *1*(3), 255–272.

Weber, K. (2001). Outdoor adventure tourism: a review of research approaches. *Annals of Tourism Research*, *28*(2), 360–377.

Weed, M. (2001). Towards a model of cross-sectoral policy development in leisure: the case of sport and tourism. *Leisure Studies*, *20*(2), 125–141.

Weed, M. (2002). Organisational culture and the leisure policy process in Britain: how structure affects strategy in sport-tourism policy development. *Tourism, Culture and Communication*, *3*(3), 147–163.

Weed, M. (2003). Why the two won't tango! Explaining the lack of integrated policies for sport and tourism in the UK. *Journal of Sport Management*, *17*(3), 258–283.

Williams, P., & Fidgeon, P.R. (2000). Addressing participation constraint: a case study of potential skiers. *Tourism Management*, *21*(3), 379–393.

Williams, S.D., & Gibson, H.J. (2004). The attraction of Switzerland for college skiers after 9/11: a case study. *Tourism Review International*, *8*(2), 85–99.

Woodside, A.G., Spurr, R., March, R., & Clark, H. (2002). The dynamics of traveler destination awareness and search for information associated with hosting the Olympic Games. *International Journal of Sports Marketing and Sponsorship*, June/July.

PART TWO

Understanding the sports tourist

EDITOR'S INTRODUCTION

MANY TEXTS FOCUSING ON THE RELATIONSHIP between sport and tourism commence with a discussion of impacts. In fact, for some texts, the impacts of linking sport and tourism are the primary focus, however, the approach taken here is different, being derived from a view that an understanding of participation and behaviours in sport and tourism is fundamental to any attempts to generate impacts, to formulate policy, or to make provision for sport and tourism (Weed, 2006). Consequently, as the first Part of the Reader to address substantive issues in sport and tourism, this Part focuses on the people who generate impacts and for whom policy and provision are made – the sports tourists themselves.

As Chapters 1, 4 and, in particular, Chapter 6 in the previous Part have noted, there is something of a paradox in relation to research on behaviours in sport and tourism. On the one hand, the systematic review in Chapter 6 showed that behaviours and profiles in sport and tourism formed the most featured topic for research into a range of activities. This would seem to indicate that the field is well served in terms of developing an understanding of the sports tourist. However, in Chapter 1 the claim is made that:

> policy, provision and impacts are all derived from participation, and it is to
> the detriment of the subject area as a whole that there is, as yet, only a very
> limited understanding of sports tourism participation.

Why, then, if the most featured topic in sport and tourism research is that relating to behaviours and profiles, is understanding of participation in sport and tourism 'very limited'? The answer is provided by the meta-evaluation aspect of Chapter 6, which notes that much of this work is fairly basic and provides profiles of, rather than explanations for, sports tourists' behaviours. This is something that has been noted elsewhere, with Gibson (2004) being critical of the tendency for researchers to focus on the 'what' of behaviours (i.e. providing profiles and descriptions) rather than attempting to understand the 'why'. The Editorial Introduction to Part One of this Reader highlighted an issue raised by the meta-evaluation in Chapter 6, concerning the pervasive use of positivist approaches to collect and analyse quantitative data, and called for greater methodological diversity in the study of sport and tourism. This issue is particularly problematic in relation to behaviours in sport and tourism, where the application of positivist quantitative methods to profile and describe sports tourism behaviour has left the field with only limited understanding of 'why sport tourists do what they do' (Gibson, 2004). In Part Four of this Reader, Downward (Chapter 23), will reinforce the view that a more detailed explanation of participation is important in understanding the impacts derived from such participation and in informing policy and provision decisions. In this respect, Downward notes that 'explanations require "ontic depth", that is moving beyond the level of events towards an understanding of the processes that produce them'.

In order to highlight the need for understanding processes that underpin behaviours, rather than straightforward descriptions of such behaviours, this part has been titled 'Understanding the sports tourist' rather than 'Sports tourism participation' or 'Sports tourism behaviours'. Furthermore, this theme was a key feature of the special issue of *European Sport Management Quarterly* (*ESMQ*) from which this Reader was conceived. As such, this Part commences with three papers that emerged from that special issue.

The first chapter in this Part (Chapter 7) is by **Tom Hinch** and **James Higham** and is entitled *Sport, Tourism and Authenticity*. As the title suggests, this paper discusses the search for authenticity in sports tourism experiences. It is a particularly useful chapter with which to start this Part as it has clear implications for understanding the sports tourism experience as related to, but more than the sum of, sport and tourism. Hinch and Higham discuss the nature of sports tourism attractions and, in particular, events as sports tourism attractions. In doing so, they invoke the work of Nauright (1996) to reinforce their view that sports events and the reactions they engender are the 'clearest manifestations of culture and collective identities in a given society'. Consequently, the sports tourist attending such an event is not only a sports spectator, but a consumer of local culture and, as such, the primacy of either the sport or tourism element (if, indeed, it is possible or desirable to separate such elements) cannot be established. Hinch and Higham's view of authenticity is an experiential one rather than being related to any objective judgement of what is and what is not authentic. They believe that many sports tourists are engaged in a search for meaningful experiences and seek to enter an 'authentic state of being'. Their discussions of this aspect of authenticity are, therefore, particularly useful in deepening our understanding of the sports tourism experience.

Chapter 8, from the *ESMQ* special issue, is a really useful example of how an in-depth understanding of the nature of sports tourism participation can lead to a clearer understanding of how impacts are generated, and to a more efficient policy. **Carla Costa** and **Laurence Chalip's** chapter, *Adventure Sport Tourism in Rural Revitalisation – An Ethnographic Evaluation* uses detailed ethnographic data on the nature of participation in paragliding by sports tourists in a small Portuguese village to show that the popular perception that paragliding has a positive impact on the village is flawed. Costa and Chalip argue that if the village wishes to generate positive impacts then specific leveraging strategies need to be developed by local policy-makers and providers. The focus on leveraging benefits, rather than simply expecting that they will come, is something that will be discussed further in Part Three. It emerges here because Costa and Chalip's chapter is an excellent example of a holistic piece of research that seeks to develop policy and provision through a knowledge of impacts that is derived from an understanding of the behaviours that generate such impacts. As such, this chapter would sit equally comfortably in Part Three (impacts) or Part Four (policy and provision) of this Reader. However, it has been included here as a clear demonstration of the fundamental nature of knowledge about sports tourism participation necessary to gain an understanding of impacts and for policy-making and provision.

The third chapter in this Part, by **Heather Gibson** and **Lori Pennington-Gray**, also emerged from the call for papers for the *ESMQ* special issue, but was received too late for inclusion and so was published in the subsequent issue (vol. 5, no. 4). *Insights from Role Theory: Understanding Golf Tourism* uses golf tourism to illustrate the utility of role theory in understanding sports tourism participation, something that has been a core part of Gibson's work for some years. One of the assumptions of role theory is that people enact different roles at different times in different situations. In relation to sports tourism, Gibson and Pennington-Gray suggest that at one extreme there is a 'sportlover' or 'sports junkie' role that people enact for the duration of their trip, leaving little room for any other tourism activities. For other people (in varying degrees) the sports tourist role is one among a number of tourist roles that might be enacted on any one trip. The implications of this, therefore, may be that the view in the literature that sports tourism can be categorised by 'trip purpose' may be flawed, and that a more complex understanding of the way in which sports tourism behaviours interact with other forms of tourism behaviours during any one trip may be needed.

The fourth chapter in this Part is *An Examination of the Determinants of Golf Travelers' Satisfaction* by **James Petrick** and **Sheila Backman**, also discusses golf tourism. Like Gibson's sustained interest in role theory, Petrick and Backman have conducted a number of studies into golf tourists, focusing on the related issues of satisfaction, perceived value and loyalty. A problem identified by Petrick and Backman in researching satisfaction is that it is very subjective and may be interpreted differently by each individual. As such, previous research has often focused on satisfaction as a result of a comparison between expectations and outcome. However, Petrick and Backman note that experiences are more complex than this and, in many cases, what is desired from an activity is not apparent until the participant realises that it is not there. Consequently, more recent research on satisfaction has compared outcomes with desires (some aspects of which participants may not realise in advance). Given this approach to satisfaction, their findings are revealing in that it is less often the golfing aspect of the experience that determines levels of satisfaction, but rather aspects of the resort experience. Perhaps because it was a conscious part of pre-trip desires and expectations, the golf aspect was almost always satisfactory. This would suggest that these golf tourists were looking for a form of 'luxury sports tourism' in which the attendant facilities and levels of service can be as important to the experience as the activity itself (Weed and Bull, 2004). It also suggests, drawing on Gibson's paper (Chapter 9), that these golf tourists were enacting multiple tourist roles during their golf tourism trips.

My systematic review and meta-evaluation of the area (Chapter 6) notes that research into outdoor and adventure activities that fell within the parameters used for the review was dominated by research on behaviours. Furthermore, behavioural research in this area tended to be much more clearly grounded in theory than did the rest of sport and tourism research into behaviours. Consequently, the next three chapters in this Part all focus on behaviours in the area of outdoor adventure activities. While the context for this work may be outdoor and adventure activities, much of the comment on the nature of behaviour is of broader relevance to understanding behaviours in sport and tourism in general.

Paul Beedie's chapter, *Mountain Guiding and Adventure Tourism: Reflections on the Choreography of the Experience*, discusses the role of mountain guides in providing adventure tourism as 'adventure education'. In this respect, novice adventure tourists are seen as needing clear guidance in the mountain setting, and this is the initial role of the mountain guide. However, Beedie notes that such tourists often wish to make the transition to greater independence and set a course towards 'becoming a mountaineer'. Somewhat paradoxically, to gain greater independence, the rules of engagement with the mountains (which might be seen as constrictive) become more important, with mountain guides trying to ensure that such rules are internalised. As such, mountain guides seek to encourage individuals to move from being dependent tourists to becoming independent mountaineers through the internalisation of the 'rules' of mountaineering and mountain engagement. However, at the same time, the increasing 'touristification' of mountains and the mountaineering experience leads to many adventure tourists leaving the mountains with what Beedie claims Hamilton Smith (1993) would label as a shallower experience. In this respect, the paper concludes by approaching issues of commodification, which links into the next chapter in this Part.

Package Adventure Tours: Markers in Serious Leisure Careers by **Maurice Kane** and **Robyn Zink** examines the tension between the idea of a package tour and the concept of adventure through ethnographic research on a fourteen-day white-water kayaking package. The research reveals that participants on this tour were seeking 'capital' within the kayaking world. The tour was linked to a well-known and celebrity- (i.e. elite kayaker) endorsed part of the tour ('Heli-kayaking'). Kane and Zink note that the gaining of this capital was enabled by the 'packaged' nature of the tour, which guaranteed 'safe success', something that is highly regarded within the kayaking world due to the nature of the activity. Conversely, however, Kane and Zink recognise that the participants were also well aware that any 'capital' among non kayaking peers would be in relation to the adventurous elements of the trip, and the packaged nature of such adventure would not be important. For the participants themselves, who were identified as having 'serious leisure careers' in white-water kayaking, the packaged aspect of the tour was not significant – it was the kayaking experience that contributed to identity formation.

Taken together, Beedie's, and Kane and Zink's papers have important things to contribute in relation to both the commodification of experience and the longevity of the experience. In the first respect, commodification, which is often viewed pejoratively, allows certain groups of mountain adventure tourists (Beedie) and white-water kayakers

(Kane and Zink) to gain access to experiences that they would not otherwise have been able to enjoy. In both papers, 'safe success' can be highlighted as significant in allowing individuals to have 'developmental' experiences. In the second respect, longevity of experience is provided either by the educational aspect that would not have been possible without the 'choreography' of the guides, or the kayaking capital gained that would not have been possible without the packaged nature of the tour. The implication, therefore, for research into sports tourism behaviours more generally is that commodification, rather than resulting in a substandard experience (as implied by those who view commodification pejoratively), can be enabling in that it allows access to experiences that can be part of longer-term sports tourism careers.

The third of the outdoor and adventure activities papers derives its approach from consumer behaviour research. **Heidi Sung's** paper, *Classification of Adventure Travelers: Behavior, Decision Making, and Target Markets* is an interesting chapter to compare with Gibson and Pennington-Gray's chapter on role theory (Chapter 9). Sung uses a different disciplinary language to Gibson and Pennington-Gray, but identifies six adventure traveller sub-groups: general enthusiast, budget youngsters, soft moderates, upper high naturalists, family vacationers, and active soloists. An interesting question here might be how far Sung's sub-groups might be legitimately described as adventure tourist roles, based as they are on a profile of activity-related behaviours. A key challenge for research aimed at understanding the sports tourist is to assess the extent to which research rooted in different disciplinary traditions might be addressing similar issues, and how an understanding of such issues might be addressed through interdisciplinary collaboration.

The issue of the evolving nature of a particular sports tourism resource, and its implications for participation experiences, is the subject of Chapter 14, *Recreation Conflict among Skiers and Snowboarders* by **Jerry Vaske, Pam Carothers, Maureen Donnelly** and **Biff Baird**. At first glance this chapter may appear to relate to a resource utilisation problem and the suitability of snowboarders and skiers sharing a resource designed specifically for skiing. However, Vaske *et al.* note that much of the conflict is at least magnified by the clash of 'styles' or 'identities' between the two groups derived from the visual difference in clothes, language, and on-slope behaviour. They also suggest that 'place attachment', which has been little considered in previous work on recreation conflict, may be a factor in creating perceived conflict.

This study would seem to reinforce the Weed and Bull (2004) conceptualisation of the sports tourism experience as arising from the interaction of activity, people, and place. In this example it would appear that the two activities struggle to coexist because of the way in which the activities interact with the people who participate in them (who each have very different lifestyle approaches) and the place (both in terms of identity and attachment, and in terms of the way it is utilised for the activities). As such, Vaske *et al.*'s study into how the different participants experience conflict provides some illuminating insights into the nature of the experiences themselves.

The final chapter in this Part switches the focus to sports fans rather than active participants. *In Search of Relived Social Experience: Group-Based Nostalgia Sport Tourism* by **Sheranne Fairley** focuses on nostalgia as a key part of the fan experience. Research in sport and tourism has often classified travelling sports fans as 'passive' sports tourists while, as noted in the introduction to Part One, Gibson (1988) has suggested that as well as active and passive sports tourism, there is a third form: nostalgia sports tourism. It has also been suggested more recently (Weed, 2006), that nostalgia sports tourism is a form of vicarious participation. Vicarious participation implies a more active engagement with the event than the traditional view of fans as 'passive' sports tourists. Regardless of which of these schema are used, it seems somewhat incongruous to view the fanatical engagement of many sports supporters as a 'passive' activity.

Fairley's chapter is interesting because it focuses not only on the attendance of fans at the event, but also their trip to the event. As such, in addition to the destination experience, there is a place experience of the bus journey itself, where past, present, and future interact in an experience drawn from reliving the past (previous trips), enjoying the present (current trip), and anticipating the future (the rest of the trip). This interaction is rooted in the past, which frames the participants' engagement with the present and future, Fairley's study is unique in focusing on the broader sports tourism experience, rather than simply on the attendance at the event, and this could have wider implications for understanding behaviours. Weed (2001; 2002), for example, has hinted that this could be a useful way of understanding football hooligan behaviour. However, it certainly provides a clearer insight into the nature of the experience of sports fans than the more pervasive narrow focus on the event itself.

It is intended that the chapters within this Part should give an insight into the sports tourism experience in a range of different settings. However, many of the issues are relevant beyond the immediate setting in which they have been researched. Role theory, for example, is generically relevant to understanding sports tourism experiences, whilst issues of identity, serious leisure, and 'capital' can inform our understanding of experiences in a range of settings. The final chapter in this Part on sports fans or spectators, which is clearly a significant sports tourist group, forms a useful final note. However, the following Part on impacts focuses largely on sports events and contains much that is relevant to understanding the fandom or spectating experience. Chapters 20 (Green) and 21 (Gibson, Willming and Holdnak) are particularly relevant in this respect.

REFERENCES

Gibson, H.J. (1998) 'Sport Tourism: A Critical Analysis of Research', *Sport Management Review*, 1 (1): 45–76.

Gibson, H.J. (2004) 'Moving Beyond the "What Is and Who" of Sport Tourism to Understanding "Why"', *Journal of Sport Tourism*, 9 (3): 247–65.

Hamilton-Smith, E. (1993) 'In the Australian Bush: Some Reflections on Serious Leisure', *World Recreation and Leisure*, 35: 10–13.

Nauright, J. (1996). 'A Besieged Tribe? Nostalgia, White Cultural Identity and the Role of Rugby in a Changing South Africa', *International Review for the Sociology of Sport*, 31 (1): 69–89.

Weed, M. (2001) 'Ing-ger-land at Euro 2000: How "Handbags at 20 Paces" Was Portrayed as a Full-Scale Riot', *International Review for the Sociology of Sport*, 36 (4): 407–24.

Weed, M (2002) 'Football Hooligans as Undesirable Sports Tourists: Some Meta Analytical Speculations', in S. Gammon and J. Kurtzman (eds), *Sport Tourism: Principles and Practice*. Eastbourne: LSA.

Weed, M. (2006) 'Sports Tourism and the Development of Sports Events', Keynote paper to Sport, Tourism and City Marketing conference, Malmo, Sweden, September.

Weed, M. and Bull, C.J. (2004) *Sports Tourism: Participants, Policy and Providers*. Oxford: Elsevier.

Chapter 7

Tom Hinch and James Higham

SPORT, TOURISM AND AUTHENTICITY

Introduction

ONE OF THE FUNDAMENTAL CRITICISMS of tourism is that it leads to pseudo-events that fail to reflect the true culture of a place (Boorstin, 1964). This criticism suggests that in the process of catering to the visitors' needs and wants, tourism operators create packages and foster experiences that corrupt the cultural essence of the attraction. In effect, the destination becomes a stage featuring performances by hosts that are removed from their real lives, their real homes, and their real culture.

Destination hosts try to balance their tourism performances with their private lives by spatially and temporally structuring their communities into a series of front stages where they perform and back stages where they escape from the visitors (Goffman, 1959). As the destination progresses through its tourism development lifecycle, this balancing act becomes increasingly difficult. Ultimately, a destination can be destroyed by its own success as more and more tourists arrive, resulting in a community dominated by a front stage with the cultural uniqueness of the destination being lost to visitors and hosts. At this point, Plog's (1972, p. 4) warning that "destination areas carry with them the potential seeds of their own destruction" is apposite.

This line of argument suggests that the commodification process destroys, or at least significantly alters, the culture of a destination community. In doing so, the authenticity of culturally-based tourism products and attractions at the destination is compromised or lost (MacCannell, 1976). As tourists begin to sense this loss, they will substitute other types of products or other destinations in their search for authenticity. From the perspective of the hosts, the loss of cultural authenticity is also destructive as it is tied closely to their collective identity. Under these conditions, tourism activity in the destination is likely to be unsustainable.

Clearly, if the residents of a destination want to avoid this course of development, they need to adopt strategies that protect their cultural integrity. This is particularly challenging in destinations where cultural attractions are positioned as important draws to the region. However, not all cultural attractions are equally sensitive. In fact, sport attractions may be more robust than other types of cultural attractions in the face of this challenge (Hinch & Higham, 2004). This thesis is explored by examining the advantages of positioning sport as a cultural tourist attraction in the context of authenticity.

Sport as a tourist attraction

Sport represents a unique type of cultural tourist attraction (Higham & Hinch, 2003). Leiper's (1990) widely cited paper on tourist attraction systems is used as the basis for considering sport as an attraction. While Leiper did not focus on sport, he presented a general framework for attractions that is theoretically sound and which facilitates empirical measurement for research and practice. At the heart of his framework is the definition of a tourist attraction as:

> a system comprising of three elements: a tourist or human element, a nucleus or central element, and a marker or informative element. A tourist attraction comes into existence when the three elements are connected.
>
> (Leiper, 1990, p. 371)

From a sport perspective, the human element includes travellers whose trips were motivated by sport or who are involved in sport while travelling. Such travellers include elite athletes and their entourages, spectators, officials, media and others. Similarly, recreational athletes pursuing their sport interests away from their home environment are a major part of this human element.

Markers are described as "items of information, about any phenomenon that is a potential nuclear element in a tourist attraction" (p. 377). For sport attractions, such markers would range from explicit advertisements that encourage travel to: (1) attend major events such as European and world championship sports events; (2) visit specific destinations such as resorts in the French and Swiss Alps to snowboard; or (3) visit sports attractions such as the Olympic Museum in Lausanne, Switzerland. Even more pervasive markers are the broadcasts of sporting events that highlight the place where the event is occurring. References to sporting places in the popular media, inclusive of movies and literature, also serve as powerful tourist attraction markers.

Finally, the nucleus of the attraction is where the tourist experience is manufactured and consumed, therefore, making it the focal point of tourism. Leiper (1990) describes the nucleus as any feature or characteristic of a place that a traveller contemplates visiting or actually visits. In terms of sport tourism, the question then becomes one of "What features or characteristics can be classified as sport in a destination?" While it is easy to answer this question at the level of specific sports, it is more challenging at the level of sport in general.

In this paper sport tourism is defined as: "sport-based travel away from the home environment for a limited time, where sport is characterized by unique rule sets, competition related to physical prowess and play" (Hinch & Higham, 2001, p. 49). This definition articulates the concept of sport in tangible terms. In the context of the attraction nucleus, the place-based features that define sport are unique rule sets, competition related to physical prowess and a playful nature. These dimensions are seen as continuums that range from informal to formal rules, recreational through to elite sport and frivolous through to serious play. They complement a full range of sport tourism typologies such as the popular classifications of event, active and nostalgia (Gibson, 1998).

While the forgoing discussion has, in effect, argued that sport is a unique type of tourist attraction, it is not meant to suggest that sport tourism is a narrow or homogeneous concept. Clearly, the complexity of sport when combined with the complexity of tourism leads to countless diverse variations of the sport tourism phenomenon. This heterogeneity is reflected in a broad range of sport tourism frameworks, models and typologies found in the literature (see Gibson, 1998; Standeven & De Knop, 1999; Robinson & Gammon, 2004). Similarly, the view that sport tourism is a large and important tourism market niche (Delpy, 1997) has been replaced in the literature with the perspective that "sport tourism is really a collection of separate niches" (Bull & Weed, 1999, p. 43). The unique context of each sport tourism attraction, therefore, needs to be considered when assessing the authenticity of sport tourism attractions. For example, there are many types and scales of sporting events. Elite sporting events or events that are very competitive in nature are likely to draw more spectators than recreational events.

Similarly, urban-based sports may function differently as attractions than rural based sports for a variety of reasons, including their relative proximity to markets and the nature of the resources upon which they are developed (Hinch & Higham, 2004). In urban settings there has been criticism of the increasing standardization of sports stadia (Bale, 1989) but over the past two decades several new stadiums have been built with a retro design in an attempt to foster the feeling of a traditional facility. While not authentic in an objective sense, these stadiums have created a nostalgic atmosphere that has been appreciated and enjoyed by the fans (Fainstein & Judd, 1999)

In contrast, destinations that exploit the natural resources and/or natural beauty of their surroundings (for instance, for the pursuit of sports such as skiing, snowboarding, mountain climbing and kayaking) create issues relating to compromising the naturalness of the venues for these sports. Despite differences between the commodification of sports that take place in built facilities and natural areas—which certainly merit closer consideration—a common characteristic of sport tourism attractions is that they tend to embody a genuine form of local culture that is accessible to visitors.

Sport as a cultural tourist attraction

Bale (1994) suggests that all sports, both urban and nature-based, are cultural manifestations. He argues that sports are not natural forms of movement but rather form part of a cultural landscape. So, even sports that take place in supposedly natural environments actually take place in environments that are subject to cultural modification. Golf courses, for instance, which are very "green" in appearance, are clearly part of a cultural landscape (Priestley, 1995).

A sport attraction is also a cultural attraction to the extent that sport identities are a reflection of the culture in a place. These identities represent the way communities are perceived and are projected based on prevailing social and ideological values and practices

(McConnell & Edwards, 2000). In his book *Travels with Charley*, novelist John Steinbeck (1963) suggested that visitors could obtain a sense of local culture by going to a local pub on a Saturday night or to a church service the next day. In both cases the visitor would be able to share in local celebrations that reflect an important dimension of the culture of a place. The pub and the church service function as recognized "windows" or perhaps even "portals" into the backstage of a destination. A similar argument has been made for sport events and activities as sport is clearly one of the ways that humans develop their personal and collective identities, Nauright (1996) goes as far as to claim that in "many cases, sporting events and people's reactions to them are the clearest public manifestations of culture and collective identities in a given society" (p. 69). For example a visitor will experience a significant aspect of Canadian culture by attending a ice hockey game while in Canada (Gruneau & Whitson, 1993). More generally, visitors who attend local sporting events, participate in local sport activities, or visit local sites to venerate sports/people are afforded a unique opportunity to access the backstage of a destination. Furthermore, their visit is not likely to be as intrusive as visits to many other cultural sites because these elements of sport experience, despite their cultural significance, tend to be viewed as being within the public rather than private domain.

Commodification

Tourism is a business. While some academics may take issue with this claim, there is little doubt that tourism operators, governments, local hosts and tourists tend to rationalize their decisions in economic terms and behave as actors in a common market (Pearce, 1989). The fundamental rationale for tourism development tends to be an economic one; destinations and providers of tourism goods and services seek net economic gains. Tourism activities can therefore be considered as commercial exchanges.

Destination resources such as attractive climates, beautiful landscapes, and unique local cultures are packaged in a multitude of ways that are designed to provide leisure experiences for visitors. These experiences are exchanged for the visitors' economic resources, which are usually collected through an assortment of fees charged for tour packages, attractions, accommodation, food and beverages, transportation, souvenirs and other visitor related products and services as well as through avenues of government taxation. Cohen (1988) described this exchange as a form of commodification or:

> a process by which things (and activities) come to be evaluated primarily in terms of their exchange value, in a context of trade, thereby becoming goods (and services); developed exchange systems in which the exchange value of things (and activities) is stated in terms of prices for a market.
>
> (Cohen, 1988, p. 380)

Commodification has drawn considerable attention from critics of tourism who suggest that selling landscapes and culture in this type of exchange is somewhat akin to prostitution in that through engaging in these transactions, the destination is sacrificing part of its soul (Greenwood. 1989). The commodification of local culture is seen as especially challenging given the intrusive nature this can have in terms of the backstage of a destination.

Sport is rapidly moving toward a similar degree of commodification as reflected, for example, in the trends toward professional competition, increased media involvement and the emergence of transnational sport equipment manufacturers. McKay & Kirk (1992, p. 10) argue that "whereas cultural activities such as sport once were based primarily on intrinsic worth, they are now increasingly constituted by market values". Sport tourism represents but one of the many ways in which sport is being commodified. The question remains, however, whether this commodification is destroying the cultural meaning of sport in tourism destinations. Stewart (1987) suggests that this is the case by arguing that:

> Social hegemony of the commodity form is apparent as the practice of sport is shaped and dominated by the values and instrumentalities of the market . . . the idealized model of sport, along with its traditional ritualized meanings, metaphysical aura, and skill democracy, is destroyed as sport becomes just another item to be trafficked as a commodity.
>
> (Stewart, 1987, p. 172)

From this perspective, recent developments such as the professionalization of Rugby Union and the associated introduction of substantive rule changes in the Super 12 rugby competition in the southern hemisphere (Higham & Hinch, 2003) would seem to compromise the integrity of the sport. Yet rugby union is more popular than ever in the participating nations of South Africa, New Zealand and Australia despite the sport being subjected to considerable changes in recent years. The professional Rugby Super 12 competition is branded as fast, skilful and entertaining, in contrast to the competitions that preceded it which centred on values of tradition and loyalty. However, the sport has certainly not been destroyed if high levels of spectator and player support for the new professional competition are used as an indicator (Higham & Hinch, 2003).

In summary, while recognizing the potential negative impacts of the commodification of culture for tourism, the process itself is not automatically destructive. This view is consistent with that of Cohen (1988) who argues that:

> Commodification does not necessarily destroy the meaning of cultural products, neither for the locals nor for the tourists, although it may do so under certain conditions. Tourist-oriented products frequently acquire new meanings for the locals, as they become a diacritical mark of their ethnic or cultural identity, a vehicle of self-representation before an external public.
>
> (Cohen, 1988, p. 383)

These observations resonate particularly well in the context of sport-based attractions. Notwithstanding the globalization of many sports, attractions based on local sporting events, activities and nostalgia tend to reflect local culture whether it is manifest in unique playing styles, emotions, or fundamental values, For example, tourists attending an amateur thakrow competition in a Thai village achieve first hand insights into local styles of play, just as those experiencing the sport of Thai boxing are ruthlessly exposed to unique local values and emotions. The same may be said of most sports, from village cricket in rural England to Melbourne's Australian Football League (AFL) competition.

In contrast to many types of cultural attractions, those based on sport tend to be more robust and resilient to the processes of commodification. For instance, one of the characteristics of sport is that the display of physical prowess is an integral part of many sporting activities (Loy, McPherson, & Kenyon, 1978). Display suggests that in addition to the athletics producing live sport, there is an audience that views or consumes it. Spectatorship, therefore, is a natural part of sport events, especially at more competitive levels. This is not to suggest that spectatorship is universal. There is, in fact, a broad range of spectator interest in events. Events that are recreational in nature or which are being contested by players in their early stages of skill development are likely to attract fewer spectators than elite competitions. Yet even these types of events can attract a loyal following of family and friends. Carmichael & Murphy (1996) provide clear evidence of high levels of spectator travel for youth, recreational (non-competitive) and non elite sports in Canada. Furthermore, the suggestion that the locals tend to view tourist-oriented products as diacritical marks of their cultural identity fits very well with the view that sport is a major determinant of collective and place identity (Bale, 1989; Nauright, 1996). In hosting visiting spectators and sports enthusiasts, the collective identity of the locals may be used by tourism marketers to influence destination image (Whitson & Macintosh, 1996). Finally, despite the challenges of commodification in terms of the changes that it inevitably brings to the meaning of these tourism products, it is unlikely to destroy the authenticity of sport given the uncertain outcomes associated with sporting competitions. Sport attractions, therefore, offer the promise of authenticity that is increasingly rare in other types of cultural attractions.

Authenticity

The role of authenticity in tourism has been a subject of interest to academics for over four decades, Boorstin's (1964) criticism that tourism fostered pseudo-events highlighted the issue of the real versus the fake in tourism. This was followed by a body of work by MacCannell (see 1973, 1976) in which he argued that the search for authenticity is one of the main motivations for travel. His contributions included the concept of staged authenticity based on Goffman's (1959) idea of the front versus back regions of social places. An example of this form of authenticity is an organized tour of a sports stadium or arena that provides access to the players' changing rooms (for instance tours of Wembley Stadium, Wimbledon Lawn Tennis Club). While giving the impression that these tours provide a glimpse into to the backstage of a destination, the management of these tours really means that the locker rooms are extensions of the front stage at least at the time of the tour.

Taylor (2001, p. 10) captures the essence of this view of authenticity in his suggestion that tourists "are driven by the need for experiences more profound than those associated with the 'shallowness' of their [modern] lives". They are searching for real things, real people, and real places. Unfortunately, the paradox inherent in tourism is that genuine authenticity is virtually impossible to find as the very presence of a tourist destroys the purity of the toured object whether it be a thing, a person or a place (Cohen, 2002). All tourist attractions are, therefore, contrived to some extent although this disturbance would seem to be mitigated somewhat in the case of objects for which public display is a core component.

An interesting variation of the basic concept of authenticity is emergent authenticity. Cohen (1988, p. 379) describes this as "a cultural product . . . which is at one point generally judged as contrived or inauthentic may, in the course of time, become generally recognized as authentic". Disneyland is a good example, as it initially was viewed as being inauthentic, but then "emerged" as an authentic representation of American culture (Johnson, 1981).

Increasingly, the view that most tourists seek objective authenticity is being challenged. It is argued that rather than seeking authentic objects tourists tend to be seeking enjoyable and perhaps meaningful experiences (Cohen, 1995; Urry, 1990). Often the search for objective authenticity seems to fall outside of the motivation for mass tourism associated, for example, with visiting beach resorts or joining ocean cruises (Wang, 1999). These popular forms of travel are more about entertainment and pleasure seeking. The extent that authenticity is important to the tourist depends in a large part on their personal perspective (Boniface & Fowler, 1993). The focus in the literature is changing from the authenticity of the toured object to the authenticity of the experience of the tourist.

At the same time that it was being recognized that there were a broad range of travel motivations beyond the "search for authenticity" postmodern scholars were also questioning the very concept of authenticity itself. Harvey's (1990) discussion of simulacra—as a copy of the original that never existed—highlights this perspective, as does Baudrillard's (1983) concept of hyperreality in which the real and the fake are indistinguishable. The arguments of these authors suggest that it is unrealistic to expect that truth or knowledge can be objectively assessed in terms of time and place. For example, Featherstone (1991, p. 99) argues that the postmodern city is one of 'no-place space' in which the traditional senses of culture are decontextualized, simulated, reduplicated and continually renewed and recycled". Notwithstanding these fascinating intellectual perspectives, even a superficial read of various travel guides such as the *Lonely Planet* series suggest that there remains a genuine quest in the "real".

Wang's (1999, 2000) review of authenticity in a tourism context recognizes the criticisms of postmodern scholars while at the same time offering a constructive perspective of authenticity as tourists experience it. He provides a pragmatic framework that is used to consider the merit of sport as a tourist attraction for the balance of this paper. His framework has been adopted for two key reasons. The first is that Wang recognizes the criticisms of postmodern scholars. Rather than abandoning the concept of authenticity, Wang has developed a typology that includes "existential authenticity". This form of authenticity is concerned with the state of being of the tourist rather than the object of the tourist visit. Tourists judge authenticity on the basis of their experience. The second reason for adopting Wang's framework is that it provides an intriguingly good fit for the examination of sport as an attraction. It serves as useful heuristic to gain insight into sport attractions that, to this point, have not been highlighted in the literature.

Wang (1999) suggests that there are at least three different ways of thinking about authenticity in a tourism context. The first type of authenticity is labelled "objective authenticity" in reference to the authenticity of the original. This is the type of authenticity on which Boorstin's (1964) critique of tourism was based. It is best illustrated by the example of a museum curator who verifies whether a particular artefact is genuine or not. Similarly, a painting may be objectively judged to be real or fake.

While this type of authenticity has application in the realm of sport museums (for instance whether a uniform on display at the *World of Rugby* museum in Cardiff was actually worn by a specific individual in a particular championship game), it is of limited value in the context of contemporary sport. The fact that sporting codes are dynamic means claims that the objective authenticity of a sport has been corrupted due to a break from tradition must be viewed in a relative sense. There are few situations in which the toured object (i.e., sport) can be objectively judged in terms of authenticity.

The second type of authenticity in Wang's (1999) framework is labelled constructive authenticity. This refers to:

> the authenticity projected onto toured objects by tourists or tourism producers in terms of their imagery, expectations, preferences, beliefs, powers, etc. There are various versions of authenticities regarding the same objects. Correspondingly, authentic experiences in tourism and the authenticity of toured objects are constitutive of one another. In this sense, the authenticity of tourism objects is in fact symbolic authenticity.
>
> (Wang, 1999, p. 352)

Constructive authenticity recognizes that tourists adopt different meanings of reality based on their particular contextual situation, "Authenticity is thus a projection of tourists' own beliefs, expectations, preferences, stereotyped images, and consciousness onto toured objects, particularly onto toured Others" (p. 355). Rather than searching for authenticity in the "originals" under this interpretation, tourists are searching for "symbolic" authenticity. Toured objects are viewed as authentic because they are seen as signs or symbols of the real. This distinction accounts for the influence of tourism promotions and the preference of most tourists for a nostalgic or sanitized version of reality. Constructive authenticity, while still focused on the toured object, provides a broader interpretation of authenticity and allows its application across a wide range of tourism activities. From a sport attraction perspective, it helps to explain the influence of mass media and tourism marketing. Attendees at sporting events seek the symbolic authenticity that has been projected by the media prior to the event. The media tends to confirm these symbols during their subsequent coverage of the event. For example, visitors to the Olympic Games may achieve a sense of authenticity when they see the Olympic flame with all of its associated symbolism as represented in the media. Similarly, active sport tourists assess authenticity based on the expectations fostered through the promotional messages of equipment manufacturers and destination marketers. Finally, sport tourists judge the authenticity of sports halls of fame based on imperfect memories from their youth in combination with nostalgic narratives found in the popular media, and the interpretive statements of the museum curators.

Wang's (1999) last type of authenticity is presented in direct response to the dismissal of the concept by postmodernist writers. Rather than judging authenticity on the basis of the toured object (for instance, sport attractions), authenticity is assessed on the basis of the reality of the tourist experience. It is this engagement in experience that makes sport such a robust type of attraction, Wang calls this existential authenticity, which he describes as referring:

> to a potential existential state of Being that is to be activated by tourist activities. Correspondingly, authentic experiences in tourism are to achieve this activated existential state of Being within the liminal process of tourism. Existential authenticity can have nothing to do with the authenticity of toured objects.
>
> (Wang, 1999, p. 352)

While there is no unified postmodern critique of authenticity, Eco's (1986) discussion on "hyperreality" is typical of this position. By deconstructing the boundaries between the copy and the original, Eco undermines the central arguments of Boorstin and MacCannell in relation to objective authenticity. Eco argues that Disneyland was born out of fantasy so that there is, in effect, no "original" upon which to make an assessment of authenticity. Others have observed that in a postmodern world, tourists seem to be more interested in seeking authentic experiences than authentic objects or Others (Cohen, 1995; Butler, 1996), Wang (1999) proposes existential authenticity as a concept that can provide insight into the motives of tourists in a postmodern world. He describes existential authenticity as a "special state of Being in which one is true to oneself, and acts as a counterdose to the loss of 'true self' in public roles and public sphere in modern Western society" (p. 358). Tourists search for this "true self" in travel settings where they are less constrained by the "roles" that they must play in other dimensions of their postmodern lives.

Tourism allows individuals to transcend their daily lives The examples of tourism activities that Wang (1999) used to pursue this type of authenticity include mountaineering and adventure travel, the former which is a particular type of sport and the latter which is infused in many sports. One of the things that makes sport a likely activity for tourists to have authentic experiences is its high propensity for engagement. Examples of this engagement range from "flow experiences" often associated with sport (Csikszentmihalyi, 1975), to the engagement that comes with being a member of a sport fandom (Jones, 2000). Sport attractions are also distinctive given their emphasis on performance, competition, and uncertain outcomes. From an experience perspective, these characteristics mean that each sporting event and activity has the potential to be unique and engaging in its own right.

Wang (1999) describes two additional dimensions of existential authenticity that have relevance for sport tourism. The first is intra-personal and the second is inter-personal in nature. Intra-personal authenticity is expressed in part through bodily feelings. The body is both used in the "display" of personal identity in terms of health, vigour, movement, and other physical characteristics and in ill sensory perception. Lefebvre (1991) uses the example of individuals on a beach to illustrate that this space serves to alter routine experience through recreation and playfulness thereby fostering existential authenticity. Other sport spaces provide comparable opportunities for tourists to have authentic existential experiences in terms of bodily feelings. This is true both in terms of the relevance of display in sport and its kinaesthetic nature. Tourists who are normally confined to sedentary jobs where their bodies may be ignored, have a much greater opportunity to experience intense feeling of bodily awareness when they are involved in active sport while on their vacations.

Another variation of intra-personal authenticity is "self-making". This form of authenticity concerns tourist experiences that build self-identity and are most often associated with adventure travel. In this case, adventure is used to compensate for the boredom often found in ordinary life. Once again, sport offers an attractive opportunity as a tourist activity due to the risks associated with unknown outcomes and the competition that is inherent within sport. While mountaineering is a classic example of this type of tourist activity (Wang, 1999), a broad range of extreme sports could be included. It is also important to note that different individuals will perceive risk and adventure in different ways. Thus the risk for a novice skier on the "bunny slope" may serve the same function in terms of facilitating an authentic existential experience as a technically challenging climb for an experienced mountaineer.

Wang (1999) described interpersonal authenticity in terms of family ties and touristic communitas. In the case of the former, he argued that the classic family vacation provides the opportunity to strengthen the social bonds between parents and their children and between siblings. Vacations take the family away from the routine of work and school thereby affording the opportunity to play with each other away from the home environment. Sport based tourist attractions represent a unique opportunity to explore these bonds whether it is through the informal sharing of sport passions or the more formal generational transfer of sport skills.

In the case of touristic communitas, the advantages of sport are even clearer. Wang (1999) draws a parallel between touristic communitas and pilgrimage. He argues that just as pilgrims confront one another as social equals based on their common humanity, there are other types of tourism activities that promote a similar type of experience. He uses Lett's (1983) ethnographic study of charter yacht tourism in the Caribbean to illustrate his claim. In this sport example, it is argued that the social hierarchies found in the regular day to day lives of these individuals do not dictate the inter-relationships between members of this subculture. There are numerous other examples of these types of sport subcultures that are closely tied in sport attractions, particularly those associated with "participation and pleasure" sports (Coakley, 2004), as opposed to "power and performance" sports. The subcultures associated with the sports of snowboarding (Heino, 2000) and windsurfing (Wheaton, 2000) serve to illustrate this view. It should be recognized, however, that while these sport subcultures may not have the same hierarchical social structures as found in other dimensions of their members' lives, there is often a unique hierarchy that exists within the subculture itself (Donnelly & Young, 1988). The key point, however, is that these sport subculture hierarchies are in fact distinct, thereby allowing an individual who may be frustrated in terms of his/her community membership in their ordinary life to feel that membership of a sport subculture community provides personal identity and meaning for his/her life.

Conclusion

The objective of this paper was to demonstrate that sport based tourist attractions have unique advantages over other types of cultural attractions in the face of issues associated with commodification and authenticity. Positioning sport as a tourist attraction is a form of commodification but the natural role of display in sport and the ability of sport attractions to align collective identity and destination image appeared to protect sport's cultural "soul". Similarly, an assessment of sport in terms of Wang's (1999) three types of authenticity suggests that sport attractions have distinct advantages in terms of constructive or symbolic authenticity as well as existential or experience based authenticity. Uncertainty of outcomes, the role of athletic display, the kinaesthetic nature of sport activities, and the tendency for strong engagements in sport represent some of the key characteristics of sport that protect cultural authenticity. To the extent that sport attractions can facilitate authentic cultural experiences, the likelihood that tourism and, more importantly, local culture an be sustained in a destination is greatly enhanced.

It is hoped that the observations provided in this discussion will serve to stimulate additional work in the area of sport tourism and authenticity. A good starting point would be the introduction of other theoretical perspectives related to authenticity. While Wang's framework is firmly positioned in a tourism-based sociological perspective, it would be useful to expand the examination in terms of a sport-based sociological perspective. This broader theoretical framework would help in the examination of concepts such as entertainment and how these concepts relate to commodification and authenticity in sport and tourism. There is also a need to explore the relationship between the collective identity of the host and destination image. For example, how are sport identities exploited by tourism marketers and what effect do these activities have on the way that potential visitors view the destination?

From an applied perspective, the argument presented in this paper suggests that sport attractions offer a useful tool for the strategic development of a destination. They offer visitors authentic cultural experiences in destination spaces that seem to function simultaneously as front and back stages. While destination managers have long capitalized on sports as tourist attractions, by considering the points raised and discussed in this paper, they may be more strategic in their use of sport as a cultural tourist attraction.

References

Bale, J. (1989). *Sports geography*. London: E & FN Spon.

Bale, J. (1994). *Landscapes of modern sport*. Leicester: Leicester University Press.

Baudrillard, J. (1983). *Simulations*. New York: Semiotext.

Boniface, P., & Fowler, P. (1993). *Heritage and tourism in 'the global village'*. London: Routledge.

Boorstin, D.J. (1964). *The image: A guide to pseudo-events in America*. New York: Atheneum.

Bull, C., & Weed, M. (1999). Niche markets and small island tourism: The development of sports tourism in Malta. *Managing Leisure, 4*, 142–155.

Butler, R.W. (1996). The role of tourism in cultural transformation in developing countries. In W. Nuryanti (Ed.), *Tourism and culture: Global civilization in change* (pp. 91–101). Yogyakarta: Gadjah Mada University Press.

Carmichael, B., & Murphy, P.E. (1996). Tourism economic impact of a rotating sports event: The case of the British Columbia Games. *Festival Management and Event Tourism, 4*, 127–138.

Coakley, J. (2004). *Sports in society: Issues and controversies*. Boston: McGraw Hill Higher Education.

Cohen, E. (1979). A phenomenology of tourist experiences. *Sociology, 13*, 179–201.

Cohen, E. (1988). Authenticity and the commoditization of tourism. *Annals of Tourism Research, 15*, 371–386.

Cohen, E. (1995). Contemporary tourism—trends and challenges: Sustainable authenticity or contrived postmodernity? In R. Butler, & D. Pearce (Eds), *Tourism: People, places, processes* (pp. 12–29). London: Routledge.

Cohen, E. (2002). Authenticity, equity and sustainability in tourism. *Journal of Sustainable Tourism, 10*, 267–276.

Csikszentmihalyi, M. (1975). *Beyond boredom and anxiety*. San Francisco: Jossey-Bass.

Delpy, L. (1997). An overview of sport tourism: Building towards a dimensional framework. *Journal of Vacation Marketing, 4,* 23–38.

Donnelly, P., & Young, K.M. (1988). The construction and confirmation of identity of sport subcultures. *Sociology of Sport Journal*, *5*, 223–240.

Eco, U. (1986). *Travels in hyperreality*. London: Picador.

Fainstein, S., & Judd, D.R. (1999). Global forces, local strategies, and urban tourism. In D.R. Judd, & S.S. Fainstein (Eds), *The tourist city* (pp. 1–17). New Haven, CT: Yale University Press.

Featherstone, M. (1991). *Consumer culture and postmodernism*. London: Sage Publications.

Gibson, H.J. (1998). Sport tourism: A critical analysis of research. *Sport Management Review*, *1*(1), 45–76.

Goffman, E. (1959). *The presentation of self in everyday life*. Harmondsworth: Penguin.

Greenwood, D.J. (1989). Culture by the pound: An anthropological perspective of tourism as cultural commodification. In V.L. Smith (Ed.), *Hosts and guest: The anthropology of tourism* (pp. 17–31). Philadelphia: University of Pennsylvania Press.

Gruneau, R.S., & Whitson, D. (1993). *Hockey night in Canada: Sport, identities and cultural politics*. Toronto: Garamond Press.

Harvey, D. (1990). *The condition of postmodernity*. Oxford: Blackwell.

Heino, R. (2000). What is so punk about snowboarding? *Journal of Sport and Social Issues*, *24*(1), 176–191.

Higham, J.E.S., & Hinch, T.D. (2003). The tourism impacts of Super 12 Rugby in New Zealand. *Journal of Sport Management*, *17*(3), 235–257.

Hinch, T.D., & Higham, J.E.S. (2001). Sport tourism: A framework for research. *The International Journal of Tourism Research*, *3*(1), 45–58.

Hinch, T.D., & Higham, J.E.S. (2004). *Sport tourism development*. Clevedon: Channel View Publications.

Johnson, D.M. (1981). Disney World as structure and symbol: Recreation of the American experience. *Journal of Popular Culture*, *15*, 157–165.

Jones, I. (2000). A model of serious leisure identification. The case of football fandom, *Leisure Studies*, *19*, 283–298.

Lefebvre, H. (1991). *The production of space*. Oxford: Blackwell.

Leiper, N. (1990). Tourist attraction systems. *Annals of Tourism Research*, *17*, 367–384.

Lett, J.W. (1983). Ludic and liminoid aspects of charter yacht tourism in the Caribbean. *Annals of Tourism Research*, *10*, 35–36.

Loy, J.W., McPherson, B.D., & Kenyon, G. (1978). *Sport and social systems: A guide to the analysis of problems and literature*. Reading: Addison Wesley.

MacCannell, D. (1973). Staged authenticity—arrangements of social space in tourist settings. *American Journal of Sociology*, *79*(3), 589–603.

MacCannell, D. (1976). *The tourists: New theory of the leisure class*. New York: Schoken.

McConnell, R., & Edwards, M. (2000). Sport and identity in New Zealand. In C. Collins (Ed.), *Sport and society in New Zealand* (pp. 115–129). Palmerston North: Dunmore Press.

McKay, J., & Kirk, D. (1992). Ronald McDonald meets Baron De Coubertin: Prime time sport and commodification. *Sport and the Media*, Winter, 10–13.

Nauright, J. (1996). "A besieged tribe?" Nostalgia, white cultural identity and the role of rugby in a changing South Africa. *International Review for the Sociology of Sport*, *31*(1), 69–89.

Pearce, D.G. (1989). *Tourism development*. Harlow: Longman Scientific & Technical.

Plog, S. (1972). *Why destination areas rise and fall in popularity*. Paper presented at the Southern California Chapter of the Travel Research Bureau, San Diego, October 10.

Priestley, G.K. (1995). Sports tourism: The case of golf. In G.J. Ashworth, & A.G.J. Dietvorst (Eds), *Tourism and spatial transformations: Implications for policy and planning* (pp. 205–223). Wallingford: CAB International.

Robinson, T., & Gammon, S. (2004). A question of primary and secondary motives. *Journal of Sport Tourism, 9*, 221–233.

Standeven, J., & De Knop, P. (1999). *Sport tourism*. Leeds: Human Kinetics.

Steinbeck, J. (1963). *Travels with Charley: In search of America*. New York: Bantam Books.

Stewart, J.J. (1987). The commodification of sport. *International Review for the Sociology of Sport, 22*, 171–190.

Taylor, J.P. (2001). Authenticity and sincerity in tourism. *Annals of Tourism Research, 28*, 7–26.

Urry, J. (1990). *The tourist gaze*. London: Sage Publications.

Wang, N. (1999). Rethinking authenticity in tourism experience. *Annals of Tourism Research, 26*(2), 349–370.

Wang, N. (2000). *Tourism and modernity: A sociological analysis*. Amsterdam: Pergamon.

Wheatson, B. (2000). "Just do it?" Consumption, commitment, and identity in the windsurfing subculture. *Sociology of Sport Journal, 17*(3), 254–274.

Whitson, D., & Macintosh, D. (1996). The global circus: International sport, tourism and the marketing of cities. *Journal of Sport and Social Issues, 23*, 278–295.

Chapter 8

Carla A. Costa and Laurence Chalip

ADVENTURE SPORT TOURISM IN RURAL REVITALISATION
An ethnographic evaluation

Introduction

THE WORLD IS BECOMING increasingly urban, and the pace of urbanisation continues to accelerate (Golden, 1981, United Nations Centre for Human Settlements, 1996). One of the side effects is a growing imbalance in the economic and social development of rural regions relative to urban centres. In recent years, some rural regions have enjoyed a degree of new development, particularly when industry in the region has been fostered through subsidy or relocation (Pickles, 1991; Skuras, Dimara, & Stathopoulou, 2003), or when the region has become a bedroom or holiday home location for urban workers seeking a rural lifestyle (Eastman & Krannich, 1995; Vogt & Marans, 2004). Elsewhere, the imbalance between urban and rural regions has become self-amplifying as younger and better educated rural residents move from rural areas to cities where opportunities are thought to be greater (Lijfering, 1974; Black, 1992), This has two immediate effects. First, the social fabric of rural communities is eroded. Second, rural areas become less desirable places to live or work, with the result that their economic base deteriorates.

Governments throughout the world have increasingly sought to find means to revitalise rural communities. Although a number of tactics have been tried, the introduction or elevation of tourism has become a common tactic to increase rural revenue (Luloff, Bridger, Graefe, Saylor, Martin, & Gitelson, 1994; Kneafsey, 2000), with recreational sport serving as a key tourist attraction (Roberts & Hall, 200]). This trend has accelerated over the past two decades, particularly in Europe, as policymakers have sought to capitalise on the worldwide growth of tourism to attract new spending to rural economies (Edwards & Fernandes, 1999; Hall, 2004). As rural locations position themselves as tourism destinations, they become new product for a tourism industry that is constantly seeking fresh places to sell. As marketers promote rural destinations, they are finding market segments that are attracted to rural locales.

There are two primary reasons that recreational sports have been used to reposition some rural communities as tourist destinations. First, rural communities' low levels of crowding and natural local amenities (mountains, open spaces, waterways) serve as attractions because they lend themselves to recreational sports (Chambers, 1994; Roberts & Hall, 2001). Second, many recreational activities require particular natural conditions (such as mountains, winds, waterways), so rural communities in which the required conditions prevail become attractive sites for repeat visitation by recreational sporting enthusiasts (Fishwick & Vining, 1992; Bricker & Kerstetter, 2000). When a rural community's local environment enables a popular recreational sport, the opportunity to engage in that sport becomes an attractive activity for promoting tourism.

A number of sports that make use of outdoor amenities surrounding rural communities have long histories. These include surfing, rock climbing, white water kayaking, and skiing. However, recent decades have witnessed the emergence of a new array of sports sometimes called "action sports", "extreme sports", or "adventure sports", such as wind surfing, snow boarding, and paragliding. These have been enabled by new technologies, and have emerged from a cultural ethos that venerates fun and excitement (Midol, 1993; Bennet, Henson, & Zhang, 2003). The rapid growth of these sports has required some sport providers to redesign their programs and their marketing (Bynum, 2004), and has bolstered the rapid growth of adventure tourism (Nelson, 7002; Swarbrooke, Beard, Leckie, & Pomfret, 2003). A clear indication of the significance of the adventure tourism market emerged from the 2002 UK Tourism survey, which found that almost 6,000 visitors per month to Scotland undertake an adventure sport activity (Killgore, 2003).

Paragliding is one among an array of adventure sports that has enjoyed substantial growth in popularity since it was first introduced at the World Hang Gliding Championships in 1979. The sport requires a rectangular parachute that is inflated as the user runs down a hill. Lift is produced by baffles that are sewn into the leading edge. Toggles attached to the parachute's lines are grasped in each hand and used for steering. The sport is now promoted as a tourism attraction in locales as diverse as the Venezuelan Andes (Minder, 2004) and the South Island of New Zealand (Attractions almost endless, 1998). Tourism promoters in destinations as diverse as Wales (Devine, 2004) and the Canadian Rockies (Crush, 2004) are advocating development of paragliding sites as a means to build local tourism.

The proliferating use of tourism, including adventure sport, as an instrument for rural economic development, has been criticised on a variety of grounds. In many instances the benefits that rural communities obtain from tourism are far less than had been hoped or expected (Ribeiro & Marques, 2002). As a result, local support can decline (Johnson & Snepenger, 1994), causing a decrease in tourism planning and development (McGchee & Andereck, 2004).

There are several structural factors that may contribute to the limited benefits that rural communities obtain from tourism. Rural communities often lack persons with sufficient expertise to market their community (Gilbert, 989) or to provide services to tourists who visit (Thomas & Long, 2001). Consequently, they rely on intermediaries, such as public agencies, membership organisations, or private companies, to facilitate access to tourism markets (Forstner, 2004). As outsiders to the community, these intermediaries typically lack the networks and local knowledge that would optimise marketing communications or facilitate integration of tourism services. Further, they may import seasonal labour, and thereby further reduce the distribution of benefits to locals.

Rural tourism that relies on one or more sporting activities can be particularly prone to local disappointment as a consequence of seasonal variations in demand. The employment generated by a sport will be proportional to the number of participants to be served. If participant demand waxes and wanes with the seasons, so will employment and cash flow, causing considerable fiscal stress in conununities that rely on visitors who come to participate in a locally provided sport (Keith, Fawson, & Chang, 1996). As a result, sporting activities may be insufficient to arrest rural out-migration or economic decline.

In order for a sporting activity to contribute to the overall tourism development of a host destination, that activity must be integrated with other tourism products and services available at the destination (Chalip, 2001; Harris, McLaughlin, & Ham, 1927). Tourists who participate in a sport require a number of tourism services, including accommodation, meals, and shopping. They may desire activities for family members who accompany them but who do not participate in the sport. They may seek additional activities for themselves in order to enhance their overall experience. However, sport organisations typically lack the networks, structures, and skills required to work effectively with tourism providers (Weed, 2003). This can serve to further weaken the value of sport to the rural community's economy.

A great deal of what has been said in the literature about rural tourism and about the uses of sport to promote rural tourism has been speculative as it has been based on anecdotal evidence or has been deduced from attitude surveys or aggregate economic and industry data The study that follows examines paragliding in Linhares da Beira, Portugal in order to identify and explore factors that facilitate or inhibit effective inclusion of an adventure sport in a rural community's tourism mix. The gap between economic conditions in Lisbon and those in rural Portugal has made rural development a particularly salient concern (Rita & Mergulhão, 1997), Entrepreneurship of the kind enabled by paragliding has been advocated as a necessary means for economic revitalisation of Portugal's rural communities (Ferrão & Lopes, 2003).

The following section describes the community and the role of paragliding as a tourism attraction The methods used to evaluate the sport's value for tourism are then described. Results are elaborated first by describing the contribution that paragliding makes to the community, and then by considering the underlying social and cultural dynamics that may inhibit better integration of paragliding into the community's tourism marketing. The paper concludes by considering implications for theory, practice, and future research.

Linhares da Beira

Linhares da Beira is a rural community in central northern Portugal. In the vernacular, it is simply called "Linhares". The community is 1.5 kilometres square, and is surrounded by hills and grazing land. The 2001 census reported the population as 337, although the number of residents in the summer is higher as family members return home to visit. The population of the community has been steadily declining (485 in 1981, and 1,016 in 1960). In its *Detailed plan for revitalisation of Linhares da Beira* (Câmara Municipal de Celorico da Beria, 1990–1991), the regional government noted that those who leave the community are among the youngest, most highly skilled, and best educated. The *Plan* established revitalisation of the community as a national policy objective. That objective has since also been adopted, in part, by the European Union, which has provided €4,939,599 for redevelopment of the community's historical infrastructure (under FEDER—European Fund for Regional Development).

Redevelopment of the community receives mixed reviews from local residents. They complain about the quality of the local economy, and comment on the need for it to improve. This concern is common among young and old alike. As one 19-year-old girl put it when interviewed for this study:

> There are no opportunities here. Even if I stay, I'll have to commute to other communities to work [which is] what my friends are doing. I'm trying to stay, but there need to be new opportunities.

A local entrepreneur said "My, children had to leave. The local economy is not strong enough for them to live here. They would come back if the economy could be improved". The owner of a local cafe, but who was otherwise retired, commented:

> Unless you have an outside income, Linhares is only a place to visit, not a place to live. My cousin and his wife are hoping that [the growth of tourism] will create new jobs [so they can stay]. . . . Paragliding could be a good source [of tourism development, because] it brings people and colour. You can't help but look up to see them [the paragliders] sailing through the sky.

The community's surrounding hills and breezes make it an ideal site for paragliding. A Portuguese paragliding web site observed: "We cannot speak of paragliding in Portugal without mentioning Linhares da Beira, a twelfth century village that has made history even in this sport" (Silva, n.d.). The community's web site comments, "It is not without reason that they call Linhares the 'Capital of Paragliding'" (Câmara Municipal de Celorico da Beira, 2001).

There is no record of when recreational paragliders first began using the hills around Linhares da Beira, but formal usage around the community dates from 1990 when the national paragliding coach identified the community as an ideal paragliding site. In an interview for this study, he said, "Linhares has perfect winds, especially during the late afternoon, the people are friendly, and access to the village and takeoff points [for paragliding] are excellent". Establishment of the sport in Linhares da Beira is characterised in three ways: (1) paragliders come to the community (particularly from Portuguese cities, but also from elsewhere in Europe) to practice their sport, especially in the summer; (2) a week long international paragliding competition has been staged in the community' during August since 1992; (3) the community has had a paragliding school offering training since 1993 and a paragliding specialty store since 2002. Paragliding paraphernalia can be purchased in the store, but nearly all paragliders brought and maintained their own equipment.

Paragliders take off from the side of a hill to the east of the community, glide over the community, and land on an open area to the west of the community. Both the take-off point and the landing site are privately owned, each by a different local resident. The use by paragliders is welcomed and permitted without charge. Paragliders shuttle up the hill in cars and vans for takeoff, typically leaving their car or truck at the landing site. One or two cars or trucks will be used to shuttle up the hillside for takeoff.

When the winds are favourable, paragliders are clearly visible in the skies over the community. The strong presence of the sport in the community has been widely cited by observers as an example of effective application of sport tourism for the economic regeneration of a rural region. When encouraging us to undertake the study reported here, a Portuguese professor who has done research in the community said, "Paragliding has changed Linhares. It's a success story showing how sport can be used for economic development". The national coach noted in an interview, "Paragliding is helping to promote everything else Linhares is trying to do [for tourism]. The media likes to cover paragliding, so it shows off the community". A monograph describing the community concludes:

> Linhares has a future, and the installation of a paragliding school was the first step for attracting youth of all kinds and all social strata. They pass by each other on the streets; they frequent coffee shops; they occupy the restaurant; they give life, movement, colour and joy to the old village almost forgotten and abandoned that now gets renovated and revitalised.
>
> (Abrantes, 1998, p. 263)

Paragliding is one element in a larger mix of tourism products and services offered by the community. Marketing brochures promoting tourism to Linhares da Beira call the community an "Open Air Museum". A walking tour is described in several brochures, featuring 27 points of interest to be visited—the primary attraction being a castle dating from the twelfth century. Adventure opportunities extend beyond paragliding as the local hills allow rock climbing, and are honeycombed with trails for hiking, horseback riding, and mountain biking. At the time of this study (Summer 2003), accommodation was plentiful as there were two licensed bed and breakfast facilities, three houses offering apartments to tourists, a camp ground, and a dormitory style accommodation intended primarily for paragliders. Food was available at three cafes, two restaurants, one small market, and a butcher. Hair services were provided by a local entrepreneur. Gifts and souvenirs were sold through two local handicraft stores. There was an outdoor swimming pool available at an entry fee of €2, and a soccer field. A tourist information centre offered information about attractions and services. All but one of these businesses (one of the handicraft stores) was locally owned, so money spent by tourists generally benefited the local economy.

In order to serve tourists, whose numbers base been expected to grow as a consequence of the community's heritage and adventure tourism, a four star hotel and resort has been under development since the European Union redevelopment money enabled refurbishment of the community's historical infrastructure. The facility was due to open in August 2004, but at the time of this writing it had not yet been completed.

Other than shopping or visiting heritage sites on the walking tour, activities while staying in Linhares da Beira must be prearranged. One can rent a horse, but it must be booked several days in advance. One can rent a mountain bike, but prior arrangement is required to assure that the shop will be open. There are insufficient bikes available for large groups, so if a group wants to mountain bike, bookings must be made in advance to allow sufficient time for the local provider to bring more bikes into town. There is a simulated hunting activity, but it must be booked several days in advance. Archery is available but it, too, must be booked in advance.

Method

Fieldwork for this study was conducted during June and July, 2003. This study was the first in a project envisaged to enhance the quality of development activities in the region. Our objective was to obtain ethnographic information that could inform subsequent development planning and programs (cf., United States General Accounting Office, 2003). We sought detailed qualitative information about the ways that residents of Linhares da Beira experience the presence of paragliders and paragliding in their community. Although the methods, data, and analyses are ethnographic in character, the collection and analysis of data were more focused than in traditional ethnography (cf., Dobbert, 1982; Sands, 2002) insomuch as the intent was to obtain and explore information specific to the presence and impact of paragliding. Ethnographic methods have a long tradition in evaluation research (see Caro, 1969; Schwartzman 1983; Patton, 2002); the targets of ethnographic scrutiny can include the organisation delivering a developnient programme, the interactions among stakeholders, and/or the persons at whom a particular programme is targeted. This study's focus was Linhares da Beira, so the community and its residents were examined. Since the presence of paragliding was the matter of interest, paragliders were among those about whom data were collected.

Data gathering included observation, interviews, and review of archival materials. The two authors took separate roles (Adler & Adler, 1987). The first author conducted the interviews and made detailed on-site observations; the second author provided the viewpoint of an outsider, commenting on observations and interviews as the study progressed, and discussing interpretations as the data were analysed. For this paper, Portuguese quotes and the title of one development plan have been translated into English by the first author, who is a native speaker of continental Portuguese. A description of how each research technique was applied during fieldwork follows.

Observation

The first author observed the daily life of Linhares da Beira. This included mingling with crowds around paraglider landing sites, attending the local church, eating in local restaurants and cafés, and socialising informally with locals and paragliders. The objective was to join into the life of the community in order to obtain a sense of community life from the standpoint of community residents. Observations were logged in a research journal.

Interviews

Informal socialising with paragliders and community residents was complemented with formal interviews. Two sets of interviews were obtained.

One set consisted of detailed interviews with key informants (6 females and 3 males). Informants who were identified as "key" were either leaders of local paragliding or played a central role in the political and economic life of the community. These included owners of the four largest local businesses, the national paragliding coach (who visits the community to train paragliders), the sports coordinator responsible for paragliding, the information coordinator for the local tourism information centre, and the former mayor. Key informant interviews lasted between one and two hours. As informants preferred not to be taped, detailed notes were kept during and after each interview. Each key informant was interviewed at the beginning of fieldwork and again at the end. The initial interview asked informants to describe the community, their role, and their thoughts and opinions about paragliding. Probes were used to explore their ideas and insights. The final interview was used to check data obtained during participant observation and to inform interpretation of the data. Fieldwork had provided substantive detail about paragliding and community life. Thus, questions were formulated that reflected tentative conclusions or emergent issues. Questions were tailored to the particular expertise or experience of the informant. Probes were used to explore their ideas and insights. Three of the business owners and the sports coordinator were also formally interviewed midway through the fieldwork. These four individuals were selected for an additional interview in order to answer questions arising from ongoing observation of the community and paragliding.

The second set of interviews was conducted throughout the fieldwork as opportunities arose. Paragliders (n = 15) and local residents (n = 27) were approached at routine gatherings in public places (castle grounds, steps of the church, a cafe, or paraglider landing sites) and were asked to participate in "a short interview". Interviews were semi-structured, and lasted from 20–40 minutes. Respondents were asked about their activities in the community, the community's needs and future, and the place of paragliding in community life. Notes were taken during and after each interview.

Archival materials

Published materials and unpublished reports were obtained in order to gather background data on Linhares da Beira and its tourism marketing. These included one monograph, a report on development of historical sites throughout the region, a tourist guidebook, three city planning documents and five brochures promoting tourism to the community. Census data were taken from government records. In addition, the community's official web site and four paragliding sites that mention the community were visited and printed. All materials were reviewed, and notes were made of key points, quotes, and themes. These were cross-referenced with the notes from interviews and observations in order to add depth and specificity to time findings.

Results

Findings are presented with reference to two related facets of paragliding's place in the community's tourism marketing mix. The first facet explores the impacts of paragliding on the community. The second facet examines the social and cultural forces that constrain those impacts.

Paragliding in the tourism marketing mix

Although there is no official count of the number of paragliders who visit the community, on days when the winds were favourable (particularly on weekends), the sky above Linhares da Beira was filled with them. Nevertheless, observation of paragliders during the fieldwork for this study suggested that paragliding was not well positioned to contribute substantially to the local economy. Although paragliders sometimes gathered in one of the local cafes, they did not spend much money locally, except during the one-week tournament in August, when local accommodation and restaurants were filled with competitors, spectators, and their families. Otherwise, on weekdays most Portuguese paragliders were day trippers. During the weekend, some might stay a night, but if so they typically chose the dormitory, where they could stay for a mere €15. Paragliders from other countries generally chose to camp or to stay in the dormitory. Restaurants in Linhares da Beira were rarely chosen by paragliders, even for dinner. Rather, paragliders would eat food they had brought with them, commute to other local communities to eat, or return home. They were not seen to engage in heritage tourism, and they did not shop for souvenirs.

Local business people volunteered similar observations when interviewed. A sales-person in one of the handicraft stores commented, "We see them [paragliders] in the sky, but not in the store". The owner of one of the restaurants observed, "They come here to paraglide not to eat". An entrepreneur who created a bed and breakfast said, "I expected they [paragliders] would stay overnight, but they don't. When they do, they stay at the dormitory because it's cheap". The attendant at the castle noted, "Paragliders see the castle from the sky [while they are gliding, so] they don't visit".

Paragliders' descriptions of their own behaviour are also consistent with these observations. They are there to paraglide and to share time with other paragliders. Heritage tourism, restaurant dining, or souvenir hunting are not on the agenda. As one paraglider put it: "When we come as a group, we like to stay at the dormitory. We share food, and learn new skills from each other. We come to relax. It's great to get away from the city".

A weekend visitor commented:

> I normally come on my own, so I stay in the dormitory. It's cheap and convenient. At night it is fun because we [other paragliders and I] can barbeque our own sausages and talk about the day and our plans for tomorrow.

A paraglider who comes as a day tripper said:

> I leave work early, and come to paraglide in the afternoon. Since I have to drive more than an hour and a half each way, I pack my own food. That leaves me the most time for paragliding.

A paraglider who often stays overnight observed: "The restaurants in Linhares are overpriced. We can get as good a meal cheaper by driving to [nearby communities]. So, that's what most of us do".

This is not to say that paragliders could not bring more business into the local economy. Paragliders who stay for two or more days noted that there needed to be activities in which they can participate when the winds are not favourable for paragliding.

This view was succinctly summarised by a paraglider who visited frequently during the summer:

> You can arrange for things to do here, but there are no activities that are ready to go if the winds are not right [for paragliding]. So, instead of doing something, we just wait [for the winds to improve]. I hope that someday they will have activities ready, so we don't have to plan for them in advance. Then we would do them when the winds are bad.

Several wanted to bring family, but felt there was too little for them to do in Linhares da Beira. As one observed: "I hope they can create more things to do here. After you have been here once, there is nothing new to do. My wife likes the peace and quiet, but only once in a while".

In fact, paragliders with families were particularly anxious for the community to do more to appeal to their families. When families were mentioned during interviews, paragliders also commented about the difficulties of leaving the family for days at a time in order to participate in their hobby. They talked about their desire to spend more time in Linhares da Beira, which they felt would be easier to justify if their families could come along without being bored.

These latter comments demonstrate that there is some potential to create added tourism by providing activities and by catering to accompanying markets. However, local residents, including local business people did not recognise these opportunities. In fact, throughout the interviews the lack of business from paragliders was treated as a given, rather than as a marketing challenge. It was as if the existing situation was a natural and unchangeable state of affairs to which residents were resigned.

Nevertheless, the strategic challenges are apparent. The key challenge is to develop attractions and activities that will appeal to paragliders (particularly those who are repeat visitors) and their accompanying markets. The heritage sites are not conducive to repeat visitation, the handicrafts in local shops are not appealing to paragliders, local restaurants are not competitively priced, and activities other than paragliding cannot be booked on the spur of the moment. It is not clear whether any of the current range of activities (such as mountain biking, horseback riding, hunting, archery) would appeal to paragliders (on days with bad winds) if they could be arranged without advance bookings. Nor is it clear whether casually available activities (soccer, swimming, rock climbing, or hiking) would be appealing if actively promoted to paragliders. However, without market research or promotion of these activities to paragliders, there is no way to tell. Indeed, therein lies the heart of the problem. Local business people have made no effort to determine what activities, menus, pricing, or merchandise would appeal to paragliders or persons who might accompany them.

Marketing to paragliders is not the only strategic challenge. As several interviewees pointed out, paragliders themselves could become a tourist attraction, and could generate media attention to help build the community's tourism brand. The marketing collateral for Linhares da Beira is produced by national and regional tourism marketing organisations, and frequently features images of paragliders. However, the community's tourism brand is founded on heritage tourism, not paragliding. There is nothing in the imagery or narratives of brochures or advertisements for Linhares da Beira that indicates how paragliding might complement the community's overall brand. Indeed the pictures of paragliders seem dissonant with the historical attractions that are the focus of community marketing communications. The inconsistency of the branding is exacerbated by the lack of any narrative or commentary suggesting why tourists might want to visit the community to see paragliders.

The businesses in Linhares da Beira are small and undercapitalised (like the community itself). Local business people lack the skills and the capital necessary to undertake market research. There is no local economic development authority or business alliance that could provide the skill base, coordination, and returns-to-scale that would be necessary to undertake that effort. Consequently, the information base required to undertake the strategic planning necessary to capitalise on the paraglider market is missing, and the coordination required to undertake any community level strategic planning is missing. The result is that activities, menus, retail, and pricing are neither designed nor promoted in a manner that appeals to paragliders. Revitalisation efforts are planned and coordinated federally or regionally without reference to or involvement by locals. Since revitalisation has been focused on renovation of the historical infrastructure, scant attention has been given to integration of the community's range of tourism products and services into a comprehensive brand.

It is not clear whether a planning effort could formulate an effective leveraging strategy. On the other hand, it is clear that without such an effort, the paragliding market cannot serve the economic development objectives that have been claimed for it. This is not to suggest that a coordinated effort to leverage the paragliding market would be easy to establish. In fact, participant observation and interviews suggest that there are significant social and cultural barriers to strategic planning that would need to be overcome.

Social and cultural barriers to strategic planning

The social organisation and cultural practices of the community have a lengthy history and a firm tradition, despite the contemporary diaspora. This characteristic of rural communities has been well demonstrated (Rogers & Burdge, 1972; Black, 1992; Flora, Flora, & Fey, 2003). It has been shown that the culture and organisation of rural communities can play a significant role in enabling or constraining development (Foster, 1972; Doughty, 1965; Wilson & Lowery, 2003). The consequent challenge is to map the behaviours, values, and beliefs that can affect community development initiatives.

The most obvious effect of community decline over the past half century has been the out-migration of the young and the well-educated (Abrantes, 1998). Despite the fact that this effect has been well documented in the regional government's plan for revitalisation of the community (Câmara Municipal de Celorico da Beira, 1990–1991), there have been no systematic efforts to stem the tide. The effect has been twofold: first, community residents generally lack skills or training in business or community development. There is no local business association, and no forum via which to initiate or implement development planning. Second, many of the residents have retirement incomes—even some who own local businesses. They are comfortable. Although they say they would like things to get better, they do not see a substantial personal benefit from exerting effort to foster or nurture community development. Their small pensions are sufficient for them to live as they are used to living.

There is scant in-migration, with the exception of older former residents who return, typically bringing some retirement income with them. For those who stay and those who return, the community's unchanging stability is an attractive source of the familiar. Throughout interviews, both those who had remained and those who had returned talked about their connection to the community as a place that is "home". The comnnmunity's traditional look-and-feel were comfortable to those who had remained, and an attraction back for those who had left. The community is characterised by a rhythm of routines. Locals know when they and their neighbours will be at work in the fields, when they will meet over lunch, and where they can socialise in the evening. Although returning residents have sought to establish new businesses, they typically lack entrepreneurial experience, and they have been frustrated by the community's relaxed pace, even though the relaxed pace had initially attracted them home. As one returnee put it, "People here don't really know how to work, if you want to do anything, you have to do it alone".

The routine rhythms and social traditions of the community are reinforced by a social climate that frowns upon public criticism, entrepreneurial individualism, or blatant zeal for change. It was as if the community's social fabric required quiet resignation to the status quo. Throughout the interviews, any critical comment was prefaced by a request that we not tell anyone else what had been said. Whenever an interviewee suggested someone else we might talk to about a topic, they would also ask that we not tell them who had suggested that they be contacted. Returnees who showed entrepreneurial ambition were quietly (and confidentially) criticised. For example, the first author was having coffee with local residents when one of the local entrepreneurs left the café. The four women remaining at the table she had left spent the next several minutes commenting to one another that the entrepreneur had enough money and really should not be working so hard to build her business. Quiet backbiting of this kind about entrepreneurs was, in fact, common. If a local person publicly and strongly advocated change, the suggested change was rejected on the grounds of tradition. For example, it is widely recognised that paragliders go out of town for dinner or eat at the dormitory. One local resident suggested (during conversations in a local café) that more should be done to cater to their tastes and preferences in order to keep then in town. Others present rejected the idea, arguing that paragliders should instead accept the menus and prices the town has to offer. The prevailing notion was that visitors should adapt to the community, not the other way around.

The small size of the community also contributed to the rejection of change, as it allowed residents to become familiar with many details of each others' lives. Consequently, they are often aware of the benefits each might accrue from any change. Advocacy of change could therefore be heard as promotion of personal or family advantage, rather than as an expression of community spirit.

The foregoing description sketches the picture of a community that lacks the human capital required to capitalise on the development opportunities represented by paragliding. The lack of human capital is underpinned by a social climate that clings to established ways and that resists change. Nevertheless, residents bemoan the out-migration of their families and friends, and they speak openly of their desire for greater economic well being. Yet they do not see any contradiction between their desires for a more prosperous community and their resistance to change. In fact, they are overtly sceptical about efforts to foster economic development There are two explicit sources of scepticism:

• First, some expressed doubt that economic development initiatives would have any observable impact. Almost everyone could describe at least one past initiative that had failed. With reference to paragliding, most residents seemed happy to have the paragliders decorating their skies, but few felt that paragliders were benefiting the community economically. This was accepted as the way that things are, and there was no thought that a more strategic effort to market to paragliders might change the situation.

- Second, residents expected that any successful economic development initiative would benefit others, but not themselves. They were acutely aware of their lack of business acumen, and they were aware that only a few locals had the resources to capitalise on new development initiatives. Further, they had experienced development grants that had been made available to individuals to refurbish their homes (in order to enhance the ambiance of the community as an historical attraction). The benefits, it was widely argued, were realised by those individuals in a position to take advantage of the opportunity. There was no sense that the community benefited as a whole. Thus, it seemed reasonable to community residents that economic development could exacerbate economic differences among community residents—something that would threaten the smooth social fabric that has for centuries been a feature of life in Linhares da Beira.

The prevailing resistance to change and scepticism about development combined with the lack of local expertise to foster development planning that was essentially exogenous to the community. Development rested in the hands of outside authorities (federal and regional government), or was initiated by a few local entrepreneurs who remained frustrated by the lack of local enthusiasm or support for their initiatives. The vision of local entrepreneurs did not inform government planning because local entrepreneurs were not consulted. Neither government nor local entrepreneurs visions for development were welcomed by residents, perhaps because local residents were never participants in economic planning or programme implementation. Their opinions were never solicited when others undertook policy formulation or implementation on their behalf.

Their exclusion from the processes of planning or implementing development served to reinforce residents' scepticism about development. Government plans made with the best of intentions might nonetheless be ignorant of local conditions or prevailing social attitudes, with the result that they would be doomed to failure when implemented. Failures of government-initiated development efforts were regularly recounted as evidence of the futility of economic development, and the sense of futility was generalised to development efforts by local entrepreneurs. The consequent cycle of social forces is diagrammed in Figure 8.1.

Discussion

A sport that appeals to tourists clearly has the potential to contribute to the economic development of a rural community. In the case of Linhares da Beira, paragliding attracts repeat visitation, and paragliders are certainly willing to purchase food, activities for family who accompany them, and activities for themselves. However, the presence of the activity in the community is inadequately leveraged. Paragliders are, at present, a low yield market. They often entertain themselves or leave town when dining out. They rarely bring family because there is too little for them to do. Consequently, the amount

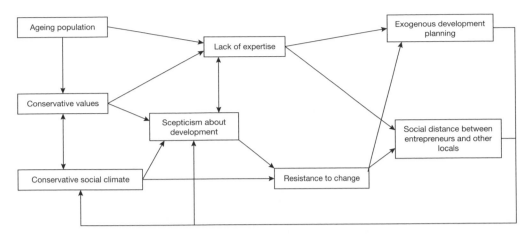

Figure 8.1 Community social forces

that paragliders spend locally is minimal, and the consequent economic benefit is small. There is no coordinated planning to create synergies between paragliding and other elements of the community's product and service mix. In the absence of that kind of planning, the potentials engendered by the sport's presence in the community remain unexploited.

The lack of coordination is but one example of the lack of community based development planning. The social and cultural conditions do not readily lend themselves to a planning effort that incorporates and energises locals. Yet, leaving them out of the planning loop reinforces the very conditions that work against effective development. This is, in fact, consistent with findings elsewhere in the community, tourism, and economic development literatures (Hirshman, 1967; Alexander & McKenna, 1998; Swanson, 2001).

Nevertheless, community participation is merely a *necessary* condition for appropriate planning; it is not a *sufficient* condition. As the foregoing analysis demonstrates, there is no consensus within the community, about its future or even the causes of its present condition. Without local agreement about the community's current status or its most desirable future, there is no starting point, and no direction for development. Without government and/or business support, the necessary resources for development cannot be marshalled. The ends and means of development are inherently political matters that call for both exogenous and local voices in planning, as well as expanded capability for local and external networks (Terluin, 2003; Shortall, 2004). This represents a more pluralistic (and potentially more acrimonious) approach to development planning than has heretofore been employed in rural Portugal.

The fact that the current social climate is not conducive to participatory planning is a disincentive to bring locals together for planning, but it is not a barrier. The challenge is to disrupt homeostatic feedback loops in the current social system. There is a substantial literature on the means by which to do precisely that (Freire, 1970; Borman, 1979; Chambers, 1994; Singer, 1994; Frisby & Millar, 2002). Although specific tactics vary, the fundamental principles are common: capitalisation on a felt sense that things should be better, facilitation of dialogue among locals, creation of a shared vision, and empowerment through skills and social networks. There is every reason to expect that tactics such as these could be effective in Linhares da Beira. Residents have a strong desire for things to be better; there are broad social ties through which to create dialogue and build a vision; the community's size makes coordination less cumbersome than in larger communities; and there are people (particularly those who would like to remain with or return to their families) who would like to build new skills that they could apply for the betterment of their community. What is required is the requisite facilitation to catalyse the intended planning.

That begs the essential question: Is paragliding potentially leverageable? Could strategic planning formulate strategies that would increase the total yield? The fact that paragliders themselves mention their desire for activities that would enable them to bring family members and for activities they could book on the spur of the moment (when the winds are not conducive to paragliding) suggests that there is a demand for which there is currently no supply. It is also significant that paragliders socialise with one another when not paragliding. Although they come to Linhares da Beira to paraglide, the winds and hills are not the only attraction. Paragliders are also attracted by other paragliders. This has been shown elsewhere to be a characteristic of sport tourism (Arnould & Price, 1993; Green & Chalip, 1998). It suggests that environments where paragliders can share and celebrate their identities as paragliders would become attractive places to socialise, drink, and dine (Price, Arnould, & Tierney, 1995; Green, 2001). Appropriate theming of local restaurants and cafés, as well as the creation of entertainments geared toward the paragliding subculture could go a long way toward attracting the patronage of paragliders.

The more difficult challenge will be to find the means to integrate paragliding into the community's brand. It seems probable that paragliding and heritage tourism appeal to separate market segments (cf., Kastenholz, Davis, & Paul, 1999). If so, then marketing communications targeted at heritage tourists and marketing communications targeted at paragliders should be devised and distributed separately. The current practice of focusing on heritage tourism but showing pictures of paragliders is not coherent. On the other hand, simply separating communications intended for the two markets does not address the fundamental challenge of creating an integrated brand. Recent models of destination branding (Cai, 2002; Brown, Chalip, Jago, & Mules, 2004) contend that brands can consist of multiple elements. The trick is to get the elements to fit together. The historical attractions of Linhares da Beira and the colourful adventure of paragliding seem to be in stark contrast—a new and technological sport silhouetted against the community's ancient architectural heritage. Perhaps that contrast is itself the basis for a brand—the new silhouetted against the old, or the old as a home for the new.

Whether a joint brand will be acceptable to the market is an empirical question, but the need to create such a brand is clear. Linhares da Beira is a heritage site. It is recognised as such by the national government, and it is a key attraction in a regional tour of Portuguese historic villages. However, it has also become the unofficial national capital of paragliding. The two—paragliding and heritage tourism—sit side-by-side as key attractions. They need to be represented jointly in the community's brand.

This is not to suggest that the two have comparable potential for the economic development of Linhares da Beira. Heritage tourists to the community are plentiful, but they rarely stay overnight, preferring instead to leave their vehicles for a quick walk through the castle or an even quicker walk through the town. Few return for a second look. Their consequent economic impact on the community is negligible. On the other hand, paragliders often stay overnight, and sometimes for several days. Their sport brings them back to the community again and again. If the two are to be compared for their potential to contribute to the economic regeneration of this rural community, paragliding seems to offer more. In order for it to reach its potential, much more needs to be done to capitalise on the opportunities it enables.

One reason so little has been done to leverage paragliding is that paragliding officials, economic development pundits, and scholars have described paragliding in Linhares da Beira as an unqualified success. Yet there has been no systematic evaluation of the sport's impact on the community, and the voices of locals who claim that the impact is slight have remained unheard. The rush to positive judgement has itself been a barrier to systematic evaluation and planning. If paragliding is thought to be an unqualified boon, then it would seem that little more needs to be done. However, that conclusion could be damaging if, as is the case here, much more remains to be accomplished.

Why, then, has paragliding in Linhares da Beira been seen to be such a success story? There are several possible answers. In the first place, paragliding represents effective exploitation of the community's natural competitive advantage—something that place marketers prescribe for the economic development of communities (Kotler, Haider, & Rein, 1993). Secondly, the ubiquitous presence of paragliding makes it easy to believe that the sport contributes appreciably to the local economy—a belief that remains unchallenged so long as there is no empirical basis for any counterclaim. It is a belief that will be attractive to politicians and paragliders. Politicians need successes that they can claim. Paragliders benefit from the support to which they lay claim on the basis of their asserted value to the economy. The unfortunate side effect is that the empirical evaluation and strategic initiatives that should consequently be mandated are thereby overlooked.

The story of paragliding in Linhares da Beira resonates with a great deal of other work on rural societies, rural economic development, and sport tourism. The conservative nature of rural communities, particularly those in decline, has been widely observed (Rogers & Burdge, 1972; Kahn, 1985; Flora et al., 2003). The benefits of involving locals when planning for rural development (Humphrey & Wilkinson, 1993; Wilson, Fesenmaier, Fesenmaier, & van Es, 2001; Davis & Morais, 200), and the disappointing effects of uncoordinated or exogenously driven development efforts (Hirschman, 1967; Pressman & Wildavsky, 1984; Doeringer, Terkla, & Topakian, 1987) have been well described. The failure to plan for strategic leverage of sport tourism (Chalip & Leyns, 2003; Weed, 2003; Bramwell, 1997) and the potential benefits of leveraging (Chalip, 2001, 2004) have also been documented. The tourism marketing opportunities engendered by sport subcultures have also been articulated (Green, 2001; Green & Chalip, 1998). Thus, findings from this case have apparent relevancy for other settings where a sport is part of a rural community's tourism product mix. The key lessons are summarised in Table 8.1.

Despite a substantial volume of work on the uses of tourism for rural economic development (Luloff et al., 1994; Edwards & Fernandes, 1999; Hall, 2004; Kneafsey, 2000) and the uses of sport in economic development (Crompton, 2000; van den Berg, Braun, & Otgaar, 2000; Gratton & Henry, 2001), there has so far been little research on the uses of sport tourism as a tool for rural economic development. The ways in which this study resonates with other work on rural development and sport marketing suggests that current theories of rural development and sport marketing will provide useful foundations for models depicting the uses of sport tourism in rural revitalisation. Nevertheless, the lessons summarised in Table 8.1 are speculative insomuch as they derive from the single case described here. Further work is needed that explores other examples

Table 8.1 Summary of key findings

- The presence of sport tourists does not necessarily deliver substation economic gain in the host rural community
- Unevaluated claims of benefits from sport tourism can hinder strategic use of sport tourism
- In the absence of a coordinated destination marketing strategy, sport tourists can be a low yield market
- Sport that is a key tourist attraction should be integrated into the community's tourism brand
- The culture and social organisation of a rural community may raise barriers to coordinated leverage of sport tourism
- Social distance between local entrepreneurs and other residents may be a barrier to coordinated leverage of sport tourism
- Planning and coordination for rural sport tourism leverage requires community involvement and commitment, which may need to be facilitated using participatory intervention techniques
- The presence of sport tourists in a rural community may itself be an attraction if appropriately leveraged

---

of rural sport tourism, and that articulates findings with theories of rural development and sport marketing. By so doing, the study of sport tourism can contribute new insight to the study of tourism behaviours, sport consumption, and economic development. It is clearly a fruitful realm for future research.

Acknowledgement

The authors thank Professor Antonio Serôdio for his help and encouragement throughout this study.

References

Abrantes, L. (1998). *Linhares: Antiga e nobrea vila da Beira museu de arte da Serra da Estrela.* Viseu, Portugal: Eden Gráfico.

Adler P.A., & Adler, P. (1987). *Membership roles in field research.* Newbury Park, CA: Sage.

Alexander, N., & McKenna A. (1998). Rural tourism in the heart of England. *International Journal of Contemporary Hospitality Management, 10,* 203–207.

Arnould, F.J., & Price, L.L. (1993). River magic: Extraordinary experience and the extended service encounter. *Journal of Consumer Research, 20,* 24–45.

Attractions almost endless (1998, September 25). *The Press,* p. S24.

Bennett, G., Henson, R.K., & Zhang, J. (2003) Generation Y's perceptions of the action sports industry segment. *Journal of Sport Management, 17,* 95–115.

Black, R. (1992) *Crisis and change in rural Europe: Agricultural development in the Portuguese mountains.* Aldershot: Avebury.

Borman, L.D. (1979). Action anthropology and the self-help/mutual aid movement. In R. Hinshaw (Ed.), *Currents in anthropology* (pp. 487–513). The Hague: Mouton.

Bramwell, B. (1997). Strategic planning before and after a mega-event. *Tourism Management*, *18*, 167–176.

Bricker, K.S., & Kerstetter, D.L. (2000). Level of specialization and place attachment: An exploratory study of whitewater recreationists. *Leisure Sciences*, *22*, 233–257.

Brown, G., Chalip, L. Jago, L., & Mules, T. (2009). Developing brand Australia: Examining the role of events. In N. Morgan, A. Pritchard, & R. Pride (Eds), *Destination branding: Creating the unique destination proposition* (pp. 279–305). Amsterdam: Elsevier.

Bynum, M. (2004). Action and reaction. *Athletic Business*, *28*(5), 50–58.

Cai, L.A. (2002). Cooperative branding for rural destinations. *Annals of Tourism Research*, *29*, 720–742.

Câmara Municipal de Celorico da Beira (1990–1991). *Plano de Pormenor de Recuperação de Linhares de Beira*. Celorico da Beira: Câmara Municipal de Celorico da Beira.

Câmara Municipal de Celorico da Beira (2001). Freguesias: Linhares da Beira. Retrieved May 15, 2003, from www.cm-celoricodabeira.pt/concelho/freguesia09.asp.

Caro, F.G. (1969). Approaches to evaluation research: A review. *Human Organization*, *28*, 87–99.

Chalip, L. (2001). Sport and tourism: Capitalising on the linkage. In D. Kluka, & G. Schilling (Eds), *The business of sport* (pp. 77–88). Oxford: Meyer & Meyer.

Chalip, L. (2004). Beyond impact: A general model for sport event leverage. In B.W. Ritchie, & D. Adair (Eds), *Sport tourism: Interrelationships, impacts and issues* (pp. 226–252). Clevedon: Channel View Publications.

Chalip, L., & Leyns, A. (2003). Local business leveraging of a sport event: Managing an event for economic benefit . *Journal of Sport Management*, *16*, 133–159.

Chambers, R. (1994). The origin and practice of rural appraisal. *World Development*, *22*, 953–969.

Cromton, J.L. (2000). Designing golf courses to optimize proximate property values. *Managing Leisure*, *5*, 192–199.

Crush, K. (2004, 26 November). Sky's the tourism limit: Paragliding presents great economic opportunity for region, says enthusiast. *Daily Herald Tribune*, p. 125.

Davis, J.S., & Morais, D.B. (2004). Factions and enclaves: Small towns and socially unsustainable tourism development. *Journal of Travel Research*, *43*, 3–10.

Devine, D. (2004, 15 June). Wales goes for the action. *The Western Mail*, p. B4.

Dobbert, M.L. (1982). *Ethnographic research: Theory and application for modern schools and societies*. New York: Praeger.

Doeringer, P.B., Terkla, D.G., & Topakian, G.C. (1987). *Invisible factors in local economic development*. New York: Oxford University Press.

Doughty, P.L. (1965). The interrelationship of power, respect, affection and rectitude in Vicos. *American Behavioral Scientist*, *8*(7), 13–17.

Eastman, C., & Krannich, R.S. (1995). Community change and persistence: The case of El Cerrito, New Mexico. *Journal of the Community Development Society*, *26*(1), 41–51.

Edwards, J., & Fernandes, C. (1999). Emigrants and espigueiros: Tourism activities in a peripheral area of Portugal. *International Journal of Tourism Research*, *1*, 329–340.

Ferrão, & Lopes, R. (2003). Zones rurales et capacité entrepreneuriale au Portugal: practiques, representations, politiques. *Géographie Économie Société*, *5*, 139–160.

Fishwick, L., & Vining, J. (1992). Toward a phenomenology of recreation place. *Journal of Environmental Psychology*, *12*, 57–63.

Flora, C.B., Flora J.L, & Fey, S. (2003), *Rural communities: Legacy and change*. Boulder, CO: Westview Press.

Forstner, K. (2004). Community ventures and access to markets: The role of intermediaries in marketing rural tourism products. *Development Policy Review, 22*, 497–514.

Foster, G.M. (1972). *Traditional cultures and technological change.* Boston: Houghton Mifflin.

Freire, P. (1970). *Pedagogy of the oppressed.* New York: Seabury.

Frisby, W., & Millar, S. (2002). The actualities of doing community development to promote the inclusion of low income populations in local sport and recreation. *European Sport Management Quarterly, 2*, 209–233.

Gilbert, D. (1989). Rural tourism and marketing: Synthesis and new ways of working. *Tourism Management, 10*, 39–50.

Golden, H.H. (1981). *Urbanization and cities: Historical and comparative perspectives on our urbanizing world.* Lexington, MA: D.C. Heath.

Gratton, C., & Henry, I. (Eds). (2001). *Sport in the city the role of sport to economic and social regeneration.* London: Routledge.

Green, B.C. (2001). Leveraging subculture and identity to promote sport events. *Sport Management Review, 4*, 1–19.

Green, B.C., & Chalip, L. (1998). Sport tourism as the celebration of subculture. *Annals of Tourism Research, 25*, 275–292.

Hall, D. (2004). Rural tourism development in southeastern Europe: Transition and the search for sustainability. *International Journal of Tourism Research, 6*, 165–176.

Harris, C.C., McLaughlin, W.J., & Ham, S.H. (1987). Integration of recreation and tourism in Idaho. *Annals of Tourism Research, 14*, 405–419.

Hirschman, A.O. (1967). *Development projects observed.* Washington, DC: Brookings Institution.

Humphrey, C.R., & Wilkinson, K.P. (1993), Growth promotion activities in rural areas: Do they make a difference? *Rural Sociology, 58*, 75–189.

Johnson, J.D., & Snepenger, D.J. (1994). Residents' perceptions of tourism development. *Annals of Tourism Research, 21*, 629–642.

Kahn, J.S. (1985). Peasant ideologies in the Third World. *Annual Review of Anthropology, 14*, 49–75.

Kastenholtz, E., Davis, D., & Paul, C. (1999). Segmenting tourism in rural areas: The case of north and central Portugal. *Journal of Travel Research, 37*, 353–363.

Keith, J., Fawson, C., & Chang, T. (1996). Recreation as an economic development strategy: Some evidence from Utah. *Journal of Leisure Research, 28*, 96–107.

Killgore, J. (2003, 11 January). The risk factor. *The Scotsman*, p. 10.

Kneafsey, M. (2000). Tourism, place identities and social relationships in the European rural periphery. *European Urban & Regional Studies, 7*, 35–50.

Kotler, P., Haider, D.H., & Rein, I. (1993). *Marketing places: Attracting investment, industry, and tourism to cities, states, and nations.* New York: Free Press.

Lijfering, J.H.W. (1974). Socio-structural changes in relation to rural out-migration. *Sociologia Ruralis, 14*, 3–14.

Luloff, A.E., Bridget, J.C., Graefe, E.R., Saylor, M., Martin, K., & Gitelson, R. (1994). Assessing rural tourism efforts in the United States. *Annals of Research, 21*, 46–64.

McGehee, N.G., & Andereck, K.L. (2004). Factors predicting rural residents' support of tourism. *Journal of Travel Research, 43*, 131–140.

Mdol, N. (1993). Cultural dissents and technical innovations in the "whiz" sports. *International Review for the Sociology of Sport, 28*, 23–33.

Minder, R. (2004, 6 March). Flying high, but mind the bugs. *Financial Times (Leisure Travel Supplement)*, p. 5.

Nelson, K. (2002). Going to extremes. *Sports Travel, 6*(7), 8–11, 14.

Patton, M.Q. (2002). *Qualitative evaluation and research methods.* Thousand Oaks, CA: Sage.

Pickles, J. (1991). Industrial restructuring, peripheral industrialization, and rural development in South Africa. *Antipode*, *23*(1), 68–91.

Pressman, J.L., & Wildavsky, A. (1984). *Implementation*. Berkeley: University of California Press.

Pressman, J.L., Arnould, E.J., & Tierney, P. (1995). Going to extremes: Managing service encounters and assessing provider performance. *Journal of Marketing*, *59*, 83–97.

Ribeiro, M., & Marques, C. (2002). Rural tourism and the development of less favoured areas: Between rhetoric and practice. *International Journal of Tourism Research*, *4*, 211–220.

Rita, J.P., & Mergulhão, L.F. (1997). Inovação organizacional e desenvolimento nas regiões pobres. *Sociologia—Problemas e Práticas*, *25*, 101–123.

Roberts, L., & Hall, D. (2001). *Rural tourism and recreation: Principles to practice*. Oxford: CABI.

Rogers, F.N. & Burdge, K.J. (1972). *Social change in rural societies*. New York: Appleton Century Crofts.

Sands, R.R. (2002). *Sport ethnography*. Champaign, IL: Human Kinetics.

Schwartman, H.B. (1993). The ethnographic evaluation of human services programs: Guidelines and an illustration. *Anthropological Quarterly*, *56*, 179–189.

Shortall, S. (2004). Social or economic goals, civic inclusion or exclusion? An analysis of rural development theory and practice. *Sociologia Ruralis*, *44*, 109–123.

Singer, M. (1994). Community-centeted praxis: Toward and alternative non-dominativve applied anthropology. *Human Organization*, *53*, 336–344.

Silva, J.C. (n.d.). Linhares da Beira: A cathedral do parapente. Retrieved June 3, 2003, from www.nca.pr/havefun/plinhar.html.

Skuras, D., Dimara, E., & Stathopoulou, S. (2003). Capital subsidies and job creation in rural areas: A Greek case study. *International Journal of Manpower*, *24*, 947–963.

Swanson, L.E. (2001). Rural policy and direct local participation: Democracy, inclusiveness, collective agency, and locally-based policy. *Rural Sociology*, *66*, 1–20.

Swarbrooke, J., Beard, C., Leckie, S., & Pomfret, G. (2003). *Adventure tourism: The new frontier*. Oxford: Butterworth-Heinemann.

Terluin, I.J. (2003). Difference in economic development in rural regions of advanced countries: An overview and critical analysis of theories. *Journal of Rural Studies*, *19*, 327–344.

Thomas, R., & Long, J. (2001). Tourism and economic regeneration: The role of skills development. *International Journal of Tourism Research*, *3*, 229–240.

United Nations Centre for Human Settlements (1996). *An urbanizing world: Global report on human settlements*. Oxford: Oxford University Press.

United States General Accounting Office. (2003). *Federal programs: Ethnographic studies can inform agencies' actions*. Washington, DC: Author.

Van den Berg, L., Braun, E., & Otgaar, A.H.J. (2000). *Sports and city marketing in European cities*. Rotterdam: Euricur.

Vogt, C.A., & Marans, R.W. (2004). Natural resources and open space in the residential decision process: A study of recent movers to fringe counties in southeast Michigan. *Landscape and Urban Planning, 69*, 255–269.

Weed, M. (2003). Why the two won't tango! Explaining the lack of integrated policies for sport and tourism in the UK. *Journal of Sport Management*, *17*, 258–283.

Wilson, P.A., & Lowery, C. (2001). Building deep democracy: The story of a grassroots learning organization in South Africa. *Planning Forum*, *9*, 47–64.

Wilson, S., Fesenmaier, D.R., Fesenmaier, J., & van Es, J.C. (2001). Factors for success in rural tourism development. *Journal of Travel Research*, *40*, 132–138.

Chapter 9

Heather J. Gibson and
Lori Pennington-Gray

INSIGHTS FROM ROLE THEORY
Understanding golf tourism

I N RECENT YEARS, the tourism industry has become increasingly specialized, and a new range of tourism products has emerged, including ecotourism, heritage tourism, and sport tourism. Despite the apparent innovative nature of these new types of tourism, academics have long recognized the existence of a range of tourism types and various tourist role typologies have been developed in an attempt to classify and explain these various modalities (e.g., Cohen, 1972; Pearce, 1985; Smith, 1977; Yiannakis & Gibson, 1992). Indeed, Cohen (1974) argued that it is futile to think that there is only one type of tourist. However, enduring questions posed by these typologies are how well they categorize tourist behavior, and whether individuals engage in more than one type of tourist role while on vacation.

Similarly, in sport tourism there has been an ongoing debate as to how to define and classify sport tourists. This debate has generally centred on the issue of active and passive involvement in sport tourism, active referring to taking part in sport while on vacation and passive referring to watching sport (e.g., Hall, 1992; Hinch & Higham, 2001; Standeven & De Knop, 1999). A third form of sport tourism, that of nostalgia sport tourism was hypothesized by Redmond (1991) and refers to visits to such locations as sports halls of fame, stadium tours, or sports themed cruises. Thus, Gibson (1998a) proposed that sport tourism encompasses three types of behaviour and can be defined as "leisure-based travel that takes individuals temporarily outside of their home communities to participate in physical activities [Active Sport Tourism], to watch physical activities [Event Sport Tourism], or to venerate attractions associated with physical activities [Nostalgia Sport Tourism]" (p. 49). Nonetheless, while the discussion over definitions of sport tourism seems to have declined somewhat, an issue that needs to be addressed in this next stage of sport tourism research is how we might better understand and explain sport tourism? Gibson (1998, 2002, 2004) has suggested that one way to achieve this goal is to frame future studies in theories and concepts from relevant disciplines, including sociology, social psychology, consumer behavior, and the like. A related approach suggested by Weed (2005) is to work inductively and develop grounded theory from our studies of sport tourism. Both inductive and deductive approaches work together and are necessary as we move forward in the next phase of sport tourism scholarship.

In this paper we address the issue of how we might classify and understand different types of sport tourist. We draw upon role theory from sociology and its subsequent use in tourism studies; we link this work on tourist roles to wider concepts in sociology, social psychology, and life span developmental psychology; and suggest a framework that could be used to identify and explain different types of sport tourist. To provide some empirical illustration as to how such a framework might be applied to sport tourism, we examine one form of active sport tourism—the golf tourist–with a view to finding out how golf travel relates to other travel preferences. Is there a pure sport (golf) tourist? Is sport (golf) for some tourists one vacation activity among many? Can role theory and its application to tourism be used to help us better understand and explain different levels of participation in sport tourism?

Conceptual framework

Role theory

Role theory is one of the oldest paradigms used to understand society. Examples of work that have addressed various issues related to roles exist in anthropology, sociology, and social psychology. The term role is borrowed from the theatre. Shaw and Constanzo (1982) explain, " a role referred to the characterization that an actor was called upon to enact in the context of a given dramatic presentation" (p. 296). While an extensive body of writings exist that have been framed in role theory, there has been a growing realization that little consistency exists in the conceptualization and operationalization of the term "role" (Biddle, 1986; Handel, 1979; Hilbert, 1981; Turner, 1979/80). Biddle suggests that much of this confusion exists because the term was not used consistently by the early role theorists (e.g., Linton, 1936; Mead, 1934) and that the legacy of this is still evident today. He further explains that to some, a role was used to refer to a collection of behaviours associated with a social status (e.g. Linton, 1936; Parsons, 1951). Others used the term role to refer to a social position (e.g., Winship & Mandel, 1983) whereas, others conceptualized roles in terms of expectations for behaviour (e.g., Zurcher, 1979). This paper will be largely grounded in sociological conceptions of role theory where the debates over the influence of agency and structure have been central to the discussions in this area. In line with this thinking, and with Shaw and Constanza's conclusion that, "almost all definitions of role universally acknowledge that it pertains to the behaviours of particularized persons" (p. 304), we work from the idea that a role refers to a collection of behaviours that are influenced by the interaction of agency and structure.

In sociology, traditionally there have been two perspectives on role theory, one from a largely functionalist perspective and one from a largely symbolic interactionist position. Functionalist role theory generally adopts a deterministic position in relation to roles (e.g., Linton, 1936; Parsons, 1951). Roles are regarded as a collection of behaviours that are associated with a social position. These behaviours are largely governed by norms and social expectations and the individual role incumbent is expected to conform and to play a role rather than actively shape it in any way. Thus, as Birenbaum (1984) explained, roles are frequently regarded as prescriptive and constraining behaviour; indeed, as Gerhardt (1980) pointed out, roles can be regarded as agents of social conformity.

In contrast, a symbolic interactionist approach to role theory has been described as being more focussed on role making rather than role playing (Turner, 1979/80). In line with the basic tenets of symbolic interactionism, role incumbents are thought to shape a particular role through their interactions with others in a particular social context (e.g., Mead, 1934; Sarbin, 1982; Goffman, 1959; Zurcher, 1979). Thus, while roles are still associated with patterns of behaviour and norms, individuals take a much more active part in creating a role as Biddle (1986) explains, symbolic interactionists largely regard norms as merely providing "a set of broad imperatives within which the details of roles can be worked out" (p. 71). Nonetheless, some of the critiques that have plagued symbolic interactionism generally, such as imprecise definitions, a failure to clearly articulate the place of society in their explanations, and a tendency to ignore the wider body of empirically based knowledge in sociology, Biddle suggests has led to a tendency to denigrate their version of role theory. Callero (1994) asks if role theory has been plagued with such inconsistencies and has been subjected to such harsh critique, then why do sociologists continue to use the concept? In turn, why then are we suggesting that it might be useful in a sport tourism context? The answer is that the concept still has utility in helping us to understand patterns of behaviour and their relationships to norms and preferences, other roles, and society in general. Callero suggests that "the emerging consensus among sociologists is that society consists of both powerful, determining structures and actors that possess a degree of efficacy, freedom and creative independence" (p. 228), Indeed, in line with this general trend in sociology of placing more emphasis on individuals as active agents, Turner (1979/80) proposed that enacting roles might be better conceptualized as describing consistency in behaviours rather than absolute conformity to external expectations. Thus, a role can be defined as a collection of behaviours that have some sense of cohesiveness and relatedness to a social position. Indeed, as Goffman (1974) explained, the role incumbent is not totally constrained or totally free, but there is an interaction between agency and social structure in shaping the behaviours associated with particular roles, or what he called the person-rote formula.

This recognition of the influence of both agency and structure in explaining behaviour has led to calls for an integrated role theory (Biddle, 1986; Callero, 1994; Turner, 1979/80). Indeed, Handel (1979) suggested that functionalist and interactionist approaches to role theory are not that disparate and it would be possible to develop "a more general theory" that "would need to incorporate both modes of analysis in a unified conceptual framework" (p. 877). While Handel doubted that a completely new theory could be developed, others have been more optimistic. Biddle (1986) postulated, "perhaps role theory needs to adopt its own distinctive theoretical orientation, one that stands apart from the theoretical perspectives with which it has been historically associated" (p. 70). In line with this thinking, he proposed that an integrated role theory would need to incorporate ideas related to agency and structure, not just in the traditional sense of norms and expectations, but one that accounts for changes in society whereby preferences shaped by the media are accorded more importance in shaping behaviours associated with roles (ideas also proffered by Turner [1976] and Zurcher [1977]). He also suggested that attention to the influence of the media might also lead us to understand other social changes such as the loss of social capital and the need for self-validation. by seeking alternative sources of identity (Goffman, 1974; Zurcher, 1979). Certainly, in the realm of leisure, sport and tourism ideas related to preferences are central to the underlying ideas of choice related to these domains (e.g., Kelly, 1999) as well as the tradition of looking at leisure roles as an important source of identity (e.g., Haggard & Williams, 1992; Shamir, 1992).

Another idea that has become part of more recent conceptualizations of role theory is the place of power. Traditional functionalist conceptualizations, of roles legitimated inequality by suggesting that roles were allocated based on skills, birth rite, class, and so forth (Durkheim, 1893/1984; Parsons, 1951). Interactionists largely ignored social inequality in their theorizing. However the legacy of conflict, and more recently critical theorizing has led us to an era where discussions about social inequality are pervasive. Turner (1979)/80) in his discussions of an integrated role theory suggests that we need to address two considerations related to role allocation, the "fit" between individuals and a role, and the fact that roles differ in what he calls their desirability, that is the power and status associated with them. Callero (1994) develops these ideas further by adopting a resource perspective to theorizing about roles whereby he indicates there is an inherent need to understand the differential access that certain roles have to economic and social capital. Thus, it appears that newer conceptualizations of role have not just merged the tenets of structuralism and interactionism, but they have integrated a more critical approach to understanding role taking and role making.

In this light, Turner defined a role as "a comprehensive pattern for behaviour and attitude, constituting a socially identified part in social interaction and capable of being enacted recognizably by different individuals" (p. 123). Moreover, Callero suggests that by regarding roles as a cultural object that is both virtual (i.e. underpinned by cultural assumptions) and visible (i.e. serves as a source of power—money, respect, etc.), we can understand how agency and structure result in both intra- and inter-role variation.

Tourist roles

Role theory has been applied to tourism behaviour since the 1970s. Cohen (1972) first used the concept of role to distinguish four types of tourist: the organized mass tourist, the independent mass tourist, the explorer, and the drifter. His underlying premise was that each of these tourist roles was associated with a consistent desire for novelty or familiarity in a vacation setting. Thus, organized mass tourists who prefer the highest level of familiarity when they travel engage in a consistent set of behaviours that "protect" them from too much novelty in their food, accommodations, transportation type, and their interactions with the host community. In complete contrast, those enacting the drifter role tend to disdain the mass tourism experiences of their organized counterparts in favour of experiences away from the main tourist routes. This distinction between mass and alternative tourism experiences led to a further tourist typology from Cohen (1979). In response to the academic debate over the authenticity of tourist experiences regarding the increasing predominance of mass tourism destinations, Cohen suggested, in contrast to the likes of MacCannell (1976), that not all tourists are motivated by the search for authenticity. He suggested that five different modes of tourist experience could be distinguished by the extent to which the tourist was motivated by "a quest for centre". He suggested that for some tourists recreation or diversion might be the purpose of their trip, whereas for others experimental or existential types of vacations are sought. In Cohen's (1972) conceptualization of tourist roles, while the focus appears to be on role as a collection of similar behaviours, the other central assumption is the role of agency—that is, the tourist chooses a certain style of travel based on his or her preferences. This idea of agency is developed further in his 1979 phenomenological approach, which distinguished tourists more by the degree to which they felt alienated (or not) from their own society. Thus, the idea of agency within a social context (i.e. the influence of society) was postulated as a way of explaining differences in touristic preferences.

Since the 1970s, scholars have extended Cohen's work by developing several tourist role typologies (e.g., Pearce, 1982, 1985; Mo. Howard & Havitz, 1993; Yiannakis, 1986; Yiannakis & Gibson, 1992), largely based on the idea of role as a collection of behaviours. Pearce used quantitative methods to verify the distinctiveness of 15 travel related roles. With a sample of 100 participants he asked them to suggest which behaviours were most associated with each of the travel roles. He found that some of the roles were not as distinctive as others. Pearce also used multidimensional scaling to find out which of the roles were most closely related. The 15 roles clustered into five types: Environmental Travel; High Contact Travel; Exploitative Travel; Pleasure First Travel; and Spiritual Travel. The roles of international athlete and migrant failed to cluster with any of the other roles. Thus, in this way Pearce was the first to empirically test the supposition that tourist roles are both distinctive and interrelated. In so doing he partly answered the enduring questions regarding whether there are different types of tourist roles and which roles are likely to be enacted by the same individual during one vacation. Yiannakis and Gibson (1992) extended this work further by developing a typology that included only tourist roles—that is, those that are leisure roles rather than including general travel roles as in the case of Pearce's typology.

Working from the premise that tourism is a special form of leisure (Cohen, 1972; Smith, 1977), Yiannakis (1986) developed the first version of the Tourist Role Preference Scale (TRPS). Tourist roles in the TRPS are operationalized as statements that identify the primary behaviours associated with a particular tourist role. For example, the sportlover role (which has subsequently been renamed the active sport tourist [Gibson & Yiannakis, 2002]), is measured by the statement, "When I go on vacation I like to stay physically active and to take part in my favourite sports". Over the past 20 years, the TRPS has been refined and currently measures 16 roles (e.g., Gibson, 1989, 1994; Murdy, 2001; Yiannakis & Gibson, 1988, 1992). In 1992, Yiannakis and Gibson, like Pearce, tested the distinctiveness and interrelatedness of the tourist roles contained in their typology. They found that the roles could be distinguished according to three underlying dimensions: a preference for familiarity or novelty; a preference for tranquility or stimulation; and a preference for structure or spontaneity. Using a three-dimensional model it was possible to see both the distinctiveness and interrelatedness of the tourist roles. Thus, while Cohen (1972) and Ryan (1997) have suggested that it is likely that individuals enact more than one role on a trip, Gibson and Yiannakis (2002) found that while this may be so, individuals appear to choose roles with similar characteristics such as novelty, risk, and spontaneity, and that it is usually possible to identify a dominant role characterizing a particular vacation. Thus, being able to identify the underlying dimensions of tourist roles, it is possible to distinguish those roles that are likely to cluster together.

This type of logic can also be applied to sport tourism, as we know that some sport tourists are uni-dimensional in their tourist behaviour—those that Faulkner et al. (1998)

called the "sport junkies"—whereas others take part in other non-sport related behaviours while attending sports events (Gibson, Willming & Holdnak, 2003; Ritchie, Mosedale, & King, 2000). Indeed, Gammon and Robinson (1997)/2003) suggested that the importance of sport to a trip can be used to distinguish two types of sport tourists. They proposed that sport tourists are those individuals for whom sport is the primary reason for the trip, whereas tourism sportists describes those individuals for whom sport is a secondary activity and may include those individuals who are more likely to take part in a range of activities during the one trip. In relation to golf tourists, Priestly (1993) identified three types of golf tourist based on their preference for either a budget or upscale style of vacation or their nostalgic motivations to embark on a pilgrimage to visit the famous courses in Scotland, particularly the Mecca of golf at St Andrews. Similarly, Robinson and Gammon (2004) show how their Sport Tourism Framework can be applied to identify the different sport tourism attractions associated either with a particular destination or a particular sport. They applied their framework to golf and showed how it is possible to distinguish different styles of golf tourism from what they call golf sport tourism, which includes (i) watching or participating in a competitive golf tournament or (ii) active participation in recreational style golf and golf tourism sport, which includes active or passive participation in golf, either as a one off round or golf attractions such as mini golf or visiting golf halls of fame and museums. The underlying premise to their Sport Tourism Framework is motivation, both in the form of primary and secondary needs and push and pull factors. Perhaps by paying attention to the underlying dimensions of tourist roles (both motivations and preferences) it might be possible in sport tourism research to understand the primacy of sport to some tourists but not to others, and also why some sport tourists prefer mass tourism style vacations and others are more adventurous and seek out destinations that are less familiar than their home environments. Indeed, we know that the type of tourist role chosen, and also the degree of risk and thrill preferred, appears to be linked to life stage, gender, social class, and motivation (Cohen, 1984; Gibson, 1989, 1994, 1996; Gibson & Yiannakis, 2002). Certainly, in the realm of golf tourism, Petrick (2002) found that younger golfers seek more novelty in their golf vacations than their older counterparts.

Tourist roles and the life course

In 1984, Cohen suggested that motivation for tourism should be contextualized within a perspective that takes into account an individual's life long plans and needs. Since that time, various scholars have applied the family life cycle to understanding touristic behaviour and more recently life span and life course models have been used. Lawson (1991), using a modernized family life cycle model to examine tourism behaviours, found that among international visitors to New Zealand, travel styles changed over the eight stages of the family life cycle. For example, couples with young children preferred visiting relatives and staying in one place, whereas once the children were older and more independent, vacations became more active. Among couples that had launched their children, a preference for historical and cultural vacations in more upscale surroundings was evident. Overall, Lawson concluded that presence and age of children and amount of discretionary income appeared to be quite influential in shaping touristic styles. Bojanic (1992) concurred with Lawson's findings in his study of 2,000 Americans who had visited

Europe. Among the Americans, age of children and discretionary income were related to vacation behaviours. In work with Warnick (Bojanic & Warnick, 1995), they found that ski resorts could be segmented according to family life cycle stage. For example, the ski resort they studied in New England was particularly attractive to parents under 45 years with young children. This finding lends support to the widely held notion that particular destinations become associated with certain life stages and or socioeconomic groups. Ryan (1995) further investigated this proposition in a study of British tourists and their holidays on small islands. He found that family life stage was an important predictor of choice, but he also advocated the use of a motivation framework to identify the primacy of certain motives during each life stage. Using Beard and Ragheb's (1923) leisure motivation scale, he found motives not only changed with the presence of children and discretionary income, but marital status and social class were also influential.

While, the use of a modernized family life cycle model accounts somewhat for the diversity of family forms which have become more pervasive over the past fifty years, some scholars have suggested that individual life course or life span models might be more useful in societies where increasingly more people are single and or traditional gender roles are not as influential. In Gibson's work with Yiannakis (e.g., Gibson, 1989, 1994; Gibson & Yiannakis, 2002; Yiannakis & Gibson, 1988, 1992) Levinson et al.'s model of the adult life cycle has been used to understand change and stability in tourist role preference (Levinson, Darrow, Klein, Levinson & McKee, 1978; Levinson, 1996). In these studies they discovered three general trends in tourist role preference over the life course. For some roles, particularly those characterized by culture, history, and familiarity, preference seems to increase over the life course; in contrast, roles characterized by risk, thrill, and physicality seem to decrease in popularity; and some roles seem to vary in popularity over the life course, these being roles such as the independent mass tourist and the escapist. In line with Levinson et al.'s contention that an individual's life structure is shaped by psychological needs, his or her roles in life, and the society in which he or she lives, they examined the influence of gender, social class, and socio-psychological needs within a life span context on tourist role preference. Like Ryan (1995) they found that socio-psychological needs were linked to tourist role preference for men and women at different life stages (Gibson & Yiannakis, 2002). Thus, these studies lend support for the contention that to understand sport tourism behaviour we need to address both agency (including motivations) and structure. Certainly, in understanding participation in sport and tourism, the influence of social structure, particularly gender, is also important.

Gender and sport and sport tourism

In most societies sport has generally been regarded as a male domain (Guttman, 1988; Snyder & Spreitzer, 1987). While the history of sport shows evidence of female partici-pation, even today in twenty-first century American women still tend to participate in sport and physical activity less frequently than men (*Participation U.S. research menu*, www.sbrnet.com/Research/Research.cfm?subRID=457). Much of the early work investigating the patterns of participation (and non-participation) in sport among girls and women was grounded in role theory. The thesis underlying much of this work was that males and females were socialized into gender appropriate roles and sport—

particularly contact team sport—was not deemed appropriate for girls and women (Greendorfer & Lewko, 1978). As a consequence, because sport participation involved taking part in behaviours that were not socially sanctioned it was also thought that female athletes experienced role conflict and that role conflict also served as a deterrent to participation for many girls and women (Sage & Loudermilk, 1979). In the mid 1980s, more critical perspectives were used to explain women and girls' lower participation rates (e.g., Birrell & Richter, 1987; Cole, 1993; Hargreaves, 1994; Lenskyj, 1994). These studies led to an understanding as to how unequal participation patterns were maintained through ideologies pervasive in socialization, education, and the media, among others. These ideologies served to marginalize female participation in sport to socially acceptable "body projects", such as aerobics or gymnastics and ice skating, which are deemed as sufficiently feminine; or, if girls and women did take part in team sports, unequal access to facilities, equipment, and media coverage was common (Kane, 1989; Frederick, Havitz & Shaw, 1994; Markula, 1995).

In tourism, there is also evidence to suggest that men and women experience travel differently and choose different activities (e.g., Butler, 1995; Jordan & Gibson, 2005; Kinnaird & Hall, 1994, McGehee, Loker-Murphy & Uysal, 1996; Squire, 1994). For example, Nichols and Snepenger (1988) found that vacations planned by men were more likely to involve physical activity than those planned by women. Likewise, McGehee *et al.* in a study of Australian's tourism preferences, found that the women in their study reported a higher preference for cultural experiences and family-time on holiday, whereas the males in their study reported that they liked to take part in sport and adventure activities while on vacation.

These results are further supported in Wilson's (2004) study of nostalgia sport tourists on a tour of Wrigley Field (home of the Chicago Cubs baseball team) whereby men reported that visiting the stadium and its historic importance were most influential in their decision to visit, whereas women cited the opportunity for family time accorded by the trip. In other sport tourism research, most of the studies that have addressed gender have focused on skiing. Williams and Lattey (1994), Hudson (2000), and Williams and Fidgeon (2000) used a constraints framework to examine women's participation (and non-participation) in skiing. The women in these studies consistently reported that intrapersonal constraints such as perceptions that the sport is too dangerous or an aversion to the cold were cited most often.

Sport, roles and life stage

Apart from the use of role theory in the early work on women and sport, the approach taken in tourism studies whereby different tourist roles have been identified has not been that widely developed in sport studies, Yiannakis (nda) did some preliminary work looking at the idea that different members of a sports team enact informal roles in the organization of a team. For example, players take on the roles of enforcer or joker. There has also been some work looking at the different roles played by individuals within a group of football hooligans (Giulianotti & Armstrong, 2002). Within studies on sport subcultures there is evidence of differential membership within these groups (e.g., Donnelly & Young, 1988). However, no formal study exists framing such investigations within role theory, although the issue of degree of involvement in a sport and contribution such membership makes to an individual's identity, which has been studied, could be approached through interactionist perspectives of role theory (Goffman, 1974; Zurcher, 1979).

In regards to the influence of life stage on sport participation, some early cross-sectional studies reinforce somewhat the patterns found in relation to active sport tourism (Gibson & Yiannakis, 2002)—that of a decline in active participation over the life course among both men and women. McPherson (1984) and Rudman (1986) both found a negative association between age and sport participation. Both of these studies are from the early 1980s and we could postulate that—perhaps with changing social expectations pertaining to older adults and participation in sport and physical activity—some of these patterns of decline may not be as sharp as in the past. Certainly, there are more opportunities for involvement in competitive sports for individuals over the age of 50 through the Masters' and Senior game's organizations (Dionigi, 2002; Gibson, Ashton-Shaeffer, Green, & Kensinger, 2002; Stevenson, 2002). We could also point to the popularity of golf, especially among retirees in the US, where such (middle-class) participation patterns have led to the rapid expansion of retirement housing situated around golf courses. But in all reality, national participation data for most western countries still shows that as people age they are less likely to take part in sport (e.g., Gratton & Kokolakakis, 2005; *Participation U.S. research menu*, www.shrnet.com/Research/Research.cfm?subRID= 457). While active participation in sport and sport tourism has been tracked over the life course, passive participation in sport in the form of spectating or nostalgia sport tourism has not been formally studied. The few studies on sport halls of fame provide some evidence of the inter-generational transmission of sporting history in particular between fathers and sons, and grandfathers and grandchildren (Newman, 2002; Snyder, 1991), and studies of Gator football fans at the University of Florida show that for the majority being a Gator fan is a life long activity and source of identity. Similar to nostalgia sport tourism, there is also evidence of inter-generational transmission of the values, rituals, and practices associated with being a fan (Gibson, Willming, & Holdnak, 2002).

Thus, in developing a framework to understand and explain different types of sport tourism behaviour, we suggest that role theory, life stage, and gender may be a useful starting point in developing an appropriate framework. To illustrate these ideas we use data from a secondary data source and examine one of the most popular forms of active sport tourism, travelling to play golf. Specifically, we investigate the preferences for and attitudes towards pleasure travel of these golf tourists with a view to exploring some of the persistent questions in sport tourism research, such as: (i) Is there a pure sport (golf) tourist? (ii) Can different types of sport (golf) tourist be distinguished based on their preferences and attitudes towards pleasure travel? (iii) Is there a relationship between type of sport (golf) tourist and socio-demographic variables (e.g., life stage, gender, marital status, income, and education)?

Methods

Data collection

We used secondary data collected by Coopers & Lybrand Consulting for the Canadian Tourism Commission (CTC) in September and October 1995. The objective of the

Domestic Tourism Market Research Study was to examine in detail the preferences, attitudes and perceptions of Canadians about tourism, travel opportunities, and destinations. While it is recognized that there are limitations associated with using secondary data for a purpose other than that for which it was originally intended, we feel that for the objective of illustrating the main intent of our paper (that is, proposing that role theory might have utility in sport tourism research), that the use of these data is appropriate in this instance.

The sample is comprised of 3,356 Canadians. The data were weighted so that each age, gender, and province was representative of the entire population. The CTC used a combination of telephone (n = 1,899) and in person (n = 1,457) interviews to collect the data. For this study a sub-sample of 492 respondents who indicated that golf was an important part of their travel were analysed.

Participants

The sub-sample ranged in age from 15 to over 65 years of age. More than half (58%) had some post-secondary education from vocational school to terminal degrees. Over 50% (55%) reported an annual household income higher than $50,000 (CDN). Almost three quarters (70%) are currently married or living with someone, and slightly more than half (53%) were male. Information on the racial and ethnic background of the participants was not collected. Approximately 98% of the respondents indicated that they had taken a pleasure trip in the last year, and the majority (84.9%) had travelled with one or more persons.

Operationalizing the variables

For the purpose of this study two scales from the overall questionnaire were used in addition to five demographic items, and one item that distinguished golf tourists from other types of tourist. One scale measured general travel preferences and the other measured attitudes towards travel.

Sport (golf) tourists. One question on the survey was used to isolate Canadians who indicated that golf is very important to their travel. Respondents who answered, "strongly agree" to the statement "How important on a scale of 1 to 4, where 1 is never important and 4 is very important, is golf when deciding on a destination for vacation" was used for this study. A total of 492 people responded to this question.

General pleasure travel preferences. Forty-one items were used to measure general travel preferences. Respondents were asked to indicate how important each travel item was on a scale of 1 to 4, where 1 meant "never important" and 4 meant "always important".

Pleasure travel attitudes. Twenty-two items were used to measure attitudes towards pleasure travel. Respondents were asked to rate the degree to which they agreed or disagreed about holiday travel related statements using a four point Likert type scale where 1 represented "disagree" and 4 referred to "agree".

Demographics included age, gender, income, education, and marital status, and were measured using a fixed choice format.

Data analysis

Data were analysed using the Statistical Package for the Social Sciences. Initially, descriptive statistics were computed to describe sport (golf) tourists. Second, responses to the list of preferences for travel were analysed using two types of cluster analysis (hierarchical and non-hierarchical). In order to further clarify the results of the cluster analysis, analysis of variance and discriminant analysis were used. Finally, attitudes towards pleasure travel and demographics were examined in relation to the resultant clusters.

Identification of clusters. Cluster analysis was used to identify different types of sport (golf) tourist based on similar responses to the forty-one travel preference statements. Initially, a Ward's hierarchical clustering method was used to determine the number of clusters. Examination of the dendrograms and agglomeration coefficients suggested four clusters. This number of clusters was used a priori in a follow-up non-hierarchical (K-means) cluster analysis. The results of an analysis of variance (ANOVA) revealed that the four clusters were statistically different from each other in terms of travel preferences (Table 9.1).

Discriminant analysis. In order to further clarify the results of the cluster analysis, discriminant analysis was used. Discriminant analysis was performed on the four clusters in an effort to identify which preferences best discriminated among the four clusters. A three canonical discriminant function was statistically significant as measured by the chi-square statistic. Function 1 explained 68.2% of the total variance and had an eigenvalue of 3.78. Function 2 explained 25.4% of the variance and had an eigenvalue of 1.41. Function 3 explained 6.4% of the variance and had an eigenvalue of 0.35. Classification matrices were also examined to determine whether the functions were good predictors. The overall classification rate was 96.4% which indicates a high degree of classification accuracy.

In order to better understand the four clusters, Chi-square and ANOVA were used to determine if there were any statistically significant differences among the four cluster groups in terms of travel attitudes and demographics.

Results

Sport tourist.   Cluster I was comprised of tourists who were more likely express a preference for destinations that provided value for money ($M = 2.05$) and budget accommodations ($M = 2.87$), including staying at campgrounds and trailer parks ($M = 2.35$) than respondents in Cluster II or III (Table 9.1). These tourists were also more likely than their counterparts to place importance on sporting activities such as alpine skiing ($M = 2.10$), water sports ($M = 2.82$), and hunting/fishing ($M = 2.29$) when traveling for pleasure. Other favourite vacation activities included casinos/gambling ($M = 2.05$) and nightlife entertainment ($M = 2.91$). The correct classification rate for this cluster was 98.9%. In terms of travel attitudes (Table 9.2), the sport tourist tends to vacation during the summer ($M = 3.58$), is more likely to be male (57.8%), and aged

Table 9.1 Cluster analysis of travel preferences

		Sample mean score N = 491	Cluster I Sport tourist N = 90	Cluster II Discerning tourist N = 118	Cluster III Resort tourist N = 104	Cluster IV Reluctant tourist N = 128	F-ratio
1	First class hotels and resorts	2.34	2.13	2.11	2.70	2.01	13.11
2	Budget accommodations	2.76	2.87	2.50	2.76	2.66	7.83
3	Campgrounds and trailer parks	2.05	2.35	2.19	1.34	1.35	76.75
4	High quality restaurants	2.30	2.38	2.44	1.61	1.71	36.92
5	Inexpensive restaurants	2.58	2.49	2.27	2.81	2.28	11.84
6	Availability of pre-trip info.	2.85	1.95	2.94	3.30	2.56	29.25
7	Availability of package trips	2.27	1.99	1.88	2.72	1.76	26.10
8	Outstanding scenery	3.20	2.70	3.53	3.36	2.47	20.88
9	Nice weather	3.54	3.30	3.53	3.76	3.19	15.01
10	Personal safety	3.58	2.81	3.70	3.88	3.50	33.28
11	Environmental quality	3.20	2.34	3.49	3.48	2.74	36.34
12	Standards of hygiene	3.68	3.25	3.73	3.90	3.54	26.54
13	Arts and cultural attractions	2.50	2.06	2.43	2.58	2.06	35.33
14	Museums and art galleries	2.26	1.74	2.43	2.27	1.79	23.40
15	Local cuisine	2.73	2.57	2.76	2.75	2.22	11.42
16	Interesting and friendly locals	3.26	2.86	3.27	3.41	2.72	29.06
17	See or experience aboriginal	2.30	1.81	2.41	2.22	1.59	60.63
18	See wildlife, birds and flowers	2.96	2.44	3.31	2.89	2.06	38.07
19	National or provincial parks	2.86	2.58	3.16	2.64	2.01	42.45
20	Alpine skiing	1.92	2.10	1.58	1.89	1.41	24.52
21	Water sports	2.58	2.82	2.07	2.76	1.53	83.05
22	Hunting or fishing	2.03	2.29	1.77	1.71	1.37	39.13
23	Activities for entire family	3.05	2.92	2.87	3.43	2.16	29.91
24	Outdoor activities	2.61	2.48	2.64	2.45	1.76	62.63
25	Spectator sporting events	2.54	2.68	2.07	2.76	2.07	23.48
26	Shopping	2.86	2.60	2.47	3.35	2.60	22.56
27	Variety of short guided tours	2.24	1.75	2.06	2.62	1.71	53.32
28	Theme parks and amusement	2.41	2.55	1.99	2.58	1.71	47.60
29	Nightlife and entertainment	2.52	2.91	1.89	2.67	2.00	25.76
30	Casinos and other gambling	1.85	2.05	1.46	2.04	1.41	13.63
31	Cruises of one or more nights	1.87	1.78	1.44	2.07	1.43	26.76
32	Visiting remote coastal attractions	2.23	1.91	2.19	2.11	1.59	40.86
33	Beaches for sunbathing and swimming	2.93	2.99	2.56	3.22	2.26	45.71
34	Modern cities	2.53	2.58	2.11	2.76	2.19	15.78
35	Historical places or buildings	2.74	2.12	2.89	2.85	2.22	30.11
36	Variety of things to see and do	3.38	3.14	3.43	3.63	2.74	32.57
37	Opportunity to increase one's knowledge	3.20	2.53	3.35	3.40	2.72	42.98
38	Having fun/being entertained	3.45	3.47	3.32	3.68	2.85	23.07
39	Destinations that provide value for $	3.47	2.05	1.46	2.04	1.41	15.91
40	Easy access to good health care	3.18	2.68	3.31	3.51	2.38	35.07
41	Taking advantage of currency rate	2.93	2.32	2.85	3.43	2.19	46.04

Notes: Items measured on a four point scale, where 1 = always important and 4 = never important.
* Significant differences among clusters for all travel preference items existed at the .05 level.

Table 9.2 Attitudes towards travel by cluster of tourists

	Cluster I Sport tourist	Cluster II Discerning tourist	Cluster III Resort tourist	Cluster IV Reluctant tourist	F-ratio	Sig. level
I travel for leisure whenever I can afford to	3.58	3.62	3.66	3.53	0.76	0.55
For me, money spent on travel is very well spent*	3.44	3.68	3.60	3.53	2.30	0.06
I generally take one or two trips of a week or more each year	3.01	3.33	3.18	2.97	1.73	0.14
I generally take frequent short trips of a few days each year	3.42	3.37	3.29	3.18	0.83	0.51
I prefer to go on escorted tours when taking a longer trip*	1.78	1.83	2.23	1.90	4.11	0.00
It is important that people speak my language*	2.04	1.77	2.21	1.82	2.58	0.04
Getting value for my holiday money is very important to me	3.45	3.80	3.76	3.63	0.30	0.88
I generally like to go to the same place every year for my holiday*	2.21	1.98	2.12	2.25	4.23	0.00
I enjoy making my own travel arrangements	3.44	3.57	3.36	3.51	1.46	0.21
Once I get to my destination I stay put	2.35	2.29	2.54	2.48	1.18	0.32
I like to travel on all-inclusive package holidays	2.25	2.04	2.35	2.08	1.55	0.19
I do not really like to travel*	1.21	1.27	1.19	1.38	2.62	0.03
Long distance travel is a hassle*	1.63	1.63	1.72	1.88	2.67	0.03
I often take winter holidays	2.64	2.69	2.63	2.67	1.15	0.33
I take short trips to a lake or cottage	2.88	2.31	2.54	2.21	1.95	0.10
I prefer travelling overseas	2.23	2.12	2.19	1.76	0.07	0.99
I take holidays in the summer*	3.58	3.39	3.29	3.10	8.55	0.00

Notes: Items measured on a four point scale, where 1 = disagree and 4 = agree. * Significant differences among clusters existed at the .05 level.

between 30 and 39 years, with annual incomes between $30,000–$50,000 (CDN) (26%) or over $100,000 bracket (CDN) (19%) (Table 9.3). While not statistically significant different characteristics, sport tourists are also more likely to be college educated, married, and under the age of 50.

Discerning tourist. Cluster II tourists on the other hand, were more likely than members of the other clusters to prefer high-quality restaurants ($M = 2.44$), outstanding scenery ($M = 3.53$), environmental quality ($M = 3.49$), outdoor activities ($M = 2.64$), national or provincial parks ($M = 3.16$), museums and art galleries ($M = 2.49$), local cuisine ($M = 2.76$), seeing wildlife, birds and flowers ($M = 2.41$), visiting remote coastal attractions ($M = 2.19$), and historical places ($M = 2.89$) during their pleasure travel (Table 9.1),

Table 9.3 Demographic characteristics of tourists by cluster

Demographics	Cluster I Sport tourist	Cluster II Discerning tourist	Cluster III Resort tourist	Cluster IV Reluctant tourist
Age *				
15–19	7.8	2.5	8.7	6.3
20–24	12.2	5.1	14.4	5.5
25–29	16.7	8.5	17.3	9.4
30–34	21.1	11.0	15.4	15.6
35–39	16.7	10.2	11.5	12.5
40–49	17.8	26.3	16.3	21.1
50–59	6.7	20.3	10.6	13.3
60–64	0.0	5.1	2.9	7.0
65 and over	1.1	11.0	2.9	9.4
Education				
Primary school (grades 1–7)	0.0	0.0	1.0	0.8
Some high school	13.3	10.3	15.4	13.4
Graduated high school (grade 12)	31.1	20.5	26.0	33.9
Graduated technical or vocational school	7.8	6.8	11.5	9.4
Some college or university	18.9	27.4	15.4	14.2
Graduated college or university	4.4	6.0	11.5	9.4
Bachelor's degree	20.0	22.2	13.5	15.0
Masters or Doctorate	4.4	6.8	5.8	3.9
Gender				
Female	42.2	53.4	52.9	57.8
Male	57.8	46.6	47.1	42.2
Marital status				
Single	26.7	19.7	27.9	18.0
Married or living with someone	65.6	72.6	61.5	74.2
Separated or divorced	6.7	2.6	8.7	4.7
Widow/widower	1.1	5.1	1.9	3.1
Income				
Less than $20,000	9.5	3.0	9.9	1.7
$20,001 to $30,000	11.9	20.2	16.8	15.1
$30,001 to $50,000	26.2	18.2	23.8	23.5
$50,001 to $70,000	26.2	31.2	30.7	31.1
$70,001 to $100,000	7.1	15.2	7.9	17.6
Over $100,000	19.0	12.1	10.9	10.9

Note: Significant differences among clusters existed at the .05 level.

The correct classification rate for this cluster was 92.4%. In terms of attitudes towards travel they felt that money spent on travel was money well spent ($M = 3.68$) (Table 9.2). The discerning tourist tended to be aged 40 and above, college educated with 22.2% having earned a bachelors degree and 6.8% a masters or doctorate degree (Table 9.3). Incomes ranged from $20,000 to $30,000 (CDN) (201%) or $50,000 to $70,000 (CDN) (311%). The majority is married although just over 5% are widowed.

Resort tourist. Cluster III tourists placed more importance on a range of activities while on vacation. These golf tourists reported opportunities for arts and cultural attractions ($M = 2.58$), spectator sporting events ($M = 2.76$), shopping ($M = 3.35$), beaches and sunbathing ($M = 3.22$), and theme parks ($M = 2.58$), were important. These tourists were more likely to prefer package trips ($M = 2.72$) and the availability for activities for the entire family was an important consideration ($M = 3.43$) (Table 9.1). The correct classification rate for this cluster was 97.1%. The family nature of these tourists' travel may also account for the importance they placed on the availability of pre-trip information ($M = 3.30$), nice weather ($M = 3.76$), personal safety ($M = 3.88$), and standards of hygiene ($M = 3.90$). They also reported that they would take advantage of currency rates ($M = 3.43$), possibly indicating they might consider vacationing abroad. (For Canadians the strength of the Canadian dollar against the US dollar is a consideration in their travel choices.) In relation to travel attitudes their penchant for safety and familiarity are reinforced as they reported preferring escorted tours when travelling long distance ($M = 2.23$), and being around people who speak the same language ($M = 2.21$) (Table 9.2). Resort tourists tend to be younger than the other types of golf tourist, aged between 15 and 29 years, although tourists of this type are found among those in their 30s and 40s (Table 9.3). A higher percentage are single (27.9%) compared with the other clusters; however, although some are separated or divorced (8.7%), the majority report that they are married. Just over 15% have graduated from high school, 11.5% are technical school graduates and 11.5% are college graduates. Their annual income tends to be moderate, with most reporting incomes between $30,000 to $70,000 (CDN), although slightly more than any of the other cluster members reported incomes less than $20,000 (CDN) (9.9%).

Reluctant tourist. Cluster IV tourists rated all travel preferences lower than any of their counterparts in the other clusters (Table 9.1). The correct classification rate for this cluster was 97.7%. In terms of travel attitudes, they reported that they liked to go to the same place every year for a vacation ($M = 2.25$), they really do not like to travel ($M = 1.38$), and in fact they regard long distance travel as a hassle ($M = 1.88$) (Table 9.2). Reluctant tourists tend to be middle-aged or older, with more members aged between 60 and 64 years (7%) than the other clusters (Table 9.3). Reluctant tourists are more likely to be female (57.8%) and married (74.2%). Just over one-third are high school graduates (31.9%) and most report annual incomes over $30,000, with 17.6% earning between $70,000 and $100,000 (CDN).

Discussion

The overall purpose of this paper was to suggest a theoretical approach that could be used to increase our understanding of sport tourism behavior. Using role theory and tenets from sociology and life span theory, we proposed a framework that could be used to address some of the unanswered questions that have emerged in sport tourism research, notably: (i) is it possible to identify a pure sport tourist? (ii) Do these roles provide insight into other preferences and activities that sport tourists are likely to participate in while on vacation? (iii) Are these preferences and patterns of behaviour associated with particular stages in the life course, gender, and other socio-demographics?

The answer to all three of these questions is basically "yes". In answering the first question—"Is there a pure sport tourist?"—it appears that, rather than identifying one pure sport tourist role, we have identified one type of sport tourist where sport predominates. This is in line with Cohen (1972) and Ryan's (1995) supposition that it is likely that individuals take part in more than one role while on vacation—or, perhaps more to the point, Gibson and Yiannakis' (2002) idea that for Cluster I, sport tourist is the dominant role, and for the others, sport is secondary and is one of various roles. Perhaps among the Canadians who indicated golf is an important component of their vacation, we identified what Faulkner et al. (1998) called the "sports junkie". Secondly, in support of Gibson and Yiannakis' work on the generic active sport tourist, there also appear to be differences by activity preference and vacation style by life stage and gender. In line with the purpose of this paper, which was to explore the application of role theory and its applications in tourism studies to the next stages of sport tourism research, rather than focusing our discussion on an interpretation of the clusters per se, we will answer the question, "So how can role theory be applied to sport tourism?".

Gibson (2004) has called for sport tourism research to go beyond profiling the sport tourist into explaining why different participation styles exist. If we look to traditional applications of role theory in tourism studies, we can see evidence of two primary uses: (i) to distinguish different tourist roles, and (ii) to identify the concepts underlying these roles to explain tourist role preference. In this paper, we were able to identify four different sport tourist types. As we noted earlier, in line with work on event sport tourists, among active sport tourists there does seem to be a collection of behaviours and preferences which have a sport orientation. While, the data did not contain motivational items, the attitudes and preferences expressed seemed to be suggestive of sport tourist types where sport was accorded more importance in a vacation than others (Robinson & Gammon, 2004). We can also draw upon other work in tourism studies that has used multidimensional scaling to suggest what types of tourist behaviour are similar or dissimilar from each other (Pearce, 1985; Yiannakis & Gibson, 1992). In sport tourism research, we have often tried to identify those sport tourists who might be more likely to take part in non-sport related activities during their trip (Garnham, 1996; Gibson et al., 2003; Nogawa, Yamguchi, & Hagi, 1996). For communities who have used sport tourism as an economic development tool, it is very valuable to be able to predict demand for other tourism related services when hosting an event, or indeed to understand how best to leverage a sport tourism event (Chalip & Leyns, 2002). Thus, in the clusters identified in this paper, we can see evidence of other tourist behaviours and preferences among the four clusters, but particularly among the discerning tourists who seem to prefer a more upscale, cultural, and environmentally oriented vacation experiences, compared to the resort tourists who typify Cohen's (1972) organized or individual mass tourists and seek a range of activities in a familiar tourist centred locale. The discerning and the resort tourists can be distinguished still further from the reluctant tourists, who seem to prefer a vacation that is hassle-free and in a familiar environment. Thus, it appears that in sport tourism research we may be able to apply role theory in the same way that general tourism researchers have practised to develop sport tourist role typologies, that in turn may be linked to gender and life stage. While this is a valuable application and certainly may provide a way of answering some of the lingering questions (such as "Is there a pure sport tourist?"), we would like to suggest that the utility of role theory could go much further than this.

Moving beyond the idea that a role is a collection of behaviours into an understanding of the dimensions underlying these behaviours may provide some further insights for sport tourism research. For example, Cohen's (1972) classic use of role theory to identify four tourist roles is under pinned by the idea that some tourists seek familiarity in their vacation experiences, while others seek novelty. The issue of novelty and familiarity has attained heightened relevance over recent years, as it appears that the degree of preference for these two characteristics seems to be an indicator of the degree of risk individuals perceive in a destination (Lepp & Gibson, 2003). Thus, for example, drifter tourists appear to seek out riskier destinations than organized mass tourists. This has relevance to sport tourism in that the threat of terrorism has become particularly pertinent with respect to event sport tourism over the last five years (Kim & Chalip, 2004; Toohey, Taylor & Lee, 2003). For event organizers, understanding which tourists are likely to attend an event where terrorism may be a threat and which tourists are likely to cancel is crucial to the success of an event, and may help them in shaping strategies to counter such negative images. Moreover, when events are held in less familiar destinations, such as the 2008 Olympic Games in China, event organizers will need to implement marketing campaigns that showcase accommodations, food, and transportation that are more akin to Western tastes to counteract the psychological distance associated with China as perceived by the majority of Western tourists (who tend to be independent mass tourists and as such are risk averse).

Another potentially interesting application of role theory is drawn from the symbolic interactionist tradition. There is already a small body of work in sport tourism that has used such concepts as involvement (e.g., McGehee, Yoon, & Cârdenas, 2003), social worlds (e.g., Papadimitriou, Gibson, & Vasioti, 2005), subcultures (e.g., Green & Chalip, 1998), and serious leisure (e.g., Gibson et al., 2002). As we discussed earlier, role theorists have examined the centrality of a particular role to an individual's sense of identity (Goffman, 1974; Sarbin, 1982; Zurcher, 1979). The existing work in sport tourism has found preliminary support for ideas that have been explored extensively in leisure studies, that leisure participation—or, in our case, sport tourism-might be linked to the degree to which individuals are involved or specialized in a particular sport tourist role. This is not only valuable from the point of view of being able to explain differential patterns of sport tourism participation, but it is linked to the wider goal of work in sport, tourism, and leisure studies which is understanding how these domains contribute to the health and well-being of individuals. Thus, perhaps, Zurcher's (1979) concept of an ephemeral role might be useful in this regard. An ephemeral role is a temporary role that provides a break from the demands and constraints of everyday roles and may provide a sense of satisfaction and balance that may be missing from ordinary life. The concept of ephemeral roles has already been applied to bowling (Steele & Zurcher, 1986) and tourism (Yiannakis, 1986) and might provide a way to understand the significance of golf tourism or serious fandom to individuals in societies which have lost many of the traditional sources of both personal and social identity (Putnam, 2001). This might have particular significance to sport and tourism identities that are increasingly shaped by media images. Certainly, in tourism studies, the importance of the media is well documented in its influence on destination image and choice (e.g., Urry, 1990; Watson & Kopachevsky, 1994) and likewise role theorists such as Zurcher (1977) and Turner (1976) have postulated that the media may be more influential in shaping roles today than in the past.

Finally, the issue of inequality is not that well developed in sport tourism (Gibson, 1998b) and may possibly be explored within the context of role theory. As discussed earlier, Turner (1979)/80) proposed that in terms of role selection, we need to pay attention to role fit and role desirability, and Callero (1994) suggested that role incumbents have differential access to economic and social capital. Certainly, in sport tourism, studies on skiing have uncovered gender differences in relation to participation in the sport and have largely explained the differences using a constraints framework (e.g., Hudson, 2000; Williams & Lattey, 1994; Williams & Fidgeon, 2000). Perhaps understanding the influence of both agency and structure in relation to role choice, or participation in different types of sport and sport tourism, might be aided by an understanding that roles differ in the power accorded to them, and that access to the more desirable roles (skier or golfer) might not be just a matter of individual choice (i.e. agency), but based on social structural forces such as gender, race, class, and age.

Conclusion

In summary, it appears that the tenets of role theory, particularly the idea of an integrated role theory (Biddle, 1986; Callero, 1994; Turner, 1979/80) hold some potential for both identifying and furthering our understanding of different types of sport tourist. Sport tourist role typologies can be used both as a classificatory tool and as a way of understanding behavioral choices. We would suggest that the latter usage should be emphasized in future sport tourism research. Gibson (2004) suggested that it is time to move beyond developing profiles in sport tourism research to understanding why people do what they do. Thus, our hope in writing this paper is that the different types of sport (golf) tourist derived from our analysis are not regarded solely as profiles, but that our use of socio-psychological factors and the underlying dimensions of tourist role theory to propose an explanation for these different sport (golf) tourist styles is taken as a starting point for future work in sport tourism research of this sort.

Acknowledgements

The data used for this study were made available by the Canadian Tourism Commission. The data for Canadian (1995) Domestic Tourism Market Research Study was originally prepared by Coopers & Lybrand Consulting. Neither the preparer of the original data nor the Canadian Tourism Commission bears any responsibility for the analysis or the interpretations presented here.

References

Beard, J., & Ragheb, M. (1983). Measuring leisure motivation. *Journal of Leisure Research*, *15*, 219–228.

Biddle, B. (1986). Recent development in role theory. *Annual Review of Sociology*, *12*, 67–92.

Birenhaum, A. (1984). Toward a theory of role acquisition. *Sociological Theory*, *2*, 315–328.

Birrell, S., & Richter, D.M. (1987). Is a diamond forever? Feminist transformations of sport. *Women Studies International Forum*, *10*, 395–409.

Bojanic, D. (1992). A look at a modernized family life cycle and overseas travel. *Journal of Travel and Tourism Marketing*, *1*(1), 61–79.

Bojanic, D., & Warnick, R. (1995). Segmenting the market for winter vacations. *Journal of Travel and Tourism Marketing*, *4*, 85–96.

Butler, K. (1995). Independence for western women through tourism. *Annals of Tourism Research*, *22*, 487–489.

Callero, P. (1994). From role playing to role using: Understanding role as resource. *Social Psychology Quarterly*, *57*, 228–243.

Chalip, L., & Leyns, A. (2002). Local business leveraging of a sport event: Managing an event for economic benefit. *Journal of Sport Management*, *16*, 132–158.

Cohen, E. (1972). Toward a sociology of international tourism. *Social Research*, *39*, 164–182.

Cohen, E. (1974). Who is a tourist?: A conceptual clarification. *Sociological Review*, *22*, 527–555.

Cohen, E. (1979). A phenomenology of tourist experiences. *Sociology*, *13*, 179–201.

Cohen, E. (1984). The sociology of tourism: Approaches, issues and findings. *Annual Review of Sociology*, *10*, 373–392.

Cole, C. (1993). Feminist cultural studies, sport and technologies of the body. *Journal of Sport and Social Issues*, *17*, 77–97.

Coopers & Lybrand (1995). *Domestic Tourism Market Research Study*. Ottawa: The Canadian Tourism Commission.

Dionigi, R. (2002). Leisure and identity management in later life: Understanding competitive sport participation among older adults. *World Leisure*, *3*, 4–15.

Donnelly, P., & Young, K. (1988). The construction and confirmation of identity in sport subcultures. *Sociology of Sport Journal*, *5*, 223–240.

Durkheim, F. (1893/1984). *The Division of Labor in Society*. Trans. W. Halls. New York: Macmillan.

Frederick, J., Havitz, M., & Shaw, S. (1994). Social comparison in aerobic exercise classes: Propositions for analyzing motives and participation. *Leisure Sciences*, *16*(3), 161–176.

Faulkner, W., Tideswell, C., & Weston, A. (1998). *Leveraging Tourism Benefits from the Sydney 2000 Olympics*. Keynote presentation at Sport Management: Opportunities and Change, Fourth Annual Conference of the Sport Management Association of Australia and New Zealand, Gold Coast, Australia, 26–28, November.

Gammon, S., & Robinson, T. (1997/2005). Sport and tourism: A conceptual framework. *Journal of Sport Tourism*, *8*, 21–26.

Garnham, B. (1996). Ranfurly Shield Rugby: An investigation into the impacts of a sporting event on a provincial city, the case of New Plymouth. *Festival Management and Event Tourism*, *4*, 145–249.

Gerhardt, U. (1980). Toward a critical analysis of role. *Social Problems*, *27*(5), 556–569.

Gibson, H. (1989). Tourist roles: Stability and change over the life cycle. Unpublished master's thesis, University of Connecticut, Storrs.

Gibson, H. (1994). Some predictors of tourist rule preference for men and women over the adult life course. Unpublished doctoral dissertation, The University of Connecticut, Storrs.

Gibson, H. (1996). Thrill seeking vacations: A lifespan perspective. *Loisir et Societe/Society and Leisure, 19*(2), 439–458.

Gibson, H. (1998a). Sport tourism: A critical analysis of research. *Sport Management Review, 1*, 45–76.

Gibson, H. (1998b). Active sport tourism: Who participates? *Leisure Studies, 17*(2), 155–170.

Gibson, H. (2002) Sport tourism at a crossroad? Considerations for the future. In S. Gammon & J. Kurtzman (Eds), *Sport Tourism: Principles and Practice* (pp. 123–140). Eastbourne, UK: LSA Publications no. 76.

Gibson, H. (2004). Moving beyond the "What is and Who" of sport tourism no understanding "why". *Journal of Sport Tourism, 9*, 247–265.

Gibson, H., & Yiannakis, A. (2002). Tourist roles: Needs and the adult life course. *Annals of Tourism Research, 29*, 358–383.

Gibson, H., Ashnon-Shaeffer, C., Green, J., Kensinger, K., (2002). "It wouldn't be long before I'd be friends with an undertaker:" What it means to be a senior athlete. Paper presented at the Leisure Research Symposium, National Recreation and Park Associations Congress, Tampa, FL, October 16–49, 2002.

Gibson, H., Willming, C., & Holdnak, A. (2002). "We're Gators not just a Gator fan:" Serious leisure, social identity and University of Florida football. *Journal of Leisure Research, 14*, 397–425.

Gibson, H., Willming, C., & Holdnak, A, (2003). Small-scale event sport tourism: College sport as a tourist attraction. *Tourism Management, 24*, 181–190.

Giulianonti, K., & Armstrong, G. (2002) Avenues of contestation. Football hooligans running and ruling urban spaces. *Social Anthropology, 10*(2), 211–238.

Goffman, F. (1959). *The Presentation of Self in Everyday Life.* Garden City, NY: Doubleday.

Goffman, E. (1974). *Frame Analysis: An Essay on the Organization of Experience.* New York: Harper & Row.

Gratron, C., & Kokolakakis, T. (2005). Trends in sports participation in Britain: 1977–2002. *The Power of Sport.* Book of abstracts of the 13th congress of the European Association for Sport Management/75th ISRM annual conference, 7–10 September 2005 (pp. 121–122), Newcastle Gateshead, UK.

Green, B., & Chalip, L. (1998). Sport tourism as the celebration of subculture. *Annals of Tourism Research, 25*, 275–292.

Greendorfer, S., & Lewko, H. (1978). Role of family members in sport socialization of children. *Research Quarterly, 49*, 146–152.

Graburn, N. (1983). The anthropology of tourism. *Annals of Tourism Research, 10*, 9–33.

Guttman, A. (1988). *Whole New Ball Game: An Interpretation of American Sports.* Chapel Hill, NC: University of North Carolina Press.

Haggard, L., & Williams, C. (1992). Identity affirmation through leisure activities: Leisure symbols of the self. *Journal of Leisure Research, 24*, 1–18.

Hall, C. (1992). Adventure, sport and health tourism. In B. Weiler & C.M. Hall (Eds), *Special Interest Tourism* (pp. 141–158). London: Belhaven Press.

Handel, W. (1979). Normative expectations and the emergence of meanings and solutions to problems: Convergence of structural and interactionist views. *The American Journal of Sociology, 84*, 855–881.

Hargreaves, J. (1994). *Sporting Females: Critical Issues in the History and Sociology of Women's Sports.* London: Routledge.

Hilbert, R. (1981). Toward an improved understanding of role. *Theory and Society, 10*, 207–226.

Hinch, T., & Higham, J. (2001). Sport tourism: A framework for research. *International Journal of Tourism Research, 3*, 45–58.

Hudson, S. (2000). The segmentation of potential tourists: Constraint differences between men and women. *Journal of Travel Research*, *38*(4), 363–369.

Iso-Ahola, S. (1983). Toward a social psychology of recreational travel. *Leisure Studies*, *2*, 45–56.

Jordan, F., & Gibson, H. (2005). "We're not stupid . . . but we'll not stay home either": Experiences of solo women travelers. *Tourism Review International*, *9*, 1–17.

Kane, M.J. (1989). The post Title IX female athlete in the media. *Journal of Physical Education, Recreation and Dance*, *60* (March), 58–62.

Kelly, J. (1999). Leisure behaviors and styles: Social, economic, and cultural factors. In C. Jackson, & T. Burton (Eds), *Leisure Studies: Prospects for the Twenty-first Century* (pp. 135–150). State College, PA: Venture Publishing.

Kim, N., & Chalip, L. (2004). Why travel to the FIFA World Cup? *Tourism Management*, *25*, 695–707.

Kinnaird, V., & Hall, D. (Eds). (1994). *Tourism: A Gender Analysis*. Chichester: Wiley.

Lawson, R. (1991). Patterns of tourist expenditure and types of vacation across the family life cycle. *Journal of Travel Research*, *21*, 12–18.

Lenskyj, H. (1994). Sexuality and femininity in sport contexts: Issues and alternatives. *Journal of Sport and Social Issues*, *18*, 356–376.

Lepp, A., & Gibson, H. (2003). Tourist roles, perceived risk and international tourism. *Annals of Tourism Research*, *30*, 606–624.

Levinson, D., Darrow, C., Klein, C., Levinson, N., & McKee, B. (1978), *The Seasons of a Man's Life*. New York: Knopf.

Levinson, D. (1996). *The Seasons of a Woman's Life*. New York: Knopf.

Linton, R. (1936). *The Study of Man*. New York: Appleton-Century.

MacCannell, D. (1976). *The Tourist: A New Theory of the Leisure Class*. New York: Schocken Books.

Markula, P. (1995). Firm but shapely, fit but sexy, strong but thin: The postmodern aerobicizing female bodies. *Sociology of Sport Journal*, *12*, 424–453.

McGehee, N.G., Loker-Murphy, L., & Uysal, M. (1996). The Australian international pleasure travel market: motivations from a gendered perspective. *The Journal of Tourism Studies*, *7*(1), 45–57.

McGehee, N., Yoon, Y., & Cárdenas, D. (2003). Involvement and travel for recreational runners in North Carolina. *Journal of Sport Management*, *17*, 305–324.

McPherson, B.D. (1984). Sport participation across the life cycle: A review of the literature and suggestions for future research. *Sociology of Sport Journal*, *1*, 213–230.

Mead, G. (1934). *Mind, Self and Society*, Chicago, IL: University of Chicago Press.

Merton, R. (1957). The role-set: Problems in sociological theory. *British Journal of Sociology*, *8*, 106–120.

Mo, C., Howard, D., & Havitz, M. (1993). Testing an international tourist role typology. *Annals of Tourism Research*, *20*, 319–335.

Murdy, J. (2001). Predicting Tourist Roles Across The Life Course. Unpublished doctoral dissertation, The University of Connecticut, Storrs, CT.

Newman, R. (2002). The American church of baseball and the National Baseball Hall of Fame. *Journal of Baseball History and Culture*, 46–63.

Nichols, C. & Snepenger, U. (1988). Family decision-making and tourism behaviour and attitudes. *Journal of Travel Research*, Spring, 2–6.

Nogawa, H., Yamguchi, Y., & Hagi, Y. (1996). An empirical research study on Japanese sport tourism in Sport-for-All Events: Case studies of a single-night event and a multiple-night event. *Journal of Travel Research*, *35*, 46–54.

Papadimitriou, D., Gibson, H., & Vasioti, E. (2005). *Applying the concept of social world to the study of winter sport tourists*. Book of abstracts of the 13th congress of the European Association for Sport Management/75th ISRM annual conference, 7–10 September 2005 (pp. 215–216), Newcastle Gateshead, UK.

Parsons, T. (1951). *The Social System*. Glencoe, IL: Free Press.

Participation U.S. research menu: Total participation by age group, by sport (n.d.). Retrieved May 2, 2004 from http://www.sbrnet.com/Research/Research.cfm?subRID=457.

Pearce, P. (1982). *The Social Psychology of Tourist Behaviour*. Oxford: Pergamon.

Pearce, P. (1985). A systematic comparison of travel-related roles, *Human Relations*, *38*, 1001–1011.

Petrick, J. (2002). An examination of golf vacationers' novelty. *Annals of Tourism Research*, *29*, 381 400.

Priestley, G. (1993). Sports tourism: The case of golf. In G.J. Ashworth, & A.G.J. Dietvorst (Eds). *Tourism and Spatial Transformations: Implications for Policy and Planning* (pp. 205–223). Wallingford: CAB International.

Putnam, R. (2001). *Bowling Alone: The Collapse and Revival of American Community*. New York: Simon & Schuster.

Rapoport, R., & Rapoport, R. (1975). *Leisure and the Family Life Cycle*. London: Routledge & Kegan Paul.

Redmond, C. (1991). Changing styles of sports tourism: Industry/consumer interactions in Canada, the USA and Europe. In M. Sinclair, & M. Stabler (Eds), *The Tourism Industry: An International Analysis* (pp. 107–120). Wallingford: CAB International.

Riley, P. (1988). Road culture of international long term budget travelers. *Annals of Tourism Research*, *15*, 313–328.

Ritchie, B., Mosedale, L., & King, J. (2000). Profiling sport tourists: The case of Super 12 Rugby Union in Canberra. In B. Ritchie & D. Adair (Eds), *Sports Generated Tourism: Exploring the Nexus* (pp. 57–67). Proceedings of the first Australian Sports Tourism Symposium, October 5–7, 2000, Canberra, Australia.

Robinson, T., & Gammon, S. (2004). A question of primary and secondary motives: Revisiting and applying the sport tourism framework. *Journal of Sport Tourism*, *9*(3), 221–233.

Rudman, W.J. (1986). Life course socioeconomic transitions and sport involvement: A theory of restricted opportunity. In B.D. McPherson (Ed.), *Sport and Aging: The 1984 Olympic Scientific Congress Proceedings*, Vol. 5 (pp. 25–36). Champaign, IL: Human Kinetics.

Ryan, C. (1997). *The Tourist Experience: A New Introduction*. London: Cassell.

Ryan, C. (1995). Islands, beaches and life-stage marketing. In M. Conlin, & T. Baum (Eds), *Island Tourism: Management Principles and Practice* (pp. 79–93). New York: John Wiley & Sons.

Sage, G., & Loudermilk, S. (1979). The female athlete and role conflict, *Research Quarterly*, *50*, 88–96.

Sarbin, T. (1982). A preface to a psychological theory of metaphor. In V. Allen & K. Scheibe (Eds), *The Social Context of Conduct: Psychological Writings of T. R Sarbin* (pp. 233–249). New York: Praeger.

Shamir, B. (1992). Some correlates of leisure identity salience: Three exploratory studies. *Journal of Leisure Research*, *24*, 301–323.

Shaw, M., & Costanzo, P. (1982). *Theories of Social Psychology*. New York: McGraw Hill.

Smith, V. (Ed.) (1977). *Hosts and Guests: The Anthropology of Tourism*. Philadelphia, PA: University of Pennsylvania Press.

Snyder, E. (1991). Sociology of nostalgia: Sports halls of fame and museums in America. *Sociology of Sport Journal*, *8*, 228–238.

Snyder, E., & Spreitzer, E. (1987). Change and variation in the social acceptance of female participation in sports. In A. Yiannakis, T. Mcintyre, M. Melnick, & D. Hart (Eds), *Sport Sociology: Contemporary Themes* (3rd edition). Dubuque, IA: Kendall/Hunt.

Squire, S.J. (1994). Gender and tourist experiences: assessing women's shared meanings of Beatrix Potter. *Leisure Studies*, *13*, 195–209.

Standevan, J., & De Knop, P. (1999). *Sport Tourism*. Champaign, IL: Human Kinetics.

Steele, P., & Zurcher, L. (1986). Leisure sports as "ephemeral roles": An exploratory study. In A. Yiannakis, T. McIntyre, M. Melnick, & D. Hart (Eds), *Sport Sociology: Contemporary Themes* (pp. 265–269). Dubuque, IA: Kendall/Hunt.

Stevenson, C. (2002). Seeking identities: Toward an understanding of the athletic careers of master's swimmers. *International Review for the Sociology of Sport*, *37*(2), 131–146.

Toohey, K., Taylor, T., & Lee, C. (2003). The FIFA World Cup 2002: The effects of terrorism on sport tourists. *Journal of Sport Tourism*, *8*, 167–185.

Turner, R. (1976). The real sell: From institution to impulse. *American Journal of Sociology*, *84*, 1–23.

Turner, R. (1979/80). Strategy for developing an integrated role theory. *Humboldt Journal of Social Relations*, *7*(1), 123–139.

Urry, J. (1990). *The Tourist Gaze: Leisure and Travel in Contemporary Societies*. London: Sage Publications.

Watson, G., & Kopachevsky, J. (1994). Interpretations of tourism as commodity. In Y. Apostolopoulos, S. Leivadi, & A. Yiannakis (Eds), *Sociology of Tourism* (pp. 281–300). London: Routledge.

Weed, M. (2005). A grounded theory of the policy process for sport and tourism. *Sport in Society*, *8*(2), 356–377.

Wilson, A. (2004). The relationship between consumer role socialization and nostalgia sport tourism: A symbolic interactionist perspective. Unpublished master's thesis, University of Florida, Gainesville.

Williams, P., & Lattey, C. (1994). Skiing constraints for women. *Journal of Travel Research*, *32*, 21–25.

Williams, P., & Fidgeon, P. (2000). Addressing participation constraint: A case study of potential skiers. *Tourism Management*, *21*, 379–393.

Winship, C., & Mandel, M. (1983). Roles and positions: A critique and extension of the blockmodeling approach. In S. Leinhardt (Ed.), *Sociological Methodology 1983–1984* (pp. 314–344). San Francisco, CA: Jossey-Bass.

Yiannakis, A. (1986). The ephemeral role of the tourist: Some correlates of tourist role preference. Paper presented at the NASSS Conference, Las Vegas, Nevada, October, 1986.

Yiannakis, A. (n.d.a.) Informal roles on sport teams. Unpublished manuscript, University of Connecticut, Storrs, USA.

Yiannakis, A., & Gibson, H. (1988). Tourist role preference and need satisfaction: Some continuities and discontinuities over the life course. Paper presented at the Leisure Studies Association Conference, Brighton, England. 29 June–3 July, 1988.

Yiannakis, A., & Gibson, H. (1992). Roles tourists play. *Annals of Tourism Research*, *19*, 287–303.

Zurcher, L. (1977). *The Mutable Self: A Self-Concept for Social Change*. Beverly Hills, CA: Sage.

Zurcher, L. (1979). Role selection: The influence of internalized vocabularies of motive. *Symbolic Interaction*, *2*, 45–62.

Chapter 10

James F. Petrick and
Sheila J. Backman

AN EXAMINATION OF THE
DETERMINANTS OF GOLF
TRAVELERS' SATISFACTION

WHILE LITTLE CHANGE has occurred in the total number of golfers in the United States over the past decade, the number of golf courses is quickly increasing (A. Crocco, personal communication, March 3, 1997). Since 1990, the total number of golfers has decreased from 27.8 million to 26.5 million, while the number of golf courses has increased from 12,846 to 14,602 (National Golf Foundation 1998). Furthermore, 1998 saw an estimated all-time high of 485 new courses completed (Dye 1998).

Conversely, the market of traveling golfers has been steadily increasing. In 1989, there were approximately 8 million golf travelers compared to 10.5 million in 1994, a compound annual growth rate of nearly 6% (National Golf Foundation 1995). Furthermore, golfers who travel on business have been shown to have a greater economic impact on the hotel industry than nongolfers who travel on business. Golfers travel more frequently, stay longer, and spend more money than nongolfing business travelers (National Golf Foundation 1995).

Since the traveling golfer market has been shown to be increasing and substantial, it appears relevant for resort managers to examine the variables that influence traveling golfers to use and return to their facilities. A variable that has been shown to be related to purchase intentions and repeat purchase behavior is consumer satisfaction (Spreng, Mackenzie, and Olshavsky 1996; Williams 1989).

Background

Numerous studies have examined the relationship between tourists' satisfaction levels and their intentions to repurchase the experience (Barsky 1992). The underlying assumption of these studies is that if an experience has a positive affect on an individual, he or she is more likely to repeat the activity enjoyed. While there is no guarantee that a satisfied consumer will be a repeat visitor, quite often a dissatisfied customer will not return (Dube, Renaghan, and Miller 1994). If management knows how the components of a product or service affect consumers' satisfaction today, the challenge of planning for future consumers may be limited almost exclusively to adapting current products and services to match the current "customer satisfaction forecast" (Barsky and Labagh 1992).

With the concept of satisfaction being interpreted differently by each individual, the definitions given are quite varied. Most academician definitions involve a comparison between expectations and experience. One of the most widely cited definitions in recreation satisfaction research is that of Bultena and Klessig (1969). They stated that a satisfactory experience "is a function of the degree of congruency between aspirations and the perceived reality of experiences" (p. 349). From a purely cognitive outlook, Hunt (1977) stated that "satisfaction is not the pleasurableness of the experience, it is the evaluation rendered that the experience was at least as good as it was supposed to be" (p. 459). Yet, others have argued that satisfaction is nothing more than brand attitude (LaTour and Peat 1979). Similar to recreation satisfaction, consumer satisfaction has been conceptualized as a cognitive appraisal of the degree to which a product or service performs relative to a subjective standard (Williams 1989).

"The dominant conceptual model in the satisfaction literature is the disconfirmation of expectations paradigm" (Patterson, Johnson, and Spreng 1997, p. 5). The disconfirmation paradigm is a contrast approach in which satisfaction is a function of an initial standard or reference point and some discrepancy from the initial reference point (Williams 1989). The contrast model most frequently used by tourism researchers was developed by Oliver (1980). According to his model, feelings of satisfaction arise when consumers compare their perceptions of a product's performance to their expectations. Thus, if perceived performance is greater than expectations (termed a positive disconfirmation), they are satisfied. Conversely, if one's perceived performance is less than their expectation, negative disconfirmation (or dissatisfaction) occurs.

Although central to the disconfirmation paradigm, the effects that expectations have on satisfaction have been argued (Barsky 1992; Spreng, Mackenzie, and Olshavsky 1996; Williams 1989). According to Barsky (1992), while expectations have been generally accepted as affecting satisfaction, there is not conclusive evidence that they directly lead to satisfaction or dissatisfaction. One problem with the model is that as expectations decrease, satisfaction inevitably must increase. Thus, the model suggests that if a consumer expects and receives poor performance, he or she will be satisfied (LaTour and Peat 1979).

Another problem is that recreation product attributes are ambiguous in their character (Barsky 1992; Williams 1989). For this reason, several studies suggest that a leisure product's performance may be the crucial determinant of future purchase intentions and good word of mouth instead of expectations or disconfirmation (Levitt 1981; Olshavsky and Miller 1972; Whipple and Thatch 1988). It has further been suggested by LaTour and Peat (1979) that consumers' evaluations of product attributes themselves may account for more of the variability in satisfaction than would the confirmation or disconfirmation of expectations about those attributes.

Recent research has suggested that the comparison of desires to performance (desires congruency) should be used in conjunction with a measure of the disconfirmation of expectations (Spreng, Mackenzie, and Olshavsky 1996). Desires are defined as "the attributes, levels of attributes, and benefits that the consumer believes will lead to or are connected with higher-level values" (Spreng and Olshavsky 1993, p. 171). Similar to disconfirmation of expectations, Spreng, Mackenzie, and Olshavsky (1996) used the comparison of desires to performance. The outcome of this comparison is termed *desires congruency* and is conceptualized as a distinct construct that represents the consumer's subjective assessment of how well the performance of a product or service matches one's desires.

While expectations can only be affected by attributes or characteristics that a consumer is aware of prior to use, the desires model allows satisfaction to be affected by any aspect of a product. According to Levitt (1981),

> the most important thing to know about intangible products is that customers usually don't know what they're getting into until they don't get it. Only then do they become aware of what they bargained for; only on dissatisfaction do they dwell. Satisfaction is, as it should be, mute. Its existence is affirmed only by its absence.
>
> (p. 96)

Thus, a measure of desires may be more accurate for intangible products (i.e., a golf vacation).

Past research has operationalized satisfaction at both the global (overall satisfaction) and attribute (attribute satisfaction) levels. Attribute satisfaction has been defined as "the consumer's subjective satisfaction judgment resulting from observations of attribute performance" (Oliver 1993, p. 421). It has been suggested that it is important to maintain a distinction between attribute satisfaction and overall satisfaction since overall satisfaction is based on the overall experience, not just the individual attributes (Spreng, Mackenzie, and Olshavsky 1996). Furthermore, attribute-specific satisfaction is not the only antecedent of overall satisfaction.

Another recognized antecedent of overall satisfaction is information satisfaction. Using a marketing perspective, Spreng, Mackenzie, and Olshavsky (1996) have shown that satisfaction with the information provided prior to purchase explains a significant amount of the variance in consumer satisfaction and that attribute satisfaction does not. Information satisfaction is defined as a subjective satisfaction judgment of the prepurchase information used in choosing a service (Spreng, Mackenzie, and Olshavsky 1996). While consumers form expectations about a destination from several sources, of particular interest to the recreation professional are those expectations controlled through marketing. Because a great deal of physical and monetary effort is given to the marketing of a destination, it is believed that this dimension is important to analyze.

Past research has shown that marketer-supplied information is compared to product performance when a consumer assesses their level of satisfaction. According to Gardial *et al.* (1994), 18% of the reasons respondents give for attributing an experience as either satisfying or dissatisfying are related to prepurchase, marketer-supplied information. Thus, satisfaction with a product or service is more than an affective reaction to the attributes of the product or service itself and includes a reaction to marketed information.

When a consumer uses information in choosing a destination to visit, the information forms expectations about the experience. When these expectations are disconfirmed, the consumer can be satisfied or dissatisfied with the experience itself, and the information provided, prior to the experience. For example, if a golf resort markets information that is inaccurate, the golf traveler will most likely be dissatisfied with the information used to select their destination. This process will inevitably affect the consumer's perception of satisfaction with the entire experience. Therefore, in following the work of Gardial *et al.* (1994) and Spreng, Mackenzie, and Olshavsky (1996), information satisfaction is proposed as a key mediating construct for the prediction of overall satisfaction.

While there are likely to be other antecedents to overall satisfaction, it is believed that the tangibility of both attribute and information satisfaction makes them important to golf resort management. Less tangible antecedents would include personal attitudes and values. While part of the satisfaction process, these antecedents cannot be controlled as easily by management. With the identification of tangible antecedents, resort management is more capable of altering the golf traveler's experience to maximize satisfaction. Thus, from a managerial standpoint, it is important to identify how both the attributes of the destination and the information provided contribute to a consumers' overall satisfaction.

The current model proposes that expectations congruency has a positive effect on attribute satisfaction since consumers assess at the attribute level whether a product or service has performed as expected. Furthermore, the current model proposes that expectations congruency has a positive effect on information satisfaction. Thus, if a consumer is told that a destination will provide certain amenities (e.g., has an indoor pool) and this attribute is negatively disconfirmed, then the consumer is likely to be dissatisfied. Therefore, the current study postulates that golf travelers' satisfaction is composed of disconfirmation of expectations as antecedents of attribute and information satisfaction, which inevitably predict overall satisfaction.

Purpose of the study

With an increasing competition for attracting golf travelers to individual sites, it is becoming more important for managers to identify the variables that assist in the attraction and/or retention of golf travelers. Research has shown that satisfaction is an important predictor of intention to revisit. Yet, relatively little is known about the determinants of, and best way to measure, golf travelers' satisfaction. Thus, the purpose of the present study was to investigate the determinants of golf travelers' overall satisfaction.

Three research questions, with subsequent hypotheses, were developed to guide this study:

1   Can the variables of expectations congruency, desires congruency, attribute satisfaction, and information satisfaction be effectively used to predict golf travelers' satisfaction?

> *Hypothesis 1*:   Attribute congruency will have a positive effect on attribute satisfaction, information congruency will have a positive effect on inform-ation satisfaction and attribute satisfaction, and both attribute and information satisfaction will be positively related to overall satisfaction.

2   What attributes of a golf vacation are best at predicting golf travelers' satisfaction?

> *Hypothesis 2*:   Attributes related to the golfing experience will be better predictors of overall satisfaction, followed by attributes related to the resort and attributes related to information provided.

3   What is the correlation between golf travelers' satisfaction and their intention to revisit?

> *Hypothesis 3:* Golf travelers' satisfaction will be positively correlated to intentions to revisit.

Research method

Pilot test

A pilot test of all the proposed variables was done by systematically distributing the proposed survey to resort visitors. In all, 49 questionnaires were distributed, and 41 were returned. Results from the pilot test ($n = 41$) helped to create the attributes of satisfaction and examined the reliability of the instrument's scales.

Similar to Spreng, Mackenzie, and Olshavsky (1996), desires congruency and expectations congruency were measured in the pilot test to investigate the utility of both measures in the overall model. It was found that measuring both expectations and desires congruency was taxing on respondents. Numerous respondents ($n = 27$) complained about the length of the survey and/or the redundancy of the measures of desires and expectations congruency. Results revealed that for all six attributes, expectations congruency was more highly correlated with overall satisfaction than was desires congruency. Therefore, the measures of desires congruency were not included in the current analysis, making the model more parsimonious and less taxing on respondents.

Sample and questionnaire

For the overall study, subjects ($N = 1,000$) were selected using a stratified, systematic sampling procedure. This was done by using the resort's database of visitors that booked a golf vacation during the fall season. Fall season was defined by changes in pricing rates. Strata by geographic location were created by ordering golf travelers by zip code in the database. The sample was also proportionately selected by week of visit.

Using a modified Dillman (1978) technique, 448 of 877 (123 bad addresses) questionnaires were returned for a response rate of 51.1%. A non-response check was conducted at the conclusion of data collection and found no significant ($p < .05$) differences on any of the variables examined (demographics, satisfaction, perceived value, and intentions to revisit). Of the golf travelers who participated, the average age was 51.9, median household income was $50,000 to $74,999, 94.8% were male, and 57.8% had completed 4 years of college.

Similar to Spreng, Mackenzie, and Olshavsky (1996), satisfaction was operationalized using measurements of expectations (four items) and information (two items) congruency (expectations minus performance), attribute satisfaction (four items), information satisfaction (two items), and overall satisfaction (four items). Overall satisfaction was measured by asking subjects about their overall experience. Four 10-point Likert-type scales anchored by *very dissatisfied/very satisfied, very displeased/very pleased, frustrated/contented,* and *terrible/delighted* were used. Respondent's score for overall satisfaction was determined to be the sum of all four scales.

Attribute and information congruency were operationalized by measuring respondents' expectations and perceived performance for each of the attributes used in the study. Attributes were derived through discussion with resort management and with the aid of an open-ended question ("What aspects of your golf vacation most influenced your overall satisfaction?") during the pilot test. The attributes used were the following: "resort facilities." "resort service," "quality of golf courses," "number of golf courses," "information about the resort," and "golf information." Expectations for the four attributes comprising attribute expectations and two attributes comprising information expectations were measured by asking respondents what they expect from each of the attributes on their next vacation at (the test resort). The six items were placed on a 7-point Likert-type scale anchored by *highly unexpected* and *highly expected.*

Performance of each of the attributes was measured by asking respondents how they would rate the performance of each of the attributes. The six items were placed on a 7-point Likert-type scale anchored by *extremely, poor performance* and *extremely good performance.*

Attribute congruency was the resulting difference from the scores on performance of the four attributes related to golf and the resort minus the scores on the expectations of the four attributes related to golf and the resort. Information congruency was similarly operationalized with the use of the two attributes related to information.

Satisfaction with each of the golf course and resort attributes chosen for the study and the information provided was measured by asking, "Thinking just about each of the following attributes, how satisfied were you with it," followed by a listing of the attributes. Ten-point scales were used, anchored *by very dissatisfied* and *very satisfied.* Attribute satisfaction was the sum of the attributes related to the golf courses and the resort, while information satisfaction was the sum of the attributes of information provided.

Similar to Grewal, Monroe, and Krishnan (1998), intention to repurchase was operationalized with a two-item, 5-point scale anchored by 1 (*very low*) and 5 (*very high*). The first item stated, "If I were to purchase a golf vacation, the probability that the vacation would be at the XYZ Resort in (name of city) is . . ." The second item stated, "The likelihood that I would consider purchasing a golf vacation to the XYZ Resort again is . . ." The respondent's score for intention to visit was the sum of both items.

Results

To examine the reliability of the scales used in the study, Cronbach's alpha coefficients were calculated. All scales were found to have Cronbach's alphas greater than 0.70 and were thus deemed acceptable (see Table 10.1).

Path analysis, using SAS system's proc calis statement with maximum likelihood estimation, was used to examine the first hypothesis. As suggested by Hu and Bender (1998). multiple fit indices were used, fit indices greater than 0.90 would suggest a good fit of the data, and fit indices greater than 0.95 would suggest an excellent fit of the data.

It was hypothesized that attribute congruency would have a positive effect on attribute satisfaction, information congruency would have a positive effect on information satisfaction, information satisfaction would be positively related to attribute satisfaction, and both attribute satisfaction and information satisfaction would be positively related to overall satisfaction. The hypothesized paths originated from Spreng, Mackenzie, and Olshavsky

Table 10.1 Reliability coefficients of scales used in the study

Variable	Number of items	Reliability coefficient
Intention to revisit	2	0.90
Overall satisfaction	4	0.96
Attribute satisfaction	4	0.81
Information satisfaction	2	0.88
Attribute performance	4	0.71
Information performance	2	0.78
Attribute expectations	4	0.82
Information expectations	2	0.83
Attribute congruency	4	0.74
Information congruency	2	0.76

(1996) and Oliver (1980). Contrary to Spreng, Mackenzie, and Olshavsky, desires congruency was not included in the model. Results of the pilot test suggested that desires congruency was not related to overall satisfaction. Furthermore, respondents found its measurement to be cumbersome. Attribute congruency and information congruency served as exogenous variables, while all other variables were endogenous.

Table 10.2 reveals the results of the chi-square analysis and the fit indices of the proposed model. The chi-square statistic analyzes the fit of the overall model. A small chi-square value reflects that the model provides a good fit. Literature has suggested that goodness-of-fit indices more accurately reflect a model's goodness of fit for the value of chi-square is inflated with sample sizes greater than 250 (Hu and Bentler 1998). Hu and Bentler (1998) further suggested that to better represent a model's goodness of fit, multiple indices should be used. Results of all three fit indices suggest that the model is an excellent fit of the data. The measurement model displayed values greater than 0.95 on Bentler and Bonett's (1980) normed-fit index, the Lisrel goodness-of-fit index, and Bentler's (1989) comparative fit index. Therefore, the model was tentatively accepted, pending further tests to examine its reliability and validity.

Standardized factor loadings (path coefficients) are shown in Figure 10.1. The SAS system's proc calis procedure further provides large-sample t-tests of the null hypothesis that each of the coefficients are equal to zero. The t values (displayed in parentheses in Figure 10.1) for all path coefficients were significant ($p < .05$), suggesting that all hypothesized paths are assisting in the prediction of overall satisfaction. These results

Table 10.2 Goodness-of-fit indices: satisfaction formation model

Model	N	Chi-square	df	p	NFI	GFI	CFI
Satisfaction formation	448	30.25	4	<.01	0.970	0.971	0.974

Note: NFI = normed-fit index; GFI = goodness-of-fit index; CFI = comparative fit index.

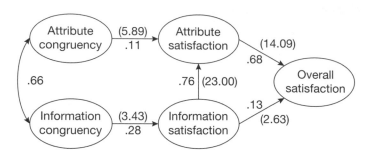

Figure 10.1 Results of satisfaction formation model

provide evidence that supports the convergent validity of the indicators (Anderson and Gerbing 1988).

A considerable amount of the variance was explained for overall satisfaction (62%) and attribute satisfaction (61%), while less variance was explained in information satisfaction (11%). The amount of the variance explained reflects the amount of variance captured by a construct compared to the variance due to random measurement error (Tabachnik and Fidell 1996). Since the variance explained in the dependent variable is considerably high (> 40%), the model demonstrates acceptable reliability (Fornell and Larcker 1981).

Combined, these findings support the reliability and validity of the hypothesized model (Hatcher 1996). Since the overall model was found to be an excellent fit of the data (fit indices > 0.95) and all paths were found to be significant ($p < .05$), the null hypothesis was rejected. Therefore, current results suggest that attribute congruency, information congruency, attribute satisfaction, and information satisfaction are good predictors of overall satisfaction. Furthermore, the model has shown that information satisfaction explains a unique portion of the variance in overall satisfaction while aiding in the prediction of attribute satisfaction. This finding suggests that the measurement of information satisfaction is important in predicting overall satisfaction.

To investigate which attributes of a golf vacation are best at predicting golf travelers' overall satisfaction (hypothesis 2), stepwise multiple regression was employed. In this type of regression analysis, the independent variable that explains the most variance in the model is entered first, followed successively by each independent variable explaining the most variance not explained by those prior. Each independent variable is assessed in terms of what it adds to the equation at its point of entry. Independent variables that do not add significantly to the variance explained are not added to the equation. Thus, this method starts with no variables in the model. Stepwise was chosen for it was the intent of this hypothesis to determine which variables are best at predicting overall satisfaction, not to build the best model for predicting overall satisfaction.

Table 10.3 presents the results of the stepwise multiple regressions. In order of importance, the variables of satisfaction with resort facilities, resort service, and golf information were found to be the best predictors of overall satisfaction. Since it was the goal of the analysis to find which attributes were best at predicting overall satisfaction instead of model building, multicollinearity between items was not considered to be a problem.

Table 10.3 The predictability of overall satisfaction with vacation attributes

Step number	Variable entered	R^2	Increase in R^2
1	Resort facility satisfaction	0.631	0.631
2	Resort service satisfaction	0.694	0.063
3	Golf information satisfaction	0.705	0.011

Note: Golf quality, golf quantity, and resort information were not significant ($p > .05$).

Resort facilities was entered in the first step and resulted in a significant model, $R2 = .63$, $F(1, 408) = 696.13$, $p < .001$. Satisfaction with resort service was entered in the second step, $R2 = .69$, $F(2, 408) = 459.56$, $p < .001$. In the third and final step, satisfaction with golf information was added, resulting in a final model with $R2 = .70$, $F(3, 408) = 322.41$, $p < .001$. The variables of satisfaction with quality of golf courses, number of golf courses, and resort information were not found to significantly ($p < .05$) add to the model.

The standardized regression coefficients are reported for the independent variables (Table 10.4). The regression coefficients represent the expected change in the dependent variable (overall satisfaction) for each unit increase in the independent variable when all independent variables have been standardized (Tabachnik and Fidell 1996). Therefore, according to the standardized regression coefficients of the final model, for each one-unit increase in satisfaction with resort facilities, overall satisfaction increased 0.44 units. For each unit increase in satisfaction with resort service, the dependent variable increased 0.35 units. Finally, for every one-unit increase in golf information satisfaction, overall satisfaction. increased 0.13 units.

In sum, the overall model was found to be significant and explained 70.5% of the variance in the dependent variable. The attributes of resort facilities, resort service, and golf information were, respectively, found to be the best predictors of overall satisfaction. Since attributes related to the resort were found to be the best predictors of overall satisfaction, instead of attributes related to golf, the researchers accepted the null hypothesis. Therefore, attributes related to golf are not the best predictors of overall satisfaction with a golfing experience.

These results suggest that golf resort management can most easily differentiate itself in the market by providing better resort facilities and service than their competition.

Table 10.4 Regression coefficients for the attributes predicting overall satisfaction

Variable	Standardized regression coefficient	F ratio	Standard error	p
Resort facilities	0.44	696.13	0.143	< .001
Resort service	0.35	459.56	0.353	< .001
Golf information	0.13	322.41	0.132	< .001

It also suggests that the golf courses played are possibly a core attribute and, while an important part of the vacation, are less likely to differentiate the resort from the competition.

To determine the correlation between visitors' overall satisfaction and intentions to revisit (hypothesis 3), simple bivariate correlation was employed. The analysis indicated that overall satisfaction is highly correlated ($r = 0.64$, $p < 0.001$) with intentions to revisit. This finding suggests that satisfaction leads to repurchase intentions and amplifies the importance of measuring visitor satisfaction.

Discussion and conclusions

Since the current state of the golf industry has created a very competitive market, it is essential for resort owners to examine the variables related to golf travelers' satisfaction and intentions to revisit. It is thus believed that results of the current study will be useful to golf resort management. The present study demonstrates that overall satisfaction can be effectively predicted with information and attribute satisfaction and that information satisfaction is an antecedent to attribute satisfaction. These findings indicate that Oliver's (1980) model may be improved with the inclusion of information satisfaction.

Results further suggest that golf resort management needs to be cognizant of not only the performance of service at the attributional level but also of the information provided about the vacation and the information's effect on golf travelers' expectations. Since attribute and information congruency were shown to aid in the prediction of golf travelers' overall satisfaction, results of the current study propose that golf travelers' expectations are integral in the formation of over-all satisfaction.

In addition, information satisfaction was shown to be a good predictor of both attribute and overall satisfaction. This finding suggests that golf resort management needs to accurately market the golf vacation experience to potential golf travelers to maximize attribute and information satisfaction to inevitably affect overall satisfaction. Moreover, results suggest that high expectations have a negative effect on attribute satisfaction and information satisfaction. Therefore, golf resort management must be careful not to inflate potential visitors' expectations with the information provided.

Results also suggest that attributes related to the resort have a greater impact on overall satisfaction than attributes related to the golfing experience or the information provided. It is postulated that this result is due to the fact that the attributes related to the golfing experience were rated as most satisfactory by the respondents. Since the majority of golf travelers believed that the attributes related to the golf experience were satisfactory, these variables did not distinguish satisfied travelers from dissatisfied travelers. Thus, attributes related to the resort, which had a larger standard deviation, were better predictors of overall satisfaction.

This finding suggests that for golf resort management to have satisfied guests, they should be most concerned with providing both superb resort facilities and excellent resort service. Yet, even though the attributes related to the golf experience were not found to be good predictors of overall satisfaction, it is believed that these variables are a very important aspect of the golf vacationers' experience. According to Gale (1994), those attributes that are most important to clientele are termed "basic attributes" and are expected by one's clientele to be present. The only time these products are postulated to be important is when they are unsatisfactory or are missing (Reichheld 1996). Thus, golf course management should not disregard the effects of the golfing experience, even though they were not found to be good predictors of overall satisfaction.

Finally, it was found that customer satisfaction is highly correlated with intentions to revisit. This result amplifies the importance of measuring overall satisfaction and its determinants. By knowing what factors influence overall satisfaction, golf resort management should be better equipped to alter the vacation experience to maximize satisfaction and increase intentions to revisit.

Further research is necessary to determine whether measures of desires congruency aid in the prediction of overall satisfaction. It is also recommended for future research that attribute importance be included in future models predicting satisfaction. It is believed that measures of importance and desires congruency may assist in the prediction of overall satisfaction and will advance the understanding of satisfaction formation.

Due to limitations, caution should be given with the generalizability of the current results. The study was limited by not randomly selecting destinations and by analyzing golf travelers during one season (fall) at one golf resort. Thus, the addition of at least one more golf resort would have increased the study's external validity. The measurement of golf travelers during all four seasons also would have increased the generalizability of the results. Moreover, the study was limited by analyzing only golf travelers. Thus, further research is necessary to determine if the results of this study are representative of other golf travelers and travelers not on a golf vacation.

Yet, since the current study is the first to analyze the proposed model, it is believed that results have important theoretical and managerial implications. By understanding how satisfaction is formed and how vacation attributes affect this formation, it is believed that management will be better equipped in their decision-making processes for the best allocation of organizational resources and for marketing techniques. It is also believed that utilization of the current results extends well beyond the promotional implications to program development, pricing, and distribution strategies. Furthermore, results have theoretical implications for the field of tourism in regards to the formation of and prediction of visitor satisfaction.

References

Anderson, J.C., and D.W. Gerbing (1988). "Structural Equation Modeling in Practice: A Review and Recommended 'Two-Step Approach'." *Psychological Bulletin*, 103: 411–23.

Barsky, J.D. (1992). "Customer Satisfaction in the Hotel Industry: Meaning and Measurement." *Hospitality Research Journal*, 16 (1): 51–73.

Barsky, J.D., and R. Labagh (1992). "A Strategy for Customer Satisfaction." *Cornell Hotel and Restaurant Administration Quarterly*, 33 (5): 32–40.

Bentler, P.M. (1989). *EQS Structural Equations Program Manual.* Los Angeles: BMDP Statistical Software.

Bentler, P.M., and D.G. Bonett (1980). "Significance Tests and Goodness-of-Fit in the Analysis of Covariance Structures." *Psychological Bulletin*, 88: 588–606.

Bultena, G.L., and L.L. Klessig (1969). "Satisfaction in Camping: A Conceptualization and Guide to Social Research." *Journal of Marketing Research*, 24: 305–14.

Dillman, D. (1978). *Mail and Telephone Surveys.* New York: John Wiley.

Dube, L., L.M. Renaghan, and J.M. Miller (1994). "Measuring Customer Satisfaction for Strategic Management." *Cornell Hotel and Restaurant Administration Quarterly*, 35 (1): 39–47.

Dye, A.D. (1998). "1998 Looming as Banner Year for Golf Course Construction." *Golf Market Today*, 38 (2): 1–5.

Fornell, C., and D.F. Larcker (1981). "Evaluating Structural Equation Models with Unobservable Variables and Measurement Error." *Journal of Marketing Research*, 18: 39–50.

Gale, B.T. (1994). *Managing Customer Value: Creating Quality and Service That Customers Can See*. New York: Free Press.

Gardial, S.F., D.S. Clemons, D.W. Schumann, and J.M. Burns (1994). "Comparing Consumers' Recall of Prepurchase and Postpurchase Product Evaluation Experiences." *Journal of Consumer Research*, 20 (March): 548–60.

Grewal, D., K.B. Monroe, and R. Krishnan (1998). "The Effects of Price-Comparison Advertising on Buyers' Perceptions of Acquisition Value, Transaction Value and Behavioral Intentions." *Journal of Marketing*, 62 (April): 46–59.

Hatcher, L.H. (1996). *A Step by Step Approach to Using the SAS System for Factor Analysis and Structural Equation Modeling*. Cary, NC: SAS Institute.

Hu, L., and P.M. Bentler (1998). "Fit Indices in Covariance Structure Modeling: Sensitivity to Underparameterized Model Misspecification." *Psychological Methods*, 3 (4): 424–53.

Hunt, H.K. (1977). "Cs/d . . . Overview and Future Directions." In *Conceptualization and Measurement of Consumer Satisfaction and Dissatisfaction*, edited by H. Hunt. Cambridge, MA: Marketing Science Institute, pp. 455–88.

LaTour, S.A., and N.C. Peat (1979). "Conceptual and Methodological Issues in Consumer Satisfaction Research." *Advances in Consumer Research*, 6: 431–37.

Levitt, T. (1981). "Marketing Intangible Products and Product Intangibles." *Harvard Business Review*, May–June: 94–102.

National Golf Foundation (1995). *Golf Travel in the United States,* Jupiter, FL: National Golf Foundation.

—— (1998). *Trends in the Golf Industry*, Jupiter, FL: National Golf Foundation.

Oliver, R.L. (1980). "A Cognitive Model of the Antecedents and Consequences of Satisfaction Decisions." *Journal of Marketing Research*, 17: 460–69.

—— (1993). "Cognitive, Affective and Attribute Bases of the Satisfaction Response." *Journal of Consumer Research*, 20 (December): 418–30.

Olshavsky, R.W., and J.A. Miller (1972). "Consumer Expectations, Product Performance and Perceived Product Quality." *Journal of Marketing Research*, 9: 19–21.

Patterson, P.G., L.W. Johnson, and R.A. Spreng (1997). "Modeling Determinants of Customer Satisfaction for Business-to-Business Professional Services." *Journal of the Academy of Marketing Science*, 25 (1): 4–17.

Reichheld, F.F. (1996). *The Loyalty Effect: The Hidden Force Behind Growth, Profits, and Lasting Value*. Boston: Bain.

Spreng, R.A., S.B., Mackenzie, and R.W. Olshavsky (1996). "A Reexamination of the Determinants of Consumer Satisfaction." *Journal of Marketing*, 60: 15–32.

Spreng, R.A., and R.W. Olshavsky (1993). "A Desires Congruency Model of Consumer Satisfaction." *Journal of the Academy of Marketing Science*, 21 (3): 169–77.

Tabachnick, B.G., and L.S. Fidell (1996). *Using Multivariate Statistics*, 3rd edn. New York: HarperCollins College.

Whipple, T.W., and S.V. Thatch (1988). "Group Tour Management: Does Good Service Produce Satisfied Customers?" *Journal of Travel Research*, 27 (2): 16–21.

Williams, D.R. (1989). "Great Expectations and the Limits to Satisfaction: A Review of Recreation and Consumer Satisfaction Research." USDA Forest Service Gen. Tech. Report SE-52. In *Outdoor Recreation Benchmark 1988: Proceedings of the National Outdoor Recreation Forum,* edited by A.E. Watson. January 13–14, Tampa. FL, pp. 422–638.

Chapter 11

Paul Beedie

MOUNTAIN GUIDING AND
ADVENTURE TOURISM
Reflections on the choreography
of the experience

Introduction

THIS PAPER HAS EMERGED from a period of research into the contributions
mountain guides may be having to the emergence of mountain based adventure
tourism. In the early stages of the project it became obvious that the author's own
mountaineering experience, which has included guiding work, was both providing the
impetus for an academic exploration of the role of the guide and informing the reading
of that literature. Preliminary theorizing drawn from the work of Goffman (1959) on
social interaction and Jenkins (1996) on identity construction led to a focus on rules, an
under-explored perspective raised by Rojek and Urry's suggestion (1997, p. 55) that:

> How we pattern tourist experience and what rules we use when we engage
> in 'escape' activity are much more important than is generally recognized.

The first part of the paper explores these theoretical dimensions and demonstrates the
limitations of such theory when set in a context of adventure tourism. In particular, the
similarities, but also the differences, between a mountain guide and a tourist guide will
be discussed using Edensor's (1998) work as a starting point. This develops the focus to
guiding in mountains, the subject of the data collection evidenced in the middle section
of the paper. Thereafter, the discussion returns to a more theoretical dimension as the
conclusion suggests a framework for illuminating how mountain based adventure holidays
in general, and perceptions of identity in particular might fit into a broader context of
leisure.

It will be suggested that there are rules that mountain guides adhere to in carrying
out their work and that have emerged from a traditional approach to mountaineering.

Guides are experienced mountaineers whose training and experiences are a product of the structure, that is the British Association of Mountain Guides (BMG), that validates their status. As professionals they must perform their work following rules set out by this and other institutions of mountaineering such as the Mountain Leader Training Board (MLTB) and the Association of Mountaineering Instructors (AMI). The clients, that is people who buy mountain based adventure holidays, for whom the guides are responsible have the opportunity through their involvement in the physical world of mountains to internalize these rules, and thereby develop the potential to operate independently as mountaineers. In this respect the issue of identity, as in 'being a mountaineer' becomes a central concern and it is guides that are positioned to shape the experiences of their clients in their own image as 'traditional mountaineers'. In this respect the 'rules' and 'traditional mountaineering practice' might be seen as virtually synonymous. However, the possibility remains that clients may interpret these rules in their own way, in so far as they might be allowed to by guides, and that the emergence of mountain based adventure tourism may influence future developments in mountaineering. The paper, therefore, addresses a number of questions. These include, what are the rules the guide follows? Are these rules a reflection of established mountaineering practice? How might clients internalize these rules, if at all, and how might the client-guide relationship affect such a process. Finally, what is the mediating influence of the inherent danger of the activity?

A theoretical framework

This research project began with a review of theories pertinent to identity construction as the aim was to more fully understand the relationship between being a mountaineer and having a mountaineering experience through buying a mountain based adventure holiday. The starting point of this exploration of identity was an interest in how behaviour might be determined by rules. According to Goffman (1959), behaviour is based on knowledge of how to 'perform' in different social settings. He suggests (1959, p. 13):

> When an individual enters the presence of others, they commonly seek to acquire information about him [sic] or to bring into play information about him already possessed. They will be interested in his general socio-economic status, his conception of self, his attitude towards them, his competence, his trustworthiness etc. Although some of this information seems to be sought almost as an end in itself, there are usually quite practical reasons for acquiring it. Information about the individual helps to define the situation, enabling others to know in advance what he will expect of him. Informed in these ways, the others will know how best to act in order to call forth a desired response from him.

When Goffman says information 'helps to define the situation' he is implying what I have termed the 'frame' of a setting. A frame is based on knowledge and experience and it helps people understand 'how best to act in order to call forth a desired response'. Goffman's (1959) analysis suggests that conversations, cues, hints and body language all play a part in how people become socialized. The reflexive mechanisms of social interaction become important to identity construction, a perspective developed by Jenkins (1996).

Jenkins (1996) argues that identity formation results from, 'the internal-external dialectic of identification' (Jenkins 1996, p. 20), Jenkins suggests that the reflexive nature of social relations creates social identity which is about meaning. Furthermore, he continues, because meanings are innovated, agreed and shared in the social world, identity becomes negotiable to a certain extent. He goes on to argue that we have a plurality of roles or identities, and that these are constantly being revised. Jerkins (1996) argues that all social activity is a process of stabilization in so much as the dynamic component of identity formation, combined with the multiple roles demanded by everyday life, can lead to social disorientation and self-confusion. Identity, then, emerges as a central concern in the social world. This validation of identity through the presentation of self in a social setting clearly stems from Goffman (1959). The extent to which a performed identity is accepted or rejected is a function of how well one has understood the rules of department (e.g., gesture and body language), display (e.g., clothing and insignia) and communication (particularly language) in that setting. Goffman (1959) suggests that, when facing other people in a social setting people perform as actors, responding to hints, cues and gestures in order to gain knowledge (and therefore advantage) to enhance their performance. Such a metaphor presupposes a script that defines how people should behave in a particular setting. Even when the social setting is new, Goffman suggests: 'the individual will already have a fair idea of what modesty, deference, or righteous indignation looks like, and can make a pass at playing these bits when necessary' (1959, p. 79). He goes on to suggest that social experience provides tools to improvise if necessary. The strength of such an argument lies in the intimation that identity is not a material thing but rather a pattern of appropriate conduct. In the performance metaphor people become actors, social space becomes a stage and the enactment therein results from learning the rules. From this perspective mountaineering, like theatre (Goffman, 1959) has a human interface and a social dynamic (Jenkins, 1996) that reflects real life. The process of constructing a moun-taineering identity may be usefully explored using the principle ideas outlined here.

There are, however, limitations of such a framework. When endeavouring to understand the rules that determine behaviour in a mountaineering setting, it is precisely this context that makes the direct application of such theory problematic. Goffman is an 'urban' theorist; much of his micro-sociology is based on quotidian performances in ordinary everyday life which, for most people, means routines of work and home life in the civilization of built up areas. Mountaineering may not be 'ordinary' for most people and it takes place in a wild and potentially dangerous setting that may demand different, or even unprecedented behaviour. Thus, one limitation of the theory promoted by Goffman and Jenkins, is that it assumes an everyday setting for its subjects. A further limitation in its application to this investigation is that the adventure tourist setting, like any holiday experience, is characterized by relatively short periods of time during which a 'holiday-mindset' may well be prevalent making any identity construction through rule bound behaviour a temporary phenomenon. It is these limitations that are expanded upon below when the discussion develops the concept of a rule bound frame of reference.

Guides are experienced mountaineers with a breadth of orographic knowledge and accumulated skill and expertise in mountaineering activities. Clients buy this expertise, increasingly through the company structures offered by adventure tourism. Adventure and tourism have grown closer in recent times as the propensity to package adventure holidays has increased (Christiansen, 1990; Trauer 1999), a development monitored closely by established mountaineers many of whom deplore the commercial developments which appear to directly or indirectly impact 'their' domain (Hoyland, 2002). Such a conflation has placed mountain guides in a unique position. As professionals they make a living through their employment as mountain experts by adventure companies and their clients. However, to become guides they must have served an apprenticeship comprising an incremental accumulation over many years of the skill and knowledge that defines their profession. They will have learnt the rules that define what it means to be a mountaineer and understand that mountaineering is a potentially dangerous undertaking that might be described as 'serious leisure' in Hamilton Smith's (1993) terminology. Mountain guides, therefore, are both guardians of the tradition that has established them as professionals and the medium through which adventure tourists, that is people who buy adventure holidays, experience mountains. Experience of mountaineering offers a frame of reference through which people can make sense of being a mountaineer. Guides will have an established frame whilst clients, who recognize their limitations as independent mountaineers by employing guides, are more like to bring degrees of framing to their adventure holidays. The following section explores how frames may emerge.

In mountaineering, the frame relates to physical and the social components of that setting. In a physical sense, to 'know' the mountains equates to having spent time in them undertaking walking, scrambling and/or climbing activities. Through such immersion people are likely to become familiar with a variety of rugged terrain, for example, the difference between a maintained footpath and sliding across unconsolidated scree.[1] Similarly, people are likely to have experience of a variety of weather conditions and the ways different mountain aspects might affect these, for example, sheltered valleys will be less windy and warmer than exposed ridges. Finally, experience of mountaineering is likely to lead to an appreciation of degrees of visibility depending upon the cloud level and variations in weather that can range from hot sunshine to blizzards. The unpredictability of mountains means that, in one sense, people can never really 'know' mountains, but can only draw upon similar experiences in order to formulate behaviour. Such experience of the physical is likely to lead to behaviour that is a common sense rational response to such conditions. For example, if the wind is strong people are likely to move away from exposed ridges, put on windproof jackets and take more care when moving across rugged terrain. The greater a person's depth and breadth of physical experience in mountains then the easier it becomes for that person to frame a response to the physical demands of that setting. The same deconstruction can be applied to the social setting.

In a social sense, to 'know' the mountains is to have experience of time spent with other mountaineers. This is not restricted to mountains, although this is clearly the fundamental reference point, but encompasses peripheral spaces where mountaineers gather. These include club meeting rooms, pubs, equipment shops, mountain huts, audio-visual presentations from adventure tourist companies and famous mountaineers, symposia and conferences. To spend time with mountaineers is to absorb patterns of behaviour relating to what to talk about, how to talk about it, how to dress and what mountaineering objectives one should aspire towards. Over time this imbues a process of inoculation that in turn will generate its own forms of behaviour. Armed with this theoretical framework, and cognisant of the limitations outlined above, I entered the mountains as a social researcher.

A mountaineer as social researcher

Following a qualitative methodology (Hammersley and Atkinson, 1995), I set out to understand: 'a particular social situation, event, role, group or interaction' (Creswell, 1994, p. 161). The subject groups were paying clientele from two adventure tourism companies and I was able to gain access to such people because I am a mountain guide and could offer my services to these companies, I have been strongly influenced, and therefore socially constructed, by the mountaineering world of people and places I move within. The values of this world have become my own. I value physical challenges, I place a value on the conservation of mountain environments and I believe that mountain adventures are educational in the broadest sense of the term. I see mountains as places to escape to from towns and I enjoy the sense of freedom that I feel out in the wind, rain, sun and snow. I enjoy living 'on the edge' whereby my skills and equipment are engaged and tested by mountaineering, but I am not reckless. I have a considered approach to mountaineering based on a confidence drawn from many years of experience and I retain a great *enthusiasm* for mountains. I have served a mountaineering apprenticeship. It is this background of experience and values that I have brought to this study. From such a position I have come to appreciate that mountaineering is governed by rules.

Using such a perspective, the rules of mountaineering form a reference point from which participants formulate meaning about what they do. Far from being an eccentric and incomprehensible pastime that, to the non-participant, appears to be characterized by risky endeavour and voluntary exposure to objective dangers such as avalanches, rock falls and extreme weather, mountaineering has emerged as rule bound but thereby predominantly rational. To be a mountaineer means learning the rules and it is guides, who are by definition experienced mountaineers, who have an important role as teachers. A modern framework of rationality is expressed in the rules defining what it means to be a mountaineer. These rules involve knowing about planning, clothing, training and styles of ascent. Mountain expeditions of whatever scale (a day out on the local hills or the ascent of a Himalayan giant), are carefully planned with due reference to existing maps and information, weather patterns and the logistics of travel to and through mountains. In addition, clothing and other specialist equipment is used to maximize comfort, training techniques are put into practice and ascents or journeys meticulously documented, not only with respect to height and distance but also to style. The rules include the following. First, serve an apprenticeship, thereby, gaining experience of mountains and knowledge and skills from those already experienced. This will facilitate the development of fitness and mountaineering competence. Second, have the right equipment and know when and how to use it (if in doubt defer to a guide or undertake a training course). Third, attend to energy requirements particularly concerning diet and pacing through the mountains. Fourth, maximize appreciation of mountains by forming only small groups (or go alone). Fifth, always rely upon your own physical efforts and respect the environment.

Operating through two Sheffield based adventure tourism companies I worked on adventure holidays in the Cuillin mountains on Skye (twice), Naranjo de Bulnes in Northern Spain, the English Lake District and the English Peak District. In these locations I worked with a total of 39 clients over a period of 25 mountain days and several nights. 'Mountaineer' is a term I use to identify people who have knowledge, skills and experience that facilitate apparent 'freedom' from quotidian routine in urban life through climbing and walking. Mountaineers are most likely to operate independently when doing their activities, Adventure tourists buy adventure holidays and, therefore, are apparently 'constrained' though their dependency upon the guides they employ. The term 'client' is used for this group of people. Data were collected using participant observation techniques, recording observations of actual client and guide behaviours in the 'natural settings' of these five adventure holidays. Conversations and reflections upon the data were also recorded during fieldwork and face to face interviews and those by telephone were conducted as follow up strategies. Thus, verbal and visual evidence, using these ethnographic methods, prompted me, as a relatively inexperienced social researcher, to reflect upon my role as experienced mountain guide in tourist adventure settings. Periods of time between each mountaineering holiday aided this reflective process in ways that facilitated progressive focusing around the role of the guide in directing client experiences.

Hamilton-Smith (1993) suggests that wilderness activities undertaken by people who live in developed countries today have become characterized by a shallowness of experience that has been, at least partly, caused by a process of commodification of wild places. Wild for Hamilton-Smith, writing about the Australian outback, means rugged terrain, cliffs, crags and a relatively remote setting away from civilization, epitomized by urban centres. Mountains are a form of landscape that is often associated with the term 'wilderness'. In its purest atavistic state, wilderness is a landscape that has not been subjugated by human intervention. It is where people are not, or 'earth-sans-man' [sic] (Walter, 1982). The debate concerning the definition of wilderness revolves around the degree to which places are more or less encroached upon by urban characteristics. Mountains visited on adventure holidays are more usually wild than wilderness as clients and the companies that provide for them encourage characteristics of tourism, such as roads, hotels, signposts and other aspects of civilization, to the setting. The way mountaineering and tourism appear to be merging arguably generates a tension between freedom and constraint. As the characteristics of tourism begin to change wild places, so it becomes more difficult for anyone, even experienced mountaineers, to operate independently in mountains. However, guides may be uniquely positioned at the interface of the two social worlds of mountaineering and tourism, to have potential to influence the scope and direction of developments.

Mountain based holidays are part of adventure tourism, itself a growing industry which utilizes the traditional spaces of mountaineering. Evidence for this is provided by Deegan's (2002) book, *The Mountain Traveller's Handbook* subtitled 'your companion from city to summit'. Such books are published because of a market demand for the information they contain. More significantly, however, as the publishers are the British Mountaineering Council, the book marks recognition of a broadening participation in mountain travel. Such developments may indicate a change in the way travel is experienced and point to one of the ways adventure tourism might be influencing mountaineering. Rubens (1999), for example, suggests that the way people experience adventure is becoming more concentrated. He uses a similar conceptualization to Hamilton-Smith (1993) when he describes adventurous activities as comprising either the 'broad' view or the 'narrow' view. The broad view encompasses activities such as multi-day trekking journeys which make sustained physical demands on the participant and in which the adventure element is sustained at a relatively low level. The narrow view is exemplified by activities such as abseiling which offer an intense, highly charged but short lived experience. In Hamilton-Smith's (1993) terminology the former might be considered the more 'serious' form of leisure. Adventure tourism embraces both broad and narrow activities, but the suggestion from Rubens is that even broad activities are now scheduled to create a greater intensity of experience. Without the 'deep' immersion required for independent operation in mountains, as is the case with serious mountaineers who have served an apprenticeship over many years, clients are likely to become more dependent upon their guides. What has not been examined is how the identity of the adventure tourist relates to the concept of the mountaineer, previously an exclusive, hard-earned identity, shaped by the experiences of self reliance in inhospitable terrain, without the amenities of transport, shelter, food provision and warmth, provided usually by urban living. The adventure tourist and the seasoned mountaineer both temporarily relinquish the routine comforts of everyday life, the former paying substantially to holiday in mountains. British mountains represent an escape location that is advertised as offering excitement, stimulation and potential adventure (Foundry Mountain Activities brochure, 2000). Adventure tourism offers adventure holidays. Clients are 'tourists' in so much as they buy an experience that is usually packaged for maximum efficiency. Existing tourist theory purports to explain tourist behaviour in relation to 'mass tourism' (MacCannell, 1976; Urry, 1990; Rojek and Urry, 1997) leaving the contemporary adventure tourist scene under researched, although studies are emerging (for example Cloke and Perkins, 1998). Given that adventure holidays are commodities which promise an experience, to succeed they need to be rationalized, standardized, efficient products, marketed sophisticatedly for profit (Smart, 1992). As such, their relationship with established traditions of mountaineering is likely to promote tension for guides who are positioned as a bridge between mountaineering and tourism.

Mountains and guiding

Experts such as guides are gatekeepers to the world of mountaineering. Giddens (1990) recognizes the emergence of experts, and our inclination to place ourselves in their hands, throughout all aspects of the social world in late modernity. In mountain regions, as the focus of mountaineering shifted from an exploratory and scientific rationale to one of sport and recreation, it was hunters and farmers who emerged as the earliest guides (Frison-Roche with Jouty, 1996). These people possessed local knowledge, and gradually, through physical engagement with walking and climbing, they also developed a rudimentary technical expertise. Gradually, the process of becoming a guide evolved into a 'recognisable' form of behaviour constructed around a consistent performance predicated on rules and institutionalized by the formation of the Union Internationale des Associations des Guides de Montagne (UIAGM) to which the BMG became affiliated in 1977 (Milburn, 1996, pp. 219–224). Fieldwork observations would suggest that, today, guides characteristically have expert knowledge in the form of mountain experience and local detail. They have the technical know how in equipment and rope choice and use; knowledge related to map reading, route finding, general safety and survival, self-reliance and sufficiency: and are familiar with traditions of the mountains in terms of icons, myths and folk-lore. As I became more deeply immersed in this subject of study, I was struck by differences between being a tourist guide and being a mountain guide. This was because ensuring the well being of clients and dealing with issues of safety resulting from the physical dangers associated with the wild terrain was an ongoing responsibility.

Edensor (1998) develops the idea of the tourist guide as choreographer of the tourist experience in his analysis of visiting the Taj Mahal. He bases the analysis on Goffman's (1959) dramaturgical metaphor. There are a number of differences between these two guiding settings. Of particular note are the differences relating to the physical setting, that is the inherent danger of mountains. Clients have to learn how to cope with exposure to such dangers and the mountain guide has a responsibility to teach skills to achieve this end. In doing so, clients must become more like independent mountaineers. It is this 'adventure education' purpose that Nichols (2002) alludes to when he suggests people who undertake adventure activities can achieve higher levels of satisfaction by coping with more technically challenging situations. Differences between guiding tourists around the Taj Mahal and in mountains include exposure to the elements, isolation and a requirement for self-sufficiency in the latter. All of these make for a dependency of adventure tourists on the mountain guide, which is arguably greater than that of tourists to a tour guide. Edensor (1998), however, identifies team performance, tourist performances, improvization and a circumscribed stage as key concepts which, I shall argue, will help uncover the 'rules' of adventure tourist guidance. I have observed that mountain guides have a certain status that has a hearing on the client experience. The extent to which the guide is seen as an expert (Giddens, 1990) is revealed in the next section.

The guide as choreographer

Despite being widely feared as the abode of evil, there is historical evidence to suggest that mountains have been climbed throughout history (Bernstein, 1989). The motivation for climbing mountains, from a contemporary perspective on these early accounts, was usually functional (Frison-Roche with Jouty, 1996, pp. 17–25). A mountain guide, in its most basic definition, is therefore someone with local knowledge of a mountain or range of mountains. This knowledge equates to experience gained first hand through days (and sometimes nights) spent in this area, The motivations for people as 'guides to be', who ventured into mountains in the past, varied but were commonly economic: chamois hunting and crystal collecting are two examples. Indeed, although mountain recreation has now emerged as an end in itself, an escape from the functional demands of a work environment for many of us, there are examples of people who have begun their mountaineering 'careers' by crystal hunting (Diemberger, 1983). The connection between guiding and economy has a long tradition.

When the Western sport of mountaineering was 'invented' it was local people who had knowledge to sell. Arrangements were struck up between visitors with aspirations to climb and local 'guides' that were mutually beneficial. Most early guiding activity took place in the European Alps and was particularly focused on those valleys located beneath the bigger or more spectacular mountains. Thus, the towns of Chamonix, Zermatt and Grindlewald became centres of social activity focused on the mountains of Mont Blanc, the Matterhorn and the Eiger respectively (Bernbaum, 1997, p. 21). However, this is an over simplification of a complex picture. There was, for example, usually a class distinction with the employer being typically upper class, educated, socially sophisticated, moneyed, with a lot of leisure time and commonly English (Moore, 1867/1939). The employee was typically poor and living a frugal and basic life in a small agricultural village, generally uneducated and with limited social opportunities. However, the mountain experience transcended these differences and, to the extent that a hierarchy existed, in a way reversed the positions of power. Local knowledge was crucial to the experience and, to a large degree, the outcome of a climb was literally in the hands of the guide. This was whether a successful ascent was made and a safe return completed or some 'fate' overtook the group as clearly happened to Whymper and his team on the first ascent of Matterhorn in 1865. On this occasion three mountaineers and one guide of Whymper's party were killed when a slip sent them down the north face as they descended the mountain. But it is more than this because, as the Alps were explored and the mountains 'opened up' to the sport of mountaineering, the target of reaching summits became the challenge which defined the activity. Many guides had not been to the actual tops of 'their' mountains because their original economic activity did not require this. Mountaineering in the Alps, certainly in the Golden Age of the 1860s, was about getting to the top (Frison-Roche with Jouty, 1996). Mountains and buildings such as the Taj Mahal might both be thought of as monuments to be consumed via 'the gaze' (Urry, 1990). However, tourist guides do not require technical competence from their parties in order to perform their guiding role amidst buildings. Many tourists will also consume mountains visually, but for those who engage more directly with mountains through adventure holidays, the relationship between client and guide becomes more significant.

Early guiding was something of a shared adventure between guide and clients. That idea remains central to adventure tourism today. Out in the mountains, in spite of the promise of the 'freedom' adventure promises, the contemporary guide of the tourist adventure choreographs the detail of the experience. My fieldwork observations reveal that this occurs by his or her selecting where to walk, when to stop to admire the view, how the group are positioned on and off the rope, how to walk and conserve energy, how to move around obstacles and so forth. All adventure tourist clients need some experience of walking in mountains. But as a mountain guide I set a pace that was sustainable for a long period of time, and, therefore, usually led from the front at the beginning of the day when the route is usually uphill to some extent. In most British mountains, leaving the valley at the start of the day usually means following a path of some description. The guide makes the choices and tends to follow the easiest line up a slope, zig-zagging if necessary to find grass amidst scree slopes for example. He or she will walk round marshy sections, stopping at places that command good views or interesting focal points as in rock formations or the first sight of the objective of the day. An actual example occurred as I was leading a walk to Coire na Banachdich on one adventure holiday to Skye. The walk passes a hidden valley called Eas Mor. Although not far from the main valley, this gorge-like feature is notable for a steep waterfall that empties into the upper end and a range of vegetation, including deciduous trees, which cling to its steep walls. One client, a forester by profession, became very animated, and several others reached for their cameras. One said it was: 'beautiful, beautiful, beautiful' and someone else likened the scene to Rider-Haggard's *The Lost World*.

Possibly the best example I observed of a guide using local knowledge to maximize the spectacular impact of a mountain, occurred on the walk to Naranjo de Bulries, a spectacular mountain in Northern Spain reminiscent of the Matterhorn. The walk began so early that it was still pitch dark, a fact that disguised details of the landscape obvious by day. The guide stayed in front and would not allow any stops, despite several clients finding the going very tough, until finally, conning round a corner just as dawn was breaking, he said: 'we can rest here for a few minutes'. Above, bathed blood red in the early morning sun was the mountain. It looked steep and formidable. Out came the cameras. All four clients referred to this moment in subsequent interviews. One added: 'and I hadn't realized what a spectacular and beautiful valley we had approached the mountain through until we walked back down again in daylight'.

So, in an adventure holiday setting, clients follow the guide who knows the safest route in hazardous terrain. He or she can find their way in the dark, taking clients into the adventure of a perceived unknown through his or her unique grasp of where to go. It is part of the guide's job to point out spectacular views. Setting up extraordinary aesthetic experiences, like sunrise over the mountains, can be consciously accomplished by the guide insisting on a pace that will enable arrival at a certain point to view a particular panorama. Framing the visual in the presentation of sublime subject matter also follows rules. So naturalized has the breathtakingly, extraordinarily beautiful, high or far distant shot of mountain peaks or valleys become, that taking one's own photographs as a record of the real experience is likely to conform to the visual composition of unity of form and composition. This seems to correspond to rules perpetuated through the tradition of *National Geographic*, mountaineering magazines and television wildlife programmes. In such presentations litter and other eyesores are carefully omitted as the camera focuses on pristine and aesthetically attractive mountains, particularly those of spectacular shape. Wells, for example, (2001, p. 7) suggests that, after Everest, the Matterhorn is probably the most famous mountain in the world because 'it represents the very idealized picture of a mountain that a child might draw'. Thus, in the rule taking, standards of photography frame the choice of subject matter and the composition of the shot in line with a more broadly constructed understanding of mountains.

Edensor (1998) likens the tourist itinerary and habitual conduct to a script and makes the point that the ensuing social drama may be designed for a number of purposes, but in this case the idea that it may reinforce communal solidarity is of interest. The route is tightly directed ostensibly for safety purposes. It is repetitive to the extent that it is probably a well trodden path. Movement is specifiable and timing is important to provide space for contemplation. The performance of the guide does try to communicate meaning and identity dependent on the audience understanding the social message, for the danger of the terrain provides a rationale for a narrow range of ways of behaving. Paraphrasing the quote from Bennett's (1995) museum example cited in Edensor (1998, p. 65), the well trodden path on the wild mountain becomes a stage for the rehearsal of performances of patterns of locomotion derived from following and observing the guide. Also it involves witnessing and capturing first hand the aesthetic experience so many times rehearsed second hand. In discussing the scripted team performance achieved in the rituals of tourist behaviour, Edensor (1998) plays up the performance of a role, and plays down the degree to which some clients may consciously wish to adopt the behaviour of the guide. This is where the tourist guide, in Edensor's sense (1998), and the mountain guide again may differ in their purposes. The tourist guide orchestrates a group of people in showing them around a tourist site, and does have to consider their welfare in a rudimentary sense. For the mountain guide, safety is not only a priority, communicating survival skills are at the heart of the performance. The risk, on which adventure tourism is based, is associated with the hostile terrain in which the tourist is dependent on the guide for safety, but in a crisis in the isolated location, he or she may have to summon their own resources (learnt from guides) to survive. This is linked to Edensor's (1998) second point about improvisation.

In a choreographic role I have implied improvisation in that the guide makes decisions along the route. But, leading does not always take place from the front. With a group, for example, the only place from which it is possible to see everyone is the rear. However, the guide will lead all technical passages of scrambling or climbing, protecting the clients by positioning and physically holding or by using the rope as appropriate. On the other hand there are clients who always choose to follow and these are characteristically those who have the most to learn. Some will always take that role, while others may plan to move on to more independence once they have acquired the knowledge needed. But the control of an experience can slip out of the hands of a guide. Group interaction and client expectation and response clearly shape what is experienced. Guides can have bad experiences with clients where the expectations of client and guide are not matched. The tension created because guides and clients may have different perceptions of what is possible in the mountains is shown by the following comment from a guide noted in my fieldwork observations:

> When a client is paying to achieve a specific aim in the mountains, and the weather is good, they never experience the down side of the mountains – like bad weather that prevents you getting up. So they don't appreciate it in the same way we do. They have no real experience as a yardstick. They don't understand why you can't just go and do anything in the mountains.

Performance scripts are played out at different levels by clients. Departures from the script, requiring improvisation, are more likely to be accomplished by those with more experience in mountains. Yet, there is a contradiction here, which the following example may illuminate. One night in Arenas de Cabrales in Spain at the end of the Naranjo de Bulnes holiday, an unplanned gathering of clients from two different companies occurred. Conversations between guides suggested that some clients were 'good' and some were 'bad'. One guide said: 'some groups gel and some don't'. Another said: 'All groups are hard work. You have to be a leader all the time, in the mountains and in the bar. You are there to answer questions and to guide, that's what they want.' He went on to explain that he had tried to give himself a break from some of his groups by suggesting that, as a more gentle alternative to a big mountain day, they could walk a sign-posted 'nature trail'. But they refused to do this without their guide even though there was little technical difficulty and virtually no physical risk. The guide concluded: 'It's as if they have paid for a service and they expect value for money.'

It appears that clients who follow unquestioningly do replicate patterns of behaviour and language that guides exhibit. But, they do so in a reactive way because it is required for the situation they are in. I observed clients who wanted to learn and progress as mountaineers to be more proactive in their interaction with guides, so that they actually imitated more closely guides' behaviours. An example illustrates this difference. One client said: 'I hope you're not expecting me to retie that knot', after he had been untied from a rope. This client may not have seen himself as a climber, but another, who had some climbing experience, clearly wanted to further this. Thus, he was prepared to tie himself into his harness provided it was checked by the guide. To explore the matter of improvisation further the role of the guide will now be examined in more detail.

The role of the guide

Continuing my reflections on fieldwork notes, for some clients, their desire to develop an identity as mountaineer was shown by a conscious replication of the guide's behaviour in mountains. But more importantly, because those who have physical co-ordination, balance and poise appear to move more effortlessly through mountainous country than others, positions such as 'assistant leader' become socially acceptable, a circumstance, one would assume, of no relevance to being guided around the Taj Mahal. To assume the role is, to a large degree, to be the guide. Moreover, part of this is expressed in a desire to 'look the part' and, therefore, the clothing and equipment used by guides become an important reference point. This is one reason why famous guides can gain lucrative sponsorship deals with equipment manufacturers. There are other ways of becoming like a guide, and hence constructing an identity as 'mountaineer', that I noted operating in the field. Some examples are: telling anecdotes about trekking and climbing experiences at home and abroad; sitting in the front of the minibus with the guides or sitting at the 'instructors' table in the centre; buying drinks for the guides. Other examples are: organizing personal mountain routes on the recommendations of guides (assuming that you haven't already done the route, if you have then your status is assured); taking on specific responsibilities such as carrying some group emergency kit or carrying and uncoiling the rope when it is needed.

The following example illustrates the point about replicating behaviour. A young male client was enthusiastic and keen to impress. On one mountain day it was very wet, with continuous light rain and cloud. I was walking without wearing over-trousers. This client took his over-trousers off despite the rain. Furthermore, he would engage enthusiastically in conversations that involved the guide and other clients in the group and would ask lots of questions. Whilst keen to impress, such behaviour actually demonstrated his inexperience, a point noted by myself and possibly by the more experienced members of the group. In the more reflective times the group walked without talking. This client would often take a tangent, as if locating himself outside the group. The same client had clearly learnt postures, gestures, group positioning and language and was experimenting with these. In the course of an hour he had enthusiastically drawn attention to, caterpillars (twice), fungi (three times), and several soaring birds. He alternated between animated excitement (for example finding some ruined huts that were marked on the map) and being aloof, 'cool' and detached, with a far off look in his eye. Additionally, although he may have learnt such behaviour from any one of the guides he had been with over the week, or a significant other in the mountains, he did two things in direct imitation of me as the guide. First, he took every opportunity to take up a position at the rear of the group, a position that I was increasingly occupying because the visibility had improved. Second, he walked with his hands in his pockets, something that I do. This client appeared to be making a conscious effort to internalize the 'hints, cues and gestures' (Goffman, 1959) he observed guides using.

So the role of the guide as choreographer comes down to minute detail of being a leader or a follower or taking up a position at the back of the walking party. Group positioning is one point. Another is attitude, gaining autonomy in decision-making or not, learning the confidence to lead a route, to wean oneself from independence from the guide, by imitating his or her behaviour and picking up his or her expert knowledge. Further, beyond dress and equipment, posture and gesture signify 'credible and knowledgeable mountaineer' or not. One difference between being a mountaineer and being a tourist is knowing that mountaineering means taking the good and the bad. For the guide as choreographer, to have to cope with the adverse reactions of clients when weather is poor, is tied up with clients' expectations of getting value for money. Value for money is defined as a pleasurable experience with all the positive characteristics that mountaineering can offer.

Opportunities for improvisation among clients might also be usefully discussed in relation to guidebooks. Mountaineering guides have characteristically been the ones who have written guidebooks and these scripts will be improvised on most often by the guides themselves. Clients have riot welcomed encouragement to improvise in the examples above. Far from this context offering opportunities for 'more amorphous and open-ended' performances (Edensor, 1998, p. 66) there is an agenda linked to the traditional apprenticeship system of becoming a credible mountaineer. Thus, some clients take on board the broad experience that Rubens (1999) talks about and engage in 'serious leisure' (Hamilton-Smith, 1993). So, mountaineering performances in the adventure tourist context are imitative for some clients who emulate the guide: a broad, take all weathers and conditions learning experience. Others do not want to acknowledge or do not realize that mountaineering is deadly 'serious leisure' which is much deeper than for pleasure. They are the tourists, from the guides' perspective. The playfulness of a self conscious 'negotiated form of tourism' (Edensor, 1998, p. 66) which parodies the role of the tourist has little place in the mountains. But some clients do take a shallower approach than others as Hamilton-Smith (1993) contends. In contrast to other tourist guiding scenarios a tacit purpose of the tourist mountain guide's performance is a didactic one, based on a rationale of teaching safe walking, climbing and scrambling techniques that will aid survival.

The Lake District fieldwork provided some interesting data, partly because the group was big and there were four guides, and partly because the weather was not good and this tested the resolve of guides and clients alike. The holiday was aimed at those who wanted to improve their mountain navigation and rope-work skills. The role(s) of the guide are well illustrated by the following description. The evening before a day of rock scrambling the clients were given an indoor rope work session. The purpose here was to teach the clients how to tie certain knots so that they could operate more efficiently and with greater confidence, and therefore safety, in the exposed situations they were likely to find themselves in during the following day. There was a range of responses to this teaching input. Although everyone was able to tie the knots by the end of the session some clients wanted to learn more, and were, for example, given an impromptu lesson in rope coiling and care. Others walked away from the room content in the knowledge they would be 'looked after' the following day as they had been on previous days. The rope is a symbol of the mountaineer. The following morning, when sorting out kit for the scrambling day one enthusiastic young male client in my group strapped the rope to his rucksack. This was not an act negotiated with others in the group. To this client, the hardship of carrying the extra weight up the mountain was obviously outweighed by the symbolic identification with the status of mountaineer. Improvisation of performance (Edensor, 1998) in this context is experimentation with the script of the lead actor.

The didactic nature of the lead actor's role operates at two levels. At one level, clients have to be able to perform simple tasks in order to complete routes. Thus, the guide will teach a client to keep his or her heels down when walking up steep ground because this takes the strain off the calf muscles and so preserves energy, an important requirement in the unpredictable mountains. Or, the guide will make sure that a client knows how to adjust the strapping systems of modern rucksacks for the most comfortable and efficient use of this piece of equipment. Energy preservation and comfort can make an important contribution to the successful completion of a route. At another level, however, the guide can teach skills that are transferable to non-guided mountain recreation. The correct way to use and tie into a harness is an example as is an understanding of appropriate mountaineering footwear. The intricacies of foot and finger work on rock climbs is another. How to use a map and compass is yet another example. Some clients were content to let the guide tie them in and to do the navigation. Others wanted to improve their own level of skill by learning from the guide and putting this into practice. Practical engagement with mountains demands the use of certain practical skills. It is part of the guide's role to teach these. There is, therefore, an educational element to mountain based adventure tourism that lends some support to the model of adventure as education promoted by Nichols (2002). The 'lessons' are not formal as they are in schools but the mountains do become a 'classroom' from this perspective and the guide a teacher.

A further example of this is moving over rocky ground. In the valley this is not usually a problem although the guide looks for the best route, meaning the most efficient in terms of time and energy expenditure. However, in positions of exposure the mind controls motility in different ways, usually, in the inexperienced, by increasing the level of conscious movement. Conscious of the exposure, fear makes movements become awkward and jittery, security may be thought to be found close to the rock. A nervous client was told by another client to: 'stop making love to the rock', when the group were on the summit ridge of Sgurr nan Gillean on Skye. At this specific moment one client has taken on the role of the guide in relation to another client. This illustrates the way in which the performance of a mountain guide is replicated by a client who is demonstrating knowledge of the guiding script. By way of contrast, another client, talking of an experience in Snowdonia, recounts how he was left to his own devices to scramble nervously round: 'a huge boulder in a precarious and exposed place by a guide who simply did not see this feature as an impediment to progress!' This client was so far from internalizing the script of mountaineer that he felt indignant at the distance, both metaphorical and physical, between himself and his guide.

Guides working together or in small teams do discuss their clients' performances. Such dialogues commonly occur towards the end of the day. One such sharing of observations occurred as myself and another guide descended the well worn path to the Sligachen hotel on Skye at a distance behind the clients who were racing ahead to reach the bar. Such a circumstance is one of the few opportunities for guides to take a Goffman-esque (1959) backstage position in that performance in front of clients is dropped. But the role of guide is not entirely relinquished. The day's objectives, the summits of two Munros[2] (Sgurr nan Gillean and Am Basteir) reached via some exposed rocky passages high on each mountain, had been achieved. As the first mountain day on this particular holiday, tourist performance (Edensor, 1998) had been a useful indicator of the clients' capacity to achieve comparable objectives over the following days.

The more experienced clients moved with a sense of rhythm and were not put out by some of the exposed positions. The case of several less experienced clients was, however, discussed in greater detail. One guide explained how he had found a client: 'sprawled on the rock like a jelly' despite suggestions, and demonstrations, that it is safer and more efficient to walk or climb as upright as possible keeping weight over the feet. This may have been what the client knew he was supposed to do but he clearly *felt* much safer with as much of his body in contact with the rock as possible. I concurred with this and explained that I had had a similar experience with one of my clients. Another client, I was told, had apparently needed coaching to improve scrambling technique. The guide said:

> He was a liability because his technique was bad but this didn't stop him jumping and lunging for holds. He took a lot of controlling, particularly where the holds aren't big anyway he's a very big man, and he was leaping around like a man possessed. He was very keen to get to the top.

In these examples the guide is teaching the client because it will make the ascent safer for them both. In this respect the performance of the script reinforces the position of responsibility the guide has to the client and the client expects from the guide.

Guiding means that the risk of danger in the mountains is controlled like a circumscribed stage (Edensor, 1998). That is, the guidebook script imposes a safe stage upon the uncertainties of the environment. The choreographing of the required movement on this stage, however, is much more like the direct teaching of a dance where the choreographer teaches set steps and motifs (i.e., sequences of movements) than a general performance such as Goffman (1959) and Edensor (1998) discuss. Physical coordination and confidence, rhythmical sure-footedness and balance are all part of the body being choreographed to act as a functional and effective instrument for achieving the goal of reaching a summit or a destination. The ultimate adventure tourist performance, from the guide's point of view, is when the client dances like the guide and becomes recognizably a mountaineer.

What this identification of rules does not do is to consider the arguably unconscious motivations that shape clients' aspirations in mountaineering. This relates to Chaney's (1993) point quoted by Edensor (1998, p. 64) 'Chaney remarks that as tourists "we are above all else performers in our own dramas on stages the industry has provided".' Brochures are an important attention catching reference point for all adventure tourists. When people buy a holiday they are paying for the expectation that they will gain something: a suntan, greater knowledge, new experiences and new (perhaps temporary) social identities are examples. But the freedom to explore such possibilities in mountain holidays is tempered by the controls operated by guides who not only contribute to brochures, but to guidebooks and videos too. With specific reference to adventure tourism the guidebook, an institution in mountaineering culture, has shifted from an expressive form often like a novel or a personal journey (for example Littlejohn, 1979). Its replacement has become more zappy and catchy with more photographs and diagrams still conveying a general feel for what is involved, often for a specific activity within mountaineering. Williams' (1994) guide to bouldering[3] in the Peak District is an example. Videos can be categorized as the educational video on safety in the mountains and some skill input, and entertainment videos often set themes that become popular like sport climbing.[4]

Guides again can be seen to have a central role in writing, appearing as the stars' of the educational and entertainment videos and also as the testers of equipment produced for the exploits promoted. One might argue that beyond the choreographic rules, identified above, to do with the scripted route and aesthetic experience, clothing and equipment, posture and gesture, rules of performance are carried as a mindset from mountaineering commodities giving information and invitations to take part. An example from guidebooks will illustrate this point. When mountaineers visit an area of which they have no local knowledge the guidebook becomes an important reference point as a descriptor of the climbing, scrambling and walking in the area. The guidebook writer, usually a local expert, may have highlighted certain routes via a star system or some other mechanism to direct activity towards the 'best' objectives. Such foci will adhere to the broader rules in so much as the 'best' routes will have the most aesthetically pleasing vistas and require the application of accepted mountaineering techniques to meet the challenge. Guidebooks also set out the degree of difficulty of a challenge through grading systems. These exist for walking and scrambling but are most fully developed in the context of climbing (for example, Milburn, 1993). Graded lists of climbs offer a ladder of progression which is 'ascended' (and the related status assimilated) by 'ticking' challenges at the different levels. Grades are allocated by the experts that make the first ascent. These are then moderated through subsequent ascents so that a consensus emerges. Guides, however, remain the central driving force behind this process. It is the social construction of this scene setting that reveals the choreographic influence on tourist performances.

Conclusion

I have identified that the choreographic metaphor for tourist performance has indicated the influence that the mountain guide wields at several levels of the adventure tourist industry. Additionally I have found that rules exist that are implemented through the guide operating as a choreographer. In contrast with the kinds of tourist guides Edensor (1998) discusses, mountain guides script their own performances and keep tight control of the drama on a circumscribed stage leaving little scope for improvisation. The essentially didactic nature of the guide's performance has been illustrated through the identification of rules patterning the client experience, namely the governing concern for safety in the choice of equipment and ways of moving. Guides are independent and self-reliant mountaineers and the seriousness of the setting in which they are operating determines their role as teacher. The recipients of this 'education', that is the clients, are engaging in developmental leisure, which is a form of adventure education. As Nichols (2002) argues, adventure settings offer the potential for participants to progress to higher levels of satisfaction by coping with more technically challenging situations. This is both educational and developmental from the perspective of the client and a much 'deeper' (and possibly more enduring) engagement, because of the mountain setting, than that experienced by tourists at the Taj Mahal. This means that some clients will begin to operate independently in mountains, thereby constructing an identity of mountaineer based on performance of the rules.

If such a perspective is correct, it also means that all clients undertaking adventure holidays can not by virtue of the dangers inherent in the setting remain at the same level of performance that they start from. The accumulation of skill and experience is ongoing as the rules do not permit a blasé or 'shallow' approach to mountaineering. The role of the guide in the risk society identified by Nichols (2002) tends towards an approach that manages the mountain stage in a way that limits improvisation but controls potential dangers. Using Nichol's (2002) view that in adventure education the greatest risks are social because the stage is managed so efficiently as a reference point, the role of the guide can be further illuminated by considering the people being guided as locatable on an identity continuum. In Edensor's (1998) conventional human constructed settings the guide is dealing with tourists who are encouraged to follow a script where the risks or dangers are minimal. This might locate the left side of the continuum. As one moves rightwards, the setting becomes less obviously human constructed, wilder, closer to a natural landscape where the 'monuments' are not temples or historic buildings but mountains. The risks and dangers of operating in such places become greater and the management response to this is expressed in the generation of rules designed to rationalize those dangers through appropriate preparation, planning and performance. Being a tourist is no longer acceptable, and progress has to be made towards becoming a mountaineer the further one moves to the right of the continuum. Not all clients who buy adventure holidays will have the same expectations of their experiences. Some will want to remain close to their comfort zones and allow themselves to be guided through the mountains but others, further right again, will aspire towards greater independence. At the right end of the continuum are 'real' mountaineers. Guides may be further right again by virtue of their greater depth of skill and experience but they clearly have an important role to play in positioning the clients who employ them. Guides encourage a movement from left to right across the continuum although once minimum standards of competence are achieved, clients can then determine whether to be proactive in seeking out further knowledge and expertise to move themselves further rightwards.

A further dimension of such a model is the extent to which the whole continuum might be moving from right to left because of more generic changes to mountains and mountaineering resulting from 'touristic evolution'. The emergence of roads, airports, hotels, satellite communication systems, more detailed guide-books and instruction manuals, the infrastructure of adventure tourism companies and many other developments operate to reduce remoteness and bring urban characteristics to hitherto wild mountains. So, the dynamic component suggested by utilizing a model based on a continuum allows for a potential movement of people from left to right at the same time as the whole continuum might be moving from right to left.

Guides have a dilemma: they have to choreograph client performance to the point where each is 'developed' enough to cope with the seriousness of mountains, but the ultimate projection of this advance would leave clients as independent mountaineers in no need of mountain guidance. The physical demands of mountains places the balance of power in the guide-client relationship with the guide but this relationship is constantly evolving in a way that has the potential to empower clients. The analysis suggests that the traditions of mountaineering are currently being sustained through the expertise of guides and that adventure tourists are engaging at varying levels with the established ethos. Its reproduction continues through clients learning to perform like guides. Its challenge comes through the larger number of adventure tourists who not only have access to the previously select mountaineering culture but who take away an experience which Hamilton-Smith (1993) would label as a shallower experience. This is because the traditional mountaineering apprenticeship generates an ethos of independence based on self reliance. From the guide's point of view such an ethos is changing and the control indicated by the analysis above perhaps over emphasizes the influence of the guide in slowing this process. As the industry continues to grow, it is possible that adventure tourism might become a more clearly defined route to 'become' a mountaineer. Moreover, if the position of authority that guides hold is compromised by economic pressures upon them to adapt to adventure tourism it is possible they might have to accept alternative interpretations of 'their' rules. This avenue of investigation is beyond the scope of the discussion here, but it raises intriguing questions about how mountaineering might develop in the years ahead. The rapid growth of adventure tourism has already accelerated the process by which mountains are commodified, a position that might be fruitfully explored through a perspective of leisure as consumption. Almost anyone who has determination, a reasonable degree of physical co-ordination and the right income can buy into the mountaineering culture.

Arguably, on the one hand, this is to by-pass the usual introductions required by a mountaineering apprenticeship. On the other hand, the guiding tradition analysed in this paper offers a contribution to mountaineering self-reliance for those who seek it. There is, therefore, a tension for the guide between the monetary opportunities which more guiding work offers in adventure tourism and retaining the old traditions. Therefore, the mountain guide is a choreographer only to the extent that he or she accommodates the adventure tourist whose performance might fall short of the script which generations of mountaineers have performed.

Notes

1   Scree is unconsolidated rocks of all sizes. Scree results from processes of weathering in mountains and gravity operates to roll larger pieces further down the mountain. Scree collects on mountain slopes but is particularly common in gullies which act as funnels through which these rocks will slide. Crossing them demands judgement, concentration and skill.
2   Named after Sir Hugh Munro, a Munro is a Scottish mountain over 3,000 feet.
3   Bouldering is climbing without any aids such as rope, harnesses, partner or protective liardwear. It usually takes place on small outcrops, and has become a popular from of climbing with its own guidebooks.
4   Sport climbing uses fixed bolted protection points to protect the person leading the climb. Bolts minimize the risks of physical harm from falling. Climbers distinguish between this form and 'adventure climbing', with the latter form engaging to a greater extent with the uncertainty of outcome commensurate with adventure.

Acknowledgements

I would like to thank Dr Joyce Sherlock for her support, guidance and proof reading of this paper.

References

Bernbaum, E. (1997) *Sacred Mountains of the World*, University of California Press, London.

Bernstein, J. (1989) *Ascent: The Invention of Mountain Climbing and Its Practice*, Simon & Schuster, New York.

Christiansen, D. (1990) *Adventure Tourism*. In *Adventure Education* (edited by J. Miles and S. Priest), Venture Publishing, State College, PA, pp. 365–382.

Cloke, P. and Perkins, H. (1998) Cracking the canyon with the awesome foursome: representations of adventure tourism in New Zealand, *Environment and Planning D: Society and Space*, 16, 185–218.

Creswell, J. (1994) *Research Design: Qualitative and Quantitative Approaches*, Routledge, London.

Deegan, P. (2002) *The Mountain Travellers Handbook*, BMC, Manchester.

Dieniberge K. (1983) *Summits and Secrets*, Hodder & Stoughton, London.

Edensor, T. (1998) *Tourists at the Taj*, Routledge, London.

Foundry Mountain Activities (2000) *Brochure*, Sheffield.

Frison-Roche, R. with Jouty, S. (1996) *A History of Mountain Climbing*, Flammarion, New York.

Giddens, A. (1990) *The Consequences of Modernity*, Polity Press, Cambridge.

Goffman, E. (1959) *The Presentation of Self in Everyday Life*, Penguin, Harmondsworth.

Hamilton-Smith, E. (1993) In the Australian bush: some reflections on serious leisure, *World Recreation and Leisure*, 35, 10–13.

Hammersley, M. and Atkinson, P. (1995) *Ethnography: Principles in Practice*, Routledge, London.

Hoyland, G. (2002) The Seven Summits, *High Mountain Sports*, 239, 1.

Jenkins, R. (1996) *Social Identity*, Routledge: London.

Littlejohn, P. (1979) *South-West Climbs*, Diadem, London.

MacCannell, D. (1976) *The Tourist: A New Theory of the Leisure Class*, Macmillan, London.

Milburn, G. (1993) *On Peak Rock*, BMC, Manchester.

Milburn, G. (1997) *The First Fifty Years of the British Mountaineering Council*, BMC, Manchester.

Moore, A. (1867/1939) *The Alps in 1864*, Blackwell, Oxford.

Nichols, G. (2002) Risk and adventure education, *Horizons*, 18, 13–20.

Rojek, C. and Urry, J. (1997) *Touring Cultures*, Routledge, London.

Rubens, D. (1999) Effort or performance keys to motivated learners in the outdoors, *Horizons*, 4, 26–28.

Smart, B. (1992) *Modern Conditions, Postmodern Controversies*, Routledge, London.

Trauer, B. (1999) Conceptualising Adventure Tourism and Travel in an Australian Context, unpublished paper, University of Lancaster.

Urry, J. (1990) *The Tourist Gaze*, Sage Publications, London.

Walter, J. (1982) Social limits to tourism, *Leisure Studies*, 1, 295–304.

Wells, C. (2001) *A Brief History of British Mountaineering*, BMC, Manchester.

Williams, A. (1994) *Bouldering in the Peak District*, OTE Media Services, Buxton.

Chapter 12

Maurice J. Kane and
Robyn Zink

PACKAGE ADVENTURE TOURS
Markers in serious leisure careers

Introduction

THE PHRASES 'PACKAGE ADVENTURE tourism' and 'serious leisure' are similar in that within each phrase there is inherent tension. 'Adventure' and 'serious' indicate excitement, uncertainty, involvement and consequence, while 'package tourism' and 'leisure' indicate organization, structured, insulated experience and relaxation. This paper suggests that the relationship between these phrases is more than a similarity in semantic contrasts and provides scope for understanding a complex tourist experience.

Tourists' experiences are diversely understood and are often linked to the description or structure of the tourist product. In this study the tour product is described as both an adventure and a package tour. Adventure tourism is defined and most commonly marketed as involving experience of risk, danger and adrenaline (Hall 1992; Sung, Morrison and O'Leary 1997; Millington, Locke and Locke 2001; Swarbrooke *et al.*, 2003). Conversely, the organized routine and structure of package tourism is conceptualized as passive, safely insulated, experience (Schmidt, 1979; Schuchat, 1983; Quiroga, 1990).

The apparent contradictions within a package adventure tour have led to a search beyond tourism theory to interpret the experience of the participants on this tour. This paper explores the potential for understanding the experience of package adventure tourism from a leisure perspective, utilizing the construct of serious leisure (Stebbins, 1982, 1992, 1999). Serious leisure is presented as the dominant 'field' or 'way of thinking' for the participants in this complex tour experience (Bourdieu, 1993). The interpretation is grounded in the tour experience, participants' understandings and their observed behaviours. It is argued that the contrasting understandings of a package adventure tour are negotiated and negated by participants' focus on advancing their serious leisure careers in white-water kayaking. To ground this paper, a description of the context, participants and theoretical concepts will follow.

Tour and participants

The guided or package tour has been described as 'insulated adventure' where 'the tourist exchanges some of the freedom that would be available to him [her] in other traveller roles (and hence opportunities for adventurism) for the relatively problem-free situation provided by the guided tour' (Schmidt, 1979, p. 446). This aptly describes the structure and organizational situation of this tour. The tour was conducted in the South Island of New Zealand over a two-week period in February (summer) 2002. It was an all-inclusive tour (food/accommodation/equipment) for nine clients (plus one researcher) staffed by two kayaking guides and two cooks/drivers. The tour followed a circular route from Christchurch, the largest South Island city, around two-thirds of the island, travelling approximately 1,500 km. We kayaked for between two and eight hours on eleven of the fourteen days, on thirteen different rivers. The central focus of the tour was the prestigious helicopter accessed kayaking (heli-kayaking) on the West Coast, although only two days in the middle of the tour were scheduled for this activity. The prestige of heli-kayaking came from adventure videos and articles that presented the West Coast of the South Island as, 'the hottest extreme kayaking destination on the planet' (Canard, 2001, p. 15). This prestige can be attributed to three factors: the quality of the kayaking; the novelty of helicopter access; and especially the endorsement of the elite kayaking heroes featured in articles and videos (Kane, 2002).

All nine clients on the tour were participants in this research. They were citizens of the USA, two women and seven men, with dispersed home residences in the states of California, Georgia and Florida. They ranged in age from 32 to 55 years, with three under 35 and five between 42 and 48. They had all attended some form of tertiary education (university), and their financial position would be described as middle class and higher. All had been on this type of kayaking tour before, with four of the participants having been on over five such tours. Five participants had also met on a previous tour in 2000. They seldom kayaked together in their home localities, primarily due to distance, but had influenced each other in deciding to come on this tour. There was a wide range of kayaking experience and skill levels. One participant had only been on one previous beginners kayaking tour, while one had kayaked at a national level and had been involved in kayaking for 35 years. All, however, shared a commitment to kayaking, which had provided the impetus to travel halfway round the world for this tour. It is this level of commitment to kayaking that suggests, for these participants, that it is serious leisure.

Serious leisure

Commitment, belonging and the ethos of a defined culture are at the core of the concept of serious leisure. A strong commitment to a form of recreation was initially theorized by Bryan (1977). He provided a framework that outlined a 'developmental process whereby people progressed to higher stages of involvement the longer they participated in a leisure activity' (Scott and Scott-Shaffer, 2001, p. 320), Involvement and progression in the form of a career is the focus of the serious leisure theory, initially proposed by Robert Stebbins in 1982 and subsequently refined into the following abbreviated definition:

> The systematic pursuit of an amateur, hobbyist, or volunteer activity that participants find so substantial and interesting that, in the typical case, they launch themselves on a career centred on acquiring and expressing its special skills, knowledge, and experience.
>
> (Stebbins, 1992, p. 3)

The factor that Stebbins promoted was that the leisure activity was an integrated and important signifier of the person's identity; in essence what a person identifies himself or herself as. Stebbins (1982, p. 251) viewed serious leisure as an 'intermediate position . . . contrasted throughout with unserious or casual leisure, on the one hand, and work, on the other'. He drew on the features and components of work to illustrate the commitment and identity individuals were deriving from their serious leisure involvement. The increasing importance of leisure provided an avenue to create identity stories that were comparable to, but not based on, the work-focused social world. People could, dependent on the social world they chose to focus on, create an identity that was oriented to the values of that social world.

Of the three forms of participation in serious leisure, the first two (amateur and hobbyist) are defined primarily by the leisure activities and the participants' relationship to its professionals. The participants in this study are amateurs with a complex and mutual relationship with professionals. They viewed themselves as having a vocation in the activity, aligning themselves with professionals and distinct from the non-activity involved public. Hobbyists have no such alter ego relationship with professionals. For many there are no or few professionals in their activity. The last group, the volunteers, are focused on involvement in a helping activity with varying relationships to professionals.

Amateurs, hobbyists and volunteers are all distinguished by six qualities that define participants' systematic pursuit of a serious leisure career. The qualities are intertwined but can be defined as:

- perseverance – conquering some adversity and gaining positive feelings
- effort to acquire knowledge, training, or skills
- finding a career marked by turning points and stages of achievement
- obtaining durable benefits and rewards
- identifying strongly with the activity
- a unique ethos constructed around the serious leisure activity.

(Stebbins, 1999)

These qualities create social worlds for participants in serious leisure that have 'unique sets of special norms, values, beliefs, styles, moral principles, performance standards, and similar shared representations' (Stebbins, 1999, p. 71). It is the uniqueness, constructed around leisure activity, which provides the ability for participants to create distinct identity and social stratification within their serious leisure social world. The uniqueness of, for example, playing chess, writing poetry or marathon running, indicates how the six qualities can manifest differently creating distinct social worlds. Research into recreational participation in climbing, rugby, skydiving, windsurfing and endurance racing has highlighted similar qualities and theories on identity, subculture and 'career stages' (Donnelly and Young, 1988; Green and Chalip, 1988; Celsi et al., 1993; Ewert, 1994; Wheaton, 2000; Kay and Laberge, 2002a,b).

Kay and Laberge (2002a,b) describe the participation and experience of a specific recreational leisure using the sociological theories of Pierre Bourdieu. Bourdieu (1993) provides a theoretical framework in how experiences are practised and understood, through his concepts of 'field' and 'habitus'. The experience of an adventure tour can be related to many 'fields', but the kayaking focus indicates that serious leisure has potential in adding to the understanding of this adventure tour.

The 'field' of serious leisure

Bourdieu's interest was in understanding and interpreting the practices of social interaction. A 'field' was not a concept to group or define people such as serious leisure kayakers, but a way of analysing their practices and interactions in terms of a 'way of thinking'. Central to a 'field', how it functions and is defined, are 'stakes and interests' which are represented by 'capital' specific to that field. 'Capital' is dynamic within a 'field' as participants compete to gain, retain and re-enforce the value of the 'capital' they possess. This 'capital' indicates the power relationships and distributions within the 'field'. One 'way of thinking' about this tour is that the serious leisure of kayaking, its uniqueness and ethos, delineates the 'capital'. Although there is 'capital' related to adventure, tourism, package tours, etc., the dominant competition focus in this instance is on 'stakes and interests' related to the kayaking social world.

The 'capital' that is most prized on this tour is the experience, or stories, of West Coast heli-kayaking. These will provide participants with experience stories, a form of 'symbolic capital', of experience similar to the kayaking elite. The professional or elite hero kayakers, who have the most capital, and corresponding hierarchy in the serious leisure social world of kayaking, define the field's 'capital'. It is a 'capital' based on the continually changing experience and skill of professionals. In social interactions and kayaking practice the participants were competing for 'capital' utilizing their understanding of kayaking ethos, or in Bourdieu's (1984) terms, their 'habitus' or 'feel for the game'. This 'feel for the game' is a tacit feeling, an understanding of the uniqueness of the kayaking social world, which produces the practice of being a kayaker. The greater the participants' 'feel for the game', the greater the ability to gain and transfer 'capital' thus retaining or improving their 'stakes and interests', their status in the kayaking social world.

Although one 'field' or 'way of thinking' may be dominant, there are always competing 'fields' that influence how an experience is understood and recounted. In this study serious leisure is presented as a competing 'field' to the dominant adventure and tourism 'ways of thinking' about the complex experience of an adventure tour. The openness to a different 'way to thinking' is mirrored in the methodological approach taken to research participants' experience of this adventure tour.

Methodology

Tourism research has been dominated by positivistic methods and assumptions that have marginalized divergent methodologies at the expense of greater explanatory potential (Walle 1997; Ryan 2000: Botterill 2001). This study's interpretation was developed from a strategy of inquiry that sought to 'stud[y] behaviour from inside a system', focused on tourists' experience (Weber, 2001, p. 372). As a group tour it was a shared experience, including the guides, drivers, the first named researcher, and other kayakers and non-kayakers encountered during the tour. The information gathered, analysis and the interpretation focused on the participants' experiences. The primary method was observation of participation, which facilitated and was complemented by unstructured conversations and more structured, individual, interviews through the tour experience.

The term 'observation of participation' indicates my role as researcher was negotiated with participants. I had the local knowledge and skills of a guide, often participating like a tourist, yet focused on research. It had been five years since I had kayaked consistently but my previous experience was from a professional perspective, as a paid kayaking instructor, video participant and guide. I had a high level of kayaking skill, knew 'elite hero kayakers' and prestigious destinations and therefore had a degree of 'capital'. Kayaking however, was not now my work or a committed leisure-time activity. It was no longer serious leisure for me. I could participate with an understanding of the kayaking social world and 'field', yet not be dominated by the ethos of the serious leisure of kayaking.

I travelled with the participants, sharing accommodation, meals, social events and kayaking rivers. Observation involved noting expressions, actions, nonactions and comments of individuals and recording these in notes, usually at day's end, but also as things transpired. Conversations were similarly noted down. The more structured 'individual interviews' were conducted and audio taped at convenient times through the tour, from day three to day twelve. The interviews, as Maykut and Morehouse (1994) advised were, 'conversation [s] with a purpose . . . [and with a] format consisting of a detailed set of questions and probes' (1994, p. 79, 83). The questions sought to identify the participants' understandings of adventure and adventure tourism, focused on this tour experience but realizing past experiences would influence their understandings. There were no direct questions as to whether participants felt their kayaking was serious leisure. The interviews allowed ideas and thoughts to be explored, especially in the probing section where the interviewee often asked me questions. In this way it was a stimulating process where knowledge was constructed in collaboration (Holstein and Gubrium, 1997).

Through the research process I contributed to the participants' experience, their conversations and their process of understanding. The participants' experiences were contrasted to others involved on the tour, guides, myself and also with the other participants, in a continual process of understanding. My interpretation and analysis of information was also a continual process through the tour, yet much of this paper's interpretative formulation was from transcribed notes and audiotapes subsequent to the tour. This post tour analysis involved repeated readings and comparison of participants' interviews, which were related to field note conversations, observations and memory. Through this process themes of understanding and abstract constructs were identified (Ryan and Bernard, 2000). It was an art of choice, like finding meaning in poetry, where meanings were both found and discarded (Rose and Webb, 1998).

This paper presents the way things were understood by participants, yet these understandings are really just the sense I, as the researcher, have made of them, and the voice given to this interpretation of experience (Crotty, 1998). This voice reflects my tour experience, yet is not focused on my reflexive experience, but rather on the interpretation of the nine participants' experiences of adventure tourism. It is to this interpretation of the tour experiences that the paper now turns its focus. The tour experience was much like kayaking a new river, the initial novelty is compared, an understanding of the river is developed and the stories of the river are formed. In this paper the novelty is compared to previous tours and tourism research, a dominant understanding is framed within the 'field' of serious leisure and both the stories told and untold will be discussed.

The tour experience

Just a bunch of kayakers

Cara's description of the group to an outsider as *just a bunch of kayakers* reflects the focus of much of the social discussion, and the currency of identity formation within the group. Making comparisons was common over the first few days of the tour, as unknown rivers and new environments were explored. For example Robert said, *that looks a lot like northern California*, and others said *it looks the same size/ colour/ level as the '—' river*. These comparisons increasingly focused on experiences on other package kayaking tours, with comments such as, *that river looks just like down in Chile* by Shane. This corresponds to a feature described in many studies where although 'tourists often find themselves in conversations with each other about home . . . A more acceptable topic of conversation among tourists is their experience as tourists' (Schmidt, 1979, p. 461; Dann, 1996; Pearce, 1991; Ryan, 1995; Selwyn, 1996). The acceptable topic of conversation on this tour was kayaking.

It was through this discussion of kayaking experiences and consequently kayaking tour experiences, that participants defined intra-group identity and status. There was limited discussion about general society's status building signifiers, such as wealth, official title or education, As Bruce expressed one evening, *how did I do this trip with you for 3 days and not know what you do [your profession]*.

In terms of previous tourism research this is indicative of Foster's (1986) 'short-lived society' where limited time and a packaged daily routine narrowly focuses social interaction. Foster's research focused on the influence of the structure and physical constraints of small cruise ship tours. He found the tourists' common interest was the previous tours in terms of structures and constraints, rather than diverse tourism experience. Although similarly guided and packaged, the participants on this tour shared a defined single focus: kayaking. The tourism, structure and constraints were not significant aspects of their kayaking tours. Rather, the focus was on the prestige of the kayaking that each destination offered. The tour environment did however, constrain behaviour and structured functional roles, which contrasts to the uncertainty and freedom of kayaking.

The participants negotiated this complexity of experience in relation to their commitment and strength of identity derived from the activity of kayaking. They were not guided tourists, they were *travelling adventure kayakers*, an oft-heard self-definition emphasizing their specialized and serious leisure.

Serious leisure identity

It's like now my life is being driven by, what big trip are we doing this year? What river are we going to do this year? It's like, completely changed! (Rachel)

Rachel's comments on the effects of a previous kayak tour to Costa Rica were an illustration of the centrality of kayaking and kayak tours to the participants' understandings of who they were. One of the ways participants displayed this kayaking identity was wearing logo bearing clothing both specific to kayaking and to kayaking destinations. This display was principally for intra-group and other kayakers' viewing, as a level of knowledge is required to distinguish the 'symbolic capital' these items inferred. This kayaking social world knowledge, embedded in the participants' kayaking 'habitus', extended to unique phrases, body language and conversations in the group and with other kayakers.

To distinguish themselves in the non-kayaking world, where this 'symbolic capital' did not have any meaning, the participants had to rely on more overt differentiation. This included the vans loaded with kayaks and by starting conversations with statements such as *we've come over to do some kayaking . . . here to kayak*. The promotion of kayaking as central to who the participants were was exhibited in responses to the initial context-setting interview question; 'Tell me a little bit about yourself?' David, Bruce and Cara offered kayaking identities, with no information as to their wider life. David's first statement, *I'm probably the least experienced kayaker on the trip*, displays the importance of kayak experience as 'symbolic capital' in signalling group hierarchy. Both Bruce and Cara established and sought to maintain their prominent positions in the group hierarchy through the telling and retelling of their extensive kayaking experience. The other participants detailed their age, employment or family members before lengthy descriptions of beginning kayaking and the extent of their experience. Allan and Shane, the only two with young children, had to be prompted to describe their extensive kayaking experience, although both had mentioned their introduction to other outdoors activities that led them to kayaking.

Kayaking was the participants' recreational specialization; they saw themselves as kayakers and it was how they wanted to be seen by others (see Stebbins, 1992; Bryan, 1977). They demonstrated and established their kayaking identity both within the group, via stories, clothing and skills demonstration and for non-kayakers directly in conversations, equipment displays and actions. This kayaking identity made them distinctive from other tourists and from the general public. It also signalled to other kayakers their involvement in the serious leisure of kayaking. Displaying and establishing identity was one of the 'stakes or interests' for which they were competing in the social world of kayaking. Their ability to display identity, especially to other kayakers, reflected their 'habitus' or their 'feel for the game' of kayaking. The 'game' of this tour was for these kayaking amateurs to seek 'symbolic capital' that identified them with the elite and professional kayakers.

Amateur kayakers

An amateur involvement in serious leisure involves an entwined alter-ego relationship with the professionals of that leisure activity, Stebbins (2002) defines this relationship in a professional–amateur–public (P–A–P) system. There are monetary, intellectual, organizational and technical relationships between amateurs and professionals, with professionals benchmarking the prestigious activity standards while constantly being scrutinized by the amateurs. The public is differentiated from both through lack of activity involvement and knowledge and, in this way, either amateurs or professionals can 'serve' the public through displays of their leisure activity.

When Cara stated that they were *just a bunch of kayakers*, she was including the professional guides in the bunch. The relationship between the participants and guides was an involved two-way relationship, with participants both seeking and providing knowledge. Participants, especially those with vast experience, offered the tour kayaking guides opinions on kayaking products, kayaking destinations or kayaking history. On many of the rivers most of the participants' kayaking skills were at such a level that they did not require guides. The guides co-ordinated the logistics with the drivers and managed the equipment, but on the river became part of the group, albeit high status and highly skilled members of the group. For the majority of the tour, when the kayaking was less challenging, Cara's statement *just a bunch of kayakers*, reflected the tour atmosphere and relationships within the whole group.

The differentiation between amateur/professional and tourist/guide, however, was perceivable and maintained in the tour structure. The guides were considered by the participants to have expert status, local specialist knowledge and organizational authority. In its simplest form, the guides were questioned about the rivers, for example, *how cold will the water be?* They also had the 'symbolic capital' of close acquaintance to other professionals or elite kayakers and more recent kayaking experience as they followed the summer season around the world. This 'symbolic capital' gained authority and physical status through the confidence and kayaking skills the guides displayed as the difficulty of the kayaking increased.

On the focal heli-kayaking on the West Coast there was a clearly demarcated division in the roles of tourist/guide, amateur/professional. Although the heli-kayking rivers were at low water levels and less challenging then expected, these rivers were formally guided. There was a structured order to progressing down the river and the guides made all the rapid route selections. Uncertainty was moderated and freedom curtailed. This segmentation of roles extended to a separation in socializing after these heli-kayaking rivers but soon transformed back into all being *just a bunch of kayakers*. The last five days of kayaking were, with the exception of one river, less challenging. As a result, the tour structure and organizational authority roles were re-negotiated to provide an image of a group of adventure kayakers.

Kayaking career

The participants' relationships both with the professionals and any other kayakers were grounded in their shared identity as kayakers. They competed for kayaking's 'capital', seeking to gain hierarchical status in their serious leisure social world. It was a focus or 'way of thinking' that differentiated the tout experience from that of other tourists and the non-kayaking public. For the participants as amateurs, displaying the qualities of perseverance, skills progression and commitment was an avenue to demonstrate their current 'capital' or status in the kayaking world. This package adventure tour provided the opportunity to increase this 'capital', and advance their career as amateur kayakers (Stebbins, 1982, 1989, 1999).

Acquisition of knowledge, training and skills, perseverance and stages or turning points are characterized as signifiers in a commitment to a career in serious leisure (Stebbins, 1992). Three participants, Shane, Rachel and Robert, referred to seeking training and skills through the use of professional kayaking centres/schools (k c/s), Shane provided an example of the importance of this training:

> We realized we were pretty crappy boaters [kayakers], so we decided to go take some lessons, we went down to Nantahala [k c/s]. We went took the beginner, intermediate and advanced courses at Nantahala for three different years and that opened up the South East [of America].

Shane also followed a progression in his first international kayaking package tour with this centre. *I kind of worked my way up from the intermediate trip to the advanced trip down there [Costa Rica]*. As all other participants had taken previous trips with the Nantahala Centre it was likely that some form of training was provided as a prerequisite.

As Shane stated, training and skills advancement was a sought after and valued part of the ethos of the participants' kayaking experiences. This training or skills achievement was often presented as a memorable turning point in the participant's kayaking career. In Shane's case it was a negative experience that indicated a lack of skill. Participants initial kayaking experiences were often characterized by lack of skill, knowledge or control and described in terms of 'swimming' and 'beatings'.[1] Robert recounted his first attempt to paddle a rapid:

> We built a boat and actually did about a class three plus rapid[2] without any life jackets or anything and just really enjoyed that. We got beat up pretty bad but!

One of Phil's early non-package trip experiences was a virtual folk legend for the trip participants. As Phil recounted:

> I shouldn't have been there – a guy was taking me down. I went through ah, a thing called 'Hydro-electric' and in the book [guidebook] it says a swim here will probably be your last!

Phil has swum this rapid twice and was viewed by the participants as heroic for persevering but lacking in skill. In the 'field' of kayaking, skills have higher 'capital' value than heroics.

Combined with these 'beatings' and disappointments were the factors constraining kayaking participation, such as time, family, money and, especially in Phil's case, distance:

> It's very difficult [to kayak]. I travel about a twelve-hour drive [each way] once a month.

Yet the participants, like Phil, had persevered with this leisure activity after 'beatings', and logistical and practical difficulties. Rachel and Shane described making this form of packaged tour experience a significant feature of their kayaking career, as the tours provided one mechanism for participants to persevere with kayaking, develop their skills and define marked achievement in their serious leisure.

This perseverance is marked by positive turning points, significant events or milestones, often in the form of first time events or the mastering of some skill. Robert recalled an early successful river trip as:

> A weird experience . . . almost like a vision, I knew right away that I loved this sport and it was a sport, you know, for me.

Phil celebrated his first kayak surf in the ocean on this tour with exuberant joy, while David, the least experienced kayaker, gained the congratulations of all for completing his first mid-rapid Eskimo Roll.[3] Such events were significant in the participants' kayaking skills progression and kayaking career. Recognition of such events and how they increased status has been observed in other adventure sport groups (Celsi *et al.*, 1993; Donnelly and Young, 1988).

A kayaking ethos

Stebbins (1999) identified three beneficial qualities of serious leisure. These are: a unique ethos or social world; an individual's strong identity associated with the leisure activity; and the durable benefits (skills and success) that participants gain. Although the participants gained benefits in multiple ways, there was some commonality in these benefits. Rachel aptly described one significant feature of this tour for her:

> I want it to be something that I have my friends with me, that we all like share in it, otherwise it just becomes meaningless.

This need to share with the *good old boys* or *kayaking buds* from home, extended to any kayakers that shared the kayaking ethos or social world. The only significant socializing the participants did on the tour outside the tour group was with other kayakers, usually also overseas tourists. Shane described how:

> . . . kayakers like to sit around and talk about: where have you been? what rapids have you done? what, you know near escape from the jaws of death have you encountered? It's part of the experience.

The durable benefits of kayaking and this adventure tour were most often described as an activity that allowed stress relief and achievement. Eric saw it:

> as a stress relief mechanism for something, that . . . ah, I feel much, much better physically and mentally after I do.

For Allan:

> . . . it's just a way to get away, have some good times with some friends . . . and just forget about work for a while.

Shane stated more clearly both what he was after and what kayaking and adventure tours provided relief from:

> With kids and work I need to fit in a lot of fun into a short period.

This adventure tour was viewed as separate from the other social worlds that the participants inhabited. The benefits, however, transcended the kayaking world into their wider social lives. As Robert stated he *kayaked to refresh his soul*.

Bruce and Robert saw the benefits in the uncertainty of participating in the challenges of kayaking. Robert suggested:

> . . . there is something extremely rewarding and gratifying about coming up to a rapid and almost piecing the puzzles together.

While similarly Bruce saw positive benefits in the success when *he picks out the line*[4] *and hits exactly that line*. Rachel expressed the beneficial feelings of this aspect of kayaking and of this tour:

> Afterwards there has to be a sense of accomplishment, something that you feel like, 'all right I did that one!' its off your life's list . . . things you are going to tell, when your kids don't want to listen to you anymore.

These benefits, the sense of achievement, are treasured by participants in relation to the 'capital' of kayaking, what was or was not challenging as established by the professional elite kayakers. The participants, as Rachel suggested, will present their own 'symbolic capital' claims through stories of this tour experience. The creation of these stories became prominent after the mid-tour experience of the prestigious heli-kayaking rivers. These stories perpetuated the adventure image for the general public (non-kayakers) and the prestigious kayaking destination image for kayaking peers. In neither of these stories did, and I suggest will, the packaged routine and guided structure of the tour be a feature. For the participants, a package adventure tour was a mechanism that allowed the freedom to be travelling adventure kayakers.

Symbolic stories of adventure and kayaking

The increased focus on the creation of tour stories before the tour was complete is indicative of the participants' serious leisure social ethos, and within this, the prestige of one part of the tour destination and the longer-term impetus for involvement on the tour. As tourists they were consuming activity, involving effort and risks, which were moderated by a package tour structure and guides, With the prestigious heli-kayaking safely concluded the participants could produce their symbolic stories of challenging effort and adventurous experience. The symbolic stories would become the valued and enduring product of the tour experience.

For an audience of the participants' non-kayaking peers, their stories of this kayaking tour presented an image of adventure, uncertainty and/or a journey into the unknown. As Phil suggested:

> I don't look at myself as, you know, as an adventurer, ah . . . but I know because of where I go and what I do I would be looked upon in that way.

Kayaking was the dominant signifier of adventure for those outside the kayaking social world. The participants universally agreed that non-kayakers could not understand the experience of this, or previous package adventure tours. The participants felt their non-kayaking peers saw them as:

> Probably more like a complete nut. (Robert)

> Oh they think I'm insane. (Phil)

> They . . . like think I'm crazy. (Rachel)

> Oh my work peers think I'm as nutty as a fruitcake. (Eric)

> Non-kayaking peers see it as risk and a danger. (Cara)

> I think they view it as a very dangerous sport and some wild streak in me. (Shane)

These negative descriptors were actually considered positively by participants. It differentiated them, characterized their identity and association with a distinct social world (Celsi et al., 1993; Kay and Laberge, 2002a,b). This adventurous social world and identity descriptor was also re-enforced by the distant, international travel aspect of this tour. The 11 September terrorist attacks were prominent and recent memories, and travel outside of the USA at this time was characterized as potentially uncertain and risky.

The participants' positive differentiation can be attributed to their commitment to kayaking, and their 'way of thinking' was that non-kayakers envied their experiences. Rachael was confident in her non-kayaking peers envy:

> Oh yeah Rachel went to such and such, Oh she was stupid to do that, but you know she went! They want to live vicariously through me.

Several participants suggested non-kayaking peers often say 'Oh I'd love to do that'. The influence and value of the views of non-kayaking peers corresponded to the participants' hierarchy in the kayaking social world. David, with the least 'capital' thought:

> . . . anybody that's on this trip is adventurous.

while Eric, one of the more experienced participants commented:

> . . . this has been a very pleasant adventure but I wouldn't call myself an adventurer.

For Eric, identity came from kayaking peers rather than from how non-kayakers viewed him. It was this audience, kayaking peers, whose 'way of thinking' could comprehend the tour stories as 'symbolic capital' who authorize increased kayaking status. The stories for non-kayakers were within the discourses of adventure; stories for kayakers are within the ethos and language of kayaking.

Shane anticipated his kayaking peers would respond as they have in the past on his return from kayak tours:

Everybody's antenna goes up and they start grilling you about what it was like.

The tour's prestigious destination was high in both 'stakes and interest', providing the opportunity for prestigious stories with valued 'symbolic capital'. This prestige came from the heli-kayaking on the West Coast. After this part of the tour, participants' socializing focused on a routine of scripting, telling and re-scripting their tour stories focused on heli-kayaking. Digital photos were reviewed, selected and exchanged. The unique feature of helicopter access could be verified in digital images, becoming a central feature of the narrative. As Shane described:

> I mean helicopter kayaking I've never had a helicopter pick me up and drop me off on a creek run before.

This 'symbolic capital' in stories and images was not guaranteed to provide increased status, as this came with the authorisation of their' peers, most notably those with more capital and hierarchy. Participants understood they had not experienced extreme, elite, kayaking as the rivers were low, just as they were not insane, crazy adventurers as imaged in the non-kayaking world. Their stories of 'symbolic capital' had to reflect their 'capital' or experience and the hierarchal relationship they had with each audience. The participants' kayaking 'habitus' was critical to the success of their stories. The stories had to demonstrate the qualities of serious leisure, especially advancing career through perseverance and gaining skills, but also be believable in relation to their present 'capital'. The participants' 'habitus' guided their tour experience and the promotion of specific storied images or the discounting of others.

Un-told package tour stories

The serious leisure qualities of commitment, perseverance, improving skills and the beneficial qualities of identity, rewards and shared ethos have been the features interpreted in the participants' experience of this packaged adventure tour. An example of the interrelationship between these features is how the elite kayakers who determine 'capital' maintain their position as elite kayakers. It is not through insane risk taking, but through successful skill demonstration. As in other activity focused social worlds, failure at any level is equated to lack of skill, or 'feel' (Celsi et al. 1993). This 'feel' is in the physical activity decisions, as Shane suggested:

> . . . at my level, I try to ride the fine line [between failure and success].

The 'feel' is also intrinsic to the participants' choice of a package adventure tour as a mechanism to advance their kayaking career. As Cara succinctly commented:

> . . . somehow it seems safer to do adventure tourism than it does to do adventure on our own.

The un-told story is the importance of the packaged and guided structure of this tour to the participants' success. Success not only in safely experiencing New Zealand kayaking, but also in gaining successful stories of 'symbolic capital'. As Cara suggested, the participants knowingly choose the organized structure and restrictions on freedom that a package tour dictates. In stories to be retold, what will not feature are comments such as Bruce's, that:

> . . . it makes it relatively tame as adventure goes, to have somebody who can tell you for every rapid go right, go left.

Bruce, and other participants, will emphasize the positive aspects of the tour:

> on the other hand I'm quite satisfied with it, I've had a great time and danger actually, we really try specifically to avoid.

Negotiating the contrasting images between a packaged (guided), insulated tour and a dangerous, risk oriented adventure tour was part of the participants' 'riding the fine line'. Participant stories will not feature their expectations that the guides would insulate them from adventure experience likely to be a failure or risky. As Allen states:

> . . . they'd be irresponsible if they put us in a risk position.

The participants' choice of a package adventure tour acknowledges the implicit guarantee of safety and success that accompanies such a tourism product. As Bauman (1996, p. 29) suggests:

> In the tourist world the strange is tame, domesticated and no longer frightens; shocks come in a package deal with safety.

The tour was a consumable package of perceived safe experience from which participants could produce stories of adventure, implying unsafe experience. Specifically in their 'way of thinking' a package adventure tour was a mechanism to increase experience and critically create stories of 'symbolic capital', with the potential to improve their status in their serious leisure of kayaking. The prestigious 'capital' value of this tour destination, and of participants' previous tours indicate that, for the participants, package adventure tours were markers in their serious leisure career.

Conclusion

This paper commenced by comparing the similarity in semantic contrasts within the terms adventure tourism and serious leisure. It has sought to explore the extent to which the theory of serious leisure could be a useful concept for understanding the complex experience of a package adventure tour. Predominantly, adventure tourism experience is contrastingly and divergently defined as either packaged safe tourism, or risky uncertain adventure. The inquiry strategy recognized this theoretical contrast and through a focus on the tourists' understandings sought to interpret how they negotiated their tour experience.

Observation of and discussion with the tour participants revealed that their kayaking involvement, inclusive of this tour, demonstrated many of the qualities and attributes of serious leisure. Kayaking was far more than the activity focus of this tour, but underpinned the participants' behaviours and understanding of the tour experience. Within the context of the tour they presented themselves through language, interaction and performance as 'just a bunch of kayakers'. They exhibited a 'field' – ('way of thinking') and 'habitus' – ('feel for the game') distinctive to the kayaking social world. For the duration of this tour the participants were not accountants, police chiefs, engineers or tourists, but kayakers with a 'habitus' that produced practice oriented to their serious leisure social world.

The tour enabled them to demonstrate and have authorized their serious leisure qualities of perseverance, skill acquisition, identity, career commitment and ethos of kayaking. These qualities of their amateur career could be practised, performed, compared and tested against the professional guides. Defining and setting the benchmark for these qualities, what can be termed 'capital' in the kayaking social world, were the oft-mentioned elite professional kayakers. It was the professionals' endorsement of West Coast heli-kayaking that made it the 'capital' laden main focus of the tour. This was the critical tour experience from which participants could potentially gain the most 'capital' and corresponding status in their kayaking social world. The realizing of this 'capital' and status would be through stories of these experiences, stories of 'symbolic capital' that would become prominent in the later stages of the tour. The most valued stories would be authorized by the participants' peers, who shared their 'way of thinking' and knowledge of kayaking 'capital'. The participants would also gain status in wider social 'fields' where the attributes of adventure are commonly positively regarded.

Although the participants' dominant demonstration was of involvement in the serious leisure of kayaking and its 'way of thinking', they were not unaware of other interpretations of their experience. The most apparent of these was the package and guided nature of their tour. The participants negotiated the structure and concepts of this tourist product, emphasizing the opportunities it provided in accessing safe and successful kayaking experiences. Safety and success are implicitly guaranteed in the tourism world or tourism 'way of thinking', especially in the packaged, guided product. It was this implicit guarantee that influenced the participants' choice of this tour structure, as 'safe success' is valued 'capital' in the kayaking social world. The adventure focus of the tour, the novelty of New Zealand, and the distinction of the kayaking activity also influenced the way participants and others interpreted the tour. In the participants' non-kayaking social worlds, tour stories would be predominantly perceived in reference to the attributes of adventure, with little understanding of the skills, safety and success of kayaking. The negotiation of this experience of a package adventure tour was the negotiation of 'fields' or 'ways of thinking'. The interpretation of this paper is that the participants' experience was within the 'field' of their serious leisure social world of kayaking. Within this 'way of thinking' this package adventure tour was a significant moment, a marker in their serious leisure career.

Notes

1   Swimming and beating occur when you lose control of your kayak, often parting company with it.

2   Rivers are rated on a scale from 1 for still water to 6 for un-kayakable rapids.
3   Skill in being able to turn the kayak, with yourself still in the correct position up right when you have capsized.
4   A line is the route the kayaker follows through the rapid, or disturbed water.

References

Bauman, Z. (1996) From pilgrim to tourist: Or a short history of identity, in *Questions of Cultural Identity* (edited by S. Hall and P. du Gay), Sage Publications, London, pp. 18–36.

Botterill, B. (2001) The epistemology of a set of tourism studies. *Leisure Studies* 20, 199–214.

Bourdieu, P. (1984) *Distinction: A Social Critique of the Judgement of Taste* (translated by R. Nice), Routledge & Kegan Paul, London.

Bourdieu, P. (1993) *In Other Words: Essay Towards a Reflexive Sociology* (translated by M. Adamson), Stanford University Press, Stanford, CA.

Bryan, H. (1977) Leisure value systems and recreational specialisation: The case of trout fishermen. *Journal of Leisure Research* 9(3), 174–187.

Canard, H. (2001) Tourism, conservation and recreation, in *Managing New Zealand's Wildlands* (edited by K. Lloyd), Federation of Mountain Clubs of New Zealand, Rotoiti, New Zealand, pp. 15–21.

Celsi, R.L., Rose, L.R. and Leigh, T.W. (1993) An exploration of high-risk leisure consumption through skydiving. *Journal of Consumer Research* 20, 1–23.

Crotty, M. (1998) *The Foundations of Social Research: Meaning and Perspective in the Research Process*, Allen & Unwin, St Leonards, NSW.

Dann, G. (1996) *The Language of Tourism: A Socio-Linguistic Perspective*, CAB International, Wallingford, UK.

Donnelly, P. and Young, K. (1988) The construction and confirmation of identity in sport subcultures. *Sociology of Sport Journal* 5, 223–240.

Ewert, A.W. (1994) Playing the edge: Motivation and risk taking in a high altitude wilderness like environment. *Environment and Behaviour* 26(1), 3–24.

Foster, G.M. (1986) South seas cruise: A case study of a short-lived society. *Annals of Tourism Research* 13, 215–238.

Green, D.C. and Chalip, L. (1988) Sport tourism as the celebration of subculture. *Annals of Tourism Research* 25(2), 275–291.

Hall, C.M. (1992) Adventure, sport and health tourism, in *Special Interest Tourism* (edited by B. Weiler, and C.M. Hall), Belhaven, London, pp. 141–158.

Holstein, J.A. and Gubrium, J.F. (1997) Active interviewing, in *Qualitative Research: Theory, Method and Practice* (edited by D. Silverman), Sage Publications, London, pp. 113–129.

Kane, M.J. (2002) Niche image: The touchstone to destination image, in *Proceedings of the International Tourism Student Conference: New Zealand Tourism Hospitality Research* (edited by W.G. Croy), School of Tourism and Hospitality, Waiariki Institute of Technology, Rotorua, New Zealand, pp. 15–23.

Kay, J. and Laberge, S. (2002a) The 'new' corporate habitus in adventure racing. *International Review for the Sociology of Sport* 37(1), 17–36.

Kay, J. and Laberge, S. (2002b) Mapping the field of 'AR': adventure racing and Bourdieu's concept of field. *Sociology of Sport Journal* 19(1), 25–46.

Maykut, P. and Morehouse, R. (1994) *Beginning Qualitative Research: A Philosophic and Practical Guide*, The Falmer Press, London.

Millington, K., Locke, T. and Locke, A. (2001) Adventure travel. *Travel and Tourism Analyst* 4, 65–97.

Quiroga, I. (1990) Characteristics of package tours in Europe. *Annals of Tourism Research* 17, 185–207.

Pearce, P.L. (1991) Travel diaries: an analysis of self-disclosure in terms of story structure, valence and audience characteristics. *Australian Psychologist* 26(3), 172–175.

Rose, K. and Webb, C. (1998) Analysing data: Maintaining rigour in a qualitative study. *Qualitative Health Research* 8(4), 556–562.

Ryan, C. (1995) Learning about tourists from conversations: the over-55s in Majorca. *Tourism Management* 16(3), 207–215.

Ryan, C. (2000) Tourist experiences, phenomenographic analysis, post postivism and neural network software. *International Journal of Tourism Research* 2, 119–131.

Ryan, G.W. and Bernard, H.R. (2000) Data management and analysis methods, in *Handbook of Qualitative Research*, 2nd edn (edited by N.K. Denzin and Y.S. Lincoln), Sage Publications, Thousand Oaks, CA, pp. 764–802.

Schmidt, C.J. (1979) The guided tour: insulated adventure. *Urban Life* 7(4), 441–467.

Schuchat, M.G. (1983) Comforts of group tours. *Annals of Tourism Research* 10, 465–477.

Scott, D. and Scott-Shafer, C. (2001) Recreational specialization. *Journal of Leisure Research* 33(3), 319–343.

Selwyn, T. (1996) *The Tourist Image: Myths and Myth Making in Tourism*, Wiley, Chichester.

Stebbins, R.A. (1982) Serious leisure: A conceptual statement. *Pacific Sociological Review* 25, 251–272.

Stebbins, R.A. (1992) *Amateurs, Professionals, and Serious Leisure*, McGill Queen's University Press, Montreal.

Stebbins, R.A. (1999) Serious leisure, in *Leisure Studies: Prospects for the Twenty-first Century* (edited by E.L. Jackson and T.L. Burton), Venture Publishing, State College, PA, pp. 69–79.

Stebbins, R.A. (2002) *The Organizational Basis of Leisure Participation*, Venture Publishing, State College, PA.

Sung, H.H., Morrison, A.M. and O'Leary, J.T. (1997) Definition of adventure travel: Conceptual framework for empirical application from the providers' perspective. *Asia Pacific Journal of Tourism Research* 1(2), 47–67.

Swarbrooke, J., Beard, C., Leckie, S., and Pomfret, G. (2003) *Adventure Tourism: The New Frontier*, Butterworth Heinemann, Oxford.

Walle, A.H. (1997) Quantitative versus qualitative tourism research. *Annals of Tourism Research* 24(3), 524–536.

Weber, K, (2001) Outdoor adventure tourism: A review of research approaches. *Annals of Tourism Research* 28(2), 360–377.

Wheaton, B. (2000) 'Just do it': Consumption, commitment, and identity in the windsurfing subculture. *Sociology of Sport Journal* 17, 254–274.

Chapter 13

Heidi Sung

CLASSIFICATION OF ADVENTURE TRAVELERS
Behavior, decision making, and target markets

Travel and tourism markets are changing. Sociodemographic changes marked by an active aging population, two-income families, childless couples, and a rising population of single adults have led to substantial changes in travel and leisure demand and in patterns of travel markets (Chon and Singh 1995; Loverseed 1997; Morrison *et al*. 1996; Ross 1999). The emergence of the special interest tourism segment, for instance, has been driven by market demand to cater to today's travelers who are pursuing special interests in more diversified categories than in the past (Hall and Weiler 1992). By definition, special interest tourism refers to "the provision of customized leisure and recreational experiences driven by specific interests of individuals and groups" (Derrett 2001, p. 3). In this, satisfaction and self-actualization appear to be crucial in understanding a traveler's engagement with an activity or a product for a distinct and specific purpose to satisfy his or her particular interests and needs (Hall 1989; Loverseed 1997; Sorensen 1993). Examples of special interest tourism include ecotourism. (Boo 1990; Cater and Lowman 1994), nature tourism (Whelan 1991), and adventure tourism (Christiansen 1990; Hall 1992), just to name a few.

Adventure travel has been developed out of a broader growth of traditional outdoor and wilderness recreation (Ewert 1989). It has broadened its scope and appeal among travelers who want to "experience" a vacation by participating in specific activities (Black and Rutledge 1995; Madrigal 1995; Vellas and Becherel 1995) that are adventure based (Ewert 1987; Hall 1989). According to Sung, Morrison, and O'Leary (1997), the notion of adventure from past leisure and recreation studies can be linked to a tourism perspective in defining adventure travel as "a trip or travel with the specific purpose of activity participation to explore a new experience, often involving perceived risk or controlled danger associated with personal challenges, in a natural environment or exotic outdoor setting" (p. 66).

Although the exact size of the adventure travel market is still debatable due to the lack of a standard definition to measure the market, it is generally agreed that adventure travel is a newly emerging, fast-growing sector in the tourism industry (Sorensen 1993; Loverseed 1997; Fluker and Turner 2000). A survey of adventure travelers in the United States reports that nearly one-half of U.S. adults, or 98 million people, have taken an adventure trip in the past 5 years (Travel Industry Association of America [TIA] 1998). Similarly, about 45% of Canadian residents engaged in various outdoor adventure activities during their trips in 2001, which was overall ranked as the second most popular type of travel behavior following visiting friends and relatives (Canadian Tourism Commission [CTC] 2002).

Unlike ecotourism or nature-based tourism in which a number of definitions have evolved for conceptual development of each discipline, adventure travel, adopted from outdoor adventure or risk recreation, appears to be heavily oriented to the industry. This is particularly true in North America, where travelers' specific interest in experiencing "active" holidays has been matched with the rapid growth in commercial operators (Hall 1992). Thousands of small operators or outfitters are now offering an enormous variety of adventure activities ranging from hiking to skydiving in conjunction with a wide range of professional expertise such as guide services, equipment manufacturing or rentals, accommodations, or specific travel arrangement (Mallett 2002; CTC 2002; Carrera 1995; Eagles and Cascagnette 1995; Ewert 1989; Hall and Weiler 1992; Jackson 1994).

Despite its growing popularity and expansion in the travel and tourism industry, little scholarly investigation has been attempted in adventure travel (Fluker and Turner 2000; Walle 1997; Weber 2001). Moreover, such diversified products and services in adventure travel have attributed to a great complexity for business entities in developing, delivering, and packaging product offerings to today's marketplace (Loverseed 1997; Ross 1999). While both active holidays and value for money have become key factors in selecting an adventure vacation (Hall 1992; Oden 1995), it is challenging for adventure travel practitioners to match the enormous variety of adventure travel products and/or services with diversified consumer demands. Following this line of reasoning, Sung *et al.* (1997) suggested that research in adventure travel should start from understanding two dimensions: (1) the distinct notion of adventure that had been often referred to as "outdoor adventure recreation" or "risk recreation" in past leisure studies and (2) the travel components in serving the movement of individuals for specific activity participation.

Furthermore, understanding adventure travelers should be centered on distinct travel psychographics emphasizing specific needs, motivations, and expectations (Fluker and Turner 2000) or individuals' subjective experiences and perceptions of adventure need (Weber 2001). In travel and tourism marketing, analyzing travelers' decision-making process generally aims at obtaining two lines of information: (1) traveler characteristics and (2) their consumer and travel behavior. As Swarbrooke and Homer (1999) claimed, today's marketing is based on the idea that knowing your customers and then anticipating and meeting their needs is the key to success. The current business and industry trend toward increasing diversity in travel demands and travel-related products requires tourism marketers to identify detailed, specific characteristics of travelers and their travel behavior to effectively pinpoint their target segments (Kotler, Bowen, and Makens 2002; Middleton 2001; Morrison 2001). To enhance the effective strategy formulation for adventure travel providers and marketers, this study aims to improve understanding of distinct adventure traveler subgroups through development of a classification construct with specific focuses on (1) traveler characteristics, (2) trip-related factors in the decision-making process, and (3) perception of the adventure components.

Conceptual framework

Adventure travelers in consumer behavior research

A discussion of consumer behavior research might start with its conceptual linkage to leisure involvement originally reported by Sherif and Cantril (1947) in ego involvement theories. Selin and Howard (1988) further developed this and identified five components comprising ego involvement: (1) centrality, (2) importance, (3) pleasure, (4) interest, and (5) self-expression. Studies (Dimanche and Havitz 1994; Havitz and Dimanche 1990, 1995, 1997) have also explored the concept of involvement as an explanatory, psychological variable to understand individual leisure behavior, where leisure involvement refers to "individual's involvement with various recreation activities and associated products, leisure service agencies, or settings" (Havitz and Dimanche 1997, p. 246).

Involvement in consumer behavior research has been generally acknowledged as a major factor in the decision-making process between the choice of purchase or not. From a tourism, perspective, the same decision can be applied to whether participating in a particular form of tourism is undertaken. It can be seen that consumer behavior research in tourism is primarily to explore the relationship between the involvement components with the inclusion of tourist behavioral variables specific to the research focus. Linking this to ego involvement, an individual's leisure involvement occurs when he or she expects personal meaning (importance) in leisure pursuits (interests) and realizes rewards (pleasure) from such involvement, where the amount of pleasure appears to have a positive relationship with the level of importance and interest (Havitz and Dimanche 1997; Selin and Howard 1988; Sung et al. 2001).

The main focus of involvement theory is on the individual. From the travel and tourism marketing perspective, such an individual has his or her own needs, taste, or attitude and is in a distinctive mode of living or lifestyle (Mill and Morrison 1998). More specifically, a lifestyle would be "a way of living characterized by the manner *(centrality)* in which people spend their time (for *pleasure*), what things they consider important *(importance* and *interests),* and how they feel about themselves *(self expression)*" (Mill and Morrison 1998, pp. 41–45). Such individual lifestyle or psychographics are primarily based on a personal value system (Hsu, Kang, and Wolfe 2002; Keng and Cheng 1999), the structural relationship of which could possibly explain how and why (or why not) an individual gets involved in leisure products or activities.

The underlying proposition is that an involved consumer is more likely to understand and memorize promotional stimuli and to purchase the product or service that raised his or her level of involvement (Havitz and Dimanche 1997). The structural relationship between factors associated with psychographies or personal value needs to be further explored as to how such distinctive individual behavior can be explained and how an individual's level of involvement in tourism activities can be increased. Given this, studies in travel and tourism marketing widely suggest use of psychographics or behavior variables to formulate preference functions in travelers' decision-making process often in conjunction with sociocultural and/or demographic variables to profile distinctive lifestyles or benefits sought (Bieger and Laesser 2002; Hsu, Kang, and Wolfe 2002; Hvenegaard 2002; Mill and Morrison 1998; Moscardo, Pearce, and Mossiron 2001; Plog 2002).

Among five components of ego involvement, Havitz and Dimanche (1995) argued that importance, interest, and pleasure might fall under an attraction facet in the leisure and tourism context. Sung, Morrison, and O'Leary (1997) reported activity, environment, experience, motivation, risk, and performance as the key elements to define adventure travel. Of those, activity, experience, and environment can be suggested as the major attraction of adventure travel. That is, an individual would be engaged in adventure travel for the purpose of gaining pleasure and personal meaning (experience) through participation in leisure pursuits (activities) in a specific setting (environment). Such conceptual linkage between adventure travel and leisure involvement can be also seen in Havitz and Dimanche's (1997) review of 50 past studies of leisure involvement: with only few exceptions, importance, pleasure, and interest loaded together and produced the highest mean scores among participants in the activity context.

Iso-Ahola (1982) identified two dimensions to explain why people engage in outdoor recreation: an attempt to achieve something and an attempt to avoid something. Similarly, Selin and Howard (1988) reported that "commitment to leisure activities could occur when the behavior would express the need of the individual" (p. 240). This is one of the key assumptions of the self-expression facet to explain the participant's development of attachments to certain types of leisure activities. Manning (1986) reported that motives for participation in outdoor recreation generally consisted of a desire for achievement, affiliation, control, escape, and self-awareness. In a more comprehensive manner, Hall (1992) tried to categorize the motivations associated with adventure travel into risk seeking, self-discovery, self-actualization, contact with nature, and social contact. It is noticeable that these motivations can be clearly grouped into two involvement domains. The first group, including self-awareness, self-discovery. achievement, and self-actualization, is central to the individual's value system (centrality), whereas control, affiliation, and social contact fall into the expression category of individuals' self-concept (self-expression). Likewise, adventure travel, is associated with specific activities as a primary motive for trips, as well as the expected outcomes (rewards) from the participants' experiences in particular environments.

Havitz and Dimanche (1990), in their study of an empirical testing of the involvement constructs in the recreational and tourist context, discussed that individuals' leisure and touristic experiences should also involve interactions from all behavioral components. Activity in adventure travel, for example, has proven to be the primary domain and is closely interrelated with experience and environment (Sung, Morrison, and O'Leary 1997, 2000). However, this does not mean that activity alone can legitimately represent the entire scope of adventure travel. By the same token, a "leisure equals activity" conceptualization appears to be fir from an adequate explanation or interpretation of the complex context of leisure.

While it is the activity that primarily attracts individuals as participants in adventure recreation (Ewert 1989; Hall 1992), traditional forms of adventure recreation usually involved elements of skill in a specific outdoor setting. According to Iso-Ahola (1980), the challenging nature of adventure experiences should be derived from the "interaction of situational risk and personal competence." The degree of risk taking appears to have a positive correlation with the level of experience and skill of the participant. That is, performance in adventure travel would be consistently associated with skill level (Ewert 1987, 1989; Martin and Priest 1986). The notion of performance in adventure participation appears to share important criteria with the importance facet in the ego involvement context.

Traditional risk recreation theories have broadly conceptualized the outdoor adventure experiences in view of two constructs: perceived risk and perceived competence. The importance of risk for the notion of adventure has been recognized as an important element in distinguishing outdoor adventure activities (Ewert 1987, 1989; Ewert and Hollenhorst 1994; Hall 1992; Meier 1978; Weber 2001). Havitz and Dimanche (1997) also found that centrality items have performed well in adventure and risk recreation settings, producing strong factor loadings and reliability scores. Noticeable is that activity is recognized as a core concept for experiencing risk-taking adventure with varying degrees of the enduring risk involved (Walle 1997).

It is interesting that among the six major components of adventure travel reported by Sung, Morrison, and O'Leary (1997)—activity, experience, environment, motivation, risk, performance—only risk does not appear to adequately fit in the context of leisure involvement. As Ewert (1989) argued, risk might be a completely additional dimension specific only to risk recreation, distinguishing this from other types of recreation. It is the complex nature of risk recreation that makes it difficult to identify and understand underlying factors to influence enduring involvement in risk recreation activities (Robinson 1992). McIntyre's (1992) adventure model appears to be a challenging attempt in exploring relationships between involvement with motivations, experiences, and level of engagement in risk recreation. The remaining question is how an individual's attachment to participation or the involvement level might provide a more appropriate basis for assessing the levels of engagement in future risk recreation involvement.

Consumer involvement with products is now widely recognized as a significant variable in marketing studies. By the same token, tourism researchers have focused on tourist behavior for better understanding patterns in consuming tourism products and services as well as for contributing to the practice of tourism marketing. Linking the behavioral aspects of adventure travelers to the leisure involvement domain, consumer involvement in leisure can be integrated in people's participation (activities) in leisure experiences that are interrelated with multidimensional behavioral components: centrality, importance, pleasure, interest, and self-expression (adopted from Selin and Howard 1988). This supports that the six major components of the notion of adventure—activity, environment, experience, risk, motivation, and performance (Sung, Morrison, and O'Leary 1997)—could be used as a set of powerful explanatory factors that might explain travelers' specific behavior in different adventure trip participation.

Research objectives

According to one general assumption for market segmnentation research in travel, and tourism, travelers with particular travel or consumer behavior are likely to be different from others who are engaged in different behavior (Jeffrey and Xie 1995; Kashyap and Bojanic 2000; Moscardo et al. 2000). Those who go camping in a neighborhood state park, for instance, might behave differently on their trip from those who are on safaris in Kenya. Stated differently, segmenting a market is targeting specific customers with homogeneous (Andereck and Caldwell 1994) characteristics or behaviors, so that marketers can focus their marketing attention on selective groups of customers (Kotler, Bowen, and Makens 2002; Middleton 2001; Morrison 2001).

Attempts to define tourist types or to develop a traveler typology have been understood as segmentation, classification, or clustering (Hvenegaard 2002). In this study, using traveler and consumer characteristics for market segmentation purposes can be seen as one way to classify traveler sub-group segments to develop a traveler typology. Looking at the vast variety of adventure travel and participation levels, not all adventure travelers are, hypothetically, alike. One important question is how to identify significant factors that are presumably related to distinctive travel and consumer behavior in classifying different group memberships.

The varied activities that constitute adventure travel accommodate a number of different demographic and socio-economic segments. Although subject to debate, studies of ecotourism or nature tourism have reported that these travelers in general are likely to be men, middle aged, well educated, engaged in managerial or professional occupations, and affluent (Higgins 1996; Loverseed 1997; Silverberg, Backman, and Backman 1996; TIA 1998; Wight 1996). This general profile appears to be the case for adventure travelers (Sung 2001) but is of limited value in explaining distinctive travel behavior to formulate strategies for different target segments. Moreover, the demographic and socioeconomic profile of adventure travelers may differ from activity to activity (e.g., from camping to hot air ballooning) and from location to location (e.g., from Brown County State Park to Mt Kilimanjaro), and their consumer and travel behavior is also affected by a changing marketing environment in the travel industry (Ewert and Hollenhorst 1994; Hall 1992; Oden 1995; Ross 1999; Sorensen 1993; Sung, Morrison, and O'Leary 2000; TIA 1998; Weber 2001).

In explaining variances among different travel behavior and understanding travelers' decision-making process, various trip-related characteristics appeared to receive increased research attention in recent tourism studies (Chandler and Costello 2002; Dolnicar and Leisch 2003; Horneman *et al.* 2002; Kemperman *et al.* 2003; Moscardo, Pearce, and Morrison 2001; Prebensen, Larsen, and Abelsen 2003). The uses of psychographics such as activities, interests, preferences, benefits, or opinions have mainly looked to identify influential factors on the travel decision-making process (i.e., participation in a specific type of adventure travel or not). Some examples related to decision making might include traveling companion, the most influential entity in making travel decisions, and information source.

As discussed earlier, adventure travel appears to be experiential and participatory in nature. This involves several additional behavioral components to explain travelers' participation in adventure trips. Travelers' preference of a specific adventure activity type and the likelihood of taking an adventure trip, for instance, might reveal some patterns about how different adventure traveler subgroups are associated with different levels of involvement (participation) in taking trips. The underlying reasoning is that there might exist a relationship between and individual's past experience and his or her future levels of involvement in purchasing leisure products or services (Dimanche and Havitz 1994). Other variables specific to adventure travel can be adventure trip arrangement, adventure vacation destination, number of adventure trips per year, and so forth.

Activity, experience, environment, motivation, risk, and competence (Sung, Morrison, and O'Leary 1997) were identified as primary dimensions that might represent the travelers' perception of adventure travel. According to Plog (2002), individuals' perceptions of adventure travel would affect their subjective experience of adventure. The examination of perceived importance of adventure travel components by different adventure traveler subgroups could explain some underlying factors in adventure travelers' different involvement levels in selecting different trips. For adventure travel providers and marketers, such psychographics of adventure traveler subgroups might suggest ways to develop and deliver adventure travel products with improved customer appeal in the travelers' decision-making process.

This study proposes a behavioral analysis to classify how distinctive groups of adventure travelers might be associated with their demographic (D), socioeconomics (SE), trip-related characteristics (TR), and perception of adventure travel (P) in travel decision making. Those factors could explain their travel behavior in purchasing and consuming adventure travel products and services, representing distinctive traveler subgroups with different behavioral characteristics. The conceptual model proposed for the subgroup formation can be generally written as Cluster formation = f D, SE, TR, P, and the error term a). Once identified, adventure traveler subgroups are further examined to determine any meaningful association with their perception of adventure travel, linking the involvement in the adventure constructs to target segments. The classification and understanding of adventure travelers in this study, for effective segmentation purposes, has the following specific research objectives:

1   to classify adventure traveler subgroups based on their traveler characteristics and consumer and travel behavior in adventure travel decision making,
2   to understand how the classified adventure traveler subgroups might perceive adventure travel differently, and
3   to discuss how adventure travel products and services could be developed and delivered to target segments.

Research methods

Sample

The participants for this study were adventure travelers in the United States defined as *those who have taken adventure trips or who are interested in taking adventure trips.* This was similar to the participants in the TIA's (1998) study, those who had been on an adventure trip in the past 5 years or who would like to take one in the next 5 years. It should be noted that some of the instruments in the current study were measured not in terms of respondents' past travel behavior but with their preferences to represent future involvement in adventure travel. Included were (1) the most preferable adventure activity type, (2) the most preferable adventure travel arrangement, (3) preferable adventure vacation destination, and (4) trip expenditure for the next trip. This was mainly due to the justification of defining adventure travelers not only by having taken an adventure trip in the past but also including those who are interested in taking a trip but have not taken one yet. As no significant differences between these two groups were expected, questions were designed not to limit individuals' past travel behavior but to avoid any systematic exclusion of those who had never been on an adventure trip from the sample.

The study used the mailing list of the Adventure Club of North America (ACONA), a nationwide association of 60,000 active adventure travelers, to serve as the sampling frame. Being a primary association of the largest membership of adventure travelers in the United States, ACONA issues and distributes a bimonthly members-only magazine, *Outdoor Adventure*. The membership also provides members with a wide range of services such as field-testing privileges of new equipment, escorted outings, and product and travel discounts by cooperating with a number of industry providers. Therefore, this membership group can be considered as actively involved or at least interested in taking adventure trips, representing not necessarily the entire population in the United States but adventure travelers in general.

The stratified random sampling method was based on ACONA's membership distribution in nine census regions within the United States. The confidence interval approach using the 95% level of confidence yielded a computation of a sample size of 1,067 to claim $\pm 3\%$ accuracy. According to Burns and Bush (2003), for a sample size of 1,000 or more, only very little gain in accuracy occurs even with doubling or tripling the sample. Given this and the estimated p to be 50% in the population, the sample size ($N = 1,067$) appears to be reasonable for this study both in terms of accuracy and cost-effectiveness. Targeting the response rate of 50% or more to the survey, the sampling frame should have at least 2,000 names.

Using the census region classification as a basis for stratification, each population member was sorted by the assigned random number within the stratum. In drawing 2,000 names from ACONA's 60,000 membership subscription, the sampling frame selected every 30th member in each stratum. As shown in Table 13.1, the proportion of strata sample sizes by stratified random sampling appears to be faithful to their relative sizes in the circulation of ACONA's membership subscription by region.

Data collection

A three-phase mail survey was employed for data collection between June and August 1998. A total of 2,000 surveys was sent out initially and was followed by the same number of postcard reminders 10 days later. Of those, 22 mailings were returned for incorrect or unreachable addresses. The response rate of the initial mailings was 39.1% with 773 valid, completed questionnaires collected. The follow-up mailing was sent out to every nonrespondent to the initial survey. A total of 260 completed surveys were additionally collected out of 1,261 valid mailings, providing 20.6% of the response rate. Overall, the response rate to this mail survey reached 52.3%, or a total of 1,033 completed surveys.

Survey instrument

An eight-page, self-administered questionnaire consisted of questions about traveler and trip characteristics that are considered to be critical for participating in adventure trips. In classifying adventure travelers, the factors examined were (1) traveler's demographic characteristics (i.e., age, gender, marital status, household size, number of children younger than 12 years, and region of residence), (2) socioeconomic backgrounds of the respondents (i.e., occupation, education, income, number of income earners), (3) trip-related factors in decision making (i.e., preference of adventure activity type, likelihood of taking an

Table 13.1 Sample distribution by stratified random sampling

Region	ACONA membership			Sample distribution		
	n	%	Total (%)	n	%	Total (%)
Northeast						
New England	5,124	8.5		96	10.8	
Middle Atlantic	8,178	13.6	22.1	104	11.7	22.5
South						
West south central	3,942	6.6		59	6.6	
East south central	2,694	4.5		35	4.0	
South Atlantic	9,696	16.2	27.3	110	12.3	22.9
Midwest						
West north central	3,954	6.6		76	8.5	
East north central	9,408	15.7	2.3	154	17.3	25.8
West						
Pacific	10,440	17.4		158	17.7	
Mountain	6,564	10.9	28.3	100	11.1	28.8
Total	60,000		100.0	892		100.0

adventure trip, trip arrangement, destination, number of trips per year, trip length, trip expenditures, traveling companion, influential person, and travel information source), and (4) perceived importance of adventure travel components (i.e., activity, environment, experience, motivation, risk, and performance. as reported by Sung, Morrison, and O'Leary 1997). Among the trip-related characteristics, adventure activity types (soft nature, risk equipped, hard challenge, rugged nature, and winter snow) were adopted from Sung, Morrison, and O'Leary (2000) in grouping adventure activities reported by industry providers in terms of the level of agreement in belonging to the adventure travel category.

As Creswell (2003) suggested, pilot testing is important to establish the face validity of the questionnaire and to improve questions, format, and the scales of the instrument. Lauer and Asher (1988) reinforced the importance of the pilot test in developing new questions and suggested using pilot samples of the population of interest to review initial responses to the questionnaire with accuracy. This study chose the 1998 International Adventure Travel and Outdoor Show, one of the major trade shows of its kind, at the Rosemont Convention Center in Rosemont, Illinois, as the location for the pilot study.

This show was set within a confined location and restricted period of time, providing easy access to large numbers of people who were actively participating in adventure travel or interested in taking adventure trips. A total of 185 completed survey questionnaires were collected through the pilot study during February 21 and 22, 1998, with a response rate of 52.9% (185 responded out of 350 distributed). The completed questionnaires, 1.85 in total, were reviewed focusing on directness, simplicity, and clarity of the questions. No indication of problems was present, concluding that the pilot questionnaire could be used for the main survey without major editorial or content change.

Findings and discussion

Cluster formation

The first research objective of classifying adventure traveler subgroups was based on the proposed conceptual model: Cluster formation = f(D, SE, TR, P, and the error term ε). Of the 1,033 respondents to the survey, 892 cases were included in the analysis after excluding surveys with one or more missing values in any clustering variable. Among various multivariate analysis techniques, cluster analysis has often been used to classify subgroups of individuals or objects into a small number of mutually exclusive groups based on a set of specified homogeneous characteristics among the individuals or objects (Arimond and Elfessi 2001; Grant and Weaver 1996; Lang, O'Leary, and Morrison 1997; Sirakaya, Uysal, and Yoshioka 2003).

This study employed the K-means method to cluster cases. Unlike hierarchical cluster procedure, the results of this method can be less sensitive to the outliers in the data and more appropriate in analyzing very large samples with 200 or more cases (Churchill 1999; Hair *et al.* 1998; Kinnear and Gray 2000). Although this method can be used to analyze various types of data, it is important that variables are measures on comparable scales. For example, variables with a 1 to 7 scale have larger standard deviations than do variables with a 1 to 3 scale, affecting the final similarity value. The value of each interval, metric, or categorical data in this study was standardized on comparable scales (i.e., transformed z scores) prior to the cluster analysis to avoid misinterpretation of the calculations of distance measures caused by the scale difference.

In line with Hair *et al.* (1998), the focus of cluster analysis in this study was on the comparison of objects (cases) according to the natural relationships between the hypothesized factors, it is considered an objective methodology to quantify the structural characteristics of a set of observations, constructing typology for classifying distinct adventure traveler subgroups with homogeneous traveler characteristics and travel behavior. As the main objective of K-means cluster analysis in this study was data simplification in which all of the observations can be viewed as members of a cluster and profiled by its general characteristics, many variables (both scale and categorical) were used in the cluster analysis as collapsed data. Age, for example, was used as a nominal variable with six categories (19–24, 25–34, 45–54, 55–64, and older than 65) and grouped into three: generation X (age 19–34), baby boomers (35–54), and seniors (55 years or older).

In this case, not for confirmatory but for exploratory purposes, the selection of clustering variables should be based on theoretical and conceptual as well as practical considerations (Churchill 1999), so that the number of clusters should be specified by the researcher. As there is no clear-cut standard to determine the optimal number of clusters, several techniques were examined in deriving cluster solutions and assessing overall fit. Taking into account practical considerations for segmenting the adventure travel market, the study findings appeared to be more manageable and easier to communicate if it was three to six adventure traveler sub-groups. Solving for this number of clusters and selecting the best solution depended on several factors such as distances between final cluster centers, iteration history, final cluster centers, number of cases in clusters, and an ANOVA table. As a result, a six-cluster solution was proposed.

Table 13.2 Cluster size and distances between final cluster centers

Cluster	1	2	3	4	5	6	Total
n	243	193	84	128	119	125	892
%	27.2	21.6	9.4	14.3	13.3	14.0	100.0
1		3.141	4.865	2.954	3.167	3.286	
2	3.141		3.979	3.519	4.372	2.911	
3	4.865	3.979		3.415	3.62	3.912	
4	2.954	3.519	3.415		3.004	2.963	
5	3.167	4.372	3.62	3.004		4.233	
6	3.286	2.911	3.912	2.963	4.233		

Distances between final cluster centers can be the most popularly used measure to determine the similarity of the clusters. These are actually a measure of dissimilarity, with greater values denoting lesser similarity (Hair *et al.* 1998). As shown in Table 13.2, the means of cluster 1 and cluster 3 were furthest apart (4.865), while cluster 2 and 6 were closest to each other (2.911). Overall, cluster 3 appeared to be furthest from all other clusters (ranges = 4.865 and 3.620), whereas cluster 4 was relatively close to other groups (ranges = 3.415 and 2.963). Looking at cluster size, it appeared that cases were not equally distributed across clusters; there were relatively fewer cases in cluster 3 (n = 84) but more in cluster 1 (n = 243). Assuming that each cluster represents a type of adventure traveler, it can be said that there might be more travelers of the type represented by cluster 1 (27.2%) than the type found in cluster 3 (9.4%). The results of cluster analysis are summarized in Table 13.2 with cluster sizes.

The size of the overall F statistics in K-means' one-way ANOVA was useful for identifying variables that contribute to the clustering and also those that differ little across the clusters. Shown in Table 13.3 is a one-way ANOVA result, using the final clusters as groups, computed for each variable individually. The means of number of people in the household (F = 237.444) and number of income earners (F = 213.932) differed the most, indicating a basis for a great deal of the difference between the clusters. Other significant demographic and socioeconomic variables included household disposable income (F = 96.006), number of children younger than 12 years (F = 61.060), and marital status and age category (F = 59.373 and 43.274, respectively). On the other hand, the means of region of residence (F = 22,587) differed little across the six clusters (F = 2.587).

The results (see Table 13.3) also pointed out that all six of the perceived importance variables appeared to make considerable contributions in characterizing clusters (F ranges from 45.433 for environment to 92.321 for risk). For trip-related characteristics, adventure trip arrangement (F = 43.594), likelihood to take an adventure trip (F = 39.458), and traveling companion (F = 36.012) had sizeable differences, whereas adventure vacation destination did not contribute greatly to differences between the clusters (F = 3.667).

One remaining question was how valid the classification might be. Assessing classification accuracy typically involves the use of discriminant analysis (Churchill 1999; Hair *et al.* 1998), which can be done once the clusters are identified. Using the categorical dependent variable a priori–defined six-cluster solution, the result of discriminant analysis

Table 13.3 K-means ANOVA for clustering variables

Variable	Cluster		Error			
	M	df	M	df	F	Significance
Perceptions of major components						
Importance of activity	55.417	5	0.627	886	88.396	.000
Importance of experience	49.407	5	0.709	886	69.637	.000
Importance of environment	35.478	5	0.781	886	45.433	.000
Importance of motivation	50.110	5	0.700	886	71.632	.000
Importance of risk	60.916	5	0.660	886	92.321	.000
Importance of performance	48.817	5	0.715	886	68.234	.000
Demographic						
Gender	12.575	5	0.926	886	13.584	.000
Age category	34.972	5	0.808	886	43.274	.000
Marital status	44.750	5	0.754	886	59.373	.000
Household size	101.435	5	0.427	886	237.444	.000
Number of children younger than 12 years	45.443	5	0.744	886	61.060	.000
Region of residence	2.509	5	0.970	886	2.587	.025
Socioeconomic						
Current occupation	3.096	5	0.934	886	3.314	.006
Highest level of education attained	16.248	5	0.902	886	18.006	.000
Household annual disposable income	62.092	5	0.647	886	96.006	.000
Number of income earners	97.617	5	0.456	886	213.932	.000
Trip related						
Preference of adventure activity type	8.755	5	0.842	886	10.393	.000
Likelihood of taking an adventure trip	30.581	5	0.775	886	39.458	.000
Adventure trip arrangement	34.323	5	0.787	886	43.594	.000
Adventure vacation destination	3.621	5	0.987	886	3.667	.003
Number of trips per year	19.980	5	0.886	886	22.539	.000
Length of adventure vacation	14.501	5	0.926	886	15.657	.000
Travel expenditure per person	12.111	5	0.930	886	13.019	.000
Traveling companion	30.769	5	0.854	886	36.012	.000
Influential person or entity	14.886	5	0.906	886	16.436	.000
Information source	7.116	5	0.967	886	7.360	.000

Note: The significance levels should be ignored here since these *F* statistics are not to test significance of a model but to describe the contribution of each variable in cluster formation. The clusters have been chosen to maximize the differences between cases in different clusters, and the observed significance levels are not corrected for this. Therefore, the significance levels cannot be interpreted as tests of the hypothesis that the cluster means are equal.

Table 13.4 Evaluation of cluster formation by classification results

Cluster case	Predicted group membership						
	1	*2*	*3*	*4*	*5*	*6*	*Total*
Count							
1	237	1	0	1	1	0	240
2	8	179	3	1	0	2	193
3	0	3	78	2	0	1	84
4	6	4	2	109	1	4	126
5	8	1	0	1	108	0	118
6	6	9	0	2	0	108	125
Percentage							
1	98.8	0.4	0.0	0.4	0.4	0.0	100.0
2	4.1	92.7	1.6	0.5	0.0	1.0	100.0
3	0.0	3.6	92.9	2.4	0.0	1.2	100.0
4	4.8	3.2	1.6	86.5	0.8	3.2	100.0
5	6.8	0.8	0.0	0.8	91.5	0.0	100.0
6	4.8	7.2	0.0	1.6	0.0	86.4	100.0

Note: $n = 886$ (from $n = 892$ for cluster analysis) after excluding 6 cases with one or more missing discriminating variable. Of the original grouped cases, 92.4% were correctly classified.

revealed significant differences between the group characteristics. The classification results (see Table 13.4) were used to determine how successfully the discriminant function could work. Among those who belonged in cluster 1 ($n = 240$), for instance, a total of 98.8% (or 237 cases) were classified correctly, leaving only 3 cases (1.2%) misclassified. Overall, 92.4% of the cases (819 out of 886) were assigned to their correct groups, validating the results of cluster analysis for useful classification of adventure traveler subgroups based on their traveler and consumer characteristics.

Profile of the respondents

The summary statistics in Tables 13.5 and 13.6 clearly indicate that the respondents were demographically distinctive. They tended to be younger (49% are 19–34 years old), and most (83.5%) had no children younger than 12 years old. Adventure travel was more popular among men (67.6%), singles (54.5%), and those who lived in the West (28.8%). As for socioeconomics, respondents were more likely to work in professional or managerial occupations (44.2%), be well educated (92.4% with more than high school education), and be more affluent (46.1% with annual income of $50,000 or higher).

As shown in Table 13.7, almost all of the respondents (95.4%) would be either highly likely (66.1%) or likely (29.3%) to take adventure trips in the foreseeable future, emphasizing the high growth potential of this market. Almost every other adventure traveler (53.5%) preferred partial arrangement of trips through a travel agency plus activities with an operator or traveling on their own. Among destinations, the popularity of American destinations (60.9%) among the North American adventure travelers (Loverseed 1997;

TIA 1998) was clearly evident in the study results. A total of 85% of the respondents were likely to take an adventure trip at least once a year. Friends seemed to be the most preferred companion for adventure travelers, and adventure travelers tended to be mostly self-oriented (61.5%) in making travel decisions. The length of travel or travel expenditure per person for the next adventure trip did not vary greatly among adventure travelers. Instead of relying heavily on any specific source, respondents would rather use various information sources in their adventure travel planning (see Table 13.7).

The "soft nature" activities such as camping or hiking appeared to be most popular (31.8%), followed by "hard challenge" (26.1%) or "rugged nature" (24.7%) types. Although travelers' preference of an adventure trip did not seem to make a significant contribution to clustering adventure travelers, nearly all (99.3%) respondents indicated their preference for adventure activity types among one of the five given types. This ensured that the suggested groupings of adventure travel activities initially reported by Sung, Morrison, and O'Leary (2000) could represent the entire range of adventure activities available in the U.S. market. Summary statistics of all activity types are exhibited in Table 13.7.

Perception of adventure travel by traveler subgroups

The second research objective was to understand perceptions of adventure travel across the classified adventure traveler subgroups. Among six major elements composing the notion of adventure, activity was perceived most importantly in taking adventure trips followed by experience and environment in terms of mean values (M = 6.06, 5.79, and 5.70, respectively, with 1 = *least important* and 7 = *extremely important)*. Motivation, performance. and risk appeared to be relatively less important across all the clusters (M = 5.25, 4.93, and 4.34, respectively). This pattern was the most evident in cluster 4 (see Figure 13.1), in which means of the upper three components were clustered close to the extremely important level leaving the other three at far less important levels.

The ANO VA results (see Table 13.3) showed substantial variation in terms of the level of importance among six components across all six clusters classified. The presentation in Figure 13.1 also indicated risk to be perceived the least important, which was consistent among all six clusters. Although risk can still be considered an important factor in adventure travel (Fluker and Turner 2000; Weber 2001; Sung, Morrison, and O'Leary 1997), care should be taken to clarify the degree or amount of risk to be involved.

The fact that cluster 3 appeared to be most distinct from all other clusters (see Table 13.3) can also be seen in Figure 13.1. Travelers in this group seemed to assign less importance to the six components (means between 2.96 for risk and 5.13 for environment) than other groups. Cluster 1 travelers appeared to be the most positive about all six components (ranges = 5.67 for risk and 6.54 for activity). Members in clusters 2 and 6, on the other hand, tended to be very close in their perception of adventure travel both with activity the highest and risk the lowest. Cluster 5 travelers perceived most of the components as somewhat. important. but identified activity as extremely important (M = 5.86).

A correlation analysis further revealed significant structural relationships between adventure traveler subgroups and the perceived importance of adventure travel components. All six subgroups were highly related to six major components. Both clusters 3 and 5 were significantly distinct from the other four traveler groups as to how importantly they would perceive those components for their adventure trips. Adventure travel overall was

Table 13.5 Demographic segmentation of adventure travelers by clusters

| Summary statistic | | | Segmentation by adventure traveler subgroup (%) | | | | | | | |
Demographic factor	n	%	GE	BY	SM	UHN	FV	AS	χ^2	Significance
Gender									63.511	.000
Male	603	67.6	79.8	69.9	45.2	53.1	80.7	57.6		
Female	289	32.4	20.2	30.1	54.8	46.9	19.3	42.4		
Age category									184.175	.000
19–34	439	49.2	61.3	80.3	32.1	23.4	38.7	25.6		
35–54	400	44.8	36.6	19.7	56.0	62.5	57.1	62.4		
55 and older	53	5.9	2.1	11.9	14.1	4.2	12.0			
Marital status									223.866	.000
Single/not married	486	54.5	47.7	91.7	63.1	28.9	16.8	66.4		
Married	406	45.5	52.3	8.3	36.9	71.1	83.2	33.6		
Household size									646.298	.000
1	321	36.0	0.8	83.4	63.1	14.1	0.8	68.8		
2	284	31.8	36.2	11.9	29.8	71.9	24.4	21.6		
3 or more	287	32.2	63.0	4.7	7.1	14.1	74.8	9.6		
Children (< 12 years old)									228.596	.000
None	746	83.6	72.8	99.0	100.0	96.9	44.5	93.6		
1 or more	146	16.4	27.2	1.0		3.1	55.5	6.4		
Region of residence									32.592	.005
Northeast	201	22.5	21.4	16.6	32.1	21.1	21.8	29.6		
South	204	22.9	23.5	21.8	22.6	20.3	21.8	27.2		
Midwest	230	25.8	27.6	31.6	13.1	20.3	33.6	20.0		
West	257	28.8	27.6	30.1	32.1	38.3	22.7	23.2		

Note: GE = general enthusiasts; BY = budget youngsters; SM = soft moderates; UHN = upper high naturalists; FV = family vacationers; AS = active soloists.

Table 13.6 Socioeconomic segmentation of adventure travelers by clusters

Summary statistic			Segmentation by adventure traveler subgroup (%)							
Socioeconomic factor	n	%	GE	BY	SM	UHN	FV	AS	χ^2	Significance
Occupation									33.860	.004
Managerial/professional	394	44.2	36.2	39.9	47.6	59.4	42.0	50.4		
Technical/sales/operational	193	21.6	23.5	25.4	14.3	15.6	26.1	19.2		
Service/self-employed	213	23.9	25.1	25.4	27.4	18.0	21.0	25.6		
Retired/other	92	10.3	15.2	9.3	10.7	7.0	10.9	4.8		
Education									108.789	.000
High school	68	7.6	10.7	9.8	8.3	1.6	8.4	3.2		
Some college	298	33.4	46.5	31.6	26.2	13.3	37.8	32.0		
College complete	326	36.5	29.2	47.2	39.3	39.8	31.9	33.6		
More than college	200	22.4	13.6	11.4	26.2	45.3	21.8	31.2		
Household income									326.866	.000
Low (<$30,000)	200	22.4	8.6	61.7	39.3	3.9	3.4	14.4		
Middle ($30,000–$49,999)	281	31.5	32.9	33.7	28.6	24.2	27.7	38.4		
High (>$50,000)	411	46.1	58.4	4.7	32.1	71.9	68.9	47.2		
Income earners									487.885	.000
1	434	48.7	9.1	93.3	77.4	30.5	14.3	88.8		
2 or more	458	51.3	90.9	6.7	22.6	69.5	85.7	11.2		

Note: GE = general enthusiasts; BY = budget youngsters; SM = soft moderates; UHN = upper high naturalists; FV = family vacationers; AS = active soloists.

Table 13.7 Travel characteristics segmentation of adventure travelers by clusters

Summary statistic			Segmentation by adventure traveler subgroup (%)							
Trip-related factor	n	%	GE	BY	SM	UHN	FV	AS	χ^2	Significance
Preference for activity[a]									124.482	.000
Soft nature	284	31.8	18.9	22.8	66.7	40.6	41.2	29.6		
Risk equipped	80	9.0	9.1	9.3	9.5	7.8	6.7	11.2		
Hard challenge	233	26.1	35.8	33.2	6.0	14.8	20.2	27.2		
Rugged nature	220	24.7	26.3	23.3	14.3	32.0	18.5	28.8		
Winter snow	69	7.7	8.6	11.4	3.6	3.1	12.6	3.2		
Other	6	0.7	1.2			1.6	0.8			
Likelihood of taking a trip									161.240	.000
Unlikely to take	41	4.6	17.3	1.0	21.4	28.1	10.1	7.2		
Likely to take	261	29.3		23.3	50.0		44.5	34.4		
Highly likely to take	590	66.1	82.7	75.6	28.6	71.9	45.4	58.4		
Trip arrangement									190.808	.000
Inclusive	166	18.6	12.8	4.1	16.7	14.8	18.5	57.6		
Partially inclusive	477	53.5	56.4	49.2	59.5	63.3	56.3	37.6		
Self-arranged	249	27.9	30.9	46.6	23.8	21.9	25.2	4.8		
Vacation destination									21.231	.020
America	543	60.9	61.3	57.0	75.0	46.3	69.7	52.8		
Europe/Africa	110	12.3	11.9	11.9	10.7	22.2	10.1	12.0		
Asia/Pacific	239	26.8	26.7	31.1	14.3	31.6	20.2	35.2		
Frequency of trip per year									109.733	.000
< Once	134	15.0	8.2	5.7	28.6	20.3	26.9	16.8		
Once	348	39.0	33.3	28.0	46.4	50.0	39.5	50.4		
> Once	410	46.0	58.4	66.3	25.0	29.7	33.6	32.8		

	n								χ²	Sig.
Trip length									72.417	.000
< 7 nights	410	46.0	51,9	57.5	35.7	17.2	60.5	39.2		
> 7 nights	482	54.0	48.1	42.5	64.3	82.8	39.5	60.8		
Trip expenditure									88.570	.000
Undecided	229	25.7	25.9	33.2	23.8	21.1	30.3	15.2		
< $1,000	299	33.5	39.5	44.0	31.0	20.3	37.0	17.6		
> $1,000	364	40.8	34.6	22.8	45.2	58.6	32.8	67.2		
Traveling companion									285.272	.000
Alone/group	153	17.2	11.5	9.8	25.0	10.9	2.5	54.4		
Family	143	16.0	19.8	2.1	13.1	25.8	27.7	11.2		
Friends	284	31.8	27.2	58.0	29.8	25.8	12.6	26.4		
Family and friends	312	35.0	41.6	30.1	32.1	37.5	57.1	8.0		
Influential person(s)									125.570	.000
Self	549	61.5	64.6	68.4	59.5	59.4	23.5	84.8		
Spouse	198	22.2	21.0	11.4	26.2	31.3	47.1	5.6		
Friends and relatives/others	145	16.3	14.4	20.2	14.3	9.4	29.4	9.6		
Information source									85.337	.000
Agent/operator/destination marketing organizations	204	22.9	16.0	11.9	31.0	18.8	26.9	48.0		
Friends and relatives	235	26.3	24.3	39.9	25.0	24.2	23.5	15.2		
Internet	194	21.7	25.1	21.2	16.7	25.0	21.0	16.8		
Magazine/others	259	29.0	34.6	26.9	27.4	32.0	28.6	20.0		

Note: GE = general enthusiasts: BY = budget youngsters; SM = soft moderates; UHN = upper high naturalists; FV = family vacationers; AS = active soloists.

[a] Sample activities for each type were listed in the survey questionnaire as follows: soft nature = hiking, nature trip, bird watching, bicycling, camping; risk equipped = paragliding, hang gliding, windsurfing, sailing; hard challenge = mountain climbing, sea canoeing, kayaking; rugged nature = jungle exploring, safari, arctic trips, trekking, rafting; winter snow = skiing, snowshoeing.

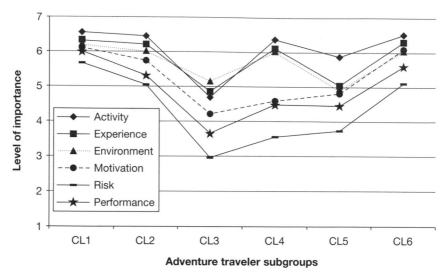

Figure 13.1 Perception of adventure travel by clusters

Note: Level of importance: 1 = least important, 7 = most important.

less importantly perceived by these two groups than by the other four, clearly indicating different levels of involvement in adventure trip participation. Also noticeable was that to upper high naturalists, activity, experience, and environment were more important than were motivation, risk, and performance.

Classification of adventure traveler subgroups

For market segmentation purposes, profiling the cluster solutions should lead toward a classification, scheme through describing the characteristics of each cluster to explain how they might differ on relevant dimensions. To interpret the meaning and patterns of clusters, Tables 13.5, 13.6, and 13.7 display a breakdown of each variable by cluster membership.

General enthusiasts (cluster 1: n = 243, 27.2% of the respondents)

Travelers in this type appeared to be enthusiastic fans of adventure travel, in general. They had the most positive perception for all six components of adventure travel and were most likely to take adventure trips (see Table 13.7 and Figure 13.1). The experiential and participatory nature of adventure travel appeared to be the most evident among these travelers. They were largely male travelers (79.8%) with some college education. Most of them had two or more wage earners (90.9%) in the household, and their household income was mostly at the high (58.4%) or at least the middle-income level (32.9%). Married or not, there was at least two persons (99.2%) in the household, and some (27.2%) had children younger than 12 years old.

Adventure travelers in this group might take at least one adventure trip per year (91.8%), mostly (88.5%) with friends and/or family members in the travel party. As both activity (89.3%) and experience (86.4%) were perceived very importantly in their taking trips, they preferred hard challenge (35.8%) or rugged nature (26.3%) rather than soft nature (18,9%) types of adventure activities. They also preferred trips to American destinations (61.3%) that could be partially arranged (56.4%) or fully inclusive (18.6%) through travel agencies or adventure tour operators. Familiarity appeared to be dominant in adventure trip participation, but some members preferred the hard challenge (35.8%) type of trips for mountain climbing or sea kayaking that might be self-arranged (30.9%) in non-American destinations such as Asia/Pacific (26.7%).

Budget youngsters (cluster 2: n = 193, 21.6% of the respondents)

A typical traveler of this type would be a young (80.3% are between 19 and 34 years of age) and single (9 1.7%) person earning relatively low income (61.7%) by himself or herself. Being so young and price sensitive, these travelers would try to arrange trips by themselves (46.6%) as much as possible, and they least preferred (4.1%) all-inclusive trips. At the same time, however, about every other traveler in this group also preferred partially inclusive trips (49.2%) for professional expertise in escorted guide services or equipment arrangement. This might be particularly true with some of them (33.2%) who wanted to ensure the desired level of perceived risk and competence for the hard challenge activities that would be relatively challenging and demanding.

The budget youngsters appeared to be highly self-oriented (68.4%) in making travel decisions. Unlike the active soloists, they wanted to take trips with friends (58.3%) rather than traveling alone (9.8%). Interestingly enough, they were least likely (2.1%) to take an adventure trip with family members. They would take trips most frequently (94.3% are likely to take at least one adventure trip) and likely to American destinations (57.0%). Primarily due to their budget trip expenditures, Europe or Africa appeared to be the least popular (11.9%) destination among them.

Soft moderates (cluster 3: n = 84, 9.4% of the respondents)

On average, this type of traveler was the most distinct from all other clusters and accounts for the smallest membership (9.4%; see Table 13.3). Here, travelers seemed to be relatively moderate in their likelihood of taking trips and perception of adventure travel (see Figure 13.1 and Table 13.8). A representative profile for this type of traveler could be a middle-aged (56.0%; 35–54 years) woman (54.8%) who would be less likely to live in the Midwest region (13.1%). Although well educated, her disposable income was relatively low (39.8%) because there was only one wage earner (77.4%) in the household. Married or not, she did not have a child younger than 12 years of age.

These travelers clearly preferred the soft nature type of adventure activities (66.7%) such as hiking, nature trips, or camping in mostly American destinations (75.0%). Although travelers in this group seemed to take trips less frequently than other groups (28.6% would take fewer than one per year), they largely preferred to purchase all-inclusive or partially inclusive packages (16.7% and 59.5%, respectively) and to use travel agents or operators as the most popular travel information source (31.0%). Here, familiarity was at a maximum with almost no risk or nothing unusual desired in making travel decisions.

Table 13.8 Correlation between adventure components and traveler subgroups

Coefficient						
Component	CL1	CL2	CL3	CL4	CL5	CL6
Activity	.149**	.119**	.547**	.105**	−.111**	.131**
Experience	.219	.112**	−.344**	.125**	−.355**	.096**
Environment	.251 **	.047	−.200**	.083**	−.359**	.059
Motivation	.293**	.121**	−.323**	−.264**	−.178**	.193**
Risk	.392**	.129**	−.331**	−.291**	−.201**	.113**
Performance	.366**	.068*	−.325**	−.203**	−.196**	.120**

*Significant at the .05 level (2-tailed). **Significant at the .01 level (2-tailed).

Upper high naturalists (cluster 4: n = 128, 14.3% of the respondents)

Similar to soft moderates in cluster 3, travelers in this group did not strongly perceive risk or performance as being important for adventure travel (see Figure 13.1). Instead, they would be rather closely attached to the great outdoors for soft or rugged nature types of activities (40.6% and 32.0%, respectively). Being middle-aged (62.5%) in the 35–54 year old category) and married (71.1%), these travelers largely resided in the western region (38.3%) and had professional or managerial occupations (59.4%) to earn high income (71.1%). Female travelers made up a considerable part of this group (46.9%), and they would like to travel with family members and/or friends. Most of them had dual income earners (71.9%) in the household but no children younger than 12 years old (96.9%). They had a high socioeconomic profile (see Table 13.4).

Being the most affluent, travelers in this group appeared to be seeking novelty. For instance, their preference for more exotic destinations such as Europe/Africa (22.2%) or Asia/Pacific (31.6%) was much stronger than the other groups. While they would take trips once a year on average (50.0%), they would like to stay longer (82.8% would stay longer than 7 nights) and spend more than the other groups (58.6%) would spend more than $1,000 per person per trip) (see Table 13.7). For such upscale trips, the role of tourism establishments might be greatly significant in making sophisticated travel arrangements and in ensuring the quality of services desired. Familiarity is still present, but the experience of novelty is greater among this type of adventure travelers.

Family vacationers (cluster 5: n = 119, 13.3% of the respondents)

Overall, travelers in this group did not seem to be greatly excited about taking adventure trips as general enthusiasts of cluster 1. Unlike those in the budget youngsters group, a typical traveler of this type appeared be a household head who was married (83.2%) and male (80.7%). Having completed at least some college education (91.6%), many of them (42.0%) were engaged in professional or managerial occupations. There were at least two income earners in the household (85.7%), so that their disposable income could be higher than the average (68.9% with $50,000 or more). With one or more children younger than 12 years old, most had more than three persons in the household (74.8%).

Travelers in this group seemed to be very family oriented in making travel decisions and taking trips. Their adventure trips were likely to be to familiar destinations such as the American continent (69.7%) including South and Central America (see Table 13.7). Without having any specific preference for the type of adventure activities, they appeared to participate in adventure trips as if they had been on vacation with family members. They would rather have tourism establishments to make partial (56.3%) or even all-inclusive arrangement (18.5%) for their carefree vacations. Familiarity was still dominant but not at a maximum level as in the soft moderates, as they preferred to travel farther than the soft moderates.

Active soloists (cluster 6: n = 124, 14.0% of the respondents)

Activity was extremely important for this group of travelers ($M = 6.47$). Unlike other groups, they considered motivation as being highly important ($M = 6.10$) for adventure travel, and some of them (11.2%) even preferred risk-equipped activities such as hang gliding or windsurfing. Since they would rather travel alone or as a member of organized packages (54.4%), they appeared to be naturally self-oriented (84.8%) in making travel decisions. Although they were relatively well educated, they had more members in the middle-income range (38.4%) than did upper high naturalists or family vacationers (24.2% and 27.7%, respectively), who had more than two earners. A traveler of this type did not have children younger than 12 years (93.6%) and seemed to be a single income earner in the household (88.8%).

Travelers in this group distinctively preferred all (57.6%) or partially inclusive (37.6%) travel arrangements by adventure tourism establishments and sought travel information largely from travel agencies or destination organizations (48.0%). This group could clearly represent the most institutionalized form (see Cohen 1972 for further discussion) of tourists who would heavily depend on an organized establishment in making travel arrangements. Their travel expenditures were higher than the others (the highest distribution, 67.2%, for more than $1,000 per person per trip), and some (35.2%) of them preferred the Asia/Pacific region for their adventure vacation destinations. Novelty appeared to be important to a great extent among this type of travelers when selecting exotic destinations.

Limitations

The structural limitations of this study included (1) the limited amount of literature directly associated with adventure travel and, as a consequence. (2) some challenges in adopting past leisure/recreation or consumer behavior theories to the context of adventure travel, due to the structural differences between these areas. Adventure travel has been heavily industry driven, so that the importance of theoretical constructs might not have been fully recognized while much more attention has been paid to the empirical applications. Leisure/recreation studies, on the other hand, appear to find a theoretical tradition in a social science perspective. This suggests that exchanging research terms or application practices may take extra caution not to violate assumptions across these two areas.

With regard to research methodology, sampling of participants from ACONA's membership subscription might possibly cause an issue in terms of representativeness. It was noted earlier that the respondents ($N = 1,033$) were drawn from an a priori known group, presumably having a similar interest in adventure travel. By subscribing with a paid membership, those respondents are considered more actively involved in adventure travel. As a result, they might have unique group characteristics or travel behavior associated with adventure travel than the general population does. Nevertheless, the target population of this study was not the general public in the United States. Rather, it was adventure travelers who would be interested in taking an adventure trip (whether they have been on a trip or not). The extension or generalization of the study results to the general public, therefore, should be treated with a degree of caution.

Conclusions and implications

The classification of adventure travelers developed in this study presented a challenging but worthy task, particularly when little systematic research has previously been reported on the subject to date. The unique classification approach to market segmentation in this study was to establish classification constructs of adventure traveler subgroups across the hypothesized factors (demographic and socioeconomic measures, trip-related factors, and perception of adventure) in the multivariate analysis, which has rarely been attempted or fully developed. The results of this study will fill these gaps in the literature by providing a meaningful explanation of consumer and travel behavior of adventure travelers. Clearly, adventure travelers are distinct in terms of some traveler and consumer characteristics and therefore have specific needs and demands for travel and tourism products and services. For effective target market purposes, the current hypothesized relationship with greater reflection on the study findings may suggest some additional development in understanding factors relevant to adventure travelers' travel decision making.

The first research objective of classifying distinctive adventure traveler subgroups: emphasizing traveler characteristics and consumer and travel behavior was accomplished. The empirical research identified a six-cluster solution labeled as (1) general enthusiasts, (2) budget youngsters, (3) soft moderates, (4) upper high naturalists, (5) family vacationers, and (6) active soloists. Although the primary purpose of using a cluster analysis in this study was not to identify individual relationships of each variable associated with the cluster solution, some factors appeared to have significant impacts on cluster formulation. Household size and number of income earners had the greatest variation across clusters; both household disposable income and number of young children showed a somewhat similar pattern.

The classified adventure traveler subgroups were then tied to their perception of adventure travel, addressing the second research objective. Overall, the relative importance of activity, experience, and environment perceived by adventure travelers appeared to have an almost identical pattern with what had been reported by Sung, Morrison, and O'Leary (1997) in defining adventure travel with providers. As shown in Table 13.8, travelers' perceptions of adventure travel across all the six components appeared to be significantly relevant to the identified traveler subgroups. Linking to the leisure involvement theories, it was likely that the general enthusiast type of travelers would be more positive in their adventure participation than those of the soft moderate type, where the notion of adventure was less significantly perceived. The inclusion of perception of adventure travel in the analysis suggests to practitioners how adventure travel products and services should be developed with the appropriate level of involvement to improve customer appeal.

The results of this study also suggest ways to discuss practical recommendations as to how adventure travel products and services might be developed and delivered to target segments. For effective use of marketing resources, marketers and industry providers should warrant an extensive attention to institutionalized tourists who would prefer all or mostly inclusive travel arrangements. For instance, the general enthusiasts subgroup clearly appears to be the biggest segment in terms of both the market share (27.2%) and the market potential with strong involvement level. Their willingness to participate in challenging adventure activities suggests that they would prefer high or hard experiences in their adventure trips rather than stay safe in familiarity. Targeting those who belong in the upper high naturalists group will be a good strategy for providers who offer a well-organized itinerary in exotic destinations such as safaris in Kenya or arctic trips on tall sailboats. Although this segment is not as big as the general enthusiasts in terms of the market share or potential, travelers in this group appear to be most affluent and willing to pay for novelty trips where they can enjoy such exotic destinations at an upscale comfort level. For the active soloists, distinct in their strong preferences of organized packages, both high activities and socializing would be key elements to a successful itinerary.

On the other hand, those who belong in the budget youngsters group tend to be at some distance from the institutionalized segments. Not every traveler in this type can afford organized packages. Instead, most of them would rather make travel arrangements by themselves. Targeting the family vacationers might also be challenging since these travelers do not show any specific preference for adventure activity types. Alternatively, they can be easily satisfied as long as their trip is well, organized and offers something for every family member. Although those who are in the soft moderates category tend to keep their involvement with the tourism organizations at a minimum level, they appear to be more approachable and easy to pinpoint due to their strong preference of the soft nature trip type in American destinations. An ecotrip to Costa Rica at an affordable price, for instance, would be an appropriate product match with this group. However, marketers still need to make extra efforts to offer strong motivation to take a trip that interests this group of travelers.

The distinctive group characteristics from the classification of adventure traveler subgroups have significant implications to revisiting Cohen's (1972) classic typology of four tourist groups and their involvement with institutions in making travel arrangements. As discussed in studies of tourist typology (Basala and Klenosky 2001; Hvenegaard 2002; Keng and Cheng 1999; Lee and Crompton 1992; Moscardo et al. 2000; Snepenger 1987; Smith 1990), Plog's (1974) cognitive-normative tourist typology focuses on travel motivation (allocentries, midcentrics, and psychocentrics), while Cohen's (1972) typology is activity oriented and emphasizes behavioral constructs and/or psychographics of travelers. Although Cohen's original study focus was on different roles of tourist types (i.e., the organized mass tourist, the individual mass tourist, the explorer, and the drifter) in the host community, his novelty versus familiarity grid appeared to be a good fit in market positioning of adventure traveler subgroups.

The exploration of the classified adventure travel sub-groups reported in this study is expected to make a meaningful contribution to understanding distinct adventure traveler subgroups and measuring travelers' involvement as to how they would purchase and consume adventure travel products and/or services. Examination of key dimensions of the notion of adventure (Sung, Morrison, and O'Leary 1997) in this study was the first attempt in identifying the conceptual linkage between consumer behavioral aspects of adventure travelers and leisure involvement theories from a tourism perspective. The results provide an improved understanding of adventure traveler subgroups and suggest a comprehension of involvement constructs, which will help adventure travel marketers and practitioners' determine their roles particularly in the strategy formulation process to match available marketing resources with target segments. Future research could include more behavioral components and/or psychographics such as needs, motivations, or benefits in the analysis to provide reliable, useful information about consumer behavior specific to particular travel participation.

References

Andereck, K.L., and L.L. Caidwell (1994). "Variable Selection in Tourism Market Segmentation Models." *Journal of Travel Research*, 33 (2): 40–46.

Arimond, G., and A. Elfessi (2001). "A Clustering Method for Categorical Data in Tourism Market Segmentation Research." *Journal of Travel Research*, 39 (4): 391–397.

Basala, S.L., and D.B. Klenosky (2001). "Travel-Style Preferences for Visiting a Novel Destination: A Conjoint Investigation across the Novelty-Familiarity Continuum." *Journal of Travel Research*, 40 (2): 172–182.

Bieger, T., and C. Laesser (2002). "Market Segmentation by Motivation: The Case of Switzerland." *Journal of Travel Research*, 41 (1): 68–76.

Black, N., and J. Rutledge (1995). *Outback Tourism: The Authentic Australian Adventure,* North Queensland, Australia: James Cook University Press.

Boo, B. (1990). *Ecotourism: The Potentials and Pitfalls*. Baltimore: World Wildlife Fund.

Burns, A.C., and R.F. Bush (2003). *Marketing Research: Online Research Applications*. 4th edn. Upper Saddle River, NJ: Prentice Hall.

Canadian Tourism Commission (2002). "Canadian Tourism Facts & Figures 2001." Canadian Tourism Commission. Retrieved May 20, 2003, from http://ftp.canadatourism.com/ctsuproads/en.publication/tourism2002.pdf.

Carrera, N. (1995). "Rapid Growth: Consultant Helps Develop Adventure Travel Opportunities." *Denver Business Journal*, 46 (36): 19–20.

Cater, E., and G. Lowman (1994). *Ecotourism: A Sustainable Option?* New York: John Wiley.

Chandler, J.A., and C.A. Costello (2002). "A Profile of Visitors at Heritage Tourism Destinations in East Tennessee According to Plog's Lifestyle and Activity Level Preferences Model." *Journal* of *Travel Research*, 41 (2): 161–166.

Chon, K.S., and A. Singh (1995). "Marketing Resorts to 2000: Review of Trends in the USA." *Tourism Management*, 16 (6): 463–469.

Christiansen, D.R. (1990). "Adventure Tourism." In *Adventure Education,* edited by J.C. Miles and S. Priest, pp. 433–442. State College, PA: Venure.

Churchill, G.A. (1999). *Marketing Research: Methodological Foundations*. 2nd edn. Fort Worth, TX: Dryden.

Cohen, E. (1972). "Toward a Sociology of International Tourism." *Social Research*, 39 (1): 164–182.

Creswell, J.W. (2003). *Research Design: Qualitative, Quantitative, and Mixed Method Approaches*. 2nd edn. Thousand Oaks. CA: Sage.

Derrett, R. (2001). "Special Interest Tourism: Starting with the Individual." In *Special Interest Tourism: Context and Cases*, edited by Norman Douglas, Ngaire Douglas, and R. Derrett, pp. 1–22. New York: John Wiley.

Dimanche, F., and M.E. Havitz (1994). "Consumer Behavior and Tourism: Review and Extension of Four Study Areas." *Journal of Travel and Tourism Marketing*, 3 (3): 37–57.

Dolnicar, S., and F. Leisch (2003). "Winter Tourist Segments in Austria: Identifying Stable Vacation Styles Using Bagged Clustering Techniques." *Journal* of *Travel Research*, 41 (3): 281–292.

Eagles, P.F., and J.W. Cascagnette (1995). "Canadian Ecotourists: Who Are They!" *Tourism Recreation Research*, 20 (1): 22–28.

Ewert, A. (1987). "Recreation in the Outdoor Setting: A Focus on Adventure-Based Recreational Experiences." *Leisure Information Quarterly*, 14 (1): 5–7.

—— (1989). *Outdoor Adventure Pursuits: Foundation, Models and Theories*. Columbus, OH: Publishing Horizons.

Ewert, A., and S. Hollenhorst (1994). "Individual and Setting Attributes of the Adventure Recreation Experience." *Leisure Sciences*, 16: 177–191.

Fluker, M.R., and L.W. Turner (2000). "Needs, Motivations, and Expectations of a Commercial Whitewater Rafting Experience." *Journal of Travel Research*, 38 (2): 380–389.

Grant, Y., and P.A. Weaver (1996). "The Meeting Selection Process: A Demographic Profile of Attendees Clusters by Criteria Utilized in Selecting Meetings." *Hospitality Research Journal*, 20 (1): 57–71.

Hair, J.F., R.E. Anderson, R.L. Tatham, and W.C. Black (1998). *Multivariate Data Analysis*. 5th edn. Upper Saddle River, NJ: Prentice Hall.

Hall, C.M. (1989). "Special Interest Travel: A Prime Force in the Expansion of Tourism?" In *Geography in Action*, edited by R. Welch, pp. 81–89. Dunedin, New Zealand: University of Otago Press.

—— (1992). "Adventure, Sport and Health Tourism." In *Special Interest Tourism*, edited by B. Weiler and C.M. Hall, pp. 141–158. London: Belhaven.

Hall, C.M., and B. Weiler (1992). "What's Special about Special Interest Tourism?" In *Special Interest Tourism*, edited by Weiler and C.M. Hall, pp. 1–4. London: Belhaven.

Havitz, M.E., and F. Dimanche (1990). "Propositions for Guiding the Empirical Testing of the Involvement Construct in Recreational and Tourist Context." *Leisure Sciences*, 12 (2): 179–196.

—— (1995). "How Enduring Is Enduring Involvement in the Context of Tourist Motivation?" *Journal of Travel and Tourism Marketing*, 4 (3): 95–99.

—— (1997). "Leisure Involvement Revisited: Conceptual Conundrums and Measurement Advances." *Journal of Leisure Research*, 29 (3): 245–278.

Higgins, B.R. (1996). "The Global Structure of the Nature Tourism. Industry: Ecotourists, Tour Operators, and Local Businesses." *Journal* of *Travel Research*, 35 (2): 11–18.

Horneman, L., R.W. Carter, S. Wei, and H. Ryus (2002). "Profiling the Senior Traveler: An Australian Perspective." *Journal of Travel Research*, 41 (1): 23–37.

Hsu, C.H., S.K. Kang, and K. Wolfe (2002). "Psychographic and Demographic Profiles and Niche Market Leisure Travelers," *Journal of Hospitality and Tourism Research*, 26 (1): 3–22.

Hvenegaard, Glen T. (2002). "Using Tourist Typologies for Ecotourism Research." *Journal of Ecotourism*, 1 (1): 7–18.

Iso-Ahola, S. (1980). *The Social Psychology of Leisure and Tourism*, Dubuque, IA: William C. Brown.

—— (1982). "Towards a Social Psychological Theory of Tourism Motivation: A Rejoinder." *Annals* of *Tourism Research*, 9 (2): 256–262.

Jackson, E.L. (1994). 'Activity-Specific Constraints on Leisure Participation." *Journal of Park and Recreation Administration*, 12 (2): 33–49.

Jeffrey, D., and Y. Xie (1995). "The UK Market for Tourism in China." *Annals of Tourism Research*, 22 (4): 857–876.

Kashyap, R., and D.C. Bojanic. (2000). "A Structural Analysis of Value, Quality, and Price Perceptions of Business and Leisure Travelers." *Journal of Travel Research*, 39 (1): 45–51.

Kemperman, A., A. Borgers, H. Oppewal, and H. Timmermans (2003). "Predicting the Duration of Theme Park Visitors' Activities: An Ordered Logit Model Using Conjoint Choice Data." *Journal of Travel Research*, 41 (4): 375–384.

Keng, K.A., and L.L. Cheng (1999). "Determining Tourist Role Typologies: An Exploratory Study of Singapore Vacationers." *Journal of Travel Research*, 37 (4): 382–390.

Kinnear, P.R., and C.D. Gray (2000). *SPSS for Windows Made Simple: Release 10*. East Sussex: Psychology Press.

Kotler, P., J. Bowen, and J. Makens (2002). *Marketing for Hospitality and Tourism*. 3rd edn. Upper Saddle River, NJ: Prentice Hall.

Lang, C.T., J.T. O'Leary, and A.M. Morrison (1997). "Distinguishing the Destination Choices of Pleasure Travelers from Taiwan." *Journal of Travel and Tourism Marketing*, 6 (1): 21–40.

Lauer, J.M., and J.W. Asher (1988). *Composition Research: Empirical Designs*. New York: Oxford University Press.

Lee, T.H., and J. Crompton (1992). "Measuring Novelty Seeking in Tourism." *Annals of Tourism Research*, 19 (4): 732–751.

Loverseed, H. (1997). "The Adventure Travel Industry in North America." *Travel and Tourism Analyst*, 6: 87–104.

Madrigal, R. (1995). "Personal Values, Traveler Personality Type, and Leisure Travel Style." *Journal of Leisure Research*, 27 (2): 125–142.

Mallett, J. (2002). *The Evolution of Adventure Travel*. Adventure Travel Society, Colorado. Retrieved June 7, 2003, from http://adventuretravelbusiness.com/index.php/research.

Manning, R. (1986). *Studies in Outdoor Recreation*. Corvallis: Oregon State University Press.

Martin, P., and S. Priest (1986). "Justifying the Risk to Others: The Real Razor's Edge." *Journal of Experiential Education*, 10 (1): 16–22.

McIntyre, N. (1992). "Involvement in Risk Recreation: A Comparison of Objective and Subjective Measures of Engagement." *Journal of Leisure Research*, 24 (1): 64–71.

Meier, J. (1978). "Is the Risk Worth Taking?" *Leisure Today*, 49 (4): 7–9.

Middleton, V.T. (2001). *Marketing in Travel and Tourism*. 3rd edn. Avon: Bath Press.

Mill, R.B., and A.M. Morrison (1998). *The Tourism System: An Introductory Text*. 3rd edn. Dubuque, IA: Kendal/Hunt.

Morrison, A.M. (2001), *Hospitality and Travel Marketing*. 3rd edn. Albany, NY: Delmar.

Morrison, A.M., P.L. Pearce, G. Moscardo, N. Nadkarni, and J.T. O'Leary (1996). "Specialist Accommodation: Definition, Markets Served, and Roles in Tourism Development." *Journal of Travel Research*, 35 (1): 18–26.

Moscardo, G., P. Pearce, and A.M. Morrison (2001). "Evaluating Different Bases for Market Segmentation: A Comparison of Geographic Origin versus Activity Participation for Generating Tourist Market Segments." *Journal of Travel and Tourism Marketing*, 10 (1): 29–50.

Moscardo, G., P. Pearce, A.M. Morrison, D. Green, and J.T. O'Leary (2000). "Developing a Typology for Understanding Visiting Friends and Relative Markets." *Journal of Travel Research*, 38 (3): 251–259.

Oden, W. (1995). "Adventure in Colorado." *Colorado Business Magazine*, 22 (5): 56–61.

Plog, S.C. (1974). "Why Destination Areas Rise and Fail in Popularity." *Cornell Hotel and Restaurant Administration Quarterly*, 14: 55–58.

—— (2002). "The Power of Psychographics and the Concept of Venturesomeness." *Journal of Travel Research*, 40 (3): 244–251.

Prebensen, N.K., S. Larsen, and B. Abelsen (2003). "I'm Not a Typical Tourist: German Tourists' Self-Perception, Activities, and Motivations." *Journal of Travel Research*, 41(4): 416–420.

Robinson, D.W. (1992). "A Descriptive Model of Enduring Risk Recreation Involvement." *Journal of Leisure Research*, 24 (2): 52–63.

Ross, K. (1999). "Exploring the World of Adventure Travel." *HSMAI Marketing Review,* 16 (2): 10–13.

Selin, S.W., and D.R. Howard (1988). "Ego Involvement and Leisure Behavior: A Conceptual Specification." *Journal of Leisure Research*, 20 (3): 237–244.

Sherif, M., and H. Cantril (1947). *The Psychology of Ego-Involvement*, New York: John Wiley & Sons.

Silverberg, K.E., S.J. Backman, and K.F. Backman (1996). "A Preliminary Investigation into the Psychographics of Nature-Based Travelers to the Southeastern United States." *Journal of Travel Research*, 35 (2): 19–28.

Sirakaya, E., M. Uysal, and C.F. Yoshioka. (2003). "Segmenting the Japanese Tour Market to Turkey." *Journal of Travel Research*, 41 (3): 293–304.

Smith, S.L. (1990). "A Test of Plog's Allocentric/Psychocentric Model: Evidence from Seven Nations." *Journal of Travel Research*, 28 (4): 40–43.

Snepenger, D.J. (1987). "Segmenting the Vacation Market by Novelty Seeking Role." *Journal of Travel Research*, 26 (3): 8–14.

Sorensen, L. (1993). "The Special Interest Travel Market." *Cornell Hotel and Restaurant Administration Quarterly*, 34: 24–30.

Sung, H.H. (2001). "Adventure Travelers: Who Are They and What They Do On Their Adventure Vacations?" In *Trends 2000: Shaping the Future. Proceedings* of *the 5th Outdoor Recreation & Tourism Trends Symposium*, 348–359. East Lansing: Michigan State University.

Sung, H.H., A.M. Morrison, G.S. Hong, and J.T. O'Leary (2001). "The Effects of Household and Trip Characteristics on Trip Types: A Consumer Behavioral Approach for Segmenting the U.S. Domestic Leisure Travel Market." *Journal of Hospitality & Tourism Research*, 25 (1): 46–68.

Sung, H.H., A.M. Morrison, and J.T. O'Leary (1997). "Definition of Adventure Travel: Conceptual Framework for Empirical Application from the Providers' Perspective." *Asia Pacific Journal of Tourism Research*, 1 (2): 47–67.

—— (2000). "Segmenting the Adventure 'Travel Market by Activities: From the North American Providers' Perspective." *Journal of Travel and Tourism Marketing*, 9 (4): 1–20.

Swarbrooke, J., and S. Homer (1999). *Consumer Behavior in Tourism*, Oxford: Butterworth-Heinemann.

Travel Industry Association of America (1998). *The Adventure Travel Report*. Washington, DC: Travel Industry Association of America.

Vellas, F., and L. Becherel (1995). *International Tourism: An Economic Perspective*. New York: St. Martin's.

Walle, A.H. (1997). "Pursuing Risk or Insight: Marketing Adventures." *Annals of Tourism Research*, 24 (2): 265–282.

Weber, K. (2001). "Outdoor Adventure Tourism: A Review of Research Approaches." *Annals of Tourism Research*, 28 (2): 360–377.

Whelan, T. (1991). *Nature Tourism: Managing for the Environment*. Washington, DC: Island.

Wight, P.A. (1996). "North American Ecotourism. Markets: Market Profile and Trip Characteristics." *Journal of Travel Research*, 35 (2): 2–10.

Chapter 14

Jerry J. Vaske, Pam Carothers, Maureen P. Donnelly and Biff Baird

RECREATION CONFLICT AMONG SKIERS AND SNOWBOARDERS

WHEN VISITORS WITH DIFFERING VIEWS on how to use a recreation resource interact with each other, conflict may occur (Adelman, Heberlein, & Bonnicksen, 1982; Jackson & Wong, 1982; Jacob & Schreyer, 1980; Knopp & Tyger, 1973). Recreation conflict is often asymmetrical, where the physical presence or actions of one group interfere with the goals (motivations) of another group, but the reverse does not hold true (Gibbons & Ruddell, 1995; Lucas, 1964; Ramthun, 1995; Watson, Niccolucci, & Williams, 1994; Watson, Williams, & Daigle, 1991). This phenomenon typically occurs when people engaged in traditional activities (e.g., skiers) interact with those using newer technologies (e.g., snowboarders). Other studies (Thapa, 1996; Thapa & Graefe, 1998, 1999), however, have shown goal interference conflict between individuals engaged in the same activity (i.e., ingroup conflict).

Jacob and Schreyer's (1980) goal interference model identifies four major factors that contribute to recreation conflict: (a) the meaning individuals attach to the activity, (b) the significance of the resource to the individual, (c) the extent to which the individual is focused on the environment or activity, and (d) the users' acceptance of different lifestyles. Although this model has provided the framework for most conflict studies (Schneider, 2000; Watson, 1995), other concepts have been proposed. For example, when multiple groups share the same physical space, safety concerns may influence conflict (Blahna, Smith, & Anderson, 1995), especially for high-speed activities that attract large numbers of participants in relatively confined areas such as ski resorts (Finley, 1990; Hughes, 1988).

Alpine skiing has traditionally dominated North America's ski slopes. In recent years, however, ski area managers have expressed concern over declining skier numbers and sought ways to recruit new participants. Snowboarding, with its youth appeal (Baird, 1993; Thapa, 1996), created a new market segment for these resorts. Although snowboarding has witnessed phenomenal growth, thus diversifying the use of ski areas, questions have arisen regarding the compatibility of the two activities sharing a resource designed specifically for skiing. Newspaper accounts (Hughes, 1988; Meyers, 1991), as well as some empirical evidence, have suggested that skiers have not always willingly embraced this new activity (Thapa & Graefe, 1998, 1999; P.W. Williams, Dossa, & Fulton, 1994).

The study reported here examined both out-group and in-group recreation conflict among skiers and snowboarders. Bivariate analyses were used to compare individuals engaged in these two activities relative to the traditional indicators of conflict (activity style, resource specificity, mode of experience, lifestyle tolerance), as well other conflict-related variables (e.g., safety). Multivariate analyses were then used to evaluate the relative impact of these predictors on both out-group and in-group beliefs about unacceptable behaviors associated with skier and snowboarder interactions.

Defining conflict

Despite the volume of conflict-related research, "there has never been agreement on how recreation conflict should be measured" (Watson, 1995, p. 237). Some studies (Thapa & Graefe, 1999; Watson et al., 1994). for example, have examined the extent to which visitors find encounters with others to be desirable or undesirable. A more direct measure of goal interference asks respondents to indicate the extent to which encounters with others interfere with their enjoyment (Thapa & Graefe, 1999; Watson et al., 1991). Other researchers (Blahna et al., 1995; Carothers, Vaske, & Donnelly, in press; Ramthun, 1995; Vaske, Donnelly, Wittmann, & Laidlaw, 1995) have focused on the social acceptability of specific behaviors (e.g., feeding wildlife, mountain biking out of control, discourteous skier behavior). Defined in this manner, conflict essentially becomes a normative (Ruddell & Gramann, 1994) as opposed to a motivational (goal) issue. Norms are evaluative beliefs (standards) regarding acceptable behavior in a given context (see Vaske, Shelby, Graefe, & Heberlein, 1986; Shelby, Vaske, & Donnelly, 1996, for reviews). In this article, we focus on skiers' and snowboarders' normative beliefs about unacceptable behaviors as indicators of recreation conflict.

There are at least two sources of unacceptable behavior: those resulting from interactions with other individuals involved in the same activity (in-group conflict) and those associated with interactions with other individuals involved in different activities (out-group conflict), Whereas most research has focused on out-group conflict (Adelman et al., 1982; Devall & Harry, 1981; Watson et al., 1991, 1994; P.W. Williams et al., 1994), some investigations have explored beliefs about unacceptable behavior occurring as a result of in-group interactions. Studies by Todd and Graefe (1989) and Thapa and Graefe (1998, 1999), for example, found that goal interference was more likely to be attributed to in-group than to out-group conflict. In general, however, the conflict literature has shown that recreationists are more tolerant of individuals engaged in the same activity as themselves than they are with those engaged in a different activity (Jackson & Wong, 1982; Gibbons & Ruddell, 1995; Knopp & Tyger, 1973; Lucas, 1964). We therefore hypothesize

H_1:   Skiers and snowboarders will report more out-group than in-group unacceptable behaviors (conflict).

Sources of conflict

Jacob and Schreyer (1980) proposed four major classes of determinants (activity style, resource specificity, mode of experience, lifestyle tolerance) that influence recreation conflict. Activity style refers to the personal meaning individuals assign to the activity. These individual meanings, not the activity itself, contribute to conflict evaluations. The more intense an individual's activity style, the greater the likelihood that contact with less intense participants will result in conflict. Intensity of participation has been operationalized relative to an individual's level of involvement in a sport (e.g., total years of participation, days of participation per year). P.W. Williams *et al.* (1994), for example, compared skiers and snowboarders at 16 ski resorts in British Columbia, Canada. Results indicated that, as a group, the skiers had pursued their sport for significantly more years and were more likely to take advantage of the services offered at the resort (e.g., lessons) than were the snowboarders. On the other hand, the snowboarders reported more overnight trips per year and more days of participation per year than the skiers. Taken together, the findings from the P.W. Williams *et al.* study showed that skiers were more involved with their activity based on years of participation, whereas snowboarders were more involved on the basis of amount of participation per year. Because these findings do not indicate a clear pattern of activity style differences between skiers and snowboarders, we hypothesize

> H_2:   Skiers and snowboarders will not differ in the importance they attach to the activity.

Resource specificity relates to the significance recreationists attach to a specific resource. Those less attached to the resource are seen to disrupt the traditional uses (Jacob & Schreyer, 1980). Hiking, for example, represents a traditional activity on most trails, whereas mountain biking is a relatively new sport (Chavez, 1999; Woodward, 1996). Hoger and Chavez (1998) have shown that hikers view mountain hiking as intrusive and are concerned with the impact mountain biking has on the environment. These findings, as well as those of other researchers (Watson, Zaglauer, & Stewart, 1996), indicate that individuals engaged in more traditional activities may place greater significance on the resource than those participating in nontraditional recreation pursuits.

Relative to skiers and snowboarders, skiing represents the traditional activity on most North American slopes. The empirical evidence supporting greater resource specificity among skiers, however, has shown a mixed pattern of results. P.W. Williams *et al.* (1994), for example, suggested that skiers saw themselves as more attached to the resource than the snowboarders. The skiers viewed the snowboarders as intruding on the pristine quality of the resort, exhibiting little respect for the natural beauty of the environment. The snowboarders, on the other hand, also expressed a closeness to the natural environment but were more concerned about the freedom to pursue their activity without restrictions on where they could snowboard. In other words, snowboarding was not allowed on all trails. Overall, the P.W. Williams *et al.* study revealed few differences in resource specificity between the two groups. Participants in the two activities attached importance to the ski resort, but for different reasons. Therefore. we hypothesize

> H_3:   Skiers and snowboarders will not differ in the importance they attach to the resource.

Jacob and Schreyer (1980) described *mode of experience* as a continuum ranging from unfocused to focused. "As the mode of experiencing the environment becomes more focused, an individual produces more rigid definitions of what constitutes acceptable stimuli and is increasingly intolerant of external stimulation" (Jacob & Schreyer, 1980, p. 375). Snowboarders in the P.W. Williams *et al.* (1994) investigation were focused on technical and competency-related issues. Alternatively, the skiers were more focused on the natural features of the environment and often complained about the snowboarders scraping and rutting the trails and ruining the moguls. Similar to the above logic, both groups appear to be focused, but for different reasons. We hypothesize

H₄: Skiers and snowboarders will not differ in their mode of experience.

Lifestyle tolerance refers to the tendency to accept or reject lifestyles different than one's own (Jacob & Schreyer, 1980). As noted by Ivy, Stewart, and Lue (1992), tolerance is typically associated with beliefs about a particular group rather than reactions to specific behaviors. When recreationists encounter others, a cognitive processing of information occurs. This action often results in the categorization of others according to some group membership, which helps to simplify and order environmental stimuli. Differences in lifestyles are often communicated through visual cues such as the equipment used by recreationists engaged in different activities (e.g., guns for hunting vs. binoculars for wildlife viewing; Vaske *et al.*, 1995). "Recreation in-groups and out-groups represent categories an individual establishes on the basis of perceived or imagined lifestyle similarities and differences" (Jacob & Schreyer, 1980, p. 376). Though useful for maintaining a view of the world, it can also lead to unjustified generalizations about other groups (Baron, Kerr, & Miller, 1992; Ramthun, 195). Those who demonstrate low tolerance for persons with differing lifestyles will be more likely to experience conflict.

P.W. Williams *et al.* (1994) suggested that skiers and snowboarders have differing views of each other. Skiers felt threatened by the snowboarders' different approach; they evaluated the language, clothes, and on-slope behavior of snowboarders as intimidating and had the perception that snowboarders purposely created conflict situations. Snowboarders, on the other hand, perceived skiers as predictable and showed less concern for their presence on the slopes. The British Columbian snowboarders, however, were more willing to share the resource with skiers than the skiers were with snowboarders (P.W. Williams *et al.*, 1994). These group differences may increase the potential for a culture clash between skiers and snowboarders (Hughes, 1988).

H₅: Skiers will be less tolerant of the snowboarders' lifestyle than vice versa.

Although not explicitly addressed by Jacob and Schreyer (1980), safety concerns represent a potential indicator of conflict. Skiers and snowboarders often share the slopes with large numbers of fellow recreationists. Participants in each group traverse the slopes at high speeds. Speed, when combined with large numbers of recreationists, can lead to potentially dangerous situations (Finley, 1990).

In 1985, only 6% of Colorado ski areas allowed snowboarders to ride their lifts (Meyers, 1991). Safety was the major consideration in these early bans on snowboarding, as ski area managers questioned whether they could coexist with skiers (Asher & Markels, 1992; Finley, 1990). To some extent, these concerns were legitimate, as early snowboards lacked steel edges, retention devices, and sidecuts, making control difficult. Insurance carriers declined to place these early boards in the category of "directional devices" and refused to issue coverage to ski areas that allowed the sport (Aitkens, 1990).

Although improvements in snowboard-manufacturing technology (leading to improved control) have played a role in the current near-unanimous acceptance of snowboarding at Colorado ski resorts, skiers may still perceive snowboarders as reckless individuals and feel threatened by their presence on the slopes (Meyers, 1991). Such safety concerns may be attributed to beliefs about unacceptable behaviors such as unsafe jumping or riding out of control (White, 1990). Taken together, these observations suggest

H_6:   Skiers will perceive more safety-related problems associated with snow-boarding than vice versa.

Conceptual model

All hypotheses proposed thus far have suggested bivariate relationships among the variables. To address the combined influence of these variables on out-group and in-group beliefs about unacceptable behaviors, we developed a multivariate conceptual model. On the basis of the research and popular literature summarized above, the model predicts that activity style, resource specificity, mode of experience, and safety concerns will increase the likelihood of conflict (both out-group and in-group). Lifestyle tolerance, on the other hand, should be negatively associated with perceived conflict. These relationships are shown in Figure 14.1 and a stated formally as hypotheses below.

H_7:   As the importance attached to the activity increases, out-group and in-group beliefs about unacceptable behaviors (conflict) will increase.

H_8:   As the importance attached to the resource increases, out-group and in-group beliefs about unacceptable behaviors (conflict) will increase.

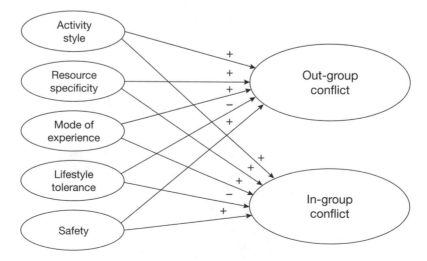

Figure 14.1 Expanded conflict model

H$_9$: As the mode of experience increases (becomes more focused), out-group and in-group beliefs about unacceptable behaviors (conflict) will increase.

H$_{10}$: As tolerance for lifestyle diversity increases, out-group and in-group beliefs about unacceptable behaviors (conflict) will decrease.

H$_{11}$: As perceptions of safety-related problems increase, awareness of out-group and in-group beliefs about unacceptable behaviors (conflict) will increase.

Method

Study locations and sampling

Date were collected from five Colorado ski areas (Arapahoe Basin, Copper Mountain Eldora, Winter Park, and Steamboat Springs)[1] between December 1992 and February 1993. Mail-back surveys were distributed on randomly selected days at lift lines and ski area restaurants. At the lift lines, every 10th individual was selected. In the restaurants, an individual was selected at random from every 5th table. Of the 1,252 surveys distributed on site, 595 usable questionnaires were mailed back (response rate = 48%). Funding constraint did not allow for any additional follow-up to nonrespondents. The sample consisted of 38 skiers and 212 snowboarders.[2]

Variables measured

Conflict

A multiple-item index was created to measure observed unacceptable behaviors (conflict) between skiers and snowboarders. Specific items asked if skiers/snowboarders (a) failed to be aware of others around them, (b) were not keeping an adequate distance from others, (c) failed to yield the right of way to the downhill skier/snowboarder, (d) behaved in a discourteous manner, (e) cut others off, and (f) failed to be aware of and yield to less-advanced skiers/snowboarders. Respondents indicated how often these behaviors were seen. Response categories were *never* (1), *rarely* (2), *sometimes* (3), *frequently* (4), and *almost always* (5).

Predictors of conflict

An activity style scale was created that reflected investment in the sport. Respondents reported the number of days per year skied/snowboarded (responses ranged from 1 to 5 to more than 50); the number of skis/snowboards owned (zero to more than three); the approximate amount of money invested in equipment, clothing, and accessories ($0–$100 to more than $3,000); number of years skiing/snowboarding (1 to more than 20); and a rating of their skiing/snowboarding ability (beginner to expert). For *resource specificity*, respondents indicated their agreement with the following place attachment statements (D. Williams & Roggenbuck, 1989): (a) "this ski area means a lot to me,"

(b) "a lot of my life is organized around this ski area," (c) "this ski area is the best place for what I like to do," and (d) "I identify strongly with this ski area." Responses were coded on 5-point scales ranging from *strongly disagree* (1) to *strongly agree* (5). A *lifestyle tolerance* index was created by asking the respondents to agree or disagree that snowboarders and skiers have similar (a) lifestyles, (b) levels of education, (c) incomes, (d) attitudes toward the environment, and (e) feelings about the value of this area. Five-point Likert scales ranging from *strongly disagree* (1) to *strongly agree* (5) were used to measure responses to these variables.

Mode of experience was measured with a single item. Individuals indicated the extent to which they agreed or disagreed that they focused most of their attention on their skiing/snowboarding skills. Responses were coded on a 5-point Likert scale ranging from *strongly disagree* (1) to *strongly, agree* (5).

Safety was also measured with a single-item statement (again using the 5-point Likert disagree-to-agree scale) that it is not safe to have snowboarders and skiers share the same trails.

Analysis

Reliability analyses were used to determine the internal consistency of each of the scaled measurement items. Confirmatory factor analyses examined the extent to which the four Jacob and Schreyer (1980) determinants of conflict and safety provided a good fit to the data. We used *t* tests to analyze bivariate differences between skiers and snowboarders and structural equation path analyses to address the predictive validity of the models. LISREL 8.14 (Jöreskog & Sörbom, 1993) was used for this analysis.[3]

Results

Reliability and confirmatory factor analyses

Tables 14.1 and 14.2 show the reliability and confirmatory factor analyses for the items in the skier indices, and Tables 14.3 and 14.4 provide the same information for the snowboarders. The primary dependent variables in the models, out-group and in-group conflict, were computed from six beliefs about unacceptable behaviors associated with skiing (Table 14.1) and snowboarding (Table 14.3). For the skiers, the reliability coefficients for the two indices were .93 (out-group) and .88 (in-group). The reliability coefficients for the snowboarders were .87 (out-group) and .83 (in-group). The confirmatory factor analyses demonstrated that the data provided an acceptable fit for both the skiers (factor loadings $\geq$ .68; $SE \leq$ .048) and snowboarders (factor loadings $\geq$ .61; $SE \leq$ .069).

Cronbach's alphas for the items in the skiers' activity style (.79), resource specificity (.79), and lifestyle tolerance (.80) indices are given in Table 14.2. The alphas for the snowboarders (Table 14.4) were similar: activity style, .85; resource specificity, .76; and lifestyle tolerance, .75. For both the skiers and snowboarders, the standardized factor loadings ($\geq$ .48 in all cases) and standard errors ($SE \leq$ .074 in all cases) provided additional support for combining these items into their respective latent constructs.

Table 14.1 Skier indices for in-group and out-group conflict

Statement	M	Standardized factor loading	SE	t^{a}	Cronbach's α
Unacceptable snowboarder behavior (out-group conflict)[b]					.93
Fail to be aware of others	3.41	.81	.046	17.45	
Not adequate distance	3.34	.86	.045	18.87	
Fail to yield right of way to downhill user	3.24	.86	.045	18.94	
Behaves in a discourteous manner	2.99	.81	.046	17.56	
Cuts others off	3.13	.85	.045	18.65	
Fails to yield to the less advanced user	3.11	.82	.046	17.73	
Unacceptable skier behavior (in-group conflict)[b]					.88
Fail to be aware of others	3.23	.74	.047	15.71	
Not adequate distance	3.31	.77	.046	16.78	
Fail to yield right of way to downhill user	3.11	.81	.045	18.03	
Behaves in a discourteous manner	2.67	.71	.047	15.00	
Cuts others off	3.05	.75	.047	16.01	
Fails to yield to the less advanced user	2.88	.68	.048	14.21	

a   All *t*s significant at $p < 001$.
b   Variables coded on a 5-point scale ranging from *never* (1) to *almost always* (5).

Bivariate analyses

Consistent with Hypothesis 1, we found significant differences between skiers ($M = 3.20$) and snowboarders ($M = 3.05$) for unacceptable snowboarder behaviors, t (592) = 258, $p = .010$, and for unacceptable skier behaviors ($M = 3.04$ and 3.56, respectively), t (591) = 8.90, $p < .001$. These findings indicate that skiers reported more unacceptable behaviors for snowboarders than for fellow skiers. Similarly, snowboarders identified more out-group than in-group conflict.

Skiers and snowboarders were predicted to be similar in activity style (Hypothesis 2) resource specificity (Hypothesis 3), and mode of the experience (Hypothesis 4). The Colorado data failed to support any of these hypotheses; significant differences ($p < .001$ between skiers and snowboarders were observed for all three constructs. The skiers in this sample attached more importance to the activity than did the snowboarders. Conversely, the snowboarders rated the resource more highly and were more focused on their activity that were the skiers.

We predicted that skiers and snowboarders would differ in their tolerances to each other's lifestyles (Hypothesis 5) and their perceptions of safety-related beliefs (Hypothesis 6). Both of these hypotheses were supported by the data (Table 14.5). The average scores for the lifestyle tolerance index indicated that snowboarders were more likely than skiers

Table 14.2 Skier indices for activity style resource specificity, and lifestyle tolerance

Statement	M	Standardized factor loading	SE	t^a	Cronbach's α
Activity style[b]					.79
Days per year skied[c]	2.75	.65	.051	12.85	
Pairs of skis owned[d]	2.41	.69	.049	14.18	
Money invested in skiing[e]	3.00	.63	.050	12.58	
Number of years skiing[f]	5.09	.61	.052	11.84	
Rating of skiing ability[g]	3.62	.78	.047	16.64	
Resource specificity[h]					.79
This area means a lot to me	3.70	.68	.050	13.57	
Lots of my life is organized around this area	2.22	.67	.051	13.21	
This area is best for what I like to do	3.06	.64	.051	12.58	
I identify strongly with this area	2.81	.79	.049	16.28	
Lifestyle tolerance[h]					.80
Skiers and snowboarders have similar:					
Lifestyles	2.59	.72	.049	14.67	
Education	2.68	.72	.049	14.47	
Income	2.92	.71	.049	14.42	
Attitudes toward the environment	2.45	.48	.055	8.70	
Feelings about the area's value	3.33	.60	.051	11.71	

a   All *t*s significant at $p < .001$.
b   Because the items in the activity style index used different response scales, all variables were standardized before computing the index.
c   Variable coded on a scale ranging from *1–5* (1) to *> 50* (8).
d   Variable coded on a scale ranging from *0* (1) to *> 3* (8).
e   Variable coded on a scale ranging from *$0 to 100* (1) to *> $3,000* (8).
f   Variable coded on a scale ranging from *1* (1) to *> 20* (8).
g   Variable coded on a scale ranging from *beginner* (1) to *expert* (8).
h   Variables coded on a scale ranging from *strongly disagree* (1) to *strongly agree* (5).

to perceive the two groups to be similar. Compared with the snowboarders, however, the skiers reported more unacceptable safety-related behaviors.

Multivariate analysis

The overall fit of the skier and snowboarder models was assessed using five indicators: chi-square, chi-square/degree of freedom, goodness-of-fit index (GFI), comparative fit index (CR), and root mean square residual (RMR; Table 14.6). Although both models produced a significant chi-square, sample size tends to inflate this statistic. Consequently, Marsh and Hocevar (1985) suggested that the chi-square should be evaluated in relation to the model's degrees of freedom, with a χ^2/df ratio of 2:1 to 5:1 indicating an acceptable

Table 14.3 Snowboarder indices for in-group and out-group conflicts

Statement	M	Standardized factor loading	SE	t^a	Cronbach's α
Unacceptable snowboarder behavior (in-group conflict)[b]					.83
Fail to be aware of others	3.19	.63	.069	9.14	
Not adequate distance	3.06	.73	.067	10.94	
Fail to yield right of way to downhill user	3.13	.75	.066	11.28	
Behaves in a discourteous manner	3.02	.65	.068	9.55	
Cuts others off	2.99	.66	.068	9.69	
Fails to yield to the less advanced user	2.94	.61	.069	8.81	
Unacceptable skier behavior (out-group conflict)[b]					.87
Fail to be aware of others	3.72	.74	.065	11.40	
Not adequate distance	3.56	.71	.066	10.83	
Fail to yield right of way to downhill user	3.66	.70	.066	10.52	
Behaves in a discourteous manner	3.40	.74	0.65	11.39	
Cuts others off	3.61	.82	.064	12.84	
Fails to yield to the less advanced user	3.42	.66	.067	9.93	

a   All ts significant at $p < .001$.
b   Variables coded on a 5-point scale ranging from *never* (1) to *almost always* (5).

fit. This ratio for both the skier ($\chi^2/df = 2.75$) and snowboarder $\chi^2/df = 1.68$) models fell within this range. Values for the GFI and CFI ranged from 91 to 93, also indicating an acceptable fit for the two models (Bollen, 1989). Finally, the RMRs, which measure the average discrepancies between the observed and the model-generated covariances, were less than or equal to .061 for both skiers and snowboarders, suggesting a close fit of the data (Church & Burke, 1994).

Skier path model

Consistent with Hypothesis 7, a significant and positive relationship between activity style and out-group ($\beta = 0.23$, $p < .05$) and in-group ($\beta = 0.27$, $p < 05$) conflict was observed in the skier model[4] (Figure 14.2). Resource specificity, however, did not significantly influence beliefs about either out-group ($\beta = 0.08$, ns) or in-group ($\beta = 0.06$, ns) unacceptable behavior as predicted by Hypothesis 8. Hypothesis 9, which predicted a positive relationship between mode of experience and the two conflict constructs, was only partially supported. Similarly, the predicted influence of lifestyle tolerance on perceived conflict received only partial support (Hypothesis 10). In-group conflict increased for skiers who were focused on their activity ($\beta = 0.14$, $p < .05$), but the relationship between out-group conflict and mode of the experience was not significant ($\beta = 0.00$,

Table 14.4 Snowboarder indices for activity style, resource specificity, and lifestyle tolerance

Statement	M	Standardized factor loading	SE	t[a]	Cronbach's α
Activity style[b]					.85
Days per year snowboard[c]	4.82	.72	.064	11.33	
Snowboards owned[d]	2.29	.76	.060	12.62	
Money invested in snowboardinge[e]	2.86	.61	.065	9.41	
Number of years snowboarding[f]	2.26	.76	.063	12.07	
Rating of snowboarding ability[g]	3.52	.84	.058	14.55	
Resource specificity[h]					.76
This area means a lot to me	3.79	.78	.067	11.70	
Lots of my life is organized around this area	2.92	.67	.069	9.67	
This area is best for what like to do	3.13	.53	.072	7.36	
I identify strongly with this area	3.11	.68	.069	9.93	
Lifestyle tolerance[h]					.75
Skiers and snowboarders have similar					
Lifestyles	2.93	.60	.072	8.39	
Education	3.27	.52	.074	7.01	
Income	3.12	.69	.070	9.80	
Attitudes toward the environment	2.73	.50	.074	6.73	
Feelings about the area's value	3.64	.68	.070	9.76	

a   All *t*s significant at $p < .001$.
b   Because the items in the activity style index used different response scales, all variables were standardized before computing the index.
c   Variable coded on a scale ranging from *1–5* (1) to > *50* (8).
d   Variable coded on a scale ranging from *0* (1) to > *3* (8).
e   Variable coded on a scale ranging from *$0 to 100* (1) to > *$3,000* (8).
f   Variable coded on a scale ranging from *1* (1) to > *20* (8).
g   Variable coded on a scale ranging from *beginner* (1) to *expert* (8).
h   Variable coded on a scale ranging from *strongly disagree* (1) to *strongly agree* (5).

n.s). Although significant paths between the tolerance variable and out-group ($\beta = 0.28$, $p < .05$) and in-group ($\beta = 0.16$, $p < .05$) conflict were observed, only the negative relationship was predicted by theory. Finally, safety concerns (Hypothesis 11) influenced out-group conflict ($\beta = 0.42$, $p < .05$) but had no effect on beliefs about in-group unacceptable behavior ($\beta = 0.10$, *ns*).

Taken together, three of the five predictor variables (activity style, lifestyle tolerance, safety) accounted for 44% of the variance in skiers' reported unacceptable behavior with snowboarders (out-group conflict). Of these, safety concerns had the largest relative influence. Three variables also explained skiers' evaluations of conflict with other skiers

Table 14.5 Bivariate analyses comparing skiers and snowboarders

Skier	Snowboarder			
Variable	(M; N = 383)	(M; N = 212)	t	p
Unacceptable snowboarder behavior[a]	3.20	3.05	2.58	.010
Unacceptable skier behavior[a]	3.04	3.56	8.90	.001
Activity style[b]	4.45	4.11	3.22	.001
Resource specificity[c]	2.95	3.24	4.23	.001
Mode of experienced[d]	3.81	4.24	6.36	.001
Lifestyle tolerance[e]	2.79	3.15	6.16	.001
Safety[d]	2.86	1.83	10.47	.001

a   Six-variable index coded on a 5-point scale ranging from *never* (1) to *almost always* (5).
b   Five-variable standardized index.
c   Four-variable index coded on a 5-point scale ranging from *strongly disagree* (1) to *strongly agree* (5).
d   Single-variable coded on a 5-point scale ranging from *strongly disagree* (1) to *strongly agree* (5).
e   Five-variable index coded on a 5-point scale ranging from *strongly disagree* (1) to *strongly agree* (5).

(in-group), but it is important to note the following: First, although lifestyle tolerance significantly influenced in-group conflict, the positive relationship was opposite that predicted by theory. Second, the in-group model accounted for only 10% of the variance in conflict.

Snowboarder path model

Figure 14.3 diagrams the findings from the snowboarder path model.[5] Three variables (activity style, $\beta = 0.22$, $p < .05$; resource specificity, $\beta = 0.23$, $p < .05$; lifestyle tolerance, $\beta = -0.33$, $p < .05$) significantly influenced snowboarders' beliefs about unacceptable skier behavior (out-group conflict) and accounted for 23% of the variance in the criterion construct. All relationships were in the predicted directions. Relative to snowboarders' evaluations of other snowboarders (in-group conflict), only activity style ($\beta = 0.40$, $p < .05$) had a significant influence, accounting for 21% of the variance.

Overall, these findings are consistent with Hypothesis 7 but provide only partial support for Hypotheses 8 and 10. The mode of experience (Hypothesis 9) and safety (Hypothesis 11) relationships were not supported for either out-group or in-group conflict.

Table 14.6 Goodness-of-fit statistics

Measure	Skier model	Snowboarder model
Chi-square	318.66	195.35
Degrees of freedom	116	116
Chi-square/degrees of freedom	2.75	1.68
Goodness-of-fit index	.92	.91
Comparative fit index	.91	.93
Root mean square residual	.059	.061

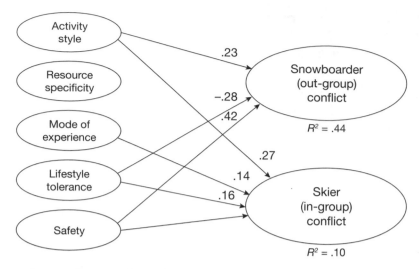

Figure 14.2 Skier conflict model. Only significant paths (*p* < .05) are shown

Discussion

Recent advances in technology such as snowboards and mountain hikes have changed the way people recreate in the outdoors and have introduced new challenges to land management agencies and researchers (Hendricks, 1995). When these new interest groups share the same resource with traditional recreationists, the potential for conflict increases. This study has highlighted the complexities in understanding and predicting both out-group and in-group conflict. The findings reinforce some aspects of previous research, raise questions about other predicted relationships, and suggest other constructs worthy of future investigation.

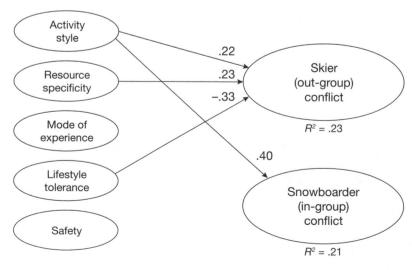

Figure 14.3 Snowboarder conflict model. Only significant paths (*p* < 05) are shown

As noted by Watson (1995), there has been little agreement regarding the definition of recreation conflict. Jacob and Schreyer's (1980) concept of goal interference is at least partially derived from motivation theory. As defined here, conflicts can also arise when groups do not share the same norms (Ruddell & Gramann, 1994). In other words, conflict may occur when individuals perceive the behavior of others to be unacceptable. Although the findings here are consistent with norm theory, more work is needed to explore the relationship between traditional definitions of conflict and the one used in this article.

Contrary to past research (Adelman *et al.*, 1982; Gibbons & Ruddell, 1995; Watson *et al.*, 1991, 1994), data reported here do not support an asymmetrical relationship between user groups. Although skiers reported more unacceptable behavior with snowboarders than with fellow skiers, snowboarders also identified more out-group than in-group conflict. As suggested earlier, the visual differences in clothes, language, and on-slope behavior of the participants in these two activities may serve to magnify the potential for conflict.

The analyses presented here were primarily based on variables suggested by Jacob and Schreyer (1980) 20 years ago. These determinants, along with other sources of conflict (e.g., safety), are still pertinent today. The skiers and snowboarders in this sample varied in terms of activity style, resource specificity, mode of experience, lifestyle tolerances, and concerns with safety. The skiers, for example, attached more importance to the activity than did the snowboarders. Data reported by F.W. Williams *et al.* (1994) indicated that the British Columbian skiers were more involved in their activity than were snowboarders on the basis of years of participation, findings that probably reflect the recent emergence of snowboarding as an activity. The snowboarders, on the other hand, were more involved on the basis of frequency of participation per year. The Colorado data produced exactly the same pattern of findings (see Tables 14.2 and 14.4). We hypothesized that when these items were combined into a single activity style index, the differences in years versus days would cancel each other out and there would be no differences between skiers and snowboarders relative to activity style. Contrary to the hypothesized relationship, the results demonstrated activity style differences regardless of whether single-item or latent constructs are used. Over time, if snowboarders continue to participate as frequently as noted here, the importance they attach to the activity may be greater than that reported by the skiers.

The P. W. Williams *et al.* (1994) study suggested few differences in resource specificity between skiers and snowboarders, leading to the hypothesis here that the two groups would not differ on this concept. In the Colorado data, the snowboarders rated the resource more highly than the skiers did. This difference in findings between the two studies may reflect the situational specifics between the British Columbian and Colorado resorts. Until recently, relatively few Colorado ski areas allowed snowboarders. Individuals who have been constrained from participating in their activity may place greater importance on the resource once such restrictions have been lifted.

These findings, similar to those reported by Gibbons and Ruddell (1995), suggest expanding the scope of conflict research to include the notion of place attachment. Place attachment is typically operationalized using two concepts—place dependence and place identity (D.R. Williams & Patterson, 1999). Place dependence (a functional attachment) reflects the importance of the resource in providing amenities necessary for desired activities. This functional attachment is embodied in the area's physical characteristics (e.g., length and steepness of ski trails) and can increase when the resource is close enough to allow frequent participation (Vaske & Kobrin, in press). Place dependence thus suggests an ongoing relationship with a particular setting. Place identity (an emotional attachment), on the other hand, is not a direct result of any one particular experience (Porshansky, Fabian, & Kaminof, 1983) but rather a psychological investment with the setting that has developed over time (D.R. Williams & Patterson, 1999). A history of repeat visitation due to place dependence may lead to place identity (Moore & Graefe, 1994; Vaske & Kobrin, in press). Similar to the resource specificity hypothesis, this suggests a relationship between place attachment (dependence–identity) and perceived conflict. Theoretical and empirical work is needed in this area.

Mode of experience, a third determinant of conflict identified by Jacob and Schreyer (1980), was predicted here to be similar for skiers and snowboarders. This hypothesis was based on findings reported by P.W. Williams *et al.* (1994), who found that skiers focused on natural features of the environment, whereas snowboarders focused on improving their skills, in essence, the mode of experience for both groups was focused (rather than unfocused), but for different reasons. As operationalized in this article, mode of experience emphasized the importance of developing snowboarding/skiing skills. Consistent with the British Columbia snowboarders, the Colorado snowboarders were more focused on developing their skills than were the skiers. Unfortunately, the data reported here do not permit an examination of the extent to which the skiers focused on other aspects of the experience. This remains a topic for future study.

The average scores for the lifestyle tolerance index indicated that snowboarders were more likely than skiers to perceive the two groups to be similar. Given that many of the snowboarders (*n* = 194) were also skiers and only 13 of the skiers had snowboarded, such findings are as expected. Research is needed, however, to understand this lifestyle tolerance relationship with conflict. Snowboarders, on average, tend to be younger than skiers. Consequently, some of the differences in tolerance observed here could be a function of differences in age. Similarly, Thapa and Graefe (1998) showed differences both between and within skier and snowboarder groups on the basis of the participants' level of expertise. Low-skilled skiers and snowboarders experienced more conflict and were less tolerant than high-skilled skiers and snowboarders.

The two path models presented here suggest concepts that are more or less likely to influence beliefs about unacceptable behavior. Of Jacob and Schreyer's (1980) four determinants of recreational conflict, only activity style significantly influenced both out-group and in-group conflict in both the skier and the snowboarder path models. Resource specificity influenced snowboarders' perceptions of conflict with skiers (out-group) but had no effect on conflict with other snowboarders (in-group) and did not enter either of the skier equations (out-group or in-group). Mode of experience predicted in-group conflict in the skier model, but not out-group conflict, and had no effect in either of the snowboarder equations (out-group or in-group). For the skiers, lifestyle tolerance predicted both out-group and in-group conflict, but the positive path coefficient was opposite that predicted by theory for the in-group conflict equation. Finally, safety only predicted skiers' perceptions of conflict with snowboarders and had no influence in the other three equations. Taken together, these patterns of relationships highlight the complexity of predicting perceived conflict. It remains for future research to support or refute the generalizability of these findings.

The two path models also highlight the distinction between out-group and in-group conflict. The snowboarder path model accounted for virtually the same amount of variance in the out-group (23%) and in-group (21%) equations. Because many of the snowboarders were also skiers, the perception of out-group and in-group differences may have been minimized. The skier path model, however, explained 44% of the variance in out-group conflict and only 10% of that in in-group conflict. These findings may suggest that Jacob and Schreyer's (1980) determinants of conflict are better suited to addressing conflict between activities rather than within activities. Differences in activity style, resource specificity, mode of experience, and lifestyle tolerance may be minimal within a given activity but relatively large between activities. To address within group conflict, research should focus on additional factors such as age, gender, and skill-level differences (Thapa & Graefe, 1998, 1999).

The distinction between out-group and in-group conflict has implications for management. For example, in both the skier and the snowboarder path models, lifestyle tolerance was negatively related to perceived out-group conflict. This suggests that physically separating the two activities by developing specific trails or attraction areas (half-pipes) for each group would help to reduce some of the negative interaction that occurs and may minimize safety concerns.

Coping with in-group conflict, however, raises a different set of issues to be resolved. In part, such problems may stem from skiers'/snowboarders' level of expertise in their respective activities. As noted above, Thapa and Graefe (1999) found that relatively unskilled skiers and snowboarders experienced more conflict than those with more expertise. These results may be explained by novices' lack of experience in avoiding problems associated with high-speed activities. Designating trails for beginner, intermediate, and advanced skiers/snowboarders and placing warning signs at trailheads about the dangers associated with more difficult trails has helped reduce some of these problems. Improved education efforts emphasizing proper etiquette and behavior for both skiers and snowboarders may serve to further minimize the potential for in-group conflict. For example, in response to increasing complaints about snowboarder behavior from both snowboarders and skiers, the Copper Mountain ski resort initiated an education program called "Shrediquette" (*shredding* is slang for snowboarding). Along with the Skier's Responsibility Code, a variety of rules and suggestions specific to snowboarding were printed on brochures and distributed (Baird, 1993). These educational efforts address specific issues and concerns so that recreationists may share the resource.

Overall, this study has attempted to identify the determinants of both out-group and in-group conflict among skiers and snowboarders. The two structural equation models highlight the complexities involved in predicting the occurrence of reported unacceptable behavior. Although our findings have helped to clarify some of the interrelationships among the variables, the lack of previous research specific to these two activities limits their generalizability. Such a limitation, however, can only be addressed through future research.

Notes

1   Ancillary analyses indicated that respondents from the five different ski areas were similar on items of concern to this article.

2   Recognizing that recreationis may participate in multiple activities, skiers were asked if they had ever snowboarded and snowboarders were asked if they had ever skied. Each was then asked to indicate if they still participated in the other activity. As the

number of skiers that still snowboarded was low ($n = 13$), and many ($n = 194$) snowboarders were once skiers, all respondents were kept in their assigned categories.

3   When using LISREL, the error variance must be assumed for single-item indicators of latent constructs. Following the recommendation of Hayduk (1987, pp. 119–123), the error variance for the mode of experience and safely concern constructs was set at 10 (reliability = .90) for all analyses presented here. Use of other error variance values (.05, .15) provided similar solutions.

4   The average correlation among the predictor variables in the skier model was .16 and ranged from .03 to .52. Only two of the correlations were above .15. The correlation between resource specificity and activity style was .33, and the correlation between safety and lifestyle tolerance was −.52. These findings indicate that multicollinearity among the latent constructs was not an issue.

5   In the snowboarder model, the average correlation among the latent variables was .14 and ranged from .01 to .41. Only three of the correlations were above .15. Similar to the skier analyses, the largest correlation was between safety and lifestyle tolerance ($r = -.41$). Resource specificity was correlated with activity style ($r = .28$) and with lifestyle tolerance ($r = .26$), findings that again suggest collinearity among the predictors was minimal.

References

Adelman, B.J., Heberlein, T.A., & Bonnicksen, T.M. (1982). Social psychological explanations for the persistence of a conflict between paddling canoeists and motor craft users in the Boundary Waters Canoe Area. *Leisure Sciences, 5*, 45–62.

Aitkens, M. (1990). Have snowboard will soar. *The Physician and Sports Medicine, 18*, 114–120.

Asher, W., & Markels, A. (1992). When snowboards and skis collide. *Snow Country, 5*, 22–23.

Baird, W. (1993). Recreation conflict between skiers and snowboarders. Unpublished master's thesis, Colorado State University, Fort Collins.

Baron, R.S., Kerr, N.L., & Miller, N. (1992). *Group processes, group decisions, group actions.* Belmont, CA: Brooks/Cole.

Blahna, D.J., Smith, K.S., & Anderson, J.A. (1995). Backcountry llama packing: Visitor perceptions of acceptability and conflict. *Leisure Sciences, 17*, 185–204.

Bollen, K.A. (1989). *Structural equations with latent variables.* New York: Wiley.

Carothers, P., Vaske, J.J., & Donnelly, M.P. (2001). Social values versus interpersonal conflict between hikers and mountain bikers. *Leisure Sciences, 23*(1), 471–6.

Chavez, D.J. (1999). Mountain biking—A rapidly growing sport. In K. Cordell (Ed.), *Outdoor recreation in American life: A national assessment of demand and supply trends* (pp. 245–246). Champaign, IL: Sagamore.

Church, A.T., & Burke, P.J. (1994). Exploratory and confirmatory tests of the big five and Tellegen's three- and four-dimensional models. *Journal of Personality and Social Psychology, 66*, 93–114.

Devall, B., & Harry, J. (1981). Who hates whom in the great outdoors: The impacts of recreational specialization and technologies of play. *Leisure Sciences, 4*, 399–418.

Finley, B. (1990, October 21). Snowboarding in safety fight. *Denver Post*, p. P-1.

Gibbons, S., & Ruddell, E.J. (1995). The effect of goal orientation and place dependence on select goal interference among winter backcountry users. *Leisure Sciences, 17*, 171–183.

Hayduk, L.A. (1987). *Structural equation modeling with LISREL*. Baltimore: Johns Hopkins University Press.

Hendricks, W.W. (1995). A resurgence in recreation conflict research: Introduction to the special issue, *Leisure Sciences, 17*, 157–158.

Hoget, J.L., & Chavez, D.J. (1998). Conflict and management tactics on the trail. *Parks and Recreation, 33*, 41–56.

Hughes, K. (1988, March 22). Surfboarding shifts to the ski slopes, and cultures clash. *Wall Street Journal*, p. 1.

Ivy, M.I., Stewart, W.P., & Lue, C. (1992). Exploring the role of tolerance in recreational conflict. *Journal of Leisure Research, 24*, 348–360.

Jackson, E.L., & Wong, R. (1982). Perceived conflict between urban cross-country skiers and snow-mobilers in Alberta. *Journal of Leisure Research, 14*, 47–62.

Jacob, G.R., & Schreyer, R. (1980). Conflict in outdoor recreation: A theoretical perspective. *Journal of Leisure Research, 12*, 368–380.

Jöreskog, K.G., & Sörbom, D. (1993). *LISREL 8: Structural equation modeling with the SIMPLIS command language*. Hillsdale, NJ: Erlbaum.

Knopp, T.B., & Tyger, J.D. (1973). A study of conflict in recreational land use: Snowmobiling versus ski touring. *Journal of Leisure Research, 5*, 6–17.

Lucas, R.C. (1964). Wilderness perception and use: The example of the Boundary Waters Canoe Area. *Natural Resources Journal, 3*, 394–411.

Marsh, H.W., & Hocevar, D. (1985). Application of confirmatory factor analysis to the study of self-concept: First and higher order factor models and their invariance across groups. *Psychological Bulletin, 97*, 562–582.

Meyers, C. (1991, January 23). All aboard? The battle over down time mounts between skiers and snowboarders, *Denver Post*, p. D–1.

Moore, R.L., & Graefe, A.R. (1994). Attachments to recreation settings: The case of rail-trail users. *Leisure Sciences, 16*, 17–3 1.

Porshansky, H.M., Fabian, A.K., & Kaminof, R. (1983). Place identity: Physical world and socialization of the self. *Journal of Environmental Psychology, 3*, 57–83.

Ramthun, R. (1995). Factors in user group conflict between hikers and mountain bikers. *Leisure Sciences, 17*, 159–169.

Ruddell, E.J., & Gramann, J.H. (1994). Goal orientation, norms, and noise-induced conflict among recreation area users. *Leisure Sciences, 16*, 93–104.

Schneider, I.E. (2000). Revisiting and revising recreation conflict research. *Journal of Leisure Research, 32*, 129–132.

Shelby, B., Vaske, J.J., & Donnelly, M.P. (1996). Norms, standards, and natural resources. *Leisure Sciences, 18*, 103–123.

Thapa, B. (1996). The role of tolerance in recreation conflict: The case of adult skiers and snow-boarders. Unpublished master's thesis, Pennsylvania State University, University Park.

Thapa, B., & Graefe, A.R. (October 1998). *Level of skill and its relationship to conflict and tolerance among adult skiers and snowboarders*. Paper presented at the National Recreation and Park Association Leisure Research Symposium, Miami Beach, Florida.

Thapa, B., & Graefe, A.R. (1999). Gender and age group differences in recreational conflict and tolerance among adult skiers and snowboarders (pp. 219–226). In *Proceedings of the 1998 North-eastern Recreation Research Symposium* (Tech. Rep. NE–255). Radnor, PA: U.S. Department of Agriculture, Forest Service, Northeastern Research Station.

Todd, S.L., & Graefe, A.R. (1989). Level of experience and perception of conflict among canoeists on the Delaware River. In Northeast Forest Experiment Station, *Proceedings of the 1989 North-eastern Recreation Research Symposium* (Gen. Tech. Rep. NE–132, pp. 147–156). Burlington, VT: U.S. Department of Agriculture Forest Service.

Vaske, J.J., Donnelly, M.P., Wittmann, K., & Laidlaw, S. (1995). Interpersonal versus social-values conflict. *Leisure Sciences*, *17*, 205–222.

Vaske, J.J. & Kobrin, K.C. (in press). Place attachment and environmentally responsible behavior. *Journal of Environment Education*.

Vaske, J.J., Shelby, B., Graefe, A.R., & Heberlein, T.A. (1986). Backcountry encounter norms: Theory, method, and empirical evidence. *Journal of Leisure Research*, *18*, 137–153.

Watson, A.E. (1995). An analysis of recent progress in recreation conflict research and perceptions of future challenges and opportunities. *Leisure Sciences*, *17*, 235–238.

Watson, A.E., Niccolucci, M.J., & Williams, D.R. (1994). The nature of conflict between hikers and recreational stuck users in the John Muir Wilderness. *Journal of Leisure Research*, *26*, 372–385.

Watson, A.E.,Williams, D.R., & Daigle, J.J. (1991). Sources of conflict between hikers and mountain bike riders in the Rattlesnake NRA. *Journal of Park and Recreation Administration*, *9*, 59–71.

Watson, A., Zaglauer, H., & Stewart, S. (1996). Activity orientation as a discriminant variable in recreation conflict research. In *Proceedings of the 1995 North-eastern Recreation Research Symnposium* (Gen. Tech. Rep. NE–21 8). Saratoga Springs, NY: U.S. Department of Agriculture Forest Service, Northeastern Forest Experiment Station.

White, D. (1990). Alpine systems come up to speed: Snowboards. *Skiing*, *43*, 196–199.

Williams, D.R., & Patterson, M.E. (1999). Environmental psychology: Mapping landscape meanings for ecosystem management. In H.K. Cordell & J.C. Bergstrom (Eds), *Integrating social sciences and ecosystem management* (pp. 141–160). Champaign, IL: Sagamore.

Williams, D.R., & Roggenbuck, J.W. (October 1989). *Measuring place attachment: Some preliminary findings*. Paper presented at the Symposium on Outdoor Recreation Planning and Management, NRPA Symposium on Leisure Research, San Antonio, TX.

Williams, P.W., Dossa, K.B., & Fulton, A. (1994). Tension on the slopes: Managing conflict between skiers and snowboarders. *Journal of Applied Recreation Research*, *11*, 191–213.

Woodward, B. (1996). *Sports Illustrated mountain biking: The complete guide*. New York: Winner's Circle Books.

Chapter 15

Sheranne Fairley

IN SEARCH OF RELIVED
SOCIAL EXPERIENCE
Group-based nostalgia sport tourism

NOSTALGIA HAS BEEN DESCRIBED as a yearning to return to or relive a past period (Havlena & Holak, 1991; Holbrook, 1993). It has received wide attention in a variety of disciplines including psychology (Castelnuovo-Tedesco, 1998; Ross, 1991), sociology (Davis, 1979; Stauth & Turner, 1988), anthropology (Graburn, 1995; Stewart, 1988), and history (Fritzsche, 2001; Lowenthal, 1985). The broad interest in nostalgia among social scientists has led to work in consumer behavior that examines the roles of nostalgia in consumer attitudes and choice. Nostalgia has been shown to be an effective segmentation variable (Holbrook & Schindler, 1996). It has been used in marketing and advertising appeals to generate positive emotional responses to "what once was" (Havlena & Holak, 1991; Holak & Havlena, 1998) in order to encourage consumption of goods and services (Holbrook, 1993; Pascal, Sprott, & Muehling, 2002). Sporting goods manufacturers, including NIKE, and sport teams, like the Baltimore Orioles and Cleveland Indians, have used nostalgic appeals to promote their products and services (Howell, 1991; Naughton & Vlasic, 1998). Research linking sport and nostalgia has focused on museums and sport halls of fame (Redmond, 1991; Snyder, 1991). Similarly, research linking nostalgia and tourism has focused on the tourism generated around sites of historical importance, including museums, heritage sites, and attractions (Chhabra, Sills, & Rea, 2000; Goulding, 1999, 2001; Peleggi, 1996). Although these studies have generated some interest in nostalgia sport tourism, the topic has received comparatively little research attention.

Gibson (1998) identified nostalgia sport tourism as one of three types of sport tourism (along with active sport tourism and event sport tourism). She defined nostalgia sport tourists as those who travel to visit sport museums, halls of fame, and stadia, or who participate in themed cruises. Note that the elements identified as being the focus of nostalgia sport tourism are physical entities to which society is said to attribute special meaning (or multiple meanings) and that are associated with sport. These entities include places of historic and symbolic importance, or those that house and showcase symbolically significant artifacts that are linked in some manner to the culture or heritage of one or many sports or events. In other words, nostalgia sport tourism has been linked to the cultural heritage of sport.

Consequently, work on nostalgia sport tourism has focused on sport sites or artifacts thought to represent an aspect of the culture or heritage of one or more sports or events. While this is consistent with research on sport consumers which suggests that identifying with a particular sport, team, or athlete affects sport consumption (Chalip, 1997; Kahle, Kambara, & Rose, 1996; Underwood, Bond, & Baer, 2001), it does not take into consideration the well demonstrated finding that sport consumption is a fundamentally social experience (Green & Chalip, 1998; Holt, 1995; Rothenbuhler, 1988). Therefore, it is reasonable to expect that sport nostalgia can derive from group (or social) experiences which themselves become the basis for tourism. Thus, the focus of some sport tourism may be on the travel group itself and therefore on reliving a sport-based group (social) experience, rather than on visiting a particular site or destination.

This paper suggests that the two other types of sport tourism identified by Gibson (1998)—active sport tourism (travel to take part in a sport event) and event sport tourism (travel to spectate at a sport event)—may engender memories that motivate subsequent sport tourism, and that those memories become meaningful and motivating because of the social experiences through which they are engendered. This is consistent with Chalip (2001) who suggests that all three types of sport tourism identified by Gibson (1998) are potentially complementary insomuch as each can foster or facilitate the other. This paper argues, therefore, that nostalgia sport tourism need not rely exclusively on place or artifact. Rather, the paper suggests that the source of nostalgia can be memories derived from sport-based social experience—specifically that of groups that travel together.

The phenomenon of group travel in sport tourism has not been previously explored. Similarly, group travel has received relatively little research attention in the tourism literature, with the few existing studies focusing on organized package and guided tours (e.g., Crompton, 1981; Gorman, 1979; Holloway, 1981; Schmidt, 1979; Schuchat, 1983; Thomson & Pearce, 1980; Quiroga, 1990). These studies suggest that guided and package tours provide added security and require less planning by trip participants. The groups studied were not preexisting ones; rather, they were groups that came together expressly for the purpose of travel. These studies illustrate how people from diverse backgrounds with seemingly nothing in common (other than their participation on a trip) momentarily neglect their differences, accept each other as social equals, and come to behave as a unitary group—exhibiting what Turner (1974) refers to as a liminoid state of communitas. In his work on rites of passage and transition, Turner defines liminality as "any condition outside or on the peripheries of everyday life" (p. 47). During liminal or liminoid periods, "the usual cultural values of competition are subordinated to values of cooperation, and the roles and statuses connected with class and gender in larger society are not operative" (Kemp, 1999, p. 81). In other words, in such situations (or transitions) there is a temporary distancing from everyday life, often indicated by an absence of everyday rules and social status differences. The absence allows individuals to treat one another as social equals. This form of anti-structure was defined by Turner (1977) as "a relation quality of full, unmediated communication, even communion, between definite and determinate identities, which arise spontaneously in all kinds of groups, situations, and circumstances" (p. 46). This is communitas.

Other work on the sociology and anthropology of tourism (Gottlieb, 1982; Graburn 1977, 1983; Lett, 1983; Wagner, 1977) suggests that tourism fosters liminoid experiences that in turn facilitate communitas. Liminoid is similar to but distinct from liminal. While liminal experience includes such things as tribal and agrarian ritual and myth, liminoid experience is associated with leisure activities. In other words, liminal experiences have a sacred component, whereas liminoid experiences do not. Studies of liminoid tourist experiences have tended to examine how tourists fit in to their host destinations (and interact with the locals at the destination), or how tourists interact with one another at a host destination (Lett, 1983), rather than focusing on the interaction between participants of group tours through the course of a tour. However, the theory suggests the value of also studying how group travelers interact with one another during such a travel experience (cf. Kemp, 1999; Turner, 1974, 1977, 1982).

This study uses an inductive methodology to examine the experiences and motivations of a small travel group. Nostalgia was identified as a common (and prominent) theme. This paper suggests ways that identification with a small group, such as a travel group, can generate nostalgia-based sport tourism. It argues that theorizing about nostalgia sport tourism should be expanded to include the contribution that social groups can make to the nostalgia that motivates some sport tourism. Further, it suggests that integrating nostalgic appeals into marketing communications may foster repeat sport tourism.

Nostalgia

In order to have nostalgic feelings (i.e., yearning for the past), individuals must have memories of the past, whether they be lived or learned. It is typically argued that individuals cannot have nostalgic feelings for periods during which they were not alive (Davis, 1979; Havlena & Holak, 1991). Although other authors admit learned memories about periods before one was born into their definitions, they nonetheless contend that the source of nostalgia is generally an individual's personal memories. Thus, Holbrook and Schindler (1991) define nostalgia as "a preference (general liking, positive attitude or favorable affect) towards objects (people, places or things) that were more common (popular, fashionable, or widely circulated) when one was younger (in early adulthood, adolescence, in childhood, or even before birth)" (p. 330).

Notice the definitional restrictions in the foci of one's preference, the frequency (or prevalence) of the object, and the temporal frame. In particular, note that the focus of one's preference is restricted to "objects (people, places or things)." While this may cover goods and services, the third point of reference recently integrated into consumer research—namely, experience (Pine & Gilmore, 1999)—is not covered. It could be argued that an individual may yearn to relive a particular experience in order to obtain feelings that are associated with that experience (Holak & Havlena, 1998).

Restrictions of time and frequency placed on nostalgia are also apparent in the Holbrook and Schindler (1991) definition insomuch as it restricts the objects of preference to those that were "more common (popular, fashionable or widely circulated) when one was younger (in early adulthood, adolescence, in childhood or before birth)" (p. 330). It is possible that "the object(s)" may be just as prevalent now as when "one was younger" and might yet have nostalgic value. For example, individuals might go on the same holiday now as they did when they were younger because of the nostalgic feelings that are evoked.

Further, although when "one was younger" is a dimension that is self-evidently relevant to nostalgia (as a yearning to return to or relive a past period), "early adulthood" may not be the oldest age for which one can feel nostalgic. Older generations might sometimes yearn to relive experiences that occurred during earlier periods of their adulthood, such as middle age.

Havlena and Holak's (1991) definition is more general than Holbrook and Schindler's (1991). Havlena and Holak suggest that nostalgia refers to "an earlier period in the individual's life and draws on biased or selective recall of past experiences" (p. 323). Notice that Havlena and Holak do not specify what an earlier period refers to, although they do suggest (concurring with Davis, 1979) that nostalgia must be related to the period in which one has lived. They therefore do not believe that any events before birth are relevant.

Holbrook (1993) disagrees. While an actual object or event may have occurred pre-birth, if the object or event is embedded within a culture (surrounding the object or event), then it is likely that it can be a focus for nostalgia. Given that modern technology allows the portrayal of different periods, eras, cultures, and events, one may develop a sense of nostalgia for times past though not experienced. The experiences for which one feels nostalgic may include those that have been learned vicariously through portrayals of experiences from times prior to one's own experience—learning which may occur through socialization or through media. This is arguably the case for sport *per se* insomuch as the folklore of many sports links them to historic, symbolic, spiritual and/or sacred elements (Slowikowski, 1991).

Given the arguments above, this paper uses a modified version of Holbrook and Schindler's (1991) definition. Nostalgia is defined here as a preference (general liking, positive attitude or favorable affect) towards objects (people, places, *experiences* or things) from when one was younger or from times about which one has learned vicariously, perhaps through socialization or the media.

Healey (1991) found that memories of sport (whether they derive from personal experience or have been passed down) signify important events in people's lives and include the group relationships with which they are associated. From the standpoint of nostalgic reflection, sport may simply provide occasions through which liminoid social experiences are lived, remembered, and felt. Consequently, the focus of associated memories may not be on the sport itself, but on the important social (or group) relationships that one has shared and the experiences thereby engendered.

Nostalgia, memory, and identity

One cannot have feelings of nostalgia without memory (or perceptions) of how things used to be (Holak & Havlena, 1998). In other words, nostalgia and memory are inextricably linked. Further, memories of group experiences are related to one's identity. Collective memory refers to recollections that belong to a group as a whole—a shared memory of past events held by members of a social group (Blockland, 2001). However, Healey (1991) suggests that while fragments of a group social experience reside in individual group members' memories, the collective memory only becomes cohesive when the fragments coalesce. That is, by coming together as a group and reliving past group experiences, collective memories become more cohesive (or salient) as various fragments are placed back together through communication. Similarly, Slowikowski (1991) suggests that feelings of nostalgia are inherent in ceremonial gatherings (e.g., the unification of group members who share an experience), emphasizing that the unification of a group with a common identity generates feelings of nostalgia.

Our memories not only act to remind us of our past identities, and reinforce our current identities, but also hold within them the experiences that led to the construction, the rebuilding, or the confirmation of our identities (Barcley & DeCooke, 1988; Stewart, 1988). Thus, the feeling of nostalgia, by bringing specific memories of related identities to the forefront, allows individuals who are disenchanted with an aspect of a particular identity to escape to a more positive aspect of that identity (Aden, 1995). In other words, positive associations of one's identity in one's memory may be used to reinforce or maintain a threatened identity. Similarly, liminal (and liminoid) states and communitas that individuals have experienced are also likely to be stored as memories and may be a source of comfort during times of disenchantment arising out of overly structured and mundane lives.

Sport tourism seems an apt context through which to study nostalgia given the demonstrated links of (a) nostalgia with identity, (b) identity with sport related consumption, and (c) identity with tourism. Nostalgia has been shown to implicate a sense of who we are (Davis, 1979)—that is, the individual's self-concept and sense of identity. Previous research on sport consumers illustrates that individuals incorporate elements of sport participation (Donnelly & Young, 1999; Green & Chalip, 1998) and/or sport fanship (Holt, 1995; Laverie & Arnett, 2000; Wann, Melnick, Russell, & Pease, 2001) into their self-concept and, by extension, into their self and/or social identities. Similarly, Chon (1992) and Sirgy and Su (2000) demonstrate a link between self-image, destination-image, and travel behavior. Thus, sport consumption and tourism choices each affect and are affected by the consumer's sense of self. Green (2001) argues that sport tourism allows individuals to celebrate and parade identities they share with others who also have an interest in a particular sport or event. Therefore, it is reasonable to expect that nostalgia will be generated from individuals' past experiences (liminal or otherwise) in relation to celebrating and parading their particular identities via sport tourism, and that nostalgia can catalyze the effort to relive those experiences (cf. Holbrook & Schindler, 1996; Pascal, Sprott, & Muehling, 2002).

The current literature on identity and collective memory focuses on society as a whole and on small groups. However, work on nostalgia in both the tourism and sport literatures has focused primarily on manifestations in society as a whole, with little consideration of the ways that nostalgia manifests itself in smaller social groups. Given that memories of sport have been found to include images of important group relationships, including friends, family, and teammates (Healey, 1991), it makes sense to consider sport-based nostalgia with reference to group experiences. Consumers may sometimes seek occasions through which to relive previous group experiences (especially liminoid experiences), including those involving sport tourism, rather than to make nostalgic contact with a sport place or artifact. Further, the nostalgia thus generated may foster repeat patronage (or repeat consumption) as the consumer seeks to relive those experiences once again and/or return to a liminoid state. This study explores that possibility through participant observation with a group that travels to follow a professional team.

Method

In order to investigate the motives and experiences of those who travel to follow a professional sport team, it was useful to seek a group that had done the trip more than once in order for some structure (or consistency) to develop. This would allow any consistencies across trips to be compared and contrasted. An article that appeared on a professional football team's official website described one such group: the Bus Trekkers. That group was selected for further study.

Participants and setting

The Bus Trekkers are a group that travels annually to follow one team in the Australian Football League (the AFL). The AFL is Australia's largest professional sporting league with sixteen teams dispersed throughout five of the eight states and territories. The Bus Trekkers were organized by a group of fans and were not an official activity of the football club. Since its inception in 1997, the group has traveled annually by bus to follow the team to a competition in a neighboring (but nonetheless distant) state. The average travel time is 36 hours each way (including stops). The trip consists of travel to and from the destination (with stops approximately every two hours) and two days at the destination. The trips attract between 20 and 40 participants each year. On-board entertainment consists of watching videos and playing various trivia games. Time at the destination includes both organized group activities (e.g., the game itself, group tours, and meals), as well as informal recreation time, which generally becomes an opportunity for impromptu group activities. The destination and the mode of transport have remained the same each year, as have many of the activities in which the group partakes.

The team that the travel group follows does not have a history of on-field success. For example, prior to the trip that took place during the seventh game of the season, the team had not won a single game. In fact, at the time of this study, the team had never won a game to which the group had traveled. However, the travel group is not particularly concerned with the on-field success of the team and continues its annual trip despite the team's dismal win/loss record. Given the history of the group participating on the trip, consistencies in the trip elements, and the lack of concern about the on-field success of the team, it was expected that elements of nostalgia might be relevant to the group.

Bus Trekker members vary greatly in terms of their involvement with the football club, as well as their interest in the team and home match attendance. The group itself does not sit together at home games. However, various Bus Trekker members meet at a local hotel to watch the team's away games together (except, of course, the ones to which they travel). A number of the members volunteer at the club in various capacities (e.g., preparing lunch for the team after training sessions, compiling a database of members, and help with mail outs). Others are involved in (and/or are members of) various groups associated with the club, including "The Harbourmasters" (foundation club members), as well as "The Sirens" (a group designed to attract women to the football club). There are also Bus Trekker members for whom involvement with the football club is not possible due to financial or temporal constraints, or other commitments.

Design and procedure

Participant observation and interviews were conducted during the Bus Trekkers' fifth annual trip during the 2001 AFL season. The 2001 trip attracted 22 participants (not including the researcher) of whom 15 were repeat trip participants. For reasons that included ill health, financial constraints, and work restrictions, a number of participants who had previously traveled with the group were unable to attend in 2001. The group was comprised of 15 females and 7 males.

The trip organizer was contacted by phone and informed of the research plan in order to gain access to the group with the purpose of becoming a full participant in the travel experience. The trip organizer responded favorably. In order to become familiar with the trip organizer and participants before the trip began, I traveled to the home city of the Bus Trekkers two days prior to the group's departure. During that time, an unstructured interview was conducted with the trip organizer and her partner, who had both been on the trip a number of times. The interview lasted 45 minutes and was audio-taped and transcribed for subsequent analysis.

During the days leading up to the trip, I stayed in the trip organizer's home, which made it possible to collect further information via informal conversations (from which notes were taken). The trip organizer was very open in her communications with me in relation to the group itself, as well as the trip. The trip organizer also (very generously) gave me a team shirt, scarf, and football so that I would have something to remember them by. These props came in very handy at the game, allowing me to visually fit in to the group and garner "authentic" reactions from both fans of the Bus Trekkers' team and fans of the opposing team. During the period before the trip, I visited the football team's club, where I met other trip participants and conducted informal interviews with three individuals who had been on the trip before, two of whom were going on the impending trip. Notes were taken during each of these interviews, which ranged between 15 and 30 minutes in length. These trip participants also helped introduce me to others during the trip.

The trip organizer made participants aware prior to the trip that I would be there to conduct research. Participants were reminded again on commencement of the trip. During the trip, I participated fully in all group activities and was treated as one of the group. Field notes were taken after each group activity. Interviews were also conducted with 20 of the 22 trip participants and one of the two bus drivers during the trip. All interviewees were assured that their anonymity would be protected. The interviews ranged between 20 and 40 minutes in length and were conducted on the bus (as there was ample time) and during the longer trip stops. The interviews were semi-structured and were used to identify motives, key experiences, and the norms and rituals of those who travel to follow the team. Each interview concluded with a prompt encouraging interviewees to describe what they felt to be pertinent elements relating to the group or the trip that were not otherwise covered during the interview. Interviews became sequentially more structured. After each interview, the interview questions were adapted to further explore experiences and ideas described in previous interviews. As the trip progressed group members became more open with the information that they would divulge, perhaps because I was accepted as a group member who adhered to all of the group's norms and participated in group rituals. During the trip, interview notes were taken. All interviews were also audio-taped and subsequently transcribed to allow more detailed analysis.

Analysis

In order to facilitate analysis, all field notes and interview transcripts were entered into NUD*IST so that themes and their structure could be explored and described. A constant comparative method was adopted, allowing the researcher to develop the analysis inductively (Glaser & Strauss, 1967). Data were analyzed for themes, categories, and patterns and were coded using standard protocols for analysis of qualitative data (Spradley, 1980; Weiss, 1994). Reading through the interview transcripts and field notes, the researcher first coded all phrases and opinions from the transcript. This was repeated on three separate occasions, with the researcher working dialectically between the data and the literature to further develop, compare, and contrast the codes and themes identified. Specific quotes have been chosen for presentation in the following section because they best represent the views of trip participants.

Results

Although all trip members were aware of my agenda for participating on the trip, I was fully accepted into the group as soon as I arrived at the trip departure point and was welcomed and included in all group activities, as were all other participants (new and old). My status as a researcher did not seem to affect the way that I was treated. The interviews that I conducted while on the trip were informal and offered trip participants the opportunity to talk about their experiences during their trip. Thus, the questions were neither obtrusive nor out of context.

Trip participants made note of the fact that the group is diverse, but is united by a common element: their support for a team—a fact that makes other differences irrelevant during the trip. As one participant put it:

> People from all walks of life, with all different interests, with one interest in common—we're all mad [team] supporters. You don't get much of that these days.

As this quote illustrates, the liminoid sense of communitas that pervades the trip is enabled (at least in part) by the group's shared fanship for the team. Shared fanship provides an immediate common focal point. What is also significant here is the quote's contrast between the group and what "you don't get much of . . . these days." That contrast represents an aspect of the group's sense of special difference—an implicit nostalgia for a kind of shared group fanship that is not common today, but by implication may be thought to have been present in past eras.

Nostalgia related to the liminoid state of communitas clearly emerged as the superordinate theme. Five key roles of nostalgia were identified: nostalgia as motive, norms and rituals as objects of nostalgia, best experience as objects of nostalgia, nostalgia as a basis for trip suggestions, and nostalgia through socialization. Each of these five themes is described below.

Nostalgia as motive

Given that the trip's stated objective was to attend the team's game, it seemed reasonable to expect that games would have a significant place in the recollections of trip participants. That was not the case. In fact, participants were eloquent about the irrelevance of the team's lack of on-field success. Accordingly, they stressed that despite the team's losing record, the trip was important to them. One participant put it this way:

> It's a pretty unusual thing . . . [to] drive 2700 kilometers [1678 miles] to watch a footy team play. . . . I don't think that people would understand. There's a mob of people who just travel all that way to see them [the team] lose, and I don't think there's anyone who is particularly disappointed with the trip. That sort of thing is hard to explain to someone who is not involved.

As this quote illustrates, the Bus Trekkers believe that their trip would be viewed as inexplicable by non-participants. They see the trip as a distinctive point of difference— one that separates the group's key activity from everyday life. This perception seems appropriate. When I first learned of the group and its seemingly grueling trip, it seemed odd to me. When I have described the group's annual trip to friends and colleagues, they too have been incredulous.

When asked why they were traveling to follow the team, several participants responded by reminiscing about those things they found to be particularly attractive or important from past trips. For example, one foundation member of the group who had been on every Bus Trekker trip said, "We have a lot of fun on the bus as a group." Another said, "[It's] the interaction, I think—everybody on the bus. It's a group going over and a group coming back."

Another participant described the important role that making friendships played in his decision to make the trip:

> You're probably making friends here that you don't necessarily have to see throughout the year, but you can see again on the next trip and still pick-up where you left off. It's a different sort of friendship and a different sort of bonding. It's not like your mate [Australian slang for good friend] who you see every week. It's just a totally different experience. . . . For these few days you're with a group of people who accept you at face value. You're not here for any other reason. . . . I think you'll find that there is not much that would ever end up resembling this trip for the reasons or the way people are together. I don't think that there's anything that could emulate what we do here.

Notice the emphasis placed on the uniqueness of the social experience achieved through the trip—the claim that it could not be obtained through an alternative activity. The participant is drawing on feelings relating to past trip experiences. Similarly, others (especially the older members of the group) talk of the cohesiveness of the group, breaking through age differences, on previous trips. Note also that the respondent emphasizes that in the group you are accepted at face value and are not judged in terms of everyday social roles thus, exhibiting characteristics of communitas. The quote above is certainly consistent with my own experience of the trip. Although different subgroups existed, the boundaries between the subgroups were indistinct and permeable—individuals (including myself) were able to move and communicate freely among subgroups. One participant described it well: "We get on so well together. Being different age groups, there's oldies and middle aged and youngies and all sorts. Because we all get on so well together and it just makes it a great trip." Throughout the interviews, references to the social aspects are not limited to the current trip; rather, the importance of the social is reflected, to some degree at least, in nostalgic reminiscences about past trips.

Participants indicated that photos were taken to reinforce memories of trip experiences. This was especially true for the foundation members of the group who had participated on all trips since the group's inception:

> We have loads of fun and we've got photos to prove it and we put them in our album. We've been doing it for like five years now, and the photos are just added and added on. Something happens different every year. It's never the same.

Photos can act as catalysts for nostalgia by reminding individuals who look back over them of good times had. In other words, the photos provide tangible evidence of the importance of reminiscing and proof to oneself that an anti-structured experience took place. Before the trip, while I was staying with the trip organizer, I was shown a number of photo albums full of photos from previous trips. Each photo was explained to me in terms of the people in it, the place where it was taken, as well as stories of group significance and ritual that were associated with each photo. A second point also stands out in the quote above. The participant indicates that the trip experiences differ from year to year. No two trips are ever identical. However, while each trip offers something different, it became apparent that various rituals and repeated activities were in place-rituals and activities that had emerged from memorable experiences on past trips. While it was my first (and only) trip with the group, it was clear that certain rituals had particular significance to the group, reinforcing the liminoid state of communitas that was achieved.

Norms and rituals as objects of nostalgia

The trip itself can be seen as something akin to a ritual. Participants noted that the trip had become "a prophecy." In essence, the trip is the focal activity that legitimizes the Bus Trekkers as a group. The mode of transport the group uses (a bus), albeit not the most comfortable or rapid choice, is one of the most apparent group rituals. It is treated like an annual rite of passage, which is a transition from everyday structured life that allows individuals to be part of the group, beginning at the departure point and concluding on arriving home. One participant described it by comparing the bus trip to travel by air:

> [We go by bus] because that's how it started—going by bus, the camaraderie of going by bus. I know to some extent there was friction by going by plane and some going by bus. I thought I wouldn't meet any of these people if I didn't go by bus. People who fly don't sit near each other. We don't go to the same functions [as people who fly].

The bus seems to have symbolic importance in itself. The previous year, the fact that a few group members chose to fly rather than to go by bus had caused friction within the group. Clearly taking the bus is a rite of passage. Those who do not travel on the bus are not easily accepted by the group unless they can offer what the group deems to be a legitimate reason. One couple who did not travel by bus was widely accepted by the group because health problems had militated against the arduous bus trip. Once everyone had arrived at the destination, the couple was integrated into group activities. However, others who did not travel by bus but who met with the group at the destination were not accepted as part of the group. The fact that I traveled on the bus made me one of the group and is the key reason that I was treated as a fully fledged group member.

Camaraderie, meeting people, and social interaction are key factors in the ritual of bus travel. The stops along the way to and from the destination and the activities at each stop have become rituals in themselves. When approaching stops, repeat group members would discuss things that were done and things that happened at the stops on past trips, often in anticipation that they would relive those experiences. The conversation and expectations focused on activities (such as kicking the football around, buying particular objects), incidents (especially encounters with famous people), and meals (which had become something of a ritual at particular stops). The following field note illustrates this point:

> There were a lot of stops that have become something of a ritual for the trip. For example, everyone was talking about stopping in Ceduna for a meal of King George whiting, and Southern Cross as the place for the last hurrah on the way home. There was also constant reference to "dressing the bus up" when they drive into [the destination].

Further, the ways that certain group members act during the course of the trip (both at stops and at the destination) are not necessarily consistent with what they would do in their everyday lives. For example, given the anonymity that one may assume during a trip, the way that individuals react and/or communicate with strangers may not be consistent with how they act at home. One trip member in particular, was known to be very quiet and reserved "back home" in his everyday life. During the trip he became outspoken, talking to other group members, people at the stops, and people at the destination. Similarly, group members are more open to trying food and beverages that they would not normally eat or drink during their everyday lives. These differences in behavior reinforce the liminoid character of the trip in that the social conventions present in everyday life are suspended in the liminoid state allowing individuals the chance to take on other personas.

One group ritual involves displaying team-related paraphernalia throughout the bus so that displays are visible from the outside when the bus arrives at the destination. This is what is referred to as "dressing up the bus." As part of this ritual, the team song is generally played loudly through the bus stereo and the group sings along as they drive into the main street of the destination.

All participants who had been on previous trips would continuously make reference to past trips and to those elements that had become rituals. One participant described the following:

> We've got to listen to [a certain group member's] jokes—big ritual that one. I tell you what, we've got some people here that entertain and they do it every year and they do a good job. . . . Then we go to Southern Cross—we have our inaugural break up at Southern Cross. That's when we all sort of have our last beer together, last feed together. And obviously, that night where we go out for a feed down in [a suburb of the destination], we've made a tradition of it over the years—all sit at a table together and have a feed. It's like the Last Supper. We've done that every year. We've religiously done that and gone to Hahndorf. I don't know why but we go to Hahndorf every year.

Phrases like "Last Supper" and words like "religiously" suggest that there is a sense in which these activities have a sacred meaning for the group. Actively participating in these rituals, as well as visiting those places where the rituals take place, serves to remind group members of past trip experiences by evoking memories and their associated effect. Further, stopping at different places along the way, or driving past particular places, creates discussion about past experiences. The telling and retelling of stories such as these evokes nostalgia in a manner that solidifies group bonds.

Best experience as object of nostalgia

Near the end of the trip, I asked participants to describe their best experiences of this or any trip. Many responded by reflecting on the entirety of their trip experiences, including previous trips, rather than solely on experiences from the current trip. The current trip became blended with reminiscences about past experiences. The game itself was acknowledged as one venue for best experience:

> I think the best experience is the game itself. Everybody is doing it [cheering] the whole game instead of waiting for something to happen. It's just the camaraderie at the games. It's almost like a power trip because you're there against 39,000 throats—and it's just like, yeah, we are here. That's the buzz for me. At home games you cannot get a response from anyone around you who is a [team] supporter like you have there.

A closer examination of the responses above suggests that it is not actually the on-field action that is of prime importance, but the feelings of camaraderie among the group members at the game. During the game, we were seated in a cornered off area behind the goal posts (the traditional supporter group area). We were surrounded by security guards that I was told is an artifact of happenings on previous trips where the opposition's fans had been abusive towards the group and thrown things at them. Being surrounded by security guards, in addition to the similar colors and paraphernalia in which the group dressed certainly emphasized the fact that we were the minority at the game. Being the minority at the game makes it considerably different from attending team home games— a feature which adds to the group experience.

Although the game is one place where camaraderie is particularly salient, the sense of camaraderie pervades the entire experience—a fact that several noted by naming camaraderie itself as the best experience. One said, "I think it's when you reach that point when everybody in the group is together. . . . [We're] all together eating, and it's sort of like a Last Supper." Another described it this way:

> I think [camaraderie] would be the biggest part in my eyes. The fact that you have the bonding. And the good thing that I find about it is that there are differences within the group, but we are all part of the group.

Camaraderie and group experience were common referents throughout responses. Sport or team-specific references were noticeable by their absence. The social element became a basis for nostalgic reminiscences about each trip. The nostalgia does not reference the sport or the team, but rather the social experiences obtained as part of the group. This is further demonstrated by the fact that most of the photos taken at the game are of the group rather than of the game. Uniting as a group and participating in the trip allows individuals to reminisce about previous trips. Rituals and trip occurrences become part of the group's folklore. By talking about the past experiences of the group on each trip, the collective memory becomes more cohesive as group members remind each other of experiences that some may have forgotten—making nostalgic thoughts more prominent. There are constant comparisons from trip-to-trip, which became even more evident when individuals were asked if there was anything about the trip that could be changed to improve the trip.

Nostalgia as a basis for trip suggestions

While all trip participants expressed satisfaction with their trip, when asked if there was anything about the trip that could be changed to improve the trip, all responses made comparisons to previous trips. For example, on all previous trips there had been a designated coordinator on the bus to organize games and entertainment during the bus ride. However, for the trip on which I traveled, although one group member emerged as an impromptu coordinator, there was no one officially designated for that role. Many group members had positive recollections of the coordinator and suggested that the role should be reinstated as an official one. One foundation member summarized this view: "I would have liked to have a coordinator on the bus that actually coordinated a little more fun times. Every other year we've had one."

Other departures from the ways things were done on previous trips were also noted with the suggestion that a previous way of doing things should be reinstated. These suggestions were generally related to being able to spend more time doing particular group activities that participants enjoy, such as having "traditional" meals at different venues, and spending more time at "traditional" stops throughout the bus trip. For example, the day after the game, the group generally goes by coach to a small village. However, this time our coach driver had organized to pick up another tour group and take them as well. The seating arrangements in the bus were therefore changed to accommodate the other group. During this period the dynamics of the group changed given that others now occupied (some of) the group's space. Similarly, time at the village was minimized to cater for the new group, so the Bus Trekkers did not have time to partake in group rituals that had occurred on previous trips. Afterwards, the group members said that they liked the people in the other tour group, but that they had no place on "our bus." This was not a mere conservative resistance to change. The suggestions were framed as means to make it possible to relive the good times that each recalled from previous years.

Nostalgia through socialization

The value placed on relived experience might lead one to expect that first time trip participants would have little in common with those whose motives were unabashedly nostalgic. However, given the emphasis on group camaraderie and the constant references by experienced trip participants to happenings on previous trips, first timers had the opportunity to relive past trips vicariously. From the information that group members passed on to newcomers (including me), I became aware of the rituals and other trip elements that are important to the group. When asked to describe activities that are central to the group, one first time participant responded, "They've got some things happening on past trips that we don't know about, but they usually tell us what it was so we can see the funny side of it." In short, socializing during the trip became the means by which new participants were integrated into the group.

This was clearly reflected in the first timers' suggestions for improvements. Their suggestions were similar to those of seasoned group members, reflecting nostalgia for experiences they had only heard about. This highlights the potent role played by norms of camaraderie, group rituals, and (especially) the group's folklore in socializing new participants into the group. In fact, by the end of the trip, new participants' descriptions of the group mirrored those of long-time members—so much so that newcomers could recount experiences from previous years as if they had been there. An element of nostalgia had been implanted through the group's processes of socialization.

Discussion

Nostalgia's role in sport tourism is not evoked solely by famous sporting attractions or the artifacts resident in museums or halls of fame. While venues, museums, and halls of fame are obviously nostalgic attractions, not all sport nostalgia is focused on the history or traditions of sport. Nor is nostalgia necessarily grounded in sport's wide social appeal. The findings of this study show that nostalgia can arise in relation to identification with a relatively small social group (in this case, a travel group) that uses sport as a context through which to create a liminoid space in which to celebrate their identity as a group. Further, nostalgic elements are not confined to the destination or to the event itself. Rather, the travel experience, including the stops along the way, acts as a focus for nostalgia. For group-based sport tourism experiences, nostalgia is represented by the effort to relive liminoid group experiences.

The memories that generate nostalgia were centered on the norms and rituals of the group. These come to represent the group as a distinctive identity. Interestingly, memories of past experiences were related to the group itself and the camaraderie members have shared. Salient memories had little to do with the team, the sport, or the game itself. While the experience of camaraderie at the game (being the minority group) was considered to be a key experience of the trip, watching the game was not the important feature. In fact, game-specific memories were never discussed. It is as if the team (or, perhaps, the sport) is merely a vehicle through which to build friendships and celebrate a common group identity.

Photos and souvenirs from the trip represented tangible evidence to group members of their trip and subsequent experiences. Belk (1990) and Csikszenmihalyi and Rochberg-Halton (1981) each discuss the importance of possessions in maintaining a sense of the past. For group members, photos are key possessions—souvenirs from the trip that act as visual catalysts for memories and the effect those memories evoke.

Memories of the past, and a yearning to relive that past, were motives for traveling to follow the team. Those memories were, however, avowedly social and had little to do with the team *per se*. The focus of group members' identification is the group itself, rather than the team or any related aspect (e.g., players, coaches). Consequently, nostalgic feelings have to do with the group, rather than the team or the sport. Previous work has noted the vital role of social interaction in fan behavior (Holt, 1995; Rothenbuhler, 1988), but most work on fan motivation presupposes that the team or the sport is nonetheless the pivotal object of identification (Underwood et al., 2001; Wann et al., 2001). The findings here suggest that identification with the team may be neither necessary nor sufficient to generate fan support, but that social bonding with other fans is sufficient to generate support and team-related consumption.

Snyder (1991) suggests that sport museums and halls of fame "selectively preserve and thus create the past that is appropriate for nostalgic feelings" (p. 237). So too does the travel group, in that the group continues to refine the trip elements based on previous trips, retaining in collective memory and in practice what is enjoyable and central to the identity of the group. As a result, the norms and rituals of the group that are facilitated by liminoid space are often the focus of nostalgia. Similarly, through the telling and retelling of stories about past trips, the group's folklore preserves and reinforces a collective sense of group nostalgia.

Research in sport tourism has generally examined the features that make a particular activity, event, or destination attractive. Little attention has been paid to the act of traveling. Yet, in the example studied here, traveling to the game plays a vital role in creating the social climate that makes sport tourism attractive enough for participants to undertake the trip and then to repeat it year after year. The collective memory of the group becomes more cohesive when the group reunites for the trip because group members' memories are allowed to collate (also see Healey, 1991). The group interactions make memories salient and amplify the effect associated with each memory. The travel provides ample opportunity to relive previous trips. The social interactions throughout the trip foster new experiences that can be added to the collective memory and provide new opportunities for relived experience during future trips.

The trip, then, is more than a mere rehearsal of past experience. While past trips are being relived, the current trip is being lived for the first time. This is, in fact, part of the attraction. The group makes ongoing comparisons between the past and the present. This fortifies the sense of nostalgia while, at the same time, making each trip something new—something to be savored.

It also reinforces the group's identity. Nostalgic recollections remind members of the positive things that are associated with their identities as members of the group. Reminiscing about good times, participating in group rituals, and visiting sites that have become significant to the group evoke memories which bind the group together as a unique whole. In this context, negative experiences—like the fact that the team is a losing one—are reframed as positive opportunities that may be worthy of nostalgia.

In the anthropological literature, there has been substantial analysis of the communitas that is engendered by rituals, festivals, and special events (DaMatta, 1986; Turner, 1982). There is a sense during these events that the normal social boundaries no longer apply—a feature that makes them attractive to those who participate. That was certainly the case for the Bus Trekkers, as many commented about the ways that social distinctions evaporated as the group came together for its trip. The process was enabled by the sense of celebration and the rituals shared by the group. Celebration and ritual were, in turn, reinforced by the group reminiscences, which gave the celebrations and rituals their special meaning. Thus, nostalgia was not merely an evoked emotion; it was an essential component of the group's sense of unity.

The impact extends to newcomers. Through the socialization which occurs throughout the trip, with repeat group members sharing the group's folklore, first time trip participants are able to live past group experiences vicariously, thereby sharing the group's nostalgia. This was enabled by the trip's length and the shared rigors of travel by bus. The trip may constitute what Graburn (1983) calls rite of passage tourism whereby individuals endure an arduous journey as a transition into another life phase, or in this case membership into the group. It also suggests the value of opportunities to socialize as means by which to foster socialization of new members into the group.

From a practical standpoint, the findings here recommend greater attention to the group experiences which sport fanship enables. Activities shared among fans can become the basis for nostalgic appeals designed to foster repeat purchase behaviors. Each new consumption occasion then provides new stories and images through which to reinforce the nostalgia and associated consumption. If appropriately devised, tourism affords an ideal opportunity to foster the requisite group experience.

Limitations and future directions

The results derived here were obtained from an analysis of a particular group, following a particular team, participating in a particular sport tourism experience, at a particular time. As the findings here indicate that theorizing about nostalgia sport tourism needs to be widened to include nostalgia generated by objects other than those that are historically or culturally related to the sport *per se*, further forms of nostalgia-based tourism should be sought. Longitudinal work examining different types of groups and individuals who participate in different kinds of sport tourism experiences would help to elaborate models of the ways that nostalgia becomes manifest and the impacts it subsequently has. That work should explore the ways that different trip elements (e.g., mode of transport, frequency of trip, destination) affect the manifestation and impact of nostalgia. Similarly, sport trips should be compared to other forms of repeat group travel to determine the degree to which the findings here are general or specific to sport.

At a practical level, this study recommends fostering group-based fan travel and creating marketing communications that appeal to resultant nostalgia. At this stage, those implications are speculative. Nevertheless, the effort to make practical use of insights from research provides a unique opportunity to test new ideas and to discover the boundaries of their impact (Argyris, Putnam, & Smith, 1985; Berg & Smith, 1985). Thus, efforts to build fan groups and then to use group nostalgia as a marketing lever should be evaluated in order to obtain new insight into the phenomena described here. The current study has addressed collective nostalgia that is based on collective memories. It may be useful to explore and contrast collective nostalgia with private nostalgia. In particular, the ways that group memories and individual nostalgia affect one another should be explored. In this study, the team that the group traveled to follow provided a rationale for the trip, but was by no means as central to the group's identity as much of the literature on fanship would lead one to expect. Indeed, once members were socialized into the group, it would seem that identification with the group played a more pivotal role in their decision to travel in support of the team than did identification with the team itself. Nevertheless, participants were fans of the team whose game they traveled to see. It is as if there were two foci of identification: the team and the group. Future work should explore the distinctions and potential synergies between these two foci of identification.

References

Aden, R.C. (1995). Nostalgic communication as temporal escape: "When it was a game's" reconstruction of a baseball work community. *Western Journal of Communication*, 59(1), 20–38.

Argyris, C., Putnam, R., & Smith, D.M. (1985). *Action science.* San Francisco; Jossey-Bass.

Barcley, C.R., & DeCooke, P. (1988). Ordinary everyday memory: Some of the things of which selves are made. In U. Neisser & E. Winogard (Eds), *Remembering reconsidered: Ecological and traditional approaches to the study of memory* (pp. 91–125). New York: Cambridge University Press.

Belk, R.W. (1990). The role of possessions in constructing and maintaining a sense of past. *Advances in Consumer Research*, 17, 669–676.

Berg, D.N., & Smith, K.K. (Eds) (1985). *Exploring clinical methods for social research.* Beverly Hills, CA: Sage.

Blockland, T. (2001). Bricks, mortar, memories: Neighbourhood and networks in collective acts of remembering. *International Journal of Urban and Regional Research*, 25, 268–283.

Castelnuovo-Tedesco, P. (1998). Reminiscence and nostalgia: The pleasure and pain of remembering. In G.H. Pollock & S.I. Greenspan (Eds), *The course of life: Completing the journey* (Vol. 7, pp. 110–130). Madison, CT: International Universities Press.

Chalip, L. (1997). Celebrity or hero? Toward a conceptual framework for athlete promotion. In D. Shilbury & L. Chalip (Eds), *Advancing management of Australian and New Zealand sport* (pp. 42–56). Melbourne, Australia: SMAANZ.

Chalip, L. (2001). Sport and tourism: Capitalising on the linkage. In D. Kiuka & G. Schilling (Eds), *The business of sport* (pp. 77–89). Oxford: Meyer & Meyer.

Chhabra, D., Sills, E., & Rea, P. (2000). Nostalgia for old world in heritage tourism. In N.P. Nickerson, R.N. Moisey, & K.L. Andereck (Eds), *Lights, camera, action: Spotlight on tourism in the new millennium* (pp. 339–334). Boise, ID: Travel and Tourism Research Association.

Chon, K. (1992). Self-image/destination-image congruity. *Annals of Tourism Research*, 19, 360–363.

Crompton, J. (1981). Dimensions of the social group in pleasure vacations. *Annals of Tourism Research*, 8, 550–568.

Csikszentmihalyi, M., & Rochberg-Halton, E. (1981). *The meaning of things: Domestic symbols and the self.* Cambridge: Cambridge University Press.

DaMatta, R. (1986). *Carnival as a cultural problem: Towards a theory of formal events and their magic.* Notre Dame, IN: Helen Kellogg Institute for International Studies.

Davis, F. (1979). *Yearning for yesterday: A sociology of nostalgia.* New York: Free Press.

Donnelly, P., & Young, K. (1999). Rock climbers and rugby players: Identity construction and confirmation. In J. Coakley & P. Donnelly (Eds), *Inside sports* (pp. 67–76). London: Routledge.

Fritzsche, P. (2001). Specters of history: On nostalgia, exile, and modernity. *American Historical Review*, 106, 1587–1618.

Gibson, H. (1998). Sport tourism: A critical analysis of research. *Sport Management Review*, 1, 45–76.

Glaser, B., & Strauss, A. (1967). *The discovery of grounded theory.* Chicago: Aldine.

Gorman, B. (1979). Seven days, five countries: The making of a group. *Urban Life*, 7, 469–491.

Gottlieb, A. (1982). Americans' vacations. *Annals of Tourism Research*, 9, 164–187.

Goulding, C. (1999). Heritage, nostalgia, and the "grey" consumer. *Journal of Marketing Practice: Applied Marketing Science*, 5, 177–199.

Goulding, C. (2001). Romancing the past: Heritage visiting and the nostalgic consumer. *Psychology & Marketing*, 18, 565–592.

Graburn, N. (1977). Tourism: The sacred journey. In V. Smith (Ed.), *Hosts and guests* (pp. 17–31). Philadelphia: University of Pennsylvania Press.

Graburn, N. (1983). The anthropology of tourism. *Annals of Tourism Research*, 10, 9–33.

Graburn, N. (1995). Tourism, modernity, and nostalgia. In A.S. Ahrned and C.N. Shore (Eds), *The future of anthropology: Its relevance to the contemporary world* (pp. 158–178). London: Athlone.

Green, B.C. (2001). Leveraging subculture and identity to promote sport events. *Sport Management Review*, 4, 1–19.

Green, B.C., & Chalip, L. (1998). Sport tourism as the celebration of subculture. *Annals of Tourism Research*, 25, 275–291.

Havlena, W.J., & Holak, S.L. (1991). The good old days: Observations on nostalgia and its role in consumer behavior. *Advances in Consumer Research*, 18, 323–329.

Healey, J.F. (1991). An exploration of the relationships between memory and sport. *Sociology of Sport Journal*, 8, 213–227.

Holak, S.L., & Havlena, W.J. (1998). Feelings, fantasies, and memories: An examination of the emotional components of nostalgia. *Journal of Business Research*, 42, 217–226.

Holbrook, M.B. (1993). Nostalgia and consumption preferences: Some emerging patterns of consumer tastes. *Journal of Consumer Research*, 20, 245–256.

Holbrook, M.B., & Schindler, R.M. (1991). Echoes of the dear departed past: Some work in progress on nostalgia. *Advances in Consumer Research*, 18, 330–333.

Holbrook, M.B., & Schindler, R.M. (1996). Market segmentation based on age and attitude toward the past: Concepts, methods, and findings concerning nostalgic influences on consumer tastes. *Journal of Business Research*, 37, 27–39.

Holloway, C. (1981). The guided tour: A sociological approach. *Annals of Tourism Research*, 8, 377–402.

Holt, D.B. (1995). How consumers consume: A typology of consumption practices. *Journal of Consumer Research*, 22, 1–16.

Howell, J. (1991). "A revolution in motion": Advertising and the politics of nostalgia. *Sociology of Sport Journal*, 8, 258–271.

Kahle, L.R., Kambara, K.M., & Rose, G.M. (1996). A functional model of fan attendance motivations for college football. *Sport Marketing Quarterly*, 5(4), 51–60.

Kemp, S.F. (1999). Sled dog racing: The celebration of co-operation in a competitive sport. *Ethnology*, 38(1), 81–95.

Laverie, D.A., & Arnett, D.B. (2000). Factors affecting fan attendance: The influence of identity salience and satisfaction. *Journal of Leisure Research*, 32, 225–246.

Lett, J. (1983). Ludic and liminoid aspects of charter yacht tourism in the Caribbean. *Annals of Tourism Research*, 10, 35–56.

Lowenthal, D. (1985). *The past is a foreign country*. Cambridge: Cambridge University Press.

Naughton, K., & Viasic, B. (1998, March 23). The nostalgia boom. *Business Week*, pp. 58–64.

Pascal, V.J., Sprott, D.E., & Muehling, D.D. (2002). The influence of evoked nostalgia on consumers' responses to advertising: An exploratory study. *Journal of Current Issues and Research in Advertising*, 24(1), 39–49.

Peleggi, M. (1996). National heritage and global tourism in Thailand. *Annals of Tourism Research*, 23, 432–448.

Pine, B.J., & Gilmore, J.H. (1999). *The experience economy: Work is theatre & every business a stage*. Boston, MA: Harvard Business School Press.

Quiroga, I. (1990). Characteristics of package tours in Europe. *Annals of Tourism Research*, 17, 185–207.

Redmond, G. (1991). Changing styles of sports tourism: Industry/consumer interactions in Canada, the USA and Europe. In M.T. Sinclair & M.J. Stabler (Eds), *The tourism industry: An international analysis* (pp. 107–120). Wallingford, UK: CAB International.

Ross, B.M. (1991). *Remembering the personal past: Descriptions of autobiographical memory*. New York: Oxford University Press.

Rothenbuhier, E.W. (1988). The living room celebration of the Olympic Games. *Journal of Communication*, 38, 61–81.

Schmidt, C. (1979). The guided tour: Insulated adventure. *Urban Life*, 7, 441–467.

Schuchat, M. (1983). Comforts of group tours. *Annals of Tourism Research*, 10, 465–477.

Sirgy, M.J., & Su, C. (2000). Destination image, self-congruity, and travel behavior: Toward an integrative model. *Journal of Travel Research*, 38, 340–352.

Slowikowski, S.S. (1991). Burning desire: Nostalgia, ritual, and the sport-festival flame ceremony. *Sociology of Sport Journal*, 8, 239–257.

Snyder, E.E. (1991). Sociology of nostalgia: Sport halls of fame and museums in America. *Sociology of Sport Journal*, 8, 228–238.

Spradley, J.P (1980). *Participant observation*. New York: Holt, Rinehart and Winston.

Stauth, G., & Turner, B.S. (1988). Nostalgia, postmodernism and the critique of mass culture. *Theory, Culture & Society*, 5, 509–526.

Stewart, K. (1988). Nostalgia: A polemic. *Cultural Anthropology*, 3, 227–241.

Thompson, C.M., & Pearce, D.G. (1980). Market segmentation of New Zealand package tours. *Journal of Travel Research*, 19(2), 3–6.

Turner, V. (1974). *Dramas, fields, and metaphors*. New York: Cornell University Press.

Turner, V. (1977). Varitions on a theme of liminality. In S.F. Moore & B.G. Myerhoff (Eds), *Secular ritual* (pp. 36–52.). Assen, Netherlands: Van Gorcum.

Turner, V. (Ed.) (1982). *Celebration: Studies in festivity and ritual*. Washington, DC: Smithsonian Institution Press.

Underwood, R., Bond, E., & Baer, R. (2001). Building service brands via social identity: Lessons from the sports marketplace. *Journal of Marketing Theory and Practice*, 9(1), 1–13.

Wagner, U. (1977). Out of time and place: Mass tourism and charter trips. *Ethnos*, 42, 28–52.

Wann, D.L., Melnick, M.J., Russell, G.W., & Pease, D.G. *(2001). Sport fans: The psychology and social impact of spectators.* New York: Routledge.

Weiss, R.S. (1994). *Learning from strangers: The art and method of qualitative interview studies.* New York: Free Press.

PART THREE

Impacts of
Sport & Tourism

EDITOR'S INTRODUCTION

AS NOTED IN THE EDITORIAL INTRODUCTION to the previous Part, the structure of this Reader has been based on the view that a full understanding of impacts is dependent on an understanding of the behaviours that produce those impacts. This is why, perhaps somewhat unconventionally, the Part on 'Understanding the sports tourist' precedes this Part on the 'Impacts of Sport & Tourism'. This process of understanding, from participation to impacts to the development of policy and provision was excellently highlighted in Chapter 8 by Costa and Chalip in the previous Part. In fact, several of the chapters in the previous Part might have appeared in this Part insofar as they provide the requisite knowledge to understand impacts. Similarly, a number of chapters in this Part could have been located in the previous Part as they contain insights into sports tourist behaviour. And, of course, this blurred distinction between research into behaviours and research into impacts serves to highlight further the fundamental link between the two.

However, not all research into the impacts of sport and tourism is clearly grounded in an understanding of behaviours. With some notable exceptions, much previous research on the impacts of sport and tourism has been a relatively simplistic 'end result' assessment, rather than an assessment of the processes that generate such impacts, and this has been a particular feature of research into event impacts.

Event impact assessment has almost become an industry in its own right, with public sector research departments, consultants and academics all producing reports of the actual or potential impacts of sports events. While the findings of these reports are interesting for the hosts or sponsors of the event in question, they add little to our theoretical knowledge or understanding of the subject. Nevertheless, many such reports have been published in academic journals with little consideration by the authors of how they contribute to the development of knowledge in the field as a whole (see discussion in Chapter 6). Some authors would argue that the contribution such studies make is to understanding the nature and extent of the economic impacts of sports events by building a larger volume of evidence. However, as the first three chapters in this Part show, this claim is undermined by variations in study methodology (and, in some cases, poor methodological practices), by the lack of post-event evaluations, and by a failure to understand the nature of the behaviours that create such economic impacts.

The lead chapter in this Part, from the *European Sport Management Quarterly* special issue, is by **Holger Preuss** and discusses *The Economic Impact of Visitors at Major Multi-Sport Events*. Like the two chapters that follow, each of which are also concerned with economic impacts, Preuss's paper does not present the results of an economic impact study, rather it outlines methodological considerations in understanding economic impacts. Preuss's chapter makes a contribution to a small but growing body of literature that has been concerned with ensuring that economic impact assessments are methodologically robust and theoretically meaningful. Taken together, the first three chapters in this Part provide a very useful set of considerations and caveats for anyone reading reports of the economic impacts of sports events.

Preuss discusses the economic impact of 'event-affected' people at major sports events. This includes not only visitors, but also residents whose spending and/or travel patterns may be affected. As such, Preuss presents a model which illustrates a range of movements of people in and out of event host cities. This model has not only a geographic dimension (i.e. movement in and out of a host city/region), but also a temporal dimension (i.e. switching of plans to coincide with or avoid the event). Preuss's chapter, therefore, demonstrates the need to understand the movements of a range of categories of 'event-affected' people if accurate economic impact assessments are to be made.

The second chapter in this Part, by **Evangelia Kasimati** focuses on the biggest of sports events, the Summer Olympic Games. In *Economic Aspects and the Summer Olympics: A Review of Related Research*, thirteen studies of the actual or potential impacts of the Olympic Games since 1984 are compared. Kasimati notes that these studies vary in that they use different models that employ a range of different assumptions. Furthermore, all are *ex ante* studies that seek to forecast economic impacts, and the majority 'were commissioned by proponents of the Olympic process . . . potentially motivated to come up with a favourable result'. The key conclusion of Kasimati's chapter is that, although the studies may be potentially positively motivated, if the assumptions and methods are transparent, then they are reliable (in that they measure what the assumptions indicate they measure). However, they are not *comparable*, and the assumptions used may be those that cast the impacts of the Games in the best light. The question of assumptions and methodology is taken further by the next chapter in this Part.

Ian Hudson's chapter, *The Use and Misuse of Economic Impact Analysis* is one of the chapters in this Reader that is not *about* the relationship between sport and tourism, but is highly *relevant to* research in the area. Hudson uses meta-analysis to examine the variation in the economic impacts assigned to a range of US professional sports teams.

Hudson identifies seven 'moderators' – factors that might explain differences between what should be very similar accounts of economic impact. Somewhat worryingly, only three of these moderators are substantive sources of difference (different sports, geographical differences, and standard of stadia). Whereas the inconsistent application of multipliers, failure to differentiate between additional and displaced spending, failure to allow for time-switchers and inconsistent consideration of geographical boundaries are identified as moderators resulting from, at best, methodological variance and, at worst, poor methodological practice. Hudson's empirical exposure of these shortcomings further reinforces the discussions in Preuss's and Kasimati's chapters, and should be a reminder to us all that we cannot always take the results of economic impact assessments at face value.

The next chapter in this Part moves away from an overt focus on economic impact to focus on the impact sports events can have on marketing of the host city. *Marketing the Host City: Analysing Exposure Generated by a Sport Event* by **Christine Green, Carla Costa** and **Maureen Fitzgerald** examines the most effective way in which cities can benefit from media coverage of events which they host. Through an analysis of the televised event coverage of the NCAA Women's Final Four Basketball Tournament, Green *et al.* show that mentions or imagery of the host city are relatively rare. However, the authors also note that iconographic images with a clear association with the host city can be very effective in promoting that city. In contrast, coverage of cityscapes rarely carries with it any place identity and thus has limited city marketing utility. The authors conclude by suggesting that if events are to be effective tools for marketing particular places, then hosts must take steps to ensure that iconographic images with distinctive associations are incorporated into event related materials such as event logos.

While Green *et al.* discuss the impacts of sports events, those impacts do not fall within the traditional framework of economic, social, cultural, and environmental impacts. In certain situations, the effective marketing of cities may impact on all of these areas (positively or negatively) and may, in turn, impact upon residents as well as visitors. As such, there may be a suggestion here that a framework that considers impacts may be a little outmoded and, as a number of authors have argued (for example, Green (2001), Chapter 20; Chalip, 2006), a more fruitful approach may be one that focuses on *leveraging* rather than impacts:

> Unlike impact assessments, the study of leverage has a strategic and tactical focus. The objective is to identify strategies and tactics that can be implemented prior to and during an event in order to generate particular outcomes. Consequently, leveraging implies a much more pro-active approach to capitalising on opportunities, rather than impacts research which simply measures outcomes.
>
> (Chalip, 2004)

The fifth chapter in this Part takes such a leveraging approach, but rather than focusing on leveraging economic aspects as most previous leveraging research has done, it examines the ways in which participation preferences can be leveraged. *Leveraging*

Subculture and Identity to Promote Sport Events by **Christine Green** examines the relationship between the event consumer (whether participant or spectator) and the subculture or identity formation connected with the event (note the similarities here with Kane and Zink's discussion of kayaking 'capital' in Chapter 12). Green discusses the role of subculture in transmitting consumption values and highlights the ways in which this can be capitalised upon (leveraged) to promote sports events. Focusing as it does on the way in which behaviours can be leveraged to provide positive outcomes, this paper further demonstrates the fundamental link between behavioural and impacts research.

The focus on sports events is retained in the sixth chapter in this Part (Chapter 21) by **Heather Gibson, Cynthia Willming** and **Andrew Holdnack**, but it considers tourism to more regularised small-scale events. *Small-Scale Event Sport Tourism: Fans as Tourists* examines the potential of college sports events in the US to generate benefits for local communities (with the suggestion that similar conclusions could be drawn about similar scale events in other countries). The assessment of the likelihood of such benefits is derived from a detailed examination, using both quantitative and qualitative approaches, of the behaviours of travelling sports fans. What is interesting about Gibson *et al.*'s paper is that the travelling fans considered are supporters of the home team, yet have travelled an average of 142 miles to see the game. Furthermore, the 'tail-gaiting' element of the event is seen as a key part of the experience, thus reinforcing the need to broaden the research focus beyond a simple study of attendance at the event (compare Fairley's paper, Chapter 15). In terms of impacts, the fact that the sports tourism experience is more complex than simply attending the event may mean that more significant benefits are forthcoming for the local community, particularly because the fans, as supporters of the home team, often feel a place affinity with the local area.

The final chapter in this Part examines in greater detail the impacts of sports tourism on local communities, focusing particularly on non-economic impacts. In *Host and Guest Relations in Sport Tourism* **Eizabeth Fredline** explores some of the ways in which social impacts of tourism on host communities have been examined. In particular, Fredline discusses the differences between extrinsic models, which tend to regard host communities homogenously and focus on changes in attitudes over time, and intrinsic models, which examine the reasons for differing attitudes to tourism development within host communities. Following the presentation of four case studies of sports events, Fredline calls for a focus on developing holistic models that can provide an overall assessment of tourism development which will then contribute to decisions about the most appropriate forms of sports tourism development for particular destinations.

While this Part has focused on impacts, it should be apparent that it provides a clear link between the previous Part on 'Understanding the sports tourist' and the next part on 'Policy and management considerations in Sport & Tourism'. As noted in a number of other places, the chapters in this Part derive their assessments of impacts from understandings of behaviour (or advocate doing so) and they each have implications for policy and management. That such links are a feature of the chapters in this Part is an indication of good scholarship and of the location of their work by the authors in the body of knowledge relating to the relationship between sport and tourism. As such, they are indicative of how good quality research into sport and tourism should be conducted.

REFERENCES

Chalip, L. (2004) 'Beyond Impact: A General Model for Sport Event Leveraging', in B. Ritchie and D. Adair (eds), *Sport Tourism: Interrelationships, Impacts and Issues*. Clevedon: Channel View.

Chalip, L. (2006) 'Towards Social Leverage of Sport Events', *Journal of Sport & Tourism*, 11 (2): 109–27.

Chapter 16

Holger Preuss

THE ECONOMIC IMPACT OF VISITORS AT MAJOR MULTI-SPORT EVENTS

Introduction

CITIES AND REGIONS ARE INVESTING billions of dollars in major multi-sport events such as the Olympic Games, Commonwealth Games, Pan American Games and Asian Games. The main economic benefit for a region derives from the consumption by visitors during the event and increased tourism in the post event period. Preuss & Weiss (2003) calculated that, for the national Olympic bid city Frankfurt Rhein/Main 2012, the regional tourism related impact had an importance of over 40% of the total economic impact for the region over the 17 years under consideration.

Literature shows that one of the main hurdles in determining the economic impact of major multi-sport events on a city or region is the lack of knowledge on consumption patterns of visitors and the number of persons that are visiting the event. Empirical research showed that the consumption of visitors during the 2002 Commonwealth Games in Manchester was not the same than that of "usual" tourists visiting the city. In addition it was also found that the consumption patterns of residents visiting the events of the 2002 Commonwealth Games changed (Preuss, 2005).

Keeping this lack of knowledge in mind, it is interesting to note that the calculation of economic impacts of major multi-sport events and navel on a host city/region has been a focal research activity over the past 20 years. The research resulted in an increased ability to assess the economic impact of travel and tourism along with a proliferation of methods, models and procedures. However, one must question the value if the primary impact is still not precisely calculated. There are a number of questions that regional tourism leaders continue to ask about assessing the primary economic impact of major multi-sport events and travel to their city/legion. These include:

- How can we conduct a precise tourism economic impact analysis?
- What persons affected through the event have to be considered in that analysis?

- How can the number of affected persons be measured?
- What are the consumption patterns of these affected persons and what part of this consumption has to be considered?

To answer these questions a theoretical framework has to be developed. This is necessary to formulate the questions for this empirical research.

Literature review

A substantial amount of research about the economic impacts of sporting events has been conducted in recent years. However, there are often mistakes and misunderstandings in interpreting and calculating the economic impact from event-affected persons. In 2002 Norman, Backman, and Backman identified several shortcomings on the evaluation of tourism impacts. These included:

- A confusion of the economic impacts with benefits different groups.
- An appropriate impact region missing.
- A confusion to separate "new" dollars from outside the area from local spending.

This paper arms to clarify these obscurities. Furthermore the complexity of the calculation of the primary impact from event-affected persons will be shown.

An economic impact analysis helps policy analysts and decision-makers to evaluate current and proposed multi-sport events by providing estimates that are measurable and comparable. Tourism industries need support from the local community, as tourism activities affect the entire community. Recreation and tourism development are regarded as attractive investments because they can lure new businesses and visitors to the region (Chang, 2001, p. 4). Major multi-sport events develop tourism products and increase the awareness of the city/region as a potential tourism destination (Ritchie & Smith, 1991; Keller, 2002). Furthermore, and importantly, the events often generate a better image.

For the calculation of the overall economic impact driven from spectators of the host city/region many models are available. All of them consider the consumption of tourists as a part of the overall economic impact. It is interesting that the consumption pattern of tourists visiting a major multi-sport event is often not precisely evaluated. The consumption pattern and the right determination of money streams from event affected persons are the base for a reliable calculation of the overall impact. This paper will provide recommendations to calculate the regional primary impact from event-affected persons, which could be used as a base for one of the following models.

Burns, Hatch, & Mules (1986) did some pioneer work when they measured the economic impact of the 1986 Adelaide Grand Prix. Following them a variety of models were developed; to name just the most famous there is the TEIM (Travel Economic Impact Model) (Frechtling, 1994); RIMS (Regional Input–Output Modelling System) (Wang 1997; Donnelly, Vaske, DeRuiter, & Loomis, 1998); TDSM (Tourism Development Simulation Model) (Donnelly et al., 1998); RIMS II (Wang, 1997) and finally the very often used IMPLAN (Impact Analysis for PLANing) (Dawson, Blahna, & Keith, 1993; Donnelly et al., 1998; Wang, 1997). Lately the Australians, particularly Dwyer, Forsyth

& Spurr (2003), emphasized the Computable General Equilibrium (CGE) model in order to better consider local effects, Preuss (2004b) developed a new model to calculate the regional economic impact. This model will be used in this paper.

Regarding major multi-sport events most of the studies available investigated the effects on the economic activity in the host region, including the tourism industry (Schulmeister 1976; Kirchner 1980; Brönnimann 1982; Kang & Purdue 1994; Krajasits 1995; Teigland 1996; Spilling, 1998; Andranovich, Burbank, & Heying, 2001; Chalip, 2002; Jones & Munday, 2004; Preuss, 2004a). However, not necessarily using an economic impact model many authors considered the tourism impact of major sport events.

Only two major empirical studies focused specifically on the event time consumption pattern of visitors. A research group from Texas investigated the consumption of tourists at 16 smaller festivals. Crompton (1999) and Gratton, Dobson & Shibli (2000) looked at the regional effects of six sports events in the ILK. They compared the economic impacts of differently sized sports events.

Theory

The primary economic impact of major multi-sport events basically stems from three sources (Preuss, 2004b):

* Consumption of the organizing committee.
* Tourism and exports.
* Investments in infrastructure.

Both, export and tourism are exogenous and bring "new" dollars into a regional economy. Therefore, visitors that come to see the beauty and experience the culture of a country can be joined in one group with exports of sport and event know how. Tourism provides the main stream of autonomous money during a major multi sport event. A well-planned tourism strategy can leverage post-event tourism (Chalip, 2002), because it is not the new sport facilities that motivate thousands of tourists to visit the city after the event. It is rather a better and attractive image of the host city, region or even country mixed with new tourism products that were established through the event impact and pre-event accelerated development. Worldwide coverage of a major multi-sport event stress positive attributes and often enlightens the city in the minds of the world population. This awakens the desire to visit the city in the future (Morse, 2001, p. 11; Rivenburgh, Louw, Loo, & Mersham, 2003).

Major multi-sport events trigger tourism based economic impacts all around the world. Nevertheless, the strongest impact occurs in the host city/region. It is obvious that the calculation of the tourism impacts, for example, the 2002 Manchester Common-wealth Games do not have to consider the payments to travel agencies in Australia or those tourists buying air tickets from Malaysian Airlines. However, the calculation of the tourism related impact becomes complex when effects such as the change of tourism infrastructure in the host city have to be considered. In this paper tourism related infrastructure will be excluded. The focus will be put on the consumption of all event-affected persons.

The regional event-affected persons' economic impact can be described by the following equation.

$$\Delta Y = X_a - X_b + \Delta X_K + \Delta X_{H,G} \tag{1}$$

The regional event-affected persons' economic impact (ΔY) can be described by the consumption of all additional persons (X_a) in the city/region minus the missed consumption of crowded out-visitors and persons leaving the city due to the event (opportunity costs) (X_b) plus the change of endogenous consumption of residents (ΔX_k) and the change of exogenous consumption of visitors that would have been in the city anyhow ($\Delta X_{H,G}$). In more detail the export (X) in Equation I can be described by the number of days (t) times the number of visitors (x) times the consumption pattern (CP).

$$\Delta Y = CP_a * t_a * X_a - CP_b * t_b * X_b + \Delta CP_K * t_K * X_K + \Delta CP_{H,G} * t_{H,G} * X_{H,G} \tag{2}$$

Empirical data collected in Manchester during the 2002 Commonwealth Games indicate that there are different groups of persons entering and leaving the region (i). These groups have different consumption patterns (j). Figure 16.2 (see later) describes the groups of persons that have to be considered (A, B, C, D, E1, E2, C, H, K).

$$\Delta Y = \sum_{i=A}^{C} \sum_{j=A}^{J} CP_{(i,j)} * t_{(i,j)} * X_{(i,j)} - \left(\sum_{i=D}^{E1} \sum_{j=1}^{J} CP_{(i,j)} * t_{(i,j)} * X_{(i,j)} \right)$$
$$+ \Delta \sum_{j=1}^{J} CP_{K(j)} * t_{K(j)} * X_{K(j)} + \left(\Delta \sum_{i=E}^{H} \sum_{j=1}^{J} CP_{(i,j)} * t_{(i,j)} * X_{(i,j)} \right) \tag{3}$$

The equation shows the impact (ΔY) change on consumption of residents during the event might be compensated in post-event periods due to saving or extra consumption. In the long-term marginal consumption rate might not change and therefore the residents are not in the centre of focus here.

The following section will introduce a model in order to identify the streams of money entering and leaving a city/region through the consumption of multi-sport event affected persons. This part is based on a model of Preuss (2004b).

Evaluation of the regional economic impact through event-affected persons

In order to isolate the regional primary economic impact from the primary national impact each flow of event-affected person's money has to be analysed.

Figure 16.1 shows how to calculate the regional primary impact (Y_R). Event affected person's expenditures (E) for each consumption category c = {1, 2, . . ., k} can be regionalized by Equation 4. The categories are, for example, expenditures for accommodation, transport, entertainment or food.

$$Y_R = \sum_{c=1}^{k} E_c * (a * R_c - r * M_c) \tag{4}$$

		Destination of funds	
		Host city/region (R)	Import (M)
Origin of funds	Autonomous (a)	Benefit (a * R)	Neutral (a * M)
	Region (r)	Reallocation (r * R)	Costs (r * M)

Figure 16.1 Matrix to identify the regional impact

For a better understanding of the calculation of the regional primary economic impact Figure 16.1 can be read as such: a Canadian Commonwealth Games tourist spends money in a restaurant in Manchester. The tourist's expenditure (F) for food (c = 1) is autonomous (a) and therefore creates a regional benefit, because "new" dollars enter Manchester (R). The origin ((a)utonomous or (r)egional) and destination ((R)egion or (I)mport) of each expenditure determines whether an economic impact occurs and therefore becomes "regional effective". Using the terminology of cost-benefit analysis the expenditures can create one of the four effects:

Benefits. Autonomous funds which stay in the city/region (a * R). These create macroeconomic benefits in terms of additional income.

Costs. Regional funds which are used for imports (r * M). These create macroeconomic costs, because money is leaving the city/region and cannot be earned by citizens. However, follow up costs and benefits occur by the structure that was built through the imports. The costs and benefits of the new infrastructure will have to be considered in the post-event period.

Reallocations. Regional funds which are spent in the region (r * R). Reallocations can also create costs and benefits. In case regional funds are spent in another industrial sector other than the event and if that sector has another creation of value then benefits or costs occur. This might become important for the residents visiting the event and changing their consumption pattern.

Neutrals. Autonomous funds which are used for imports (a * M), To be precise, neutrals can also indirectly create costs and benefits. Neutral just means that autonomous money is directly spent for imports and never becomes income in the city/region. However, two effects have to be considered. First, something gets imported and that may create costs and benefits in the post-event period. For example a multipurpose exhibition hall financed by the state of federal government and constructed by a foreign company is a neutral stream of money for a city. After the event the hall entertains residents and tourists but also has to be maintained. These effects are considered in the post-event period. Second, tourists that planned to visit the city/region, but avoid coming at event time create opportunity costs.

It becomes clear that the analysis of money streams has to consider the pre- and post-event period. For major multi-sport events both the tourism related pre-event effects (up to five years before the event) and the post-event tourism effects (up to 10 years after the event) have to be evaluated to determine the long-term regional economic impact through event-affected persons. Therefore each event-related stream of spectator money as well as that of other event-affected persons has to be distinguished into the four above-mentioned effects for each period. The sum of benefits, costs, value increasing/decreasing part of the reallocations and opportunity costs of the neutrals form the so-called "regional effective" primary economic impact of event-affected persons.

The identification and precise calculation of the primary impact is the base for most of the above-mentioned input–output models. These models can be used to determine the induced impacts and to finally calculate the overall economic impact.

Categorization of event-affected person movements

The previous section displayed the model to identify the "regional effective" streams of money through event affected persons. Before examining the groups of persons that have to be considered for the regional economic impact a few definitions must be presented.

Although tourism is a growing industry with significant effects on a regional economy, researchers have not worked out how to define tourism or event visitors. From the perspective of its demand side, tourism could be defined narrowly as only a segment of the travel market that comprises "free and independent travellers", excluding business travellers, etc. Alternatively, it can be defined more broadly to include business travellers, volunteers from abroad or members of the sport federation such as athletes etc. In the end, we can include all persons that are affected by the event. Before measuring the impact of event-affected persons on a regional economy, the elements to be measured must be clearly identified.

- Event-affected persons are persons that get attracted by the event (such as spectators, staff in tourism industry) but also those persons that avoid the event by leaving or not entering a city/region.
- Spectators are persons that attend sessions of the event. They are persons without work commitments during the event and can be residents, tourists and day tourists.
- Tourists and day tourists are persons that do not live in the city/region.
- Tourists' stay a night or longer in the host city/region, while day tourists enter and leave the city/region just for one day.
- Residents are persons that permanently stay in the city/region.

Figure 16.2 gives an overview of the movements of event-affected persons to and from a host city/region. In the literature there is often a lack of differentiation between the several groups and some of them are overseen.

"Extentioners" (A), "Event visitors" (B) and "Home stayers" (C) are the event visitors that spend autonomous money and create a significant economic impact. Group (C) creates an import substitution (Cobb & Weinberg, 1993).

Concerning the residents, the avoiding group has to be distinguished by "Runaways" (D) and "Changers" (F). The Changers switch their holiday trip to the period of the event. Therefore they do not carry more money out of the city/region than they would

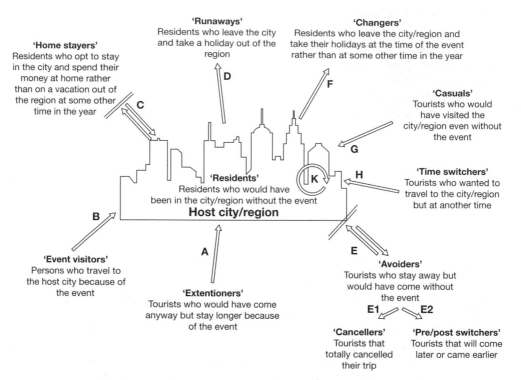

Figure 16.2 Movements of event affected persons during event-time

have done anyway over the year. The "Runaways" create opportunity costs because they plan an additional holiday trip and spend money abroad that would usually have been spent in the city/region. To give some empirical data: in Barcelona, 16% of the people interviewed in a survey six months prior to the Olympics stated that they considered spending their holidays outside the city during the Games (Brunet, 1993), In Sydney 2000 the Traveland Survey suggested that a proportion of residents (18%) intended to leave Sydney and travel abroad (TFC, 1998). The risk is that "Runaways" and "Changers" may discover new holiday destinations and decide to return there in the future. For Athens 2004 this was not a problem. During August the majority of citizens usually leave the city during the summer heat. In 2004 quite the contrary occurred. The Olympic Games made many Athenians stay at home, either to see the Games or work at the Games or in tourist related industries ("Home stayers" (C)). Only 23.2% actually wanted to leave Athens during the Games (MRB, 2004).

"Casuals" (G) and "Time switchers" (H) are groups that are not often considered in economic impact studies. The expenditures of "Casuals" would have occurred without the event and the "Time switchers" would have come to the city/region as well, but at another time. So the income generated by the expenditures of these two groups should not be attributed to the event. But there is another reason why these groups must be considered. During the event "Casuals" and "Time switchers" spend their money and time on event-related activities rather than on everyday tourist attractions It is also likely that this group spends more money than it would have without the event. For example, in

Los Angeles attendance figures at popular tourist destinations were down 30–50% during the 1984 Olympics (ERA, 1984). Therefore, the change of their consumption has to be considered. Later on, the additional importance of "Time switchers" will be explained.

"Avoiders" (E) create opportunity costs, because tourists that planned to visit the city/region stay away due to the event. For example, the 1999–2000 Utah Skier Survey found nearly 50% of non-resident skiers indicated that they would not consider skiing in Utah during the 2002 Olympic Winter Games. When questioned as to the reason, respondents indicated that crowds (76%) and higher prices (20%) were the primary deterrents (GOPB, 2000). Another example is that 66% of Danish tourists avoided the Lillehammer region during the 1994 Olympic Winter Games (Getz, 1997). In July and August 1992 the Costa Brava region lost part of its high summer seasonal demand due to the 1992 Games in Barcelona (Ministerio de Economíca, 1991–1993; Ministerio de Industria, 1990). A similar situation occurred during the 1984 Olympics in Los Angeles concerning theme park hotel owners (ERA, 1984) and in 1988 at Calgary with skier visits (GOPB, 2000), Group (E) has to be distinguished in two subgroups: The "Pre-/ Post-switchers" (E2) are those that will come sometime during the pre- or post-event period. The "Cancellers" (El) are those that will not come at all and are therefore lost as tourists. For a positive long-term effect new tourists and MICE tourists (Meetings–Incentives–Conventions–Events) attracted by the multi-sport event have to over compensate subgroup (El) as well as the group that "lose their interest" in travelling to the host city/region due to subjective negative image.

Figure 16.3 shows the movements of event-affected persons between pre-, post- and event period. Here the different meaning of groups El and E2 becomes clearer. Positive for the pre-event period are those that avoid the event-time and visit the city earlier (E2 "Pre-switchers"). It is important to see that not all "Avoiders" create opportunity costs. Under the assumption that hotel capacity is a limited resource at major multi-sport events "Avoiders" of type (E2.) create a rather positive effect by keeping hotel capacities free and the other way round. "Time switchers" (H) that postpone their trip to see the event get lost in pre-/post-event periods and fill the hotels during event time. In a long-term consideration there also might be some "Pre-avoiders" during the pre-event period due

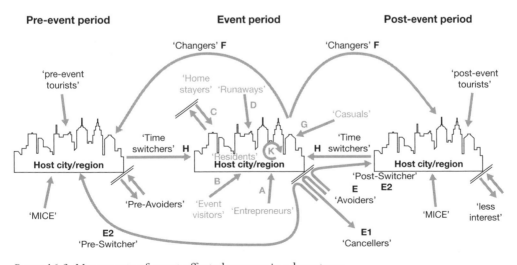

Figure 16.3 Movements of event-affected persons in a long-term

to the often-massive construction and renovation of tourist attractions during the years before the event. For the pre-event period there usually will be an increase of the MICE tourists (McCay & Plumb, 2001). These are, for example, athletes, federations, sponsors, media, sport and tourism conferences, experts and guests of the organizing committee that have to meet, organize and prepare for the multi-sport event (Preuss, 2004a). They are all additional visitors that bring "new" dollars to the city/region. During the post event period the number of MICE tourists as well as normal tourists will probably increase. Tourists become interested because the event increased the awareness of the destination through media, stories from returning tourists (Preuss & Messing, 2002, p. 225) as well as upgraded or new tourism products and infrastructure (Keller, 2002). The benefits to the convention sector are not confined to the years immediately surrounding the event. For example, "the growth in facilities (both convention and hotel) and exposure has long-term payback benefits with Barcelona achieving a 21% per annum compound growth in international convention delegates between 1992–1997" (McCay & Plumb, 2001).

Finally each city/region also runs the risk that the event is not successful and the media spreads a negative message that makes the destination less attractive ("group less interest"). In that case the event creates "Avoiders" for the post-event period. For example, Australia's image was apparently damaged in South Africa through the Olympics. This occurred because of the way in which the Aboriginal issue was highlighted and portrayed by the South African media in 2000 (Rivenburgh et al., 2003).

Event-affected persons of multi-sport events can be divided into four groups. The first group is based on reallocation of money and due to the change of the consumption the group might add 'new" dollars to the city/ region (E2, G, H and K). The second group brings autonomous money into the city/region (A, B, C), The third group carries out money that would have been spent in the city/region without the event (E1, D). Finally group F ("Changers") does not need to be considered, because it is a neutral group in the long-term. This raises the question whether an event in its overall effect leads to additional consumption and creates an economic impact at all.

$$(A + B + C) - (D + E1) + \Delta(E2 + G + H + K) = ? \tag{5}$$

Transformed in equation (3) the economic impact can be calculated by summing up groups A to C minus groups D to F plus the changes of group F to K:

$$\Delta Y = \sum_{i=A}^{C} \sum_{j=A}^{J} CP_{(i,j)} * t_{(i,j)} - (\sum_{i=D}^{E1} \sum_{j=1}^{J} CP_{(i,j)} * t_{(i,j)} * X_{(i,j)})$$

$$+ \Delta \sum_{j=1}^{J} CP_{K(j)} * t_{K(j)} * X_{K(j)} + (\Delta \sum_{i=E2}^{H} \sum_{j=1}^{J} CP_{(i,j)} * t_{(i,j)} * X_{(i,j)}) \tag{6}$$

Many of the economic impact analyses of past major multi-sport-events lack a differentiation between the various movements of event-affected persons. Some of them simplified their analyses by considering all tourism related consumption expenditures. Then expenditures of the "Casuals" (C) and the "Time switchers" (H) are wrongly included. Furthermore the streams of "Runaways" (D) or crowded out visitors ("Avoiders" E) are not considered in economic impact studies (Baade & Matheson, 2004).

Transfer of the theoretical approach into the evaluation of data

The previous section showed the theoretical framework and what/who needs to be evaluated for the calculation of the regional primary economic impact from event-affected visitors. How can this complex theory be used? This section will suggest how almost all the movements of economically relevant event-affected persons (groups in Figure 16.2) can be evaluated through empirical research.

Table 16.1 shows the possibility of evaluation of the respective groups that need to be considered. It divides the groups into those that can be evaluated by surveys during the event and those that have to be evaluated before or after the event. Table 16.1 also distinguishes the place where the visitors of events are staying during the event. This is important to calculate the opportunity costs of group E. Therefore the number of event-affected persons using hotel accommodation is needed, Group E "Avoiders" cause some problems, which will be focused later.

While the evaluation of the size of each group and the duration of stay is the same for all groups the type of consumption pattern needs to be differentiated. For example, from "Time switchers" we need the difference of their consumption during the event to that of another time when they would have visited the region. From "Event visitors" and "Home stayers" we need the total consumption pattern, because all money that they spend is new and from "Runaways" we just need their pattern of normal life in their home city (home pattern). Finally it has to be considered that in the long run the average consumption of some groups might be the same even if they spend more money during event time, This is due to the constant marginal consumption rate. They might save that money in the pre or post-event period. However some also might be time switching "Home stayers". This group saves money they would have spent outside the region (holiday) in pre/post event periods and prefer to spend this additional money during the event time in the city/region.

Table 16.1 An overview of the possibility of evaluation and the data needed for the calculation of the economic impact

	Groups									
	A	B	C	D	El	E2	F	G	H	K
Possibility of evaluation										
During event	X	X	X	–	–	–	–	X	X	X
Pre-/post-	–	–	X	X	–	(X)	X	–	–	X
Staying during event time										
At home	–	–	X	–	–	–	–	–	–	X
With friends/relatives	X	X	–	–	–	X	–	X	X	–
In hotels etc	X	X	–	–	–	X	–	X	X	–
Consumption pattern										
Change of pattern	–	–	–	–	–	X	–	X	X	X
Total pattern	X	X	X	–	X	–	–	–	–	–
Home pattern	–	–	–	X	–	–	–	–	–	–
In long-term neutral	–	–	–	–	–	–	X	–	–	(X)

Table 16.2 Groups of visitors to the Commonwealth Games in Manchester 2002

% in venues		Group related to Figure 16.2
15.6	(C)	*Home stayers*: "I am resident and abstained from my vacation in order to attend the Games"
4.9	(H)	*Time switchers*: "I am a tourist who wanted to travel to Manchester anyhow this or next year"
17	(G)	*Casuals.* "I am a tourist and would have visited Manchester even without the Games" and "I am a tourist who wanted to travel to Manchester anyhow this or next year"
46	(B)	*Commonwealth games visitors*
	(A)	*Extentioners*
16.5	(K)	*Residents*: Citizens living less than 50 km around main stadium

It becomes obvious that the evaluation of the right primary economic impact of event affected persons is difficult. It is quite easy to gather data from all persons that attend the events. Groups A, B, C, C, H and K can be evaluated by a questionnaire or interviews. Data from a survey during the 2002 Commonwealth Games in Manchester ($n = 1,196$ spectators) give evidence that there have been all different groups in the stadiums.

It is more difficult to evaluate the opportunity costs that are created through group D "Runaways" and E "Avoiders". The only way to estimate the size of group D is by running a pre-/post-event questionnaire among the residents of the city/region. However, this method has a lack of validity because of the unknown gap between those that have a pre-event willing to leave a city and the realization of a holiday during the event. Furthermore the "Runaways" (D) have to be distinguished from "Changers" (F).

Another major problem is the evaluation of group F. This group is often overseen, because the visitors do not appear during event time and therefore cannot be evaluated. Also pre/post-evaluation is impossible, because some visitors (E1) will not be at all in the region but others E2 will be there, although at different times. Here only a logical calculation can help to estimate the opportunity costs that have to be considered.

Model to evaluate opportunity costs of "avoiders" at event period

The following model offers a way to calculate the opportunity costs caused by the group E "Avoiders". The opportunity costs have to be subtracted from the impact described above, however, there is a limitation to the model by four premises:

1   Group F "Avoiders" are tourists staying in hotels and not day tourists or tourists staying with friends and relatives.
2   Visitors interested in travelling to the host city/region book accommodation in advance and travel only if accommodation is available.
3   The number of crowded out tourists (F "Avoiders") is larger or equal to that of group G "Time switchers".
4   The average occupancy rate of hotels during the event can be predicted reliably.

Premise 1 is set, because avoiding day tourists and tourists staying with friends and relatives cannot be identified Premise 2 is based on the assumption that major multi-sport events (hallmark events) attract a large number of tourists to one city (Hall, 1992). Therefore the main limiting resource is hotel capacity. Athletes, media representatives, team and technical officials, sport federations, VIPs, etc., pre-book large contingents of hotel beds, which often results in a shortage of available accommodation for tourists. Evidence can be found by the growth of hotel capacity in Olympic cities. Table 16.3 shows that despite the fact that the hotel market increased dramatically the post-Olympic year it did not have a significant decrease in occupancy rates. That indicates that the market develops on a long-term demand and not on the event short-term peak demand. Therefore the thousands of event visitors will most probably fill all available hotels during the short period of the event.

Premise 3 is not needed if the long-term impact is considered. The number of "Time switchers" (H) at the event period will be equalized in pre-/post-event periods. "Avoiders" (F) during event-time might come during pre-/post event periods (E2). Premise 3 is most likely to be given in reality due to the fact that there seem not to be too many "Time switchers" (see Table 16.2) while the number of "Avoiders" appear to be rather high (Preuss 2004a, pp. 53–54).

Concerning Premise 4 the occupancy rate during major multi-sport events is very high. Due to speculation of the local hotel industry (high prices and late reservations) and the difficulties to reallocation (if tourists do not show up) a host city can expect occupancy rates of 90% to 95% during event-time. This figure highly depends on the supply of hotels in the city/region. If the occupancy rate during the event-time can be

Table 16.3 Hotel industry changes in Olympic host cities

	Munich 1972	L.A. 1984	Seoul 1988	Barcelona 1992	Atlanta 1996	Sydney 2000	Athens 2004	Beijing 2008
Games-related increase in the number of hotel rooms (%)	12.2*	58	41.9–48	38	10–13	40	N/A	62.5
Hotel occupancy rate during Olympic year	N/A	75	72	65	68	49	N/A	N/A
Change in occupancy rate one year after the Games compared to Olympic year (%)	N/A	−1	−2	−5	−3	−3	N/A	N/A

Sources: Bidding Committee Beijing 2008 (2001); Brown (1997); Brunet (1993); Carswell (1996); Davidson Peterson Associates Studies (1996); EP (1984); Kim *et al.* (1989); Statistisches Landesamt München (1973), Australian Bureau of Statistics (2004), McCay/Plumb (2001), Property Council of Australia (2003).

Notes: *Calculation to year preceding the Games; **three years after the Games.

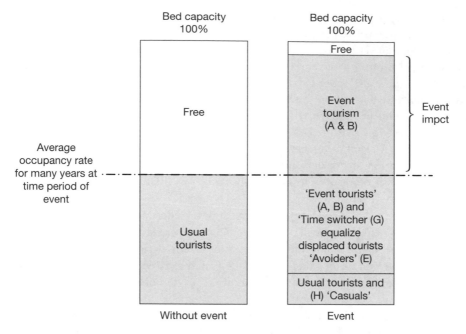

Figure 16.4 Assignment of event-affected groups to accommodation capacity

estimated reliably (Premise 4) the size of group E "Avoiders" (under the Premise 1 and 3) can be calculated as illustrated in Figure 16.4.

For the calculation of the regional primary economic impact from event-affected persons three sets of data are needed. First the long-term (several years before the event) average occupancy rate during the event-time must be found. Secondly, the total capacity of hotel beds must be determined, Thirdly, the (estimated) occupancy rate during event-time must be calculated.

The right bar in Figure 16.4 shows how the categorized event-affected persons (Figure 16.2) fill the hotels during event-time. The left bar shows the long-term average occupancy rate of the hotels in the city/region. Under Premise 3 the "Event visitors" (A and B) and "Tune switchers" (G) will crowd out tourists (E). Part of the hotel capacity is still booked by usual tourists such as business people that work during event-time or ordinary tourists that are not interested in the event. Tourists that are in the city during the event and might visit some events ("Casuals") complete this group.

To determine the impact during event-time only those tourists that overcompensate the average number of tourists will be considered. The impact effective number of visitors is the event occupancy rate (EOR) minus the average occupancy rate (OR) times the overall hotel capacity of the region/city (CAP_{Hotel}) times the duration of the event (t). Therefore the number of event effective tourists $Y_{Tourist}$ is:

$$\text{Number } Y_{Tourist} = (EOR - OR)*CAP_{Hotel}*t \tag{7}$$

This is the number of tourists that create the regional primary economic impact. The number has to be split in groups A, B, G and H by percentage, for example those given in Table 16.2.

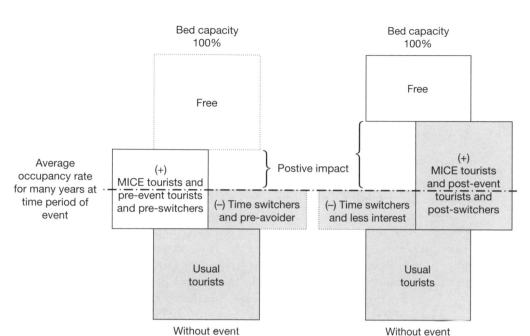

Figure 16.5 Assignment of even affected groups to accommodation capacity at pre- and post event periods

Model to evaluate opportunity costs of "Avoiders" at pre-/post-event periods

The calculation of the regional economic impact becomes more complex by considering the long-term impact. Then the pre and post-event period has to be implemented in the model. Figure 16.3 displayed the movements of groups that have to be considered in the long-term. Figure 16.5 translates these movements into numbers.

The positive impact of the pre-/post-event period can be determined by subtracting the negative (−) from the positive (+) movements. Here again only the impact above the average occupancy rate has to be considered However, the limitation of this model is that no other tourism impact (besides direct and indirect event impacts) should occur. These, such as terrorist attacks, Tsunamis, tourism crises, etc., also have influence on the occupancy rates. In a final step the net results from pre/post-event periods have to be added to the event period impact.

Discussion

Most cities and regions planning to bid for a major multi-sport event face immense investments in their leisure and general infrastructure. Therefore the citizens and politicians have a high interest in reliable information about the economic impact the event will have for them. The main part of benefits for the city/region derives from "new" dollars carried into the city/region by persons affected by the event.

In the past years much research has been done on models to calculate the economic impact of major events. To date, it is argued that limited effort has been put into a detailed measurement of the regional primary impact. In addition, the correctness of money streams that have to be considered is lacking. This paper presented two theoretical models. First, a model to determine whether or not a person affects the regional impact. Second, a model to evaluate opportunity costs. Both models presented some findings that have to date been overlooked in many papers:

1   For an event economic impact it is not enough to only consider the consumption of tourists that visit the event. Depending on the size of the region under investigation there are many other event-affected persons that have to be considered. Their different consumption patterns or the changes of their consumption pattern have to be evaluated and considered as primary economic impact.

2   Nearly all persons visiting events—even the residents—have to be considered as adding to the impact. There is only one group—the "Changers" (F)—that do not need consideration Even if they leave the city/region due to the event and carry money out of the region they do not create opportunity costs, because they would have travelled anyway.

3   The theoretical approach to consider the precise visitor impact in this paper has to be distinguished from efficient field research. Therefore it is enough to evaluate consumption patterns of groups staying at different levels (hotels, bed and breakfast, friends and relatives, at home) and to consider the major groups displayed in Table 16.2. Groups with similar consumption patterns and small groups do not need to be considered. Therefore even if this paper is very detailed the empirical research done is not necessarily wrong.

4   Cities expecting to have the tourism expenditures as their main economic event impact have to consider that the hotel capacity is a limiting resource and therefore the event impact is limited to the capacity over the average occupancy rate. "Time switchers" (H) may fill up the remaining hotel capacity and therefore reduce the potential long-term economic impact, because the "Time switchers" stay away in pre-/post-event periods and fill up the capacities at event time. The consumption of the event time is different than at pre-/post-periods.

5   Superficial "Avoiders" create opportunity costs, because the money they would carry in the city/region will not be spent. However, partly the "Avoiders" are pre-/post-"Time switchers" (E2) and just come to the city at another period. The other part of the "Avoiders" (E1) is limited to those planning to stay in hotels, because someone who has "friends and relatives" in the city/region will come to visit them at another time and therefore belongs to group E2. As long as the hotel capacity is a limiting resource due to the "Event visitors", "Extentioners", "Casuals" and "Time switchers" and the hotels are filled, the "Avoiders ' (E1) are not reducing the potential economic impact. Then it is the additional demand under the restriction of limited hotel capacity that crowds out all groups that plan to stay in hotel.

6   There often is an argument that crowded out visitors that come on a constant basis might get lost as tourists to the city/region due to the experience they make travelling to another destination for one season. This might be true. However, new visitors exploring the city/region due to the event and the worldwide broadcast of the event might replace them. The long-term occupancy rates of cities that have hosted

the Olympic Games show increasing rates in the post-Olympic period and therefore show an overcompensation of the lost tourists.

This paper described the complexity of evaluating the regional primary economic impact of event-affected persons. Two facts made it particularly difficult to calculate this impact: First, if an appropriate impact region is missing, it creates a confusion to separate "new" dollars from outside the area from local spending. A basic approach to overcome the obstacle of determining "regional effective" streams of money was explained. Second, the evaluation of the number of games-affected peons and their different consumption patterns needs to be further investigated. In addition the missed consumption of crowded out visitors has to be considered. The model to calculate the long-term opportunity costs of group E1 is based on the availability of hotel occupancy rates at pre- and post-event periods. In practice these data are very difficult to gather.

Acknowledgements

I would like to thank Markus Kurscheidt and the two blind reviewers for their valuable comments on an earlier draft.

References

Andranovich, G., Burbank, M.J., & Heying, C.H. (2001). Olympic cities: Lessons learned from mega-event politics. *Journal of Urban Affairs*, *23*(2), 113–131.

Australian Bureau of Statistics. (2004). Overseas arrivals and departures, 3401.0, monthly report.

Baade, R., & Matheson, V. (2004). An economic slam dunk or march madness? Assessing the economic impact of the NCAA basketball tournament. In J. Fizel, & R. Fort (Eds), *Economics of college sports* (pp. 111–133). Westport, CT: Praeger Publishers.

Bidding Committee Beijing 2008. (2001). Bidbook: Beijing.

Brönnimann, H, (1982). *Die touristische bedeutung von wintersport-grossveranstaltungen*. Bern: Max Bronnimann (Eigenverlag).

Brown, G. (1997). Anticipating the impact of the Sydney 2000 Olympic Games. In Department of Tourism Studies (Ed.), *The impact of mega events*. Papers of the 'Talk at the Top Conference, July 7–8, typescript.

Brunet, F. (1993). *Economy of the 1992 Barcelona Olympic Games*. Lausanne: International Olympic Committee.

Burns, J.P.A., Hatch, J.H., & Mules, T.J. (1986). An economic evaluation of the Adelaide Grand Prix. In G. Syme, B. Shaw, P.M. Shaw, P.M. Fenton, & W.S. Mueller (Eds), *The planning and evaluation of hallmark events* (pp. 172–185). Aldershot: Avebury.

Carswell, A. (1996), Atlanta is hot. *Mortgage Banking*, *56*(4), 22–27.

Chalip, L. (2002). *Using the Olympics to optimise tourism benefits*. Centre d'Estudies Olimpics I de l'Esport (UAB).

Chang, W.H. (2001). Variations in multipliers and related economic ratios for recreation and tourism impact analysis. Unpublished dissertation Michigan State University.

Cobb, S., & Weinberg, D. (1993). The importance of import substitution in regional economic impact analysis: Empirical estimates from two Cincinnati area events. *Economic Development Quarterly*, *7*(3), 282–286.

Crompton, J.L. (1999). *Measuring the economic impact of visitors to sports tournaments and special events*. Ashburn, VA: National Recreation & Park Association.

Davidson Peterson Associates Studies (1996). *The economic impact of expenditures by tourists on Georgia*. York: ME.

Dawson, S.A., Blahna, D.J., & Keith, J.E. (1993). Expected and actual regional economic impacts of Great Basin National Park. *Journal of Park and Recreation Administration*, *11*(4), 45–59.

Donnelly, M.P., Vaske, J.J., DeRuiter, D.S., & Loomis, J.B. (1998). Economic impacts of state park: Effect of park visitation, park facilities, and county economic diversification. *Journal of Park and Recreation Administration*, *16*(4), 57–72.

Dwyer, L., Forsyth, P., & Spurr, R. (2003). *Economic evaluation of special events: A reassessment*. Research report of the University of New South Wales.

Economics Research Associates (ERA) (1984). *Community economic impact of the 1984 Olympic Games in Los Angeles*. Los Angeles: typescript.

Frechtling, D.C. (1994). Assessing the economic impacts of travel and tourism—measuring economic benefits. In J.R.B. Ritchie, & C.R. Goeldner (Eds), *Travel, tourism and hospitality research* (pp. 367–391). New York: John Wiley & Sons.

Getz, D. (1997). The impacts of mega events on tourism: strategies for destination. In Department of Tourism Studies (Ed.), *The impact of mega events*, papers of the Talk at the Top Conference, July 7–8, typescript.

GOPB (Governor's Office of Planning and Budgeting) (2000). *2002 Olympic Winter Games: Economic, demographic and fiscal impacts*. Salt Lake City: GOPB.

Gratton, C., Dobson, N., & Shibli, S. (2000). The economic importance of major sports events: a case-study of six events, *Managing Leisure*, *5*(1), 17–28.

Hall, C.M. (1992). *Hallmark tourist events, impacts, management and planning*. London: Belhaven Press.

Jones, C., & Munday, M. (2001). Evaluating the economic benefits from tourism spending through input-output frameworks. Issues and cases. *Local Economy*, *19*(2), 117–133.

Kang, Y.S., & Purdue, R. (1994). Long-term impact of a mega-event on international tourism to the host country: A conceptual model and the case of the 1988 Seoul Olympics. In M. Uysal (Ed.) *Global tourist behaviour* (pp. 205–225). New York: International Business Press.

Keller, P. (2002). Sport and tourism: Introductory report. Paper presented at the first World Conference on Sport and Tourism, World Tourism Organisation, Barcelona, Spain, 22–23 February.

Kim, J.G., Rhee, S.W., Yu, J.C., Koo, K.M., & Hong, J.C. (1989). *Impact of the Seoul Olympic Games on national development*. Seoul: Korea Development Institute.

Kirchner, C. (1980). *Auswirkungen von internationalen Großveranstaltungen auf die regionale Entwicklung. Dargestellt am Beispiel der IX. und XII. Olympischen Winterspiele Innsbruck 1964 und 1976*. Bergheim: F.L. Doepghen.

Krajasits, C. (1995). Olympische Winterspiele als Impuls für den Tourismus. In M. Steiner, & F. Thorn (Eds), *Sport und Ökonomie*, Graz.

McCay, M., & Plumb, C. (2001). Reaching beyond the gold: the impact of the Olympic Games on real estate markets. *Global Insights*, (1). Boston: Global Insights.

Ministerio de Economía y Hacienda. Instituto Nacional de Estadística. (1991). *Annuario Estadístico de España 1991*. Madrid.

Ministerio de Economía y Hacienda. Instituto Nacional de Estadística. (1992). *Annuario Estadístico de España 1992*. Madrid.

Ministerio de Economía y Hacienda. Instituto Nacional de Estadística. (1993). *Annuario Estadístico de España 1993*. Madrid.

Ministerio de Industria (1990). *Annuario de Estadística*. Madrid.

Morse, J. (2001). The Olympic Games and Australian tourism. Paper presented at the First World Conference on Sport and Tourism, World Tourism Organisation, Barcelona, Spain, 22–23 February.

MRB, Research International, & VPRC consortium (2004). *The image of the Olympic Games— Greek national survey*. Athens: MRB.

Norman, W., Backman, S., & Backman, K. (2002). *The changing face of tourism impact analysis*. Paper given at the National Extension Tourism Conference, Traverse City.

Preuss, H. (2005). Unpublished data sample of 1,196 spectators at the Commonwealth Games 2002 in Manchester, Research Team Olympia, Institute for Sport Science Johannes Gutenberg-University Mains.

Preuss, H. (2004a). *The Economics of staging the Olympics. A comparison of the Games 1972–2008*. Cheltenham: Edward Elgar.

Preuss, H. (2004b). Concept of calculating the regional economic impact of Olympic Games. *European Sport Management Quarterly, 4*(4), 234–253.

Preuss, H., & Weiss, H.J. (2003). *Torchholder value added. Der ökonomische Nutzen der Olympischen Spiele 2012 in Frankfurt Rhein/Main*. Eschborn: AWV Verlag.

Preuss, H., & Messing, M. (2002). Auslandstouristen bei den Olympischen Spielen in Sydney 2000. In A. Dreyer (Ed.), *Tourism im sport* (pp. 223–241). Wicsbaden: Deutscher Universitatsverlag.

Property Council of Australia (2003). Hotel valuation index, March 2003, typescript.

Ritchie, B.J.R., & Smith, B.H. (1991). The impact of a mega-event on host region awareness: A longitudinal study. *Journal of Travel Research, 30*(1), 3–10.

Rivenburgh, N.K., Louw, P.E., Loo, E., & Mersham, G. (2003). *The Sydney Olympic Games and foreign attributes towards Australia*. Gold Coast: CRCST Publishing.

Schulmeister, S. (1976). Olympische Spiele und Reisensverkehr. *Monatbereichte des Österreichischen Instituts für Wirtschaftsforschung, 8*, 89–97.

Spilling, O.R. (1998). Beyond Intermezzo? On the long-term industrial impacts of mega-events—the case of Lillehammer 1994. *Festival Management & Event Tourism, 5*, 101–122.

Teigland, J. (1996). *Impacts on tourism from mega-events—the case of Winter Olympic Games*. Western Norway Research Institute, Report 13/96.

Tourism Forecasting Council (TFC) (1998). *The Olympic effect*. Canberra: TFC.

Wang, P.C. (1997). Economic impact assessment of recreation services and the use of multipliers: A comparative examination. *Journal of Park and Recreation Administration, 15*(2), 32–43.

Chapter 17

Evangelia Kasimati

ECONOMIC ASPECTS AND THE SUMMER OLYMPICS
A review of related research

Introduction

THE MODERN OLYMPIC GAMES were first held in Athens in 1896. Over the years, the Games have survived many trials, including wars and boycotts, and each set of Games is held every 4 years. In recent years, the interest of countries and regions in staging a future edition of the Games has grown because of the perception that doing so would help attract tourists and generate income.

As well as the likely impacts on the socio-cultural and environmental areas, host cities place great emphasis on the economic implications of the Olympics and the tourism development. These implications have received increasing attention over the past two decades, involving economic studies to provide a measure of the net gains that hosting the Games may provide. Although economic impact analyses prepared by or on behalf of Olympic advocates have demonstrated economic advantages from hosting the Games, potential host communities pose the question of whether, in fact, the economic benefits of the Olympics are pragmatic and, if they are, the extent to which such benefits offset the costs (Haxton, 1999).

Much of the published literature on the Olympics emphasises long-term benefits such as newly constructed event facilities and infrastructure, urban revival, enhanced international reputation, increased tourism, as well as improved public welfare, additional employment, local business opportunities and corporate relocation (Ritchie and Aitken, 1985; Hall, 1987; Kang, 1988; Robin, 1988; Walle, 1996; French and Disher, 1997). In contrast, potential negative impacts include high construction costs of public sports infrastructure and related necessary investments (usually placing a heavy burden on the government budget), temporary crowding problems, loss of visitors, property rental increases and temporary increases in employment and business activities (Hiller, 1990; Darcy and Veal, 1994; Mount and Leroux, 1994; Leiper, 1997; Spilling, 1998).

The objective here is to review existing literature that focuses on the economic impacts of the Summer Olympic the Games. No economic impact studies were found for Games before Los Angeles in 1984. Seven cases of the modern Games are examined, dated between 1984 and 2012. Thirteen studies are considered that investigate various economic variables related to the hosting of the Games and they have been categorised into *ex-ante* and *ex-post* economic impact assessments.

This review does not attempt to draw any conclusion as to which Games have the most favourable economic impacts. This would require a comprehensive study involving the review, comparison and justification of the models from both theoretical and empirical standpoints. Instead, our implicit objective is more modest. The goal is primarily to provide an overview and evaluation of the different approaches and demonstrate the differences that may appear in the results.

The remainder of this article is organised as follows. It begins by explaining the link between direct, indirect and induced economic effects, which is the principal theory embraced by economic impact studies. It then goes on to examine the alternative modelling approaches taken to ascertain the economic implications generated by the Summer Olympics. Finally, the article analyses each study in turn, evaluates the assumptions made and outlines directions for further research.

Understanding the overall economic effect

When a city is awarded the Summer Olympics, a large amount of new money is expected to flow into the host economy and recirculate within it. An economic effect through hosting the Games arises because an inflow of funds, which have not been switched from elsewhere in the economy and probably would not otherwise have come without the Games, will enter the local, regional or national economy. This inflow of money stems from broadcasters, sponsors, Olympic family, athletes and dignitaries as well as non-area travellers who would be defined as 'tourists' by those in the tourism business.

There has been a tendency to assess the economic impact of Summer Olympics using the 'multiplier' concept. Briefly; a multiplier estimates the number of times a unit of currency, once spent within an economy, is respent within the borders of that economy. The overall effect of the new money on the local/regional/national economy is broken down into three major elements.

1   Direct effect: the first economic effect of the new money spent by outside visitors. As Figure 17.1 illustrates, new money is injected into the host economy in industries such as accommodation, food, transportation, etc.
2   Indirect effect: the subsequent effects of the injected money within the economy, after allowing for leakages.
3   Induced effect: the proportion of household income then respent in other businesses in the economy.

The indirect and induced effects together are collectively referred to as *secondary impact* (Crompton, 1995).

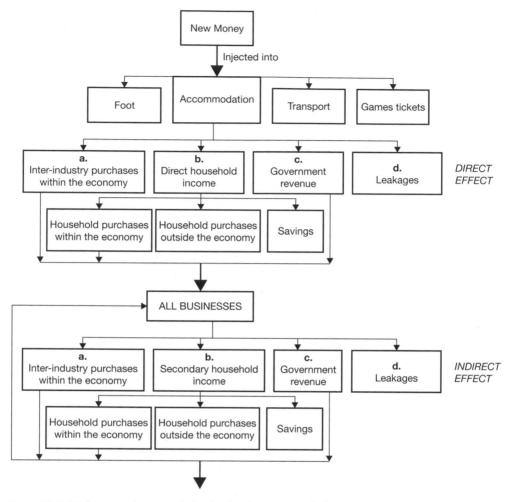

Figure 17.1 FSchematic diagram of the 'multiplier' approach, based on Liu and Var (1982) and Crompton (1995)

'Accommodation' is chosen to show how the multiplier concept operates, but should be similarly implemented for 'food', 'transport' and 'Games tickets'. The three direct recipients of the injected money, after allowing for leakages, subsequently spend this money in the same four ways, generating the *indirect effect*. Leakages occur because some money could be spent outside the host economy. Moreover, some of the household income could leak out of the economy by the purchase of products from outside, or would not stimulate economic activity because it was invested in savings.

The multiplier analysis has been a common form of estimating the respending impact of an initial inflow of money in an economy. Adopting this approach, if errors occurred in estimating the direct effect then those errors of calculation are compounded in estimating the secondary effect. Therefore, an accurate calculation of the direct spending is essential in order for the economic impact estimates to be reliable (Baade and Matheson, 2002).

The three most commonly reported multipliers are those of sales, income and employment (Crompton, 1995). *Sales or Transactions multipliers* measure the direct and secondary effect of the injected money on the business activity and turnover. *Household*

Income multipliers concentrate on the direct and secondary effects on the household income. *Employment multipliers* measure the number of new full-time jobs resu.iting from the money injected in the economy.

Although the sales multiplier is the one most often used in the economic impact studies, Crompton (1995) argues that the household income multiplier is the most relevant for assessing the economic impact of hosting a sport event. The reason for this is because it focuses particularly on the effect of the injected money on residents' income and their standard of living. In other words, the host community is not interested in knowing how many sales are attributable to the hosting of the Summer Olympics, but rather what proportion of these sales will end up as residents' income.

In contrast, the employment multipliers are the least reliable among the others (Fletcher and Snee, 1989; Crompton, 1995). Their basic assumption of full utilisation of existing employees may creates errors in calculating the increase in the level of employment, particularly for 'one-time' mega-sports events such as the Summer Olympic Games. The short duration of the Games does not necessarily justify the hiring of new employees, the generation of permanent full-time jobs and the sustainability of the employment effects. Entrepreneurs will probably exhaust other alternatives such as asking existing employees to work overtime or perform other tasks, before hiring additional work force to satisfy the temporary high demand (Crompton, 1995).

A short review of the literature reveals that the multiplier is a particularly contentious measure. A study by Hunter (1988, p. 16) argues that 'economic impact studies based on multipliers are quite clearly an improper tool for legislative decision-making'. In contrast, Crompton (1995, p. 34) comments that despite its shortcomings, this technique can be valuable 'if it is implemented knowledgeably and with integrity'.

In event economic studies, problems usually arise when researchers do not clearly identify what type of multiplier (sales or income) is used in their methodological approach, and as a result misleading conclusions can be derived from the data. Because sales multipliers include higher numbers compared with income multipliers, they tend to be attractive tools for advocates of sport events to use in their attempt to justify the economic benefits of hosting the events (Crompton, 1995). In addition, misapplication of the data may arise when spending generated by local residents or which occurred outside is included in the overall economic effect. Furthermore, it is crucial to exclude both spending by tourists who rescheduled a previously organised trip to coincide with the Games or by those who visit the host for other reasons but also end up attending from an economic impact study (Howard and Crompton, 1995).

Types of modelling approach

In order for economists to identify and quantify the economic consequences of hosting an event, such as the Summer Olympic Games, a modelling approach must be adopted. In the published literature examined, two main approaches have been used under the broad label of the input–output (I–O) and the computable general equilibrium (CGE) framework.

The I–O method is a long-established technique originated by Leontief in the 1940s and since then it has been very widely applied in economics. Classic I–O models are structured around input–output tables and their production or price categories, but make little or no use of regression-based behavioural equations. The disaggregation of classic I–O models is limited by the disaggregation of the published input–output table. As these models account for intermediate exchanges, they are useful for assessing industry level impacts for changes in final demand, indirect tax rates or commodity price shocks (West, 1995). However, projections normally are made by specifying final demands (consumption, investment, exports and imports) exogenously. Intermediate consumption, prices and income are determined with strict identities. Consequently, there is no integration between final demand and prices or income and no guarantee that there will be economic consistency among, for example, consumption, prices and income (Werling, 1992). Moreover, attempts to build 'dynamic' I–O models by endogenising investment based on the capital equipment 'requirements' for future output often lead to severe instability problems (Almon, 1966; Steenge, 1990).

Studies that adopted the I–O analysis to evaluate the total economic impact of hosting a mega sporting event made use of linear assumptions. They calculated a set of multipliers suggesting particular proportions of consuming the inputs and used them intact, regardless of the scale of the injected funds and the surge in the economic activity. As a result, they failed to take into account economies of scale, production close to full capacity and price adaptations to demand changes. Ignoring these factors tended to result in miscalculating the multiplier values.

The shortcomings described above apply to the regional input-output modelling system (RIMS II), a computer program often used by studies examined the Summer Olympics in the USA. The RIMS II has been proven to be successful for measuring effects at several levels of industrial aggregation, when initial tourist spending is known, but fails to examine the effect on nearby areas, because it is a single-region model (Humphreys and Plummer, 1995). An alternative I–O computer program, also developed in the USA, is IMPLAN (IMpact analysis for PLANning).

Although a comparatively large number of the referenced economic studies have been carried out in an I–O framework (see Table 17.1), studies of the Sydney Olympics turned towards the use of CGE models. The CGE frameworks are disaggregated representations of the economy, which use input-output structure for the production side of the economy. The CGE models include sectoral-level production functions and disaggregated demand functions for consumption, imports, investment, etc. They combine input-output structure and behavioural functions. Normally, however, behavioural parameters are not estimated with regression analysis but are deduced from the single year's set of data or specified exogenously (Werling, 1992). In the determination of prices, CGE models assume flexible prices that move to clear all the markets simultaneously (although some CGE models will assume some sticky prices, such as in the labour market).

Earlier CGE models were used to estimate different static equilibriums under Walrasian general equilibrium theory. Most contemporary CGE models have been expanded to incorporate dynamic adjustment. The MMRF (Monash multi-regional forecasting) model, used by Australian studies to measure the economic impact of the Sydney Olympics, is an example of a dynamic CGE model.

The MMRF used the so-called 'bottoms-up' approach. A number of regional economic models are included and then are linked using interregional flows of commodities, factors of production and population. The bottoms-up approach allows the modelling of economic agents' behaviour at the regional level and then their aggregation is attempted. Although MMRF explicitly distinguishes the economies of Australia's eight states and territories

Table 17.1 Economic impact studies of the Summer Olympic Games (1984–2012)[a]

State/country	Host/bid city	Year	Reference	Analysis	Type of approach
District of Columbia	Washington–Baltimore bid	2012	Fuller and Clinch, 2000	*Ex-ante*	I–O (IMPLAN)
Texas	Houston bid	2000	Airola and Craig, 2000	*Ex-ante*	I–O (RIMS II)
Greece	Athens	2004	Balfousia–Savva et al., 2001 Papanikos, 1999	*Ex-ante* *Ex-ante*	Macroeconometric Multiplier
Australia	Sydney	2000	Arthur Andersen, 1999 NSW Treasury, 1997 KPMG Peat Marwick, 1993	*Ex-ante* *Ex-ante* *Ex-ante*	CGE (MMRF) CGE (MMRF) I–O
Georgia	Atlanta	1996	Baade and Matheson, 2002 Humphreys and Plummer, 1995	*Ex-post* *Ex-ante*	Econometric I–O (RIMS II)
Spain	Barcelona	1992	Brunet, 1995 Brunet, 1993	*Ex-ante* *Ex-ante*	No modelling No modelling
South Korea	Seoul	1988	Kim et al., 1989	*Ex-ante*	No modelling
California	Los Angeles	1984	Economics Research Associates, 1984	*Ex-ante*	I–O (RIMS II)

[a]Apart from the official reports, no economic impact studies were found for Moscow (1980), Montreal (1976), Munich (1972), Mexico City (1968), Tokyo (1964), Rome (1960) and Melbourne (1956).

and generates results for all regions in a steady multiregional accounting framework, its size limitation hinders the application of a similar model to larger countries compared with Australia.

Owing to vague technical details often found in the economic studies, a deep penetration proved to be a difficult task, The economic models rely on assumptions that reduce the economy to a level of simplicity so that it can be analysed. Each technique is subject to its own limitations defined by its assumptions. Most of the theoretical assumptions used in MMRF, such as perfect competition in product markets, zero pure profits and constant returns to scale production functions, labour market equilibrium, are not always valid for the Australian States. It is therefore important to consider whether these assumptions may have a significant impact on the Games modelling results.

In the case of I–O analysis the assumption that the I–O coefficients remain unchanged or can be extrapolated into the future in a reliable manner is of particular importance. This is still more so when the I–O model is being used to analyse the impact of major structural changes or shocks such as that of hosting a mega sporting event. The import coefficients have particular relevance in this case. A further consideration, pertinent perhaps to all forms of analysis, is differentiating between the short-term and the long-term impact of hosting the Games. For example, the examination of the extent to which the employment generated is sustainable in the long run. From the short overview, however, it is our understanding that the I–O model has been comparatively more popular, because it might be cost effective and simple in comparison with CGE models.

Ex-ante and ex-post economic impact assessments

The importance of the relationship between tourism and the Summer Olympics has gained increased recognition in recent years. The tourism effect is one among several that bid and host cities seek, arguing that the international media coverage preceding and during the Games presents a tremendous opportunity to advertise themselves in the global marketplace.

In an attempt to assess the likely growth in tourism as well as other economic effects, ex-ante assessments have been carried out to forecast the impacts of the Summer Olympics. Table 17.1 shows that a number of ex-ante economic analyses have been conducted, but the research significantly lacks ex-post impact assessments. An ex-post analysis examines the economic situation of the geographical influence zone before and after the event and manages to isolate the event from other factors that may run at the same time and may have contributed to the economic impact (Baade and Matheson, 2002).

The majority of studies listed in Table 17.1 were commissioned by proponents of the Olympic process, and the reader must bear in mind that the report writers were potentially motivated to come up with a favourable result (Baade and Matheson, 2002). This interpretation could more likely be the case when reports were prepared to justify an Olympic bid. A good way to provide some balance to these views would be to read economic impact studies prepared by 'anti-Olympics' groups, but there are none currently available. There is, however, a growing non-affiliated literature that can be used as a counterweight.

For example, the anti-Olympic alliances 'Bread not Circuses' (BNC) and 'People Ingeniously Subverting the Sydney Olympic Farce' (PISSOFF), based in Toronto and

Sydney respectively, made use of the Internet to promote their Olympic critique (current addresses are www.breadnotcircuses.org and www.cat.org.au/pissoff). The main argument of BNC was that the public money spent for the Games would be taken from other more important sectors (e.g. education, health, environment, prosperity). Now with almost every potential Olympic city's bid there tends to be the creation of an anti-Olympic alliance such as the recent example from Vancouver's bid for the 2010 Winter Games. In the case of Vancouver, 'The Impact of the Olympics on Community Coalition' (IOCC) defines itself as a community watchdog rather than an anti-Olympic group and aims to ensure that the environmental, social, economic and civil rights issues remain outstanding and the Olympic benefits apply to everybody.

On the other side, the bidding process itself has gained attention. In his book, Hill (1996) described the experience of the unsuccessful bids by Birmingham and Manchester to host the 1992 and 2000 Olympic Games respectively, focusing especially on the politics involved, and Hiller (1999) has discussed the strategy used by Cape Town in its bid to host the 2004 Olympic Games. Further dimensions of the bidding process, however, have been revealed by assertions of bribery and corruption. Books such as *Lords of the Rings* (Simson and Jennings, 1992) and *New Lords of the Rings* (Jennings, 1996) criticised intensively the legitimacy of the bidding process, claiming that IOC members corruptly requested bribes and accepted generous gifts from potential host cities in return for their votes, in addition, the Salt Lake scandal further emphasised the need to address such problems (McIntosh, 2000) and virtually prompted a revamping of the IOC's rules with respect to the host-city bidding process.

The review will now analyse the studies mentioned in Table 17.1 with reference to a specific question: What are the economic implications of the Summer Games on the host?

Three studies commissioned for the Sydney Olympics predicted the event would generate substantial extra revenue for Australia, and New South Wales (NSW) in particular. Table 17.2 shows the predictions made by each study.

Although KPMG Peat Marwick (1993) adopted a different modelling approach, its figures broadly concurred with those released by Andersen (1999) and NSW Treasury (1997). The I–O framework used in the study by KPMG Peat Marwick (1993)

Table 17.2 Sydney Games impact summaries

Projected figures	Andersen[a]	NSW Treasurr[a]	KPMG[b]
Sponsor of analysis	Sydney OOC	NSW Treasury	Sydney Bid Committee
Addition to Australian GDP	A$6.5 billion	A$6.4 billion	A$7.3 billion
Addition to NSW's GDP	A$5.1 billion	A$6.3 billion	A$4.6 billion
International arrivals in Australia	1.5 million	2.3 million	1.3 million
Additional tourist spending	A$2.7 billion	A$4.3 billion	A$3.0 billion
New jobs (Australia)	90,000	98,700	156,198
Period	1994–2006	1994–2006	1991–2004

a 1996 values.
b 1992 values.

Sources: KPMG, 1993; NSW Treasury, 1997: Andersen, 1999.

ignored supply-side constraints and therefore made its estimates questionable. More specifically, supply-side constraints such as investment crowding out, price increases owing to resource scarcity and public financing of infrastructure expenditures are of great importance in the study of the Summer Olympics and the consulting firm should take this into consideration.

Investigating the tourism impacts of the Games, Andersen (1999) and NSW Treasury (1997) gave little consideration to the likely loss of visitors as a result of hosting the 2000 Games. This subject is of particular interest in light of the argument put forward by Leiper (1997), which mentions that although mega-events such as the Summer Olympics may encourage new tourists, the holiday-makers, business travellers or even local residents will be diverted elsewhere to escape expected disturbances and congestion problems.

A number of *ex-ante* studies are also available for the next Summer Olympics, which will be taking place in 2004 in Athens, Greece; prominent amongst these are the studies by Balfousia-Savva *et al.* (2001) and Papanikos (1999). Balfousia-Savva *et al.* (2001) had the advantage of utilising the most recent estimates of the direct impacts of the Games (Table 17.3), including updated estimates for the Olympics budget. However, scepticism is raised regarding data estimates related to the level, of induced tourism, total Olympic construction expenditures and Olympics operating profits.

Despite major methodological differences between the studies by Papanikos (1999) and Balfousia-Savva *et al.* (2001), their results do not differ significantly, with both suggesting growth in tourism and revenue. The macro-econometric model utilised in the Balfousia-Savva *et al.* (2001) study implied different scenarios in macroeconomic settings, but failed to take into account possible resource constraints. On the other hand, Papanikos 'borrowed' the value of multipliers from other studies in related cities. This probably happened because the direct estimation of the value could be both complicated and costly. However, it might affect his results, because economic relationships may be different between communities. Both studies make predictions on a national level and lack an explicit spatial dimension in assessing the impact of the Games. The choice of the nation as a reference area is doubtful, because as Howard and Crompton (1995) illustrated, the larger the assessed area, the smaller the leakages that are likely to happen and then the larger the multiplier is likely to be. It is noteworthy to mention that difficulties were experienced in providing a further evaluation of the Balfousia-Savva *et al.* (2001) model as there are few published details relating to its theoretical structure.

Other *ex-ante* studies that have looked at the economic impact of Summer Olympic Games are those of Brunet (1993, 1995) and Kim *et al.* (1989). Quantifiable data describing expenditures, contracts, jobs, investments and tourism were based almost exclusively on secondary research and the studies did not provide any predictions using a form of modelling. Rather they were more theoretical in their approach aiming to identify and collate evidence of the economic benefits of the Barcelona and South Korea Games respectively. It is our understanding that the studies were conducted with a view to capturing and aggregating disparate pieces of evidence regarding the economic activities flowing from the conduct of the Games.

An attempt to offer an *ex-post* economic impact analysis of the Summer Olympics was made by Baade and Matheson (2002). Their aim was to assess changes in employment in Los Angeles and Atlanta that were attributable to the staging of the 1984 and 1996 Olympics respectively. In other words, their *ex-post* approach was targeted to estimate the level of employment in the Games' absence. To achieve this, they constructed an

Table 17.3 Summer Olympics impact summaries

Summer Olympics	Sponsor of analysis	Reference	Total economic impact	Tourists	New jobs	Period
Washington–Baltimore bid, 2012	Greater Baltimore Alliance/Committee Greater Washington Board of Trade/Initiative	Fuller and Clinch, 2000	US$5.3 billion[a]	1.3 million	69,758 Washington–Baltimore metropolitan area	2012
Houston bid, 2012	None	Airola and Craig, 2000	US$4.3 billion[a]	0.8 million	64,216 Houston metropolitan area	2012
Athens, 2004	Centre of Planning and Economic Research	Balfousia-Savva et al., 2001	GRD 2,850 billion[a] (medium scenario)	4.8 million	300,400 Greece	2000–2010
	Greek Hotel Chamber's Tourism Research Institute	Papanikos, 1999	US$15.9 billion[b] (medium scenario)	5.9 million	445,000 Greece	1998–2011
Atlanta, 1996	None	Baade and Matheson, 2002	Not examined	Not examined	42,448 State of Georgia	1994–1996
	Atlanta OOC	Humphreys and Plummer, 1995	US$5.1 billion[c]	1.1 million	77,026 State of Georgia	1991–1997
Barcelona, 1992	Supreme Sports Council of Spanish Government/Olympic and Sports Studies Centre	Brunet, 1993, 1995	US$0.03 billion	0.4 million	296,640 Spain	1987–1992
Seoul, 1988	Seoul OOC	Kim et al., 1989	WON 1,846.2 billion (income effect only)	n.a.	336,000 South Korea	1982–1988
Los Angeles, 1984	None	Baade and Matheson, 2002	Not examined	Not examined	5,043 Los Angeles	1984
	Los Angeles OOC	Economics Research Associate, 1984	US$2.3 billion[d]	0.6 million	73,375 Southern California	1984

a 2000 values; b 1999 values; c 1994 values; d 1984 values.

econometric equation including as independent variables those of population, real per capita personal income, wages, taxes as well as dummy variables for the occurrence of the Olympics and the oil boom. Using standard regression analysis techniques, Baade and Matheson (2002) found that the coefficient for the Olympics variable was insignificant. The econometric equation was then used to estimate changes in employment and isolated the contribution of the Games by comparing this estimated value with the actual employment levels.

Their results for employment growth were more divergent by far than those released by *ex-ante* studies of Economic Research Associates (1984) and Humphreys and Plummer (1995) and have brought to light possible over-estimation reported by the latter studies. Another key finding was that the economy virtually returned, to its 'normal' pattern afterwards and any increase in economic activity attributable to the Games was temporary. However, Baade and Matheson's (2002) conclusions rest heavily on the model being correctly specified, which invites one to wonder how sensitive these results are to alternative specifications.

Covering the period of 1984 through to 2012, all the *ex-ante* economic studies indicate the significant role of the Summer Olympic Games in the promotion of the host economy. They highlighted the extension of the Games economic impact well beyond the actual period of the event occurrence itself. Economic growth, increased tourism and additional employment were some of their major findings.

However, the high expectations released by most of them could be considered to be potentially biased, because the ambition of those commissioning the studies is to favour the hosting of the Games. This issue has received a great deal of attention from scholars investigating the Games and other mega-events (Mills, 1993; Crompton, 1995; Howard and Crompton, 1995; Kesenne, 1999; Porter, 1999; Preuss, 2000; Baade and Matheson, 2002). Nevertheless, it is our opinion that if the estimation process is made transparent, then the findings are reliable. Taking into account the strengths. and weaknesses of all the methods and techniques used, the discussion here shows that *ex-ante* models and forecasts were not confirmed by *ex-post* analyses and this therefore prompts the need for improved theory.

Research in this field needs to further consider a substantial element, which is the opportunity cost involved in hosting the Summer Olympic Games or other mega-events. Host communities often pose the question of whether financing the Games is the most effective and efficient use of public money. In other words, if the public funds spent on the Games were used in a different way, would the host economy receive a greater return than it does when these funds are spent on Games investments? To answer this one needs to look no further than Kesenne's argument (1999) that even though a mega-event does create net benefits, public funding should occur only if the mega-event yields higher net benefits from an alternative project. In reality, of course, it is not feasible to measure the net benefits of all possible alternative projects; however, some important opportunity cost elements can be investigated further (Kesenne, 1999).

In addition, another aspect to be considered in subsequent research. is the potential economic retreat after the completion of the Gaines. When the level of income and investment falls after the event, then the multiplier also follows. To illustrate this point, findings from broader mega-event literature could be utilised to demonstrate that 'one-time' events have no lasting post-event effects in new business activities or employment (Mount and Leroux, 1994; Spilling, 1998).

It is important, therefore, that prospective researchers be inspired by a recognition of the shortcomings found in earlier *ex-ante* and *ex-post* studies and that they concentrate on areas that most need the effort. This will help planners and potential hosts of mega-events to improve their forecasting and decisions.

Acknowledgements

The author would like to gratefully acknowledge and thank Professor John Hudson, Dr Peter Dawson, Adam George-Wood, Nikos Veraros and Martha McIntosh for their helpful comments on earlier drafts of this paper. Special thanks also to two anonymous referees who provided substantial and constructive comments.

Any remaining errors or omissions are the author's alone.

References

Airola J., Craig, S. 2000. *The Projected Economic Impact on Houston of Hosting the 2012 Summer Olympic Games*. Houston Working Paper, University of Houston.

Almon C. 1966. *The American Economy to 1975*. Harper & Row: New York.

Andersen, Arthur. 1999. *Economic Impact Study of the Sydney 2000 Olympic Games*. CREA: Centre for Regional Economic Analysis/University of Tasmania: Australia.

Baade R.A., Matheson, V. 2002. Bidding for the Olympics: fool's gold? In *Transatlantic Sport: the Comparative Economics of North America and European Sports*, Barros, C.R., Ibrahimo, M., Szymanski, S. (eds). Edward Elgar: London; 127–151.

Balfousia-Savva, S., Athanassiou, L., Zaragas, L., Milonas, A. 2001. *The Economic Effects of the Athens Olympic Games*. Centre of Planning and Economic Research: Athens. (In Greek.)

Brunet, F. 1993. *Economy of The 1992 Barcelona Olympic Games*. International Olympic Committee: Lausanne.

Brunet, F. 1995. An economic analysis of the Barcelona '92 Olympic Games: resources, financing, and impact. In *The Keys to Success*, Miquel, M.D., Botella, M. (eds). Autonomous University of Barcelona: Barcelona; 203–237.

Crompton, J.L. 1995. Economic impact analysis of sports facilities and events: eleven sources of misapplication. *Journal of Sport Management* 9(1): 14–35.

Darcy, S., Veal, A.J. 1994. The Sydney 2000 Olympic Cannes: the story so far. *Australian Journal of Leisure and Recreation* 4(1): 5–14.

Economics Research Associates. 1984. *Community Economic Impact of the 1984 Olympic Games in Los Angeles and Southern California*. Los Angeles Olympic Organizing Committee: Los Angeles.

Fletcher, J., Snee, H. 1989. Tourism multiplier effects. In *Tourism Marketing and Management Handbook*, Witt, S.F., Moutinho, L. (eds). Prentice Hall. International: England; 529–531.

French, S.P., Disher M.E. 1997. Atlanta and the Olympics: a one-year retrospective. *Journal of the American Planning Association* 63(3): 379–392.

Fuller, S.S., Clinch, R. 2000. *The Economic and Fiscal Impacts of Hosting the 2012 Olympic Games on the Washington–Baltimore Metropolitan Area*. George Mason Working Paper, George Mason University.

Hall, C.M. 1987. The effects of hallmark events on cities. *Journal of Travel Research* 26(2): 44–45.

Haxton, P.A. 1999. The Perceived Role of Community Involvement in the Mega-Event Hosting Process: a case study of the Atlanta 1996 and Sydney 2000 Olympic Games. Unpublished Ph.D. thesis, Sydney University of Technology.

Hill, C.R. 1996. *Olympic Politics. Athens to Atlanta 1896–1996*. Manchester University Press: Manchester.

Hiller, H.H. 1990. The urban transformation of a landmark event: the 1988 Calgary Winter Olympics. *Urban Affairs Quarterly* 26(1): 118–137.

Hiller, H.H. 1999. Mega-events and urban social transformation: Human development and the 2004 Cape Town Olympic bid. In *The Impact of Mega-events*, Andersson, T.D., Persson, C., Sahlherg, B., Strom, L.I. (eds). ETOUR: European Tourism Research Institute, Sweden; 109–120.

Howard, D.R., Crompton J.L. 1995. *Financing Sport*. Fitness Information Technology: Morgantown.

Humphreys, J.M., Plumnner M.K. 1995. *The Economic Impact on the State of Georgia of Hosting the 1996 Olympic Games*. Selig Center for Economic Growth: Georgia.

Hunter, W.J. 1988. *Economic Impact Studies: Inaccurate, Misleading, and Unnecessary. Study 21.* Heartland Institute: Chicago.

Jennings, A. 1996. *The New Lords of the Rings: Olympic Corruption and How to Buy Gold Medals*. Pocket Books: London.

Kang, H.B. 1988. Accelerating the future-state: urban impact of hosting the 1988 Seoul Olympic Games. In: *Hosting the Olympics: the Long-Term Impact, Conference Report*. East Asian Architecture and Planning Program, MIT and Graduate School of Environmental Studies, Seoul National University: Seoul; 17–32.

Kesenne, S. 1999. Miscalculations and misinterpretations in economic impact analysis. In *The Economic Impact of Sports Events*, Jeanrenaud, C. (ed.). Centre International d'Etude du Sport: Switzerland; 29–39.

Kim, J.G., Rhee, S.W., Yu, J.C., *et al*. 1989. *Impact of The Seoul Olympic Games on National Development*. Korea Development Institute: Seoul.

KPMG Peat Marwick. 1993. *Sydney Olympics 2000: Economic Impact Study*. Sydney Olympics 2000 Bid Ltd: Sydney.

Leiper, N. 1997. A town like Elis? The Olympics: impact on tourism in Sydney. In *Proceedings of the Australian Tourism and Hospitality Research Conference*, Sydney.

Liu, J., Var, T. 1982. Differential multipliers for the accommodation sector. *Tourism Management* September: 172–187.

Mcintosh, M.J. 2000. The Olympic host city bid process: facing challenges and making changes. In *Focus on Olympism: Discoveries, Discussion, Directions*, Messing, M., Muller, N. (eds). Waila Walla Press: Sydney; 312–321.

Mills, E.S. 1993. The misuse of regional economic models. *Cato Journal* 13(1): 29–39.

Mount, J., Leroux, C. 1994. *Assessing the Effects of a Landmark Event: A Retrospective Study of the Impact of the Olympic Games on the Calgary Business Sector*. Laurentian University: Ontario.

NSW Treasury. 1997. *Research and Information Paper: the Economic Impact of The Sydney Olympic Gaines*. New South Wales Treasury and CREA: Centre for Regional Economic Analysis (University of Tasmania).

Papanikos, G.T. 1999. *Tourism Impact of the 2004 Olympic Games*. Tourism Research Institute: Athens. (In Greek.)

Porter, P.R. 1999. Mega-sports events as municipal investments: a critique of impact analysis. In *Sports Economics: Current Research*, Fizel, J., Gustafson, E., Hadley, L. (eds). Praeger Press: New York: 61–73.

Preuss, H. 2000. *Economics of the Olympic Games: Hosting the Games 1972–2000*. Walla Walla Press: Sydney.

Ritchie, J.R.B., Aitken, E.C. 1984. Assessing the impacts of the 1988 Olympic Winter Games: the research program and initial results. *Journal of Travel Research* 22(3): 17–25.

Robin, D. 1988. Hosting the Olympic Games: long-term benefits to sport and culture. In: *Hosting the Olympics: the Long-term Impact, Conference Report*. East Asian Architecture and Planning Program, MIT and Graduate School of Environmental Studies, Seoul National University: Seoul: 245–264.

Simson, V., Jennings, A. 1992. *The Lords of the Rings: Power, Money and Drugs in the Modern Olympics*. Simon & Schuster: New York.

Spilling, O.R. 1998. Beyond intermezzo? on the long-term industrial impacts of mega-events: the case of Lillehammer 1994. *Festival Management and Event Tourism* 5: 101–122.

Steenge, A.E. 1990. On the complete instability of empirically implemented dynamic Leontief models. *Economic Systems Research* 2(1): 3–16.

Walle, A.H. 1996. Festivals and mega-events: Varying roles and responsibilities. *Festival Management and Event Tourism* 3(3): 115–120.

Werling, J.F. 1992. MIDE: A macroeconomic muitisectoral model of the Spanish economy. Unpublished Ph.D. thesis. University of Maryland.

West, G.R. 1995. Comparison of input–output and econometric and computable general equilibrium impact models at the regional level. *Economic Systems Research* 7(2): 209–220.

Chapter 18

Ian Hudson

THE USE AND MISUSE OF ECONOMIC IMPACT ANALYSIS
The case of professional sports

T**HE PURPOSE OF ECONOMIC** impact analysis is to measure the change in economic activity resulting from a specific program or project. This can be a useful tool for governments when deciding between various uses for public funds. A properly designed and carefully researched study can shed considerable light on the very murky domain of economic costs and benefits for a particular region. However, the accuracy of these studies is very dependent on the methodology followed by the individual author, who is required to make numerous, often discretionary decisions that will affect the final conclusion. Needless to say, when the final results are so dependent on the decisions of the authors, the door is open to all manner of inconsistencies. In fact, these types of studies need to be read with a very critical eye before accepting their conclusions.

This note of caution is particularly relevant when analyzing the economic impact studies that have been published to examine the economic contribution of professional sports teams. Anyone with an even vaguely suspicious nature should be immediately on his or her guard when a study so dependent on the author's discretion is published or funded by one of the interested parties in a debate. The purpose of this study is to determine whether economic impact studies of sports teams tend to overstate the teams' impact.

The degree of variation between studies that are investigating similar phenomenon is quite remarkable. For example, Baade and Dye (1990, p. 6) cite the contrast between two studies on the value of National Football League (NFL) franchises in Philadelphia and Baltimore. According to one study, the Philadelphia Eagles contributed more than $500 million to the city's economy in 1983. In contrast, a study on the now relocated Baltimore Colts concluded that the team had a quite marginal economic impact, only managing to increase the economic activity of the city by $200,000 in 1 year. John Crompton (1995, p. 16) provides an equally telling example. When baseball's San Francisco Giants were considering relocating to nearby San Jose, both cities commissioned economic impact studies on the team. San Francisco, faced with the prospect of losing the team and therefore keen to downplay its economic benefit, concluded that they contributed a meager $3.1 million to the city. On the other hand, San Jose, eager to justify public spending on a new ballpark to house the team, estimated that it increased economic activity by somewhere between $50 million and $100 million each year. Only the most trusting reader would put this entire discrepancy down to the different impacts of the team in two different cities. Far more likely is that methodological differences between the two studies account for the divergent conclusions.

The purpose of this article is to examine several of the economic impact studies that have been used to determine the costs and benefits of professional sports teams in an effort to account for the variation in estimated economic impacts. It will also attempt to judge the appropriateness of the techniques used in these studies to determine the validity of their results.

Problem definition

The first step in any empirical work is to formulate a specific research question. Broadly speaking, this analysis is interested in determining the accuracy and consistency of the collected impact studies. In an effort to do this, I will first attempt to determine the extent to which these studies have followed accepted practices in conducting their studies. All assumptions are not created equal, and many of the impact analyses that have been conducted to date have been justifiably criticized for breaking some of the more generally accepted conventions of the discipline. To determine which conventions of well-constructed investigations have been flaunted by the sample studies, it will first be necessary to identify the preferred assumptions and methodologies. If it is found that many of the studies have violated standard practices in impact analysis, then the stated impacts of these studies must be viewed with some suspicion.

Furthermore, this study will use meta-analysis in an attempt to determine the causes of the variation between these studies. What is critical to determine is whether the very large observed variation in the impacts assigned to the differing teams in this study accurately reflects differing impacts or is simply a result of different assumptions. If the variation is in large part due to differing assumptions and methodologies, and especially if those assumptions and methods are somewhat questionable, then the reliability of these studies must be called into question.

Data collection

Obtaining economic impact studies on professional sports teams is somewhat more difficult than the usual gathering of published empirical work. Impact studies are usually not published in reputed journals and listed in easily accessible databases on user-friendly CD-ROMs. Instead, they are published for a very specific purpose, cited time and again by the local media and the respective lobby groups keen to sway public opinion, and then they disappear. Therefore, the search for studies was somewhat more difficult than a standard gathering of literature. After realizing the paucity of studies published in easily accessible sources, this study turned to an information request sent over the Regional

Science Information Exchange, maintained by the Regional Science Institute at West Virginia University. The response to this request was quite encouraging, with several authors sending in their own studies and other respondents providing useful bibliographies.

The second method of obtaining studies was through bibliographies of articles on related topics. Journal articles that examine how economic impact studies are used in the broader context of the debate about subsidizing professional sports were significant sources of citations. Attempts were then made to locate these documents with varying degrees of success. Although some were easily available from the local library of the city in question, others seemed to have simply vanished or were not available to the public. The total sample, then, consists of all of the available studies that could be obtained using these two methods, along with the usual search of published literature. The sample is less a representation of all of the studies that have been produced than of what was available.

Only studies that fulfilled two criteria were deemed eligible for this survey. First, the analysis had to explicitly account for the economic impart of a major league professional team. Many studies simply calculate the impact of a new stadium or arena without specifically determining the economic impact of the team playing in the facility. These were not included. After all the underlying logic behind building a stadium is not the construction of the building itself, but the impact of the new building on increasing team revenues in comparison to the existing facility. Indeed, simply looking at how the construction of an arena or stadium contributes to economic activity is quite misleading, because any number of alternative structures could have been built with the money, creating on identical economic impact. The real point is how the facility contributes to the economy once it is constructed, and, clearly, much of this is dependent on the franchise for which it is built.

Second, the studies had to follow what can be loosely described as the typical approach to economic impact studies. By this I mean the quite familiar exercise of estimating an initial or direct impact, and then determining how this first round of expenditure circulates throughout the area of the study. Other, more exotic methodologies were used in some studies, but this article is solely interested in the traditional version of the economic impact study precisely because it is the version most likely to be used. The studies that met these stringent criteria are listed in the appendix. Most interesting, only the study by Blair and Swindell (1997) was not funded by either a pro lobby interest group or a state or municipal government.

Accepted practices in economic impact studies

The next step will be to outline some of the most widely accepted practices for conducting economic impact studies in an attempt to determine the extent to which the surveyed studies conform to these procedures. In general terms, economic impact analysis attempts to calculate the total economic impact of a policy or project by determining a net initial impact by subtracting any costs imposed by the project from its total initial or "first round" benefits. This initial impact is then adjusted by a multiplier to arrive at the total economic impact. In a 1995 article, Crompton has concisely identified accepted practices in economic impact analysis by pointing out 11 frequently committed misapplications. This article will analyze the credibility of the sample study by determining the extent to which the studies commit Crompton's misapplications, all of which will inflate the estimated economic impact. Of Crompton's 11, 5 will not be extensively analyzed in this study because they were violated in all of the studies. I will first deal with these misapplications.

First, I will deal with two costs that were neglected in all of the sample studies. Crompton (1995, p. 29) argues that studies should always attempt to explicitly account for the costs of the project, including the opportunity costs of the subsidy. The presence of a professional sports facility will inevitably impose costs on the surrounding region, which should be accounted for in the initial impact assessment. For example, if a new stadium results in increased traffic congestion for a neighborhood, then this needs to be weighed against the benefits of the project. Opportunity cost, which is the value of the next best alternative, should also be explicitly calculated. This is necessary because the funds that were used for the stadium could have been spent on a convention center or highway construction. If a new stadium would generate $100 million in economic benefits each year but a convention center would have generated $200 million, the sacrifice of the convention center must be accounted for in evaluating the costs and benefits of the stadium. Crompton is quite correct in arguing that these elements should be included in a well-crafted economic impact analysis. The fact that not one of the studies in this sample accounts for either costs or opportunity costs will lead them to overstate the initial economic impact. However, because they do not explain the variation in the results, they will not be discussed further in the article.

Crompton (1995) also warns against the malleability of employment multipliers in estimating the number of full-time jobs that a project will provide. The employment multiplier assumes that an increase in visitor spending will translate into a given number of jobs, based on an assumption about the full-time pay rate. Crompton provides the example of a $1 million dollar increase in tourist spending, which would create 81 full-time equivalent jobs, based on a $12,350 per year salary (p. 22). The main problem with this is that increased spending may not translate into increased employment, especially if labor is not fully utilized. It may be possible, for example, for existing labor to work harder, rather than hiring extra people. For these purposes, this is a somewhat moot point, as only a few of the studies in this sample calculated an employment impact; therefore, I am much more concerned with the economic impact estimate.

Crompton (1995) also includes an argument by two other authors, Burns and Mules, who claim that a public funding agency should not claim the full amount of economic benefit for projects that it has only partially funded. If the government only funds one third of the project, it should only claim one third of the benefit. Crompton himself appears to be less than certain this is a valid critique, because it assumes that two thirds of the project would have occurred in the absence of government funding, which is not necessarily the case (p. 30). Crompton's skepticism is very well placed. Indeed, it is surely a mark of efficient subsidization if a government can spend as little as possible while ensuring that a project goes ahead. If the goal is to ensure that a sports team remains in a city through the construction of a new stadium, a government should not simply offer to fund the entire project, but should try to ascertain what minimum expenditure is required to keep the team. If the team would have left without the government subsidy, it seems valid for the government to claim the full economic benefits. Because this misapplication seems misplaced, it will not be further included in this study.

Crompton (1995) also argues for using an income as opposed to a sales multiplier. This is based on the seemingly incontestable assertion that local residents care about how a project will impact their personal incomes, not economic activity in a broader sense. Crompton quite correctly points out that using the larger sales multiplier can lead to spurious inferences about the income generating effects of a project. Although Crompton's insistence that studies be very explicit about just what they are measuring is, of course, justified, his point about the inappropriateness of sales multipliers is perhaps more controversial. Crompton claims that a tourist dollar spent in the local economy can be respent on any one of three local alternatives: households, interindustry spending, and government. Only the money that finally comes to rest in the coffers of households should be of interest to the researcher. If one is only concerned about the impact of the project on household incomes, then by definition, this is correct. However, it seems possible for the local economy to be improved by increased flows of foods to local government and businesses. Taking government as an example, if tax revenue is increased, this either means that households pay less tax for the same level of services or get access to more services. If more roads are repaired or libraries opened, this would seem to be of some interest to local residents, even if their incomes have not changed. As long as it is very clear that the sales multiplier does not represent an actual increase in household income, there seems to be no reason to object to its use. All of the studies in this sample use overall economic impact, Crompton's sales multiplier, to measure the impact of the team. However, as long as the study refrains from making dubious inferences about income increases, this methodology is not inappropriate. Of course, this is a very different issue from artificial inflation of whatever multiplier the study chooses to use.

Of the remaining six misapplications, all of which are present in some of the studies in this sample but not in others, I will turn first to the controversy surrounding the choice of the appropriate multiplier, which encompasses 3 of Crompton's (1995) 11-item menu. The works cited in this study use two different techniques to determine a multiplier. Most of the studies use an economic base multiplier. The assumption behind this multiplier is that when an injection of money is made into the economy it is circulated again, increasing the economic impact of the initial spending. For example, when vacationers stop by a city to sample some of the cosmopolitan attractions, they will pay for a hotel room. This money is not then hoarded by the hotel, but is spent on such things as a laundry service, wages, and groceries that further contribute to the local economy. The people that receive this money will then spend some of it on other local goods for yet another round of increased economic activity. During each of these rounds, only a portion of the income received will be spent on the local economy; the rest is said to have leaked out. If the hotel spends the initial money from the visitors on national sales tax or imported wine, then these are leakages and will not count in the next round of economic impact. What needs to be determined, for each round of spending, is the local marginal propensity to consume and the local tax rate. The reliance of this multiplier on export base theory should be quite clear from the preceding description. Only additions (experts) from the local economy serve to increase economic activity, and the growth in the region arising from the initial impact is dependent on how well the economy can create locally oriented jobs (Vias & Mulligan, 1997, p. 959). Because economic impact is determined by taking the initial spending and expanding it by the multiplier, the author's choice of this one value can have a monumental impact on the bottom line.

The second method of determining a multiplier is through input-output analysis. In input-output analysis, the initial expenditure is adjusted to account for indirect spending on the inputs needed to supply the initial impact. To do this, a fairly complex input-output table of the local economy is needed, which attempts to model the production activity in the region. Crucially, the input-output table must be able to specify linkages between the different sectors of the region being studied. For example, if one were to determine the impact of building a new arena using the input-output technique, the initial construction impact would have to be adjusted to include the extent to which the construction industry purchases from the rest of the local economy. This would depend on such factors as the percentage of materials produced locally used in construction and the percentage of labor hired locally. The patterns of expenditure in these five sectors would then have to be considered in the next impact round (Hefner, 1990, p. 7). The total economic impact of an initial expenditure is only arrived at once all of these linkages are exhausted.

For an input-output model, total output for each industry is assumed to be the sum of final demand sales and output destined as inputs into other sectors. So for each industry,

$$X_i = \sum X_{ij} + Y_i \, ,$$

where X_i is the total output for each industry, i, X_{ij} is the output of industry i used as an input in other industries, and Y_i is the output of industry i used to meet final demand. The crucial calculation for this equation is to determine how much of industry output is needed to meet the needs of other sectors. Xij can be expressed as

$$X_{ij} = a_{ij} X_j \, ,$$

where a_{ij} represents the amount of input i needed to increase the output of j by one unit, and X_j is the output of j. Combining all of the industries provides the vector

$$X = AX + Y \, ,$$

where A is a vector of all the coefficients representing the interdependence between industries (Leistritz & Murdock, 1981, p. 34). The researcher needs to estimate the coefficients that comprise A and the final demand for each industry.

The information requirements for an input-output multiplier would appear to be beyond the means of most researchers. Fortunately, the U.S. Department of Commerce maintains RIMS II, an input-output model for each state in the union. All four studies in this sample that use an input-output analysis make use of this model. Within each state, distinct multipliers are tabulated for each industry. The RIMS II multiplier is designed to take into consideration all of the leakages, taxes, imports, and earnings through input-output coefficients applied to each industry. To use the RIMS II multiplier, the researcher must correctly determine the industry that accounts for the initial impact. Sporting events are included in the "hotels and lodgings places and amusements" industry (Hefner, 1990, p. 8).

Although the two types of economic impact study multipliers may seem quite different and therefore incompatible in the same study, this is not the case. Indeed, with corresponding definitions both techniques would yield identical multipliers. If industries are divided into the expert and local sectors, then there is equivalence between input-output and export base multipliers (Merrifield, 1987, p. 653). Although the use of the RIMS II input-output multiplier does eliminate one source of discretion from the study, the other problems identified by Crompton (1995) and applied in this study are still very much applicable. Indeed, with the exception of the choice of the multiplier, the methodology applied by those studies using the RIMS II input-output and economic base multipliers is identical. In both cases, the researcher must determine the initial impact onto which the multiplier is then applied. It is this determination of the initial impact in which all of the other misapplications arise. Therefore, it is valid to use the studies that include both economic base and RIMS II methodologies in the same study.

The size of the input-output and export base multipliers crucially depends on the extent to which additional rounds of goods and services are purchased from the local economy The larger the geographical area under consideration, the less leakage. A substantial amount of spending would be conducted within a nation, less within a state or province, and less still within a city. Therefore, in general, cities should have a lower multiplier than states or provinces. The multiplier also depends on the extent to which the demand for goods and services can be met by local firms. Therefore, regions with a diverse industrial base should have higher multipliers than areas heavily dependent on goods imported into the locality. Crompton (1995, p. 29) argues that although reasonable estimates of the appropriate multipliers are available for specific regions, even for specific industries within those regions, those are often ignored in favor of overly optimistic numbers. It would be quite useful to determine the extent to which those studies have inflated their multipliers, thus overestimating the overall economic impact.

I will next address two problems that highlight the need to distinguish between gross and net impacts. Gross impacts do not account for money being substituted from one use to another, whereas act impacts attempt to count only funds that are genuinely additional. Crompton (1995) correctly insists that it is net rather than gross impacts that are appropriate, because it is additional rather than displaced money that increases economic activity in a region. The distinction between these two techniques is especially crucial, given the importance of the calculation of the initial impact in the final benefit calculation. In these studies, the initial impact is expanded by the multiplier to get a final measure of total economic impact. The overestimation resulting from using gross rather than net figures is, therefore, exacerbated as the initially inflated figures are adjusted by the multiplier.

The first distinction between net and gross impacts revolves around the inclusion of local spending. Because only spending that would not have occurred in the absence of the sports team should be included as part of the initial economic impact, any spending that is merely transferred from one local business to another should not be included. It would seem highly plausible that much of the spending on sports teams by local citizens would be spent on other local entertainment options in the absence of a team. Local expenditures should only be included if season tickets are purchased instead of an out-of-town vacation, not if they substitute for tickets to the local theatre. Although certainly some local expenditure is additional in this sense, assuming that all local spending is not substituted from elsewhere in the local economy will clearly result in an overstatement of the initial impact. Indeed, Crompton (1995, p. 26) correctly argues that only a very small portion of local spending is additional, and therefore a safer assumption is to assume that no local spending represents an increase in economic activity. This same principle should be used in dealing with any of the team's revenue sources. For example, national television revenue is additional, but local contracts are not if that money would have been spent on other local programs. Studies that insist on counting local expenditure as increasing local economic activity are undoubtedly inflating the impact of the team.

Second, not all of those from outside the city attending the sporting event should be included as additional funds coming into the region as a result of the team. There is an important distinction between travelers drawn to town because of the sporting contest and those who are attending the contest simply because they are in the area. The latter group should not be included as additional money, because they are in town for other purposes and would have spent money in the city anyway. The money they spent on tickets and concessions at the game would have likely been spent on another attraction. Certainly the amount spent on hotels and restaurants during their stay would have been spent in the absence of a sporting contest. Well-formulated studies should, therefore, have some method of identifying visitors in town only for the sporting event, as opposed to "casuals" who would have made the trip regardless of the presence of the team.

The last of Crompton's (1995) misapplications that are relevant in this context is the temptation to use a different definition of the geographic area of interest for different aspects of the analysis. It is advantageous to use a quite small area when defining locals and visitors so that as many spectators as possible are included in the latter category, making them eligible as increases in local economic activity. On the other hand, a large geographical area permits a larger economic impact, because a larger multiplier can be used. Some studies have attempted to get the best of both worlds by using a small area when defining visitors and a larger, area when applying the multiplier. For example, a study of the impact of the Commonwealth Games in Victoria, British Columbia, considered anyone from outside the city to be a tourist, but used the whole province to measure the economic impact of the games (Crompton, 1995, p. 24). Altering the geographic area of interest in this fashion is a serious flaw in the analysis, again used to inflate the economic impact.

This section should have provided the reader with some idea of how economic impact studies can diverge from accepted practice. As indicated in this section, I cannot test all of Crompton's (1995) misapplications in the following meta-analysis. This article is limited to examining those problems that have been addressed in some studies but not in others. However, this does not mean that problems like omitting opportunity costs are not important—it is simply a reflection of the information available lathe studies obtained. The next section of the analysis will attempt to determine the extent to which these problems have contributed to variations in economic impact estimates among the studies in the sample.

Analysis of the studies

The variances in all of the studies are listed in Table 18.1. Note that there is often more than one economic impact for each study, because in several studies the authors published different conclusions based on differing study areas or assumptions. For example, the Chicago study on the Cubs estimated impacts at the state and city level, with and without a newly constructed park. Of the 13 studies, 12 were financed by either prosubsidy lobby groups or the government, both with a vested interest in demonstrating the import of the subject team to the local economy. Despite the lack of difference in motivation, there

Table 18.1 Economic impact studies

Study	Geographical region	Team(s)	Sport	Impact in millions ($)
Mayor Hoffman McCann & Mid-America Regional Council (1989): Gross	Kansas City	Royals and Chiefs	MLB and NFL	200.92
Mayer Hoffman McCann & Mid-America Regional Council (1989): Net	Kansas City	Royals and Chiefs	MLB and NFL	164.91
Maryland Department of Economic & Employment Development (1987)	Maryland	Orioles	MLB	161.42
Center for Economic Education (1996)	Cincinnati	Reds and Bengals	MLB and NFL	161.11
Deloitte and Touche (1998): State	Arizona	Devil Rays	MLB	159.72
Deloitte and Touche (1993): City	Phoenix	Devil Rays	MLB	112.51
City of Chicago (1986): State, new park	Illinois	Cubs	MLB	104.67
City of Chicago (1986): City, new park	Chicago	Cubs	MLB	87.85
City of Chicago (1986): State, old park	Illinois	Cubs	·MLB	86.91
Melaniphy & Associates (1986)	Chicago	Cubs	MLB	84.76
City of Chicago (1996): City, old park	Chicago	Cubs	MLB	72.89
Silverstein (1990): Gross	Denver	Rockies	MLB	69.61
Blair and Swindall (1997)	Cincinnati	Reds and Bengals	MLB and NFL	64.75
Conway and Bayere (1996)	Washington State	Seahawks	NFL	43.88
Schaffer and Davidson (1984)	Atlanta	Falcons	NFL	36.01
Coopers and Lybrand (1990)	Winnipeg	Jets	NHL	31.92
Schaffar and Davidson (1972)	Atlanta	Falcons	NFL	31.81
Conway and Beyers 0994)	Washington State	Mariners	MLB	29.79
Silverstein (1990): Net	Denver	Rockies	MLB	29.54

Note: MLB = Major League Baseball, NFL = National Football League. Impact is based on 1983 constant dollars.

Table 18.2 Economic impact studies of major league baseball teams on a state

Study	Geographical region	Team	Impact in millions ($)
Maryland Department of Economic & Employment Development (1987)	Maryland	Orioles	161.42
Deloitte and Touche (1993)	Arizona	Devil Rays	159.72
City of Chicago (1986)	Illinois	Cubs	104.67
Conway and Beyers (1994)	Washington State	Mariners	29.79

Note: Impact is based on 1983 constant dollars.

is certainly variation in results. Although some of the contrasting conclusions can clearly be attributed to acceptable differences in the case studies, much of the variation could be due to differences in methodology. The acceptable differences should be readily apparent from a cursory examination of Table 18.1. There are differences in the number of teams being studied, the sport being played, and the geographical region in question, which should all lead to different economic impacts. This makes it difficult to make an immediate comparison between many of the studies, because the National Hockey League (NHL) Jets should have a different impact on Winnipeg than the NFL Chiefs and Major League Baseball (MLB) Royals combined in Kansas City.

However, what is equally obvious are the tremendous differences between studies that examine the same sport and similar regions. The Center for Economic Education (1996) and the Blair and Swindell (1997) studies investigate the exact same teams in the exact same cities, yet they have arrived at estimates that are remarkably far apart. The divergence in studies that only focus on baseball teams' impact on a state is also worth noting. The four studies in Table 18.2 should have less variance than the whole sample because they are all on teams in the same sport and are all at a statewide level. Although two of the studies predict a similar impact, there can be little question that tremendous variation remains between studies that should yield quite similar results. The most optimistic assessment was the Department of Economic and Community Development study, conducted to determine the economic impact of the Baltimore Orioles in their new Camden Yards home. They estimated that the team contributed $161 million (1983 constant) to the state of Maryland in 1992. At the other end of the spectrum, a study on the economic impact of the Seattle Mariners on the state of Washington arrived at the much more modest figure of $30 million (1983 constant), less than one fifth of the Maryland estimate. Despite these widely disparate numbers, both authors were able to reach the similar conclusions about the value of the franchises to their respective states. In the executive summary of the Maryland study, the authors argue that "the Orioles' 1992 home season generated substantial economic and fiscal impacts in the City of Baltimore and the State of Maryland" (Maryland, 1992, p. 1). Despite their much lower dollar figure, the study on the Mariners claims, in its very first sentence, that the team "make(s) a contribution to the Washington State, King County and City of Seattle economies" (Conway & Beyers, 1994, p. 1). The remainder of this section will start to determine what accounts for these differences, and which of the studies follow the accepted economic impact study practices.

I will first make a preliminary examination of the extent to which these studies suffer from Crompton's (1995) misapplications. The first column in Table 18.3 shows the multiplier that was used in converting the direct into the total economic impact. It is impossible to make a blanket statement about what the multiplier of cities and states should be, because this would depend on the structure of the economy in question. However, having said this, sonic of the multipliers used in these studies are clearly exaggerated. Of the 13 studies, 4 have used multipliers of 2.5 or more, which is most probably an overestimation, especially considering that Crompton (1995, p. 29) cites a University of Missouri paper that claims that 90% to 95% of U.S. county multipliers fall between 1.4 and 1.8. The Conway and Beyers (1994) study used the RIMS II multiplier, eliminating that element of discretion from their study. It is worth noting that this multiplier is at the very low end of the spectrum in the sample, at 1.5 for the state of Washington. It is also remarkable that all of the studies with multipliers of more than 2.5 are studying the impact on cities, not on states. In fact, the studies conducted on states, such as the Maryland study and those by Conway and Beyers, have been much more conservative in their multiplier estimates.

As Table 18.3 clearly shows, the vast majority of the studies use gross rather than net figures. As discussed earlier, using net figures is the correct methodology. In Table 18.3, this is captured by the middle two columns. Locals Included and Casuals Included.

Table 18.3 Analysis of economic impact studies

Study	Multiplier	Locals included	Casuals included	Area shifting
Mayer Hoffman McCann & Mid-America Regional Council (1989): Gross[a]	2.9	Yes	Yes	No
Mayer Hoffman McCann & Mid-America Regional Council (1989): Net[a]	2.9	No	Yes	No
Maryland Department of Economic & Employment Development (1987)	1.9	Yes	Yes	No
Center for Economic Education (1996)	1.7	Yes	No	Yes
Deloitte and Touche (1993): State	1.9	Yes	Yes	No
Deloitte and Touche (1993): City	1.6	Yes	Yes	No
City of Chicago (1986): State, new park	2	Yes	Yes	No
City of Chicago (1986): City, new park	1.7	Yes	Yes	No
City of Chicago (1986): State, old park	2	Yes	Yes	No
Melaniphy & Associates (1986)	3.3	Yes	Yes	No
City of Chicago (1986): City, old park	1.7	Yes	Yes	Na
Silverstein (1990): Gross[a]	2	Yes	Yes	No
Blair and Swindell (1997)	1.7	No	No	No
Conway and Bayers (1996)	1.5	No	Yes	No
Schaffer and Davidson (1984)	2.1	Yes	No	No
Coopers and Lybrand (1990)	2.5	Yes	Yes	Yes
Schaffer and Davidson (1972)	3.3	No	Yes	No
Conway and Bayers (1994)	1.5	No	Yes	No
Silverstein (1990): Net[a]	2	No	No	No

a   These studies cite gross figures and "new" money, which is more appropriate, but do so in a manner that emphasizes that the gross figure is the economic impact of the team.

Both of these items are designed to capture whether the study is only including additional money. The Locals Included column indicates whether the study has included local revenue sources as part of economic impact. A "yes" will appear in this column if locals are included. As discussed in the previous section, this indicates that gross impacts are being used, because most local spending is probably diverted from other local businesses. As can be seen from Table 18.3, most of the studies in the sample (13 of 19) do include local spending as part of economic impact. When no distinction is being made between genuine additional impact and money that would have been spent in the local economy anyway, it is very unlikely that the authors will attempt to separate tourists into these primarily in town for the game (casuals) and those who would have been visiting the city anyway. If a study made an attempt to determine whether the number of out-of-town spectators were genuine additions to the tourist population, then a "no" will appear in the Casuals included column. Table 18.3 shows that these economic impact studies were only rarely interested in making this distinction. Again, this demonstrates that many of these studies have overstated the impact of the team.

It is worth noting that all of the studios in the top half of Table 18.3, that is, with the highest economic impacts, use gross rather than net numbers, and are therefore overstating the benefits of the team. Interestingly, many of these studies made little effort to justify their use of gross rather than net impacts. For example, the study by Deloitte and Touche (1993) for the Arizona Office of Sports Development is content with stating that "a gross expenditures and economic multiplier approach was used in conducting this study, which is the most widely accepted approach in conducting these types of studies" (p. 6). Although Table 18.3 does show that this approach is the most widely used, most economists would argue that it should not be accepted.

The only area in which these studies followed widely accepted economic impact practices was in their commendable refusal to fluctuate their area of study. This is captured in the last column of Table 18.3, Area Shifting. A "yes" in this column indicates that the study has altered the area of interest for different aspects of the study, and as a result has overestimated the economic impact. Only two of the studies in the sample are guilty of this error.

What is perhaps somewhat alarming is that of the 14 studies in this sample, only the Blair and Swindell (1997) study can claim to have followed recommended practice in all four of the criteria. Their study has a much lower economic impact than most of the other studies, concluding that the Reds and Bengals combined only contributed $98 million in 1996 ($64 million in 1983 constant dollars). Although Silverstein (1990) did follow accepted methodology in estimating the net impact of the Colorado Rockies, the gross number was presented as the more plausible estimate of the team's economic impact. All of the rest of the studies have, to a greater or lesser extent, violated the practices that should be followed in conducting a sound economic impact evaluation. The next section will attempt to use a more rigorous empirical technique to analyze these studies.

Meta-analysis

This study will use the technique of meta-analysis in conducting a survey of several economic impact studies on professional sports franchises. Although meta-analysis has yet to see widespread use in economics, it is well established in other social sciences as a statistical approach to literature surveys. Meta-analysis is an empirical method of reviewing a number of studies in which the data points in a regression are the surveys themselves, as opposed to individual observations. Regressions are used to determine the causes of variation in study results by using the differing methodologies, data sets, and assumptions as explanatory variables. Although, as in all empirical work, the formulation of the model allows for considerable discretion on the part of the researcher, proponents of this method argue that it leaves less to the individual perception of the author than more traditional methods of literature surveys. Given economists' obsession with empirical rigor, it is perhaps surprising that this technique has not been more quickly

Meta-regression model

The purpose of this section of the study is to outline the specific regression model to be used. This regression will hopefully be able to determine whether the variation in economic impacts of the different studies is due to legitimate differences between studies, or due to the use of the unacceptable techniques discussed in the previous section. The regression will be performed on the following model:

$$VAL = a_0 + a_1 FOOTBALL + a_2 BASEBALL + a_3 REGION + a_4 STAD +$$
$$a_5 MULT + a_6 LOCAL + a_7 SWITCH + a_8 SHIFT$$

The dependent variable in the regression is the study's final assessment of the team's economic impact in constant dollars. FOOTBALL and BASEBALL are dummy variables set to capture the differences in economic impact between sports. There are three sports included in the studies surveyed, so if the survey studies football or baseball, the dummy variable will be set to 1. Football and baseball are expected to have a larger impact than hockey. The NFL plays only a few games each season, but generates significant revenues from national television broadcasts and merchandising. Baseball, though not so well supported by the national media compared to the NFL, plays a 162-game season, twice that of NHL teams and in larger stadia than have yet been constructed for hockey.

REGION is designed to capture the understandable difference in impact of differing geographical areas. If the region being studied is a city, the dummy variable is set to 1. For a state or province, the variable is set to 0. If the area being measured is a state as opposed to a city, a higher multiplier can be justifiably applied. However, using the larger area also means that the initial impact should be smaller because the local area is expanded, reducing the number of revenue sources that can be defined as additional.

STAD accounts for the fact that a team's economic impact is, to a certain extent, dependent on the facility in which they play. The positive sign indicates that teams playing in new stadiums and arenas attract fans simply for the curiosity value, and thus should be expected to have a larger impact than those playing in older facilities. Of course, as the tenants of the once state-of-the-art Skydome in Toronto are finding out, curiosity is soon sated and attendance tends to fall back to its historical average. In an early study on attendance and pricing, Roger Noll (1974) set about to estimate the determinates of fan attendance in the four major leagues. One of the explanatory variables used by Noll was the age of the stadium. He found that in baseball, attendance will rise immediately after the construction of a new stadium but then decline steadily, until after a decade it has reverted back to the historical average (p. 124). However, Noll found little support for the claims that new facilities could dramatically improve attendance in other sports. The variable is set to 1 if the team played in a stadium that was constructed in the 10 years prior to the impact study and 0 if they played in an older park.

MULT is designed to capture the crucial estimation of the multiplier in the study. The positive sign demonstrates the hopefully obvious fact that a larger multiplier should result in a higher economic impact. The real question is whether the multiplier chosen is artificially inflated. It is entirely plausible for a state to have a higher multiplier than a city, and this would be a completely acceptable difference in the sample studies. However, as was pointed out earlier, in this sample states do not have higher multipliers than cities; in fact, it is the cities that have a higher multiplier than the states. Therefore, variations in multipliers cannot be considered acceptable differences between the studies.

LOCAL captures whether the study has made an attempt to distinguish between revenue sources. As mentioned in the previous section, it is crucial to distinguish between funds generated inside the local area, which are likely to be displaced from spending on other local goods, and money from outside the area that is genuinely additional. For example, although a team's share of national television revenue is genuinely additional, spending by local fans is not. This variable is set to 1 if local spending is included and 0 if only revenue from outside the area is used.

SWITCH captures a difficulty in including all visitor spending. Only visitors that are drawn to town because of the sports team should be included in calculating additional impact. Surveys should always include a question such as, "What is your reason for coming to Nantucket?" SWITCH will be set to 1 for studies that do not attempt to distinguish between visitors and 0 for those that do.

SHIFT accounts for the practice of shifting the geographical area between determining revenue sources and applying the multiplier. Obviously, a thoughtful study should maintain a consistent region, but this is not always the case. SHIFT is set to 1 for studies that shift boundaries and 0 for those that remain constant.

As has already been seen, the last three variables are not acceptable causes of variation. If all of these studies were conducted according to accepted economic impact study practices, the LOCAL, SWITCH, and SHIFT variables would all be set to 0.

Empirical results

The question that this regression is attempting to answer is to determine the extent to which the misapplications cited in the previous sections are significant in explaining the variation in the economic impacts of the studies. As was mentioned earlier, the number of observations in the regression is slightly larger than the number of studies, because a few of the studies presented different economic impacts for different assumptions or areas of study. For example, the study by Chicago offered different impacts for state and local areas and was based on whether a new stadium was constructed. For studies that have done this, each economic impact number is a separate observation connected to the specific estimates and assumptions used to arrive at the estimate. There are 19 observations in the regression.

In running any cross-sectional regression, the empiricist should be vigilant for potential heteroscedasticity. The White test is the most general (and currently the most widely used) test for detecting this potential empirical entanglement. Unfortunately, with the small sample size in this study, the White test is impractical because it involves regressing the squared residuals on the independent variables, their squares, and their crossmultiples. With this many independent variables, the sample size in this study is simply not large enough to produce reliable results (Gujarnti, 1988, p. 380). As an alternative test, more amenable to the small sample size, the Spearman's rank correlation test was used. This test first ranks the absolute values of the residuals with the variable, dependent or independent, to be tested. Using this data, the Spearman's rank correlation coefficient can be calculated in the following manner:

$$rs = 1 - 6\left[\Sigma d_i^2 / n(n^2 - 1)\right],$$

where d_i is the difference in the ranks assigned to each cross-section and n is the number of cross-sections. Using the t test, the rs can be tested for significance. If the t test is above the critical value, we can consider heteroscedasticity to be present (Gujarati, 1988, p. 373). Applying this test to each of the variables, it was found that heteroscedasticity was present between the residual and dependent variable. To correct for this problem, Shazam's hetcov option was used to perform White's Heteroscedastic-Consistent Covariance matrix estimation. The results are presented below.

$$\text{VAL} = 65 + 77\ \text{FOOT} + 88\ \text{BASE} - 37\ \text{REGION} + 4\ \text{STAD} + 11\ \text{MULT} +$$
$$\phantom{\text{VAL} = 65 +}(6.2)(7.0)(-1.9)(0.9)(1.3)$$

$$38\ \text{LOCAL} + 41\ \text{SWITCH} + 10\ \text{SHIFT}$$
$$(3.5)(3.4)(0.7)$$

adjusted $R^2 = .69$, F statistic $= 5.9$.

The model seems to perform reasonably well. The adjusted R^2 of .69 indicates that much of the variation in the dependent variable can be attributed to the explanatory variables. The F statistic of 5.9 is safely above the boundary levels for the F distribution at both the 6% and 1% confidence levels of 3.07 and 5.06, respectively.

Turning to an analysis of the individual variables, the numbers in parentheses are the t statistics for the explanatory variables. The coefficients of the variables represent millions of dollars. Individually, it appears as though studies on football and baseball teams claim a substantially larger impact than hockey. Baseball's larger positive coefficient relative to football also suggests that the larger number of fans attracted to baseball creates larger impact numbers in their studies than those on football. Whether the study area was a city or state is significant at the 10% level. The negative coefficient indicates that state-level studies increase the economic impact by $37 million. There seems to be no significant connection between whether a team is playing in a new stadium and the studies' estimation of economic impact.

Of more concern to this study is the significance of the last four variables. The inclusion of local spending was both positive and significant at the 5% level. The coefficient indicates that including local spending increases the economic impact by a rather substantial $38 million. Neglecting to distinguish visitors in town for the expressed purpose of the sporting contest from the rest of the tourist population attending the game is also significant at the 5% level. SWITCH has the predicted positive sign, and the coefficient shows that out distinguishing between the two types of tourists increases the size of final economic impact estimate by $41 million, This is important for those attempting to determine the validity of these studies, as these two variables appear to positively influence the final estimate. Surprisingly, the MULT variable was insignificant, indicating that much more of the variation between the studies is accounted for by the decision to use gross or net impacts than the choice of the size of the multiplier. The SHIFT variable was insignificant.

Conclusion

This article analyzed one of the most important aspects of the subsidization debate. Economic impact assessments are an important weapon in the subsidization debate, as the protransfer lobby seeks to prove that the team has a major economic impact on the city. The purpose of this section was to determine to what extent those studios are realistic reflections of the impact of the team, or whether they have taken advantage of the amount of discretion required in economic impact analysis to manipulate the results. Somewhat disappointingly, many of the studies violated what Crompton (1995) has identified as acceptable practices in conducting these studies. The most common violation was using gross rather than net impacts, but several studies have also used inflated multipliers, and a few have even shifted the area of study to increase the impact. The meta-analysis of those studies demonstrates that the decision to use gross or net impacts is the most significant cause of the rather large variation in impacts between the studies in the sample. The studies in this sample tended to use methodologies that would inflate the economic impact of the sports team being studied.

This is crucially important to the protransfer lobbying effort, because the economic impact of the few highly paid athletes and several lowly vendors employed by most professional teams is hardly readily apparent to the public. Therefore, teams must establish that they have an impact well beyond their meager employment figures. Fortunately for those in favor of the subsidy, economic impact studies have been, with varying degrees of credibility, able to do just that by arguing that professional sports teams substantially increase the level of economic activity in the region. Therefore, they play an important role in convincing voters that the team does indeed have a sizeable economic impact. In fact, it maybe possible that one of the reasons sports teams have been successful in their lobbying activities is that they have been able to show that they are an important economic engine for the region.

Appendix

Economic impact studies surveyed

*   Blair and Swindell (1997)
*   Center for Economic Education (1996)
*   City of Chicago (1986)
*   Conway and Beyers (1994)

- Conway and Beyers (1996)
- Coopers and Lybrand (1990)
- Deloitte and Touche (1993)
- Maryland Department of Economic & Employment Development (1992)
- Mayor Hoffman McCann & Mid-America Regional Council (1989)
- Melaniphy & Associates (1986)
- Schaffer and Davidson (1972)
- Schaffer and Davidson (1984)
- Silverstein (1900)

Acknowledgements

This article was significantly improved by the helpful suggestions of James Dean and John Loxley.

References

Baade, R., & Dye, R. (1990). The impact of stadiums and professional sports on metropolitan area development. *Growth and Change*, *20*(2), 1–14.

Blair, J., & Swindell, D. (1997). Sport, politics and economics: The Cincinnati story. In R. Noll & A. Zimbalist (Eds), *Sports, jobs and taxes: The economic impact of sports teams and stadiums* (pp. 282–323). Washington, DC: Brookings Institution.

Center for Economic Education. (1996). *The effects of the construction, operation and financing of new sports stadia on Cincinnati economic growth*. Cincinnati, OH: University of Cincinnati.

City of Chicago (1986). The economic impact of a major league baseball team on the local economy. Unpublished consultant report.

Conway, R., & Beyers, W. (1994). Seattle Mariners Baseball Club economic impact. Unpublished consultant report.

Conway, R., & Beyers, W. (1996). Seattle Seahawks economic impact. Unpublished consultant report.

Coopers and Lybrand. (1990). Winnipeg Jets Hockey Club: Report of the projected economic benefits of the club's operations. Unpublished consultant report.

Crompton, J.L. (1995). Economic impact analysis of sports facilities and events. *Journal of Sport Management*, *9*(1),14–35.

Deloitte and Touche. (1993). Economic impact study of a Major League Baseball stadium and franchise. Unpublished consultant report.

Gujarati, D.N. (1988). *Basic econometrics*. Toronto, Canada: McGraw-Hill.

Hefner, F. (1990). Using economic models to measure the impact of sports on local economies. *Journal of Sport and Social Issues*, *14*(1), 1–13.

Leistritz, L., & Murdock, S. (1981). *The socioeconomic impact of resource development: Methods for assessment*. Boulder, CO: Westview.

Maryland Department of Economic & Employment Development. (1992). Economic and fiscal impacts of Baltimore Orioles' 1992 season in Maryland. Unpublished consultant report.

Mayer Hoffman McCann & Mid-America Regional Council. (1989). The economic impact of the Kansas City Chiefs and Kansas City Royals on the state of Missouri. Unpublished consultant report.

Melaniphy & Associates. (1986). Chicago Cubs economic impact analysis. Unpublished consultant report.

Merrifield, J. (1987). A note on the general mathematical equivalency of economic base and aggregate input-output multipliers: Fact or fiction. *Journal of Regional Science*, *27*(4), 651–654.

Noll, R. (1974). Attendance and price setting. In R. Noll (Ed.), *Government and the sport business* (pp. 115–159). Washington, DC: Brookings Institution.

Schaffer, W., & Davidson, L. (1972). Economic impact of the Falcons on Atlanta: 1972. Unpublished consultant report.

Schaffer W., & Davidson, L. (1984). Economic impact of the Falcons on Atlanta: 1972. Unpublished consultant report.

Silverstein, P. (1990). The economic impact of Major League Baseball in Denver. Unpublished consultant report.

Vias, A.C., & Mulligan, G.F. (1997). Disaggregate economic base multipliers in small communities. *Environment and Planning A*, *29*, 955–974.

Chapter 19

B. Christine Green, Carla Costa, and Maureen Fitzgerald

MARKETING THE HOST CITY
Analyzing exposure generated by a sport event

Executive summary

SPORT EVENTS ARE INCREASINGLY used in the marketing of cities. Cities have justified the use of sport events as a component of their marketing mix on the basis of their power to attract event visitors, and to generate media exposure for the city. The exposure generated by an event is thought to build awareness of the host city as a desirable destination. The ability of sport events to attract visitation is well documented, but there has been little work examining the impact of event media. The purpose of this research was to determine the nature and extent of the television exposure generated for the city of San Antonio by hosting the 2002 NCAA Women's Final Four basketball tournament. The ESPN coverage of the tournament was content analyzed for any verbal mentions of San Antonio or its associated images, and for the variety and duration of San Antonio imagery that appeared in the ESPN broadcast coverage. Ten programs (11 hours and 46 minutes of coverage) were analyzed: (1) the Selection Show; (2) ESPN Sports Center broadcast on the Friday, Saturday, and Sunday of the tournament weekend; (3) pre-game show for each of the semi-final games and the championship game; (4) both semi-final games; and, (5) the national championship game. Over the 12 hours of coverage, "San Antonio" was mentioned 49 times and "the Alamodome" was mentioned 42 times. Further, "'Alamo", "River Walk", and "Texas" were mentioned a combined total of six times. Two main categories of images appeared in the telecasts – images of San Antonio and of the NCAA Women's Final Four logo. Visual imagery of San Antonio appeared for a total of 209 seconds, with the dominant images being the cityscape, River Walk, Alamodome, and Alamo. The logo appeared in 13 distinct contexts for a total of 1,716 seconds. The dominant logo context was the center court logo. Overall, the findings question the value of the exposure generated by events as a tool for place marketing. However, three key findings have practical implications for potential implementation of event-based place marketing strategies: (1) the minimal exposure obtained for the host city via event telecasts; (2) relative exposure obtained by the event logo and by actual host city images; and (3) the need for cities to differentiate themselves from their competitors. It is recommended that future event logos prominently integrate host city images, and that effort should be made to link those images to televised shots of actual host city imagery, perhaps including athletes and event personalities in the context of the city's locations or cultural settings. The host city should provide video imagery to event broadcasters that showcases distinctive (i.e. iconographic) imagery, and should work to create associations within those video clips which expand the range of the host city's recognizable icons. Logos should be kept simple to maintain clarity in a variety of contexts and from a variety of camera angles. Further, the host city should create relationships with event announcers through a hospitality program, and create written materials with easy-to-use facts and stories about the city, its sport, and the event venue. Suggestions for future research to expand the effectiveness of host cities' event leveraging are included.

Marketing the host city: analyzing exposure generated by a sport event

Introduction

Sport events have become a significant component of the product mix used to market cities (Bramwell and Rawding, 1994; van den Berg, Braun and Otgaar, 2000). Events serve two purposes. They attract visitors to cities during the time that events are taking place (Getz, 1998). They are also used to build awareness of the host city through the media exposure that is obtained (Brown, Chalip, Jago and Mules, 2002). Consumer awareness is thought to be valuable because it can help to build tourist visits and business relationships.

There has been a great deal of work examining the attraction that events have for those who attend (e.g. Green and Chalip, 1998; Madrigal, 1095; Pearce, 1993), but there has been comparatively little work examining the media impacts of events. A recent experimental study (Chalip, Green and Hill, in press) reported that event media affect viewers perceptions of the host destination, but often not in ways that had been anticipated by the event hosts. The authors suggest that the effects of event exposure may depend on the type of exposure obtained. They suggest that further work is needed to examine the volume of exposure that events actually generate, and to determine the nature of that exposure. The nature and volume of exposure obtained by the host city was not, however, reported in that study.

The nature of exposure that cities obtain through sport event telecasts is of interest for two reasons. First, by mapping the nature of exposure, it should be possible to develop specific strategies to optimize the impact that events have on the city's brand (Chalip, 2001). Second, the funding that sport events obtain may be enhanced. Sport events are often made feasible as a result of the public subsidies that they obtain (Mules, 1998, Roche, 1994). Public subsidies are legitimized by the claimed benefits that events have for the host city. Media coverage of an event is claimed to enhance the tourism image of a destination resulting in long-term positive effects of tourism on the economy (Dwyer, Mellor, Mistilis and Mules, 2000; Ritchie and Smith, 1991). But several analysts have questioned whether the actual benefits are as positive as those that were claimed by event organizers (e.g. Chalip and Leyns, 2002: Putsis, 1998: Whitson and Macintosh, 1996). If the value of events to development of the city's market position can be optimized, then the support that event organizers claim for their event will be better legitimized.

This paper begins with a brief review of work on events and consumer awareness of cities. It then derives research questions, and reports a content analytic study of the exposure that San Antonio obtained by hosting the NCAA Women's Final Four basketball tournament. The paper then identifies specific tactics that city marketers can use to optimize the exposure that a host city obtains via event telecasts. It concludes by suggesting new directions for future research.

Events and consumer awareness of cities

A substantial volume of research has examined the role that product awareness plays in consumer decision making. That work finds that brands which are most salient to the consumer are most likely to be chosen (Aaker and Day, 1974; Batra and Lehmann, 1995; Hoyer and Brown, 1990). The basis for this effect has been modelled with reference to the processes by which consumers develop a product choice. That work shows that consumers first identify a pool of potential purchases that they will consider, and then evaluate the alternatives in order to make a final choice (Peter and Olson, 2001). Crompton and his colleagues (Crompton, 1992; Crompton and Ankomah, 1993; Um and Crompton, 1992) have shown that this same process drives tourists' choice of destinations.

The implications for city marketers are clear. In order to build tourism, they must first bring their city into the consideration set of potential tourists. In other words, they must enhance the saliency and attractiveness at their destination. The staging of a major sport event provides a city with a unique opportunity to reach a large national (and sometimes international) audience. To enhance the return on their investment in broadcast rights for the event, broadcasters provide lengthy coverage of events, often at peak viewing times. Thus, broadcasts of major events tend to provide extensive event coverage to a broad viewing audience. Coverage of the Olympic Games is a prime example of the effective exposure that an event can provide a city. Ritchie and Smith (1991) showed, in the case of the Olympic Games, media coverage increased the saliency and attractiveness of Calgary as a destination.

Although the demonstration of an effect of Olympic media is encouraging, there are grounds for wondering whether the effect would be comparable for other events. The Olympic Games obtain a volume of media coverage that is not typically obtained by other events, including an array of stories that go well beyond the sport competitions themselves (Real, 1989; Whannel, 1992). The vast majority of events obtain coverage of the competition itself with, perhaps, some pre and post-event color commentary about the competition. The event's host city may be only minimally featured in this coverage, and then only as background scenery.

The coverage of a city during an event does not represent a targeted message controlled by city marketers. Rather, the images and messages communicated to audiences are a haphazard collage of images gathered, selected and edited by the broadcaster. These images and messages may last for little more than a few seconds at a time. Whether they will be processed by the audience will depend on the nature of the imagery and the commentary. Iconographic images or place references are particularly likely to be recognized and remembered (Sternberg, 1997; Vivanco, 2001). Recent work in destination iconography shows that unique architecture, natural features, or place names can play a significant role in building and reinforcing the saliency a destination has for tourists (Hill, Arthurson and Chalip, 2001).

In essence, this work shows that two elements of exposure through event media are important from the standpoint of cities that seek to market themselves through events. First, it is necessary to know how often the host city is shown, mentioned, or represented. This is comparable to the measurement of exposure frequency which is standard when evaluating the effects of sponsorship (Howard and Crompton, 1995). Second, it is necessary to know what was shown or mentioned, and how it represents the city. In other words, one needs to know whether the city was shown as a distinctive entity, or merely as an indistinguishable urban backdrop to the event itself. Despite the pivotal nature of these two forms of information, the quantity and forms of host city representation have not been the focus of previous research. Rather, previous work has considered what the effects of exposures are (e.g. Chalip *et al.*, in press; Ritchie and Smith, 1991), but has not formulated a quantitative or qualitative examination of the exposures themselves.

Research questions

This study examines the nature and extent of the television exposure generated for the city of San Antonio, Texas, as a result of hosting the 2002 NCAA Women's Final Four basketball tournament. On the basis of the literature reviewed, the following research questions were formulated:

1   How extensive is the host city's exposure during the telecast of a large and nationally significant sport event?
2   What kinds of city mentions and city images occur during the telecast?

Method

A content analysis of 11 hours and 46 minutes of videotape forms the basis of this study. Five program types were included in the analysis: (1) the NCAA Women's Final Four selection show; (2) three ESPN Sports Center broadcasts (Friday, Saturday, and Sunday of the tournament weekend); (3) pre-game show for each of the semi-final games and the championship game; (4) both semi-final games and the championship game; and (5) two ESPN Spots promoting the NCAA Women's Final Four. All programs were broadcast on ESPN, and videotaped for later analysis.

Setting

San Antonio is the eighth largest city in the United States, and the second largest city in Texas. The city covers 430 square miles in South Central Texas, and boasts a population of over 1.14 million. San Antonio was once a small settlement founded by Spanish missionaries in the early 1700s, and its historical charm and grace are preserved in the Alamo and its other Spanish missions, in its historic neighborhoods, and in the River

Walk. Tourism is a key industry in San Antonio, with the city attracting close to seven million visitors a year. The city's most famous landmark is the Alamo, an old Spanish mission where, in 1836, 189 men defended the mission against 4,000 Mexican troops for 13 days. The cry "Remember the Alamo" became the rallying point of the Texan revolution against Mexico. San Antonio is so closely linked with the Alamo that the city's main indoor arena is called the Alamodome. The selection show, pre-game shows, and all basketball games for the 2002 NCAA Women's Final Four were broadcast from the Alamodome.

In more recent times, San Antonio has become famous for its River Walk – a series of cobblestone and flagstone paths which border both sides of the San Antonio River as it stretches for approximately two-and-a-half miles through the middle of the business district. The River Walk is quiet and park-like in some stretches, while other areas include European-style sidewalk cafes, specialty boutiques, nightclubs and high-rise hotels. Riverboats and barges provide a unique way to experience downtown San Antonio. Tourism marketing communications make strong use of the city's association with these two landmarks (i.e. Alamo and River Walk).

Procedure

The content analysis followed the general guidelines proposed by Neuendorf (2002) and Weber (1990). First, coders engaged in code training for both verbal mentions and imagery. During this stage, the coders developed lists of the types of verbal mentions and visual images appearing in the broadcasts. The coders shared their lists and discussed the emerging categories and assignment rules with the other coders. This initial process allowed for the clarification of some ambiguous rules, the development of more precise definitions, and the addition of new categories. Definitions for each coding category were agreed upon and compiled in a coding manual (see Appendix). Coding matrices were developed for each analysis – visual and verbal. Specific image or verbal types were listed down the left side of the matrix, and each occurrence was listed along the top. Coders then entered the duration of each occurrence by its image type.

The second phase consisted of pilot coding. During this phase, coders individually analyzed a sample of the telecasts. Inter coder reliability assessed at the pilot coding phase yielded a coefficient of reliability greater than .90 for all variables, a figure deemed "acceptable to all" by Neuendorf (2002, p. 143). Consequently, the researchers felt confident regarding the viability of the coding scheme.

In the final analysis, two researchers independently coded each telecast twice. First, the telecast was coded for the number and type of verbal name mentions of San Antonio or San Antonio-related words (e.g. Alamodome, Alamo, River Walk). In the second analysis, coders recorded the types of San Antonio-related images (i.e. what was shown), and the duration of those images (i.e. how many seconds the image appeared on the screen). The achieved coefficient of reliability was greater than .90 for a but two variables. In both cases, the broadcast was then analyzed by a third researcher. The two scores that correlated at .90 or higher were used to calculate aggregate scores. Aggregate scores were created by averaging the two researchers reports of the total time that image appeared during a broadcast.

The primary coders were aware of the purpose of the study. However, a blind coder was also used as a third coder in several telecasts with the specific purpose of checking

Table 19.1 Verbal mentions by broadcast

	Min	San Antonio	Alamo-dome	Texas	River Walk	Alamo	Total
Selection Show	55	8	0	1	1	0	**10**
Sports Center							
Friday	55	2	1	0	0	0	**3**
Saturday	55	2	0	0	0	0	**2**
Sunday	55	4	3	1	0	0	**8**
Semi-final: Duke vs Oklahoma							
Pre-game	25	4	6	0	0	3	**13**
Game	130	10	7	0	0	0	**17**
Semi-final: Tenn vs UConn							
Pre-game	25	0	3	0	0	0	**3**
Game	125	12	8	0	1	0	**21**
Championship: UConn vs OK							
Pre-game	35	1	6	0	0	0	**7**
Game	145	6	8	0	0	1	**15**
Total	**11:45**	**49**	**42**	**2**	**2**	**4**	**99**

for coding bias by the researcher-coders (Neuendorf, 2002; Sparkman, 1996). In all cases primary coders' results matched those of the blind coder (r >.90).

Results

Results are reported in three sections. The first section focuses on verbal mentions during the broadcasts; the second examines actual images of San Antonio; and the third considers images of the NCAA Women's Final Four logo. Each section reports both the nature (i.e. type) and extent (i.e. quantity) of the message or image by broadcast.

Verbal mentions

There few name mentions during the broadcasts (see Table 19.1). The majority of mentions were for the city itself and for the Alamodomo facility. Many of these mentions occurred as the broadcast segued from a commercial break to the event broadcast. There were no direct or indirect mentions of San Antonio in either of the ESPN promotional spots that were analyzed.

San Antonio imagery

San Antonio imagery appeared for a total of 209 seconds during the telecasts examined (see Table 19.2). This is nearly the equivalent of seven 30-second commercial spots. Three distinctly San Antonio images appear: the Alamo, the Alamodome, and the River Walk.

Table 19.2 Visual imagery of San Antonio (seconds on-screen)

	City-scape	Alamo-dome	River Walk	Alamo	Texas	Other	Total
Selection Show	21	3	8	2	2	0	**36**
Sports Center							
Friday	4	0	0	0	0	0	**4**
Saturday	0	0	0	0	0	0	**0**
Sunday	0	0	0	0	0	0	**0**
Semi-final: Duke vs Oklahoma							
Pre-game	1	0	34	1	0	5	**41**
Game	21	0	0	0	0	0	**21**
Semi-final: Tenn vs UConn							
Pre-game	0	0	0	0	0	0	**0**
Game	11	20	14	0	0	0	**45**
Championship: UCoun vs OK							
Pre-game	0	0	0	0	0	0	**0**
Game	25	13	3	18	3	0	**62**
Total	**83**	**36**	**59**	**21**	**5**	**5**	**209**

Note: Descriptions of the image categories appear in Appendix 1.

The River Walk received nearly one full minute of exposure, half of that appearing in the pre-game show for the first semi-final game. The exterior of the Alamodome appeared for 36 seconds, and the Alamo itself appeared for 21 seconds. These three iconic images are strongly and distinctively associated with San Antonio. The cityscape (i.e. the downtown area of San Antonio) appeared for 83 seconds. Many of these were night images, and nearly a quarter of these images included an image of the Tower of the Americas (a structure similar to Seattle's Space Needle, Toronto's CN Tower, and Sydney's Contrepoint Tower). Neither images of the cityscape nor images of the Tower of the Americas could be clearly identified by coders as an image of San Antonio. Rather, these images could have been images of any number of other urban centers. The images were matched to known San Antonio landmarks during construction of the coding manual, thus were included in the final analysis. Images representing the remaining categories, "Texas" and "other", appeared in several video montages along with images of the city and its icons. These montages nearly always appeared at the start of the broadcast.

Images of the NCAA Women's Final Four Logo

The logo (Figure 19.1) made good use of the Alamo image as a San Antonio icon, and prominently displays the words, "San Antonio." The strong San Antonio associations embedded in the logo are particularly important when considering the relative exposure of San Antonio through the logo versus through actual images of the city. Total exposure gained through San Antonio images was just 209 seconds. The logo obtained 1,716 seconds of coverage – more than eight times the exposure of actual San Antonio images.

Figure 19.1 2002 NCAA Women's Final Four logo

The logo appeared in numerous forms and contexts throughout the broadcasts (see Appendix 1 for a description of various logo forms). The most prominent logo was the center court floor logo. The exposure time for this logo is somewhat misleading. Of the 931 seconds that this logo was visible, it was the main focus of the camera shot just 10 percent of the time. At all other times (i.e. 90 percent of the total time), it was shown while players moved from one end of the court to the other during play. Not surprisingly, the clarity of the center court logo varied. Its impact was greatest when it was the sole focus of the camera shot and weakest during high speed play.

In general, the clarity and visibility of the logos varied dramatically. Depictions of large logos and close-ups of logos produced the highest level of clarity. The large logo on the exterior of the Alamodome was a powerful but rarely-shown image. Close-up camera shots of the large banner inside the Alamodome, the logos appearing on the set (especially the logo on the front of the anchor desk which appeared in the Selection Show), and the computer-generated logos (i.e. full screen, ⅓ screen, corner screen) that appeared on-screen throughout the broadcasts were the clearest and most recognizable of the logos.

The clarity of other logos varied greatly. The scoreboard logo appeared often, but mainly in the distant background of the announcer's set. Logos appearing on the scorer's table, the basket supports, and the chairbacks were never the sole focus of a camera shot. Rather, these logos appeared in the background as the camera focussed on players and coaches.

Lastly, several images were so subtle that they largely went unnoticed. In several cases, the Words "Alamodome, San Antonio, Texas" appeared at the bottom of the television screen during play. Anyone focussed on the game would have had difficulty recognizing this text. Similarly, the outline of the Alamo on the court inside the three-point line was an interesting, albeit subtle touch. The variety of the logo appearances and the duration of those appearances are shown in Table 19.3.

Discussion

One of the clearest yet most surprising finding from this study is the relative paucity of mentions or images obtained by the host city (San Antonio imagery appeared in only three-and-a-half minutes of the nearly 12 hours of coverage). The broadcaster's focus is

Table 19.3 Visual images of the NCAA Women's Final Four Logo (seconds on-screen

	Centre court	Full screen	½ screen	Corner screen	Scoreboard	Banner	Set logo	Desk logo	Scorers' table	Chairbacks	Basket support	Exterior dome	Screen words	Total
Selection Show	0	0	0	0	0	0	0	181	0	0	0	0	0	**181**
Sports Center														
Friday	12	6	0	6	0	0	0	0	0	2	2	0	4	**32**
Saturday	3	0	10	0	0	0	0	0	0	0	0	0	0	**13**
Sunday	4	0	0	0	0	0	0	0	2	0	0	0	0	**6**
Semi-final: Duke vs Oklahoma														
Pre-game	0	17	0	18	1	5	4	0	0	0	0	4	0	**49**
Game	240	6	0	0	24	5	3	0	0	0	0	0	30	**308**
Semi-final: Tenn vs UConn														
Pre-game	12	6	0	17	9	0	0	0	0	0	0	0	7	**51**
Game	230	9	0	0	18	6	0	0	0	9	6	0	47	**345**
Championship: UConn vs OK														
Pre-game	10	0	10	56	19	22	2	0	2	0	2	1	11	**135**
Game	400	10	0	37	57	29	3	0	13	17	21	2	7	**596**
Total	**931**	**54**	**20**	**134**	**128**	**67**	**12**	**181**	**17**	**28**	**31**	**7**	**106**	**1,716**

Note: Descriptions of the categories appear in the appendix.

on the competition itself, not on the city that is hosting it. Given the fact that the broadcaster is there to cover the event, and not to promote the city, this finding makes intuitive sense. Nevertheless, the zeal with which cities compete with one another to host events suggests that they expect more exposure, at least as background, than was found here, as recent studies of event and destination marketers' expectations and strategies demonstrate (Emery, 2002; Jago, Chalip, Brown, Mules and Ali, 2002). Although media exposure is only one potential objective for hosting an event, other objectives (e.g. attracting tourism, positioning the city as a site for future events) rely on media exposure to enhance viewer awareness of the city as a destination.

In fact, the total exposure obtained by San Antonio was arguably greater than might have been obtained by a host city that lacked San Antonio's distinctive iconography. The majority of the city's exposure occurred not through explicit mentions or visuals but, rather, as a consequence of a well-chosen event logo which obtained consistent exposure during the event telecast. Since the logo included the city's name and referenced the city's most famous landmark, the Alamo, its appearance gave San Antonio the lions share of its exposure. That exposure was complemented by mentions of the event venue – a venue that was named after the city's most distinctive icon, the Alamo. Consequently, mentions of the venue and visuals of the logo jointly reinforced the events connection to the Alamo, and thus to San Antonio.

The value of iconography to the total exposure is further illustrated by the finding that simple visuals of cityscapes do not seem to identify the host city. Researchers found it difficult to code images of downtown San Antonio because cityscapes without distinctive icons look very much like one another, there is nothing to clue viewers to the identity of what is being shown and there is nothing to anchor the visual in memory. Thus, even it a host city were to obtain more visual exposure during an event, there is no reason to expect that the exposure would have promotional value unless it were tied to something distinctive or readily recognizable (cf. MacInnis and Price, 1987; Potter, 1999).

The nature of icons may also be important. Although the Alamo is distinctive because of its shape and its history, River Walk is much harder to encapsulate in a short visual sequence. This is, in part, because of its geographic, size (two-and-a-half miles in length). It is also because River Walk is intended as an iconographic *experience*, rather than as an iconographic image. Experience is not easily captured in a short visual or brief mention (Pine and Gilmore, 1999; MacAloon, 1989), This suggests that the host city will be best represented when it links its events to icons that are readily captured and recognized in short televised images.

In fact, most of the visual exposures obtained by San Antonio were short (lasting only a few seconds) and were embedded in the context of event actions and activities. Given their short duration and peripheral status, they may not have been perceived by many viewers. Although there is substantial work suggesting that advertising need not be noticed in order to be effective (Debner and Jacoby, 1994; Shapiro, MacInnis and Heckler, 1997), it is not clear that these particular exposures would have value comparable to that of dedicated ads or signage.

Taken as a whole, the findings of this study question the overall value of events as tools for place marketing. This is not to say that events have no effect; rather it is to suggest that event media may not be a particularly potent source of exposure. The results of this study show that the exposure that will be generated depends not on the fact of hosting an event, but on the ways that event symbols and venues represent the host city and its distinctive icons. Thus, the value of an event as a place marketing tool depends on the ways that hosting is leveraged. The derivative implications and recommendations for effective leveraging of events by host cities are considered in the following section.

Implications and recommendations

From a practical standpoint, the findings suggest the utility of drawing implications in four areas: (1) maximizing total exposure for the host city; (2) incorporating city images into event logos; (3) considering the size, placement, and content of images; and (4) differentiating the host city. The following sections extend the findings of this study, consider practical implications, and derive recommendations for event end city marketing.

Maximizing total exposure

Effective place marketing starts with consumer awareness of a city as a destination. As with other forms of advertising and promotion, more frequent exposure results in increased awareness for a product or service (D'Souza and Rao, 1995; Krugman, 1993), in this case, the city itself. Thus, city marketers need to find ways to increase the meager exposure obtained via event broadcasts. One could negotiate with the broadcasters to include a minimum number of name mentions during an event broadcast. However, the host city is often not included in negotiations for broadcast rights. Rather, the broadcaster contracts with the event owner directly. Fortunately, this is not the only tactic available to host cities.

In the absence of a contract with the broadcaster, the host city has two indirect routes to increased exposure The first is through the event announcers. Sports announcers are often left to their own devices to fill airtime. As is sometimes painfully obvious, these people do not always have relevant information to share with the audience, and may resort to personal anecdotes and the like. Proactive city marketers could provide event announcers with a concise, easy-to-use reference book or card with interesting facts, figures, and narrative snippets about the city, its characters, and the competition venue. Further, host cities might consider hosting event announcers prior to the event in order to provide them with stories and experiences of the city. In many cases, broadcasters have little time to prepare for an event assignment. Thus cities could plan to provide broadcasters with an experience of the destination. A memorable experience may often find its way into the event broadcast, particularly when announcers are required to fill time.

Visual exposures can be increased in much the same way – by making things easy for the broadcaster. The host city can provide images to media and event owners showcasing distinctive city imagery and/or athletes and other event personalities in recognizable locations or cultural settings associated with the city. These can be provided to broadcasters in the form of video postcards, or as short montages of images.

Incorporating city images into event logos

The findings of this study show that San Antonio obtained eight times more exposure via the event logo than was obtained via actual city images. Thus, the importance of a well-designed event logo cannot be understated. The logo for the 2002 NCAA Women's Final Four worked well for San Antonio insomuch as it garnered the greatest relative exposure for the city and its primary icon. The words "San Antonio" featured prominently, and a silhouette of the Alamo was incorporated into the design. Event hosts would do well to ensure that icons, city imagery and the city name appear prominently in their event logos.

Further, it would be useful to forge positive associations among the city images, the event logo, consumers perceptions of the event, and their perceptions of the city as a destination. A good start would be to link the images provided to media and event owners to the images that appear on the logo. By assisting the audience to make associations of this type, the excitement and interest in the event can translate into increased awareness and interest in the city as a destination.

Considering the size, placement and content of images

Not all exposures of the logo are equivalent. Neither are all exposures of city images. Some logo images are larger than others; some are seen from a more favorable camera angle; some are the central focus, while some are not. In order to make the logo easily recognizable from a variety of camera angles and in a variety of contexts, event hosts should keep the logo design simple, and use colors in a way that clearly differentiates the name and imagery of the host city from their background.

This study has also highlighted the potential value of a city's iconographic images. Some San Antonio images are highly and uniquely identifiable with San Antonio, while others are not distinguishable from those of any other city. For example, the River Walk is a recognizable San Antonio image, whereas the Tower of the Americas could easily be mistaken for one of the many towers that have become common to American cities.

The River Walk, although clearly a San Antonio image, was portrayed in a piecemeal fashion. Images of parts of the River Walk were sometimes embedded in the event broadcasts. However the *experience* of the River Walk may have been better communicated through a co-ordinated series of River Walk images and sounds (e.g. a montage created with images of the canal boats, cafes, shopping, scenery, and art backed with Mariachi music). After all, experience marketing is based on the necessity of building holistic experiences through sensory, affective, and creative associations (O'Sullivan and Spangler, 1998; Schmitt, 1999).

Differentiating the host city

San Antonio's distinctive iconography – particularly the Alamo – gives it a competitive advantage when seeking to build the city's brand via an event. A great deal of the city's exposure came as a result of Alamo silhouettes and the association of the Alamo with the competition venue, the Alamodome. There were also verbal references, such as "These players sure will remember the Alamo." Whenever possible, host cities should seek to build and use the icons uniquely associated with the city in order to differentiate it as a destination. The city's iconography should appear in logos, in venue names, as names for mascots or for a group of volunteers.

Cities may also want to develop a long-term strategy to build audience recognition of two or three additional city icons in order to expand the array of potential iconographic linkages. One strategy to create associations and to expand the range of recognizable imagery of the host city is to develop short video clips for event broadcasters in which images of well known icons (e.g. the Alamo in San Antonio) segue into images of less well known features (e.g. in the case of San Antonio, the Alamodome). In this way, host cities can build the array of images which can be used to differentiate the city from other tourist destinations.

Further research

The findings from this study hint at ways in which events can be integrated into the marketing strategies of destinations. However, further research could greatly aid cities efforts to obtain the greatest impact from telecasts of the events that they host. Content analysis looks only at source characteristics. Consequently, this study identified the nature of exposure obtained through event broadcasts, but the effect of that exposure on audiences is not clear. Future research should explore the impact that short exposures of the kinds found in this study have on *audience* perceptions of the host destination (cf. Shapiro *et al.*, 1997). That work should also examine the degree to which different exposure contexts (competitive action, time outs, etc.) make a difference in the effect obtained (cf. Kumar, 2000).

Indeed, the choice of event also varies the exposure context. Events appeal to different market segments, vary in duration, and present varying opportunities for destination-specific exposure. The NCAA Women's Final Four, although growing in stature as an event, has yet to attain the same level of attention and potential for exposure that is obtained by other major events, such as the Super Bowl, the World Series, or the Olympics. Future research should compare the nature and extent of exposure generated by different events. Further, research should begin to identify the event elements that are associated with more effective exposure for the host city.

The focus of this study was on television exposure. Event telecasts, albeit important, are only one source of exposure available to host cities. It would be beneficial to extend our work by examining the quantity and types of exposure generated through a variety of distribution channels (e.g. print media, outdoor advertising, attendance, word-of-mouth, Internet).

The vital role played by a city's icons was also highlighted in this study. Yet we know very little about how icons develop, what makes one icon preferable to another, or how to use icons most effectively in city marketing. Research is needed that explores the development and application of urban icons (cf. Hill *et al.*, 2001; Sternberg, 1997; Vivanco, 2001).

In this study, the event logo obtained the lion's share of the city exposure during event telecasts. It was argued that the event logo should consequently make use of the host city icons and the host city name. Further work is needed to explore the features that help event logos to build an optimal association with the city and its desired brand. This includes the best means to incorporate the city name and images, as well as associated design characteristics, such as color, style, and layout. That work should examine the best means to combine the logos imagery with other images of the city which are likely to be televised during an event.

Concluding observation

It is clear that the advantages afforded by event media for city marketers will depend substantially on the ways that the city's distinctive names and imagery are deployed in the design of the event, its venue, and its symbols. These are matters over which event organizers have a significant degree of control. Nevertheless, this study suggests that there is a great deal more to be learned in order to optimally formulate the necessary tactical elements. Further research along the lines indicated here would provide a strengthened empirical base for the development and implementation of strategies to optimize the impact of hosting events. That, in turn, could give savvy marketers a competitive advantage.

References

Aaker, D.A. and Day, G.S. (1974), "A dynamic model of relationships among advertising, consumer awareness, and behavior". *Journal of Applied Psychology*, 59, pp. 281–286.
Batra, R. and Lehmann, D.R. (1995), "When does advertising have an impact? A study of tracking data". *Journal of Advertising Research*, (5), pp. 19–32.

Bramwell, B. and Rawding, L. (1994), "Tourism marketing organizations in industrial cities: Organizations objectives and urban governance". *Tourism Management*, 15, pp. 425–434.

Brown G., Chalip, L., Jago, L. and Mules, T. (2002), The Sydney Olympics and Brand Australia. In Morgan, N., Pritchard, A. and Price, R. (eds), Destination branding: Creating the unique destination proposition (pp. 163–185). Oxford, UK: Butterworth-Heinemann.

Chalip, L. (2001), Sport and tourism – capitalizing on the linkage. In Kluka, D. and Schilling, G., (eds), The business of sport (pp. 71–90) Oxford, UK: Meyer & Meyer Sport.

Chalip, L., Green, B.C. and Hill, B. (2003), "Effects of sport event media on destination image and intention to visit". *Journal of Sport Management*, 17(3), pp. 214–234.

Chalip, L. and Leyns, A. (2002), "Local business leveraging of a sport event: Managing an event for economic benefit". *Journal of Sport Management*, 16, pp. 132–158.

Crompton, J.L. (1992), "Structure of vacation destination choice sets". *Annals of Tourism Research*, 19, pp. 420–434.

Crompton, J.L. and Ankomah, P.K. (1993), "Choice set propositions in destination decisions" *Annals of Tourism Research*, 20, pp. 461–476.

Debner, W.A. and Jacoby, L.L. (1994), "Unconscious perception: Attention awareness, and control". *Journal of Experimental Psychology: Learning, Memory, Cognition*, 20, pp. 304–317.

D'Souza, G. and Rao, R.C. (1995), "Can repeating an advertisement more frequently than the competition affect brand preference in mature markets?" *Journal of Marketing*, 59(2), pp. 32–42.

Dwyer, L., Mellor, R., Mistilis, N. and Mules, T. (2000), "A framework for assessing 'tangible' and 'intangible' impacts of events and conventions". *Event Management*, 6, pp. 175–189.

Emery, P.R. (2002), "Bidding to host a major sports event: The local organising committee perspective". *International Journal of Public Sector Management*, 15, pp. 316–335.

Getz, B. (1998), "Trends, strategies, and issues in sport-event tourism". *Sport Marketing Quarterly*, 7(2), pp. 8–13.

Green, B.C. and Chalip, L. (1998), "Sport tourism as the celebration of subculture". *Annals of Tourism Research*, 25, pp. 275–291.

Hill, B., Arthurson, T. and Chalip, L. (2001), Kangaroos in the marketing of Australia. Potentials and practice. Gold Coast, Australia: Cooperative Research Centre for Sustainable Tourism.

Howard, D.R. and Crompton, J.L. (1995), Financing sport. Morgantown, WV: Fitness Information Technology.

Hoyer, W.D. and Brown, S.P. (1990), "Effects of brand awareness on choice for a common, repeat purchase product". *Journal of Consumer Research*, 17, pp. 141–148.

Jago, L., Chalip, L., Brown, G., Mules, T. and Ali, S. (2002), The role of events in helping to brand a destination. In Jago, L., Deery, M., Harris, A., Hede, A. and Allen, J. (eds), *Events and pace making: Proceedings of the International Event Research Conference* (pp. 111–143), Sydney: Australian Centre for Event Management.

Krugman, J. (1993, September 6), "More is indeed better". *Media Week*, 3(36), pp. 14–15.

Kumar, A. (2000), "Interference effects of contextual cues in advertisements on memory for ad content". *Journal of Consumer Psychology*, 9, pp. 155–166.

MacAloon, J.J. (1989), Festival, ritual and television. In Jackson, R. (ed.), *The Olympic movement and the mass media: Past, present and future issues* (pp. 6/21–6/40), Calgary: Hurford.

MacInnis, D.J. and Price, L.L. (1987), "The role of imagery in information processing: Review and extensions". *Journal of Consumer Research*, 13, pp. 473–491.

Madrigal, R. (1995), "Cognitive and affective determinants of fan satisfaction with sporting event attendance". *Journal of Leisure Research*, 27, pp. 205–228.

Mules, T. 'Taxpayer subsidies for major sporting events". *Sport Management Review*, 1, pp. 25–43.

Neuendorf, K.A. (2002), The content analysis guidebook. Thousand Oaks, CA: Sage Publications.

O'Sullivan, E.L. and Spangler, K.J. (1998), Experience marketing: Strategies for the new millennium. State College, PA: Venture Publishing.

Pearce, P.L. (1993), "An examination of event motivations: A case study". *Festival Management and Event Tourism*, 1, pp. 5–10.

Peter, J.P. and Olson, J.C. (2001), Consumer behaviour (6th edn). New York: McGraw-Hill.

Pine, B.J. and Filmore, J.H. (1999), The experience economy: Work is theatre & every business a stage. Boston, MA: Harvard Business School Press.

Potter, M.C. (1999), Understanding sentences and scenes: The role of conceptual short-term memory. In Coltheart, V., (ed.), Fleeting memories: Cognition of brief visual stimuli (pp. 13–46), Cambridge, MA: MIT Press.

Putsis, W.P. (1998), "Winners and losers: Redistribution and the use of economic impact analysis in marketing", *Journal of Macromarketing*, 18, pp. 24–33.

Real, M.R. (1989), Super media: A cultural studies approach. Newbury Park, CA: Sage.

Ritchie, J.R.B. and Smith, B. (1991), "The impact of mega-event on host region awareness: A longitudinal study". *Journal of Travel Research*, 30(1), pp. 3–10.

Roche, M. (1994), "Mega-events and urban policy", *Annals of Tourism Research*, 21, pp. 1–19.

Schmitt, B.H. (1999), Experiential marketing, New York: Free Press.

Shapiro, S., MacInnis, D.J. and Heckler, S.E. (1997), "The effects of incidental and exposure on the formation of consideration sets", *Journal of Consumer Research*, 24, pp. 94–104.

Sparkman, R. (1996), "Regional geography, the overlooked sampling in advertising content analysis", *Journal of Current Issues and Research in Advertising*, 18(2), pp. 70–79.

Sternberg, E. (1997), "The iconography of the tourism experience", *Annals of Tourism Research*, 24, pp. 951–969.

Um, S. and Crompton, J.L. (1990), "Attitude determinants in tourism destination choice". *Annals of Tourism Research*, 17, pp. 432–448.

Van den Berg, L., Braun, E. and Otgaar, A.H.J. (2000), Sports and city marketing in European cities. Rotterdam, The Netherlands: Euricur.

Vivanco, L.A. (2001), "Spectacular quetzals, ecotourism, and environmental futures in Monte Verde, Costa Rica", *Ethnology*, 40(2), pp. 79–92.

Weber, R. (1990), *Basic content analysis* (2nd edn), Newbury Park, CA: Sage.

Whannel, G. (1992), *Fields in vision: Television sport and cultural transformation*, London: Routledge.

Whitson, D. and Macintosh, D. (1996), "The global circus: International sport, tourism, and the marketing of cities", *Journal of Sport and Social Issues*, 20, pp. 278–297.

Appendix 1

Visual imagery of San Antonio (Table 19.2)

Cityscape	includes scenes of the Tower of the Americas in Hemisfair Park, the downtown skyline at night, and various street scenes.
River Walk	includes scenes of the restaurants and water, and of the shopping center area (with minimal water visible).
Texas	includes a plaque in the shape of Texas and the flag of Texas.
Other	includes a country scene (horses in a field) and a mariachi band.

Visual images of the NCAA Women Final Four Logo (Table 19.3)

Center Court	includes shots in passing during the game (80 percent +) and shots from the top of the arena looking down on to the logo.
Full screen	computer generated NCAA Women's Final Four logo.
1/3 screen	computer generated NCAA Women's Final Four logo.
Corner screen	computer generated NCAA Women's Final Four logo.
Scoreboard	quality/readability were an issue. The vast majority (80 percent) of the scoreboard images containing the NCAA Women's Final Four logo are viewed from quite a distance and/or serve as background for action or interview shots.
Banner	quality/readability were an issue. The vast majority (80 percent) of the banner images containing the NCAA Women's Final Four logo are viewed from quite a distance and/or serve as background for views of the whole court.
Set Logo	NCAA Women's Final Four logo which was located off to the side of the commentator's anchor desk.
Desk Logo	placed on the front of the anchor desk during the Selection Show.
Scorer's Table	logo on the banner attached to the front of the scorer's table.
Logo	It was not often shown and was typically only visible in the background when the camera focussed on the players and/or coach.
Chairbacks	logo on the backrests of the players' chairs and was not often shown. The few times it was visible were during player introductions or faintly in the background when the camera focussed on players.
Basket Support	(i.e. Basket Standard) – only ones that were readable were recorded (i.e. few were clear and/or readable).
Exterior Dome	logo on the outside of the Alamodome it was very vibrant but not often shown.
Screen Words	the words "San Antonio" occasionally appeared at the bottom of the screen and were sometimes in conjunction with Alamodome.

Chapter 20

B. Christine Green

LEVERAGING SUBCULTURE AND IDENTITY TO PROMOTE SPORTS EVENTS

S PORT EVENTS ARE NO LONGER merely about providing good sport. They have become a common tool for local and regional economic development (Getz, 1997; van den Berg, Braun, & Otgaar, 2000). As a consequence, organisers are expected to attract as many visitors as possible in order to maximise each event's economic impact. This has required event organisers to think beyond the nature and quality of sport provided; organisers have had to invent ways to make events more appealing to more people.

The result of this effort has depended, in part, on whether event organisers expect to optimise economic impact primarily through the spectators attracted or through the number of participants attracted. For example, when marketing a grand prix auto race, organisers seek to attract spectators. On the other hand, organisers of a marathon or a triathlon typically seek to attract large numbers of participants. Of course, in the case of the auto race, there may be some marketing effort to attract more participants, and in the case of the marathon, there may be substantial marketing effort to attract spectators. However, the primary marketing focus of the two kinds of events – spectator vs. participant – will typically differ.

Nevertheless, the response of event organisers in both cases has shared a common element. In the jargon of marketing, it has become common to think beyond the "actual product" (i.e., the sport competition itself). Event organisers have begun to "augment" the product through a variety of add-on activities and services. For example, the Preakness, once solely a horse race, now incorporates a week of social activities and partying. The Gold Coast Marathon, once a race for marathoners, now includes a half marathon, a 10K run, a 10K walk, plus an array of social, educational, and entertainment events in the days surrounding the run itself.

The objective of this augmentation has been to enhance and broaden the event's appeal. Advertisers can promote more than the mere competition; they can (and do) promote the partying, the activities, and special opportunities to learn from experts. In other words, they can (and do) promote the fun and excitement associated with the atmosphere engendered by the many augmentations.

This approach to event design and marketing has certainly enhanced the appeal of events. For example, the week leading up to the Preakness – once not much more exciting than any other week in Baltimore – now sees an influx of thousands of visitors ready to party (and spend accordingly). The Gold Coast Marathon, once a destination for a few dedicated runners, now attracts over 11,000 visitors from 21 countries.

However, from the standpoint of event promotion, the augmentation has typically served as a means to add lustre to the "fun" and "excitement" that potential visitors are told they can expect. Events are still advertised primarily as hedonic consumption. Although, in some instances, the inclusion of opportunities to learn (as, for example, with running clinics for marathoners), to achieve (for example, by undertaking the challenges of participating in an event), or to socialise (as, for example, with the myriad parties and festivals now associated with many events) are sometimes pitched in need fulfilment terms, these elements are nonetheless typically secondary to the hedonic opportunities afforded by attendance.

The inclusion of event augmentations represents a tacit recognition by organisers that persons who attend are making a choice about the way they will invest their leisure time. Thus, it is not uncommon for sport marketing texts (e.g., Brooks, 1994; Shank, 1999; Shilbury, Quick, & Westerbeek, 1998) to note that sport marketers should recognise that they compete with other leisure activities for their clientele. Yet, what has not commonly been introduced into this analysis is the recognition that, as a form of leisure consumption, attendance or participation in sport events represents a form of symbolic consumption (cf. Haggard & Williams, 1992; Hirschman & Holbrook, 1992; Kleine, Kleine, & Kernan, 1993; McCracken, 1988; Richins, 1994a, 1994b). In other words, the act of attending or participating encompasses a set of meanings for the attendee and the participant. As important as fun and excitement may be, the kinds of personal meanings that an event provides may be no less important.

There is substantial work demonstrating that sport consumption can be profitably understood as the expression of values associated with particular sport subcultures (e.g., Featherston & Hepworth, 1984; Lever, 1983; Pearson, 1979), and that participation in sport subcultures becomes a demonstration of personal identity (e.g., Baldwin & Norris, 1999; Donnelly & Young, 1988; Haggard & Williams, 1992; Kleiber & Kirshnit, 1991). This is consistent with work elsewhere in consumer behaviour that demonstrates the importance of subculture in transmitting consumption values, particularly in leisure contexts (e.g., Hebdige, 1979; Schouten & McAlexander, 1995; Thornton, 1996). Recent work (e.g., Green & Chalip, 1998; Green & Tanabe, 1998; Veno & Veno, 1996) suggests that by incorporating this insight into event design and promotion, the size and commitment of the event's market will be enhanced. In other words, there are demonstrable marketing benefits to be obtained by systematically incorporating insights derived from an examination of the subculture's values and the identities associated with the sport being showcased at an event. New and fruitful directions for promoting event attendance become salient.

In order to explore and demonstrate the utility of subculture and identity as targets of marketing communications, this paper first establishes the underlying conceptual rationale. The role and consequence of subculture in sport are reviewed. The relevance of subculture to identity and consumption is then described. Finally, the application of these concepts in three separate events – the Key West Women's Flag Football Tournament, the Gold Coast Marathon, and the Australian Motorcycle Grand Prix – is considered.

Subculture and sport

Subcultures can be defined as segments of society embracing certain distinctive cultural elements of their own (see Donnelly, 1981). Subcultural elements typically include a shared set of identifiable beliefs, values, and means of symbolic expression. Sport provides a highly visible, easily accessible, and particularly salient setting for the formation of subculture and the resulting expression of subcultural values. However, sport is not itself a single subculture; rather, each sport incorporates distinctive values and beliefs, and each provides varied venues for symbolic expression of those values and beliefs. As such, there has been substantial research examining a wide range of sport subcultures (e.g., Donnelly & Young, 1985; Hughson, 1998; Humphries, 1997; Klein, 1986; Pearson, 1979; Wheaton, 2000).

Sport subcultures are accessible through both direct and indirect participation. Direct participation in a subculture can include actual physical participation in the activity or competition, or it can include active participation through avenues such as rotisserie baseball or fantasy football leagues. Indirect participation can include viewing (e.g., live or televised sport), reading (e.g., about the sport, sportspersons, equipment, events), discussing with others, and purchasing products. The distinction between direct and indirect participation is useful because it conforms approximately to the distinction between doing the activity and spectating or following the activity as a fan. Obviously, the distinction is merely a heuristic one insomuch as the two forms of participation may co-occur. What the distinction highlights is that the notion of subculture can be applied when marketing to obtain spectators or when marketing to obtain participants.

Participation in a sport subculture is rarely limited to a single type of participation. Rather, each interaction with the subculture provides a slightly different venue for the expression of shared values and beliefs. For example, one may play basketball at the local gym, hold season tickets to NBA games, read the sports page of the newspaper, discuss last night's game with workmates, and purchase an officially licensed product such as a t-shirt to wear in other leisure settings. Another may collect trading cards and watch the game on television. Regardless of the ways in which people choose to participate in a subculture, the unique values and beliefs of that subculture are transmitted socially as participants or fans interact with others. Subcultural values and beliefs are learned. In other words, people are socialised into the particular sport subculture. Newcomers tend to hold stereotypical images of the ways in which subcultural participants express their values through appearance and behaviour. As one interacts with others within the subculture, these images are shaped and refined to reflect a deeper understanding of the symbolic meanings and the appropriateness of various forms of subcultural expression.

The subcultural learning that occurs through interactions with others within the subculture is not limited to personal interactions. Media can also play a part in transmitting values associated with specific sport subcultures. In fact, the success of much of our sport marketing efforts, particularly celebrity endorsement, is predicated on the ability of the media to shape and transmit subcultural values. The subcultural elements transmitted via the media, while easily accessible, tend to be fairly superficial, image-related elements rather than elements carrying deeper symbolic meaning. Nevertheless, interactions with others (be they face-to-face or mediated) are at the core of the socialisation process and provide venues through which values and beliefs come to be shared and expressed.

It is significant that participation in a subculture is socially enabled. Just as social processes teach the values and beliefs of a subculture, so do social processes reinforce those values and beliefs. Thus, continued participation is inherently a social process. Indeed, there is substantial work suggesting that these social processes not only maintain values and beliefs, they commonly become one of the pivotal attractions of participation (e.g., Anderson & Stone, 1981; Green & Chalip, 1998; Kemp, 1999; Melnick, 1993; Pearson, 1979). As we shall see, this provides an effective lever for event marketing.

Identity and consumption

As one adopts the values and beliefs of a subculture, one's identity becomes more closely associated with the subculture. Interactions within the subculture first help to construct and later confirm the identity the participant takes on by joining in (Donnelly & Young, 1988; Haggard & Williams, 1992; Holt, 1995). As the participant becomes committed to the subculture, he or she develops a sense of identification with the activity, and may incorporate the activity (whether through direct or indirect participation) into the self-concept.

Identity takes on two elements (Shamir, 1992). The first, commonly labelled self-identity, represents the degree to which the participant has incorporated the activity into his other self-concept. The second, commonly labelled social identity, represents the degree to which the participant perceives that others identify him or her with the activity.

There has been substantial work in other contexts demonstrating that identity plays a pivotal role in consumption. Kleine, Kleine, and Kernan (1993) demonstrated that people use products to enact one or more of their social identities. A subsequent study (Kleine, Kleine, & Allen, 1995) demonstrated that attachment to an object depends on the degree to which the object is consistent with one's self-identity. Hetherington (1996) showed that the choice to attend New Age festivals derives from a sense of self-identity with New Age ideologies, and that active and continued participation in those festivals depends on enactment of a New Age social identity while attending. Bhattacharya, Rao, and Glynn (1995) show that similar dynamics inhere in museum membership. Other research has shown that identity-relevant consumption is facilitated by sales interactions that reference appropriate subcultural values or beliefs (e.g., Varley & Crowther, 1998; Yoder, 1997).

Taken as a whole, this work demonstrates that products and services can enhance their appeal by projecting their consistency with self-identity and their capacity to facilitate enactment of social identity. In the case of events, this suggests that events are attractive when potential attendees are persuaded that the event is consistent with who they see themselves to be. The event will be particularly attractive if it can be shown to provide opportunities to perform activities publicly that are consistent with a social identity that the attendee values.

Interestingly, in the case of sport, it is a relatively straightforward matter to identify core elements of self-identity and the ways in which social identity is enacted. The elements of self-identity and the means of social identity enactment are learned and reinforced via sport subcultures. Sport subcultures are publicly accessible. Just as market research has demonstrated its value in the marketing of products and services, so can ethnographic research prove itself useful to the design and promotion of events. This contention is illustrated by review of research into three recent events.

The Key West Women's Flag Football Tournament

Green and Chalip (1998) examined factors that prompt women football players to participate in the annual flag football tournament in Key West, Florida. The three-day event is national in scope, attracting more than 25 teams from across the United States. It has been held on President's Day weekend in February each year since 1992. The tournament format has varied; however, all teams have been guaranteed at least two games over the three days. In addition to the competition itself, the event program includes a variety of social events (e.g., meet and greet social, dinner with live entertainment, end of tournament party).

Each team plays eight players per side. With the exception of stopping the ball carrier (which is accomplished by pulling the flag from her flagbelt), full contact is permitted, despite the prohibition against wearing padding of any kind. The physical nature of the game is an important element in the subculture of women's football. The sport of football enjoys a strong affiliation with masculinity in American society (Foley, 1990; Messner, 1989). Women who choose to play football are well aware of this association. But in fact, neither masculinity nor femininity is uniquely valued by women footballers. Rather, it is the capacity to choose and execute a fuller range of endeavours – including actions that are not readily accepted in other contexts – that draws women to the sport of football. An 11-year veteran of the game explained it this way:

> [Football] gives you a place where things you would typically apologize for, things that aren't acceptable from a woman, are OK. They're more than OK, they're glorified . . . We grew up with football in school, on TV, but it wasn't something little girls are supposed to do . . . Here we get to be macho. It's fun.

The tournament, albeit unintentionally, provides a time and a space in which participants can share and celebrate their identity as women footballers. The interactions with other women football players nurture and reinforce the values of the subculture. Key elements of the subculture are represented in the nature of conversations that take place during the event. As the tournament progresses, players devote more time to descriptions of their bruises, exhaustion, and injuries. Each becomes a symbol of the player's toughness and a recognisable expression of her identity as a football player. Each also becomes an easy starting point for conversations with other players, thus enhancing the sociability of the event.

The event includes a variety of social activities that encourage players to interact with one another. One could argue that these activities provide players with yet another venue in which to parade their identity as football players. While this is true, these formalised social events unintentionally change the focus of that identity. Players at these events identify with their individual teams, rather than with the broader subculture of women footballers. These interactions contrast with the informal interactions that occur as a consequence of chance encounters between individuals and small groups of players that occur as tournament participants wander around Key West. In other words, the formalised social events emphasise players' differences; informal social encounters emphasise players' similarities. The quarterback of a Northern California team put it this way:

> When you meet someone out in Key West – out in the town – you see them as another football player. When you see them at one of the social events, you see them as kind of the enemy – someone on another team. Because out in the town there are other people, so that's what you have in common – being a football player That brings you together. At the social events, you're divided by teams . . .

Other means of parading and celebrating subcultural values have also become important elements of the event experience. Teams attending the Key West Tournament have presented whimsical imitations of institutionalised elements associated with the professionalised male version of the game. For example, supporters for one team performed the national anthem on kazoos as a "pre-game entertainment". Another group of supporters (christened "The St. Louis Moped Mamas") has become legendary for a half-time show in which they perform precision routines on mopeds with their bras flapping from the aerials. Beyond their entertainment value and their ability to provide grist for informal conversations, these performances serve a deeper purpose. They provide stories that become the folklore which binds succeeding tournaments together, giving the event its ongoing culture.

Although the opportunities for celebrating subcultural values and parading one's identity as a women football player are unintentional (insomuch as they were not intentionally designed into the event), they are, nevertheless, effective. Participative sports events are typically planned in terms of the competitions to be provided. This research suggests that participants judge the quality of an event in far broader terms than the competition itself. In fact, participants at the Key West Tournament noted the poor quality of many of the elements of the competition. As one long-time attendee put it, "Each year the seeding is screwed up, the officiating is uneven, and nobody seems to know what's going on." However, this player and others continued to attend year after year, and continued to describe the tournament as a "good event'.

Beginning in 1996, the tournament has sought to institute policies intended to provide better football. Although the resulting atmosphere has been more businesslike, it has also curtailed the breadth and depth of subcultural celebrations. These changes have been difficult to implement because they are resisted by the players themselves, who continue to demand opportunities to share and celebrate their sport's subculture.

This study highlights the marketing potential of leveraging the sport's subculture and attendees' identification with that subculture. Two key features are illustrated.

First, opportunities for participants to parade and celebrate their identities as women footballers are vital. In particular, opportunities to share informally with other women who also identify with the subculture are important. The scheduling of formal social opportunities into the event is useful, but only given the fact that there are substantial opportunities for informal (often chance) social interactions that are facilitated by Key

West's confined geography and attractive eating and shopping venues. These interactions are not merely an opportunity to celebrate being women footballers with other women; they are an opportunity to parade the identity "women footballer" to other participants and to Key West residents and visitors.

It is of some interest that these informal opportunities are identified by the participants as core elements of the tournament's value, yet none of these has been leveraged by the event organisers. The organisers have not sought to find ways to make better use of informal as well as formal social spaces. Nor have they advertised this characteristic of the event. Rather, it is something that players discover by attending or by word of mouth from previous attendees. Indeed, the organisers have recently sought to "professionalise" the event in part by requiring all participants to stay in one of the "official tournament hotels". Not surprisingly, putting players together in this manner has reduced the range of encounters outside official tournament spaces, and has consequently accentuated team (rather than subculture) identification. This has been negatively received by the players themselves.

Second, opportunities for players and their supporters to provide performances (e.g., the kazoo pre-game show and the St. Louis Moped Mamas) that frame or celebrate the subculture are valuable. These become grist for the discussions among players who might otherwise remain strangers, thus enhancing the quality of subcultural revelry. Further, stories about these performances have given the event a sense of continuity (and value) from year to year; they render its distinctive, ongoing, and continually recreated cultural feel.

The only way this element has been put to marketing use has been via mentions of these activities in the event's newsletter. They have not, however, been built systematically into the event's other marketing communications – whether as imagery or as stories. Instead, as the event has sought to provide a more "serious" image, it has recently ceased to allow performances like those of the St. Louis Moped Mamas. This has abridged celebrations of the women's football subculture and withdrawn opportunities for supporters (i.e., non-players) to play a performative role in the event. As a consequence, teams that were once tournament regulars are now reappraising the tournament's value.

In summary, study of participants (particularly repeat participants) at the Key West Women's Flag Football Tournament demonstrates that the event's core appeal is its capacity to provide opportunities to parade and celebrate the football player identity with other women footballers. However, the event's marketing communications have focused on football competition per se, rather than on shared subcultural revelry. Meanwhile, event organisers have, like their advertising, focused increasingly on football competition rather than on the women's football subculture. It has been a marketing mistake.

The Gold Coast Marathon

The motives of entrants into the Gold Coast Marathon were studied by Green and Tanabe (1998). Having started as a single marathon race in 1979 with only 124 finishers, the event is now the second largest running event in Australia with more than 11,000 competitors. Three races have been added to the programme (half marathon, 10K run, and 10K walk), and the event has been expanded to incorporate a weeklong festival which includes a variety of social, educational, and entertainment events. In the words of the advertising brochure, the augmentations have been included to "widen the number of people able to participate in this spectacular sports week" (Gold Coast Marathon Week, 1997). In other words, the event intends to attract participants who may be seeking experiences in addition to or different from the marathon race per se. By adding to the number and types of experiences offered, event organisers can reach into market segments not obtainable with a single race event. One would expect these market segments to vary in terms of their motives and their degree of identification with running.

Green and Tanabe (1998) surveyed participants in each of the four races included on the Gold Coast Marathon programme. Participants were asked to respond to questions that included measures of motives for attending the event (viz., Beard & Ragheb, 1983), their identity as a runner (viz., Shamir, 1992), and their commitment to running (viz., Carrnack & Martens, 1979). The motivation scale measured four types of motivation – mastery, social, intellectual, and escape. Two dimensions of identity as a runner were measured – self-identity and social identity. The measure of commitment to running is unidimensional – measuring the respondent's overall commitment to the activity. In addition, respondents were given a checklist of the seventeen social, educational, and entertainment events offered as part of Marathon Week, and were asked to tick the events that they had attended or would attend.

If the event is truly reaching more runners by offering more races, then participants in the four races should differ from one another in terms of their motives and/or their identification with and commitment to running. Identification and commitment were chosen as proxies for the degree to which participants are involved in the sport's subculture. Motives were chosen as representations of runners' underlying reasons for participating in the event. It was expected that participants in the three running races would be more involved with the running subculture than were the walkers. Given the volume of training required for a marathon, it was also expected that marathoners would report higher levels of running identity (both self and social) and higher commitment to running than that reported by runners in the shorter events. For similar reasons, comparable differences in mastery motivation were expected. On the other hand, given the relatively social nature of the walking race as opposed to the running races, higher levels of social motivation were expected among the walkers than among the runners.

If the inclusion of associated activities during the week leading up to the race itself also adds value, then they should be associated with participants' motives for attending the event as well as the race in which they are participating. Thus, it was expected that activities associated with learning, such as the training seminar would appeal more to participants with higher levels of intellectual motivation, while entertainment activities, such as a production of Gilbert and Sullivan's *HMS Pinafore* would appeal to participants higher in escape motivation. Similarly, it was expected that activities associated with running, such as the traditional pre-event pasta party would appeal more to runners than to walkers; whereas social events, such as the "Last Drink Stop Party" were expected to appeal more to participants with higher levels of social identity as runners.

Participants in the four races did not differ in terms of their mastery, social, intellectual, or escape motivation. However, they did differ in terms of their commitment to running and their identity as runners. Analyses of variance using Helmert contrasts on the commitment and identity variables are summarised in Table 20.1. Inspection of Table 20.1 shows that the direction of effects is as predicted. Runners (regardless of race event) report higher levels than walkers of commitment to running, self-identity as runners,

Table 20.1 Helmert contrasts: event participants' commitment, self-identity, and social identity

Variable	Mean	1/2 Marathoners vs 10K runners	Marathoners vs other runners	Runners vs walkers
Commitment to running		0.61	2.75**	5.12*
Marathoners	7.59			
1/2 marathoners	6.70			
10K runners	5.56			
Walkers	0.57			
Self-identity as a runner		−0.33	2.11**	4.38*
Marathoners	3.54			
1/2 marathoners	2.82			
10K runners	1.61			
Walkers	0.81			
Social identity as a runner		0.41	2.17***	3.70*
Marathoners	2.44			
1/2 marathoners	2.07			
10K runners	1.33			
Walkers	−1.47			

* $p < .001$, ** $p < .01$, *** $p < .05$

and social identity as runners, Marathoners report higher levels of commitment to running, self-identity as runners, and social identity as runners than are reported by entrants in the half marathon or the 10K race, There is no difference between participants in the half marathon or the 10K on any of these variables.

There were also systematic differences in the kinds of associated activities that partcipants in the four races chose to attend. Marathoners were more likely than other participants to attend the pasta party, but walkers were more likely than the runners to attend a breakfast with the Gold Coast mayor or a production of *HMS Pinafore*. More tellingly, even when activities did not appeal differently to participants in the various races, attendance did typically vary as a function of motive, commitment, or identity. Thus, participants with higher levels of social identity such as runners, were more likely to attend a breakfast with former Olympian (and world record holder). Ron Clarke, and were more likely to attend the post-race "Last Drink Stop Party". On the other hand, participants with higher commitment to running and/or a higher self-identity as runners attended the training seminar. Participants with higher mastery motivation and/or higher social motivation attended the event's associated trade show, the Pro-Sport Expo.

These findings are consistent with the commonsensical notion that event augmentations enhance an event's appeal by broadening the range of segments for whom the event may he attractive. More importantly, these findings also highlight the relevance of subculture and identity. Although motives for participation did not differ as a function of race event, participants in each of the three running events (but not the walking event) did report substantial commitment to running and a strong identity as runners—each a proxy for their involvement with the subculture of running. As expected, the importance of these variables was greater for marathoners than for those in the shorter races.

The appeal of the various activities is also consistent with subcultural involvement. Activities that bear some relationship to running each provide a different way for participants to parade and celebrate their identity as runners. Thus, events that were more social in nature (e.g., the post-event party) appealed more to participants with a stronger social identity as runners, while those that were more associated with performance (e.g., the training seminar) appealed more to participants with a higher self-identity as runners and/or a higher commitment to running. On the other hand, events that had little to do with running (e.g., the performance of *HMS Pinafore*) added to the entertainment value of the event for those who were not invested in the subculture of running – particularly walkers.

As with the football tournament in Key West, organisers of the Gold Coast Marathon have made no systematic effort to build their marketing communications campaign with reference to runners' identities as runners or the subcultural celebrations that the event makes possible. Rather, the event has been advertised in terms of the challenge of running or the entertainment available during the week. To be sure, these seem to be appropriate appeals, particularly for those choosing to walk the 10K. However, the opportunity to appeal more directly to runners *as runners* has yet to be exploited. As we shall see in the following case, a conscientious application of subcultural focus and insight can have a dramatic effect on an event's appeal.

The Australian Motorcycle Grand Prix

Between 1985 and 1987, attendance at the Australian Motorcycle Grand Prix fell from 13,701 to 4,300. In 1988, the event was cancelled and moved from Bathurst, New South Wales, to Phillip Island, Victoria. That year, the new event organisers brought a community psychologist onto their event planning team in an effort to change the events image and its consequent appeal (see Veno & Veno, 1996 for a detailed description of the consultation). When the event reopened in 1989, it eclipsed old attendance records, attracting over 241,000 spectators. A key feature of the event's turnaround was that the consultant made extensive and explicit reference to the subculture of motorcycle enthusiasts when formulating his recommendations. Further, event organisers made use of the resulting recommendations for event design and event promotions.

During its years in Bathurst, event organisers had tried to rein in celebrations associated with the subculture of motorcyclists. Organisers sought to implement rigorous crowd control, which included extensive policing of transportation arteries, and suppression of public partying by motorcyclists attending the event. As a consequence, there was substantial tension between event security and event visitors. In 1976, 1980, 1981, 1983 and 1985, the tensions escalated into confrontations defined by the media as riots. After 1987, with event attendances plummeting and public support waning, the event was cancelled altogether. A new team of event organisers took over when the event was shifted to Phillip Island and scheduled to recommence in 1989.

As the event was being planned for its new venue, the consultant attended rallies organised by motorcyclists themselves, and also interviewed bikers to learn their values and their expectations. He noted that at events organised by motorcyclists, there was substantial self-policing and incidents of public disorder were rare. He discovered that motorcyclists seek opportunities to join together during events to parade and celebrate their identity as bikers.

The consultant brought motorcycle groups together with event security to plan a self-policing strategy for the grand prix, including cooperation and liaison between bikers and police before and throughout the event. He also worked with hospitality providers, particularly camp ground owners, to establish procedures to facilitate socialising and self-policing among visitors. He then helped with plans designed to enhance opportunities for motorcyclists to parade and celebrate themselves as bikers. The most visible element of that plan was a rally immediately prior to the grand prix competition itself.

Over 4,000 motorcyclists participated in the rally, which began in Melbourne and terminated at the Phillip Island camping areas 60 miles away. The event was highly publicised in local media and in various publications aimed at bikers and motorcycle enthusiasts. Participants assembled in central Melbourne, paraded around the city, and were escorted by police over the entire course of the rally.

The rally was designed to achieve a number of goals. First, it established a celebratory atmosphere at the event's outset. Second, it demonstrated that bikers were welcomed visitors to the event. Third, it began the event by demonstrating the cooperative relationship between police and bikers.

The rally best illustrates the degree to which the new event organisers were able to reformulate the event and thus recast its image. Rather then seeking to suppress the biker subculture, the event became, in part, an opportunity to celebrate it. Further, that feature was a consistent part of the event's marketing communications plan. In the year leading up to the event, the self-policing plans, the rally, and the quality of social opportunities the event would offer were publicised nationally in mainstream media and internationally in motorcycle media.

In order to make certain that the event's new image was accurately reported, event public relations established a media watch. On the basis of information derived from the consultant's work with bikers, event organisers concluded that the media's portrayal of motorcyclists misrepresented them. Consequently, public relations efforts sought to present a new image, not only of the event itself, but of the core audience – the bikers. Further, since the consultant's informants suggested that some reporters had actively encouraged acts of vandalism in order to obtain a story, the media watch campaign also included a watch on journalists during the event in order to intervene if and when vandalism was prompted.

By recasting the event's image, organisers also sought to broaden its appeal. The celebratory atmosphere combined with high-quality racing seemed like something that could appeal to motor sport enthusiasts more generally. In particular, organisers noted that other motor sport events appeal strongly to families. Since the biker celebrations had been recast as an integral part of the event's festival atmosphere, it became possible to design promotions that would target motor sport enthusiasts more generally, and families in particular.

The event's consequent success can be measured in more than mere attendance. To be sure, recasting the event in terms that embraced the sport's subculture increased attendance by a whopping 5,600%. But perhaps more significantly, public support for the event increased substantially. Whereas residents of Bathurst had lobbied strongly to end the event after 1987, after the event's inaugural hosting on Phillip Island, residents there voted 93% in favour of hosting the event again. The focus on subculture and identity did more than attract visitors; it made the event popular.

Discussion

Taken together, these cases illustrate the significance and utility of subculture and identity as levers for event marketing. The Key West Women's Flag Football Tournament demonstrates the central role that opportunities for subcultural revelry and socialising play in the quality of experience that participants obtain from an event. The Gold Coast Marathon shows that event augmentations permit a wider range of opportunities for participants to parade and celebrate the subculture they share. The Australian Motorcycle Grand Prix demonstrates that systematic application of insights derived from attention to subculture and identity is both practical and useful.

These cases suggest that we need to consider more deeply what our core product is when we are promoting an event. A casual examination of event advertising might suggest that fun, excitement, entertainment, challenge, or the sport competition per se are the core products. These may be important to some who participate or watch – as seems to have been the case with walkers at the Gold Coast Marathon. Yet concepts like "fun" and "excitement" are so global that they have little practical utility. By explaining everything, they explain nothing. What matters are the features and factors from which such global ascriptions derive. They are at the core of what we sell; they seem to be rooted in subculture and identity.

This is not to contend that subcultures are either unitary or monolithic. Within any sport subculture, there are likely to be variations in the ways that values, motives, and social identity are expressed – as was the case among runners at the Gold Coast Marathon. These variations are themselves a subtle form of segmentation. By identifying these variations, events can be designed to broaden their appeal by incorporating elements that are congenial to these varied forms of expression. Marketing communications can then leverage these augmentations to amplify the event's attraction.

A great deal of work in sport consumer behaviour has focused on spectators' identification with a team (e.g., Hill & Green, 2000; Kahle, Kambara & Rose, 1996; Madrigal, 1995; Warm, McGeorge, Dolan & Allison, 1994) or with particular competitors (e.g., Duret & Wolff, 1994; Lipsyte & Levine, 1995). These are demonstrably important. However, by limiting our concept of identification to identification with the performers, we have paid inadequate attention to identification with the subculture that those performers represent. More work needs to be done to explore the marketing potential of viewing teams and athletes as symbols of values and beliefs (cf. Chalip, 1992, 1997; Chalip, Green, & Vander Velden, 2000; Lever, 1983).

Although the three events reviewed here each encouraged spectators, the Australian Motorcycle Grand Prix is the only one that positioned itself primarily as a spectator event. The other two were marketed primarily for participants. Nevertheless, it is of some interest that the motorcycle event's turnaround depended on strategies to make spectators feel more like participants. Interestingly, the football tournament obtained some of its appeal for spectators and players alike by allowing opportunities for spectators to provide performances, such as those of the St. Louis Moped Mamas. Spectating and cheering are relatively passive expressions of identity. This suggests the utility of seeking ways to incorporate spectators more actively into an event's festivities (cf. Deighton, 1992; Holt, 1995).

This work suggests that market research for events will benefit by incorporating ethnographic elements. Marketers may find that their understandings of a sport's subculture or range of subcultural expressions are under-elaborated or stereotypical. Nor will it be sufficient to rely on media accounts, as these may fail to appreciate the subculture's core values and beliefs. Indeed, it is not uncommon for subcultures to define themselves in terms of their resistance to popular stereotypes and media portrayals (cf. Hebdige, 1979; Thornton, 1996). The phenomenal turnaround of the Australian Motorcycle Grand Prix depended on extended and careful ethnographic research. That research rendered insights that contradicted popular wisdom and organisers' preconceived notions. The utility of subculture and identity as marketing levers may depend on the quality of ethnographic insight that organisers and marketers are willing to obtain.

References

Anderson, D.F., & Stone, G.P. (1981). Sport: A search for community. In S.L. Greendorfer & A. Yiannakis (Eds), *Sociology of sport: Diverse perspectives* (pp. 164–172). West Point: Leisure Press.

Baldwin, C.K., & Norris, P.A. (1999). Exploring the dimensions of serious leisure: "Love me – love my dog!" *Journal of Leisure Research, 31*, 1–17.

Beard, J.G., & Ragheb, M.G. (1983). Measuring leisure motivation. *Journal of Leisure Research, 15*, 219–227.

Bhattacharya, C.B., Rao, H., & Glynn, M.A. (1995). Understanding the bond of identification: An investigation of its correlates among art museum members. *Journal of Marketing, 59*, 46–57.

Brooks, C.M. (1994). *Sports marketing: Competitive business strategies for sports.* Englewood Cliffs, NJ: Prentice-Hall.

Carmack, M.A., & Martens, R. (1979). Measuring commitment to running: A survey of runners' attitudes and mental states. *Journal of Sport Psychology, 1*, 25–42.

Chalip, L. (1992). The construction and use of polysemic structures: Olympic lessons for sport marketing. *Journal of Sport Management, 6*, 87–98.

Chalip, L. (1997). Celebrity or hero? Toward a conceptual framework for athlete promotion. In D. Shilbury & L. Chalip (Eds), *Advancing management of Australian and New Zealand sport* (pp. 42–56). Burwood, Victoria: Sport Management Association of Australia and New Zealand.

Chalip, L., Green, B.C., & Vander Velden, L. (2000). The effects of polysemic structures on Olympic viewing. *International Journal of Sport Marketing & Sponsorship, 2*, 39–57.

Deighton, J. (1992). The consumption of performance. *Journal of Consumer Research, 19*, 362–372.

Donnelly, P. (1981). Toward a definition of sport subcultures. In M. Hart & S. Birrell (Eds), *Sport in the sociocultural process* (pp. 565–587). Dubuque, IA: William C. Brown.

Donnelly, P., & Young, K. (1985). Reproduction and transformation of cultural forms in sport: A contextual analysis of rugby. *International Review for the Sociology of Sport, 20*, 19–38.

Donnelly, P., & Young, K. (1988). The construction and confirmation of identity in sport subcultures. *Sociology of Sport Journal, 5*, 223–240.

Duret, P., & Wolff, M. (1994). The semiotics of sports heroes. *International Review for the Sociology of Sport, 29*, 135–148.

Featherston, M., & Hepworth, M. (1984). Fitness, body maintenance and lifestyle within consumer culture. In *Sports et sociétés contemporaines* (pp. 441–447). Paris: Société Français de Sociologic du Sport.

Foley, D.E. (1990). The great American football ritual, reproducing race, class, and gender inequality. *Sociology of Sport Journal, 7*, 111–135.

Getz, D. (1997). *Event management and event tourism.* New York: Cognizant Communication Corporation.

Gold Coast Marathon Week. (1997). *Feature event of the Gold Coast Marathon week* [Brochure]. Southport, Qld: Author.

Green, B.C., & Chalip, L. (1998). Sport tourism as the celebration of subculture: Parading identity at a women's football tournament. *Annals of Tourism Research, 25*, 275–291.

Green, B.C., & Tanabe, L. (1998, May). Marathons, motive, and marketing: Segmentation strategies and the Gold Coast Marathon. Paper presented at the Annual Conference of the North American Society for Sport Management, Buffalo, NY.

Haggard, L.M., & Williams, DR. (1992). Identity affirmation through leisure activities: Leisure symbols of the self. *Journal of Leisure Research, 24*, 1–18.

Hebdige, D. (1979). *Subculture: The meaning of style.* London: Methuen.

Hetherington, K. (1996). Identity formation, space and social centrality. *Theory, Culture & Society, 13*(4), 33–52.

Hill, B., & Green, B.C. (2000). Repeat attendance as a function of involvement, loyalty, and the sportscape across three football contexts. *Sport Management Review, 3*, 145–162.

Hirschman, E.C., & Holbrook, M.B. (1992). *Postmodern consumer research: The study of consumption as text.* Newbury Park, CA: Sage.

Holt, D.B. (1995). How consumers consume: A typology of consumption practices. *Journal of Consumer Research, 22*, 1–16.

Hughson, J. (1998). Among the thugs: The "new ethnographies" of football supporting subcultures, *International Review for the Sociology of Sport, 33*, 43–57.

Humphries, D. (1997). "Shredheads go mainstream"? Snowboarding and alternative youth. *International Review for the Sociology of Sport, 32*, 147–160.

Kahle, L.R., Kambara, K.M., & Rose, G.M. (1996). A functional model of fan attendance motivations for college football. *Sport Marketing Quarterly, 5*(4), 51–60.

Kemp, S.F. (1999). Sled dog racing: The celebration of co-operation in a competitive sport. *Ethnology, 38*, 81–95.

Kleiber, D.A., & Kirshnit, C.E. (1991). Sport involvement and identity formation. In L. Diamant (Ed.), *Mind-body maturity* (pp. 193–211). New York: Hemisphere Publishing.

Klein, A.M. (1986). Pumping irony: Crisis and contradiction in bodybuilding. *Sociology of Sport Journal, 3*, 112–133.

Kleine, S.S., Kleine, R.E., & Allen, C.T. (1995). How is a possession "me" or "not me"? Characterizing types and an antecedent of material possession attachment. *Journal of Consumer Research, 22*, 327–343.

Kleine, R.E., Kleine, S.S., & Kernan, J.B. (1993). Mundane consumption and the self: A social-identity perspective. *Journal of Consumer Psychology, 2*, 209–235.

Lever, J. (1983). *Soccer madness.* Chicago: University of Chicago Press.

Lipsyte, R., & Levine, P. (1995). *Idols of the game: A sporting history of the American century.* Atlanta: Turner Publishing.

Madrigal, R. (1995). Cognitive and affective determinants of fan satisfaction with sporting event attendance. *Journal of Leisure Research, 27*, 205–227.

McCracken, G. (1988). *Culture and consumption: New approaches to the symbolic character of consumer goods and activities.* Bloomington, IN: Indiana University Press.

Melnick, M.J. (1993). Searching for sociability in the stands: A theory of sports spectating. *Journal of Sport Management*, 7, 44–60.

Messner, M. (1989). Masculinities and athletic careers. *Gender and Society*, 3, 71–88.

Pearson, K. (1979). *Surfing subcultures in Australia and New Zealand.* St Lucia: University of Queensland Press.

Richins, M.L. (1994a). Valuing things: The public and private meanings of possessions. *Journal of Consumer Research*, 21, 504–521.

Richins, M.L. (1994b). Special possessions and the expression of material values, *Journal of Consumer Research*, 21, 522–533.

Schouten, J.W., & McAlexander, J.H. (1995). Subcultures of consumption: An ethnography of the new hikers. *Journal of Consumer Research*, 22, 43–61.

Shamir, B. (1992). Some correlates of leisure identity salience: Three exploratory studies. *Journal of Leisure Research*, 24, 301–323.

Shank, M.D. (1999). *Sports marketing: A strategic perspective.* Upper Saddle River, NJ: Prentice Hall.

Shilbury, D., Quick, S., & Westerbeek, H. (1998). *Strategic sport marketing.* St Leonards, NSW: Allen & Unwin.

Thornton, S. (1996). *Club cultures: Music, media and subcultural capital.* Hanover, NH: Wesleyan University Press.

van den Berg, L., Braun, E., & Otgaar, A.H.J. (2000). *Sports and city marketing in European cities.* Rotterdam: Euricur.

Varley, P., & Crowther, G. (1998). Performance and the service encounter: An exploration of narrative expectations and relationship management in the outdoor leisure market. *Marketing Intelligence & Planning*, 16, 311–317.

Veno, A., & Veno, E. (1996). Managing public order at the Australian Motorcycle Grand Prix. In D. Thomas & A. Veno (Eds), *Community psychology and social change* (2nd edn, pp. 58–80). Palmerston North, NZ: Dunmore Press.

Wann, D.L., McGeorge, K.K., Dolan, T.J., & Allison, J.A. (1994). Relationships between spectator identification and spectators perceptions of influence, spectators' emotions, and competition outcome. *Journal of Sport and Exercise Psychology*, 16, 347–364.

Wheaton, B. (2000). "Just do it": Consumption, commitment, and identity in the windsurfing subculture. *Sociology of Sport Journal*, 17, 254–274.

Yoder, D.G. (1997). A model for commodity intensive serious leisure. *Journal of Leisure Research*, 29, 407–429.

Chapter 21

Heather J. Gibson, Cynthia Willming and Andrew Holdnak

SMALL-SCALE EVENT SPORT TOURISM
Fans as tourists

1 Introduction

IN RECENT YEARS, SPECIAL INTEREST tourism of various types has become increasingly popular (Weller & Hall, 1992). One form of special interest tourism which has garnered particular attention is travel related to sport or sport tourism. Most scholars agree that there is a distinction between individuals who travel to actively participate in a sport (Active Sport Tourism) and those who travel to watch a sports event (Event Sport Tourism) (Gibson, 1998a, b; Hall, 1992a; Standeven & De Knop, 1999). In the United States, event sport tourism generates an estimated $27 billion a year (Travel Industry Association of America, 2001) and more than 75 million American adults (two-fifths of the population) reported attending a sports event as either a spectator or as a participant while traveling in the past 5 years (TIA, 1999). In fact, around the world, thousands of people travel significant distances to watch their favorite sports on a regular basis.

While there have been numerous studies over the years about fans, these have generally focused on the meanings and identities associated with being a fan (Anderson, 1979; McPherson, 1975; Wann & Branscombe, 1993), or in the case of the UK, football hooliganism (Dunning, 1990; Ingham, 1978; Maguire, 1986). However, few researchers have examined the sports fan in the context of sport tourism. Indeed, the use of college sport as a community tourist attraction in the US has received scant attention (Irwin & Sandler, 1998). College-sports events have the potential to increase city revenue and community spirit, while increasing traveler's awareness of the local community (Garnham, 1996; Higham, 1999; Irwin & Sandler, 1998; Walo, Bull, & Breen, 1996). This paper reports the results of a two-part study on the tourism-related behaviors of fans who attend University of Florida (UF) football games (American football).

2   Review of literature

Much of the existing literature on event sport tourism has focused on mega or hallmark events. The term hallmark event refers to "major fairs, expositions, cultural, and sporting events of international status which are held on either a regular or one time basis" (Hall, 1989, p. 263). Hallmark events are generally thought to help position a host city as an international-tourist destination and facilitate touristic activity in the years following the event (Hall, 1992b; Ritchie, 1984). While some of the literature has characterized the impacts of hallmark events as positive (Gratton, Shibli, & Dobson, 2000; Ritchie & Smith, 1991), scholars have recognized the downsides associated with these events (Matzitelli, 1989; Hall & Hodges, 1996; Orams & Brons, 1999; Ritchie, 1999). Roche (1994) argued that mega events tend to be short lived but have long-term consequences for a community that may not always be positive. Other scholars argue that hallmark events frequently result in huge debts for host communities (Roberts & McLeod, 1989; Whitson & Macintosh, 1993), possible corruption during the bid process (Jennings, 1996), and frequently lead to the displacement of local residents because of new infrastructural improvements (Hall & Hodges, 1996; Hiller, 1998; Olds, 1998).

Given the challenges associated with hallmark events, Higham (1999) suggested that small scale-sports events might result in more positive effects for host communities. He defined small scale-sports events as "regular season sporting competitions (ice hockey, basketball, soccer, rugby leagues), international sporting fixtures, domestic competitions, Masters or disabled sports, and the like" (p. 87). Furthermore, Higham explained small-scale-sports events usually operate within existing infrastructures, require minimal investments of public funds, are more manageable in terms of crowding and congestion compared to hallmark events, and seem to minimize the effects of seasonality. Hence, ". . . it is important to recognize the need to attract or develop sporting events that complement the scale, infrastructure and resourcing capabilities of the host city" (p. 89). Perhaps, the term small scale also needs to be conceptualized in relative terms as the definitions outlined above can equally apply to sporting competitions with a small local fan base as well as sports events which draw national, and even international attention. The distinction between small scale and hallmark events is not simply related to the size of the event, but is also related to the fact that regular season games do not tax the resources of the host city in the same manner as hosting a mega event.

To date, the literature on small-scale-sport events is sparse (Garnham, 1996; Higham & Hinch, 2001; Irwin & Sandler, 1998; Walo, Bull and Breen, 1996). Irwin and Sandler (1998) were among the first to recognize the tourism-related potential of US fans traveling to watch college-sports events. In this case, they concentrated their investigation on people who attended ten US collegiate championships. Irwin and Sandler were interested in the travel planning and expenditure patterns of the fans who attended these events. They found that fans spent the most on lodging and retail shopping and fans with a particular team affiliation spent more time and money at the destination. With this finding the authors suggested that future research on college sport and tourism should segment the analysis of fan behaviors by team affiliation. Irwin and Sandler also recommended that tourism agencies in cities hosting such events should work more closely with each other and with the universities involved to actively market the event and provide more information about the destination to potential sport tourists. Indeed, Higham and Hinch investigated the symbiotic relationship between sport and tourism based on another example of small-scale event sport tourism, Super 12 Rugby in New Zealand. They found that the development of a regional destination image among tourists seemed to be related to the exposure the region received from people watching the games or from viewing media coverage about the rugby team.

Wilo, Bull and Breen (1996) investigated the economic benefits accruing from an Australian university sports event affiliated with the Northern Conference University Sport's Association Games held at Southern Cross University in July 1995. They found that the event provided an 'economic boost' to the community, with fans spending the most on food and drink. Almost two-thirds of the attendees said they would not have visited Lismore (the host community), if it had not been for the event. Moreover, there was an increased sense of community cooperation and spirit centered on hosting the event, because many of the residents volunteered with various aspects of the event operations. Likewise, Garnham (1996) examined the Ranfurly Rugby Shield located in New Plymouth, New Zealand and found that the major impact for the host community was the increase in community spirit and morale, or what Burgan and Mules (1992) called psychic income. Garnham found that the economic benefits accruing from the event were disproportionate, where some businesses in the immediate vicinity of the games such as restaurants and pubs experienced positive economic benefits, and other businesses away from the games such as retail shopping did not. Garnham suggested, "people were not in a shopping mode but in a partying mode" (p. 148). This assessment may prove to be quite insightful when examining the tourism effects of fans attending sports events. As Faulkner, Tideswell, and Weston (1998) postulated before the 2000 Olympic Games in Sydney, most international tourists attending the Games would be "sport junkies" interested in little else besides sports. One of the challenges in understanding sport tourism and traveling fans might be to recognize that for many fans, their primary motivation is to watch the sporting competition and little else. To address this challenge it might be necessary to segment fans by their length of stay within the community, as found by Nogawa, Yamguchi, and Hagi (1996) who studied a sport tourism event in Japan. They found that sport excursionists, participants who stay less than 24 h at a destination, are less likely than sport tourists (those who stay overnight), to engage in regular tourist activities such as sightseeing. In another study on active sport tourism in Key West, Florida, Green and Chalip (1998) pointed to the need to understand the subculture of the fans and participants in order to assess what they want from an event and the possibilities of enticing them to do other things in the host community.

The purpose of this two-part study was (a) to investigate the tourism-related behaviors of fans traveling from outside of Alachua County, Florida (USA) to follow the University of Florida's football team (the Gators); and (b) to investigate their fan related behaviors, specifically, their rituals and practices pertaining to following the Gators, and the meanings associated with being a Gator fan (Gibson et al., 2001). This paper focused on the sport tourism related behaviors of the fans and suggests ways in which small communities such as Gainesville, Florida can leverage the tourism related benefits associated with college sports.

3   Method

3.1 *Study site*

The UF is located in the city of Gainesville in North Central Florida approximately 80 miles (128.7 km) west of Jacksonville and 100 miles (160.9 km) north of Orlando. Gainesville is located in Alachua County and has a population of 101,405 residents (North Central Florida Almanac, 2001). During the academic year, UF has a population of over 46,000 students. The University's sports teams are called the Gators. The UF football team is a member of the South Eastern Conference (or league) and is currently one of the top teams in the country. The Gators play an average of five home games and five away games per season (autumn). If they have had a successful season, they will be invited to play in a Bowl game, which is a championship game held on or around New Year's Day. On average 84,000 fans attend home football games in Gainesville, of which, 50,000 are non-students and 21,500 are students with season tickets (University Athletic Association, 2000). Almost 80% of the non-student season ticket holders travel from outside of Alachua County to attend home games (University Athletic Association, 2000). The University of Florida also has 17 additional sports teams that attract fans to the community throughout the year, most notably men's basketball and baseball.

3.2 *Study one—fall 1999*

Using systematic-random sampling procedures, 181 Gator fans were surveyed before three home football games during the fall of 1999. In the US, fans typically tailgate for 2 or 3 h before a football game. Tailgating consists of socializing with family and friends in a car park, eating, drinking, and even barbecuing. Tailgating can be quite elaborate with satellite televisions so fans can follow the other football teams around the country, and some may be catered by professional-food-service companies. However, most consist of groups of fans sitting by their vehicles socializing and enjoying the pre-game atmosphere.

For this study, the car parks on the university campus and surrounding community were divided into three categories according to parking type: (a) recreational vehicles (RVs); (b) Gator boosters (fans who donate money to the Gators), and (c) regular fans. A grid was drawn over the map of these car parks and each resulting grid square was numbered. Using stratified-systematic-random sampling procedures, 15 grid squares were identified. The stratification was based on the three types of fans in each car-parking zone e.g., RVs, Gator boosters, and regular fans. The aim was to obtain a sample that included all types of Gator football fans as designated by their parking privileges which are linked to seniority as fans.

Two members of the research team were assigned to each grid. Using systematic random sampling with a random start and a sampling interval of three, Gator football fans were identified to complete the questionnaire. A screening question was asked to ensure that the fans being surveyed were sport tourists. The definition used by the State of Florida to identify tourists as persons who have crossed the county line in pursuit of recreation was employed. Therefore, Gator football fans who had traveled from outside of Alachua County were surveyed. The self-identified 'leader' of each travel group was asked to complete the questionnaire. The instrument consisted of 67 items, primarily closed ended, fixed choice questions that asked participants about their behavioral patterns when following the Gators. For example, how many home games they attended each year, and their behaviors as a fan such as tailgating before a game and wearing team colors. Fans also answered questions about their travel behaviors related to home football games and other sport-related events, such as length of stay, type of accommodations, and expenditures when traveling as a Gator fan. The data were analyzed using descriptive statistics. Most of the respondents were male (72%), 28% were female, and aged between 18–80 years (mean 48 years). About three-fourths were married and 88% were white. On average, these men and women had been Gator fans for almost thirty years (S.D. 14.7) and 43.6% were alumni of the University of Florida. An item on the questionnaire asked individuals to identify themselves as a particular type of fan. Seventy percent self-identified themselves as Type I (Gator football is my number one interest); 15.2% were Type II (I follow all Gator sports); 9.8% were Type III (I am a spouse or parent of Gator fan); and 3.7% were Type IV (To me the game is a social event).

3.3. Study two—fall 2000

The 1999 survey provided a valuable description of the travel-related patterns of these fans; however, it was felt additional insights could be gained by conducting a follow-up study. During the 2000 season, respondents from the 1999 survey were invited to participate in a second study. Using a process of theoretical sampling, fans who indicated in 1999 that they would be willing to take part in a follow-up interview were selected based on gender, age, type of fan (Types I–IV), length of time as a fan, and distance traveled to attend games. The aim of theoretical sampling in this instance was to include participants with a range of characteristics thought to be relevant to the study. These fans were contacted by mail and later telephoned to schedule interviews.

A total of 41 fans were invited to participate in the second part of the study. Twenty face-to-face semi-structured interviews were completed before home football games during fall 2000. The final sample does not contain any Type III fans (spouse or parent of a Gator fan), although among the fans interviewed some could be classified as a Type III, but their primary identity was a Type I (football) or II (Gator sports) fan. Reasons for not taking part in the follow-up study included being no longer interested in participating or they were unreachable by mail or telephone. An interview schedule comprised of questions pertaining to fan-related behaviors, meanings associated with being a fan, changes over time in fan behavior, and travel associated with following the team was used. The interviews varied in length from 20 to 60 min. As the interviews were completed, they were transcribed and mailed to the participants to verify transcript accuracy. Constant comparison (Glaser & Strauss, 1967; Strauss & Corbin, 1998) was employed during the interview process and analysis stages. Each member of the research team independently coded the transcripts for common patterns among the data. The researchers then met to discuss the patterns in the data, and through a process of comparing and contrasting, a series of themes and sub-themes emerging from the data were corroborated.

The sample was comprised of 16 white males and 4 white females ranging in age from 30 to 78 years (mean age of 53.8 years). The participants traveled an average of 249.6 miles (401.6 km) to attend home games. Their length of time as a Gator fan ranged from 7 (one fan) years to 51 years, with a mean of 33.8 years. Sixteen participants classified themselves as Type I fans, three as Type II fans, and one as Type IV fan. All of the respondents were season ticket holders, who attended most, if not all, home games and some traveled to away games as well.

4   Results

4.1   Study one results

The fans surveyed in study one traveled an average of 142.5 miles (229.3 km) (S.D. = 127.2; 204.7 km) to attend home football games. Sixty-six percent of them had season tickets, 64% attended at least four to five home games, and 61% attended the Orange and Blue football game in the spring (which entails another trip to Gainesville). The Orange and Blue Game is an intra-squad held every spring and provides the fans with a preview of the team for the up and coming season. Many of these fans occasionally attended other Gator athletic events (66%). Almost half of these Gator fans were likely to use vacation or annual leave to attend home and away football games. Additionally, 60% indicated that sports were somewhat to very important in their annual vacation plans.

Initially the data were analyzed according to fan type (Types I–IV). However, due to disproportionate sub-sample sizes (70% comprised of Type I football fans), as the focus of this study was on travel behavior, in accordance with Nogawa *et al.*'s (1996) suggestion, the analysis was segmented into two types of tourists, sport excursionists and sport tourists. To support this decision, cross-tabulations were run by fan type and several of the tourism related variables to establish if fan type was a significant predictor of tourist behavior. As might be expected due to their lower levels of involvement as fans, Type III fans, spouses or parents of a Gator fan were less likely to use vacation time to follow the Gators and were less likely to spend nights away from home in conjunction with attending games. However, with only 9.8% of the sample identified as Type III fans, it was felt that these results might be an artifact of a small sub-sample and might not be reliable. Cross-tabulations also showed that Types I, II, and IV fans were equally as likely to be excursionists (Type I 52.7%; Type II 52%; and Type IV 50%) as to be tourists (over night stay). Thus, a decision was made to segment the analysis by a tourism related variable, that of sport excursionist compared to sport tourist (over night stay).

Forty-seven percent of the fans stayed less than 24 h (sport excursionists) while 48% stayed at least one night (sport tourists). On average, sport excursionists traveled 94.3 (151.7 km) miles (S.D. 45.8 miles; 73.7 km) to attend home football games while sport tourists traveled 192.1 miles (309.1 km) (S.D. 162.6 miles; 261.6 km). Both excursionists and tourists were as likely to have season tickets while tourists were more likely to be University of Florida alumni.

During each football game in Gainesville, sport excursionists spent an average of $114.82 (USD) where as sport tourists spent an average of $293.38 (USD) (Table 21.1). On average, sport excursionists spent $34.12 (USD) on tailgate supplies, $34.12 (USD) on meals, and $7.38 (USD) on petrol.

The major differences between sport excursionists and sport tourists were that most sport tourists paid for accommodations (mean $76.84) and spent more on meals (mean $66.05). Regarding accommodation patterns, 35.9% of sport tourists spent the night in Gainesville. Of these, 30% stayed in hotels or motels, 13% stayed in RVs or campers,

Table 21.1 Mean expenditures per travel group for sport excursionists and sport tourists attending a University of Florida home-football game

Expenditure type	Sport excursionist ($)	Sport tourist ($)
Tailgate supplies	34.12[a]	51.13
Meals	25.68	66.05
Food & drink in the stadium	16.51	17.98
Retail shopping	4.61	17.71
Petrol	7.38	17.56
Gator souvenirs	26.52	46.11
Accommodation	0	76.84
Average game-related expenditure[b]	114.82	293.38

a Reported in US dollars.
b 90% reported that these were typical game-related expenditures.

1% stayed in bed and breakfasts, and 36.8% stayed with friends or family. Almost 14% stayed one night in Gainesville, 27.1% stayed two nights, and 7.2% stayed three or more nights. The general pattern was to arrive on the Friday before the event and stay until the Sunday after the event. In fact, some hoteliers in Gainesville have a two-night minimum stay policy. Over 90% of excursionists and tourists indicated that these expenditures were typical of their spending patterns when attending home-football games.

4.2 Study two results

Three themes emerged from the interview data related to the tourism-related patterns of these Gator football fans: (a) being a fan, (b) pilgrimages to the Mecca of Gator football, "the Swamp," and (c) on the road with the team. Two sub-themes were also identified in conjunction with being a fan and pilgrimages to the Mecca of Gator football, "the Swamp".

4.3 Being a fan

Being a Gator played a major role in the lives of these fans. They spend a lot of time following Gator football and other UF sports both in person by attending the games and through various other means including television, newspapers, and the Internet. All of them pride themselves on their loyalty and are adamant about not being "a fair weather friend" (Female 65, # 18) if their team loses. Part of the commitment to being a Gator fan involves regular attendance at the games and as such comprised the first sub-theme.

4.4 Home games

All of the fans interviewed are season ticket holders and attend most of the home football games. Indeed as one fan proudly proclaimed:

> We make all the home games. There has to be something pretty major for
> us to miss a home game. We've missed one, the Florida State game in '91,

> because we had a death in the immediate family and we couldn't make that
> one but other than that we have had our season tickets since '82 and that is
> the only home game we have ever missed.
>
> (Male 46, #21)

This sentiment is the norm rather than the exception. Another fan reported, "I have not missed a home game since we've been in Florida—that's six years" (Male 60, # 75). Thus, fans tended to visit Gainesville at least four or five times per year when attending home football games. However, football games do not tend to be the extent of their visits to Gainesville. As one fan explained:

> [I attend] every home football game. Typically, every year I take two trips
> to away football games. Probably 15 baseball games a year, home games and
> six to ten home basketball games a year.
>
> (Male 38, #87)

4.5   "I'm a Gator not a Gator fan"

The sentiment, "I'm a Gator not a Gator fan," expressed by a male fan was repeated by many of the fans and constituted the second sub-theme. The idea that a Gator is more than just a fan seems to be tied in part to whether or not they attended the University of Florida as a student. The five alumni of UF were more likely to voice this sentiment. Also, part of this identity was tied to being Type II fans, interested in more than just football. Gators attended other UF sports events, most notably baseball and basketball, which entailed additional trips to Gainesville throughout the year. As one fan explained, "I'm not just a one sport person, I'm a Gator fan period!" (Male 54, # 4). He went on to explain how he followed basketball, bringing his sons with him to the games when he could:

> I come personally to most every Gator basketball game. I might miss a Gator
> basketball game, you know if it's not a conference game or something . . .
> or if my work load, ahh, can't get out of it or something like that, but my
> sons will be with me too unless it's a game, a weekday when they got school
> (Male 54, #4).

Another fan explained, ". . .well we're basketball fans, football fans, . . . we come up for all of the games. We usually come up for Gator Growl, we participate in Home-coming . . ." (Male 55, #91). Gator Growl is an evening pep rally held in the football stadium the night before the homecoming football game. Homecoming for American universities is usually one weekend in the fall semester when the alumni of the university come back to visit. There is a homecoming parade that many of the fans talked about attending on a regular basis. At UF, the homecoming parade and Gator Growl events are held on a Friday each year. The university suspends classes for the day and many of the alumni and fans come to Gainesville 1 day early and stay all weekend. As one female fan explained, "I come, yeah, I come here for the parade! We come to watch the parade . . . I haven't missed the parades in (she paused to think) . . . except when I was out of town" (Female 65, #18).

At the start of the season, many of the UF sports teams also hold fan days where the team is present to sign autographs and to talk with the fans. The most elaborate of these is at the start of the basketball season called "Midnight Madness," which is not just a chance to meet the fans, but a full blown pep rally and is the reason fans come from out of town. One fan explained, "[w]e usually make all the fan days in football, we make the ah . . . midnight madness. . . . (Male 54, #4). The football team also holds an intra-squad scrimmage called the Orange and Blue Game in the spring that may attract as many as 40,000 fans (University Athletic Association, 2000). It is generally a chance for the fans to see how the team might perform the next season and it is also a good excuse to come to Gainesville to tailgate with friends and family, and to watch football, which many of the fans report feeling desolate without during the off season (Gibson *et al.*, 2001). Thus, even though regular season football games are the days when Gainesville has the most visitors per year, there are also a number of other occasions each year that attract these traveling-sports fans. Indeed, to prepare for the upcoming season, some fans talked of coming to Gainesville just to shop for Gator clothing and souvenirs. For example, one fan stated, "Uh, usually one time during the year we will come up and usually its just before the season starts and spend a whole wad of money on uh, new Gator paraphernalia for the new year" (Male 60, # 75).

4.5.1   Pilgrimages to the mecca of college football, "the Swamp"

For some, the trips to Gainesville each season were regarded as a pilgrimage. In line with previous research in both tourism studies (e.g., MacCannell, 1976; Moore, 1980) and sport studies (e.g., Leonard, 1993; Nixon & Frey, 1996), the idea of making a journey towards a spiritual center or in search of meaning (MacCannell) appeared to describe the behaviors of these fans. Indeed, one fan proclaimed, "It's a mecca" (Male 39, #169) when talking about his trips to Gainesville each season. On Friday afternoons and Saturday mornings before a home game, it is easy to visualize this sentiment as the roads leading to Gainesville are full of cars, trucks, and RV's with their Gator flags flying and the occupants decked out in their orange and blue Gator clothing. Unruh (1980) writes of each social world as possessing a geographical center. For Gator football the center is Gainesville and more specifically, Ben Hill Griffin Stadium or the "Swamp" (Gibson *et al.*, 2001).

The patterns associated with these pilgrimages to Gainesville comprised the second theme that emerged from the data. All of the fans spoke of planning their lives around the football schedule during the fall season. In fact, many described how they looked forward to the fall each year and often planned their trips well in advance. When asked to describe their travel patterns, as reported in the first study, the fans were either excursionists or tourists. The excursionists spoke of leaving home in the pre-dawn hours to arrive in Gainesville at least 3 h before each game. For the tourists, decisions related to choice of accommodation comprised the first sub-theme.

4.6   *Where to stay*

Most of the fans who are tourists arrive in Gainesville on a Friday and stay until Sunday. As one fan explained:

> We come up Friday and we leave on Sunday . . ., we stay in the house. Years, ahh, for quite a long time we've had a hotel room that we get every year. . . . cause we've got so many friends like [name], for example, that will come up. Uh, we may have like 20 people coming up on a weekend with us, and what we'll do is we need a hotel room cause we can't fit everybody in the house. We have a hotel room that we get every game. Plus, the house . . .
>
> (Male 49, #67)

Having a house in Gainesville to use for game days is a trend evident in the lodging-patterns data from the first study. Some fans have children who are students at the university and they have bought the house for them to live in while they are earning a degree. For others, the house is viewed as a financial investment and it is used while the fan and his or her family and friends are in town for games. For the hospitality industry in Gainesville, this trend of purchasing houses or staying with family and friends does not generally benefit city tourism; however, as the fan explained above, often the house is not big enough to accommodate all of their guests, so they still rent a hotel room for the weekend.

4.7   *While we are in town*

The second sub-theme identified in the data pertaining to the pilgrimages to Gainesville relates to what the fans actually do while they are in town. Most of the fans talked about eating and drinking in area restaurants, particularly those in the immediate vicinity of the university or those they may have patronized when they were students. As one fan explained, "[u]m, well it depends on what time we get in on Friday. We may go over to the 'Swamp' [restaurant-bar]. Most of the time we'll go to the 'Ale House', it's an old hang-out for us. But, most of the time we're here for this" (Male 49, #67). The last comment is a particularly insightful comment for analyzing the potential tourism development which might accrue from football fans in Gainesville. Among those fans interviewed, it was apparent that their major motivation for being in town was to see the game and to tailgate with their friends and family. Some spoke of doing a little shopping, "[w]ell, we go to the mall once in a while, but that's about it" (Male 79, #23) and "[o]h, go out to Butler Plaza out there and, . . . ah now and then if I get time I like to go out towards the Millhopper and see what all's happening" (both of the places she mentioned are shopping plazas) (Female 65, #18). She went on to explain, "[w]e do more of that on homecoming when I have, more time homecoming weekend", which is another key insight. Not surprisingly, the longer the fans stay in town, the more likely they are to do other things. Indeed, at the start of the season, when it is still very hot in Florida, the games are generally scheduled for the evenings, which the fans said also gave them more time to do other things like shopping. Thus as the results of our first study show, while the fans spend some money in Gainesville, generally in restaurants and a little in retail shopping, on the whole they are uni-dimensional in their motivations. They are in Gainesville to see the game and to socialize with their friends and family, thus, it would be quite a challenge to get them to visit other tourist attractions. Therefore, benefits from Gator football fans to other sectors of the tourism industry in Gainesville, like museums and parks might be limited. The key to leveraging the tourism benefits associated with UF football might rest with the away fans.

4.7.1   On the road with the team

"When I said that I went to every game, I literally mean every game . . . Not just home" explained one male fan (Male 54, # 72). Many of these fans follow the Gators on the road to attend away football games. One-third of these fans also follow the basketball and baseball teams when they play away. In fact, some of them talked about taking days off from work to follow the Gators and turning their trip into a mini vacation. As one fan said "[m]y goal is to go to every game in every city, I haven't made it yet, but that is my goal" (Male 65, #150). Another fan said "that's the only way we can get my husband to take a vacation" (Female 73, # 16) is when he travels to see the Gators play. The behaviors associated with these away games comprised the third theme that emerged from the data.

As part of this study we did not interview any away fans (i.e., non-Gator fans); however, some clues for strategies to leverage UF football to benefit the tourism industry in Gainesville might be gained from looking at the away travel behaviors of the Gator fans. While they are in Gainesville, as the results show above, it appears that the fans are interested in football, socializing, and little else. However, when they travel to watch the Gators play away games, their behavioral patterns become very different. As one fan explained, "[a]ctually, we go most places now, at least 1 day early so we can go out sightseeing . . . so we go on Thursday so we can have Friday to go sightseeing around. Take a tour. We go to Nashville, we take a tour every year on Friday" (Female 73, # 16). This female fan and her husband are retired and might be expected to have more time to turn their trip into a mini vacation. However, it seems that fans at other stages in the life course also take the opportunity to sightsee when they visit other universities to see the Gators play. While careful to emphasize the importance of seeing the game one fan explained, "[w]ell, the first thing we do is to follow the Gators . . . but then if you got time, like I've said if it's a late game, we get there early or something you know . . . it, I'd like to try and let my boys see things that they haven't never seen or something, you know" (Male 54, #4). Thus as a parent, the responsibility of exposing his children to other parts of the US also comes to the fore (Crompton, 1981) and might be capitalized upon by Gainesville regarding visiting fans. Another fan, explained while he may have been to some of the destinations a number of times over the years, this did not prevent him and his family from taking time to enjoy the sights associated with each university town. He described a typical season in terms of the away games and the tourist behaviors they might take part in while visiting a particular destination. He explained:

> We've always been big on going to see all of the um, um, tourist sights in the area like, uh, in New Orleans you have the Superdome there. We've done the tour to that. We've gone to the zoo. We've gone to the old planta-tion tours and we've taken the swamp tours. We've done the trolley car thing. Um, of course all the great restaurants. . . . You know, when we go to Tennessee, to Knoxville, we usually stay somewhere in the mountains, near the Smokey Mountains National Park and we may be in a motel or we

may rent a cabin there for a period of time. . . . Um, when we go to Kentucky, the horse farms are big deals. We uh, we've done the horse farm routine several times. Um, uh, we have only been to Athens [Georgia] once and we stayed in Atlanta then and got to experience the, uh well the night they won their World Series. We were there that night. So that was kinda neat, but, uh, the whole deal with Atlanta, we've been to Kennesaw to the battlefield there. . . . But, we try to find something that might be historical or just something kinda different to see while we are there . . .

(Male 46, #21)

Thus, extrapolating from the Gator fans' behaviors during away games, one might suggest that the major potential for tourist development for the city of Gainesville and the surrounding areas might be linked to the opposing team's fans, not necessarily their own fans as is commonly thought.

5   Discussion

The potential for college sports events to generate tourist activity is largely unrecognized in the sport tourism literature. The findings of this study suggest that college sports events attract a significant proportion of fans from outside of the local community and as such, support the growing focus within the tourism literature that small-scale-sport tourism events may hold more benefit for a community than hosting mega events (Higham, 1999). Similar to Garnham (1996) and Walo, Bull and Breen's (1996) findings, football game days in Gainesville bring a heightened feeling of community pride. Residents of Gainesville decorate their cars with flags and wear orange and blue (university colors) in much the same way as the Gator fans from out of town. However, while the results suggested that fans contribute economically to the host community through their use of food services, accommodations, and shopping related activities, it appears that further development as a tourist destination may lie in actively leveraging the opposing team's fans who travel to Gainesville. As Faulkner *et al.* (1998) postulated in relation to the 2000 Olympic Games, many of these traveling fans are "sport junkies" and they are interested in little else besides watching the game and socializing with their friends and family. Indeed, in a related study, we found that tailgating with family and friends (Gibson *et al.*, 2001) is very much an integral ritual for Gator fans and supports Green and Chalip's (1998) contention that we need to understand the subcultural values and behaviors of sport tourists if we are to adequately cater to their needs. Thus, may be it is not surprising that Nogawa *et al.* (1996) found sport tourists are more likely to engage in other tourist behaviors like sightseeing than are sport excursionists. While the results of this study support this finding, our data also seem to suggest that the away fans (non-Gator fans) who are sport tourists might be more likely to engage in other tourist behaviors than are the 'home' fans (Gator fans).

Unlike other college sports, college-football games are scheduled home and away on a 2-year cycle in the US. For example, the University of Tennessee, which is traditionally a major fixture for UF is only played in Gainesville every other year, and so, the novelty of visiting Gainesville for the visiting fans might be increased by the fact that it does not occur every year. Moreover, for some of the non-conference games (non-league games or friendlies) played at the start of the season, the fans of these teams might only visit Gainesville once, and the motivation to see the sights might be even more heightened. Thus, as Irwin and Sandler (1998) suggested, team affiliation may be crucial in understanding the tourism associated with college sports in the US. If we have correctly extrapolated from the patterns of behavior exhibited by Gator fans when they travel to away games, we would suggest that for cities like Gainesville, which host Division I college-sports teams, actively targeting the opposing team's fans might enhance the tourism benefits accruing from UF sports. Irwin and Sandler also suggested that this would require collaboration between the university and the tourism agencies in the local area. At present, there is a distinct separation between the university athletic department and the tourism agencies in Gainesville. Chalip and Green's (2001) research on the Sydney 2000 Olympics advocated that communities leverage an event. They argued that it is not sufficient to host a sports event and think that the fans will automatically take advantage of the other tourist attractions and services in the vicinity. Tourism agencies in communities need to collaborate and develop strategies whereby they target sport tourists and not merely raise awareness of what there is to see and do in a region, but should also develop special events that are likely to attract a particular target market. Perhaps, for example, in Gainesville, local restaurants, bars, or outdoor recreation areas could arrange and market sport-related social gatherings or pep rallies before and after college sport events. Since parking and traffic are often a problem on game days, local businesses could also provide transportation to and from the college sports event, which might encourage these participants to patronize their establishment before and after the game. Certainly, Chalip and Leyns (2002) in a study of the Gold Coast Honda Indy in Australia, found that businesses which hosted special events attracted more customers than those who did nothing, especially if the business was located outside the immediate vicinity of the sports event.

If Gainesville and similar college towns in the US wanted to develop sport tourism around their sports teams further, they might also think about attracting different types of sport tourism. For example, other universities around the US such as the University of Kentucky, have developed their own sports halls of fame displaying the history of their sports teams over the years. Opening a Gator hall of fame on the university campus would attract nostalgia sport tourists year round, as indeed would offering stadium tours. At present, many visitors to UF can be found walking around the stadium and taking photographs of the 'home of the Gators.' As Bale (1988) suggested, some sports stadia develop a mystique of their own. Certainly, Ben Hill Griffin Stadium (the Swamp) at UF appears to be one of these places. Another potential way of developing nostalgia sport tourism might be to offer fantasy camps where Gator fans get a chance to play with ex-players and be coached by the current football coach. Certainly, as Gammon (2001) discussed, the growth in nostalgia sport tourism based on fantasy sport camps has been quite dramatic in recent years.

6   Conclusion

The results of this two-part study suggest that college sport in the US and similar small-scale-sport events in general, holds some untapped potential for tourism development in the communities hosting them. The lessons for tapping this potential appear to be related to actively leveraging the events (Chalip & Green, 2001; Chalip & Leyns, 2002) and in the case of college sport in the US, increasing awareness of the tourism potential that such sports events hold, and increasing the collaboration between universities and community tourism agencies (Irwin & Sandler, 1998). Certainly, in studies of small-scale-sports events in New Zealand, Higham and Hinch (2001) found that the tourism associated with Rugby Super 12 games helped to establish a distinct regional image for cities hosting a professional franchise. In terms of future research, we suggest that the next step would be to investigate the tourism-related behaviors of opposing team's fans to substantiate the findings we have extrapolated from our data. Further we would recommend extending this research at other universities to better understand the tourism surrounding college sports in the US, and small-scale, sport-tourism events in general.

References

Anderson, D. (1979). Sport spectatorship: Appropriation of an identity or appraisal of self. *Review of Sport and Leisure*, 4(2), 115–127.

Bale, J. (1988). *Sports Geography*. London: E & FN Spon.

Burgan, B., & Mules, T. (1992). Economic impact of sporting events. *Annals of Tourism Research*, 19, 700–710.

Chalip, L., & Green, B.C. (2001). *Leveraging large sports events for tourism: Lessons learned from the Sydney Olympics*. Supplemental Proceedings of the Travel and Tourism Research Association 32nd Annual Conference, Fort Myers, FL, June 10–13, 2001.

Chalip, L., & Leyns, A. (2002). Local business leveraging of a sport event: Managing an event for economic benefit. *Journal of Sport Management*, 16, 132–158.

Crompton, J. (1981). Dimensions of the social group role in pleasure vacations. *Annals of Tourism Research*, 8, 550–568.

Dunning, E. (1990). Sociological reflections on sport, violence and civilization. *International Review for the Sociology of Sport*, 25, 65–82.

Faulkner, B., Tideswell, C., & Weston, A. (1998). Leveraging tourism benefits from the Sydney 2000 Olympics, Keynote presentation, Sport management: Opportunities and change. Fourth Annual Conference of the Sport Management Association of Australia and New Zealand, Gold Coast, Australia, November 26–28.

Gammon, S. (2001). Fantasy, nostalgia and the pursuit of what never was—but what should have been. Paper presented at the Leisure Studies Association Conference (Journeys in Leisure: Current and Future Alliances), University of Luton, July 17–19.

Garnham, B. (1996), Ranfurly Shield Rugby: An investigation into the impacts of a sporting event on a provincial city, the case of New Plymouth. *Festival Management and Event Tourism*, 4, 145–249.

Gibson, H. (1998a). Sport tourism: A critical analysis of research. *Sport Management Review*, 1, 45–76.

Gibson, H. (1998b). Active sport tourism: Who participates? *Leisure Studies*, 17(2), 155–170.

Gibson, H., Holdnak, A., Willming, C., King, M., Patterson, T., & Copp, C. (2001). "We're Gators . . . not just a Gator fan": Serious leisure, social identity, and University of Florida football. Paper presented at the National Recreation and Parks Association Congress, Denver, CO, October 3–6.

Glaser, B., & Strauss, A. (1967). *The discovery of grounded theory: Strategies for qualitative research*. Chicago, IL: Aldine Publishing, Co.

Gratton, C., Shibili, S., & Dobson, N. (2000). The economic importance of major sports events. *Managing Leisure*, 5(1), 17–28.

Green, B., & Chalip, L. (1998). Sport tourism as the celebration of subculture. *Annals of Tourism Research*, 25, 275–292.

Hall, C. (1989). The definition and analysis of hallmark tourist events. *Geojournal*, 19(3), 263–268.

Hall, C. (1992a). Adventure, sport and health tourism. In B. Weiler, & C.M. Hall (Eds), *Special interest tourism* (pp. 141–158). London: Belhaven Press.

Hall, C. (1992b). *Hallmark tourist events: Impacts, management and planning*. London: Belhaven Press.

Hall, C., & Hodges, J. (1996). The party's great, but what about the hangover? The housing and social impacts of mega-events with special reference to the 2000 Sydney Olympics. *Festival Management and Event Tourism*, 4, 13–20.

Higham, J. (1999). Commentary—sport as an avenue of tourism development: An analysis of the positive and negative impacts of sport tourism. *Current Issues in Tourism*, 2(1), 82–90.

Higham, J., & Hinch, T. (2001). Sport and development at tourism destinations: Exploring mutually beneficial links. Paper presented at the Leisure Studies Association Conference (Journeys in Leisure: Current and Future Alliances), University of Luton, July 17–19.

Hiller, H. (1998). Assessing the impact of mega-events: A linkage model. *Current Issues in Tourism*, 1(1), 47–57.

Ingham, R. (Ed.) (1978). *Football hooliganism: The wider context*. London: Inter-Action.

Irwin, R., & Sandler, M. (1998). An analysis of travel behavior and event-induced expenditures among American collegiate championship patron groups. *Journal of Vacation Marketing*, 4(1), 78–90.

Jennings, A. (1996). *The new lords of the rings*. London: Simon & Schuster.

Leonard, W. (1993). *A sociological perspective of sport* (4th edn). New York: Macmillan.

MacCannell, D. (1976). *The tourist: A new theory of the leisure class*. New York, NY: Schocken Books.

Maguire, J. (1986). The emergence of football spectating as a social problem 1880–1985: A figurational and developmental perspective. *Sociology of Sport Journal*, 3, 217–244.

Matzitelli, D. (1989). Major sports events in Australia – Some economic, tourism and sports-related effects. In G. Symes, B. Shaw, D. Fenton, & W. Mueller (Eds), *The planning and evaluation of hallmark events* (pp. 195–202). Aldershot: Avebury.

McPherson, B. (1975). Sport consumption and the economics of consumerism. In D. Ball, & J. Loy (Eds), *Sport and the social order* (pp. 243–275). Reading, MA: Addison-Wesley.

Moore, A. (1980). Walt Disney world: Bounded ritual space and the playful pilgrimage centers. *Anthropological Quarterly*, 54, 207–217.

Nixon, H., & Frey, J. (1996). *A sociology of sport*. Belmont, CA: Wadsworth Publishing Co.

Nogawa, H., Yamguchi, Y., & Hagi, Y. (1996). An empirical research study on Japanese sport tourism in Sport-for-All Events: Case studies of a single-night event and a multiple-night event. *Journal of Travel Research*, 35, 46–54.

North Central Florida Almanac (2001). *The Gainesville Sun*, March 25, 2001.

Olds, K. (1998). Urban mega-events, evictions and housing rights: The Canadian case. *Current Issues in Tourism*, 1(1), 2–46.

Orams, M., & Brons, A. (1999). Potential impacts of a major sport/tourism event: The America's Cup 2000, Auckland, New Zealand. *Visions in Leisure and Business*, 18(1), 14–28.

Ritchie, J.R.B. (1984). Assessing the impact of hallmark events. *Journal of Travel Research*, *23*, 2–11.

Ritchie, J.R.B. (1999). Lessons learned, lessons learning: Insights from the Calgary and Salt Lake City Olympic Winter Games. *Visions in Leisure and Business*, *18*(1), 4–13.

Ritchie, J.R.B., & Smith, B. (1991). The impact of a mega-event on host region awareness: A longitudinal study. *Journal of Travel Research*, *30*(1), 3–10.

Roberts, E., & McLeod, P. (1989). The economics of hallmark events. In G. Symes, B. Shaw, D. Fenton, & W. Mueller (Eds), *The planning and evaluation of hallmark events* (pp. 242–249). Aldershot: Avebury.

Roche, M. (1994). Mega-events and urban policy. *Annals of Tourism Research*, *21*, 1–19.

Standeven, J., & De Knop, P. (1999). *Sport tourism*. Champaign, IL: Human Kinetics.

Strauss, A., & Corbin, J. (1998). *Basics of qualitative research: Techniques for developing grounded theory* (2nd edn). Thousand Oaks, CA: Sage.

Travel Industry Association of America (1999). *Profile of travelers who attend sports events*. www.tia.org.com.

Travel Industry Association of America (2001). *Travel statistics and trends*. www.tia.org.com.

University Athletic Association (2000). Personal communication with staff in the University of Florida Athletic Association ticket office, Gainesville, Florida, September.

Unruh, D. (1980). The nature of social worlds. *Pacific Sociological Review*, *23*(3), 271–296.

Walo, M., Bull, A., & Breen, H. (1996). Achieving economic benefits at local events: A case study of a local sports event. *Festival Management and Event Tourism*, *4*, 95–106.

Wann, D., & Branscombe, N. (1993). Sport fans: Measuring degree of identification with their team. *International Journal of Sport Psychology*, *24*, 1–17.

Weiler, B., & Hall, C. (Eds) (1992). *Special interest tourism*. London: Belhaven Press.

Whitson, D., & Macintosh, D. (1993). Becoming a world-class city: Hallmark events and sport franchises in the growth strategies of western Canadian cities. *Sociology of Sport Journal*, *10*, 221–240.

Chapter 22

Elizabeth Fredline

HOST AND GUEST RELATIONS
AND SPORT TOURISM

Introduction

IT IS IMPORTANT THAT any discussion of sport tourism considers the population of the host region and takes into account how tourists' enjoyment of the sport and recreation facilities at a destination may impact upon the quality of life of local residents. As with any human activity there is a range of potential positive and negative impacts associated with sport tourism, and an understanding of these is useful in informing the tourism planning and management function within both public and private sectors.

There are two reasons why it is imperative that governments manage the impacts of sport tourism on the host community. Firstly, there is a moral obligation for governments to attempt to ensure sustainability in any activity they promote and support, and that such activity does not have negative implications for the quality of life of local residents. Secondly, and more pragmatically, local residents often play an important part in sport tourism, and in many instances, the commercial success of the product is dependant on a supportive and involved local community. Such support will wane if residents perceive the negative impacts to outweigh the positives.

A growing awareness amongst public sector managers of the need to manage social impacts has lead to the recent embracement of the concept of Triple Bottom Line reporting. This term, originally coined by John Elkington [1], refers to the importance of considering not only the economic impacts of any endeavour, but also to consider the social and environmental issues associated with it.

Empirical research on the impacts of sport tourism on host communities is limited, but substantial insight can be drawn from the literature documenting the impacts of tourism activity more generally. This essay will present a review of the social impacts of tourism literature with a view to identifying the range of potential positive and negative impacts of sport tourism. It will then examine the theoretical frameworks that have been used to explain variation in impact across and within regions.

Strategies used by hosts to deal with tourists will be explored as will the issue of user conflicts with regard to recreational facilities. Finally, the essay will conclude with a discussion of the future research needs of this emerging sub-field as it relates to the socio-cultural impacts of sport tourism.

Social impacts of tourism

Although it has not been specifically addressed in the literature, there appear to be two alternative approaches to defining the social impacts of tourism. Some authors include only the impacts that could not be regarded as fitting into any other category, that is, are neither economic nor environmental, while others more broadly consider any impact on society as being within the social domain. For example, Mathieson and Wall suggest that social impacts of tourism refer to the changes in quality of life of residents of tourist destinations' and using this definition, the social aspects of economic and environmental change must be deemed as being in scope [2]. For example, the contribution made by tourism to employment levels is typically considered to be an economic impact, but it clearly has social implications as well. Similarly, an environmental impact of tourism, such as damage to sensitive environmental areas, is also likely to affect the quality of life for local residents by reducing the amenity it provides to them.

The use of these alternative definitions seems to be related to three main assessment techniques that have been previously employed in the evaluation of social impacts. By far the most common method measures impacts through host community perceptions [3]. In this type of study, a sample of local residents is asked to report their perceptions of specific impacts of tourism on their quality of life via a questionnaire The questionnaire method allows the inclusion of a large number of impacts (within reason) and therefore these studies typically adopt the broader definition of 'social' impacts.

Another method, which has been occasionally employed, is the use of Contingent Valuation (CV) and related techniques such as Choice Modelling. These techniques attempt to assign monetary values to social impacts by asking residents about how much they are willing to pay to ensure or avoid some aspects of tourism development [4]. A quasi-experimental design is used in this type of research and thus there are limits on the number of variables (impacts) and levels of those impacts, which can be manipulated. For this reason a narrow definition of social impacts is typically adopted, and even then, only a few impacts can be tested at one time.

In an example of this type of study, Lindberg, Andersson and Dellaert modelled the impacts of new slope development in a ski resort in terms of residents' reactions to the potential social gains (increased tourism employment) and social losses (increased risk of landslides) [5]. They also took account of recreational benefits that would accrue differently across the community depending on the extent to which the residents participated in skiing as a recreational pastime. The questionnaire asked residents who perceived the proposed development positively about how much additional taxation they were willing to pay to ensure that the new slopes were developed. Where residents opposed the proposed development they were asked to nominate the level of tax cut that would be required for them to accept the new slopes. The conclusion of the study was that overall social losses outweighed potential social gains in this case study.

The final method has parallels with a technique developed in urban planning referred to as Social Impact Assessment (SIA). Originally this method was aimed at 'assessing or estimating, in advance, the social consequences that are likely to flow from specific policy actions or project development' and it is often used in justifying proposed tourism development [6]. However, examples of academic research that fit this description within the tourism literature have instead adopted a post-development evaluation perspective. They have identified key indicators of social impact and described. the changes that can be attributed to the tourism activity. For example, Hall, Selwood and McKewon documented some of the social impacts of the 1987 America's Cup in Fremantle, Western Australia, including increases in crime and prostitution [7].

However, by far the bulk of the literature has adopted the first approach, the measurement of impacts of tourism as perceived by local residents. This approach has advantages and disadvantages. First, it is clearly a subjective measure and responses to the survey will be framed within the respondent's value and attitude set. Therefore, a respondent may, either consciously or subconsciously, over or under rate the actual impacts in an effort to present a picture that is consistent with their overall representation of the tourism activity. However, many of the impacts, particularly the specifically 'social' impacts, cannot be effectively measured in any other way. As an example, there is no objective way at measuring the exciting atmosphere that is generated in a community that plays host to a major sporting event, such as the Olympic Games. Even when impacts can be objectively assessed, for example the increase in noise generated by sport tourism, any objective measure must then be compared with a researcher defined optimum level. There seems to be an assumption that the impact is uniform across the community, and that all local residents will perceive it in a similar way. However, empirical research has shown that, in some contexts, although many residents perceive increased noise as a negative impact, some actually see it in a positive light as a contribution to the excitement associated with some sporting events [8]. Therefore, use of the host community perception approach to assessing the social impacts of tourism allows exploration of the variation within a community, which can lead to a better understanding of the differential impact amongst community subgroups.

Characteristics of sport tourism

There is a broad array of activities that can be regarded as sport tourism and there are many ways to define the concept. However, in terms of the impact on the host community, it may be more useful to think of a number of different continua that can be used to describe sport related activity undertaken while away from home. And it is not only the characteristics of the sport tourism activity that will influence the level of impact on the host region. There is interplay between the characteristics of the activity and the participants it attracts, with the characteristics of the host destination. Table 22.1 presents a series of descriptors, presented as semantic differentials, which describe some of the factors that may affect level of impact.

When the activity is small scale, frequent and spatially diffuse, a low level but continual impact occurs which, over time, residents are likely to adapt to, especially if the activity is consistent with local values and residents can also gain advantage through participation. However, a large scale one off event is likely to be more disruptive, but also bring more

Table 22.1 Variables which affect the impact of sport tourism on the host community

The activity is . . .	Small scale	Large scale
	Frequent (daily or weekly)	Rare (one off event)
	Free	Expensive to participate in
	Spatially diffuse	Spatially concentrated
	Consistent with local values	Inconsistent with local values
The participants are . . .	Actively involved	Passively involved (spectators)
	Tourists and locals	Tourists only
	Non elite	Elite
	Socially and culturally similar to locals	Socially and culturally different to locals
The destination is . . .	Small, regional or rural	Large, urban
	Environmentally sensitive	Environmentally robust
	Relatively undeveloped	Relatively well developed
The tourism is . . .	Well managed	Poorly managed

economic, entertainment and excitement benefits. Intuitively, a large, well developed, urban area will cope better with the impacts of tourism; however, the residents of a small regional or rural area, which has fewer industrial bases, may be more eager to attract the economic benefits of sport tourism, and therefore he more prepared to accept any negative externalities. Management of impacts is clearly a critical component in ameliorating the costs and promoting the benefits of tourism.

Tourism impacts

Using the broader definition of social impacts referred to earlier, that is, any impact that has a social dimension, leads to the identification of an enormous array of possible effects. It is therefore useful to summarize them into a classification scheme. For some time it has been popular to think about tourism impacts in three domains: economic, environmental and social [9]; and recently, tourism researchers have borrowed the term the 'triple bottom line' from company accounting, to refer to this trilogy. Ritchie identified six impact domains in the context of event tourism, but these are also useful for examining the potential impacts of tourism more generally [10]. Recent work in the area of sport event impact assessment has merged these two approaches by examining impacts within the triple bottom line framework with an additional focus on longer term effects on image [11]. Table 22.2 summarizes the overlap between these classification schemes. Each type of impact may have both positive and negative manifestations, and the magnitude of the impact is likely to he substantially affected by management intervention. Some of the impacts of tourism may be perceived differently within a community as they effectively redistribute resources resulting in some subgroups reaping rewards at the expense of others.

Table 22.2 Classification of impacts

Triple bottom line approach[9]	Ritchie[10]	Fredline, Raybould, Jago and Deery[11]	Examples of impacts that could be classified into each category
Economic	Economic	Economic	Contribution to Gross Regional Product Generation of income Employment Changes in the structure of the local economy Stimulation of entrepreneurial activity Opportunity costs Upward pressure on prices/property values
Physical	Physical	Environmental	Pressure on sensitive natural areas Pollution and litter Pressure on existing urban infrastructure, e.g. traffic, crowding, noise, public transport Influence on new infrastructure development
Social	Socio-cultural Psychological Political	Social	Influence on social structure Influence on culture and values (Demonstration Effect) Outcomes of intercultural interaction Political outcomes Influence on individual psychological well being
	Tourism/ Commercial	Long term image • Media exposure • Destination image • Business promotion	Changes in tourism flows Changes in investment patterns and business opportunities

Sport tourism impacts

Economic

The economic impacts of sport tourism are unlikely to he substantially different from those associated with other forms of tourism, although there is some evidence to suggest that sport tourists (particularly spectating sport tourists) yield higher returns than the average 'holiday' visitor because they tend to spend more per day [12]. Some forms of sport tourism may also be more likely to deliver economic benefits to non-urban areas where regional economic development is desirable [13].

Physical and environmental impacts

Physical and environmental impacts will depend to some extent on the characteristics of the region that is playing host to the activity. Where sport is undertaken in a potentially sensitive natural area, environmental damage may result. For example bushwalking, horse or mountain bike riding, and other activities in pristine natural environments may have minimal impact if traffic is low, but as activity increases then impacts such as pollution, erosion and disruption to flora and fauna are likely to escalate. In urban environments it can be more difficult to attribute environmental and physical change specifically to tourism; however, any activity that temporarily increases the population of an area, is likely to place increased pressure on existing infrastructure such as roads and public transport, particularly in the case of a large-scale sporting event, which may also contribute to unwelcome levels of noise and crowding.

On the positive side, the growth of sport tourism in a destination can promote the development of infrastructure that may also be utilized by local residents. Large-scale sporting events tend to promote the development of new sporting venues and the longer-term benefits of these depend on the extent to which they can be effectively utilized to the advantage of locals.

Social impacts

In terms of 'social' impacts of sport tourism (using the narrower definition) the hosting of major sporting events is often associated with a sense of pride and self-actualisation amongst the resident population. They may also provide opportunities for entertainment and community or family togetherness. The demonstration effect of hosting sport activity may also be a catalyst for promoting sporting activity amongst the local community, which may have long-term implications for fitness levels and health.

On the negative side, there are examples of situations where the demonstration effect may be perceived as detrimental, for example, sport fans behaving in a rowdy or delinquent manner, which is negative in itself but may also have some affect on the behaviour of local residents. Intercultural interaction can manifest itself negatively, especially when international sporting teams are competing and nationalistic sentiments are strong. Also, individuals or community subgroups may experience reductions in their psychological well being, especially if they perceive a loss of control over their environment, and an injustice in the way tourism impacts are managed.

It is not possible to fully document the myriad of possible impacts because of the unique characteristics of each destination and sport tourism activity. It is important though to understand why some regions are differently impacted than others, and also why impacts are perceived differently amongst some communities and community subgroups. Some insight can be drawn from sociological theory.

Theoretical bases for understanding the impacts of tourism

The literature relating to the impacts of tourism on host communities has generally taken one of two approaches. The earliest studies adopted a macro perspective assuming a level of homogeneity within the resident population. These studies examine residents' reactions to tourism in terms of variables that characterize the region as a whole. This type of study has been described as 'extrinsic' because they look only at the community as a single entity [14]. In many of the more recent studies, the emphasis has switched to the exploration of the inherent heterogeneity within geographically-defined communities. These 'intrinsic' studies aim to understand why some subgroups of residents perceive the impacts of tourism differently than others.

Extrinsic models of community impact

A sub sector of extrinsic models are often also referred to as stage-based models because they describe how resident reactions to tourism change in response to changes in the magnitude and characteristics of tourism to the host region. One of the earliest models was Doxey's Irridex [15], which suggested that the attitudes of the host community toward tourists will pass through a series of stages including euphoria, apathy, annoyance and antagonism. The implication is that, over time, the hosts will be exposed to continued (and probably increasing) levels of negative impact.

Butler's well renowned Tourist Area Cycle of Evolution similarly implies that as the number of tourists increases, the impact on the host community is likely to intensify, and that escalating annoyance is a possible outcome [16]. However, he suggests that a thorough explanation of resident reaction is far more complex, and consideration must be given not only to the characteristics of the tourism, but also to the characteristics of the hosts and their region.

These early models seem to ignore the potential for residents to adapt to the impacts of increasing tourism, which appears likely given that more recent studies have found high levels of support in destinations with advanced tourism development such as Hawaii and Australia's Gold Coast [17]. However, the models are highly valuable to the extent that they have been instrumental in raising awareness of the importance of managing the impacts of tourism to avoid eventual antagonism.

In these extrinsic models, there are several variables that are considered likely to explain differences in host community perceptions of tourism. These include the stage of development; that is, whether tourism is in an exploration, involvement, development, consolidation, stagnation, rejuvenation or declining phase [18]. Also, the seasonality of the tourism activity is thought to be relevant; whether visitation levels are fairly uniform over an annual period or whether they are concentrated into specific tourism seasons. The host/guest ratio, and the cultural distance between hosts and guests are also considered to be relevant, together giving an indication of the tourism-carrying capacity of the region [19]. This is defined as the point beyond which the tourism resources of a community become overloaded and, therefore, if this point is exceeded negative impacts and negative community perceptions are likely to result [20]. Unfortunately the limited empirical work in this area has been, by necessity, case based, and frequently using substantially different methods which impedes comparison. A larger body of work exploring intrinsic variables means that this variation is better understood.

Intrinsic models of community impact

The intrinsic models attempt to explain why some residents within a community have higher levels of support for tourism activity than others. A substantial body of literature

Table 22.3 Variables which explain intrinsic variation in resident perceptions of
           impacts

Variable	Relationship
Financial benefit from tourism (through employment or ownership of a business that benefits from tourism)	Residents who benefit financially from tourism perceive higher levels of social benefit
Identification with the theme	Residents who enjoy the theme of the tourism/event perceive higher levels of social benefit
Contact (usually defined by residential proximity)	Residents who come into closer physical contact with tourism perceive both costs and benefits more highly
Values	Residents who have social values that are consistent with development tend to perceive higher levels of social benefit

has accumulated in recent decades and some of the relevant variables, have been clearly identified, as summarized in Table 22.3.

While early intrinsic studies shed substantial light on the variables that appeared to explain variance in resident perceptions of tourism, they tended to be descriptive and atheoretical, and it is only relatively recently that an attempt has been made to explain the variation in light of existing sociological and psychological theory.

Ap [21] employed social exchange theory, in an effort to understand how residents may led and behave in the context of tourism [22]. The theory describes behaviour in terms of exchanges, suggesting that residents engage in tourism exchanges such as working in or owning a business in the sector, sharing community resources with tourists, and utilizing new resources developed because of tourism. They then weigh up the costs and benefits of these exchanges and their overall perception will be the result of an internal cost benefit analysis. That is, if they believe that on balance, the benefits of tourism outweigh the costs, they will form a positive attitude toward tourism and may engage in supportive behaviours. If however they perceive the costs to outweigh the benefits, they will hold negative attitudes toward tourism and may attempt to withdraw from the relationship.

Pearce, Moscardo and Ross [23] have drawn upon social representation theory [24], which describes how values and attitudes toward a phenomenon are shared within a community. Social representations are 'systems of preconceptions, images and values' about a phenomenon [25]. Representations are the mechanisms people use to try to understand the world around them. When information on an unfamiliar object or event is encountered, past experience and prior knowledge of something that is seen as similar is used as a reference point. It is argued that representations are resistant to change, because they form a frame of reference through which new information is interpreted. Echabe and Rovira found that people had more accurate recall of facts that were consistent with their representation, and tended to 'modify' facts that were inconsistent [26].

The 'social' element refers to the fact that these representations are shared by social groups and help facilitate communication. In the context of tourism, the theory suggests that residents have representations of tourism which underpin their perceptions of impact, and that these representations are informed by direct experiences, social interaction and other information sources such as the media.

These two theories are not inconsistent, in fact there are substantial parallels, but social representation theory allows for non-rational reactions to tourism that are based on personal and social values, while social exchange tends to assume rational information processing. Social representation theory also acknowledges the fact that representations are socially transmitted making it possible for people who have less experience with a phenomenon to adopt a representation that is presented to them by their social group or through the media.

A third theory that has been advanced in this regard by Lindberg and Johnson [27] is the expectancy value model [28]. This model suggest that there is an interaction between the importance that residents place on certain outcomes (values) and the degree to which they believe tourism contributes to these outcomes (expectancy). Like social exchange, this model does not appear to allow for residents who act as cognitive misers; that is they do not care enough about an issue to think deeply about it. Rather, they assume a representation that is consistent with the norms of their social groups.

However, while social representation theory is more appealing than the alternatives in terms of its ability to accommodate different levels of interest in tourism amongst various resident sub-groups and the transmission of representations from person to person, this additional complexity also makes it far more difficult to test. There is substantial progress yet to be made in substantiating the validity and reliability of existing measures of social impact, and then in more fully understanding the variation within communities and between different communities.

The next section summarizes a series of studies that have been undertaken to explore residents' reactions to the hosting of large-scale sporting events. These studies have taken place in developed western destinations, and therefore the results cannot necessarily be generalized to other contexts, but the results nonetheless provide insight into the potential impacts of sporting events and sport tourism more generally.

Empirical research

A series of studies have been undertaken on a range of large scale sporting events in Australia using similar methods. Some of the results from four of these studies are reported here to give some insight into the range of impacts identified, and the perception of impacts of different types of event in different communities. A brief overview of the four case studies reported on is provided below.

The 2002 Australian Formula One Grand Prix. The Australian Formula One Grand Prix has been hosted in Melbourne every year sine 1996. Melbourne is a large (by Australian standards) state capital city with a population of approximately 3.6 million [29]. The event is hosted close to the city, approximately four kilometres south of the centre on a street circuit, in and around a large city park. Thus, there is substantial effort required in erection and dismantling of the necessary infrastructure. This creates substantial disruption in the vicinity and restricts access to the park for a period of the year.

The 2003 Australian Open Tennis Tournament. The Australian Open was first hosted in Melbourne in 1905, and thus it is a long-standing tradition in the city. The event is one of the Grand Slam tournaments on the international tennis circuit, and is therefore regarded as a prestigious event. It is staged in a purpose-built facility. The National Tennis Centre, close to the city and there is substantial infrastructure supporting the event precinct including parking and public transport.

The 2003 Rugby World Cup – Brisbane Matches. The Rugby World Cup is held every four years, but as it rotates between host regions it is effectively a one-off event. The 2003 event was hosted by the Australian Rugby Union (ARU) and matches were held across the nation in ten different cities. Brisbane is the capital city of Queensland and has a population of about 17 million residents [30]. The city hosted seven pool matches and two quarter finals over a period of approximately four weeks.

The 2003 Rugby World Cup – Townsville Matches. Townsville is the second largest city in Queensland situated in the north of the state, approximately 1,500 kilometres north of Brisbane. It is a much smaller city with a population of approximately 140,000 residents, and it serves as the regional centre for North Queensland, an area that is fairly reliant on agriculture and mining. The northern regions of Queensland are also important tourism destinations; however, Townsville itself attracts fewer tourists than more popular areas to the north (for example Cairns) and to the south (for example, the Whitsunday Islands, gateway to the Great Barrier Reef).

Method

In each of the case studies, a random selection of local residents was surveyed, either using a self completion questionnaire administered through the postal system or via a telephone interview. The instrument was developed over time. The earliest studies used a scale with forty-five items, but subsequent studies have used a compressed scale derived from analysis of the previously collected data. More details on the scale development process are documented elsewhere [31]. The compressed impact scale, which comprised twelve items, initially asked respondents to agree or disagree with a statement about a potential impact of the event. If they agreed, they were then asked to rate the level of impact on their personal quality of life, and the impact on the community as a whole

Results

Table 22.4 shows the mean personal and community level ratings for each of the events on each of the potential impacts. There is a fairly consistent pattern in the responses, which is to be expected given that the events were all similar in theme (that is, mainstream, large-scale, spectator sport events) and the communities examined all had similar cultural backgrounds. However, there are some differences that are worthy of further attention. The respondents in Townsville perceived a substantially higher level of community benefit from the RWC with regard to pride, entertainment opportunities, regional showcasing and economic impact. This is most likely to be related to the characteristics of this city in comparison to the other regions. Given Townsville's much smaller population, and its status as a remote regional centre rather than a state capital city, residents there would have fewer opportunities for sport-related entertainment, and feelings of pride and self-actualisation associated with playing host to a major event. Both Melbourne and Brisbane host several other international sporting events on a regular basis, thus any individual experience is less unique for residents of those communities. Also, Townsville's ambitions to attract more inbound tourism probably create awareness amongst local residents of the value of short- and long-term economic benefits of the hosting of events.

With regard to costs, none of these events attracted substantial mean ratings for any of the negative impacts except the Grand Prix, where local residents appear to be somewhat concerned about disruption, community injustice and the impact on the environment. This is likely to be a function of the fact that the Grand Prix is the only one of these events not staged in a permanent venue. The race track has to be built and dismantled for each event creating substantial disruption in the vicinity for about three months each year and denying local residents access to all important recreational venue. This undoubtedly fuels the perception that the event is unjust because those who reside further away from the event site are not as exposed to the localized negative externalities such as increased traffic congestion, parking problems and excessive noise. In terms of environmental damage, it seems logical that a motor sport event would be perceived as being more detrimental to the environment than tennis or rugby.

Strategies used by hosts to deal with tourists

At the micro, or individual level, some insight has been shed on the different ways in which residents may adapt their lifestyles to cope with tourism. Dogan suggested five behavioural responses including resistance, retreatism, boundary maintenance, revitalization and adoption, which could be employed by residents to cope with tourism activity in their community [32]. Ap and Crompton developed a simple scale for measuring residents' behavioural responses to tourism based on Dogan's categories [33]. They reduced the options to four levels because of difficulties in operationalizing the distinctions between all the responses, the eventual response options being embracement, tolerance, adjustment and withdrawal

Subsequent research suggests that residents can identify with these reactions [34]. In a case study comparison of the Gold Coast Indy Car Race 1998 and the Melbourne Grand Prix 1999, local residents reported behaviours consistent with these four responses. About one quarter of the sample reported that they embraced their event (through attending it or related functions, or by becoming involved in the public celebration). Over 40 per cent reported tolerance (which is associated with no behavioural change), and about 15 per cent reported minor adjustments to cope with the inconveniences. Finally, appoximately 20 per cent of the sample reported withdrawal which manifested itself by retreating to the confines of their homes for the duration of the event or by electing to leave the area altogether.

At a macro level, public sector tourism management organizations can employ a range of strategies to reduce the negative impacts of tourism on the host community, but only if they are aware of time issues. Until recently, such organizations have shown little interest in the evaluation of tourism impacts beyond an assessment of the economic benefits which is frequently undertaken to justify substantial public investment (particularly

Table 22.4 Comparison of perceived impacts of events

Event	Australian F1 Grand Prix		Australian Open Tennis		Rugby World Cup		Rugby World Cup	
Host Region	Melbourne		Melbourne		Brisbane		Townsville	
Year	2002		2003		2003		2003	
Frequency of Event	Annual		Annual		One-off		One-Off	
Scale	45 items#		12 items		12 items		12 items	
Administration method	Self completion postal survey		Telephone interview		Telephone interview		Telephone interview	
Sample size	279		300		306		303	
Perceived impacts	Personal	Community	Personal	Community	Personal	Community	Personal	Community
The event made local residents feel more proud of their city and made them feel good about themselves and their community	0.8#	1.2#	0.6	1.2	0.8	1.2	0.9	1.7
The event promoted development and better maintenance of public facilities such as roads, parks, sporting facilities, and/or public transport	0.7#	1.4#	0.3	0.7	0.2	0.7	0.3	0.7
The event gave residents an opportunity to attend an interesting event, have fun with their family and friends, and interact with new people	0.6#	1.3#	0.9	1.5	0.9	1.4	0.8	1.9
The event showcased the region in a positive light. This helps to promote a better opinion of our region and encourages future tourism and/or business investment	0.5#	1.4#	0.5	1.5	0.4	1.2	0.6	2.1
The event was good for the community because the money that visitors spent when they came for the event helps to stimulate the economy, stimulates employment opportunities, and is good for local business	0.4#	1.5#	0.4	1.5	0.3	1.5	0.5	2.0

The event was associated with some people behaving inappropriately, perhaps in a rowdy and delinquent way, or engaging in excessive drinking or drug use or other criminal behaviour	-0.1#	-0.3#	0.0	0.0	0.0	-0.2	0.0	-0.2
The event led to increases in the price of some things such as some goods and services and property values and/or rental costs	-0.1#	0.0#	0.0	0.0	-0.1	0.0	-0.1	0.1
The event had a negative impact on the environment through excessive litter and/or pollution and/or damage to natural areas	-0.2#	-0.5#	0.0	0.0	0.0	-0.1	0.0	0.0
The event was unfair to ordinary residents, and the costs and benefits were distributed unfairly across the community	-0.2#	-0.7#	0.0	0.0	0.0	-0.1	0.0	-0.1
The event was a waste of public money, that is, too much public money was spent on the event that would be better spent on other public activities	-0.3#	-0.4#	0.0	0.0	0.0	-0.1	0.0	-0.1
The event disrupted the lives of local residents and created inconvenience. While the event was on problems like traffic congestion, parking difficulties and excessive noise were worse than usual	-0.4#	-1.1#	0.0	-0.1	-0.3	-0.3	-0.1	-0.2
The event denied local residents access to public facilities, that is, roads, parks, sporting facilities, public transport and/or other facilities were less available to local residents because of closure or overcrowding	*	*	0.0	-0.1	-0.1	-0.2	-0.1	-0.1

these scores represent the average response to multiple items.

* no equivalent impact measured.

in large-scale sporting events). However, recent embracement of the concept of triple bottom line reporting amongst the public sector should hopefully promote more social and environmental impact assessment and extend awareness of time issues that need to be considered. Such information will be useful in informing the sustainable management of existing sport tourism activity within a region, and in selecting appropriate new forms of sport tourism to promote within a destination.

User conflicts

One of the potential impacts of sport tour hum is the impact of increased demand on natural areas and sporting and other tourism infrastructure. Beaches may become overcrowded, sporting venues, which are normally accessible to the public, may be restricted, for a specific event, and roads may be closed for a motor race or a marathon. While there is the potential that increasing demand will lead to increased supply of built facilities through public or private sector investment in sporting facilities, there is still the possibility that residents will perceive that tourism has reduced their amenity with regard to certain facilities.

The empirical research suggests that one of the important intrinsic predictors of overall perceptions of the impacts of tourism is utilization of affected recreation facilities. In the case of the Australian Formula One Grand Prix, the event takes place in a large recreational park which is the home of numerous sporting venues providing facilities for basketball, netball, badminton, squash, table tennis, cricket, football, soccer, baseball, hockey, lawn bowls and tennis. There is also a golf course and driving range, and a lake for boating. The erection and dismantling of event infrastructure restricts access to the park before, during and after the event. Residents who frequently used the park for recreational purposes (at least once a week) were found to have significantly more negative perceptions of the social impact of the Grand Prix than did those who were not frequent users of the park. This is consistent with findings from previous research by Keogh who found that residents who were frequent users of a recreational area were more concerned about tourist use of that area because of the potential reduction in amenity to them [35].

Conclusion

Given the perceived benefits of tourism, particularly the economic impacts, it is likely that tourism will continue to be encouraged in many destinations by both public and private sector organizations [36]. As noted in Table 22.1, one of the key influences on the level of impact of tourism is likely to be the management strategies employed in an effort to maximize the benefits and minimize the costs associated with the activity, and it is only through research, and an increased understanding of the most effective management techniques, that sustainability can be achieved.

Social impact assessment has progressed considerably in the last two decades and yet there is still much work to be done. More work is required to ensure the validity of the measures and this could be at least partially achieved through triangulation, by simultaneously employing more than one of the methods referred to at the beginning of this paper. Additionally, more empirical work is required, to better understand the extrinsic sources of variation in social impact.

There has been a long history of evaluation of the economic impacts of tourism, and these techniques have been embraced by government in an effort to justify the promotion of tourism. However, it is only very recently that governments have also indicated an interest in assessing the broader range of impacts including environmental, social and longer term impacts. The triple bottom line approach, represents a step forward for tourism impact management, not only because it considers broader issues, but because it can also consider the trade-offs between impacts of different types. For example, a large-scale motor sport event may attract numerous high spend international visitors leading to substantial economic benefits but may also cause extensive social disruption and environmental damage. A smaller, participant-oriented sport activity, may not generate as much revenue, but is unlikely to have the same level of social and environmental cost.

Techniques that attempt to synthesize the various impacts of tourism into an overall assessment, are in their infancy, and need substantial development. Once this has occurred they will be extremely useful in identifying the best types of sport tourism for destination managers to pursue.

Notes

[1] J. Elkington, *The Ecology of Tomorrow's World* (New York: Halsted Press, 1981).

[2] A. Mathieson, and G. Wall, *Tourism: Economic, Physical and Social Impacts* (London: Longman, 1982), p. 137.

[3] J. Ap and J.L. Crompton, 'Developing and Testing a Tourism Impact Scale', *Journal of Travel Research*, 37, 2 (1998), 120–30; C. Ryan and D. Montgomery, 'The Attitudes of Bakewell Residents to Tourism and Issues in Connnunity Responsive Tourism', *Tourism Management*, 15, 5 (1994), 358–69; E. Fredline and B. Faulkner, 'Residents' Reactions to the Staging of Major Motorsport Events Within Their Communities: A Cluster Analysis', *Event Management*, 7, 2 (2002), 103–14.

[4] K. Lindberg and R. Johnson, 'The Economic Values of Tourism's Social Impacts', *Annals of Tourism Research*, 24, 1(1997), 90–116; K. Lindberg, B. Dellaert and C. Rassing, 'Resident Tradeoffs: A Choice Modelling Approach', *Annals of Tourism Research*, 26, 3 (1999), 554–69; K. Lindberg, T. Andersson and B. Dellaert, 'Tourism Development: Assessing Social Gains and Losses', *Annals of Tourism Research*, 28, 4 (2001), 1010–30.

[5] Lindberg, Andersson and Dellaert, 'Tourism Development: Assessing Social Gains and Losses', 1010–30.

[6] R. Burdge and F. Vanclay, 'Social Impact Assessment: A Contribution to the State of the Art Series', *Impact Assessment*, 14, 1 (1996), 59.

[7] C.M. Hall, J. Selwood and E. McKewon, 'Hedonists, Ladies and Larrikins: Crime, Prostitution and the 1987 America's Cup', *Visions in Leisure and Business*, 14, 3 (1996), 28–51.

[8] E. Fredline, 'Host Community Reactions to Major Sporting Events: The Gold Coast Indy and the Australian Formula One Grand Prix in Melbourne' (unpublished doctoral thesis, Griffith University, Gold Coast, 2000).

[9] Mathieson and Wall, *Tourism: Economic, Physical and Social Impacts*; C.M. Hall, *Hallmark Tourist Events: Impacts, Management and Planning* (London: Belhaven Press, 1992).

[10] J. Ritchie, 'Assessing the Impact of Hallmark Events: Conceptual and Research Issues', *Journal of Travel Research*, 22, 1 (1984), 2–11.

[11] E. Fredline, M. Raybould, L. Jago and M. Deery, 'Triple Bottom Line Event Evaluation: Progress Toward a Technique to Assist in Planning and Managing Events in a Sustainable Manner'. Paper presented at the *Tourism State of the Art II Conference*, Glasgow, June 2004.

[12] Bureau of Tourism Research, *International Visitor Survey* (Canberra: BTR, 2003). (This conclusion is based on Australian tourism expenditure data estimates and may not be generalizable to other destinations.)

[13] For more on economic impacts see T. Mules and L. Dwyer, 'Public Sector Support for Sport Tourism Events: The Role of Cost–Benefit Analysis', *Sport in Society*, 8, 2 (2005), 338–55.

[14] B. Faulkner and C. Tideswell, 'A Framework for Monitoring Community Impacts of Tourism', *Journal of Sustainable Tourism*, 5, 1 (1997), 3–28.

[15] G.V. Doxey, 'A Causation Theory of Visitor Resident Irritants: Methodology and Research Inferences', in *Travel and Tourism Research Association Sixth Annual Conference Proceedings* (San Diego, CA: TTRA 1975), pp. 195–8.

[16] R.W. Butler, 'The Concept of a Tourist Area Cycle of Evolution: Implications for Management of Resources', *Canadian Geographer*, 24, 1 (1980), 5–12.

[17] J. Lui and T. Var, 'Resident Attitudes Toward Tourism Impacts in Hawaii', *Annals of Tourism Research*, 11, 2 (1986), 193–214; Faulkner and Tideswell, 'A Framework for Monitoring Community Impacts of Tourism', 3–28.

[18] Butler, 'The Concept of a Tourist Area Cycle of Evolution', 5–12.

[19] R.W. Butler, 'Tourism as an Agent of Social Change', *Proceedings of the International Geographical Union's Working Group on the Geography of Tourism and Recreation* (Ontario, Canada: Trent University, 1975), pp. 85–90.

[20] H. Coccossis and A. Parpairis, 'Tourism and the Environment: Some Observations on the Concept of Carrying Capacity', in H. Briassoulis (ed.), *Tourism and the Environment: Regional, Economic and Policy Issues* (Dordrecht: Kluwer Academic Publications, 1992), pp. 23–33

[21] J. Ap, 'Residents' Perceptions on Tourism Impacts', *Annals of Tourism Research*, 19, 4 (1992), 665–90.

[22] R. Emerson, 'Exchange Theory. Part 1: A Psychological Basis for Social Exchange', in J. Berger, M. Zelditch and B. Anderson (eds), *Sociological Theories in Progress* (New York: Houghton-Mifflin, 1972), pp. 38–87.

[23] P.L. Pearce, C Moscardo and G.F. Ross, *Tourism Community Relationships* (Oxford: Pergamon, 1996).

[24] S. Moscovici, 'On Social Representations', in J.P. Forgas (ed.), *Social Cognition: Perspectives on Everyday Understanding* (London: Academic Press, 1981), pp. 181–209.

[25] S. Moscovici, 'The Coming Era of Social Representations', in J.P. Codol and J.P. Leyens (eds), *Cognitive Approaches to Social Behavior* (The Hague: Nijhoff, 1982), p. 122.

[26] A. Echabe and D. Rovira, 'Social Representations and Memory', *European Journal of Social Psychology*, 19 (1989), 543–51.

[27] Lindberg and Johnson, 'The Economic Values of Tourism's Social Impacts', 90–116.

[28] A.H. Eagly and S. Chaiken, *The Psychology of Attitudes* (Orlando, Florida: Harcourt Brace Jovanovich, 1993).

[29] Australian Bureau of Statistics, *Australian Demographic Statistics* (Canberra: ABS, 2003).

[30] Ibid.

[31] E. Fredline, L. Jago and M. Deery, 'The Development of a Generic Scale to Measure the Social Impacts of Events', *Event Management*, 8, 1 (2003), 23–37.

[32] H.Z. Dogan, 'Forms of Adjustment: Sociocultural Impacts of Tourism', *Annals of Tourism Research*, 16, 2 (1989), 216–36.

[33] J. Ap and J.L. Crompton, 'Residents' Strategies for Responding to Tourism Impacts', *Journal of Travel Research*, 32, 1 (1993), 47–50.

[34] Fredline, 'Host Community Reactions to Major Sporting Events: The Gold Coast Indy and the Australian Formula One Grand Prix in Melbourne'.

[35] B. Keogh, 'Public Participation in Community Tourism Planning', *Annals of Tourism Research*, 7, 3 (1990), 449–65.

[36] For more on economic impacts see T. Mules and L. Dwyer, 'Public Sector Support for Sport Tourism Events: The Role of Cost-Benefit Analysis', *Sport in Society*, 8, 2 (2005), 338–55.

PART FOUR

Policy and management considerations for Sport & Tourism

EDITOR'S INTRODUCTION

IF THE ASSUMPTION OF THE PREVIOUS PARTS is that research on the impacts of sport and tourism is underpinned by an understanding of sports tourists' behaviours, then it should be a relatively straightforward step for managers and policy-makers to utilise this research in informing their policy and management decisions. As such, it might be expected that policy and management research in sport and tourism would focus on the most effective ways to manage impacts, and to make policy and provision for sports tourism activities. However, as a number of chapters in this Part will show, and as has been noted for some time in policy and management research in sport and tourism (see General Introduction), it is often the case that policy-makers and managers in the public sector are reluctant to collaborate on policy and management for sport and tourism.

The lack of collaboration in the public sector belies the established link between sport and tourism that many of the earlier papers in this Reader demonstrate. Whether such a link is seen as positive or negative in any given situation is immaterial, as the fact that the link exists means that there is a requirement for collaboration between sport and tourism bodies either to maximise benefits or to minimise negative impacts. As such, policy and management considerations for sport and tourism have been concerned not only with the ways in which the links between and impacts of sport and tourism should be managed, but also with the reluctance of policy-making agencies in the sport and the tourism sectors to collaborate in managing and providing for sports tourism. Consequently, the chapters in this Part focus on how policy and management in sports tourism is researched, understanding the dynamics of (and lack of collaboration in) policy-making for sport and tourism, the challenges faced by sports tourism policy-makers and managers in overcoming issues such as seasonality and participation constraint, and the ways in which sport and tourism can be managed and policy developed to encourage positive outcomes for local communities.

The first chapter in this Part, and the last in this Reader from the special issue of *European Sport Management Quarterly*, focuses not on policy-making and management per se, but on how policy and management research is conducted. In this respect, **Paul Downward**'s paper, *Critical (Realist) Reflection on Policy and Management Research in Sport, Tourism and Sports Tourism* provides a useful context for the papers that follow. Downward also usefully provides a comment on the nature of policy and management that is worthwhile noting here:

> one must view the application of management and the achievement or pursuit of policy objectives in the context of their being connected with, and deriving from, various specific institutional formations. These exist in a number of domains, such as the public or private sector. However, it remains that they are structured entities comprising internally related positions and governed in various degrees by rules, norms and trust in which obligations to act persist.

Downward's view establishes policy and management as being formed within an institutional context (e.g. National Tourism Organisation or National Olympic Committee), where there are established positions which govern potential responses (e.g. a commitment to sport for all or to social tourism) and individual behaviours (e.g. to act autonomously, or within specific guidelines, or within less specific expectations), and from which some obligation to manage or develop policy exists. However, in relation to this latter point, the obligations are usually to make policy for, or to manage, sport or tourism respectively; rarely is there an obligation to respond to sports tourism issues, and this point is addressed in the following two chapters.

The second and third chapters in this Part are by myself, **Mike Weed**, and are derived from my ongoing work on policy responses to what I have previously described as 'the sport-tourism link'. I have used this terminology, including the hyphen, as a deliberate strategy to refer to the range of issues that might legitimately be the concern of any policy collaboration between sport and tourism bodies. These might include liaison on resources and funding, policy and planning, and information and research, many of which would not be perceived to be sports tourism issues. For example, tourism organisations might be interested in collaborating with a sports body in order to use a sports stadium for a tourist event such as a rock concert. This clearly does not involve sports tourism, but it does involve a sport-tourism link.

The first of my chapters, *Towards a Model of Cross-Sectoral Policy Development in Leisure: The Case of Sport and Tourism*, discusses the structure of policy communities for sport and for tourism, and examines how these structures might effect the emergence of a sport-tourism policy network. In particular, the traditionally and historically separate development of the two sectors is perceived as having determined a separatist approach in the UK, as indeed it has done in many other countries around the world. Following up on this, the second of my chapters, *Why the Two Won't Tango! Explaining the Lack of Integrated Policies for Sport and Tourism in the UK*, identifies and examines a further six influences that interact with the structures of the sport and tourism policy communities to affect sport-tourism policy liaison and development. Taken together, the two chapters suggest that despite the wide range of evidence establishing a clear link between sport and tourism, many policy-makers are still not fully aware of the extent of the sport-tourism link, or believe it is not relevant to their work, their organisation, or their job portfolio. In this respect, in addition to the need to further educate policy-makers about the link, the papers suggest that sport-tourism policy liaison is likely to be more sustainable at the regional level, where specific aspects of the link relevant to historic, geographic, administrative, economic and structural regional contexts can be reflected in sport-tourism policy development.

This more local focus is reflected in the fourth chapter in this Part by **Christopher Hautbois** and **Christophe Durand**. *Public Strategies for Local Development: The Effectiveness of an Outdoor Activities Model* examines the ways in which the local public sector can encourage inward investment in order to reach a critical mass of concentrated activity. Hautbois and Durand use a case study based upon equestrian activities in the Basse-Normandie region of France to illustrate their discussions, in which they found that a lack of leadership and co-ordination in the public sector was a *centrifugal* force that was likely to drive investment away. Acting alongside this was a lack of organisational skill among those working in some areas of the equestrian industry that led to the local public sector being more likely to fund activities that were already well-organised, thus acting against the development of new markets. Hautbois and Durand's paper, therefore, reinforces the problems that exist in forming partnerships to develop collaborative policy for sport and tourism initiatives.

In moving from an exploration of the issues that mitigate against collaboration between sport and tourism bodies to a consideration of some of the issues that such bodies face in managing and making policy for sport and tourism, **James Higham** and **Tom Hinch** explore issues of seasonality at the intersection of sport and tourism. *Tourism, Sport and Seasons: The Challenges and Potential of Overcoming Seasonality in the Sport and Tourism Sectors* explores the nature of seasonality in sport and in tourism and its implications for sports tourism development. Tourism has long faced problems of seasonality and Higham and Hinch distinguish natural factors (e.g. the weather) from institutional factors (e.g. timing of school holidays) in causing such seasonality. In sport, globalising forces, professionalisation, and increased media and commercial interests are all cited as factors contributing to the changing of traditional seasons in sport and, in some cases, de-seasonalisation. Through a case study of the development of Rugby Union in New Zealand, Hinch and Higham show how changing seasons in sport can help alleviate some of the problems of seasonality in tourism and in the process contribute to the development of a sports tourism product.

One of the longest established sports tourism sectors is the ski industry, and the next two chapters examine issues associated with policy and management in this sector. First,

Simon Hudson, Brent Ritchie and Seldjan Timur examine the development of competitive advantage in their paper, *Measuring Destination Competitiveness: An Empirical Study of Canadian Ski Resorts*. Crouch and Ritchie's (1999) model of destination competitiveness is applied to the Canadian ski industry, which is seen as having reached a stage of maturity and consolidation and where, as such, establishing competitive advantage is particularly important. Following the approach of other chapters in this Part, Hudson *et al.* emphasise the importance of strategic policy, planning and development. They identify three resorts, all owned by one company with a reputation for extensive strategic planning, as those that score most highly on the dimensions of competitiveness identified in the model. These dimensions – supporting factors and resources, core resources and attractions, destination management, destination policy planning and development, qualifying and amplifying determinants – are shown by Hudson *et al.*'s study to form a potentially useful benchmark, not only for winter sports destinations, but for sports tourism and, indeed, tourism destinations in general.

Peter Williams and Paul Fidgeon's chapter, *Addressing Participation Constraint: A Case Study of Potential Skiers* is also based on the Canadian ski industry. Like many other chapters in this Reader, it demonstrates the inextricable link between understanding participation and developing policy and management initiatives. However, somewhat unusually, Williams and Fidgeon's paper focuses on non-participants and the factors that put off those who have never tried skiing. They suggest that non-skiers are either unaware of the benefits of the sport or, more significantly for managers and marketers, have emotional or perceptual biases that inhibit their desire to take part. While a number of strategies are suggested for managers and marketers to help overcome these inhibitions, Williams and Fidgeon strongly advocate further research that develops a more detailed understanding of the potential non-skier market and the factors that would encourage participation.

The final chapter in this Reader returns to the concept of leveraging. *Local Business Leveraging of a Sport Event: Managing an Event for Economic Benefit* by Laurence Chalip and Anna Leyns reports on four linked studies that examine the way in which local businesses in the Gold Coast attempted to leverage benefits from the Gold Coast Honda Indy motor race. Originally published in 2002, the chapter suggests that very few local businesses recognised the leveraging opportunities that the event presented, and those that did used fairly standard promotional and theming tactics. While business leaders favoured some co-ordination of leveraging efforts, they indicated that they would prefer such co-ordination to come from an existing business association rather than through government. Chalip and Leyns' chapter indicates that, even in fairly recent times, leveraging approaches are largely unrecognised and, as a result, are often underutilised. However, as sports tourism policy and management develops and matures in the future it is likely that an appreciation of leveraging approaches will become much more commonplace in both the public and commercial sectors.

The chapters in this Part have both examined the problems that mitigate against the development of collaborative approaches for sport-tourism policy partnerships, and explored some of the areas in which policy-makers and managers have been successful in developing the link between sport and tourism for mutual benefit. As more examples of the latter become known, it is possible that there will be a greater motivation among policy-makers and managers to overcome some of the issues that have led to a lack of partnership in the past. This, more than anything else, will be a clear sign of a maturing sports tourism sector.

REFERENCES

Crouch, Geoffrey I. and Brent Ritchie, J.R. (1999). 'Tourism, Competitiveness, and Societal Prosperity', *Journal of Business Research*, 44 (3): 137–52.

Chapter 23

Paul Downward

CRITICAL (REALISTIC) REFLECTION ON POLICY AND MANAGEMENT RESEARCH IN SPORT, TOURISM AND SPORTS TOURISM

QUALITY ASSURANCE AGENCY (QAA)[1] benchmarks statements suggest that sports degree programmes in the UK inherently draw upon a number of disciplines ranging from the sciences, such as anatomy, physiology and psychology; to business, such as strategy, marketing, economics, and the humanities, such as history, sociology and philosophy. The key areas of study in which these disciplines are typically applied involve: exploring the human responses to sport and exercise, the monitoring and enhancement of sporting performance, the historical, social political economic and cultural distribution and impact of sport as well as sports policy planning and management.

Likewise, tourism is typically taught within subject areas such as tourism management; tourism geography; leisure and tourism management; and tourism studies but includes specific areas of study such as sports tourism; rural tourism and sustainable tourism. Broad concern is with activities and relationships that take place away from typical places of residence. Emphasis is upon private sector activity such as tour operators, airlines and hotels as well as a quasi-public sector including agencies such as the tourist boards and regional development agencies. In addition the nature, impacts and meanings of tourism are now of direct interest. As Davies & Downward (2001) and Downward & Mearman (2004a) argue, the academic analysis of tourism has eclectic origins.

In general, this raises quite fundamental philosophical challenges for the researcher seeking to understand and to inform policy and management debates in sport, tourism and sports tourism. Likewise, these challenges are relevant for policymakers in having to digest different research findings. If one considers the interface between these two areas, then matters are clearly more complicated. This is made clear by Weed & Bull (2004) who, whilst arguing that sports tourism research needs to be more than a conflagration of issues traditionally associated with sport and tourism, cite Gibson's argument that:

the field suffers from a lack of integration in the realms of policy research and education. At a policy level, there needs to be a better coordination among agencies responsible for sport and those responsible for tourism. At a research level, more multidisciplinary research is needed, particularly research which builds upon existing knowledge bases in both sport and tourism. In the realm of education, territorial contests between departments claiming tourism expertise and those claiming sport expertise needs to be overcome.

(Gibson, 1998, p. 45)

In this paper two main related issues are addressed within the context of sports tourism. The first is to explore the basis upon which insights from different disciplines can be combined to inform research and policy, the second is to discuss what this implies about the conduct of research. To address these issues, the next section offers a brief restatement of some characteristics of the academic study of sport and tourism, before focussing on one branch of study; policy, planning and management, to reveal some implicit realist assumptions within the approach. The following sections then review some features of social science research methods, before exploring the constraints and possibilities of drawing upon different disciplines in research. It is argued that a critical realist ontology can be drawn upon to specify a coherent interdisciplinary approach to sport and tourism research and, as such, motivate a clearer understanding of sports tourism as a branch of social science.[2] An illustration of the application of these ideas then follows, before conclusions are offered.

Some features of sports and tourism study

As implied earlier, QAA benchmark statements provide a synthetic audit of the scope and content of sports study in the UK. The following three features, extracted from these statements, are worth noting, in the current context, in more detail:

1   In programmes of study with sport in the title, sport refers to personal, social and cultural activity embraced within the participation, organisation, provision, and delivery of sporting activity, as defined by the Council of Europe.
2   Their currency and diversity is demonstrated by the orientation towards sport and exercise sciences, sports coaching, sport development and sport management.
3   Sport has emerged as an academic area with a developing body of knowledge. This is characterised by a balance of discipline-based knowledge and knowledge derived from the practice of sport. With programmes adopting a multidisciplinary and/or interdisciplinary approach, the study of sport has intrinsic intellectual value.

The first of these points suggests that the unit of analysis can range from the individual to more aggregated concepts. The second point suggests that different areas of study, within which specific disciplinary and substantive contributions reside, can contribute to this analysis. In this regard a distinction is drawn between "scientific" disciplines, "sports practitioner" contributions and those from management and policy studies. One should note here that there is often a distinction drawn between "sports management" and "sports studies", with the former drawing upon economics, and the study of business functions, and the latter sociology, philosophy and history, etc. This is illustrated in drawing distinctions between journals such as *European Sports Management Quarterly*, *The Journal of Sports Management and Managing Leisure* with journals such as *Leisure Studies*, *Sociology of Sport* and the *Journal of Sports and Social Issues*. Both of these are contrasted with an experimental science approach, implied, for example in physiology, biomechanics and psychology.[3] Notwithstanding this distinction, point three emphasises that a pragmatic view is taken upon disciplinary combination.

In the case of tourism, the following issues are worth noting in relation to the disciplinary context of the subject:

1   Of the programmes with management in the title many focus particularly on business management.
2   Others are more concerned with the management of scarce resources in the community through concepts of planning and public policy.
3   Typical subject areas might include: accommodation for tourists, destination planning and development, geography of tourism, impacts of tourism, international tourism, operation of the tourism industry, passenger transportation, research methods, technology in travel and tourism, tourism and the environment, tourism economics, tourism marketing, tourism policy, tourism management, sustainable tourism.

These suggest an emphasis upon management and resource allocation specifically, but again within an eclectic approach to disciplinary context (see also Tribe, 1997). As with sports research there are distinctions within the literature. For example, at one extreme Tourism Economics draws upon the economic, business and financial disciplines, whilst a journal such as *Tourist Studies* is populated by papers drawing upon postmodernist and post-structuralist themes. Commensurate with the eclectic development of tourism and hospitality, journals such as *Annals of Tourism Research* and *Tourism Management* are populated with papers drawing upon a wide ranging set of analytical approaches. It is here that the first issue of this paper, concerned with exploring the logical basis upon which such disciplinary insights are combined, is raised.

In relation to sports tourism, Weed & Bull's (2004) recent analysis briefly discusses impacts, with which most other sports tourism texts are largely concerned (see Standeven & De Knop, 1999; Hudson, 2003) before a substantive examination of sports tourism participants, policymakers and providers. Clearly, the study of these four areas is underpinned by a range of different disciplines, and Weed & Bull (2004, p. 205) cite psychology, geography, sociology, policy studies, marketing and management, along with the use of grounded theory, as perspectives that inform their analysis. This, along with the above discussions of QAA benchmarks, partly informs the scope of the analysis in relation to the second concern of this paper, the actual conduct of research. Here, attention is focused upon policy and management for sport, tourism and sports tourism as deriving insights from the economics, policy and management literatures. Policy and management are clearly distinguishable areas of study within both sport and tourism, and Weed and Bull's analysis identifies them as key contributors to an understanding of sports tourism, particularly sports tourism policymaking and provision. Furthermore, the focus of this journal on management issues means a focus on policy and management research and practice is clearly an appropriate way to circumscribe the discussion.[4] However, there is no clear and unitary definition of the terms management and policy. In this context any specific conceptual view upon the research methods employed to generate insights within the sport, tourism and sports tourism literatures must be predicated upon that which emanates from the originating disciplinary theory or research approach. What *can* be said in a general sense however, is that, by construction, policy and management insights presuppose a realist perspective.

In its most general sense, realism is an ontological position in which "we perceive objects whose existence and nature are independent of our perceptions" (*Oxford Companion to Philosophy*, 1995, p. 746). However, as discussed later in the paper there are different variants of this position. For now, though, what matters is that the existence of objects is not simply confined to perception.

One can justify the claim that policy and management for sport, tourism and sports tourism has a realist foundation by way of a form of transcendental argument that involves answering the question, "What must the world be like in order to make possible the existence of institutions like sports and tourism organisations and their related management systems, or policy bodies and their prescriptions?"

To answer this question one must view the application of management and the achievement or pursuit of policy objectives in the context of their being connected with, and deriving from, various specific institutional formations. These exist in a number of domains, such as the public or private sector. However, it remains that they are structured entities comprising internally related positions and governed in various degrees by rules, norms and trust in which obligations to act persist. In this sense whether defined in terms of customers and sports centre service providers or tourism attractions, or policy funding and implementing bodies such as UK Sport and Sport England or Visit Britain and the Scottish and Wales Tourist Boards, the processes involved are not reducible to the unique individual *per se* but can be viewed as comprising persistent relationships that transcend the specific individual's experience and which are constituted in relation to other objects (see Lewis, 2004). In this respect relationships and processes must, by this argument, exist independently of specific individual consciousness, that is have a realist basis.

Of course, this is one form of question about reality. In this sense it produces a particular view of the nature of reality. Consequently the argument also carries with it some constraints about the presupposed nature of the world so conceived. It implies that the world is structured, potentially hierarchical and has both individual and social features. This is a social ontology in which relationships between these constituent features are causal in bringing about outcomes. The variety of units of analysis associated, for example, with the study of sports presented in Point 1 (p. 417) suggest that this approach is potentially useful.[5]

Realism does not need to rely on such a view, however. To extend the basic definition of realism above to the ideas that policy and management are causal processes simply requires a conception that the implied causal forces associated with policy or management decisions are, at least partially, independent of those conceptualising or implementing the policy. Such a more limited view, to be distinct from the account above, is conceivable in an approach in which the individual is the sole unit of analysis, which can be referred to as methodological individualism, or in which the broader identified grouping is the sole unit of analysis, which can be referred to as methodological collectivism. In this respect once again, both the individual and more collective units of analysis for sport, tourism and sports tourism, though not the combination of such units, are relevant for this perspective.

It is clear, then, that debate about the nature of realism, in connection with the nature of cause and the ways in which we can understand it, that is epistemological issues associated with research methods, is important in understanding policy and management for sport, tourism and sports tourism. The next section begins the exploration of these issues in more detail by reviewing some broad features of research in social science.

Some features of social science research and its disciplinary combination

The conception of policy and management for sport, tourism and sports tourism discussed above, as distinct from, say, the experimental and practitioner research that also populates the study of sport, is implicitly presented as social science. It follows that exploring some of the main methodological issues associated with social science research can help to refine the understanding of realism just discussed, as well as to provide a basis upon which one can assess how insights from different disciplines can be combined in management and policy decisions.

A useful starting point is to note that combining insights from different perspectives is typically referred to as triangulation (Denzin, 1970). Table 23.1 summarises an non-exhaustive, and non mutually-exclusive list of perspectives on triangulation.

As Downward & Mearman (2004b) note, there are two main arguments put forward to justify triangulation. The first is that triangulation increases the "persuasiveness" of evidence either through enhancing the empirical reliability of quantitative measures (Campbell & Fiske, 1959) or more generally enhancing the "validity" or completeness of insights (Jick, 1979; Shih, 1998). This may involve the uses of quantitative analysis to "test" the validity of qualitative insights, or to use qualitative work as preparation for quantitative work, and to elucidate a phenomenon in as much detail as possible (Danermark, Ekstrom, Jakobsen, & Karllson, 2002, p. 153). However, there is clearly an implicit argument that the data or investigations undertaken are inherently compatible. It can be shown that important philosophical issues arise here. These equally apply to the second argument for triangulation, for example, put forward by Cresswell (1995), Tashakkori & Teddlie (1998) and Bryman (2001) is that one should combine methods on typically pragmatic grounds. This can be viewed as an instrumentalist (methodological) position, which focuses upon the use of theories for practical purposes, such as prediction of outcome, but does not embrace concepts of truth. As such it rejects realism.[6]

Are there adequate philosophical grounds upon which to justify triangulation? To begin with, some social research texts, for example, Silverman's (1993), argue that quantitative methods retain a positivist perspective in which data essentially captures objective entities. In contrast, qualitative methods can be viewed as "interactionist" or "constructionist" as the interviewer, interview context and the interviewee mutually create research objects. In this respect research is inherently subjective. It follows that under this perspective realism is rejected and there is no legitimacy for triangulation.[7] However, positivism remains influential in social science as revealed in work such as Frankfort-Nachmias & Nachmias (2000).[8] Here, the stress is upon quantitative data to seek to avoid (if not eliminate) subjective values entering analysis. There is scope for triangulation under this positivist perspective, particularly where different quantitative methods are to be used (triangulation of method) and for different quantitative measures to be combined

Table 23.1 A taxonomy of triangulation

Form of triangulation	Description
Data triangulation	Involves gathering data at different times and situations, from different subjects. Surveying relevant stakeholders about the impact of a policy intervention would be an example. An alternative would be address concerns about the inadequacy of available data.
Investigator triangulation	Involves using more than one field researcher to collect and analyse the data relevant to a specific research object. Asking scientific experimenters to attempt to replicate each other's work is another example.
Theoretical triangulation	Involves making explicit references to more than one theoretical tradition to analyse data. This is intrinsically a method that allows for different disciplinary perspectives upon an issue. This could also be called *pluralist or multidisciplinary* triangulation.[*]
Methodological triangulation	Involves the combination of different research methods. For Denzin, there are two forms of methodological triangulation. *Within method* triangulation, involves making use of different varieties of the same method. Thus, in economics, making use of alternative econometric estimators would be an example. *Between method* triangulation involves making use of different methods, such as "quantitative" and "qualitative" methods in combination. It is here that the most interesting issues arise as discussed in detail in the main text

Note: *As discussed below, a key argument of this paper is that such pluralism, and that implied by other forms of triangulation, can be underpinned by a coherent ontological or epistemological position.

Source: Downward & Mearman (2004b).

(data triangulation). Here a form of realism is embraced as both data and enquiry are conceptualised as having an existence that is independent of the researcher and which transcends the context and method of investigation.

In summary, therefore, the literature suggests that instrumentalism embraces triangulation on the basis of pragmatism, which essentially sidesteps philosophical issues. Second, from a positivist-realist perspective, if the same sort of data is triangulated, then triangulation is legitimate. However, from an interactionist perspective, triangulation must be rejected. In what sense do these approaches offer different recommendations? The answer lies in the different ontological bases of the approaches. Interactionist approaches emphasise the subject of analysis, that the world cannot be independent of our understanding of it. It is a constructivist ontology. In contrast positivist approaches emphasise the independence of our understanding of the world from the objects analysed. This is a realist ontology. This dispute over ontology must, therefore, be key to understanding if and how research insights can be combined. Moreover, it follows that it provides a basis to understanding, in more detail, how this might apply to alternative accounts of realism.

Concepts of realism and ontological constraints on research

The previous section argued that a potential realist account can be constructed through reference to positivism. Yet, despite its persistence, the approach has been historically and widely criticised. The induction problem applies to enumerative forms of positivism, in which repeated observation of a phenomenon is asserted to reveal aspects of causes. Likewise, the idea that value free observation is possible has been widely challenged (for a discussion in the context of sport see Parry, 2005).

An alternative empirical approach has evolved from Popper (1972) whose falsifiability criterion bypassed these problems. This criterion argues for the *logical* demonstration of falsehood (of value-driven hypotheses) with reference to a *particular* set of (crucial) observations.[9] Amongst other contributions, Popper's work can thus be seen to be one of the underpinnings of the hypothetico-deductive approach (Blaug, 1980).[10] Crucially, it is here that positivism and deductive logic become enmeshed as deduced consequences, from statements of initial conditions and assumptions, are assessed empirically as predictions. Deduction is the process of establishing the logically correct conclusions from the components of an argument. In itself, deduction does not rely upon empirical references.

Though having distinct specific emphases, and being realist in form, the positivist and hypothetico-deductive approaches share an essential logic: explanations are presented in the form of "covering laws", that is relationships between variables that transcend space or time of the form "whenever event X then event Y". Lawson (1997, 2003) and Sayer (2000) describe the approach as "Humean" because causality is associated with the succession of events, as "correlations of a causal-sequence sort" (Lawson, 2003, P. 25). Ontologically speaking a closed-system is assumed such that causes act in a consistent manner (the "Intrinsic Condition of Closure": ICC) isolated from other causes (the "Extrinsic Condition of Closure": ECC). In such circumstances, events, our empirical description of them, and the causes of the events are conflated. Revisiting the discussion of realism above, such a perspective is entirely consistent with both methodological individualist or methodological collectivist accounts, in which, say, policy or management decision "X" purports to bring about management or policy outcome "Y". The unit of analysis of itself is not central to the structure of explanation.

In contrast critical realists would describe such (positivist) approaches as naïve, simple or empirical realism which commit an "epistemic fallacy" through conflating the subject and object of analysis. As a consequence, knowledge of phenomena is treated as logically equivalent to the phenomena. Moreover, in drawing upon a closed-system form of reasoning, the explanations offered involve the assumption that premises fully entail conclusions. Lawson (1997, 2003) describes this as deductivism, thus generalising the concept of deductive reasoning to be the organising principle of any arguments that invoke covering laws, whether they are presented as part of a specifically deductive, inductive, or hypothetico-deductive view. It is because deductive reasoning is directly concerned with, and thus can only cope with, knowledge that already exists or has been acquired, that it promotes the epistemic conflation.

The same argument can be made of interactionist and instrumental approaches. In the former case, this is naturally because the subject *is* conceived of as the object of analysis. In the instrumentalist case this follows because whichever insight is drawn upon, there is the presumption that it captures the relevant object. Table 23.2 summarises this argument where each column identifies a methodological position. The first row then indicates the focus of analysis and the last row, the direction of the subject-object conflation.

In contrast, critical realists (Lawson 1997, 2003; Sayer 2000) embrace the alternative form of realism discussed earlier, which invokes a social ontology whereby the world is structured and in which relationships between its constituent features are causal in bringing about outcomes. Critical realists argue that reality is a structured open system in which the real, the actual and the empirical domains are organically related. The real refers to the intransitive dimensions of knowledge, which exist independently of our understanding of the world, and in which actual causes, structures and powers to make things happen exist. The actual domain refers to what happens if powers and causes act. In contrast the empirical realm is where the transitive dimensions of knowledge reside because this is where the real and actual are observed, albeit filtered through the hermeneutic process and because causes act *transfactually* in the face of countervailing influences in a non-experimental context.[11] Critical realism thus combines ontological realism with epistemological fallibility.

From this point of view explanations of cause require ontic depth, that is moving beyond the level of events and/or texts towards an understanding of the processes that produce them. Importantly, the concept of cause is not linked to the succession of events but rather an evolutionary or transformational concept of emergence in which agency and institutions combine to bring about effects. Individuals are thus borne into a world of pre-existing structures and norms which help to mould but do not determine their behaviour, which is intentional and has the potential for spontaneous change (Archer, 1995; Lewis, 2000).

As Danermark *et al.* (2002) argue, in contrast to the deductivist approach to explanation, critical realism advocates retroduction, which is a conceptual process of moving between knowledge of one thing to another, for example, from empirical phenomena expressed as events to their causes. The key is that the researcher moves beyond a specific ontic context to another, hence generating an explanation that embraces ontological depth. The process of abduction, whereby specific phenomena are recontextualised as more general phenomena can be a part of this process.[12]

The literature does, however, debate the substantive application of retroduction. As Downward (2007) argues, for Lawson (1997) a mixture of forms of descriptive statistical analysis coupled with historical and case-study narrative are deemed appropriate because

Table 23.2 Subject–object conflations

Methodological position	Deduction	Interactionism	Instrumentalism	Hypothetico-deductive	Positivism
Structure of explanation	Internally consistent sequence of events	Relations between texts	Relations between texts and/or events	Sequence of deduced events empirically explored	Explore empirical sequence of events
Form of conflation	Subject → Object	Subject → Object	Subject → Object	Subject ↔ Object	Subject ← Object

Source: Downward & Mearman (2004b).

of the excessive closure assumptions implied by inferential statistical work. Quantitative methods presuppose degrees of closure. Numeric representations assume intrinsic closure and probability distributions assume extrinsic closure. This is suggestive of a limited triangulated research strategy. A less restrictive approach is broadly advocated by both Sayer (2002) and Danermark *et al.* (2002), who argue that critical realism is compatible with a wide range of methods, with the key issue being that analysis is matched to the appropriate level of abstraction and the material under investigation. Sayer (2000) distinguishes between intensive and extensive research designs. The former is what is typically thought of as social science—for instance qualitative research—in that it begins with the unit of analysis and explores its contextual relations as opposed to emphasising the formal relations of similarity between them, that is producing taxonomic descriptions of variables as is the case in the latter—for instance quantitative design. It is argued that the causal insights from extensive research will be less and it is argued that the validity of the (qualitative) analysis of cases does not rely upon quantitative evidence.

In contrast, Downward & Mearman (2002, 2003) argue that combining methods is *central* to retroductive activity as different methods will be necessary to reveal aspects of the constituency of phenomena, that is their ontic character, as well as structural, that is cause and effect, relations more broadly. In this regard the motivational (or otherwise) dimension of agency needs to be elaborated, as well as the mechanisms that facilitate action, or behaviour, coupled with the relational context of that behaviour. In addition, it can be argued that specific research methods within intensive and extensive designs differ more in emphasis than in kind through invoking degrees of closure. For example even "qualitative" methods, in collating insights and offering stylised interpretations, assume qualitative invariance or intrinsic closure; quantitative methods can also refer to different aspects of the *same* research object as qualitative methods and thus are not wedded to particular and different ontological presumptions; and finally their combination helps to raise rational belief in a set of (partial but) mutually supported propositions. In this regard statistical inference can still play a role in analysis (see also Ron, 2002).[13] Broadly speaking, thus, quantitative methods can identify partial regularities as outcomes of causal processes from which qualitative methods can investigate their causes.

There are two important features of this analysis worth noting here. The first is that critical realism provides an ontological justification for triangulation that is mixed methods. Units of analysis can thus vary as one attempts to unpick complex structured phenomena. The second point is that such combination of methods can transcend specific disciplines in as much that specific methods of analysis are often tied to specific disciplines. In this regard genuine interdisciplinary, as opposed to multidisciplinary analysis with ontological clashes, can be constructed. It follows that sport and tourism can easily unite as "sports tourism" from this perspective, with no necessary inconsistency of emphasis, implied pejorative connotation, or subordination of one to the other. Furthermore, if the focus is on disciplines or research insights rather than subject areas, it reinforces the perspective of Weed & Bull (2004), that:

> sports tourism is a unique area of study derived from the interaction of activity, people and place . . . [and] a dependence on the social institution of sport to characterise the area would be somewhat incongruous.
>
> (Weed & Bull, 2004, p. xv)

Weed and Bull's concern here is that a full understanding of sports tourism requires a recognition that it is more than the sum of its parts, and as such cannot simply be understood as a tourism market niche or a subset of sport management. In this respect, Weed and Bull see any definition of sports tourism that is dependent on definitions of the "parent" subjects (cf., Standeven & De Knop, 1999) as restricting the "ontic depth" required for a full understanding of the phenomenon. This is not to say that insights will not be partial. Partiality is a function of the need for abstraction in the light of specific enquiry, some of which is couched in terms of specific questions and conceptualisations. The emphasis upon sport or tourism, however, now becomes almost redundant, as the focus is on the combined but expanded area of sports tourism, with (partial) insights being provided by a range of disciplines, both unitarily and in combination, with the need for and extent of such combinations being a matter of (equally valid, but contingent) emphasis rather than distinction.

In summary the above discussion suggests that alternative realist perspectives, (critical-transcendental or empirical) can provide a basis for sports, tourism and sports tourism management and policy. Each can embrace different units of analysis. Each can purport to offer causal insights, and each can purport to combine methods of analysis and disciplines (as defined by methods). The final section presents an example which, it argues, suggests that the transcendental route to realism is appropriate.

Critical realism in action in sports tourism research

Weed & Bull (2004), along with most other academics in the area (Standeven & De Knop, 1999; Turco, Riley, & Swart, 2002; Hinch & Higham, 2004) see sports tourism as embracing a wide range of active and passive, competitive and recreational, and formal and informal pursuits. As such, the substantial opportunities for active informal recreational activity that have been put in place through the National Cycle Network developed by SUSTRANS, which currently offers 9,500 miles of routes in the UK, are clearly of interest to sports tourism practitioners and researchers. The goal by the end of 2005 is to extend this network to 10,000 miles, putting the majority of the UK population within two miles of the Network. A clear policy objective of the network is to provide leisure opportunities, as well as more utilitarian transport links between towns and within towns for schools and work. Consequently, drawing, again, on Weed & Bull's (2004) analysis of sports tourism stakeholders, the network can be considered as involving both sports tourism policymakers and providers. Furthermore, within the context of this paper, it provides a clear illustration of many of the issues raised in relation to policy and management research and practice.

It would seem dubious to approach evaluating the success of such a policy initiative, which has a complex structure by drawing upon a simple law-like empirical conception of use per se. For example, Downward et al. (2004) report a research project, which was a trial of an evaluation strategy assessing the direct economic impact of the route as well as profiling route users, and which drew upon ideas from critical realism to shape the research design.

Two key features of the research are particularly worth noting that reflected the principle of exploring different but important and related features of the same object.

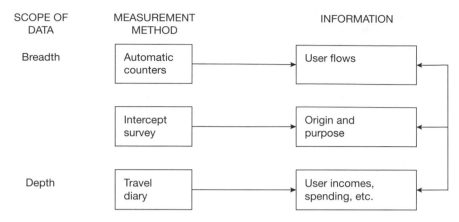

Figure 23.1 Investigating the impact and use of cycle routes

The first is that a triangulated research strategy was employed. Cycle counters were employed to measure aggregate route usage, that is the partial-regularities of cycle use. An intercept survey was then employed to capture implied causal features of these patterns. Information on numbers in user groups, ages and genders etc as well as cycling experience, purpose of journey and place of origin were investigated. The aim was clearly to identify aspects of the participants and the pattern and nature of their cycling activity. Finally, a travel diary was employed to probe in more detail aspects of cyclist profiles in which potentially sensitive questions were asked, such as to enquire about income. The diary also enabled the recording of actual distances covered and actual spending enroute rather than prior estimation, which is often used in transport and tourism surveys despite reported limitations. Figure 23.1 describes the research design.

The second point refers to the sites chosen for data collection. The study area, in essence, reflected a "necklace" of centres of gravity of different urban or locational settings. Whilst the centres of population vary in size they can be broadly characterised as large urban, small urban and smaller rural settings. It was at points of access to and egress from such sites that counters were located and surveying, etc., took place. Again, features of the object of enquiry shaped the research.

The importance of considering such ontological features of the research are important. For example, consider a simplified, but extremely typical approach to visitor spending surveys. These adopt a methodologically individualist approach and aggregate spending projections on a per capita basis. The potential problems of this approach are profound. For example, on one particular segment of the route it was established that the average spend per "respondent" was £40.47. Data counters indicated that 1992 users had been along the route over the particular time period of review. It might easily be forecast, then, that approximately £80,617 income could have been generated. However, if one recognises that the respondent is typically part of a family group of just over two people, and that the spending is *de facto* associated with the respondent group because the structure of demand reflects family activity then the forecast might be £37,135. The possibility of considerable error is clear. Likewise the implications for future sports tourism development.[14]

Of course, these are relatively simple calculations, but they illustrate the main point, which is the dangers of relying on a methodologically individualist approach and simple event regularities. This is not to say that statistical projections are of no use. The point is that their reliability can be enhanced by being constructed upon an explicit consideration of the structures that underpin behaviour. This raises the issue of whether or not complex or stratified/clustered sampling coupled with multivariate analysis are, of themselves, sufficient, say, to capture the intent of critical realist inference. The answer is clearly that they can be of more use than simple naïve empirical work when both are employed in isolation. However, caution should be emphasised here. On the one hand regression-type analysis and associated statistical inference tends to emphasise analytical focus upon regression to the mean—as a stylisation—and also the generality and robustness of the characteristics of a complex population. This can lead to an emphasis on producing "law-like" statements. In contrast policy scenarios and segmented analysis is essential for complex objects, in which there is recognition that the constituent parts may change and evolve differentially. In this respect and, on the other hand, the nature of the structures do need some explicit investigation. The main point, therefore, is that emphasis should be upon an exploratory approach to understand the structure of a phenomena as, for example, implied by Byrne (2003).

Conclusions

This paper has addressed two related issues: How insights from different disciplines can be combined to inform sport, tourism and sports tourism research, policy and management; and the implications this has for both the conduct of research, and establishing the relationship between sport and tourism and the area of sports tourism. The establishment of sports tourism as a research area in its own right is not merely a synthesis of sport and tourism. Sports tourism is clearly a synergistic phenomenon that benefits from a focus on disciplines rather than subject areas, and is most usefully thought of, as proposed by Weed & Bull (2004), as being derived from the unique interaction of activity, people and place. In seeking to inform aspects of sports tourism research, this paper has argued that policy and management is intrinsically a realist endeavour. Two varieties of realism have been contrasted as a basis for informing the issues above. The first is an empirical realism, that draws upon positivism and deductivism, and which emphasises the understanding of causes through law like expressions of covarying empirical events for a given unit of analysis. The other is critical realism that comprises a transcendental approach to understanding a structured reality, in which the triangulation of methods is required to capture a concept of cause associated with emergence out of agency and structures. Whilst ultimately the choice between these approaches is necessarily one of ontological commitment, the paper has illustrated how critical realism can be used to inform policy and management decisions in sports tourism.

Acknowledgements

An earlier version of this paper was presented at the *British Philosophy of Sport Association Conference*, 12–14 May, Louisa Centre, Stanley, County Durham. I am grateful for comments on the paper from participants at this conference and for reviewer's comments.

Notes

1   http://www.qaa.ac.uk/academicinfrastructure/benchmark/honours/hospitality.asp
    (accessed 25 April 2005).
2   These arguments draw heavily on previously published researched that explore these
    issues in the context of economics and Tourism and Hospitality (Downward, 2003;
    Downward & Mearman, 2004a). This paper is an attempt to extend these ideas to
    cover sports and their combination to tourism.
3   The implication of the current discussion for this broader context, as well as reflective
    practice in the action-based research of sports education and pedagogy is discussed in
    Downward (2005).
4   Discussion of the broader "studies" literature would involve encapsulating non-realist,
    constructivist accounts. Elements of this are discussed below. For further discussion
    see Downward & Mearman (2004a).
5   An important feature of realism is a commitment to causal explanation.
6   This approach arguably began in economics (see Friedman, 1953), with an emphasis
    upon prediction. There is an echo of positivism in the approach, in which data provides
    the arbiter in assessing the usefulness of theories. At the very least the approach is
    inductive, yet this does not imply necessarily a quest for objective truth.
7   Interactionism or constructivism so defined embraces a wide range of specific methods,
    such as content analysis, discourse analysis, grounded theory, ethnography as well as
    methodological positions including postmodernism, post-structuralism, hermeneutics
    and phenomenology. But, in general interactionism recognises hermeneutic concerns
    that social phenomena are intrinsically meaningful; that meanings must be understood;
    and that the interpretation of an object or event is affected by its context (Sayer, 1992,
    2000).
8   For a discussion of the changing conception of positivism in sociology see Halfpenny
    (1982). For a discussion in economics see Walters & Young (2001).
9   Lakatos's (1970) concept of scientific research programmes in which sophisticated
    falsification is required in the absence of crucial experiments is, in this regard, an
    extension of detail and aspiration than difference in logical position.
10 The deductive–nomological and inductive–statistical models of Carl Hempel (1965)
    can be viewed likewise as extensions of a simplistic view of positivism.
11 In social science the researcher shares the hermeneutic moment of the objects of study
    Bhaskar (1978). Indeed, Sayer (2000) argues that the social researcher operates in a
    double hermeneutic of both the scientific and objects-of-study communities. Logically
    speaking, a triple hermeneutic applies to policymakers synthesising and acting upon
    research findings.
12 Generality here refers to essential constituents rather than, say, statistical generalisation.
13 One can view statistical induction as a process of "hypothetical" triangulation. Here
    validity is sought from hypothetical repeated sampling, with ontological assumptions
    about the nature of probabilities being required to facilitate this. The usual arguments
    presented are that probabilities can act as summary indicators of the outcomes of complex
    covariation not specifically of interest to a particular study or policy outcome, for
    example as the errors of a regression model, or they can be viewed as a literal feature
    of reality (independently of their purported objectivity or subjectivity). It is clear that
    such a limited view of triangulation or validity requires the persistence of the ontological
    closure required to define probabilities. Whilst this might be useful as a vehicle for
    generating possible scenarios, for example if one argues that current structures persist,

clearly it implies a potentially fragile basis, in isolation, for inferences outside such conditions and, in particular if one rejects the concept of universal relationships because of the likelihood of changes to structures and behaviours in an open system.

14   It is worth noting at this point that there is a literature addressing concern with the conceptual measurement of economic impacts (see Crompton, 1995, 2004; Hudson, 2001). These papers focus on the technicalities of arithmetic and what to include or exclude in a calculation of the multiplier effect stemming from initial direct spending activity, as was the case in the study above. The issue being discussed in this paper concerns the logically prior question of what constitutes the nature of visitation or use of a resource, in other words the structure of demand. It is clear that a similar exercise should apply to the derived demands that form the basis of multiplier effects.

References

Archer, M.S. (1995). *Realist social theory: The morphogenetic approach*. Cambridge: Cambridge University Press.

Bhaskar, R. (1978). *A realist theory of science*. Sussex: Harvester Press.

Blaug, M. (1980). *The methodology of economics*. Cambridge: Cambridge University Press.

Byrne, D. (2003). *Interpreting quantitative data*. London: Sage.

Campbell, D.T., & Fiske, D.W. (1959). Convergent and discriminant validity by the multitrait–multimethod matrix. *Psychological Bulletin*, *56*, 81–105.

Cresswell, L.W. (1995). *Research design: Qualitative and quantitative approaches*. Thousand Oaks, CA: Sage.

Crompton, J.L. (1995). Economic impact analysis of sports facilities and events: Eleven sources of misapplication. *Journal of Sports Management*, *9*, 14–35.

Crompton, J.L. (2004). Beyond economic impact: An alternative rationale for the subsidy of major league sports facilities. *Journal of Sports Management*, *18*, 40–58.

Danermark, B., Ekstrom, M., Jakobsen, L., & Karlsson, J.C. (2002). *Explaining society: Critical realism in the social sciences*. London: Routledge.

Davies, B., & Downward, P.M. (2001). The industrial organisation of the package tour industry: Some implications for practitioners. *Tourism Economics*, *7*(2), 149–161.

Downward, P.M. (2003). *Applied economics and the critical realist critique*. Routledge: London.

Downward, P.M. (2007). Empirical analysis and critical realism. In M. Hartwig (Ed.), *A dictionary of critical realism*. London: Routledge.

Downward, P.M. (2005). *A critical realist view of sports and exercise research*. Paper presented at the ECSS Conference, Belgrade, 13–16 July.

Downward, P.M., & Dawson, A. (2000). *The economics of professional team sports*. Routledge: London.

Downward, P.M., & Mearman, A. (2002). Critical realism and econometrics: Constructive dialogue with post Keynesian economics. *Metroeconomica*, *53*(4), 391–415.

Downward, P.M., & Mearman, A. (2004a). On tourism and hospitality management research: A critical realist proposal. *Tourism and Hospitality Planning and Development*, *1*(2), 107–122.

Downward, P.M., & Mearman, A. (2004b). *Retroduction as mixed-methods triangulation in economic research: Reorienting economics into social science*. Paper presented to the Cambridge Realist Workshop, November 29.

Downward, P.M., Cope, A., & Lumsdon, L. (2004). Monitoring long distance trails: The North Sea cycle route. *Journal of Transport Geography*, *12*(1), 13–22.

Downward, P.M., Lumsdon, L., & Ralston, R. (2003). An evaluation of volunteers reflections on the experience of volunteering at the XVII Commonwealth Games, Manchester, 25 July–4 August, 2002, UK Sport.

Frankfort-Nachmias, C., & Nachmias, D. (2000). *Research methods in the social sciences*. New York: Wadsworth.

Friedman, M. (1953). *Essays in positive economics*. Chicago, IL: Chicago University Press.

Gibson, H.J. (1998). Sport tourism: A critical analysis of research. *Sport Management Review*, *1*(1), 45–76.

Halfpenny, P. (1982). *Positivism and sociology: Explaining social life*. London: Allen & Unwin.

Hempel, C. (1965). *Aspects of scientific explanation and other essays in the philosophy of science*. New York: Free Press.

Hinch, T., & Higham, J. (2004). *Sport tourism development*. Clevedon: Channel View.

Hudson, I. (2001). The use and misuse of economic impact analysis: The case of professional sports. *Journal of Sport and Social Issues*, *25*(1), 20–39.

Hudson, S. (Ed.) (2003). *Sport and adventure tourism*. Binghamton, NY: Haworth Press.

Jick, T.D. (1979). Mixing qualitative and quantitative methods: Triangulation in action. In J. Van Manen (Ed.), *Qualitative methodology*. London: Sage.

Lawson, T. (1997). *Economics and reality*. London: Routledge.

Lawson, T. (2003). *Reorienting economics*. London: Routledge.

Lewis, P. (Ed.) (2004). *Transforming economics*. London: Routledge.

Parry, J. (2005). Must scientists think philosophically about science? In M. McNamee (Ed.), *Philosophy and the sciences of exercise, health and sport: Critical perspectives on research methods*. London: Routledge.

Popper, K.R. (1972). *The logic of scientific discovery*. London: Hutchison.

Ron, A. (2002). Regression analysis and the philosophy of social science: A critical realist view. *Journal of Critical Realism*, *1*(1), 119–142.

Sayer, A. (1992). *Method in social science: A realist approach*. London: Routledge.

Sayer, A. (2000). *Realism and social sciences*. London: Sage.

Shih, F.J. (1998). Triangulation in nursing research: Issues of conceptual clarity and purpose. *Journal of Advanced Nursing*, *28*, 631–641.

Standeven, J., & De Knop, P. (1999). *Sport tourism*. Champaign, IL: Human Kinetics.

Tribe, J. (1997). The indiscipline of tourism. *Annals of Tourism Research*, *24*(3), 638–657.

Turco, D., Riley, S., & Swart, K. (2002). *Sport tourism*. Morgantown: Fitness Information Technology.

Walters, B., & Young, D. (2001). Critical realism as a basis for economic methodology: A critique. *Review of Political Economy*, *13*(4), 483–501.

Weed, M., & Bull, C. (2004). *Sports tourism: Participants, policy and providers*. London: Elsevier.

Chapter 24

Mike Weed

TOWARDS A MODEL OF CROSS-SECTORAL POLICY DEVELOPMENT IN LEISURE
The case of sport and tourism

Introduction: analysing leisure policy

ALTHOUGH LEISURE STUDIES has now become an established field of academic analysis, there is still surprisingly little literature relating to the dynamics of the leisure policy process. With the exception of work such as that by Henry (1993) on the politics of leisure policy, which focuses more on ideological concerns than the dynamics of the policy process, examples of the limited work in this area are those by Houlihan (1991, 1994, 1997) on sport, and Hall (1994) and Hall and Jenkins (1995) on tourism. However, these authors do not extend their analysis beyond sport and tourism respectively, nor do they look in any detail at cross-sectoral liaison. Work in this area would appear to be increasingly relevant at the present time as the leisure policy sectors (with the exception of countryside issues) are now located within the same government department, the Department for Culture, Media and Sport. In addition, the current government's emphasis on 'joined up thinking' and holistic approaches to policy would appear to further emphasize the relevance of such work.

Since its inception as the Department of National Heritage in 1992, the Department for Culture, Media and Sport has struggled, to a certain extent, to define a role for itself. The view of many policy makers in the leisure sectors is that it has concerned itself with directly interfering in the work of the leisure QUANGOs rather than seeking to establish those areas where it might 'add-value' to their work (Weed, 1999). It is the contention of this paper that it would be much better placed to do this if it were to take an integrated view of the leisure policy area and, in particular, to consider those areas in which the leisure sectors for which it is responsible might benefit from closer collaboration.

One such area is that of sport and tourism. Literature elsewhere documents the benefits to be gained from linking these two spheres (Redmond, 1991; Jackson and

Glyptis, 1992; Bramwell, 1997; Collins and Jackson, 1998) and these benefits are increasingly becoming more recognized. However, there are few examples where agencies responsible for sport and tourism have developed links or worked together (Weed and Bull, 1997a). Furthermore, in the few areas where links have emerged, they have done so in a piecemeal and *ad hoc* manner. Work elsewhere (Weed and Bull, 1998) has suggested that five factors can be identified – ideology, government policy, organizational structure, organizational culture and key staff – that affect the relationships between sport and tourism agencies, and that the respective influence of these factors is responsible for the limited and fragmented patterns of liaison that have emerged.

However, while the Weed and Bull (1998) analysis focuses on the factors influencing relationships between the sport and tourism sectors, it only briefly describes the structure of the policy communities for sport and tourism. While this was not a major omission, it was perhaps a lost opportunity to examine in greater depth the concept of the policy community and its utility in developing an understanding of cross-sectoral policy development in leisure.

Therefore, this paper attempts to synthesize previous research relating to the policy community in developing a descriptive model of cross-sectoral policy development. It goes on to examine the structures of the sport and tourism policy communities and analyse how such structures might affect the emergence of a sport-tourism policy network. In conclusion, consideration is given to the extent to which the model suggested here might be applicable to other areas of leisure policy.

The origins of the policy community concept

The concept of the policy community is a descendent, albeit a distant one, of the general pluralist theory of the state. Political pluralism developed as a rejection of absolute, unified and uncontrolled state power as exemplified by the absolutist monarchies of Western Europe in the eighteenth century (Skinner, 1978). The rationale for institutionalized pluralism – the separation of powers and federalism – was set out during the writing of the American Constitution by James Madison, in 'Federalist Paper No 10' (1787). Madison argued that a number of institutional checks and balances were required to prevent the abuse of power. Firstly, that the powers of the executive (the President), the legislature (Congress) and the judiciary are vertically separated and secondly, that sovereignty is horizontally divided through federalism and the provision of vetoes. In addition, Madison suggests the cultivation of an extended republic of heterogenous social groups and territorial areas in order that political factions are numerous and diverse. Dahl (1956) argues that social pluralism – non-institutionalized checks and balances on authority such as the extended republic suggested above – is as important as institutionalized pluralism. It is this idea of social pluralism that contributes to the policy community model.

A more contemporary explanation of pluralism is provided by Schmitter's (1970, pp. 85–86) particularly useful, if lengthy, definition:

> Pluralism can be defined as a system of interest representation in which the constituent units are organized into an unspecified number of multiple, voluntary, competitive, non-hierarchically ordered and self-determined (as to type or scope of interest) categories which are not specially licensed, recognized,

subsidized, created or otherwise controlled in leadership selection or interest articulation by the state and which do not exercise a monopoly of representational activity within their respective categories.

Thus the concept of pluralism involves a large number of independent interest groups interacting and competing with each other for influence over policy. The government assumes an independent and passive role, deciding on the allocation of resources to reflect the balance between interest groups in society at a particular time. However, three distinct pluralist conceptions of the 'passive state' have emerged. Firstly, the 'cipher' model, where the state is seen as a coding machine that acts as a passive vehicle through which inputs are processed (MacPherson, 1973). Secondly, the 'neutral' state as a 'mediator, balancer and harmonizer of interests' (Dunleavy and O'Leary, 1987, p. 46), acting in the public interest and playing an active role as guardians of the process, ensuring that unorganized groups do not become alienated. Finally, the 'broker' model, where public policy is the aggregation of pressure group activities within the state apparatus. In this model, state and elected officials are seen as having their own non-altruistic preferences (Selznick, 1949) and thus whilst the state acts as an intermediary or middleman, it still has interests of its own that it brings to bear on the policy making process.

The pluralist conception of the independent, passive state was seen as a major flaw by many writers (see, Schmitter, 1970, and Dunleavy and O'Leary, 1987, for discussion of this). The model of the state as a broker with interests of its own was the start of a move towards the corporatist theory where the state is cast in a more active role and as a result some players are excluded from the policy process. Again, Schmitter (1970, pp. 93–94) provides a useful definition:

> Corporatism can be defined as a system of interest representation in which the constituent units are organized into a limited number of singular, compulsory, non-competitive, hierarchically ordered and functionally differentiated categories, recognized or licensed (if not created) by the state and granted a deliberate representational monopoly within their respective categories in exchange for observing certain controls on their selection of leaders and articulation of demands and supports.

In the corporatist model the state exerts a controlling influence over the interest groups, recognizing and licensing them in return for the groups exercising moderation in their demands on the state. Thus the number of interest groups with access to the policy process is limited and the links both between groups and between the groups and government are closer. Often groups are offered incorporation within the process, but in exchange they are compelled to sacrifice their organizational muscle and to discipline troublemakers within their organizations.

More recently *neo-pluralist* writers such as Galbraith (1985) have attempted to incorporate an analysis of economic power systems – particularly the influence of business and the large corporation – into the conventional pluralist account of government-interest group relations. However, such accounts still have their flaws. In fact, the major drawback of each of these three models is their claim to provide a general view of relationships between interest groups and government when, quite patently, relations vary in different policy areas. Furthermore, it is difficult to find either pure pluralism or pure corporatism in any policy area.

The American sub-government literature, an important antecedent of the policy community approach, was also a critique of both pluralism and corporatism. However, the sub-government theory was applicable at the level of the particular policy process rather than the general level. Freeman (1955) is identified by Jordan (1990) as an important figure in the development of the sub-government literature. He emphasizes the need for the study of policy making to be disaggregated to sub-systems in which bureaucrats, Congressmen and interest groups interact. Freeman (1955, p. 11) describes such a subsystem as:

> the pattern of interactions of participants or actors involved in making decisions in a special area of public policy . . . although there are obviously other types of sub-systems, the type which concerns us here is found in an immediate setting formed by an executive bureau and congressional committees, with special interest groups immediately attached.

Sub-governments are viewed as being concerned in the main with routine areas of policy. However, the sum of these 'routine' policies represents a significant influence on public policy as a whole (Marsh, 1983). Furthermore, sub-governments will attempt to deal with as many items of policy as it is possible to reach agreement on. Failure to reach agreement will result in the drawing together of a wider audience which may impinge on the activities of the sub-government. The deliberations of such a wider audience may result in basic policy realignments that may reduce the power of, or work against the interests of members of the sub-government (Ripley and Franklin, 1980). Therefore, there is a strong incentive for sub-governments to compromise and reach agreements.

Although the influence of the sub-government literature on the concept of the policy community is indisputable, Rhodes (1981) emphasizes that the British literature owes a lot to non-American sources, particularly European work on inter-organizational theory and work by Heclo and Wildavsky (1974) on decision making in the British Treasury.

Models of the policy community

The most interesting developments in the British literature took place when, in the early 1980s, the ESRC funded two initiatives utilizing the concepts of policy community and policy networks: the inter-governmental relations (IGR) initiative focused on central–local government relations, whilst the second initiative focused on government-industry relations (GIR). The IGR studies used the Rhodes model (Rhodes, 1981) whilst the GIR studies developed a recognizably different model (Wilks and Wright, 1987). One of the major problems in comparing these two models is the different definitions used for the concepts of policy community and policy network, something which is a source of considerable confusion in subsequent literature with a number of authors confusing the models and definitions used.

Rhodes initially uses Benson's (1982, p. 148) definition of a policy network as a:

> cluster or complex of organizations connected to each other by resource dependencies and distinguished from other clusters or complexes by breaks in the structure of resource dependencies.

Table 24.1 The Rhodes model

Type of network	Characteristics of network
Policy community	Stability, highly restricted membership, vertical interdependence, limited horizontal articulation
Professional network	Stability, highly restricted membership, vertical interdependence, limited horizontal articulation, serves interests of profession
Intergovernmental network	Limited membership, limited vertical interdependence, extensive horizontal articulation
Producer network	Fluctuating membership, limited vertical interdependence, serves interests of producer
Issue network	Unstable, large number of members, limited vertical interdependence

Source: Rhodes, 1981.

However, he subsequently elaborates on this, identifying five types of networks along a continuum from highly integrated policy communities to loosely integrated issue networks. The term 'policy network' is used as the generic term encompassing all types (see Table 24.1).

A problem with the Rhodes model, later recognized by Rhodes himself (Rhodes and Marsh, 1992) is that whilst it is easy to see the policy community and issue network as opposite ends of a continuum, it is difficult see the other three models as progressive points on that continuum. It was partly in order, to address this problem that Marsh and Rhodes (1992) revised and updated the Rhodes model. The updated model continues to conceptualize the policy network as existing on a continuum, with at one end the tightly formed policy community and at the other the loosely structured issue network. However, the new model does not, as previously, include other types through the continuum, but describes five dimensions along which communities may vary, these being; membership, interdependence, insulation, resource distribution and members interests. The first four of these will change incrementally along the continuum, whilst members' interests may be either governmental, economic or professional at any point on the continuum (see Figure 24.1).

Both the updated and original versions of the Rhodes model emphasize structural relationships between institutions at the sectoral level. However, it might be argued that a significant shortfall of these models is their failure to include any analysis of relationships at the disaggregated, sub-sectoral level.

The GIR model, outlined by Wilks and Wright (1987), stresses the disaggregated nature of policy networks, using the term 'policy community' to describe interaction at the aggregate or sectoral level. A policy community is seen as having three characteristics: differentiation, specialized organizations and policy-making institutions, and interaction (Grant *et al.*, 1989). Beyond this level, sub-sectoral policy networks can be identified. Grant *et al.* (1989, p. 74) conclude that the policy community is:

> a useful conceptual tool for ordering the material . . . [but] . . . any analysis which ignored the sub-sectoral level would be incomplete.

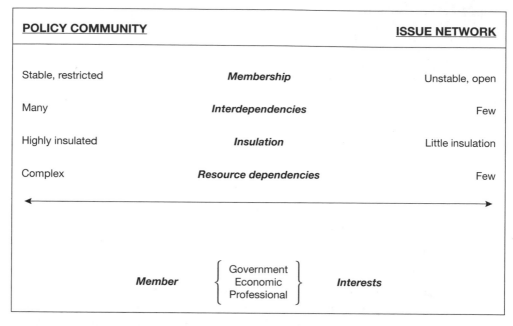

Figure 24.1 The updated Rhodes Model (Marsh and Rhodes, 1992)

The GIR model thus uses the term 'policy community' as a generic at the aggregated, sectoral level in the same way the Rhodes model uses the term 'policy network'. However, 'policy network' in the GIR model is reserved for the disaggregated, sub-sectoral level. In addition, the term 'policy universe' is used to refer to the general policy area within which activity takes place (see Table 24.2).

The groupings of these policy actors can be defined (based on Wright, 1988, p. 606) as:

- Policy universe: the large population of actors and potential actors who share a common interest in a policy area (e.g., leisure) and may contribute to the policy process on a regular basis.
- Policy community: those actors who share an interest in a particular policy sector (e.g., sport or tourism) and who interact with one another in order to balance and optimize their mutual relationships.
- Policy network: a linking process, the outcome of those exchanges within a policy community or between a number of policy communities.

Wilks and Wright (1987) argue that a major advantage of the GIR distinction between community and network is that it allows for the possibility that members of a policy network may be derived from different policy communities. This is particularly useful in examining cross-sectoral policy development such as that for sport-tourism where the sport and tourism policy communities exist within a leisure policy universe that was given a stronger collective identity by the creation of the Department of National Heritage in 1992 (since July 1997, the Department for Culture, Media and Sport). Consequently, the issues where the sport and tourism policy communities overlap is where a sport-tourism policy network should emerge.

Table 24.2 Levels in the GIR model (adapted from Wilkes and Wright, 1987)

	Policy level	*Policy actors*
Policy area	education, health, leisure, etc.	Policy universe
Policy sector	sport, tourism, arts, etc.	Policy community
Policy sub-sector	sports tourism, countryside sports, elite sport, etc.	Policy network

There is, however, a third dimension to consider, because the membership of a particular network need not come exclusively from within the policy universe (Wright, 1988). Thus it is conceivable that an interest in the sport-tourism policy network may come from, for example, the economic development or foreign affairs policy communities, it would appear that the GIR model provides the most useful framework for analysing sport-tourism relations as it focuses on relations at the sub-sectoral level. However, the updated Rhodes model (Figure 24.1) would also seem capable of offering useful insights, This may be particularly the case when examining, as is the case here, cross-sectoral liaison where it would appear that the nature of communities at the sectoral level might influence the formation of cross-sectoral networks at the sub-sectoral level. In fact, Dowding (1995), in his critique of the Rhodes model, identifies its failure to address the sub-sectoral or micro-level as a significant omission. Therefore, in addressing this criticism, and given the nature of the area under consideration here, perhaps the most productive way to proceed would be to attempt to combine the two models. In doing so, the three policy levels of the GIR model are maintained – policy universe, policy community (sectoral level) and policy network (sub-sectoral level). However, the continuum outlined in the updated Rhodes model is included at the sectoral level, thus allowing for an analysis of the influence on the sub-sectoral level of the structure and organization at the sectoral level. Combining the models in this way creates problems with terminology, with the terms community and network meaning different things in each model. As the overall framework is provided by the GIR model, the conceptions of 'policy communities' as occurring at the sectoral level and 'policy networks' as referring to the sub-sectoral level are maintained. To avoid confusion, the updated Rhodes policy community continuum (although the updated Rhodes model still uses the term 'policy network' as a generic term at the sectoral level) will be characterized as having a tightly structured policy circle (Rhodes' policy community) at one end and a loosely structured issue zone (Rhodes' issue network) at the other. The combined model is illustrated in Figure 24.2.

This combined model will now be used to examine and compare the respective structures of the sport and tourism policy communities. In the following analysis, the focus is on the extent to which these respective structures might affect the emergence of a sport-tourism policy network.

The structure of the policy communities for sport and tourism

Policy community membership varies from being fairly stable and restricted to being relatively unstable and open to a wide range of groups. Smith (1993) claims that a tightly

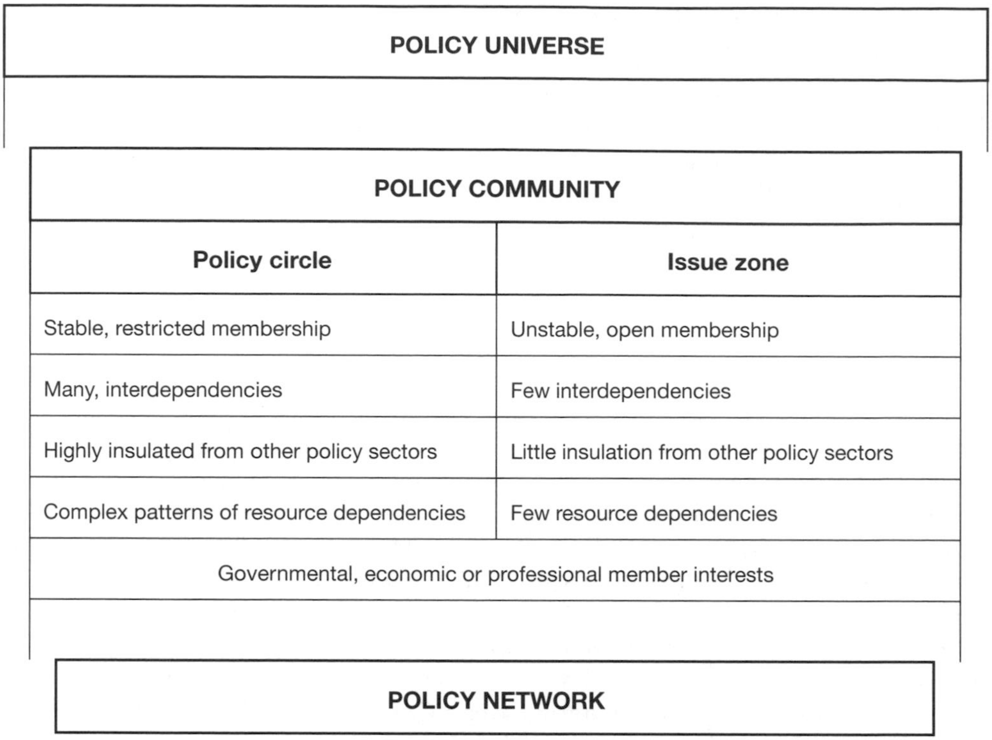

POLICY UNIVERSE

POLICY COMMUNITY	
Policy circle	**Issue zone**
Stable, restricted membership	Unstable, open membership
Many, interdependencies	Few interdependencies
Highly insulated from other policy sectors	Little insulation from other policy sectors
Complex patterns of resource dependencies	Few resource dependencies
Governmental, economic or professional member interests	

POLICY NETWORK

Figure 24.2 The combined model

formed policy circle will usually involve one government agency or section within that agency which Rhodes (1986) believes will usually give a lead to the community. However, leadership in the sport and tourism policy communities is not clear-cut. The lead government department would be expected to be the Department for Culture, Media and Sport; however, historically policy issues for sport and tourism have been devolved to the Sports Council and the English Tourist Board respectively, and this has led to a number of tensions. The Department for Culture, Media and Sport does not appear to value the role played by the English Tourist Board[1] as it has both significantly cut its resources and, more recently, shown a trend towards directly intervening in areas of the Board's work. For example, the most recent English Tourist Board strategy, 'Success Through Partnership' (DNH/ETB, 1997) was a joint publication with the Department, an unprecedented move as far as the leisure QUANGOs are concerned. Furthermore, later in 1997 the Department for Culture, Media and Sport established a Tourism Advisory Forum, made up of prominent figures from the tourism industry, to advise it on tourism matters, which is the exact role the English Tourist Board was set up to fulfil in 1969. As a result much of the Board's work has been short-circuited by government and the organization has become marginalized. The Department has also increasingly restricted the autonomy of the Sports Council, to the point where its drawn out restructure into United Kingdom and English Sports Councils and the publication by the department of the 'Sport: Raising the Game' (DNH, 1995) White Paper have forced the Sports Council and its successor bodies into a major change in policy direction that has seen it drop the promotion of mass participation from its remit.[2] The Department for Culture, Media and Sport now exerts a much greater level of control over Sports Council direction and consequently the organization has become an implementor rather than a developer of national sports policy.

It would appear, therefore, that the 'arms length' principle on which both the English Tourist Board and the Sports Council were established has gradually been eroded. This creates problems for both the sport and tourism policy communities because, as might be expected, both the Sports Council and English Tourist Board are looked to by other agencies to give a lead on national policy. Therefore, tensions are created between the government, which ultimately controls the purse strings, and the national agencies where, in theory, the expertise is invested. However, it is at this juncture that differences appear between the sport and tourism policy communities. Whilst the ETB has seen its funding cut and has become increasingly marginalized, the new English Sports Council has seen its role, as far as funding is concerned, expand. In fact, although the new English Sports Council might be regarded as less independent than its predecessor it has become more central because its role in distributing Lottery funds clearly indicates that it is now seen as having a valuable role to play by the Department for Culture, Media and Sport. Consequently, any sporting initiatives that come from government are carried out through, rather than bypassing, the English Sports Council. However, the role of the Council is now as an agent rather than an instigator of policy.

The situation in the tourism policy community is different. As discussed above, the government has marginalized the English Tourist Board which, as a result, has lost some credibility in the eyes of the wider policy community. Thus, although it still attempts to give a lead to the community, its authority to do so is questioned by the involvement of the Department for Culture, Media and Sport in tourism matters. This creates instability in the tourism policy community and a lack of clarity in the eyes of its members as to where the lead is coming from.

Laumann and Knocke (1987) believe that policy communities have primary and secondary communities. The primary core contains the key actors who set the rules of the game and determine membership and the main policy direction of the community, whilst the secondary community contains the groups that, although abiding by the rules of the game, do not have the resources or influence to greatly affect policy. It would appear that this distinction of a primary and secondary community is useful in examining the differences between the structure of the sport and tourism policy sectors. Although neither community could be said to generally have stable restricted membership, as is the case in a policy circle, the nature of the primary and secondary communities would appear to vary. The sports policy community would appear to have a fairly stable primary community that includes the Department for Culture, Media and Sport, the English and other national Sports Councils and the UK Sports Council. The secondary community, the membership of which appears to be fairly open, contains a wide range of interest groups, sports organizations and clubs and local authorities. It might be argued that local authorities, or at least their representative organizations, form part of the primary community, although evidence suggests (Weed, 1999) that they have little input into the development of national policy.

The situation in the tourism policy community appears to be different, and it may not be possible to define clearly primary and secondary communities. Whilst the marginalization of the English Tourist Board means that it is not really possible to regard it as a member of a primary community, perhaps the Department for Culture, Media and Sport and its Tourism Forum could potentially be so regarded. However, the Advisory Forum mainly comprises industry representatives who are not necessarily interested in setting an agenda across the whole range of issues. Therefore, only the government department remains, and as the Department for Culture, Media and Sport appears to be increasingly emphasizing the role of the private sector in the tourism industry, it must be assumed that it does not want to become involved in a major way. This leads to the conclusion that the tourism policy community shows more of the characteristics of an issue zone, where membership is unstable and groups join or leave the community according to the issues being discussed. This contrasts with the sports policy community which, while having a fairly open secondary community, appears to have a primary community of which membership is fairly stable and restricted, and thus, at least in comparison to the tourism sector, shows some of the characteristics of a policy circle. These differences in the basic structures of the communities clearly cause problems for sport–tourism liaison. The lack of an identifiable lead agency in the tourism policy community means that there is no organization with which sports agencies can liaise on strategic matters. Although, arguably, the Regional Tourist Boards may fulfil this lead role at sub-national level, their regional nature means that they cannot provide a lead for the tourism policy community at national level. This situation has resulted in some liaison taking place at regional level (Weed and Bull, 1997a), but a complete lack of initiatives nationally.

One of the major issues facing both the sport and tourism policy communities is the extent to which they can insulate themselves from other policy areas. Houlihan (1991) highlights the inability of the sports policy community to insulate itself from other more powerful policy areas. An example of this is the response to the problem of football hooliganism in the 1980s, where the sports policy community was overridden by the law and order policy community in defining responses to that problem. Another example would be the inner city policy area, which has often impinged on the work of the sports policy community.

Of course, the changing priorities of the inner cities also impinge considerably on the work of the tourism policy community. Often the funds that are offered to Regional Tourist Boards by the government on a competitive bidding basis are for urban regeneration purposes through the Single Regeneration Budget. Having cut the funds of the English Tourist Board, and as a result reduced the core funding of Regional Tourist Boards, the government is able to direct both the English and Regional Tourist Boards' activities towards their regeneration priorities by offering them funds with conditions attached that direct the focus of initiatives towards the economic and social regeneration of communities. The conclusion to be drawn in the instances of both the sport and tourism policy communities is that they cannot insulate themselves from other, more powerful and politically important, policy communities and thus, in this respect, they both display the characteristics of an issue zone. Perhaps the reason for this is that, in all but the smallest minority of cases, political ideologies for both sport and tourism are often linked to other policy areas rather than seeing the provision of sport and tourism as an end in itself. This obviously makes long term strategic planning difficult because political objectives for sport and tourism are liable to change in the short to medium term. This obviously does not assist in the creation of links between the sport and tourism agencies as each are dealing with more specific aims and objectives laid down by the political thinking of the time.

The level of interdependency in a policy community is often linked to resources. Resources come in a range of forms, most obvious are financial resources, but also important are knowledge, information, legitimacy and the goodwill of other groups (Smith, 1993). A policy circle has many interdependencies, and the relationships between groups are often exchange relationships. In the more loosely constituted issue zone, the relationship changes from being one of exchange to one of transmission or consultation. Regional Tourist Boards may often have to forgo their independently established strategic plans in order to tap into funds offered by the government on a competitive bidding basis – control over direction is exchanged for financial resources. To a certain extent this has also occurred with the Sports Council, which has sacrificed much of its independence (although not necessarily willingly) for a central role in the distribution of Lottery funds. There does, however, appear to be more significant interdependencies in the sports policy community than is the case with the tourism sector.

Although a complex pattern of resource dependencies are increasingly developing between the Regional Tourist Boards and the commercial sector, the government retains a privileged position due to its greater resources (Rhodes, 1988). Whilst the government may be shifting Whitehall's resources away from projects supporting tourism towards projects with regeneration as their prime aim, it is still the case that its position within the policy community is stronger than that of the other actors. Thus, despite the dominant member interests in the tourism policy community being economic, the government's 'golden share' means it is able to wield a considerable influence in the areas it considers to be important. However, the open and unrestricted nature of the community's membership means that, with the exception of that with the government, there are no major resource relationships upon which the community is dependent. The relationships are complex, but they are small, and the loss of any one of them would not greatly affect the operation of the community as a whole.

In contrast, the sports policy community, particularly since the advent of the Lottery Sports Fund, does have a range of resource relationships upon which the community is dependent. In the primary community the resource relationship between government and the Sports Councils is important as, unlike the Regional Tourist Boards, which partially operate through industry subscriptions, the Sports Councils could not survive without the government's grant-in-aid. This relationship helps ensure that the Sports Council accepts the lead of the Department for Culture, Media and Sport over general policy direction. However, the government in general does not wish to involve itself with the detail of all aspects of sports policy, and thus the Sports Councils' expertise is required to convert general policy direction into implementable specifics. It is this exchange relationship that ensures these agencies comprise the primary core of the sports policy community. Their relationship with the secondary community is as a result of the dependence of much of that secondary community on Sports Council grant aid and Lottery Sports Fund money. The actors in the secondary community do not have anything to exchange for these resources and as a result have to accept the general policy directions and terms and conditions under which they are offered.

In summarizing the nature and features of the sport and tourism policy communities it is possible to characterize the tourism policy community as showing many of the characteristics of an issue zone. It has an unstable, open membership with no clear leadership and few major interdependencies, it has virtually no insulation from other policy sectors and its members interests are mainly economic, although the government retains a privileged position as a result of its resource position. By contrast, while the sports policy community is not strong enough to be labelled so (Houlihan, 1997), it does show some of the characteristics of a policy circle, certainly in relation to the tourism community. The membership of its primary core is stable and restricted, although the secondary community is fairly open; there are a number of major interdependencies, both in terms of finance and expertise, that dictate the structure of, and relationships in the community; and its interests are mainly governmental, supplemented by professional connections. The one factor that prevents the sports policy community becoming a policy circle is its historical lack of insulation from other, more powerful, policy areas such as education and thus, at times, its inability to define its own agenda, something that Laffin (1986) sees as a significantly important variable.

However, whilst neither the sport or tourism community is able to exclude more powerful policy sectors from impinging on their respective work, they are able to define their agenda within the leisure policy universe. In fact, within the leisure area the communities are able to establish a greater degree of insulation as neither the tourism or sport sectors are seen as more politically important than each other. It is perhaps the case that, due to its greater correspondence with the features of a policy circle, the sport policy community is more able to exclude tourism interests than the tourism community is able to exclude sport. This may have a significant effect on the extent to which these two communities can generate a sport-tourism policy network, particularly as they both appear to be concerned with defining their own agenda within the leisure policy universe rather than seeking connections.

Conclusion

Historically, the sport and tourism policy sectors – and, indeed, the other leisure sectors have developed separately. Each sector has its own national agency and regional framework, and they are often located in different departments within local authorities. Furthermore, until the creation of the Department of National Heritage (DNH) in 1992, they were located in different government departments. This legacy of independent development may have created a culture of unilateral action by these agencies that has not been changed by the DNH or its successor, the Department for Culture, Media and Sport (DCMS). In fact, as mentioned earlier, rather than identifying areas in which it might add-value to the work of the national agencies, the DNH/DCMS has concerned itself with directly interfering in the work of these agencies. Furthermore, evidence suggests (Weed and Bull, 1997b) that the DNH/DCMS has done more to damage the potential for links between these two sectors than it has done to bring them together. However, notwithstanding the above, there is evidence to suggest that the sport and tourism agencies are aware of the link between sport and tourism and, indeed, are unilaterally active in the sports tourism area. A review of the activities of the regional agencies responsible for sport and tourism policy respectively revealed:

> that there exists an increasing level of sport–tourism activity . . . [which] . . . has not been matched by an increase in liaison amongst the agencies responsible for sport and tourism policies.
>
> (Weed and Bull, 1997a, p. 146)

Therefore, while the sport and tourism policy communities are aware of the links between the two areas, it would appear that they make little effort to work together in developing such links. The discussions in this paper would appear to go some way towards explaining this lack of liaison.

In highlighting some of the problems for sport–tourism liaison caused by the structure of the policy communities for sport and tourism, this paper has attempted to demonstrate the utility of the combined model of the policy community (Figure 24.2) in illuminating some of the problems of cross-sectoral liaison. In fact, a combination of this analysis with an examination of those factors that affect relationships within and between policy communities – ideology, government policy, organizational structure, organizational culture, and key staff – as identified by Weed and Bull (1998), would appear to provide a useful model of the way in which a wide range of factors affect the dynamics of liaison in particular policy sub-sectors, in this case sport-tourism.

While there are clearly some factors that have been discussed here that are specific to the sport-tourism link, a useful avenue for further investigation would be the extent to which the policy community model outlined in this paper might be applicable to other forms of cross-sectoral liaison in leisure. The art-tourism policy network, for example, appears to share many of the problems of the sport-tourism policy network – such as their differing member interests – and the factors affecting sport-tourism relationships may have the potential to offer insights into the workings of this network. In fact, it is conceivable that the model may be useful in offering insights into the dynamics of the wider leisure policy area. While this is clearly an area for substantial further research, such research would be particularly relevant now that the leisure policy sectors are all located within the same government department and given the current government imperative for 'joined up thinking'. Such research might assist in identifying those areas in which the Department for Culture, Media and Sport might 'add-value' to the work of the leisure QUANGOs by providing an integrative view of the leisure policy universe. Furthermore, a model of decision making dynamics across the leisure sectors might assist in achieving a greater understanding of the factors that contribute to the development of policy for leisure at all levels in the policy process in addition to identifying those organizations and individuals that exert most power and influence in particular policy sectors and subsectors. This is certainly something that is missing from the current literature in this area.

Notes

1   At the time of writing the government was proposing to replace the English Tourist Board with a new English Tourism Council. The exact structure and role of this new body remains unclear, however, given its establishment by the present government, it might be expected that it would have a more central role than its predecessor.

2   The Blair government (1997–present) has, to a certain extent, reversed this change in direction with the introduction of its 'social inclusion' agenda into Sports Council programmes. Nevertheless, the central point regarding the influence of the DCMS over Sports Council priorities remains and is, in fact, re-inforced by the incorporation of the language of 'social inclusion' into current Sports Council initiatives.

References

Benson, J.K. (1982) Networks and policy sectors: a framework for extending inter-governmental analysis. In *Inter-Organisational Co-ordination* (edited by D. Roger and D. Whitten), Iowa State University, Iowa.

Bramwell, B. (1997) A sport mega-event as a sustainable tourism development strategy, *Tourism Recreation Research*, 22(2), 13–19.

Collins, M.F. and Jackson, G.A.M. (1998) The economic impact of sport and tourism. In *Sport and Tourism* (edited by J. Standeven and P. De Knop), Human Kinetics, London.

Dahl, R.A. (1956) *A Preface to Democratic Theory*, University of Chicago Press, Chicago.

Department of National Heritage (1995) *Sport – Raising the Game*, HMSO, London.

Department of National Heritage/English Tourist Board (1997) *Success Through Partnership*, HMSO, London.

Dowding, K. (1995) Model or metaphor? A critical review of the policy network approach, *Political Studies*, 43(1), 136–158.

Downs, A. (1967) *Inside Bureaucracy*, Little Brown, Boston.

Dunleavy, P. and O'Leary, B. (1987) *Theories of the State*, Macmillan, London.

Freeman, J.L. (1955) *The Political Process*, Doubleday, New York.

Galbraith, J.K. (1985) *The Anatomy of Power*, Corgi Books, London.

Grant, W., Patterson, W. and Whitson, C. (1989) *Government and the Chemical Industry: A Comparative Study of Britain and West Germany*, Clarendon Press, Oxford.

Hall, C.M. (1994) *Tourism and Politics: Policy, Power and Place*, Belhaven Press, London.

Hall, C.M. and Jenkins, J.M. (1995) *Tourism and Public Policy*, Routledge, New York.

Heclo, H. and Wildavski, A. (1974) *The Private Government of Public Money*, Macmillan, London.

Henry, I.P. (1993) *The Politics of Leisure Policy*, Macmillan, London.

Houlihan, B. (1988) *Housing Policy and Central–Local Government Relations*, Avebury, Aldershot.

Houlihan, B. (1991) *The Government and the Politics of Sport*, Routledge, London.

Houlihan, B. (1994) *Sport and International Politics*, Harvester Wheatsheaf, New York.

Houlihan, B. (1997) *Sport, Policy and Politics: A Comparative Analysis*, Harvester Wheatsheaf, New York.

Jackson, G.A.M. and Glyptis, S.A. (1992) Sport and Tourism: A Review of the Literature, Report to the Sports Council, Recreation Management Group, Loughborough University, unpublished.

Jordan, A.G. (1990) Sub-governments, policy communities and networks: Refilling old bottles? *Journal of Theoretical Politics*, 2(3), 319–338.

Laffin, M. (1986) Professional communities and policy communities in central-local relations. In *New Research in Central–Local Relations* (edited by M. Goldsmith), Gower, Aldershot.

Laumann, E.O. and Knoke, D. (1987) *The Organisational State*, University of Wisconsin Press, Madison.

MacPherson, C.B. (1973) *Democratic Theory: Essays in Retrieval*, Oxford University Press, Oxford.

Marsh, D. (1983) Interest group activity and structural power: Lindblom's politics and markets. In *Capital and Politics in Western Europe* (edited by D. Marsh), Frank Cass, London.

Marsh, D. and Rhodes, R.A.W. (1992) Policy communities and issue networks: beyond typology. In *Policy Networks in British Government* (edited by D. Marsh and R.A.W. Rhodes), Oxford University Press, Oxford.

Redmond, G. (1990) Points of increasing contact: sport and tourism in the modern world. In *Sport in Society: Policy, Politics and Culture* (edited by A. Tomlinson), LSA Publication No. 43, Leisure Studies Association, Eastbourne.

Redmond, G. (1991) Changing styles of sports tourism: Industry/consumer interactions in Canada, the USA and Europe. In *The Tourism Industry: An International Analysis* (edited by M.T. Sinclair and M.J. Stabler), CAB International, Oxford.

Rhodes, R.A.W. (1981) *Control and Power in Central–Local Government Relations*, Gower/SSRC, Farnborough.

Rhodes, R.A.W. (1986) *The National World of Local Government*, Macmillan, London.

Rhodes, R.A.W. (1988) *Beyond Westminster and Whitehall*, Unwin Hyman, London.

Rhodes, R.A.W. and Marsh, D. (1992) Policy networks in British politics: A critique of existing approaches. In *Policy Networks in British Government* (edited by D. Marsh and R.A.W. Rhodes), Oxford University Press, Oxford.

Richardson, J.J. and Jordan, A.G. (1979) *Governing Under Pressure*, Martin Robertson, Oxford.

Ripley, R. and Franklin, G. (1980) *Congress, the Bureaucracy and Public Policy*, Dorsey Press, Illinois.

Schmitter, P. (1970) Still the century of corporatism, *Review of Politics*, 36, 85–96.

Selznick, P. (1949) *TVA and the Grass Roots*, University of California Press, Berkeley.

Sharpe, L.J. (1985) Central co-ordination and the policy network, *Political Studies*, 33(3), 361–381.

Skinner, Q. (1978) *The Foundations of Modern Political Thought, Volumes I–II*, Cambridge University Press, Cambridge.

Sproat, I. (1994) *Oral Statement to the House of Commons*, 8 July.

Weed, M. (1999) *Consensual Policies for Sport and Tourism in the UK: An Analysis of Organisational Behaviour and Problems* (Ph.D. thesis), Canterbury, University of Kent at Canterbury/Canterbury Christ Church College.

Weed, M. and Bull, C.J. (1997a) Integrating sport and tourism: A review of regional policies in England, *Progress in Tourism and Hospitality Research*, 3(2), 129–448.

Weed, M. and Bull, C.J. (1997b) Influences on sport–tourism relations in Britain: The effects of government policy, *Tourism Recreation Research*, 22(2), 5–42.

Weed, M. and Bull, C.J. (1998) The search for a sport–tourism policy network. In *Leisure Management: Issues and Applications* (edited by M.F. Collins and I.S. Cooper), CAB International, Wallingford.

Wilks, S. and Wright, M. (eds) (1987) *Comparative Government–Industry Relations*, Clarendon Press, Oxford.

Wilson, J.Q. (1973) *Political Organisations*, Basic Books, New York.

Wright, M. (1988) Policy community, policy network and comparative industrial policies, *Political Studies*, 36(4), 593–612.

Chapter 25

Mike Weed

WHY THE TWO WON'T TANGO!
Explaining the lack of integrated policies for sport and tourism in the UK

A N EXAMINATION OF POLICY RESPONSES to the sport-tourism link suffers from a "double death" in terms of supporting literature. While this themed edition is testament to an increasing interest in sports tourism,[1] the area of sports tourism, although growing, is not particularly well served by a significant body of literature. Similarly, although leisure studies is now a relatively established field of academic analysis, there is still surprisingly little literature relating to the dynamics of the leisure policy process. With the exception of work such as that by Henry (1993, 2001) on the politics of leisure policy, which focuses more on ideological concerns than the dynamics of the policy process, examples of the limited work in this area are those by Houlihan (1991, 1997) on sport, and Hall (1994) and Hall and Jenkins (1995) on tourism. Furthermore, while the work of these authors is useful in informing an examination of sport-tourism policy, they do not extend their analysis beyond sport and tourism respectively, nor do they look in any detail at cross-sectoral liaison.

Across the globe there are few examples where agencies responsible for sport and tourism have developed links or worked together. Furthermore, in the very few areas where links have emerged, they have done so in a very piecemeal and ad-hoc manner. This is evidenced by perhaps one of the highest profile areas of the sport-tourism link, major events. In many countries the potential of major events to attract visitors to an area is recognized; however, the partnerships that emerge are often short-term or uncoordinated, and in some cases, virtually non-existent.

Notwithstanding any reluctance among sport and tourism agencies to work together, developing policy to support the diverse nature of sports tourism is no simple task. That the development of such policy takes place against a general backdrop of indifference from many of the policy agencies that might reasonably be expected to be involved only serves to make the task more complicated. There are a number of complicating factors that contribute to such indifference. In many countries around the world the agencies and structures that exist for developing sport and tourism respectively have been established and have developed entirely separately. This separate development is often compounded by a significantly different "culture" or "ethos" in the two sectors. There is often a tradition of public sector support, subsidy and/or intervention in the sports sector (the exception, perhaps, being the USA, where the United States Olympic Committee, although granted a role via legislation, receives no public sector funding), while the tourist sector is largely seen as a private sector concern, and agencies are often limited to a marketing or business support role. These factors are further complicated by the different levels at which responsibility for policy development lies. Organizations may exist at the national, regional and/or local levels, and in countries such as the USA or Australia that have federal systems of government, the significant rule of state governments also needs to be considered. The respective responsibilities of these agencies can mean that in some instances liaison would need to take place not only across sectors, but also between levels. The relative scarcity of such liaison is a testament to the range of problems that exist.

Due to the relative lack of literature on the dynamics of the sport-tourism policy process, and that in leisure, tourism, and sports studies in general, it is useful to turn to the general body of literature in policy studies and political science to inform an understanding of policy responses to the sport-tourism link. Of particular use is literature on two related concepts: sub-governments (e.g., Jordan, 1990), which has largely developed in America, and policy communities, which has tended to develop in Europe. In the UK in the early 1980s, the Economic and Social Research Council funded two initiatives utilizing the concept of the policy community, and the related concept of the policy network. The inter-governmental relations (IGR) initiative focused on central-local government relations, while the second initiative focused on government-industry relations (GIR). Between them these initiatives generated over thirty research projects, with a number of significant theoretical developments (IGR, see Goldsmith & Rhodes, 1986; GIR, see Wilks, 1989). The models developed through these studies were utilized by Houlihan (1991, 1997) in his work on the dynamics of spoil policy and are adapted for use in understanding the response of policy makers to the sport-tourism link in this paper. Also of use in understanding the dynamics of the sport-tourism policy process are ideas associated with ideological thought (e.g., Giddens, 1977), theories of the state (e.g., Dunleavy & O'Leary, 1987), organizational structure (e.g., Mintzberg, 1979), and organizational culture (e.g., Morgan, 1986, 1997), each of which has been utilized in previous studies (see below) and are drawn on in this paper to develop an overview of sport-tourism relations in the UK.

A range of previous papers and articles has considered the sport-tourism policy process in the UK. An initial examination of the extent of liaison through a review of the strategy statements of the regional agencies then responsible for sport and tourism policy respectively (Weed & Bull, 1997a) was followed by a commentary on the influence of government policy on sport-tourism partnerships (Weed & Bull, 1997b). Theoretical development has taken place with the suggestion of a range of influences that might affect the extent to which sport-tourism partnerships may develop (Weed & Bull, 1998), and a model of the dynamics of the sport-tourism policy process has been proposed (Weed, 2001). Each of these papers has drawn on a 4-year research project in the late-1990s that assessed the potential for greater integration of the sport and tourism functions at national, regional, and local level in the UK. This paper now reports on the final conclusions of this research project and makes tentative suggestions for future development and research.

Although the research reported here was conducted in a UK context, many of the generic issues are likely to be relevant in other countries. While, clearly, there are numerous different structures for policy development around the world, many of the tensions in the policy process and problems associated with collaborative sport-tourism policy are generally applicable in many countries—for example, Canada and Australia— there is an historical institutional separation of policy-making for sport and tourism that is similar to that of the UK. Furthermore, much of the discussion in this paper that focuses on the regional level of policy making is likely to be of relevance in federal systems such as France, Canada, and Australia. The USA, while also a federal system, may be slightly different in that there is a considerable variability in attitude between states on the desirability of public sector involvement in both sport and tourism. Certainly at national level, where the national tourism organization, the US Travel and Tourism Association, was abolished in 1996 and the US Olympic Committee receives no public sector funding, there is little public sector involvement. It appears that in the USA it is the city level that is important, where over one hundred "sports commissions" have been established, often under the umbrella of Convention and Visitor Bureaus, in cities across the country (Standeven & De Knop, 1999). At the opposite end of the scale, France's tradition of providing for "social tourism" (subsidized development for the benefit of low income groups) means that there is a greater public sector involvement in the tourism sector. Such differences in tradition and structure obviously mean that no research can be wholly internationally applicable, but many issues are relevant across a range of countries, and some of these will be highlighted in the conclusion to this paper.

Sport and tourism institutions in the UK

Before embarking on a discussion of the research, some brief explanatory comments are required on the agencies responsible for sport and for tourism policy in the UK (a more detailed examination of these agencies and their interactions with each other is provided by Weed, 2001). During the period of the research, considerable change took place in the make up of the government department and agencies involved. Following a protracted debate, dating back to the late 1980s, regarding the future of the Sports Council (the UK's national agency for sport, with quasi-autonomous status and a remit to cover both English and UK-wide issues), the organization was split into UK Sport and Sport England in 1997. These organizations report to the government Department for Culture, Media and Sport (DCMS), which was established as the Department of National Heritage (DNH) by a Conservative government in 1992. and was subject to a name change following the election of a Labour government in 1997. The DCMS is also responsible for the adminis- tration of the National Lottery, the proceeds of which are distributed among a number of good causes, one of which is the Lottery Sports Fund. Also reporting to the DCMS is the English Tourism Council, a business support organization with quasi-autonomous status that replaced the English Tourist Board, which had a wider direct marketing and development remit, in 1999. Sport England has ten regional offices that roughly correspond to the areas covered by Regional Tourist Boards (RTBs) in England. The RTBs are independent, non-statutory organizations that are funded by a mixture of a direct grant from the English Tourism Council, local authority subscriptions, commercial sector memberships, and commercial income-generating activities. These organizations, along with sportsscotland and the Sports Council for Wales, and the Scottish and Wales Tourist Boards (the Scottish and Welsh equivalents of Sport England and the old English Tourist Board, respectively), were the central subjects of study during this research. Although the Sports Council was split into UK Sport and Sport England during the research, the staff interviewed all became part of the Sport England set up and, as such, the Sports Council and Sport England are used interchangeably during this paper to refer to Sport England.

Methods

Much of the research was based on dated collected from in-depth, "informed source" interviews with officers of sportsscotland and the Scottish Tourist Board, the Sports Council for Wales and the Wales Tourist Board, and Sport England and the Regional Tourist Boards in England. The purpose of such interviews is to draw on the knowledge of the most informed source in the organization or section (see King, 1994; Lowe, 1981: Lowe & Goyder, 1982, for a discussion of this technique), while also following up other sources for triangulation to ensure validity (Cassel & Symon, 1994). However, Lowe and Goyder (p. 4) also note that this approach provides insights into the "outlook and attitudes of people in such key positions which are also important facts." The officers interviewed were the Development Directors/Managers in the tourism agencies and time Senior (Regional) Planning Officers or Heads of Planning and Development in the sports agencies. In addition, a number of interviews were conducted with selected local authority leisure departments in England with Chief Leisure Officers or, in authorities where leisure and tourism functions were split, with the officers heading those sections.

The schedule of questions for the interviews was structured around seven themes: structure and communication, strategy and policy development, organizational philosophy and operations, government and political thinking/policy, recruitment and staff background, grant aid and funding, and consultancy. Each of the interviews was recorded and subsequently transcribed in order that they could be analyzed in detail. An issues analysis was conducted. The structure of the issues analysis was similar to that used by Marshall (1994) in her discourse analysis of interviews with Health Care workers. There were 25 informed source interviews conducted in total, which varied in length from just over 1 hour to around 2½ hours. Consequently the analysis focused on 25 transcripts that ranged from 15 to 34 A4 pages of single spaced script. Firstly, all the scripts were read through and checked with the tapes for both familiarization and verification. As suggested by Marshall, the scripts were then read through again and recurrent themes were identified. Initially, 21 themes were identified, which were subsequently grouped into seven main themes (see Table 25.1).

The seven main themes were used as the framework for the subsequent analysis. Each of the transcripts were read through seven times, each time highlighting those parts of the interview that discussed one of the themes. At the end of this process, there were seven copies of each transcript, each relating to one of the main themes identified. The

Table 25.1 Themes for analysis

Main theme	Sub-themes
Strategic direction	Strategy initiatives
	Policy development
	Leadership
	Vision
	Public sectorism
	Commercialism
Specificity and diversity	Regional specificity
	Diverse aims and objectives
Flexibility and change	Flexibility
	Change
	The nature of the work
Resources and funding	Resources and funding
	Service delivery
Communication and influence	Communication
	Influencing others
	Political activity
Relationships	Relationships
	Partnership and liaison
	Working together and teamwork
	Conflict
Sport-tourism	The sport-tourism concept

next stage of the analysis was to construct an index for each interview that summarized the main points of the discussion under each theme and also highlighted those areas here the themes overlapped. This resulted in 25 indices, from which the main issues were summarized under the headings "context,' "supra-setting," "setting and situated activity," and "selves" (adapted from Layder, 1993) according to the main links that emerged between the seven themes. These summaries provided the structure for the detailed discussion of the results presented in Weed (1999). Of course, in a paper such as this, space does not permit either the inclusion of the same volume of empirical data (Weed. 1999, presented over 300 extracts from these interviews) or the same level of detail in discussion. Consequently, what is presented in the following pages is only a small illustrative selection of the full volume of empirical evidence that supports the observations and conclusions made in this paper.

The interview data are supplemented by data born a number of other sources that were used to validate the information collected through the interviews. These sources include a range of preliminary and off-the-record briefings, a review of strategy documentation (partially reported in Weed & Bull, 1997a), a consultation exercise among the agencies involved in the strategy review, and three brief studies of successful partnership initiatives. The selected data is presented, in places, in the main body of the text, but largely in "tables" of representative comments from the interviews. The purpose of these tables is twofold: firstly, they allow evidence to be presented without breaking up the flow of ideas in the text and, secondly, they allow a greater volume of evidence to be presented than would have been possible if quotations had been included in the main text. The discussions and empirical evidence in the first part of the paper highlight a range of tensions in the sport-tourism policy process, and a number of problems they may cause for sport-tourism policy development. However, it is the root cause of such tensions, the influences proposed in the conceptual paper by Weed and Bull (1998) that are perhaps of most interest. These influences—political and professional ideology, government policy, organizational structure, organizational culture, and key staff—are reviewed and modified in the second part of this paper in the light of the empirically derived tensions identified in the first part, and then place in the model proposed by Weed (2001) is discussed. Finally, the paper analyzes the extent to which these revised influences affect the ability of the sport and tourism policy communities in the UK to generate a sustainable sport-tourism policy network.

Results

Tensions in the sport-tourism policy process

As mentioned above, in-depth "informed source" interviews with officers of the agencies responsible for the development of sport and tourism in the UK revealed a range of tensions that affect relationships between sport and tourism agencies. These tensions may be within or between central government and the Department for Culture, Media and Sport (the UK government department responsible for both sport and tourism), the English Tourism Council, the Regional Tourist Boards, Sport England and its regional offices, or any combination of these organizations. However, they have all been shown to affect relationships within and between the sport and tourism policy communities and are summarized in Table 25.2.

Table 25.2 lists five main tensions that this research has highlighted within the sport and tourism policy communities. Also listed are a number of subsidiary tensions related to each of the five main tensions. Of course, these tensions are by no means mutually exclusive; in fact they are inextricably interlinked. In terms of assessing the influences on relationships within and between the sport and tourism policy communities proposed by Weed and Bull (1998), these tensions are important because their root causes are the factors that exert major influence on the development of a sport-tourism policy network, and as such they are reviewed below.

It is possible to identify Sport England, based on their central role in implementing government sports policy and distributing Lottery Sports Fund money, and the Regional Tourist Boards, based on their connections with both local authorities and the private sector, as the lead agencies within the sport and tourism policy communities respectively. However, despite their unique network of connections, the Regional Tourist Boards can only sustain their leadership role through the retention of a strategic function, and they are increasingly under pressure to focus on income generation. Such tension between income generation and strategic direction is the first major tension highlighted in Table 25.2.

Table 25.2 Tensions in the sport and tourism policy communities

Income generation	.V.	Strategic direction
Resources	.v.	Knowledge
Top-down policy	.V.	Bottom-up policy
National	.v.	Regional
Imposed initiatives	.v.	Ownership of initiatives
Change	.v.	Evolution
Organization	.V.	Individuals
Professionalization	.v.	Adhocracy
Framework	.v.	Flexibility
Internal focus	.V.	External focus
Organizational survival	.v.	Future development
Project based liaison	.V.	Ongoing liaison
Initiatives	.v.	Advocacy

Income generation.   Weed (1999) describes how government uses competitive funding mechanisms to influence the strategic direction of the Regional Tourist Boards. The Boards are virtually forced into bidding for such funds, regardless of their own strategic priorities, because they need to generate income, the result being that strategic developments are increasingly secondary to the generation of funds (this is highlighted by the range of comments in Table 25.3). This means, therefore, that unless such funding mechanisms are promoting sport-tourism relationships (which is highly unlikely), this tension is likely to work against sport-tourism links because Regional Tourist Boards will not have the strategic capacity to develop such links. The subsidiary tension also works in this way because, as a range of authors have discussed (Coghlan & Webb 1990; Collins, 1991, 1992; Houlihan, 1997), the government has increasingly used its control of Sport England funding to dictate its policy direction. The tension here is between the specialist knowledge that resides in Sport England and the resource control exercised by the government (Gouldner, 1954). Weed and Bull (1997b) have discussed the effects that the various policies of the Department for Culture, Media and Sport (and its predecessor, the Department of National Heritage), the government department responsible for both sport and tourism matters, have had on sport-tourism relations—particularly its failure to take a holistic view of the leisure sector. In fact, despite being established to bring the leisure sectors together, the Department has implemented a number of policies that have served to maintain, if not increase, their segregation. Consequently, government control of Sport England direction does not assist in the development of sport-tourism relationships. However, if the government were to take a more holistic view of the leisure sector, the tensions described above would have the potential to assist rather than hinder the development of relationships between Sport England and Regional Tourist Boards.

For example, competitive funding mechanisms might include sport-tourism partnership criteria while government directives to Sport England might encourage it to develop a wider remit that recognizes the contribution that other sectors of the leisure area can

Table 25.3 Comments on need to generate income

The problem is our core binding has been cut . . . there is more money available to help with specific initiatives, but the problem with that is it creates a bit of a bottleneck, there's actually lots of scope for us to do more, but of course these funding programs don't want to contribute to core costs, they want to put something into specific projects. So we've got this balancing act of trying to sustain a strong enough core strategic operation to actually run and oversee both these programs and our overall direction. (1)

It's a simple equation—core funding cuts mean cuts in our ability to deliver all the programs we have previously been delivering. (4)

I don't think competitive bidding is good strategically. It's difficult to show what you are trying to do strategically. The bids tend to be based on that particular initiative, not on what you are seeking to achieve. That's the problem . . . [bids] don't actually show where facilities fit into the development of tourism within the area. (2)

The RTB is having to bid for this money from other sources and try to get matching funding to come in for it. Obtaining funding is very opportunistic and takes up a major segment of our time. (3)

Our work is increasingly being driven by the need to make money, frankly. We have to get out there and sell services. (5)

Note. These comments are representative examples from informed source interviews with the Regional Tourist Boards.

make to the development of sport. Alternatively, if the government were to respect the independence of both the Regional Tourist Boards and Sport England then it may be likely that they would move towards greater collaboration as they identify their own strategic priorities. In fact, there are some examples of this in some regions (see later discussions) However, the initiation of such initiatives pre-dates the establishment of the Department for Culture, Media and Sport and its predecessor, the Department of National Heritage, who showed very little interest in developing such partnerships in the regions. As one Regional 'tourism Board Development Director explained:

> When we did these joint [sport- tourism] statements and the new Department of National Heritage was set up, I actually sent these to the DNH and said "look, why can't you put some resources into getting something going down here, we've already got the thing set up". Theme was a total lack of interest on the part of the DNH, which was disappointing. There was never that feeling from them that you've got something good going here, we'll make these little pilots.

Top down policy.   The second tension highlighted in Table 25.2 is between top-down and bottom-up policy development. Obviously this is related to the previous tension as there is clearly a significant element of top-down influence from government (Collins 1991, 1992). In addition, the abolition, in 1995, of the Regional Councils for Sport and Recreation (RCSRs), bodies that brought together a wide range of sport, recreation, and countryside interests, removed a major mechanism for bottom-up policy development. Furthermore, the government was quite clear about its motives for abolishing the RCSRs,

Table 25.4 Comments on imposed initiatives and change

Whatever the project, people have to have ownership of it if it's going to be successful. You can't impose success on projects. . . . It's absolutely essential to get people to have ownership of projects. (6)	The status quo is continually changing. I would pose the question, "Do we evolve or change?" Are we evolving, which contains notions of continuity and sustainability, or changing because there are other imperatives that have been imposed on us . . . that turn over the apple cart. (7)
I think it is important that . . . [the status quo] . . . is maintained internally. Externally, it is important to take a lead in changing . . . we would rather shape the change than have the change shaped for us. (8)	It's not really the best time to be [forging sport-tourism partnerships] because there is so much change going on within the organization, apart from any other disturbances there's a lot of time being expended on re-organizing and restructuring. (9)
The demands of such [sport-tourism] partnerships on staff are likely to be unacceptable, especially during the current stage of re-organization. (10)	

Note. Comments 6 (national agency), 7 (Sports Council Region), and 8 (Regional Tourist Board) are representative examples from informed source interviews. Comments 9 and 10 are representative examples from preliminary discussions with Sports Council personnel during the winter and spring of 1995, when the intention to restructure the organization had been announced, but firm proposals had not been drafted.

claiming that their link with Sport England's predecessor, the Sports Council, was interfering with the implementation of Sports Council policy (Sproat, 1994). Consequently, Sport England now focuses on the implementation of national policy at a local level and it is aided in this by its role as a distributor of Lottery funds, because local authorities must follow Sport England direction if they wish to benefit from Lottery Sports Fund money.

Houlihan (1991, 1997) has noted that the sports policy community in general, and Sport England in particular is unable to insulate itself from the imposition of initiatives or priorities from other often more important or influential policy areas. Furthermore, it appears that the same is true of the tourism policy community and the Regional Tourist Boards. For example, much of the funding offered on a competitive bidding basis to the Regional Tourist Boards focuses on economic and social regeneration, and so many initiatives will have these priorities as their "imposed" goal. Research has shown (Clarke & Newman, 1997; Handy, 1989: Mintzberg, 1979) that initiatives or directions suggested or developed internally by organizations have a much greater chance of success than those imposed externally, and consequently it is important that both staff and organizations feel they have ownership of initiatives (see comment 6, Table 25.4). Analogous to these ideas is the differentiation that can be made between evolution and change. Several interviewees referred to evolution as a development of the organization that is usually internally instigated, whereas change was seen as being disruptive and as being externally imposed (see comments 7 and 8). Interviews with Sport England officers suggest that externally imposed change causes organizational instability—certainly in respect of this organization's recent re-organization (see comments 9 and 10)—and can often lead to an internal focus on organizational maintenance.

The consequences of these tensions are twofold. Firstly, that while the government continues to take a segregationist view of leisure, imposed or top down initiatives are unlikely to assist in developing sport-tourism partnerships. Secondly, even if the government were to attempt to impose sport-tourism initiatives on the sport and tourism policy communities, it is unlikely that they would meet with much success. Sustainable sport-tourism relationships are only likely to emerge if the organizations are encouraged to draw up their own agenda for liaison, which they feel they have ownership of. However, as the following tensions will show, other factors exist that make the development of an "owned" internal agenda for sport-tourism partnerships unlikely.

Individual and organizational factors.   Analyses of the role of individuals and organizational factors in the policy process highlight tensions between the organization and the individual (Crozier, 1964; Dalton, 1959). Morgan (1986, 1997) highlights that the extent to which this tension manifests itself will depend on the structure and culture of the organization. In fact, as both Sport England and the Regional Tourist Boards allow their staff some autonomy, the tension between individual and organization is magnified because staff has the opportunity to divert from organizational goals and priorities. However, while the professionalized structure of Sport England allows its employees autonomy within a framework, the adhocratic structure of the Regional Tourist Boards gives its employees greater flexibility (Mintzberg, 1979). Because, in many cases, relationships between sport and tourism bodies are new and therefore outside of the parameters of many organizations' structures, flexibility is a key element in developing such relationships. In fact, in the few cases where sport-tourism relationships have developed, key staff have been given the flexibility to pursue such relationships. However, interviews with both Sport England and Regional Tourist Board staff highlight that it is possible for key individuals within organizations to work outside the framework laid down by their organization if they have the seniority and inclination to do so. This is best illustrated by a detailed examination of two examples of sport-tourism liaison in the regions. In the first of these, where a joint statement was initiated by the Regional Tourist Board, the impetus came from the Development Manager at the board:

> I suppose [the initiative] came from myself. . . . Around about the same time that I was working on our strategy the Sports Council were doing theirs. I think I just suggested that we should be putting our heads together and look at areas where we could work together—that's how it started. . . . [Then] I basically wrote it and we got some comments from them.

However, while the project was initialed and driven forward by the Development Manager of the Regional Tourist Board, it was supported by the Regional Director of the Sports Council.

> The then Regional Director of the Sports Council [was] quite laid back about it I suppose. He was quite happy to see us take the lead and get on with it. If he liked what came out then he'd be happy to put his name to it. . . . [But] in fairness it was driven or led by us.

The initiative was thus driven forward by one individual in the Regional Tourist Board with the support of the Regional Director of the Sports Council. This was quite important as the then Chief Executive of the Regional Tourist Board was not particularly supportive of the initiative but, because it had the support of the Sports Council Regional Director, he was prepared to go along with it. However, after the publication of the joint policy statement there were few subsequent joint initiatives. The Regional Board Development Manager puts this down to a number of factors:

> It's certainly down to resources and, of course, the Sports Council have had their other internal problems to worry about. It's down to changing personalities —essentially, really, this was driven forward by a couple of individuals— it was certainly useful to me having [the then Sports Council Regional Director] supporting it. I don't think [the new Regional Director] is probably aware of it, I think it's probably dim and distant past there; they've probably got other things on their plate.

In this comment lies a microcosm of many of the issues outlined in this paper. A lack of resources, internal organizational problems, changing organizational priorities and personalities are all quoted as having an effect. However, the clear implication is that the failure of the initiative was due to the change of Regional Director at the Sports Council. This change, combined with the lack of enthusiasm for the project from the Regional Tourist Board Chief Executive, appears to have conspired to condemn the initiative.

This initiative, however, did inspire one other Regional Tourist Board to embark on a similar initiative, as described by the Development Manager of the above Board:

> The [Regional] Tourist Board shared an office with the regional Sports Council and the new Development Manager at the time was from a planning background, so he tends to think in these ways, and could see the sense in it. He was looking to make further strategic contacts, and using our report as a basis was a good way forward. I didn't object to it. The more we can be moving forward on that common basis—it's in all our interests.

The Development Manager of this Board saw the joint statement as a way of indicating to other organizations the importance of working together on sports tourism initiatives. As such it had a slightly different purpose than the joint statement discussed above which was written, "to anchor both organizations to some action points and get some resources." In this case, however, the statement:

> was to communicate and clarify where the overlaps were, and to identify those so we had an agenda that we could work to, so that then—in one sense it's not something we run around flashing about, but it has helped us to guide the way we respond to people. . . . I think specific initiatives tend to not necessarily be initiated by ourselves or the Sports Council, either separately or together, but by others with whom we would then get involved. So the town of [XXX] on their cycling development project are talking to us and they are talking to the Sports Council, and because we've got an understanding of the links between sport and tourism that works.

This initiative is also supported by the Regional Director of the Sports Council in this region who believes the initiative "has resulted in close cooperation between the regional sport and tourism agencies in the [region]." Again it would appear that this initiative has been driven forward by a number of key individuals. Firstly, it should be noted that had the first joint statement not been produced by the Regional Tourist Board above, it is likely that this joint statement may not have been written. As a result, a key individual is the Development Manager of the first Board. Clearly, the Development Manager of this Board, who was responsible for writing the strategy, was a key player, as was the Sports Council Regional Director. However, there do appear to be other factors that have contributed to the greater success of this initiative. The less ambitious objectives for the joint statement appear to have assisted the initiative in that it did not require any resources or additional inputs. It was seen as a way of indicating where the links are in other agencies, and as a guide for the Sports Council and Regional Tourist Board in responding to other agencies. Thus, the joint statement was used as a mechanism to develop the trust and understanding that is clearly important to the development of joint initiatives. It has been further assisted by the Regional Tourist Board sharing an office building with the Sports Council regional office. But, the significant difference between this and the first initiative is that the individuals who drove it forward still work in the same positions in the two organizations.

Internal and external foci.   Tensions between internal and external foci of organizations have already been touched upon earlier. In many cases such tensions are explicitly related to the tension between income generation and strategic direction. There is evidence of an emergent culture (Williams, 1977) of commercialism in Regional Tourist Boards that can lead to a more internal focus on organizational maintenance or "fire fighting," dealing with the day-to-day survival of the organization, rather than an external focus on future development. As already described above, Regional Tourist Boards must continue to operate strategically if they are to retain their lead position in the tourism policy community, and a requirement in doing so is an external focus and a concern for future development.

At the sectoral level, the tension between an internal and external focus exists in both the sport and tourism policy communities. Discussions have already taken place on the inability of both policy communities to insulate themselves from other policy areas (Houlihan, 1991). Jordan and Richardson (1987) describe how this may lead communities to focus on establishing a clearly identifiable policy heartland, rather than on working on areas in their policy periphery—which is where the majority of sport-tourism issues lie. Added to this is perhaps an ideology in some quarters, but certainly not the majority, of both the sport and tourism policy communities that sport-tourism issues are not a legitimate concern of either the sport or tourism policy communities, or of their organization, on in their geographical area (see comments in Table 25.5). The sum of these factors is an internal focus for both communities, whereas what is required for successful sport-tourism liaison is an external focus and a culture of developing partnerships outside immediate policy heartlands.

Liaisons.   The final tension highlighted in Table 25.2 is that between project based and ongoing liaison. Notwithstanding the discussion in the previous paragraph, there is

Table 25.5 Comments on sport-tourism liaison

We haven't got a dialogue with the sports bodies, we haven't got a natural constituency and there is nobody coming to us asking for our help. I think the sports bodies need to come to us. (11)	Contact with [the Sports Council] depends on the nature of the product. However, in this region it's often what I'd class as informal facilities like public rights of way, which have nothing to do with the Sports Council, that are important. (12)
We have initiatives that we have decided are key to us, and it's difficult to see where tourism would be part of those —I don't think there is any concerted effort to work directly with the tourist authorities. (13)	The roles of the Sports Council and the Regional Tourism Board do not coincide. What role has the Sports Council to play in inspecting Bed and Breakfasts? (14)

Note. Comments 11 and 12 (national agency) and 13 (Sports Council) are from informed source interviews. Comment 14 is a response to the Strategy Review consultation exercise. While these comments are indicative of a significant minority view, they are not representative of the majority of the sample.

a general acknowledgement within the sport and tourism policy communities that some liaison between them is desirable (although in many cases both organizations and individuals believe the responsibility for developing such liaison does not lie with them). Opinions vary as to whether ongoing strategic liaison is required, or whether liaison should take place in an ad hoc manner as and when projects arise (see comments in Table 25.6). Quite patently, those who favor a more commercial culture within their organization are likely to believe that liaison should take place in an adhocratic, project based way, while those who believe the focus should be strategic would prefer to see ongoing liaison. Evidence from the interviews suggests, as highlighted in the earlier discussion of the second of the two specific examples of sport-tourism partnerships, that perhaps a focus on advocacy and developing an agreed agenda for responding to projects proposed by other organizations might be the best way forward. Such an approach represents a compromise between the project-based and ongoing approaches and is described in greater detail by Weed (1999).

Influence on sport tourism relations and the policy community model

Weed and Bull (1998), in their conceptual paper on "The search for a sport tourism policy network," suggested a range of factors that might affect relationships within and between the sport and tourism policy communities, namely: ideology (political and professional), government policy, organizational structure, organizational culture, and key staff. It would be expected that such factors would be the root causes of the tensions discussed above. However, in the light of empirical research, a small representative selection of which has been included here, it is clear that these factors do not fully account for the tensions summarized in Table 25.2, and as such some revision of Weed and Bull's conceptually derived model is required. Six revised influences were identified in these

Table 25.6 Strategic links vs. project-based contact

For strategic links	For project-based contact
I think if we have some sort of ongoing framework, preferably quite a simple networking mechanism of some kind so there is a point of regular contact with them. (15)	Partnerships should probably be more project oriented . . . the strength of the Sports Council is the ability to comment on specific projects on the technical side. (19)
We have a sport and tourism working group set up that includes the Tourist Board, ourselves, and a few other organizations such as the Countryside Commission, to look at whether there are any particular initiatives we can take forward where sport and tourism are linked. (16)	Liaison should be on an ad hoc basis, otherwise you just have meetings and develop an agenda for the sake of it. Liaison meetings for the sake of it are really non-productive. (20)
There's a danger that, because of the current climate, future liaison may be project driven with no clear vision or direction. (17)	We have deliberately not done what some boards have done—gone round the regional organizations and write joint policy statements. . . . [That's] a half-way house between a strategy and a program. We prefer to look for an action-based approach—identify a project, fund it, do it. (21)
There should be an underlying dialogue, but its impractical to go through everything with them—we contacted the Sports Council during our strategy process. (18)	There is ongoing liaison, but I wouldn't say there were enough projects for people to meet at set times right through the year—so I think it tends to be project by project—we try to keep in touch with what each other is doing. (22)

Note. Comments 15, 18, 19, and 21 are from the Regional Tourist Board informed source interviews. Comments 16 and 22 are from informed source interviews in the Sports Council Regions. Comment 17 is from Sports Council responses to the Strategy Review consultation exercise. Comment 20 is from the National Agency informed source interviews (sports response).

data: ideology, definitions, regional contexts, government policy, organizational culture and structure, and individuals.

Ideology.   Firstly, while ideology has clearly emerged as affecting sport-tourism relationships, there appears to be little utility in retaining the distinction between political and professional ideology, ideology causes tensions at all levels of the policy process, but is particularly important at the contextual level, contributing to the environment within which policy is made. However, it has also become clear that tensions between income generation and strategy, change and evolution, organization and individuals, and organizational survival and future development are caused in some instances by conflicting ideological stances. Maintaining the distinction between political and professional ideologies does not assist in the analysis of these tensions—in fact, it may be that more personal ideologies are at work that are not necessarily professional or political. Consequently, identifying ideology generally as important is of greater value than maintaining the political/professional distinction.

Definitions. Linked to ideology in some respects is the influence wielded by individual and organizational definitions and conceptions of sport, tourism, and sports tourism. Government definitions of sport have been, to a certain extent, imposed on Sport England causing organizational instability through the changes that resulted. In the mid 1990s the government's preferred definition of sport did not include recreation, but a much more narrow concept of competitive activities, and this move away from recreational activities was at the heart of the changes in Sport England that took place during this time. Definitions and conceptions can also cause tensions between organization and individual and between internal and external foci. A more narrow definition of either sport or tourism leads to a more sharply defined policy heartland and less willingness to work in an organization's or community's periphery. This obviously has negative implications for the development of sport-tourism initiatives.

Regional contexts. Perhaps one of the most significant influences to emerge from the interviews was "regional contexts" (see comments in Table 25.7). In this respect, historic, geographic administrative, economic, structural and a whole range of other factors that vary between regions were seen as causing tensions in different ways in different regions. For example, the extent of the tension between project based and ongoing liaison is affected by regional contexts such as geographical resources for sports tourism, historical liaison (or non-liaison) between regional bodies, and the strength and structure of the regional economy. To a certain extent individuals may be seen as regional contexts as they can cause specific tensions in their region. However, the influence of individuals is also prevalent at the national level and within government and therefore perhaps still merits separate consideration. While "regional contexts" may appear a slightly eclectic label, it is nevertheless a useful one in helping to understand the variations between regional approaches to the sport-tourism link.

Government policy. Of the five influences initially proposed by Weed and Bull (1998), perhaps government policy is the one that emerges most clearly from the data as wielding the significant influence that was originally suggested. Patently, as described by Weed and Bull (1997b), government policy causes tensions between income generation and strategy and between top-down and bottom-up policy development in a number of ways. It is the only one of the original influences that does not need to be reviewed in some way.

Organizational culture and structure. Organizational structure and organizational culture were originally proposed as separate influences on relationships between sport and tourism agencies. However, while they clearly contribute to many of the tensions identified in Table 25.2, it has been almost impossible to separate them in practice. In fact, it appears that culture and structure evolve together and are inextricably inter-linked. Consequently, it is perhaps more useful to combine these factors and consider them as one.

Individuals. Individuals have already been mentioned briefly in the discussion of regional contexts. However, in the original proposals "key staff" were identified as an influencing

Table 25.7 Comments on the effect of specific regional influences on sport-tourism liaison

We have a stronger history of public intervention in Scotland than in other parts of the UK. . . . We have many organizations that are unique to Scotland . . . that tend to be based in one city—Edinburgh. Many of the staff have worked in a number of Scottish agencies and know what their limitations are. . . . There's also a greater commitment, I think, to a "Scottish identity" than you would get in England or its regions. (23)

It depends on regional characteristics. Here we've got the natural resources that can help sustain a wide range of outdoor activities such as water sports, orienteering canoeing, walking, cycling, and climbing—all of these are growth areas for tourism. More people are taking part and doing so for a longer period of their life—people in their 40s, 50s, 60s take part in quite active sports and do so on holiday that's got a very strong market significance for us. (26)

My view is that tourism has a much closer link with sport on an implementational, practical level than with economic development. . . . It depends where you are—our kind of tourism is linked to the countryside, leisure and heritage. (28)

Sport isn't important in this city because we don't need any more tourists, and they don't come here for sport. . . . here we get tourists because of what the city is, and one of the principal reasons is the arts. (30)

If you take resort towns as an example, one of the major government defined issues in [this region] is the future of the coastal resorts and their economies. . . . The future of some of those towns is a mixture of sport and tourism initiatives—how much can we afford to invest, do we have a sport project here, or a tourism project? If we have a sports facility, do we have community facilities or a regional facility that would attract more business to the town? (24)

There is close contact with tourist boards in the more metropolitan areas, because there is promotion of the individual towns and cities, not least linked to events, like Manchester and the Commonwealth Games. (25)

If this city didn't have some of the sporting facilities it has, a let of people from outlying areas wouldn't come in. That's why it's important to recognize that when we create the next generation of sports centers they're not just for local people, but an attraction in their own right. (27)

I think in the future [we] may need to get more involved with the aspirations of the professional clubs and perhaps the private sector sports facilities too. I think it's the big league that's going to do the most for the promotion of tourism. (29)

Note. Comment 23 is from the National Agency informed source interviews. Comment 24 is from the Regional Tourist Board informed source interviews. Comments 25 and 26 are from the informed source interview with the Sports Council central contact and the Strategy Review consultation exercise. Comments 27, 28, 29, and 30 are from the local authority informed source interviews.

factor on sport-tourism relationships. It is perhaps more useful to use the term "individuals" as this would also allow for the influence of, for example, significant political figures. In this respect, John Major as Prime Minister (1990–1997) had a significant influence on sport-tourism relationships because the sports policy statement, "Sport: Raising the Game" (Department of National Heritage, 1995), that contained the proposals for Sport England to withdraw from the promotion of recreational activities in order to focus more on competitive sport, is widely seen as bearing the personal stamp of the Prime Minister (Collins, 1995). Consequently, John Major was responsible for a number of tensions related to top-down policy development and organizational change and instability. However, it should perhaps be pointed out that individuals are not always aware of the wider implications and repercussions of their actions. It is unlikely that John Major gave any thought to the effect his proposals would have on sport-tourism relationships and as such the consequences for sport-tourism links were unintended.

Sport tourism policy structure

The final cause of tensions in the sport-tourism policy process that emerged is the structure of the sport and tourism policy sectors. Weed (2001) developed a policy community model that combines the models suggested by Rhodes (Marsh & Rhodes. 1992; Rhodes, 1981) and Wilks and Wright (1987). This combination allows for an analysis of the way in which the structure of the policy communities at the sectoral level (e.g., sport, tourism, arts, etc.) might affect the development of policy networks at the sub-sectoral level (e.g., sport-tourism). The model sets the sport and tourism policy communities within a broader leisure policy universe that includes other interests such as the arts, heritage and countryside recreation. Policy communities themselves are characterized as existing on a continuum from a close-knit policy circle, to a much more loose and open issue zone. The structure of such communities is seen as affecting the potential for sub-sectoral policy networks to emerge to deal with more specific areas of policy such as the sport-tourism link. A brief analysis of the sport and tourism policy communities shows that the sports policy community can be identified as having a primary core comprising key organizations such as central government, the Department for Culture, Media and Sport, and Sport England, which is fairly closed to the rest of the community, but a more open secondary community; the tourism policy community, on the other hand, is altogether more open. Although in relation to the tourism policy community, the sports policy community shows more of the features of a policy circle—and thus is perhaps more able to exclude tourism interests than vice-versa—both communities are unable to insulate themselves from other, more politically important policy areas. Consequently, tensions surrounding the imposition of initiatives and the ability to define strategic direction may be related to the structure of the two policy communities—specifically, that both policy communities are susceptible to the imposition of initiatives from other, non-leisure communities and, perhaps more significantly, that the tourism policy community might be more open to sports bodies than the sports community would be to tourism agencies.

It is possible, therefore, to draw together the above discussions and the model of the sport-tourism policy process proposed by Weed (2001) into an overall picture that might explain the extent of liaison between sport and tourism agencies in the UK. The sport and tourism policy communities exist within a leisure policy universe. The structure of the sports policy community is such that it has a tightly defined primary core, but a more open secondary community, and thus falls towards the "policy circle" end of the continuum described in the previous paragraph. Conversely, the tourism policy community has a generally more open structure and thus falls more towards the "issue zone" end of the continuum. While these respective structures exert some influence on the potential for a sport-tourism policy network to form at the point where the sport and tourism policy communities intersect, there are a further six influences (revised from those proposed in Weed & Bull, 1998) that affect the relationships between these communities and, as per the above discussion, these are:

- ideologies
- definitions
- regional contexts
- government policy
- organizational culture and structure
- individuals.

These influences, and the model of the respective structures of the sport and tourism policy communities, now provide an empirically substantiated backdrop against which the potential development of a sport-tourism policy network can be assessed in the next section.

Discussion

The potential for a sustainable sport-tourism policy network

In light of the revised influences on relationships between the sport and tourism policy communities it is useful to assess the extent to which these influences affect the ability of the sport and tourism policy communities to generate a sustainable sport-tourism policy network. Wright (1988, pp. 609–610) identifies several "rules of the game" that act as an "unwritten constitution" for the behavior of actors within policy networks. The following discussion assesses the extent to which a sport-tourism policy community might be able to live with these "rules of the game."

The first of these rules is mutuality—members believe that mutual advantages and benefits will result from their participation in the network. However, research has shown (Weed, 1999, 2001) that mutuality is not evident in all organizations. Particular ideologies, definitions of sport and tourism, and real or perceived regional contexts each contribute in some areas to the belief that sufficient mutual benefits and advantages would not result from participation in a sport tourism policy network. However, in other areas, members and potential members of a network have considered that mutual benefits would be forthcoming. A wide range of work now exists detailing the mutual benefits to be gained from linking sport and tourism (e.g., Bramwell, 1997; De Knop, 1990; Gibson, 1998; Glyptis, 1982; Jackson & Glyptis, 1992; Redmond, 1991), consequently it is perhaps awareness of the full extent of the sport-tourism link that needs to be raised among policy makers.

The willingness of agencies to consult with others, and the expectation that they will be consulted is a second rule. Jordan and Richardson (1987) describe the concept of organizational territory, and the concept of heartland and periphery in relation to an organization's policy area. The heartland comprises those policy areas that an agency considers to be solely its responsibility and it will resist invasion of this territory by other agencies. However, there is also a policy periphery that agencies recognize will involve other organizations. Most of the deliberations of a sport tourism policy network are likely to fall within the policy periphery of the agencies involved. While this is positive in that it avoids any conflict over territory, its negative side is that agencies may not wish to devote time to areas they consider to be on the periphery of their responsibility. Evidence from the interviews shows that both regional contexts and individuals are important here. There are examples where both sport and tourism policy makers have recognized that there is a link between sport and tourism, but their belief has been that developing that link is not their responsibility or is not important in their region (see, for example, comments 11 and 12 in Table 25.5, and comments 25, 27, and 30 in Table 25.7). In many cases, tourism agencies believe sports agencies should take the lead and vice-versa. However, in the regions where sport-tourism links have developed, there have been individuals in each organization who have both recognized the link and been willing to develop partnerships (see earlier discussion for two examples of such partnerships). In these cases there are examples of both sport and tourism agencies having taken the lead role.

Generally, it would be expected that leadership of a sport-tourism policy network might depend on the initiative under consideration and on the particular circumstances in that region. However, it may be that the Regional Tourist Boards are in a better position to develop priorities and suggest areas where the agencies might work together because they have a little more independence and have a slightly wider remit. Nonetheless, this would require both that the sports agencies would not see such a role as an invasion of their core territory and that the Regional Tourist Boards were prepared to take on such a rule. While it appears unlikely that such conditions would occur throughout all the regions there is also some indication, in one or two regions, that such a realignment of roles and attitudes may be possible.

Thirdly, there are often rules emphasizing informality within the network—the expectation that sport and tourism officers would feel able to communicate with each other on an informal basis. Weed and Bull (1998) suggested that informal contacts are vital to the development of a sport-tourism policy network. In one example of liaison, as discussed earlier, the departure of one member of staff led to the cessation of informal contacts and to the failure of the initiative to move beyond an initial joint policy statement. Other examples describe the contribution of informal networks, often sustained outside of the work context, to the success of initiatives. While individuals are clearly the key factors in developing such informal networks, the culture and structure of an organization also wields an important influence in creating the atmosphere in which informal links are either encouraged or discouraged.

Linked to the third rule is a fourth—that policy issues are discussed in a commonly accepted language. This may be problematic in some areas where the sport and tourism sectors may have different conceptions or definitions of sport, tourism, and sports tourism. As such this may work against the establishment of a network. However, in other areas, joint statements have indicated that the sport and tourism sectors can come to some agreement on the nature of sports tourism and what their responsibilities may be towards it.

The final network rule relates to the recourse to higher authority, or to agencies outside the policy network. This is generally because the opening up of an issue to wider debate outside the policy network will result in other organizations impinging on the network's "territory" (Jordan & Richardson, 1982, 1987: Ripley & Franklin, 1980). Consequently, as far as is possible, policy networks attempt to resolve issues within the network. It is unclear how this rule might work within a sport-tourism policy network as there is, as yet, limited evidence of sport-tourism policy partnerships. However, it may be the case that were an issue to become contentious, the sport and tourism agencies would retreat to their policy heartlands and take up fairly entrenched positions. This may result in the issue going unresolved or in it being left to either the sport or tourism agencies to resolve unilaterally. In short, rather than recourse to higher authority, the inability of a sport-tourism policy network to resolve problematic issues is likely to lead to the withdrawal of one or more agencies from the network.

Conclusion

The picture of sport-tourism relations presented through the above analysis would seem to indicate that there are areas in which there is potential for sport and tourism agencies to work together in the UK, but that such potential is not being fulfilled. The analysis perhaps serves to emphasize the major influence that regional contexts and individuals may have on the sport-tourism policy process. This is because it is these two influences that account for the variation of attitude to the sport-tourism link between regions. The obvious conclusion would seem to be that it is unrealistic within the current climate to expect a sport tourism policy network to develop at national level, despite some recent developments that indicate, on the surface, that such liaison should be developing.

In the last few years UK Sport and the British Tourist Authority, both quasi-autonomous government agencies, have each established sections relevant to sports tourism. Since July 1999, UK Sport has had the lead role as the distributor of Lottery funds for the bidding for and staging of major events throughout the UK through its Major Events Group. The Group exists to bring world class sporting events to the UK, "harnessing the benefits that major events can bring to our athletes, sports system and the country as a whole" (UK Sport, 2000, p. 4). In addition, in early 2000 the British Tourist Authority established a small Sports Tourism Department which, among a number of aims included the following:

> To raise awareness among the sports industry of the economic benefit and potential of overseas visitors.

> To contribute to the winning of major international sporting events.

> To position the BTA as the leading agency of an integrated approach to the development of sports tourism.
>
> (British Tourist Authority, 2000, p. 2)

However, despite these aims there has been very little evidence of any partnerships between these agencies, with the UK Sport Major Events Group largely concerning itself with the technical requirements of successfully bidding for events, while the British Tourist Authority Sports Tourism Department has focused largely on promoting events to visitors. The respective aims and remits of these agencies would certainly seem to suggest that there would be a great deal of mutual benefits in working together, but there has as yet, been no indication of any long-term partnerships. Furthermore, despite its stated aim to establish itself as the "leading agency of an integrated approach" (British Tourist Authority, 2000, p. 2), the British Tourist Authority's Sports Tourism Department has shown some reluctance to become involved in academic research initiatives in the sports tourism area.

However, while liaison at national level has not developed, it is already the case that networks have developed at regional level in some areas. Such networks are based on the particular needs of the region and are often driven forward by individuals who believe that mutual benefits do emerge from the sport-tourism link. It would seem that a major factor in the success of such networks is their ability to determine their own agenda according to the resources, people, and attitudes that exist in their region. In this respect, perhaps the most effective antecedent of greater sport tourism links might be, as suggested earlier, the raising of awareness of the benefits of the links among key policy makers and organizations who may then work up their own agenda for greater collaboration.

In early 2000, the Department for Culture, Media and Sport established eight Regional Cultural Consortiums (RCCs) throughout England that may have the potential to assist in raising such awareness. The RCCs aim to:

- Champion the whole spectrum of cultural and creative interests in each region, including tourism and sport.
- Forge links across this spectrum.
- Create a common vision expressed in a cultural strategy for the region.
                    (Department for Culture Media and Sport, 1999, p. 3)

The RCCs cover the same geographical areas as the government's regional offices and the Regional Development Agencies (which are currently providing administrative support). Their membership comprises nominees from the various regional "cultural sector" public bodies and other agencies (defined by government as including sports, tourism, arts, creative industries, heritage and museums, libraries, media, and archives (Burns & Booth, 2001), and as such they cover the range of issues that might be expected to comprise the leisure policy universe. While the RCCs are a top-down government imposed initiative, it appears that they are intended to operate in a similar way to the old Regional Councils for Sport and Recreation, albeit covering a much wider range of issues. If this is the case, then they may provide a very useful mechanism for bottom-up input into regional, and indeed national, strategy. In most cases the Consortiums are still in the early stages of establishing their membership and remit. They are currently engaged in writing their first regional strategies and their success is likely to depend on the extent to which the regional agencies involved feel that the work is either an important part of their agenda, or an additional piece of bureaucracy lying on the edge of their policy periphery. As such, the individuals within the regional agencies charged with responding to the RCCs will be a key determinant of their success, as will their perception of the importance of the RCCs' role within their specific regional context. That the RCCs are aligned with the Regional Development Agencies, through which much government funding is channeled will be an advantage, particularly if funding is made available for initiatives that "forge links across this spectrum" (Department for Culture Media and Sport, 1999, p. 3) while making use of the specialist knowledge that resides with the regional agencies. Tourism and sport are specifically mentioned in the first aim of the RCCs, and now further research is needed to assess the extent to which these agencies can act as a catalyst for the development of genuine regional sport-tourism policy networks.

Finally, some commentary is required on the international application of this research. While some initial comments were made earlier on international similarities and differences, it is perhaps easier to now extrapolate those areas that are likely to be generically relevant. The first part of the paper used the UK data to derive five tensions in the sport-tourism policy process and, although not empirically validated, it would appear that these tensions would be relevant in many countries around the world. In any country where there are debates about the level of public sector involvement in sport and in tourism there are likely to be tensions between income generation and strategic direction, while the existence in most countries of more than one tier of government means that tensions will arise surrounding top-down and bottom-up policy. This is particularly likely to be the case, as highlighted earlier, in countries with federal systems of government. The final three tensions, between organizations and individuals, internal and external organizational focus, and project-based and ongoing liaison, are by no means specific only to the UK. Consequently, it is reasonable to expect that the six factors identified in the second part of the paper as influencing the relationships between sport and tourism policy communities (ideology, definitions, regional contexts, government policy, organizational culture and structure, and individuals) would have some salience in a range of countries. However, the structure of the respective policy communities for sport and for tourism is likely to differ significantly between countries, and consequently the effect this will have on the emergence of a sport-tourism policy network will differ (see Weed & Bull (2004) for a more detailed discussion of the international application of this model).

Weed (2001) discusses the respective structures of the sport and the tourism policy communities in relation to the UK. The sports policy community is identified as having a dual structure with a lightly defined primary core and more open secondary community, while the UK tourism policy community is described as having a much more open structure. Such structures are likely to differ in other countries according to the level of public sector involvement, the nature of inter-dependencies and resource dependencies, and the level of insulation from other policy areas. As such, the structure and nature of the tourism policy community in the USA, where commercial interests dominate, and in France, where there is a stronger public sector tradition, will differ considerably. This will obviously mean that some of the issues surrounding the development of a sport tourism policy network will differ. However, one of the key strengths of the policy community model is that it allows for variations in structure to be accommodated within the generic model, and consequently a key area for further research would be to use the model suggested by Weed (2001) against which to conduct empirical research into the validity in other countries of the influences and tensions described here in relation to the UK.

Note

1   I would like to make some comment on the use of the terms *sport-tourism link/ partnerships/liaison and sports tourism*. This is quite deliberate and indicative of a specific difference. The term sports tourism is generally taken to refer to tourism that includes some sports participation, either active or passive. The use of the hyphen refers to the

broader concept of the "sport-tourism link." There are many issues on which there might be a profitable link between sport and tourism organizations, which would not fall within the generally accepted definition of sports tourism.

References

Bramwell, B. (1997). A sport mega-event as a sustainable develoment strategy. *Tourism Recreation Research*, 22(2), 13–19.

British Tourist Authority (2000). *Sports tourism: Trade information pack*. London: BTA.

Burns, J., & Booth, P. (2001). *North West cultural strategy: Briefing paper*. Manchester: NWCC/NWDA.

Cassell, C., & Symon, G. (1994). Qualitative research in work contexts. In C. Caswell & G. Symon (Eds), *Qualitative methods in organisational research: A practical guide* (pp 1–9). London: Sage.

Clarke, J., & Newman, J. (1997). *The managerial state*. London: Sage.

Coghlan, J.F., & Webb, I.M. (1990). *Sport and British politics since 1960*. London: Falmer.

Collins, M.F. (1991). Sport for all in government in the United Kingdom, with some European comparisons. In P. Oja & R. Telema (Eds), *Sport for all, Proceedings of the 1990 World Congress* (pp. 447–458). Oxford: Elsevier Science Publishers.

Collins, M.F. (1992). Sport and the State—the case of the United Kingdom. In F. Landry, M. Landry, & M. Yerles (Eds), *Sport . . . The third millennium, International Symposium* (pp. 261–268). Sainte-Foy: Presses de l'Universiade Laval.

Collins, M.F. (1995). Sights on sport, *Leisure Management*, 15(19), 26–28.

Crozier, M. (1964). *The bureaucratic phenomenon*. Chicago, IL: University of Chicago Press.

Dalton, M. (1959). *Men who manage*. New York: Wiley.

De Knop, P. (1990). Sport for all and active tourism. *World Leisure and Recreation Association*, 32, 30–36.

Department for Culture, Media and Sport (1999). *Regional cultural consortiums*. London: HMSO.

Department of National Heritage (1995). *Sport: Raising the game*. London: HMSO.

Dunleavy, P., & O'Leary, B. (1987). *Theories of the state*. Basingstoke: Macmillan.

Gibson H.J. (1999). Sport tourism: A critical analysis of research. *Sport Management Review*, 1, 45–76.

Giddens, A. (1977). *Studies in social and political theory*. London: Huchinson.

Glyptis, S.A. (1982). *Sport and tourism in western Europe*. London: British Travel Education Trust.

Goldsmith, M.J., & Rhodes, R.A.W. (1986). *Register of research digest on central–local government relations in Britain*. London: Economic and Social Research Council.

Gouldner, A.W. (1954). *Patterns of industrial bureaucracy*. Chicago, IL: Free Press.

Hall, C.M. (1994). *Tourism and politics: Policy, power and place*. London: Belhaven Press.

Hall, C.M., & Jenkins, J.M. (1995). *Tourism and public policy*. New York: Routledge.

Handy, C. (1989). *The age of unreason*. London: Arrow.

Henry, I.P. (1993). *The politics of leisure policy*. London: Macmillan.

Henry, I.P. (2001). *The politics of leisure policy* (2nd Edition). London: Palgrave.

Houlihan, B. (1991). *The government and the politics of sport*. London: Routledge.

Houlihan, B. (1997). *Sport, policy and politics: A comparative analysis*. London: Routledge.

Jackson, G.A.M., & Glyptis S.A. (1992). Sport and tourism: A review of the literature (unpublished report to the Sports Council). Loughborough: Loughborough University, Recreation Management Group.

Jordan, A.G. (1990). Sub-governments, policy communities and networks: Refilling old bottles? *Journal of Theoretical Politics*, 2(3), 319–338.

Jordan, A.G., & Richardson, J.J. (1982), The British policy style or the logic of negotiation? In J.J. Richardson (Ed.), *Policy styles in western Europe* (pp. 80–110). London: Allen & Unwin.

Jordan, A.G., & Richardson, J.J. (1987). *British politics and the policy process*. London: Allen & Unwin.

King, N. (1994). The qualitative research interview. In C. Cassell & G. Symon (Eds), *Qualitative methods in organisational research: A practical guide* (pp. 14–38). London: Sage.

Layder, D. (1993). *New methods in social research*, London: Routledge.

Lowe, P. (1981). *A political analysis of British rural conservation issues and policies*. Final report to the Social Science Research Council (Rep. No. HR5010). London, UK: University College London.

Lowe, P., & Goyder, J. (1983). *Environmental groups in politics*. London: Allen & Unwin.

Marsh, D., & Rhodes, R.A.W. (1992). Policy communities and issue networks: Beyond typology. In D. Marsh & R.A.W. Rhodes (Eds), *Policy networks in British government* (pp. 249–268). Oxford: Oxford University Press.

Marshall, H. (1994). Discourse analysis in an occupational context. In C. Cassell & G. Symon (Eds), *Qualitative methods in organisational research: A practical guide* (pp. 91–106). London: Sage.

Mintzberg, H. (1979). *The structuring of organizations: A synthesis of the research*. Eaglewood Cliffs, NJ: Prentice Hall.

Morgan, G. (1986). *Images of organisation*. London: Sage.

Morgan, G. (1997). *Images of organisation* (2nd Edition). London: Sage.

Redmond, G. (1991). Changing styles of sports tourism: Industry/consumer interactions in Canada, the USA and Europe. In M.T Sinclair & M.J. Stabler (Eds), *The tourism industry: An international analysis* (pp. 107–120). Wallingford: CAB International.

Rhodes, R.A.W. (1981). *Control and power in central–local government relations*. Farnborough, England: Gower/SSRC.

Ripley, R., &. Franklin, G. (1980). *Congress, the bureaucracy and public policy*. Champaign, IL: Dorsey Press.

Sproat, I. (1994). *Oral Statement to the House of Commons*, July 8.

Standeven, J., & De Knop, P. (1999). *Sport tourism*. Champaign, IL: Human Kinetics.

UK Sport (2000). *Major events: A blueprint for success—a UK policy*. London: UK Sport.

Weed, M. (1999). Consensual policies for sport and tourism in the UK: An analysis of organisational behaviour and problems. Unpublished doctoral thesis, Canterbury Christ Church University College/University of Kent at Canterbury, UK.

Weed, M. (2001). Towards a model of cross-sectoral policy development in leisure: The case of sport and tourism. *Leisure Studies*, 20, 125–141.

Weed, M., & Bull, C.J. (1997a). Integrating sport and tourism: A review of regional policies in England. *Progress in Tourism and Hospitality Research*, 4, 129–148.

Weed, M., & Bull, C.J. (1997b). Influences on sport–tourism relations in the UK: The effects of government policy. *Tourism Recreation Research*, 22(2). 5–12.

Weed, M., & Bull, C.J. (1998). The search for a sport-tourism policy network. In M.F. Collins & I. Cooper (Eds), *Leisure management: Issues and applications* (pp. 277–298). Oxford: CAB International.

Weed, M., & Bull, C.J. (2004). *Sports tourism: Participants, policy and providers*. Oxford: Elsevier.

Wilks, S. (1989). Government–industry relations. *Public Administration*, 67, 329–339.

Wilks, S., & Wright, M. (Eds) (1987). *Comparative government–industry relations*. Oxford: Clarendon Press.

Williams, R. (1977). *Marxism and literature*. New York: Oxford University Press.

Wright, M. (1988). Policy community, policy network and comparative industrial policies. *Political Studies*, 36, 593–612.

Chapter 26

Christopher Hautbois and Christophe Durand

PUBLIC STRATEGIES FOR LOCAL DEVELOPMENT

The effectiveness of an outdoor activities model

Introduction

STIMULATING THE ECONOMY has long been a major responsibility of centralized governments. In Europe, however, and especially in France, this responsibility has been shifting since the early-1980s toward local governments. Thus, economic activity has become a common concern for all levels of public management, and French local governments are now major actors in the organization of their citizens' everyday lives. Local public managers now expect to be involved in all sectors they consider important for their community. Indeed, although the laws of 1982 provided for this type of public intervention, one can now observe initiatives that exceed these provisions with local governments using direct and indirect means to stimulate local economy. This phenomenon is of great importance, because the growth of local economic activity may have repercussions on both territorial organization and the vitality of social networks: one powerful repercussion, for example, is that more citizens are given the opportunity to both live and work in the same community (Lipietz, 2001). This tendency toward work and residence in the same community is notable for its successful resistance of the powerful centripetal force that usually concentrates a population in towns and villages around a major economic pole: the city.

For these reasons, local government bodies are continuously searching for potential levers of economic development. Although public policies in Europe have traditionally looked to the industrial sector as a reliable means for development, this is no longer the case today, and other sectors are now being actively explored. One of the sectors under consideration is sports in general, and outdoor sports in particular. For the past several years the potential of sports activity to serve as an impetus for local economic growth has been the focus of study not only in France, but also throughout Europe and in the United States. This model of local economic development via outdoor sports is thus a modern approach with important theoretical and practical potentialities.

Before examining this model, a fundamental question first, needs to be addressed: exactly what should government's role be in the organization of a community's economic life? In addition to the important stakes mentioned above (i.e., providing citizens the opportunity to live and work in the same community), are there other arguments to justify public intervention in economic development? Indeed, free market economies support the least government intervention possible, trusting in the self-organizing capacities of the economic actors. Reflection today on the relationships between economic activity and public actions inevitably confronts issues of regulation. Should local economic development be regulated by public strategy?

This article is presented in two parts:

- The first part reviews the importance of the industrial sector in local development strategies. It also describes the development of a new model organized around outdoor activities.
- The second part presents an illustration of this model in action with a case study of the development of equestrian activities in the *Basse-Normandie* region. These activities provide a prism for evaluating the feasibility of this model. The effectiveness of the public strategy for local development via these outdoor activities is thus examined.

The importance of the industrial sector in public strategies of local development

Responding to an important demand of society, public policies have often been oriented toward redressing inequities between territories. The guiding principle has been to ensure identical treatment for all citizens, wherever they live. However, the mechanisms of France's central government for ensuring territorial equity are at times quite rigid, given the difficulties of discerning the specificities and needs of each territory, and local public managers often complicate matters with their own actions. This tendency has increased over the past few years and, today, local public initiatives for economic development have reached an intensified pitch because of growing competition between the territories (Davezies, 2000, 2002, 2003). In the current economic environment, where other local governments may be allies or competitors, public managers are thus compelled to think strategically. Crucial to their effectiveness is the identification of the strengths and the potentials of their territory.

The principal impetus for local economic development is still essentially industry. Public managers dispose of both direct means (financial and fiscal incentives) and indirect means (transportation infrastructures, for example) to attract businesses to their community. Once the businesses are implanted, however, local policies have to consolidate the relationship—ideally by fostering dependence—in order to ensure the territory's long-term stability. The goal in fact is to make it unnecessary or difficult for businesses to migrate to another region, and this can be accomplished by various means: offering a specialized work population, ensuring the quality of local resources, and adapting public policies to the goals of the local business community. The long-term presence of industrial partners provides a territory with the conditions necessary to develop employment opportunities and to sustain its own growth. For the industrial sector, several researchers (Corolleur and Pecqueur, 1996; Crevoisier, 1998, Baptista and Swann, 1999; Benko and Lipietz, 2000; Courlet, 2001) have hypothesized a transfer from 'upward to downward development', referring to the observation that local economic development is no longer decided by central government but is instead boosted by the local actors' initiatives.

Two recent lines of thinking have suggested that a critical density of businesses is needed to ensure a healthy territorial economy, which implies that local development is not possible with just one company, even one of big size. According to these perspectives, local growth is observed only with a concentration of many small businesses within a single territory. This concentration has to exceed a certain density (which depends on the specific characteristics of the economic sector and the territory) in order for the local development to become real, strong and durable. The first line of thinking comprises local development theories; Baptista and Swann (1999), Belleflamme *et al.* (2000), Chevassus-Lozza and Galliano (2001), Courlet (2001) and Lucas (2001). These theories specifically detail the importance of small businesses in achieving local development goals. The second is mainly an outgrowth of Krugman's works on the new economic geography; Krugman (1991a, 1991b, 1993), Krugman and Venables (1995), Duranton (1997), Jayet *et al.* (1996), Fujita and Thisse (1997, 2001), Tabuchi (19981), Hsaini (2000) and Martin and Sunley (2000). In the case of industry, for example, from this perspective the degree of business concentration (and thus of economic growth) depends on both centrifugal forces that cause the desired concentration to decrease and centripetal forces that cause the desired concentration to increase.

These two theoretical perspectives are both valuable for the construction of local economic development models organized around physical activities in general, and leisure sports in particular. In this last case, researchers need to find, test and model the centripetal forces that will ensure local growth through leisure sports. This paper presents the first step in the construction of such a model. The working hypothesis is that local public action in support of professionals (in contrast to a non-interventionist policy) is one of these forces.

Sports activities as an impetus for local development

The studies that have found sports to be an impetus for economic growth can be integrated into a major research paradigm operating not only in France, but in Europe and North America, as well. The focus to date has essentially been on professional sports, with major sports events (soccer World Cup, Olympic Games) or regularly scheduled competitive events expected to have an economic impact on the host region. Based on this assumption, local governments should be willing to finance such events in order to reap the benefits; economic growth and higher employment. Yet today there is no consensus as to the reality of this scenario, and questions about the legitimacy of public funding in this domain are rightly being raised. The following authors are some of those who have addressed these questions: Baade (1996), Barget (2001), Barget and Gouguet (2000),

Crompton (1995), Kurscheidt (2000), Porter (1999), Noll and Zimbalist (1997) and Siegfried and Zimbalist (2000).

Over the past two decades, outdoor activities and leisure sports have grown in popularity and today they have a well-defined place in the local development sports-based model. Outdoor activities seem to offer particularly strong potential for the development of territories that have undergone little urbanization, since these regions cannot envisage hosting major sports events. Moreover, two other factors support the integration of leisure sports into local public strategies. In contrast to professional sports, the installation of leisure sports is less 'traumatizing' because they do not require extensive facilities. Second, outdoor activities are riot affected by the negative overspill from professional sports; internal and external stadium security, doping, profitability pressures, and so on.

Nevertheless, despite these positive factors, the literature dealing with leisure sports, even those articles taking an economics approach, indicates that little attention has been given to these activities in the elaboration of the local development policies: De Knop (1995), Kurtzman and Zauhar (1995), Pigeassou (1997), Gibson (1998), Bourdeau and Rotillon (1999), Standeven and De Knop) (1999) and Decarnin (1999). The question is thus: how feasible is a model for local economic development that is based on outdoor sports? One way to begin to answer this would be to examine the effectiveness of a case of public strategy. The public policies implemented by a small number of local governments tend to suggest that the model is worth taking seriously; surfing in the *Aquitaine* region, sailing in *Bretagne*, and skiing in the *Alpes*. In *Basse-Normandie*, equestrian activities have greatly benefited from local government funding. Although from a theoretical point of this view this model of local development is still in construction (Hautbois *et al.*, 2004; Hautbois, 2004), in practical terms a case study seems likely to provide valuable insights into future directions.

The second part of this work presents the case of equestrian activities development in the *Basse-Normandie* region and analyzes the effectiveness of the public policies.

Case study of equestrian activities in Basse-Normandie

This paper represents a first step in the construction of a local economic development model. The working hypothesis is that public intervention is a useful centripetal force and this was tested by studying a specific case: equestrian activity. The effectiveness of public strategy was examined with an interview-based method.

An interview-based method

The *Basse-Normandie* region of France is one of the most famous regions in the world for horse-riding. In order to evaluate the effectiveness of this region's public strategy for local development, the results were measured against the declared objectives. This was accomplished with a qualitative approach based on interviews with the different actors involved.

Before explaining the method, Figure 26.1 describes line territorial organization of France.

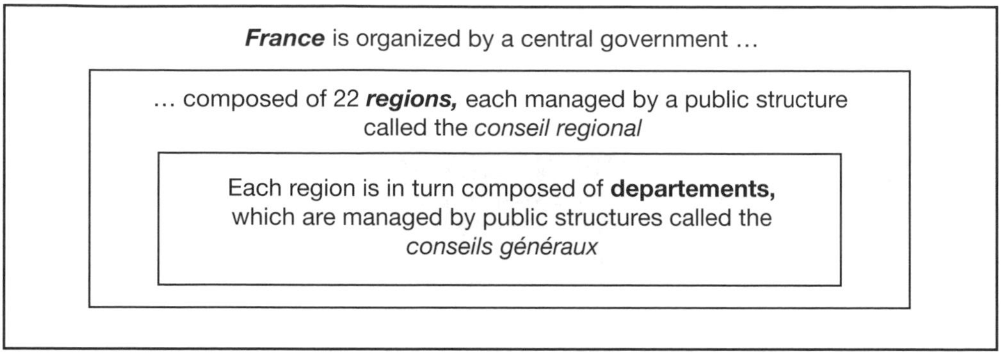

> **France** is organized by a central government ...
>
> > ... composed of 22 **regions,** each managed by a public structure called the *conseil regional*
> >
> > > Each region is in turn composed of **departements,** which are managed by public structures called the *conseils généraux*

Figure 26.1 The French territorial organization

The *Basse-Normandie* region comprises three *departements*: Calvados, Orne and Manche. The equestrian activities in *Basse-Normandie* are organized into four sectors: horse racing, equestrian sports, equestrian tourism, and equestrian-related activities. In addition to a study of all relevant documents, 68 interviews were conducted between December 2002 and January 2004 with representatives of each of these sectors and with the public managers in charge of developing equestrian activities. The interviewees were randomly chosen from each of the four sectors, although the three *departements* were equally represented. The interviews were continued until there were no more new elements to be added into the analysis. The interviews of the public managers sought out all representatives of all public structures that were in any way concerned with the development of equestrian activities. The distribution of the 68 interviews is presented in Figure 26.2 (number of interviews conducted/number of actors identified):

Two categories of actor were identified: public managers and professionals. The objectives for the interviews were adapted for each category. For the public managers, the interviews were organized around the following questions and sub-questions:

- The reason for public support (Why intervene? Why not free market organization?)
- The objectives (Were they specific to each category of equestrian activity or similiar for all?) and characteristics of the intervention (What form did it take: real or financial, short or long term?).
- The tools created to evaluate the effectiveness of the intervention (Quantitative or qualitative analysis? Will future support be dependent on the professionals' ability to reach fixed objectives?).

For the professionals, a complementary point of view was adopted and the interviews focused on three specific topics:

- is the public support accepted or rejected by the professionals? (Do they think that a free market organization would be more relevant to this economic sector? Would it be more efficient and more adapted to their activity?).
- Does the help given by public managers respond to a real need of the professionals? (Did the local government conduct a thorough study to identify the professionals' needs and wishes?).

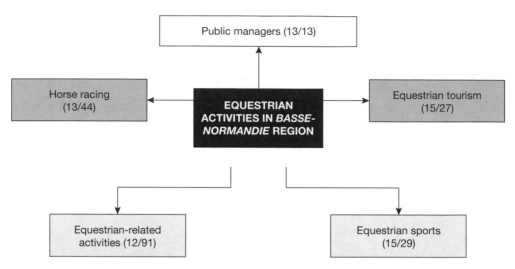

Figure 26.2 The distribution of the 68 interviews

• Were specific objectives for development (qualitative/quantitative) imposed on the professionals? (Was the public support freely given or was it conditional?).
• Is public support a necessary condition for the development of the professionals' activity?

Equestrian activities in Basse-Normandie and local public strategies: three steps to partnership

The document search and some of the interviews suggested three steps in the development of public strategy that signal a growth in public support.

1982–1989: No public participation: financial support from the local governments of *Basse-Normandie* was negligible. The *conseils généraux* and the *conseil regional* saw little potential in developing equestrian activities and thus they proposed no strategies. Furthermore, the professionals working in the four sectors made no requests for support. During this period, each sector of equestrian activity operated completely independently, with little interaction at any level.

1990–1996: A strategic opportunity became clear to local governments. In 1990, the *conseils généraux* began to strongly support policies that favoured the development of equestrian activities. Many projects were proposed to promote all activities related to horse-riding. First, the *conseil général* of *Manche* declared 1990 'The year of the horse'. Over the next 12 months, the *conseil* allocated 2,851,000 euros for equestrian events and for the construction of specific facilities. In 1995, the *conseil général* created 'Jump Manche', an international competition bringing together the world's best riders and horses. From 1991 to 1996, the *departement* of *Manche* contributed an average of 240,000 euros per year for the different equestrian activities.

In 1991, the *conseil général* of *Calvados* organized the first edition of 'Equidays', a 2-week event allowing all the equestrian professionals of the *departement* to promote their activities. Each year, thousands of tourists now attend 'Equidays', an operation that promotes *Calvados*, as well. The first year, the *conseil général* contributed 290,000 euros for the organization. In addition to supporting this event, *Calvados* also funds equine research. In the 1990's, the *conseil général* built a new laboratory and increased the number of researchers.

In 1993, two events signalled the interest of the *conseil régional* in the development of equestrian activities: funding of a study to evaluate the importance of these activities in *Basse-Normandie* and the announcement of the intent to build an international centre for equine research. These two axes of investment were complemented by financial support to breeding farms and to various equestrian events.

1997–2003: Local government became a major presence in the equestrian system of Basse-Normandie. This new direction in the public policies of the *conseil régional* became even more marked in 1997, with the *conseil's* financing of a new organization, the Normandy Horse Council. The NHC, composed of experts from the four equestrian sectors, is today at the interface between the public managers and the local professionals, with responsibilities that include the coordination of activities, the assessment of new projects, and the orientation of public funds.

Every year, the *departement* of *Manche* helps to finance the events that promote the economic activities connected to 'the horse': 53,000 euros per year for the 'Normandy Horse Show' and 41,000 euros for 'Jump Manche'. The *conseil général* of *Calvados* continues to support 'Equidays', with 365,000 euros in 2003. For equine research, the *departement* signed a contract with the AFSSA-Dozulé research centre, obligating it to 160,000 euros per year for the next 5 years.

The *conseil général* of *Orne* has been supporting the 'Festival de Ia Licorne' since its creation in 2002. It also contributes to the renovation of equestrian stadiums, horse breeding farms and the promotion of horse riding activities in the public schools.

Despite this growth in public support for equestrian activities, a review of the economic structures of the four sectors indicates major commercial funding, with public funding having only a minor role. This is a general finding based on the document search and the interviews. However, there are some differences among sectors. In *Basse-Normandie*, horse racing is the most important sector from an economic point of view (even if the turnover is very difficult to estimate). This is largely due to the commercial activity connected with betting. But this sector also receives the greatest amount of help from local governments (facilities, equestrian research, communication, and so on), reflecting the wish of public managers to reinforce the activity of this sector and thus maximize its economic potential for the region.

For the equestrian sports sector, a somewhat similar observation can be made. It is primarily up to the professionals themselves to develop their activity, and public support is reserved for only a few nationally and internationally ranked competitors. Public managers clearly want to avoid developing a sector dependent on public support.

Equestrian tourism is one of the least helped by local governments. Tourism is essentially a commercial activity but its relatively low level of development has forced some of the professionals of this sector to have a parallel activity. The findings of this study underline the fact that the commercial development of an equestrian sector is the first condition that must be met in order for the sector to be supported by local governments.

Equestrian-related activities receive the least support from the public sector. Two reasons can be underlined. First public managers do not consider these professionals as directly connected to equestrian activities but instead see them as parallel actors. They therefore do not benefit from any consequential public support. Secondly, equestrian-related businesses are essentially private enterprises. Thus, local governments consider that supporting them amounts to a marked distortion of free market organization.

The effectiveness of public policy

The actors' points of view are presented in terms of the objectives of each sector of equestrian activity described below. The analysis of effectiveness was based on the public managers' specific objectives. Finally, the limits of the system are specified.

Effectiveness according to the professionals' objectives

Horse racing: effective public intervention

The professionals of this sector judged the public intervention to be quite effective. According to the interviewed professionals, this intervention meets their needs and allows them to reach their own objectives for development. Public investment was judged to be effective on essentially three points:

- the development and maintenance of the facilities related to racing (galleries, stadiums, race tracks);
- the capacity of public managers to put potential foreign buyers in touch with professionals of the region;
- the conception and development of important research centres by local governments. These allow owners and coaches to tend to and train their champions more efficiently.

Out of 13 horse-racing interviews, 11 professionals estimated that public support has been quite effective for the three objectives. Of the two others, one thought that the help was effective only for the facilities; the other professional had no opinion because he had never met with any public managers and had never benefited from public support.

In contrast, the public policies were considered to have been nearly worthless for the professionals who specifically breed and raise race horses. Out of 13 interviews, ten professionals estimated that public efforts have been unable to directly benefit breeders, since this activity is not within the competence of government. The three others had no opinion on the question, nor could they estimate whether the creation of research centres is a useful way to help with breeding.

According to the professionals, two difficulties explain the failure to aid this sector. First, local governments lack sufficient funds to invest in a sector that has particularly high operating costs. The public managers confirmed this, stating that such investments would have been too high for regional budgets and would have forced them to discriminate between those to receive direct aid and those who would not. The other difficulty is the high fiscal burden placed on French equestrian professionals in comparison with those of other countries. However, local governments have begun to lobby at a national level to alleviate some of the burden on these professionals, in fact, this initiative recently bore fruit: legislation was passed in January 2004 to drop the main tax rate from 19.6% to 5.5%.

Equestrian sports: public support for elite sports and equestrian sports structures

The professionals of this sector were somewhat divided in their evaluation of public action. Some considered that the interventions of the *conseil régional* and the *conseils généraux* have been effective in promoting the development of equestrian sports. In contrast, others indicated that public support has had no effect on their activities. Generally, ten out of 15 equestrian sports professionals felt that public policies were effective in breeding and related matters, but only six felt that public policies were effective in marketing initiatives.

Those in support of public policies belong for the most part to an elite group (jumping competition, for example), and they particularly underlined the important role of public support for the costs of preparation, training and transportation. According to the equestrian sports shows organizers, the support of the *conseil régional* and the *conseils généraux* is quiet effective. For breeders, public investment in the horse farms of *Manche*, for example, or in the research centre in *Calvados* was also considered to be particularly useful and a boost for activity.

For the managers of the equestrian sports structures, the judgment was quite divided. In the *département* of *Orne*, the professionals benefit periodically from local public support. For many years, public managers have chosen to aid this type of structure, justifying their decision by the importance of this economic activity in the *département*. This support is efficient because it allows the professionals to reach their development objectives and to progress despite several difficulties (damages to the facilities, increasingly tighter security norms and the need for greater investment, etc.). In the other *départements* (*Manche* and *Calvados*), public support is lower for this type of structure and equestrian sports are not as important. *Calvados* is essentially an area devoted to horse racing and *Manche* is the territory of breeding farms. In consequence, since public support is a voluntary strategy and not a legal obligation, governments can decide to adapt their help to these global characteristics.

However, according to other professionals of this sector, the public policies have had little or no effect on their activities. For them, it has been difficult for local governments to finance all the professionals of the sector without creating important inequalities. These actors have thus preferred to work independently, without depending on public funding. Aid to individuals is quite rare, and local governments prefer to promote those events which benefit all the professionals of this sector.

The criticisms made by these professionals concern two aspects of equestrian sports. The first deals with horse breeding itself, especially horses for equestrian competition and leisure sports, with some professionals expressing the opinion that public managers are not aware of their needs and of the efforts they have made to organize this production; consequently public support for them is seen as non-existent or ill-adapted. Other professionals held the opinion that public support for the breeding and raising of leisure sports horses has been a direct response to the popularity of this activity, but that the help is insufficient to have a real impact on development.

The second criticism concerns the type of help given by local governments to promote equestrian production. Not enough professionals have the key-competences to sell their product: they lack training in management techniques, sales, English, and so on. In an international market, the professionals of the *Basse-Normandie* region are disadvantaged in comparison with some English, German and Nordic sellers, and for the moment local governments are unable to help them to make up for lost time.

Equestrian tourism: the dilemma

The results of this study indicated weak ties between professionals of equestrian tourism and local government bodies—only three out of 15 professionals felt that public support was effective.

Despite a strong potential for growth, equestrian-oriented tourism has not, been strongly promoted, which explains the weak public support. The local governments have preferred to concentrate their support on those sectors that are highly organized and well-positioned on the market, and that have clear objectives for development with a well-defined marketing strategy. This is not the case today for equestrian tourism. Most of the professionals of this sector are obliged to have another professional activity, especially since equestrian tourism is seasonal for the moment. Many suppliers therefore lack the professionalism needed to meet demand and cultivate the conditions for developing their activity. Furthermore, *Basse-Normandie* is still not considered an important region for equestrian tourism, as are *Ardèche* or *Drome* to the centre of France. For the French, *Basse-Normandie* is essentially a region for horse racing. The professionals of equestrian tourism would like to change this view, but so far the local public managers have not integrated this aim into their policies.

Moreover, it has been difficult for public managers to determine how to promote all the professionals of this sector and not just a certain few. Beyond projects that promote the ensemble of equestrian activities in *Basse-Normandie*, specific: projects to develop equestrian tourism are few. Yet most of the professionals of this sector (11 out of 15) agreed on one idea: the creation, renovation and maintenance of a network of riding trails would be a powerful motor for launching a campaign to bring tourists to the region. This has not been undertaken for the moment, and one may hypothesize that this kind of intervention is not visible enough.

Equestrian-related activities: a forgotten sector

The effects of public intervention on the various suppliers to the equestrian industry have been negligible. Nine out of 12 professionals interviewed from this sector think that public support is low. These actors are apparently of low priority for local public strategies. According to the suppliers themselves, local governments have neglected to consider the economic growth potential of this sector. This may very well be explained by the reticence of government bodies to engage in direct support to a private sector that is regulated by the laws of commercial competition.

However, the public policies to develop and support surfing activities in the *Aquitaine* region provide a strong example of the economic benefit to the entire local community when, directly or indirectly, surfing-related businesses are assisted. According to the professionals further development of equestrian-related activities in the *Basse-Normandie* region could generate employment and boost local economic activity. These professionals thus want to reinforce their relationship with local governments.

Effectiveness according to public objectives

Coordination of equestrian activities

In *Basse-Normandie*, the different sectors of equestrian activity remain separate because of important cultural and economic differences. These differences are rooted in history, with each sector showing a specific construction; yet today they constitute an important obstacle to coordination and to the development of a single, unified and strong equestrian economy. As a consequence, the coordination of the different sectors has become a major objective of local public policies. The professionals belonging to the four sectors need to work more closely together to improve overall quality. The professionals themselves acknowledge this, and 49 out of the 68 interviewed agree that the creation of the Normandy Horse Council was quite effective in attenuating perceptions of differences and that this offers hope that one day they will be united in a true 'equestrian community'. According to most of the professionals with whom we met, this objective of public policy has already been reached.

Nevertheless, for the moment the professionals admitted to being principally organized around their own respective activities, They found it difficult to truly unite in a common cause because of persistent and profound differences in culture and economic outlook, inked to different perceptions of the central role of the horse.

Development of the regional economy

The analysis of the impact of equestrian activities' promotion on the regional economy of *Basse-Normandie* is quite difficult. Some of the professionals interviewed declared that public policies and funding have had a direct impact on economic growth in their sector. These prolessionals essentially belong to the most supported sector: horse racing. For these actors, it is important to underline the concrete benefits of this aid: they have made great strides in reaching their objectives of economic development via more customers and bigger turnover. Others expressed reservations and doubts. These professionals essentially belong to the equestrian sports and tourism sectors. For them, public help has been an important way to boost activity but they have few detailed accomplishments to point to. Nevertheless, despite the relative lack of concrete results, it appears that public help is perceived as important for development, and the professionals expressed a strong interest in continuing to work with government bodies.

Relatively few of the interviewed actors (27 out of 68) claimed positive consequences from public support of their activities in terms of reaching their objectives. The others were unable to make the same claims because they either lacked detailed data or had never been supported by public structures.

Limits of public strategy

Two main limits to public strategy were mentioned by the interviewed professionals. The first concerns the method of intervention and the second is related to how public action is structured in France.

Method of public intervention: a lack of clear communication

First, the lack of clear communication from the various public structures was one of the most frequent reproaches from the professionals of all tour sectors, identified by 32 of the 55 interviewed from the industry. Their major concern was that a large proportion of public help is decided on without much consultation with the professionals The Normandy Horse Council should have improved communication between professionals and public managers; however, to date this organization does not seem able to ensure that public help is closely adapted to the needs of the different sectors. Also, the methods used by the Normandy Horse Council to manage some of the requests from professionals have led to criticism. If specific projects do not correspond to the agreed upon general policy, it is impossible for professionals to enlist government support and acquire funding, even when the aid can be demonstrated to be directly useful. As a consequence, the system of public aid is perceived as being too rigid to adapt to professional needs and unable to evolve. The interviewed professionals stated that this lack of communication, illustrated by the fact that the public structures sometimes decide alone on appropriate strategies, is the greatest limit to public effectiveness.

The poor distribution of public responsibility

Equestrian activity is not the responsibility of any one governing body. Thus, the central government, the *conseil régional* of *Basse-Normandie* and the three *conseils généraux* are all free to develop and implement their own policies—which they do. However, each does so from a perspective based on its particular territorial concerns (each level of government does what it wants regarding the equestrian activities on its territory) instead of on the basis of a defined area of competence (in which each level of government would be charged with managing specific aspects of time equestrian sectors). This has led to a lack of coherence between the different levels of policy and, more unfortunately, to the wastefulness of redundant initiatives and actions. The professionals noted that the public budget was not used as efficiently as it could have been.

Discussion and perspectives

The presentation of these results leads to three principal points that should be made. First, the local public structures that were studied do provide support to equestrian professionals. The support is at times substantial but it also differs for each sector: it is substantial for horse racing, reserved for only a specific category of equestrian sports professionals, and rare for equestrian tourism and equestrian-related activities.

Second, our methodological choices were adapted for a qualitative analysis of the effectiveness of public strategy. But the main limit of this methodology was its inability to measure the economic growth in *Basse-Normandie* due specifically to the public promotion of equestrian activities. Ideally, the professionals' perceptions of the effectiveness of public policies would have been complemented with a quantitative analysis to assess regional growth.

Third, despite the criticisms made by some of the professionals, they expressed the desire for closer relationships with public managers, pointing out that this was a condition for boosting their economic sector and thus the overall local economy. Nevertheless, this case study of equestrian activities illustrates how sports activities or leisure sports are managed by French government. Given the current projects to reform the organization of general public action in time country, the central government has put these activities aside. The consequence will continue to be a lack of specific competences at the different levels of local government and thus an overlap in the interventions, with an inevitable loss of efficiency and the potential waste of resources.

Conclusion

This article underlines the growth of outdoor sports as an important lever for local economic development. Outdoor activities and leisure sports offer much of value to communities seeking to develop new strategies for development. However, this case study of equestrian activities in *Basse-Normandie* illustrates some of the limits to this model, according to the professionals themselves.

First some of the professionals did not have the characteristics, particularly organizational, that are prerequisites for improving local economic development. Second

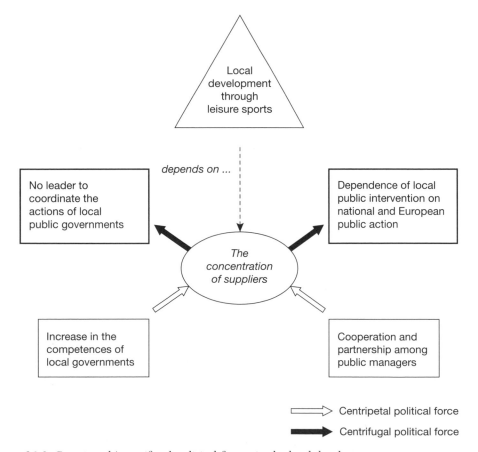

Figure 26.3 Centripetal/centrifugal political forces in the local development

the local governments seemed sensitive to this: they were more willing to support and invest in those sectors that were already well-organized and coordinated—for example, horse racing—and that had a ready-made plan of development for at least the mid term and a secure position in the leisure market. In other terms, we can see from this case study that, at least for the moment, public structures seem more willing to accompany and support a movement rather than to act as pioneers. Last, when the drive to develop and implement policies at a local level is not closely coordinated among the various levels of public structure, questions about the optimal use of public funds are raised. This appears to be the main obstacle to formulating efficient policies to support leisure sports with the aim of stimulating economic growth. This observation may be generally applicable, and not only pertinent to this case study. Time coordination of different levels of intervention is a common need in order for public action to be a centripetal force for local economic growth. The type of public support has to be much more closely attuned to the professionals expressed needs, and the different actors have to work in concert to achieve common goals, instead of continuing to operate from the perspective of separate sectors.

In terms of the model presented here, one can say that public intervention is for the moment an essential factor for growth in leisure sports. This factor is positive (a centripetal force) if the coordination between the different actors is good and if local governments have sufficient legal competence to act. Nevertheless, it could become an important limit to development if it does not correspond to the professionals' needs if coordination between the different public structures is lacking (no leader), or if the public structures have no effective means (legal or financial) to provide support. In these cases, professionals may likely leave the territory for a more welcoming one. This in fact would be an example of a centrifugal force operating to decrease the potential for local economic growth through leisure sports.

Based on both theoretical lines and a specific case study, the role of public action in the outdoor activity-based model is schematized in Figure 26.3. Economic development through leisure sports depends on an equilibrium between centripetal and centrifugal forces.

References

Baade, R. (1996) Professional sports as a catalyst for metropolitan economic development, *Journal of Urban Affairs*, 18, 23–31.

Baptista, R. and Swann, G.M. (1999) A comparison of clustering dynamics in the US and UK computer industries, *Journal of Evolutionary Economics*, 9, 373–399.

Barget, E. (2001) Le spectacle sportif ponctuel: essai d'évaluation, Doctorate dissertation, University of Limoges.

Barget, E. and Gouguet, J.-J. (2000) *Impact économique du spectacle spoitif: analyse critique de la littérature. Reflets and Perspectives: Sport et mondialisation. Quel enjeu pour le XXème Siècle?* Paris, De Boeck Université.

Belleflamme, P., Picard, P. and Thisse, J.-F. (2000) An economic theory of regional clusters, *Journal of Urban Economics*, 48, 158–184.

Benko, G. and Lipietz, A. (2000) *La richesse de regions: la nouvelle géographic socio-économique*, Paris, Presses Universitaires de France.

Bourdeau, P. and Rotillon, G. (1999) L'impact de l'escalade dans une analyse couts-bénéfices, *Revue Juridique et Économique du Sport*, 51, 7–27.

Chevassus-Lozza, E. and Galliano, D. (2001) Les déterminants territoriaux de la comepétitivité des firmes agro-alimentaires, *Cahiers d'Économie et de Sociologie Rurales*, 58–59, 193–222.

Corolleur, F. and Pecqueur, B. (1996) Les politiques économiques locales en Frances, in C. Demaziete (ed.) *Du local au global*, Paris, L'Haramattan, pp. 123–146.

Courlet, C. (2001) Les systèmes productifs localizes: un bilan de la literatre, *Cahiers d'Économie et de Sociologie Rurales*, 58–59, 81–103.

Crevoisier, O. (1998) Mondialisation et territorialisation, in M.-U. Proulx (ed.) *Territoires et développement économique*, Paris, L'Harmattan, pp. 35–62.

Crompton, J. (1995) Economic impact analysis of sport facilities, *Journal of Sport Management*, 9, 14–35.

Davezies, L. (2000) Les fondements d'une intervention publique en faveur du développement territorial, in OCDE. Paris, Territorial Outlook.

Davezies, L. (2002) La solidarité redistributive entre les territories, in S. Watcher (ed.) *Pour en finir avec la decentralization*, Paris, Editions de l'Aube, pp. 67–79.

Davezies, L. (2003) Inégalités et solidarities spatiales, le pot de fer contre le pot de terre, in S. Watcher (ed.) *L'aménagement durable: defis et politiques*, Paris, Editions de l'Aube, pp. 35–56.

De Knop, P. (1998) Sport tourism: a state of the art, *European Journal of Sport Management*, 5(3), 30–36.

Decarnin, H. (1999) Le développement local et l'escalade à Buoux, in L. Bensahel and M. Donsimoni (ed.) *Le Tourisme, Facteur de Développement Local*, Grenoble, Presses Universitaires de Grenoble, pp. 61–70.

Duranton, G. (1997) La nouvelle économie géographique: agglomeration et dispersion, *Économie et Prévision*, 131, 1–24.

Fujita, M. and Thisse, J.-F. (1997) Économie géographique, problèmes anciens et nouvelles perspectives, *Annales d'Économie et de Statistique*, 45, 223–249.

Fujita, M. and Thisse, J.-F. (2001) Agglomération et marché, *Cahiers d'Économie et de Sociologie Rurales*, 58–59, 11–57.

Gibson, H. (1998) Sport tourism: a critical analysis of research, *Sport Management Review*, 1, 45–76.

Hautbois, C. (2004) Stratégie publique de développement local par les sports de nature. Le cas du tourisme équestre en Basse-Normandie, *Les sports de nature, Cahiers Espace*, 82, 63–65.

Hautbois, C., Ravenel, L. and Durand, C. (2003) Sport tourism and local economic development: The importance of an initial diagnosis of suppliers' geographical concentration. Case study of France, *Journal of Sport Tourism*, 8(4), 240–259.

Hsaini, A. (2000) Le dépassement des economies d'agglomération comme seule sources explicatives de l'efficacité des systèmes de production territorializes, *Revue d'Economie Régionale et Urbaine*, 2, 215–242.

Jayet, H., Puig, J.-P. and Thisse, J.-F. (1996) Enjeux économiques de l'organisation du territoire, *Revue d'Economie Politique*, 106, 127–158.

Krugman, P. and Venables, A. (1995) Globalization and the inequality of nations, *Quarterly Journal of Economics*, 110, pp. 857–880.

Krugman, P. (1991) History versus expectations, *Quarterly Journal of Economics*, 106, 857–880.

Krugman, P. (1991a) *Geography and trade*, Cambridge, MIT Press.

Krugman, P. (1991b) Increasing returns and economic geography, *Journal of Political Economy*, 99, 483–499.

Krugman, P. (1993) First nature, second nature and metropolitan location theory, *Journal of Regional Science*, 33, 129–144.

Kurscheidt, M. (2000) *Poids macro-économique du sport et le spectacle sportif: méthodologie, resultants empiriques et perspectices économiques pour le cas de l'XXème Siècle?* Paris, De Boeck Université.

Kurtzman, J. and Zauhar, J. (1993) Research: Sport as a touristic endeavour, *Journal of Sport Tourism*, 1(1), 30–50.

Lipietz, A. (2001) Aménagement du territoire et développement endogène, *Aménagement du territoire, rapport du Conseil d'analyse économique*, 31.

Lucas, R. (2001) Externalities and cities, *Review of Economics Dynamics*, 4, 254–274.

Martin, R. and Sunley, P. (2000) L'économie géographique de Paul Krugman et ses conséquences pour la théorie du développement regional: une evaluation critique, in G. Benko and A. Lipietz (eds) *La richesse des régions: la nouvelle géographie socio-économique*, Paris, Presses Universitaires de France.

Noll, R. and Zimbalist, A. (eds) (1997) *Sports, jobs and taxes: the economic impact of sports teams and stadiums*, Standford, Brookings Institutional Press.

Pigeassou, C. (1997) Sport and tourism: The emergence of sport into the offer of tourism. Between passion and reason. An overview of the French situation and perspectives, *Journal of Sport Tourism*, 4(2), 24–47.

Porter, P. (1999) *Mega-sports events as municipal investments: A critique of impact analysis*, Mimeograph, Westport, CT, Praeger Press.

Siegfried, J. and Zimbalist, A. (2000) The economics of sports facilities and their communities, *Journal of Economic Perspectives*, 14(3), 95–114.

Standeven, J. and De Knop, P. (1999) *Sport tourism*, Champaign, IL, Human Kinetics.

Tabuchi, T. (1998) Agglomeration anti dispersion: A synthesis of Alonso and Krugman, *Journal of Urban Economics*, 3, 333–351.

Chapter 27

James Higham and Tom Hinch

TOURISM, SPORT AND SEASONS
The challenges and potential of
overcoming seasonality in the sport
and tourism sectors

1   Introduction

THE RELATIONSHIP BETWEEN SPORT and tourism is a subject of
increasing interest among contemporary tourism academics, Gibson (1998) reviews
a rapidly expanding literature that considers the extent to which sports people travel to
compete and, conversely, tourists engage in sporting pursuits, actively or as spectators,
while on holiday. Somewhat lacking to date has been a comprehensive analysis of the
potential links that may be forged between sport and tourism administrator's in pursuit
of mutual benefit (Higham & Hinch, 1999). This article explores the potential to modify
the seasonal distribution of tourism activity generated by the playing seasons of professional
sports. It employs a case analysis of the development of professional Rugby Super 12 in
the *Otago Highlanders* franchise region (New Zealand). Primary research methods are
applied to the collection of qualitative data via a programme of interviews. This research
assesses the changing seasonal element of the Rugby Union in New Zealand, and the
extent to which this may present opportunities to moderate patterns of tourism seasonality.

2   Tourism and sport

The links between sport and tourism have expanded considerably, and become more
clearly defined, in recent years (Gibson, 1998; Standeven & De Knop, 1999; Higham &
Hinch, 1999). The latter part of the twentieth century witnessed the rapid development
of sport and tourism (Redmond, 1991; WTO (World Tourism Organisation), 2000).
Both now stand among the largest and fastest growing industries in the global economy.
Sport and tourism have achieved mass participation in the post-war years and in many

cases, participation in sport and tourism takes place simultaneously (Higham & Hinch, 1999). This process has created new links between the sport and tourism sectors (Glyptis, 1991). Indeed, the resource and infrastructural requirements of sport and tourism are often shared (Standeven & De Knop, 1999). These include natural environments, constructed facilities, transport, services and hospitality. This shared foundation suggests the likelihood that developments in sport will affect the tourism sector, and vice versa.

While there has been a recent proliferation of sports related travel (Nogawa, Yamaguchi, & Hagi, 1996), much of the junction between sport and tourism remains unresearched (Higham & Hinch, 1999). The capacity for international sporting events to generate tourism has been widely addressed in the tourism and events literature (Getz, 1991; Hall, 1992; Williams, Hainsworth, & Dossa, 1995). However, the impacts of sporting mega-events may have been overstated in many cases (Faulkner, Tideswell, & Weston, 1998). Some mega-sports, in fact, have generated varied and severe long-term negative impacts (Olds, 1998; Hiller, 1998; Higham, 1999). While the links between high profile sports and tourism have become increasingly apparent, comparatively little attention has been paid to lower profile sports-related travel. One of the few exceptions is Irwin and Sandler's (1998) study of college sports in the USA. This indicates that local and regional sports, may, within their own geographical parameters, function in precisely the same way as mega-sports events while offering less potential for negative impacts (Higham, 1999). The democratisation of sport and tourism has resulted in most sports offering the potential to generate tourist activity. This article explores this potential by focussing on seasonal travel patterns associated with the regional level of sport.

3   Tourism and seasonality

Seasonality is one of the most prominent features of tourism, yet, paradoxically, it is also one of the least understood. The vast majority of tourism destinations are characterised by systematic fluctuations in tourism phenomena throughout the year. In particular, seasonality generally exhibits a dramatic tourism peak during the summer months. Such fluctuations in visitors and revenues are almost universally viewed as a problem by the tourist industry, which spends considerable time, money, and effort to modify these patterns through the development and implementation of strategies designed to extend the "shoulder seasons", or to create "all season" destinations.

Most of the literature describes seasonal variations in visitation that result in a number of negative effects on the destination and the people living within that destination (Allcock, 1989; Edgell, 1990; Go, 1990; Jefferson & Lickorish, 1988; Laws, 1991; Lockwood & Guerrier, 1990; Poon, 1993; Robinson, 1979; Snepenger, Houser, & Snepenger, 1990; Whelihan & Chon, 1991). This view is clearly expressed by Jefferson (1986, p. 24), who states, "whether assessed in terms of lost revenue or reflected as the enforced termination of employment, there is obviously a major economic and social dimension to these (seasonal) troughs which evidently is in no-one's interest". McEnnif (1992, p. 68) explains that tourism industry issues arising from seasonality "are chiefly concerned with off-peak underutilisation of capacity".

It is generally accepted that tourism seasonality can be attributed to two basic groups of factors, natural and institutional (BarOn, 1975: Hartman, 1986). Natural seasonality refers to regular temporal variations in natural phenomena, particularly those associated with cyclical climatic changes throughout the year, such as temperature, precipitation, wind, and daylight (Allcock, 1989; Butler, 1994). For example, climate is of fundamental importance to tourism in Canada, although it is often considered as a nuisance factor or constraint to tourist development. Kreutzwiser (1989, pp. 29–30) contends that:

> Climate and weather conditions . . . influence how satisfying particular recreational outings will be. Air temperature, humidity, precipitation, cloudiness, amount of daylight, visibility, wind, water temperature, and snow and ice cover are among the parameters deemed to be important. . . . In summer, air temperature and humidity can combine to create uncomfortable conditions for vigorous activities, while wind and temperature in winter can create a wind chill hazardous to outdoor recreationists.

Institutional factors reflect the social norms and practices of society (Hinch & Hickey, 1997). These factors are typically based on religious, cultural, ethnic, social, and economic considerations, epitomised by religious, school, and industrial holidays. At the heart of institutional factors is the prevailing mechanical perspective of time that emerged with the Industrial Revolution (Sylvester, 1999). Within this framework, leisure travel is seen to be constrained by work and other obligations. Distances travelled tend to be a function of the amount of time that is available, exhibiting a positive correlation between longer free-time slots and greater distances travelled.

Butler (1994) argues that there are three additional causes of seasonality: (1) social pressure or fashion; (2) sporting season; and (3) inertia on the part of travellers, who continue to travel at a specific time of the year even though they are no longer restricted to this particular period. If an inclusive definition of the "institutional" category of determinants is adopted, then social pressure and sporting season would seem to fit into this group.

4   Sport and seasonality

Sport is a dynamic phenomenon (Loy, McPherson, & Kenyon, 1989). The evolution of sport takes place in numerous ways, many associated with the transition from amateurism to professionalism. Avenues of sport development include but are not limited to those outlined in Table 27.1. These avenues of development are generally pursued to increase interest in sports. This outcome may be measured in terms of participation or spectatorship, sponsorship, media ratings, television audiences, and the sale of television rights, among others. These changes exist in a close relationship with the televising of sports which are characterised by low broadcast production costs. At the same time, municipal authorities have pursued the benefits that professional sport promises in terms of economic development through stadium and facility development and tourism. This is certainly the case in the United Kingdom (United Kingdom Business Information Futures, 1995), North America (Frisby & Getz, 1990), and New Zealand (Ryan, Smee, & Murphy, 1996). These developments are part of wider processes operating in the field of sports management. The globalisation and international televising of sport have brought domestic as well as international sporting competitions into the living rooms of the mass market (Standeven & De Knop, 1999). The democratisation of sport has contributed to mass participation in many sporting pursuits for a wide range of reasons including fitness, social contact, health, performance dedication to excellence and, in some cases, livelihood (Loy *et al.*, 1989).

One significant corollary has been changes in the seasonal component of sports. Numerous examples can be cited to illustrate this consequence of the development of sport. The expanded European football competition structure has taken a predominantly autumn/winter sporting code into all four calendar seasons. The global Super League competition involved the transposition of the Rugby League from a winter to a summer sport in the United Kingdom and France to align the northern and southern hemispheres sporting seasons. The development of all-season sports facilities reinforces this point. Examples include summer ski jump facilities in Lillehammer (Norway), Millennium

Table 27.1 Avenues and examples of sport development

Avenues of development	Examples
1 The development of existing sports	One-day cricket, Cricket Marx, Super Sixes, extreme skiing, night skiing, artificial ski slopes, touch rugby, doubles squash, indoor athletics championships, short course swimming, Arena Football (USA)
2 The introduction of new competitions	Rugby Super 12, Six Nations Rugby, Around Alone (yachting), European Champions League Soccer, Tri-Nations, World Cup of Test Cricket
3 The introduction of new competition rules	Bonus points (Super 12), player transfer rules, disciplinary systems, video judiciary, yellow/red card systems, third umpire (cricket)
4 The introduction of new sports rules	Strikezone Squash, Sevens rugby restart rules, triathlon cycle drafting
5. Harnessing new technologies	Floodlit night sport, replay screens, video referees, Stumpcam (Cricket), multi-angle computer generated replays, virtual advertising, referee microphones, artificial snow making
6 Sport consumption and presentation	Televising (e.g. super slow motion), team uniforms (e.g. One-Day cricket, Aussie Rules, Netball) post-match interviews, dressing room cameras (Rugby League State of Origin), referee microphones, cheerleaders, team mascots, pre-match entertainments (e.g. fireworks and concerts), team names (e.g. Chicago Bulls), electronic scoreboards/replay screens, stadium development (e.g. Corporate facilities), virtual advertising, half time/interval entertainments and competitions
7 The development of new sports (often linked to technological developments)	Mountainbiking, windsurfing, snowboarding, SCUBA, parapenting, triathlon, multidisciplinary endurance sports, trans-Atlantic rowing, mountain running, bungy jumping, jetboating

Stadium, Cardiff (Wales) and Colonial Stadium, Melbourne (Australia) which hosted the first indoor game of International Cricket in July (Southern Hemisphere mid-Winter) 2000. If sport is indeed a major tourism attraction then it is logical to assume that changes to the traditional playing seasons associated with popular sports will have a substantial impact on temporal patterns of tourist visitation.

5   The professional development of the Rugby Union in New Zealand

Rugby Union is the national sport in New Zealand. The sport has experienced unprecedented change over the last five years. In 1995, the Rugby Union abandoned the

Table 27.2 Changes to the sport of Rugby Union with the development of the professional Rugby Super 12 competition[a]

Rule structure

1	New rules designed to speed up play (e.g. substitution rules and extended half time break)
2	New rules to encourage attacking play and maintenance of possession (e.g. lineout rules)
3	New rules to promote "ball in play" time (e g. dead ball and restart rules)
4	Professional referees and touch judges directed to facilitate continuous play
5	SANZAR directive on rule interpretation to minimize stoppage of play (e.g. advantage rule)
6	Disciplinary rules introduced to eliminate illegal play
7	Development of a judicial system designed to reduce foul play

Competition

1	Points system developed to reward try scoring and encourage 80 min of intense action
2	The involvement of teams from three countries
3	Amalgamation of 27 provincial teams into five regional franchises
4	Drafting introduced to ensure that only the most talented players are selected to play Super 12
5	Audio networked referees and touch judges
6	The scheduling of pre-season warm-up games to ensure a high level of early season performance
7	The entertainment packaging of Super 12 to act as a vehicle for its branding and promotion

Professionalism and presentation

1	Professional players with greater attention paid to fitness, skills and match preparation
2	Professional management teams travelling with players
3	Enhanced public liaison through advertising, school visits competitions, and arrangements for young fans and disabled children to meet the players
4	Creation of five franchise headquarters each represented by a professional regional icon
5	Required standard of stadium facilities to act as headquarters for a Super 12 franchise. SANZAR has power to revoke or modify franchise status
6	Need for floodlighting, seating capacity and television production facilities to host professional, globally televised sport

a Source: NZRFU (1998), Higham and Hinch (1999).

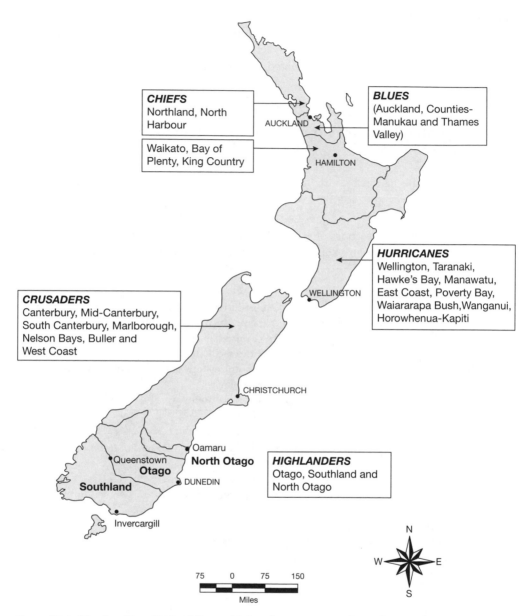

CHIEFS
Northland, North
Harbour

Waikato, Bay of
Plenty, King Country

BLUES
(Auckland, Counties-
Manukau and Thames
Valley)

HURRICANES
Wellington, Taranaki,
Hawke's Bay, Manawatu,
East Coast, Poverty Bay,
Waiararapa Bush,Wanganui,
Horowhenua-Kapiti

CRUSADERS
Canterbury, Mid-Canterbury,
South Canterbury, Marlborough,
Nelson Bays, Buller and
West Coast

HIGHLANDERS
Otago, Southland and
North Otago

Figure 27.1 The five New Zealand Super 12 franchise regions with amalgamated Provincial
Union memberships listed

amateur ethos at the elite level and became a professional sport. The professionalisation
of the Rugby Union in the southern hemisphere has been managed by the board of
SANZAR (South Africa, New Zealand, Australia Rugby). In 1995, SANZAR negotiated
with News Ltd to create two professional competitions, the Tri-Nations and Rugby Super
12. The Tri-Nations involves a mid-season series of home and away matches between
the three member nations. Rugby Super 12, by contrast, is an early season competition
for provincial/regional teams from each of the SANZAR nations. The New Zealand

Rugby Football Union (NZFRU) branding values for Rugby Super 12 centre on entertainment. It is branded as a contrast to the tradition and aura of the international competition (Tri-Nations). Rather Super 12 is branded as the "total entertainment package", a fast, skilful and spectacular form of rugby (NZRFU, 1998). SANZAR and the member national unions made several important changes to the Rugby product to fill this niche.

The development of this professional rugby competition necessitated that various changes be applied to the sport as summarised in Table 27.2. This included the amalgamation of 27 provincial unions in New Zealand into five regional teams (Figure 27.1), each selecting a squad of 25 players. A player draft scheme was also introduced to ensure the identification and selection of the most skilled 125 players in the country. Table 27.2 highlights the extent to which the rule structure, competition structure and professional presentation of the Rugby Union were developed with the advent of the Rugby Super 12 competition in 1996. These changes closely mirror the concept of commodification (MacCannell, 1973) as it has been applied to tourism attractions. The result has been the development of a sporting competition that serves as a much stronger tourist attraction than earlier versions of the sport. Methodological design took place with a view to exploring the implications of these developments vis-à-vis the seasonal dimension of tourism within a defined study area.

6   Methodology

The following methodology was designed to generate insights into the changing seasonal travel patterns associated with the development of a professional sport competition contested by regional teams from three Southern hemisphere countries (New Zealand, Australia and South Africa). The financial and logistical reasons the southern New Zealand *Otago Highlanders* franchise region constituted the subject of the study. The city of Dunedin is the headquarters of the *Highlanders* Rugby Super 12 organisation (Figure 27.2). The franchise region includes the provinces of Southland, Otago and North Otago. A qualitative research design was used to investigate the extent to which the development of the Super 12 professional rugby competition has had implications for seasonal travel patterns and preferences in southern New Zealand. The collection of qualitative primary data took place via a programme of personal interviews. Semi-structured interviews were conducted so as to follow a prescribed interview schedule while seeking to accommodate the varied fields of knowledge held by interviewees. This interview technique provided the flexibility required to conduct interviews with a diverse range of sport and tourism industry representatives each of whom brought a unique perspective to the subject of research. The interviews addressed issues such as changes to rugby introduced specifically for the purpose of the Super 12 competition, facility/stadium developments, team/competition promotion and marketing public liaison, ticketing, city promotions and related tourism development opportunities.

The interview programme took place in centres throughout the franchise region at the conclusion of the 1998 Super 12 season. Interviews were conducted with selected administrators affiliated with the sport of rugby and the regional tourism industry within the *Highlanders* franchise area (North Otago, Otago and Southland). Interviews with rugby officials included the three provincial Union Chief Executive Officers (CEOs), the Marketing Manager, Treasurer, Team Management personnel and *Highlanders* Coach.

In each instance, interviewees were required to have a minimum of 5 years administrative experience to be able to comment accurately on the transition period from amateurism to professionalism. Economic Development staff and Regional Tourism Organisation staff at local government offices within the region (Tourism Waitaki, Dunedin City Council and Invercargill City Council) were also interviewed. Economic and Tourism development staff within these government offices hold considerable knowledge of travel patterns, visitor interests and tourist expenditure patterns within the region. A list of administrators selected for inclusion in the interview programme, and their respective fields of expertise, is presented in Table 27.3.

Table 27.3 Fields of industry expertise that justified interviewee selection for the interview

Interviewee position	Fields of expertise
TLA economic development staff (Economic Development Unit, Dunedin City Council, Southland Economic Development Agency)	Experience and knowledge of local economic development potential in tourism and related sectors
RTO[a] staff (Tourism Dunedin, Tourism Waitaki Tourism Southland)	Knowledge of the changing tourism resources (and the potential for the development of tourism resources) within the region
TLA[b] tourism promotions staff (Tourism Dunedin, Tourism Waikati, Tourism Southland)	Local tourism promotions and demand for different aspects of the local tourism product. Intimate knowledge of local visitor statistics from commercial and private accommodation providers. Extensive knowledge of domestic travel patterns and tourism seasonality
TLA events staff (Tourism Dunedin, Tourism Southland)	Specific events, festival and activities and their visitor markets
Rugby Union CEOs[c] (Otago, Southland and North Otago Provincial Unions, *Highlanders* franchise)	Processes of rugby development from amateur to professional sporting code. Detailed knowledge of the development of sport stadia and other facilities. Development of the *Highlanders* brand
Rugby Union coaching staff	Changes to the rules governing the sport and their implications for the way the sport is played (e.g., entertainment values)
Otago Rugby Football Union Marketing Manager	Changing marketing mix for rugby spectatorship and the dynamics of local and non-local demand
Highlanders team manager	The relationship between team and public
Otago Rugby Football Union Treasurer	Attendance, ticketing and the relative attendance of local residents, domestic tourists and international tourists at home fixtures

a   CEO denotes Chief Executive Officer.
b   TLA denotes Territorial Local Authority (Local Government).
c   RTO denotes Regional Tourism Organisation.

Representatives of these sport and tourism offices were interviewed from each of the Rugby Unions and Territorial Local Authorities within the *Highlanders* franchise region. A total of 11 interviews were conducted. Interviews that ranged in duration from 25 to 75 min were tape-recorded with permission, and fully transcribed for the purpose of analysis. Interview transcriptions were analysed and annotated manually. "Thematic analysis" techniques (Banister, Burman, Parker, Taylor, & Tindall, 1996) were then employed in order to coherently organise interview material. This process involved the interpretation of interview transcriptions and the identification of linkages between the responses of interviewees and the themes of sport and tourism seasonality.

7   Results

The analysis of interview transcripts confirmed that the transition to professional rugby in New Zealand has presented new opportunities for tourism development at the regional level. Interviewees identified changes to the seasonal aspect of professional rugby that have held implications for the regional tourism industry. Most particularly, these changes related to the expanded sports season and the scheduling of the Super 12 competition at the beginning of the representative rugby calendar. This was seen to be associated with seasonal advantages of climate with the game now played in the weeks of late summer and early autumn. This was considered to have enhanced the entertainment values associated with Super 12 Rugby. The key results relating to changes to sport and tourism seasonality are presented sequentially, with sources referenced to interviewees in parentheses.

7.1 *The changing sport season*

7.1.1 *The expanded sport season*

Prior to 1985, the New Zealand first class (representative) rugby season spanned 4 months (June–September). By 1995, following a decade of pseudo-professionalism, the same season extended over 8 months (March–October). The 1997 rugby season immediately following the professional development of the Rugby Union in New Zealand in 1996, extended over 11 months (February–December). These sport developments were considered to have wider implications of sport-related domestic travel within the region.

7.1.2 *Changes to the scheduled rugby season*

The inclusion of the Super 12 competition at the start of the rugby calendar has effectively doubled the duration of the representative rugby season. Corroboration of this point may be drawn from New Zealand Rugby Union statistics published on a season by season basis by the New Zealand Rugby Almanac (Figure 27.2). Figure 27.2 illustrates that the professional Super 12 competition has been scheduled to precede the traditional National Provincial Championship (NPC). Rugby Super 12, therefore, takes place over 12 weeks in the summer/autumn calendar seasons (February–May) which was seen to coincide with the shoulder tourist season (Tourism Dunedin, 1999). This was considered to have contributed to extending regional domestic tourist activity at this part of the shoulder tourist season (Tourism Dunedin, 1999).

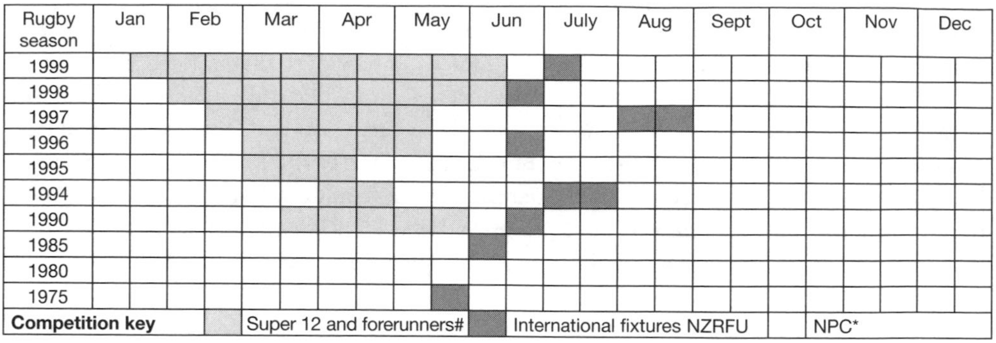

Rugby season	Jan	Feb	Mar	Apr	May	Jun	July	Aug	Sept	Oct	Nov	Dec
1999												
1998												
1997												
1996												
1995												
1994												
1990												
1985												
1980												
1975												

Competition key	Super 12 and forerunners#	International fixtures NZRFU	NPC*

Sources: New Zealand Rugby Almanac 1975–1999
Rugby Super 12 (1996–), Super 10/CANZ (1990–1995)
NPC National Provincial Championship
Note: Does not include end of season international tours (October–December)

Figure 27.2 The expansion of the New Zealand first class rugby season (1975–1999). Note years prior to 1994 not continuous

7.1.3 Seasonal advantages of climate

The entertainment value of Rugby Super 12 has, according to the Otago Rugby Football Union (1998) been enhanced by this seasonal shift. Super 12 is more likely to be played in warm conditions on a dry and fast playing surface. Atmosphere and entertainment value are promoted by weather conducive to skilful play and these factors were considered to attract "new" rugby watchers to attend games (North Otago Rugby Union 1998). This confirms Kreutzwiser's (1989) observation of the link between climate/weather conditions and levels of satisfaction with recreational outings. The expanded demographic profile of domestic and international tourists who attend Super 12 matches at this time of year has benefited levels of match attendance, atmosphere team support and sponsor/merchandising interests (Otago Rugby Football Union 1998).

7.1.4 Focus on entertainment values

The Rugby Union officials reported the deliberate development of the entertainment values associated with this early season competition. "There has been an agreement with the countries who take part to speed the game up and make it spectator friendly . . . they are not actually rule changes, but just agreement about how to use and interpret existing laws . . . so as to increase continuity in the game" (Otago Rugby Football Union 1998). The entertainment values that have been pursued through the development of this competition corroborates the view that sports may be developed to mirror the defining qualities of a tourist attraction (Leiper, 1990). "The product is still rugby but it is packaged as entertainment. Many come to see the fireworks, the bands and the hoopla. These things make it a genuine entertainment package" (Otago Rugby Football Union 1998). This was considered to have implications for distance decay thresholds associated with travel to attend sports.

7.1.5 Pre-competition warm up matches and mini tours

The early season temporal aspect of Super 12 necessitates that teams undertake pre season matches, often involving tours. This brings the rugby product into the summer season and matches are regularly hosted in tourist towns (most notably Queenstown), remote communities, or as part of mini domestic tours. The significance of this development was highlighted by the Southland and North Otago Rugby Unions. These matches were seen to offer much potential for the development of sport in the provincial unions while offering the potential to attract summer visitors.

7.2 Changing travel patterns and tourism development

The relevance of these changes for tourism was discussed with both sport and tourism administrators. Interviewees generally considered that the advent and initial success of the Rugby Super 12 competition offers tourism development opportunities that should be explored and pursued. Many related to the temporal dimension of tourism and, most particularly, to seasonal patterns of visitation. Tickets sales were reported to have indicated an increase in domestic travel and day excursions made on the part of travelling spectators from communities throughout the franchise region. Tourism administrators recognised and discussed the shoulder season tourism opportunities presented by these domestic tours and excursions these included the use of the franchise team as a marketing tool, focussed promotion of the local tourism product targeting new rugby spectator groups, and the wider use of multipurpose stadium facilities during the shoulder seasons, among others. The following subsections provide an overview of these findings.

7.2 1 Additional domestic trips and excursions within the region

The Super 12 competition was seen to attract visitors from across the franchise region to attend home matches. These travellers, according to the North Otago Rugby Union (1998), are generally not time-switching (rescheduling an otherwise planned trip to coincide with a Super 12 game), but rather are visiting more frequently, and at different times of the year, specifically to attend the Rugby Super 12 games (North Otago Rugby Union 1998). The Otago Rugby Football Union (1998) cited anecdotal evidence to suggest that the greater frequency of domestic trips associated with Super 12 brings benefits to the retail sector, food and beverage providers and tourism operators. "It is astronomical the number of people who make trips to Dunedin to watch the Highlanders in the Super 12 series, but they don't come and see a local game of rugby. Most treat it as a big family day out and sometimes make a whole weekend of it" (North Otago Rugby Union 1998).

7.2.2 New travelling groups

The commodification and positioning of Super 12 was considered to have created new travelling spectator groups (Otago Rugby Football Union 1998). Women, families and young people are more likely to travel to watch the Rugby Super 12 than the amateur rugby competitions that preceded it. The Southland Rugby Football Union (1998) stated that many "first-time rugby followers (and) many women have become interested in rugby because of Super 12". This has affected the spending patterns, entertainment preferences and wider travel motivations of these tourists. This, according to the Otago Rugby Football Union (1998), is closely linked to the seasonal context of the competition. "Different people come out (to spectate) in the summertime, particularly women . . . We've got a real emphasis on families. Many come from Central Otago and Southland and their tendency is to get here early and be in town shopping" (Otago Rugby Football Union 998). The branding of Rugby Super 12 has, therefore been effective in generating domestic tourism in the autumn quarter. "A good percentage of them stay and make a weekend out of it . . . by the time a night game has finished it is a pretty long haul home" (Southland Rugby Football Union 1998).

7.2.3 Potential to link sport attendance with the wider local tourism product

The majority of Super 12 games take place in floodlit stadia on Friday or Saturday evenings. The Otago Rugby Football Union (1998) confirmed the deliberate scheduling of matches to coincide with blocks of leisure time. This allows spectators to combine rugby spectator ship with social and other leisure activities. It also necessitates most travelling supporters to be accommodated for at least one night in the host city. This, according to tourism administrators presents the opportunity to link sport spectatorship with the wider local/regional tourism product (Tourism Dunedin, 1998) The Southland, Dunedin and North Otago Regional Tourism Organisations (RTO) recognised the tourism possibilities presented by two significant changes associated with the development of the professional Super 12 Rugby competition: (1) the spectator catchment associated with the Rugby Union has broadened, and (2) the scheduling of matches coincides with blocks of discretionary leisure time (weekends/evenings). With these changes, the potential for travelling supporters to experience the wider tourism and hospitality product in centres hosting Super 12 live sport has emerged.

7.2.4 Sport and international visitor flows in the Highlanders region

Much of the Rugby Super 12 season coincides with periods of significant international visitor activity in the nature/adventure tourism product of the southern New Zealand region. This raises the possibility that international tourists, whose visits to the southern macro-region coincide with Super 12 competition matches, may choose to visit Dunedin to experience live sport. Tourism Dunedin (1998) recognises this potential and stated an interest in pursuing the market opportunity presented by rugby as a secondary attraction for international tourists travelling within the region.

7.2.5 Shoulder season marketing tool

The Highlanders were considered to offer significant tourism marketing potential (Southland Economic Development Unit, 1998). "The team adds considerably to raising the profile of the city of Dunedin. It has become quite a statement in the Dunedin City promotions campaign" (Southland Economic Development Unit 1998). This profile is clearly the greatest during the shoulder season weeks of March–May when the Super 12 competition is actually taking place. Tourism Dunedin (1998) stated the view that "there are increasingly clear links between the Highlanders and Dunedin's identity . . . which translate . . . into value for tourism". "Indeed Super 12 offers the potential for joint ventures with other tourism administrations within the region".

7.2.6 Shoulder season domestic tourism between neighbouring franchise regions

Rugby Super 12 may also generate inter-regional domestic tourism. When neighbouring franchises meet, this potential is greatest. In March 1999, for example, the *Crusaders* (see Figure 27.1) visited Dunedin to play the *Highlanders*. The domestic travel component of this fixture was anticipated by the *Otago Daily Times* (Page, 1998) which reported that "almost 10,000 Canterbury Crusaders fans are expected to be among a crowd of 30,000 for the Super 12 Rugby match on Friday night (9 April 1999)". This observation makes no account of non-ticket holding travelling fans. In actual fact, this game produced a record crowd of 36,120 for a regular season non-international fixture. The *Star Sunday Times* (11 April 1999) reported that "on Friday afternoon the traffic was slowed to 10km/h . . . to the north of Dunedin as an estimated 8000 Canterbury fans drove south". These same teams met 5 weeks later at the same venue to contest the Super 12 final.

7.2.7 Multi-purpose stadium development

The development of multi use stadium facilities at the Highlander's franchise headquarters (Carisbrook, Dunedin) was also considered to serve the interests of the local tourism sector in terms of providing opportunities to stage major events throughout the year. This facility now has the seating capacity sufficient to successfully bid for and host various international sporting and cultural events (Otago Rugby Football Union 1998). The Otago Rugby Football Union (1998) confirmed that the redevelopment of the *Highlanders* stadium (Carisbrook) included aspects of design to promote multiple purpose utility. The staging of classical concerts and sporting events such as the Youth World Cup soccer fixtures have subsequently taken place in the shoulder seasons much to the benefit of the local tourism industry (Tourism Dunedin, 1998).

7.2 8 Facility developments in secondary centres

Facility developments have also been undertaken at secondary centres within the franchise region (such as Centennial Park, Oamaru). This initiative has taken place in order to attract pre-season games and harness their tourism potential (North Otago Rugby Union 1998). Interviews revealed that "some people travel to every single game . . . even the pre-season games in places such as Queenstown" (North Otago Rugby Union 1998). This has been recognised by the North Otago Rugby Union, which has succeeded in hosting pre-season matches involving the *Highlanders* in both 1998 and 1999. "On February 14, 1999, against the ACT Brumbies, we're expecting the crowd to be bulging at the seams . . . there are a few alterations going on at present with a view to that" (North Otago Rugby Union 1998).

   These examples suggest a multiplicity of ways that the extension of the rugby season can influence the temporal distribution of tourism within the region. However, it is difficult to be specific in quantitative terms about the causal relationship between the extension of the rugby season and tourist visitation. For example, the strength of this relationship is likely to vary depending on the opposition, current league standings, playing style and weather patterns. While ticket sale records (held by the Otago Rugby Football Union) and monthly regional visitation data (collected in different forms by Statistics New Zealand and Regional Tourism Organisations) support the results of this research the diversity and dynamics of the tourism sector are too complex to attribute changing patterns of regional visitation to a single factor. While levels of visitation to Dunedin have increased in the March–April–May quarter (1998–2000), coinciding with the annual Rugby Super 12 competition, a range of local/regional events, visitor activities, visitor promotion campaigns and such like render it impossible to generalise the relative impacts of the Super 12 competition in the absence of specific quantitative research.

8   Conclusion

Seasonality has to date been an inescapable aspect of both sport and tourism. However, in the field of sport management, the restrictions of functioning within a traditional sports season have, in many cases, been cast aside. The professional development of numerous sports, where teams compete virtually year round, has in those cases, largely eliminated the notion of sport seasonality. The development of multi-purpose indoor sports facilities and stadia with retractable all-weather enclosures cements this conclusion. Sport seasons have traditionally been determined by "natural" factors (Hartman, 1986) and this remains the case to a degree in sports such as skiing. However, the development of professional sports provides support for the viewpoints presented by Butler (1994) and Hinch and Jackson (2000) that sport seasons are determined to an increasing extent by "institutional" factors that can be moderated by sports administrators.

This scenario does not apply to the tourism sector. Seasonality in tourism remains a barrier to development and often to operational and economic viability. This article explores the possibility that changes to the seasonal aspect of spots may offer potential for tourism associated with those sports. In the case of Rugby Super 12, a regional sports competition, this scenario was upheld. Both sport and tourism administrators identified significant benefits associated with the expanded representative Rugby Union season. This scenario is likely to apply, albeit in varying degrees, to sports at national, regional and local levels of representation. However, it is noteworthy that little mention was made of the probable implications of these changes for sports that have been traditionally played in the rugby off-season. This aspect of sport and tourism seasonality justifies close examination. These conclusions support the need for a more thorough understanding of sport tourism at the regional and local levels than has hitherto been the case. It also supports a comprehensive analysis of the reciprocal potential that sports and tourism development interests may offer.

Acknowledgements

The researchers acknowledge and thank the following organisations for making staff time available for the conducting of interviews on the relationship between sport and tourism: Otago Rugby Football Union, Southland Rugby Union, North Otago Rugby Union, Dunedin City Council Economic Development Unit, Tourism Dunedin, Waitaki District Council, Invercargill City Council, Southland Economic Development Unit.

References

Allcock, J.B. (1989). Seasonality. In S.F. Wilt, & L. Moutinho (Eds), *Tourism marketing and management handbook* (pp. 387–392). Englewood Cliffs NJ: Prentice-Hall.

Banister, P., Burman, E., Parker, I., Taylor M., & Tindall, C. (1996). *Qualitative methods in psychology: A research guide*. Philadelphia, USA: Open University Press.

Baron, R.R.V. (1975). *Seasonality in tourism. A guide to the analysis of seasonality and trends for policy making*. London, England: Economist Intelligence Unit.

Butler, R.W. (1994). Seasonality in tourism: Issues and problems. In A.V. Seaton (Ed.), *Tourism: The state of the art* (pp. 332–339). Chichester, England: Wiley.

Edgell, D.L. (1990). *International tourism policy*. New York: Van Nostrand Reinhold.

Faulkner B., Tideswell, C., & Weston, A.M. (1998). Leveraging tourism benefits from the Sydney 2000 Olympics: Keynote address. *Proceedings of the fourth annual conference on sport management: Opportunities and change*, 26–28 November 1998. Gold Coast Australia: Sports Management Association of Australia and New Zealand (SMAANZ).

Frisby, W., & Getz, D. (1990). *The role of municipalities in developing festivals and special events*. Waterloo, Canada: Department of Recreation and Leisure, University of Waterloo.

Getz., D. (1991). *Festivals, special events, and tourism*. New York: Van Nostrand Reinhold.

Gibson, H.J. (1998). Sport tourism: A critical analysis of research. *Sport Management Review*, *1*, 45–76.

Glyptis, S.A. (1991). Sport and tourism. *Progress in tourism, recreation and hospitality management*, Vol. 3. London: Belhaven.

Go, R. (1990). Resorts resurgent: Shoulder and off-season expand their base. *Canadian Hotel and Restaurant*, *68*(8), 43–44.

Hall, C.M. (1992). *Hallmark tourist events: Impacts, management and planning*. London: Belhaven.

Hartsman, R. (1986). Tourism, seasonality and social change. *Leisure Studies*, *5*(1), 25–33.

Higham, J.E.S. (1999). Sport as an avenue of tourism development: An analysis of the positive and negative impacts of sport tourism. *Current Issues in Tourism*, *2*(1), 82–90.

Higham, J.E.S., & Hinch, T.D. (1999). *The development of Super 12 and its implications for tourism*. Industry report. http://www.commerce.otago.ac.nz/tourism/frst/super12/sporti.htm (25 August 2000).

Hiller, H.H. (1998). Assessing the impacts of mega-events: A linkage model. *Current Issues in Tourism 1*(1), 47–57.

Hinch, T.D., & Hickey, G.P. (1997). Tourism attractions and seasonality: Spatial relationships in Alberta. In K. McKay (Ed.), *Proceedings of the travel and tourism research association*, Canadian chapter (pp. 69–76). Winnipeg: University of Manitoba.

Hinch, T.D., & Jackson, E.L. (2000). Leisure constraints research: Its value as a framework for understanding tourism seasonability. *Current Issues in Tourism*, *3*(2), 87–106.

Irwin, R., & Sandler, M. (1998). An analysis of travel behaviour and event-induced expenditure among American collegiate championship patron groups. *Journal of Vacation Marketing*, *4*, 78–90.

Jefferson, A. (1986). Smoothing out the ups and downs in demand. *British Hotelier and Restaurateur*, July/August, 24–25.

Jefferson, A., & Lickorish, L. (1988). *Marketing tourism: A practical guide*. Essex, UK: Longman House.

Kreutzwiser R. (1989). Supply. In G. Wall (Ed.), *Outdoor recreation in Canada* (pp. 19–42). Toronto: Wiley.

Laws, E. (1991). *Tourism marketing: Service and quality management perspectives*. Cheltenham, England: Stanley Thornes Publishers.

Leiper, N. (1990). Tourist attraction systems. *Annals of Tourism Research*, *17*, 367–384.

Lockwood A., & Guerrier, Y. (1990). Labour shortages in the international hotel industry. *Travel and Tourism Analyst*, *6*, 17–35.

Loy, J.W., McPherson, B.D., & Kenyon, G. (1989). *Sport and social systems*. Reading, MA: Addison Wesley.

MacCannell, D. (1973). Staged authenticity—arrangements of social space in tourist settings. *American Journal of Sociology*, *79*(3), 589–603.

McEnnif, J. (1992). Seasonality of tourism demand in the European community. *Travel and Tourism Analyst*, *3*, 67–88.

Nogawa, H., Yamaguchi, Y., & Hagi, Y. (1996). An empirical research study on Japanese sport tourism in sport-for-all events: Case studies of a single-night event and a multiple-night event. *Journal of Travel Research*, *35*(2), 46–54.

NZRFU (1998). NZRFU broad values and positioning articulation. Unpublished report. NZRFU, Wellington, New Zealand.

Olds, K. (1998). Urban mega-events, evictions and housing rights: The Canadian case. *Current Issues in Tourism*, *1*(1), 2–46.

Page, C. (1998). Traffic strategy revised. *Otago Daily Times*, 22 October (p. 3).

Poon, A. (1993). All-inclusive resorts. *Travel and Tourism Analyst*, *2*, 54–68.

Redmond, G. (1991). Changing styles of sports tourism: Industry/consumer interactions in Canada, the USA and Europe. In: M.T. Sinclair, & M.T. Stabler (Eds), *The tourism industry: An international analysis*. Wallingford, Oxon: CAB International.

Robinson, H. (1979). *A geography of tourism*. London: MacDonald & Evans.

Ryan, C., Smee, A., & Murphy, S. (1996). Creating a database of events in New Zealand: Early results. *Festival Management and Event Tourism*, *4*(3/4), 151–155.

Snepenger, D., Houser, B., & Snepenger, M. (1990). Seasonality of demand. *Annals of Tourism Research*, *17*, 628–630.

Southland Economic Development Unit (1998). Economic impact report: Highlanders versus Golden Cats rugby match. 28 March 1998. Unpublished report. New Zealand: Invercargill.

Standeven, J., & De Knop, P. (1999). *Sport tourism*. Champaign, IL: Human Kinetics.

Sylvester, C. (1999). The western idea of work and leisure: Traditions, transformations, and the future. In E.L. Jackson, & T.L. Burton (Eds), *Leisure studies: Prospects for the twenty first century* (pp. 17–33). State College, PA: Venture Publishing.

Tourism Dunedin (1998). *Dunedin and Coastal Otago Tourism Strategy 1999*. Dunedin City Council Discussion Document. Dunedin, New Zealand.

United Kingdom Business Information Futures (1995). *Festivals and special events*. New Leisure Market Series, London: UK Business Information Futures.

Whelihan, W.P., & Chon K.S. (1991). Resort marketing trends of the 1990s. *The Cornell Hotel and Restaurant Administrative Quarterly*, *32*(2), 56–59.

Williams, P., Hainsworth, D., & Dossa, K. (1995). Community development and special event tourism: The men's World Cup of skiing at Whistler British Columbia. *Journal of Tourism Studies*, *6*(2), 11–20.

WTO (2000). IOC and WTO strengthen links between sport and tourism. http://www.world-tourism.org/pressre1/0004.27.htm (27 April 2000).

Chapter 28

Simon Hudson, Brent Ritchie and Seldjan Timur

MEASURING DESTINATION COMPETITIVENESS
An empirical study of Canadian ski resorts

Introduction

COMPETITIVE ADVANTAGE IS NOW WIDELY accepted as being of central importance to the success of organizations, regions and countries (Porter, 1980, 1990). Much management effort goes into establishing strategies and operating procedures that will lead to competitive advantage and into measuring performance against key competitors through bench marking initiatives. Destination competitiveness has become a significant part of the tourism literature, and evaluation of the competitiveness of tourism destinations is increasingly being recognized as an important tool in the strategic positioning and marketing analysis of destinations (Pearce, 1997; Faulkner *et al.*, 1999).

This particular study was an attempt to operationalize a model of destination competitiveness in order to measure the relative competitiveness of ski resorts in Canada. The skiing market has reached the maturity stage in Canada. However, despite increasing consolidation and competitive rivalry, no systematic effort has been made to compare resorts on attributes other than infrastructure (e.g. number of ski lifts) or satisfaction ratings from readers of ski magazines. Further research would offer these destinations a mechanism for analyzing, diagnosing, planning and communicating their competitive strategies.

Destination competitiveness

To compete is, most simply, 'to strive for superiority in a quality' (*Concise Oxford Dictionary*). The *World Competitiveness Yearbook*'s definition has varied somewhat over the years. For example, it has defined competitiveness as 'the ability of entrepreneurs to design, produce and market goods and services, the prices and non-price qualities of which form a more attractive package of benefits than those of competitors' (IMD, 1994, p. 49). It has also defined world competitiveness as 'the ability of a country or company to . . . proportionally, generate more wealth than its competitors in world markets' (IMD, 1994, p. 18). Competitiveness is viewed as the effective combining of both assets and processes, where assets 'are inherited (e.g. natural resources) or created (e.g. infrastructure)', and where processes 'transform assets into economic results (e.g. manufacturing)' (IMD, 1994, p. 18). The *World Competitiveness Yearbook* examines competitiveness in terms of four fundamental forces that 'are often the result of tradition, history, or value systems and are so deeply rooted in the 'modus operandi' of a country that, in most cases, they are not clearly stated or defined' (IMD, 1994, p. 48). The four dimensions used are attractiveness versus aggressiveness, proximity versus globality, assets versus systems and individual risk taking versus social cohesiveness.

Destination competitiveness has been defined as the ability of a destination 'to maintain its market position and share and/or improve upon them through time' (d'Hauteserre, 2000, p. 23); 'to compete effectively and profitably in the marketplace' (Goeldner and Ritchie, 2003, p. 417); to create and integrate value-added products that sustain its resources while maintaining market position relative to competitors' (Hassan, 2000, p. 240); and 'to provide a high standard of living – which is determined by the economic, social and environmental conditions – for residents of the destination' (Crouch and Ritchie, 1999, p. 140).

Despite the numerous definitions, few frameworks have been developed to assess the competitiveness of a destination. Some have argued that Porter's generic model of industrial competitiveness may be utilized in tourism. This framework asserts that the state of competition in an industry depends on five basic forces – the bargaining power of suppliers, the bargaining power of buyers, the threat of new entrants to the market, the threat of substitute products or services and the nature of rivalry among existing firms (or destination in tourism terms). From a tourism perspective, Bordas (1994) argues that destination competitiveness cannot be established between countries. However, competition does exist between clusters of tourism businesses. He argues that a strategic plan is required to gain competitive advantage, and he introduced three strategies – low cost, differentiation and specialization – for clusters to gain competitive advantage. A cluster is defined by Bordas as 'a group of tourist attractions, infrastructure, equipment, services and organization concentrated in a delimited geographical area' (1994, p. 3).

Evans *et al.* (1995) use the three organizational strategies identified by Porter: cost leadership strategy, differentiation strategy and focus strategy. To be competitive, the authors emphasize the significance (and role) of developing a strategy that establishes a fit between the destination's resources and opportunities in the environment. While both of the models are based on strategies from Porter's competitiveness model, the unit of analysis is different; while the focus of Bordas (1994) is on tourism clusters, Evans *et al.* (1995) focus upon destination management organizations (DMOs). They suggest that DMOs have to discover their core competencies (strengths) and then build their strategy around these competencies.

Chon and Mayer (1995) also adapted Porter's generic competitiveness model to the tourism industry. They developed a tourism competitiveness model that includes five dimensions: appeal, management, organization, information and efficiency (cited in Faulkner *et al.*, 1999). The authors incorporate tourism-specific issues such as the intangibility of the tourism product and renewability of tourism resources into their model. Faulkner *et al.* (1999), when measuring the competitiveness of South Australia, used only one of the dimensions of this model.

Pearce (1997) introduced the competitive destination analysis (CDA) tool to measure the competitiveness of tourism destinations. CDA is defined as 'a means of systematically comparing diverse attributes of competing destinations within a planning context' (Pearce, 1997, p. 16). He argues that a systematic appraisal and comparison of key tourism elements (attributes) among competitors can provide 'a more objective basis for evaluating the strengths and weaknesses of the destination, provide a better appreciation of its competitive advantage, and contribute to the formulation of more effective development policies' (1997, p. 17). He recommends that CDA be used as a tool for tourism planning and marketing techniques. CDA, which compares destinations on an element-by-element basis, is argued to be a better approach in identifying specific competitive features of the destinations.

Hassan (2000) introduced another model that examines the relationships among stakeholders involved in creating and integrating value-added products to sustain resources while maintaining market position relative to other competitors. He criticizes traditional competitiveness models (referring to Porter's five forces model) as providing limited analysis in the context of tourism. He argues that the indicators that most competitiveness models include are necessary but not sufficient to measure the competitiveness of tourism destinations because of the diverse nature of the tourism industry. According to Hassan 'the multiplicity of industries involved in creating and sustaining destinations require the development of a competitiveness model that examines the extent of cooperation needed for the future of competitiveness' (2000, p. 239).

Hassan recommends turning comparative advantages (resource-based attributes of destinations) into competitive advantage by responding to the changing nature of tourism demand. His model, for market competitiveness analysis, focuses on comparative advantage, demand orientation, industry structure and environmental commitment. He emphasizes how tourism is sensitive to and dependent on high-quality resources and underlines the need to protect the resource base. He suggests that a balance of growth orientation and environmental commitment, and partnerships among major stakeholders are required to sustain destination market competitiveness. Unfortunately, this model does not identify the key variables associated with measuring market and environmental sustainability (i.e. two major components of his model).

Finally, Crouch and Ritchie developed from the ground up a model of destination competitiveness that 'offers the tourism industry a mechanism for analyzing, diagnosing, planning, and communicating competitive strategies' (1999, p. 142). Then, over a total period of eight years, they further refined the concepts and propositions underlying the model to the point where it has matured to its present form (Ritchie and Crouch, 2003).

The goal of the model is to achieve sustainable destination competitiveness by enhancing the well-being of the residents of that particular destination (in terms of economic prosperity, environmental stewardship and resident quality of life). This competitiveness/sustainability (C/S) model (see Figure 28.1), which examines the relationship between societal prosperity and tourism, has five major dimensions: qualifying and amplifying determinants; destination policy, planning and development; destination management; core resources and attractors; and supporting factors and resources.

The qualifying and amplifying determinants dimension includes situational conditions that are often beyond the control of the tourism industry, such as location or safety of a destination. But this dimension also includes factors such as destination awareness and current image, and the cost and value for money, factors that can be influenced by the destination. The destination policy, planning and development dimension identifies processes required to create an environment within which tourism can flourish in a sustainable manner. The third dimension, destination management, deals with activities that can best adapt to the constraints imposed by the qualifying determinants (the first-mentioned dimension) and the global forces that surround the destination. Core resources and attractors are the key motivators for visit to a destination, such as physiography and climate, culture and history or special events. The fifth dimension, supporting factors and resources, consists of factors such as infrastructure and accessibility that enhance the core attractors and are required to establish a successful tourism industry for a destination.

According to the model, the environment of a destination can be categorized as global (macro) and competitive (micro). It is essential for destination managers to monitor both of the environments regularly and identify the forces that might present a risk or an opportunity to the destination. Having identified the forces driving change, destinations must either adapt to or overcome these forces if they are to remain competitive (Crouch and Ritchie, 1999).

While the latest version of the model can no doubt be improved upon with further work, the authors of this paper believe it is now arguably the most comprehensive and most rigorous of all models of this type currently available. Such a multifaceted model is necessary to help comprehend the complex, fragmented and interrelated nature of the tourism industry and the relationships that exist within it. Being a comprehensive and complex model, it reflects a wider range of issues than past models of destination competitiveness, thus assisting better understanding of the nature of the environment in which tourism destinations operate. Past models have focused on comparative measures, but a mere listing of comparative and competitive factors, no matter how comprehensive it may be, is not sufficient. It is also necessary to understand the relationship and interplay between the factors of competitiveness.

The Crouch and Ritchie model can play an important role in guiding destination managers as they seek to diagnose their competitive problems and develop sustainable solutions. However, to date, this model has not been subject to adequate empirical testing, and it is therefore the objective of this research to apply the model to one specific setting, Canadian winter sports destinations.

Canadian winter sports destinations

A winter sports destination is defined as a 'geographical, economic, and social unit consisting of all those firms, organizations, activities, areas and installations which are intended to serve the specific needs of winter sport tourists' (Flagestad and Hope, 2001, p. 449). In North America, there are nearly 800 such destinations, 244 of them being in Canada. Winter sport tourism in North America over the last decade has been characterized by diversification and consolidation (Hudson, 2003). In a mature market, where even avid skiers are typically skiing less, winter resorts have realized that they must offer a more diverse range of activities, both on-snow and off-snow. The more progressive resorts are

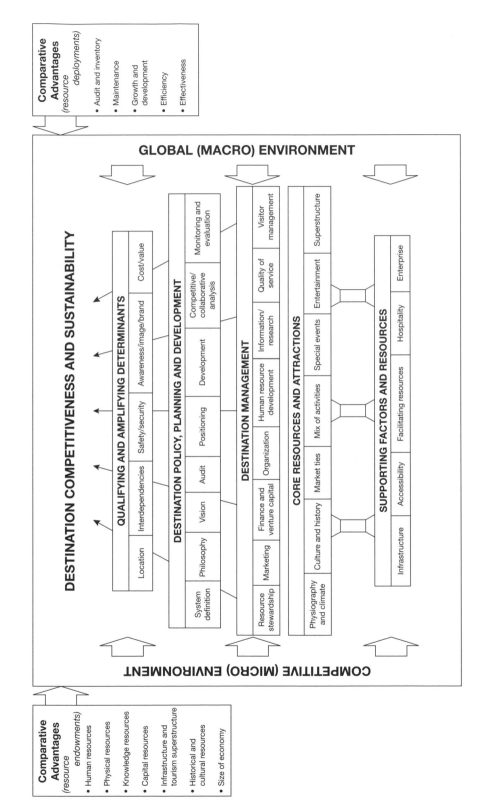

Figure 28.1 Destination competitiveness model (Crouch and Ritchie, 1999)

now treating skiing as a form of entertainment by establishing more off-slope diversions. The larger ski chains in North America are expanding the range of activities they offer, such as ice-skating, sledging and dog sledging, snowmobiling and tubing (the increasingly popular activity of sliding down the slope on the inner-tube of a lorry tire). The idea is to turn the big resorts into fully fledged winter theme parks, attracting more beginners and families to the slopes.

Consolidation has resulted in a gradual drop in the number of ski areas in the US and Canada, and the four largest resort groups in North America now account for approximately 18 million skier visits, over 25 percent of the total. Despite encouraging statistics from recent seasons, the numbers of skiers and snowboarders has been falling in the US since the early 1990s, with women skiers in particular falling off at a double-digit pace (National Ski Areas Association, 2001; Anon, 2002). The snowboard market growth is slowing as baby boomers are nearing retirement age, and there is the additional problem of a decline in leisure time. There has been an increase in the number of hours worked per household (and an increase in the number of women working) and disposable income has not increased at the same rate as hours worked. Marketing resources are also limited compared to other leisure activities, and competing activities have grown, taking market share away from winter sport destinations.

In 2003 the 244 ski areas in Canada attracted 18.8 million skier/boarder visits, a slight increase on the previous season, and, in total, 14.7 per cent of Canadians over 12 (3,935,000) participated in one or more forms of skiing (Canadian Ski Council, 2003). Mountain resorts are making heavy investments in resort real estate, and the trend to use winter sports as almost a 'loss leader' to bring in revenue from base operations continues to be the leading financial model for more and more resort operations. With three major ski center operators attempting to dominate the ski industry in Canada (Intrawest, Resorts of the Canadian Rockies and Mont Saint-Sauveur International Inc.) the market is becoming increasingly competitive, and it is therefore critical for Canadian ski areas to measure their performance against key competitors in order to discover their core competencies and relative weaknesses.

Objectives

Given the foregoing, the objectives of this research were to:

a)   develop operational measures for each of the components of the destination competitiveness model developed by Crouch and Ritchie (1999); and
b)   to use these measures to develop an index of destination competitiveness for ski areas in Canada.

Methodology

The initial stage of the research involved in-depth interviews with key ski area stakeholders in an attempt to develop a survey instrument that could measure each of the 33 components of the model. A tourism destination has many stakeholders it must seek to satisfy and the perceptions of these stakeholders are critical in understanding how destinations compete regarding the elements of the core and supporting resources, the qualifying determinants of the ski destination, the tools used for destination management practice and the policies destinations formulate for planning and development.

Previous research has identified five key stakeholders in ski destinations: ski area operators; tourism associations or destination management organizations (DMOs); accommodation owners; tour operators; and commercial enterprises (Hudson, 2000). However, in many resorts today there are other important 'resort-specific' groups, such as environmental groups or ski area consultants, that have just as much influence as the above stakeholders. It was decided therefore that the interviewees would represent the five groups above as well as one more 'resort-specific' group. For example, in Fernie, British Columbia, the former owner was perceived by many to be a key stakeholder in the resort, even though he did not represent one of the five stakeholder groups identified above. He was therefore interviewed during data collection. Likewise, in Panorama, the East Kootenay Environmental Society had a large influence on ongoing development plans, so a representative from this group was interviewed as part of the study.

After the initial interviews, it became apparent that some components of the model were going to be easier to measure than others. For example, the first factor of 'location' could be measured by asking respondents to indicate their strength of agreement/ disagreement with the following statement: 'The competitive position of your resort is strengthened by the fact that it is close to important skiing markets.' However, not all of the 33 components could be measured in one question. For instance, it required six different questions to measure the marketing tactics employed in resorts, as respondents had to comment on various elements of the marketing mix. Similarly, the 'tourism superstructure' component had to be divided into separate measures for the number of lifts, the terrain, snow quality, accommodation and dining facilities.

In total, 50 questions were developed after these initial in-depth interviews with ski area stakeholders. Once the questionnaire had been drafted, it was piloted in three separate resorts – Banff, Whistler and Fernie – and further refined. Such refinements were confined to minor changes in the wording of the individual questions as opposed to the addition or deletion of questions.

For the survey proper, at least one completed questionnaire was obtained from each of the six stakeholder groups referred to above. Given its complexity the researchers were available to explain the questionnaire, either in person or over the telephone. Due to time and cost limitations, the focus of the research was limited to ski areas in Western Canada – ten resorts were approached from British Columbia and Alberta. However, three resorts from the East – two in Quebec and one in Ontario – were also studied; for comparison purposes. Data were collected during the winters of 2001 and 2002, and ten stakeholders were interviewed in each resort, making a total sample of 130.

Results

Table 28.1 indicates the total scores and the average mean scores for each destination, while Table 28.2 shows the mean scores for each resort on individual components of the model. For the mean scores, data were weighted to account for the 33 components of the model. For example, results from the six questions used to measure the marketing

Table 28.1 Destination scores for each dimension of the model

| Ski area | Overall competitiveness (n = 130) | | Qualifying & amplifying determinants | Destinations policy, planning & development | Destination management | Core resources & attractors | Supporting factors & resources |
	Total*	Mean					
1 Whistler	248	4.97	4.56	4.90	5.11	5.18	4.75
2 Tremblant	247	4.94	5.27	4.65	5.00	4.92	5.13
3 Blue Mountain	240	4.80	5.27	4.98	4.96	4.45	4.41
4 Sun Peaks	239	4.79	4.20	4.75	5.10	4.76	4.81
5 Silver Star	229	4.58	4.58	4.38	4.79	4.41	4.86
6 Big White	228	4.56	4.47	4.60	4.88	4.41	4.47
7 Panorama	226	4.53	4.08	4.77	4.79	4.32	4.39
8 Kicking Horse	212	4.24	4.14	4.21	4.32	4.28	4.16
9 Mont St Anne	211	4.23	4.44	3.98	4.21	4.38	4.25
10 Kimberley	202	4.05	4.25	3.79	4.07	4.06	4.30
11 Banff	199	3.99	4.14	3.29	4.05	4.49	4.07
12 Jasper	199	3.98	3.42	3.95	4.19	4.20	3.64
13 Fernie	197	3.94	4.01	3.35	3.87	4.53	3.91

*Areas were ranked from 1 to 6 on 50 questions giving a total possible score of 300.

tactics employed in resorts were averaged out to give one score. Where stakeholders were over-represented (for example, three ski area managers completed surveys in Panorama), their scores were averaged. Results of a *post hoc* test (SNK test) indicate the significant differences that exist between resorts. Table 28.2 is useful for highlighting various strengths and weaknesses for particular destinations.

Areas were ranked from 1 to 6 on 50 questions, giving a total possible score of 300. In terms of overall competitiveness, Whistler received the highest score (248), closely followed by Tremblant (247) and Blue Mountain (240). All three resorts are owned by Intrawest, recognized as the most diversified and successful company in North America, which focuses on developing four-season resorts in conjunction with other partners and investors (Hudson, 2003), and invests heavily in real estate developments and tourism infrastructure.

By applying the five core dimensions of the model to Whistler, it is perhaps not surprising that the resort is ranked number one in terms of competitiveness. In terms of *qualifying and amplifying determinants* (mean = 4.56), over the past few decades Whistler has experienced unprecedented growth and rising stature as a world-class ski area. Close to Vancouver, an international destination in itself, Whistler is easily accessible, and strong growth in visitor numbers has consistently been achieved in both summer and winter, year after year. In the 2000/2001 season, total skier visits reached a North American record of 2.18 million visits and, the same winter, the number of room nights generated increased by 3 per cent to 616,201.

As for the *destination policy, planning and development* dimension (mean = 4.90), Tourism Whistler, a member-based organization, is responsible for developing co-ordinated strategies in the areas of sales, advertising, media relations and promotion of the entire resort. An all-member meeting takes place annually to review both long-range and short-term visions. Involving Whistler's 9,000 full-time residents in the planning process has been vital in achieving community cohesion and effective operations. Building partnerships has also been essential to achieving the objectives, and, working with organizations such as the Canadian Tourism Commission and the Ottawa-based Tourism Industry Association of Canada (TIAC), the group is able to maximize efficiencies.

Looking at *destination management* (mean = 5.11), Tourism Whistler's marketing team of 25 people does most of the advertising and prepares promotional material in-house to give them greater control over their image and costs. The group also regularly conducts customer surveys to gauge satisfaction levels, identify areas that need improvement and formulate strategies. Stewardship is also taken seriously when planning on-mountain development. For example, the resort has created the Habitat Improvement Team, a corps of managers and employees who help local conservation groups restore habitat for fish, wildlife and plant species in Whistler valley. Whistler is also spending $1.5 million over a five-year period for watershed restoration on its lands, in a program called Operation Green-Up.

Whistler has many *core resources and attractors* (mean = 5.18), including reliable snowfall of more than nine meters (30 feet) annually, and one of the longest seasons in North America, with the regular season stretching from November through to early June, and summer glacier skiing from June through to early August. Whistler has the most terrain (7,071 acres) and greatest vertical (5,280 feet or one mile) in North America. The resort stages annual events as diverse as the Winter Start Festival, World Ski and Snowboard Festival and the Whistler Summit Series.

Table 28.2 Destination scores for each component of the model

Individual components of the model		Mean score for each resort												P value
	Banff	Big White	Blue Mountain	Fernie	Jasper	Kicking Horse	Kimberley	Mont St Anne	Panorama	Silver Star	Sun Peaks	Tremblant	Whistler	
Location	4.38	4.63	5.50	4.57	4.00	4.14	3.66	5.00	3.37	4.17	4.50	5.33	5.00	ns
Interdependencies	3.38	4.12	5.00	3.36	3.29	2.43	3.00	2.83	3.50	4.00	3.13	5.33	5.00	<.005
Safely/security	4.07	4.35	5.50	3.53	2.92	4.00	4.10	5.08	4.41	4.91	4.31	5.66	3.65	<.005
Awareness/image/brand	4.15	5.11	5.50	4.35	3.28	4.85	3.33	4.83	4.75	4.83	4.00	5.33	5.90	<.005
Cost/value	4.77	4.88	4.63	4.71	4.14	5.14	5.33	5.17	4.38	4.67	5.00	4.33	4.20	ns
System definition	2.54	4.75	4.63	3.21	3.86	4.00	4.17	4.33	4.50	4.00	4.50	4.83	4.30	<.005
Philosophy	2.77	4.63	4.63	3.43	3.86	4.57	3.17	4.00	4.50	4.17	4.38	4.67	4.80	<.005
Vision	2.63	4.63	4.88	3.57	3.71	5.00	3.00	3.50	5.00	4.17	4.88	5.00	5.10	<.005
Audit	3.31	3.88	5.13	3.07	4.43	3.86	3.17	3.67	4.63	4.50	4.63	4.17	5.00	<.005
Positioning	3.00	4.38	5.13	3.64	4.00	4.71	3.33	4.33	4.75	4.67	4.63	4.50	4.90	<.005
Development	3.15	4.75	5.08	2.85	4.04	4.00	3.66	3.61	4.79	4.27	4.95	4.77	5.03	<.005
Competitive/collaborative	4.10	4.81	5.18	3.81	4.01	4.21	4.49	4.24	4.93	4.49	5.06	4.33	5.20	<.005
Monitoring & evaluation	3.73	4.37	4.75	3.53	3.71	3.85	4.08	3.91	4.75	4.33	4.56	4.50	470	<0.01
Resource stewardship	3.62	4.38	4.50	2.79	4.29	3.71	3.50	4.17	4.25	4.50	5.13	4.67	5.10	<.005
Marketing	4.82	5.56	5.50	4.48	4.30	4.92	4.55	4.72	5.18	5.36	5.37	5.36	5.45	<.005

Finance & venture capital	3.58	4.63	5.00	3.00	3.57	4.14	3.50	3.50	4.63	4.67	5.50	5.17	4.80	<.005
Organization	3.23	4.38	4.00	3.14	3.71	3.29	4.33	3.67	4.63	4.17	4.63	4.83	4.60	<.005
Human resource development	3.00	4.00	4.50	3.36	4.00	3.71	3.17	3.50	4.75	4.17	4.00	4.00	5.10	<.05
Information/research	2.92	3.88	4.50	3.71	4.43	3.29	3.67	3.67	4.50	3.83	4.63	4.33	4.50	ns
Quality of service	3.92	4.63	4.38	4.14	4.00	4.57	4.50	4.00	4.13	4.83	5.38	5.17	4.50	ns
Visitor management	3.77	4.25	4.75	3.36	4.71	4.00	3.00	4.00	4.38	4.00	488	4.67	5.20	<.05
Physiography & climate	5.08	4.25	4.50	5.14	4.71	5.29	4.50	3.33	4.75	4.67	5.00	3.50	5.50	<.05
Culture & history	5.38	5.25	4.88	5.43	5.43	5.71	5.17	4.50	5.00	5.00	5.50	5.67	5.80	ns
Market ties	3.88	4.06	3.50	3.82	4.07	3.21	3.08	3.91	4.06	3.91	4.12	4.25	4.90	ns
Mix of activities	4.30	4.50	4.88	4.36	3.86	4.29	4.17	4.67	4.88	4.83	5.13	5.00	5.50	ns
Special events	4.46	4.25	5.13	4.43	4.29	3.86	4.17	4.67	4.50	4.67	5.13	5.33	5.60	<.005
Entertainment	4.38	2.88	4.13	3.64	3.29	2.71	4.00	3.67	3.25	4.67	4.00	5.17	4.90	<.005
Superstructure	4.51	4.68	4.56	4.71	4.16	4.57	4.11	4.72	4.29	4.27	4.83	5.13	5.05	ns
Infrastructure	3.92	4.00	4.50	2.93	4.29	3.14	4.17	4.00	4.38	4.00	5.00	5.67	4.60	<.005
Accessibility	4.30	5.00	4.25	3.74	3.14	3.92	4.08	4.25	4.75	5.16	4.50	5.58	4.85	<.05
Facilitating resources	3.31	3.63	4.63	3.64	2.43	4.43	4.33	4.67	3.75	4.67	4.13	3.50	4.00	<.005
Hospitality	4.62	5.13	4.50	5.07	4.71	5.14	5.00	4.33	4.63	5.33	5.63	5.17	5.20	ns
Enterprise	4.00	4.13	4.38	4.36	4.14	4.43	4.17	4.00	4.13	4.83	5.13	5.33	5.00	ns
Overall mean	3.99	4.56	4.80	3.94	3.98	4.24	4.05	4.23	4.53	4.58	4.79	4.94	4.97	<.005

Whistler's *supporting factors and resources* (mean = 4.75) are impressive. Huge increases in the number of accommodation properties (the resort attracted investments totaling $550 million in construction between 1995 and 2000), retail shops and restaurants, along with extensive on-mountain improvements and expansions have followed on the heels of the growth in overall visitor and skier numbers. Since its establishment as a municipality in 1975, building investment has exceeded $2 billion. Now, with more than 55,000 pillows, and 18,000 of those within 500 meters of the lifts, Whistler boasts the most ski-in/ski-out accommodation of any mountain recreation resort in North America.

Ranked second in overall competitiveness was Tremblant in Quebec. Intrawest bought the Tremblant property in 1991, and has invested $850 million to build the first two phases of the resort. The resort currently employs up to 3,000 people in peak periods. Once the new developments are complete, the resort could handle four million visitors a year and will employ around 7,500 people. The ski area has been staging public meetings with local residents concerning a ten-year development plan that management say would triple the size of the resort. The resort also wants to add some 4,000 lodging units within the next decade, along with improvements to the current infrastructure of the resort, an increase on the current 1,700 units on the developed south side of the mountain. A CDN$75-million casino is being built, and the resort has recently added an airport able to accommodate international flights. In 2000, *Ski Magazine*'s readers rated Tremblant as the number one resort in Eastern North America (*Ski Magazine*, 2000), and in 2002 the resort won a US award for real estate development – one of eight Urban Land Institute 2002 Awards for Excellence presented during a ceremony in Las Vegas.

Blue Mountain, Ontario's largest mountain resort, was ranked third in terms of overall competitiveness, perhaps signifying the resort's success in its bid to transform a local resort into a world-class destination. In 2001, the longest season in its 60-year history helped earnings increase by 18 percent for the resort over the previous year (Stueck, 2001). Located two hours north of Toronto (perhaps explaining the highest score for location; mean = 5.50), the resort has the province's highest vertical across 235 acres of ski-able terrain. Originally conceived as a winter playground, the resort has developed into a four-season destination. When the village is complete in 2008, Blue Mountain will have 1,482 units of accommodation. Blue Mountain equaled the highest mean score for qualifying and amplifying determinants (mean = 5.27), and received the highest score for the destination policy, planning and development dimension (mean = 4.80).

While the position of Whistler in Table 28.1 is not surprising, perhaps Fernie's ranking at the bottom is unexpected. Owned by the Resorts of the Canadian Rockies (RCR), Fernie has an international reputation for powder snow, and received a record 300,000 skiers in 1999/2000. Since buying the resort in 1997, Charlie Locke, the owner of RCR, has invested millions of dollars in the ski hill and the infrastructure surrounding it. However, the survey results can probably be explained by the fact that, at the time of the research, Locke owed money to many people in the town, and eventually filed under the Companies' Creditors Arrangement Act for protection from its creditors while RCR restructured. Stakeholders who completed the questionnaire could therefore have been concerned about the future of the ski resort. Researchers also received the impression that there was some animosity between the town of Fernie, and the actual ski area, a short drive away, perhaps explaining its significantly low score for teamwork in its DMO activities (mean = 3.14, $p < .005$). Fernie's mean score regarding the deployment of resources for effective ski resort development was also significantly lower than others (mean = 2.85, $p <$ .005). Stakeholders felt that management had not developed effective marketing, financial or human resource strategies for the development of the ski resort.

The other resorts owned by RCR in the survey also received low overall scores, with Mont St Anne ranked tenth, Kimberley eleventh and Lake Louise, as part of the Banff resorts, twelfth. Again, the overriding explanation could be the precarious financial position of the company at the time of the survey, but analysis of Table 28.2 reveals more. For example, Kimberley was ranked poorly for its location (mean = 3.66), and significantly lower than others for awareness and image (mean = 3.33, $p <$ .005), resource stewardship (mean = 3.50, $p <$ .005), the ability to raise finance (mean = 3.50, $p <$ .005) and visitor management (mean = 3.00, $p <$ .05). The resort was also ranked significantly lower for all of the destination policy, planning and development components, despite having a high score for cost and value for money (mean = 5.33).

Mont St Anne was perceived to be significantly more dependent on the success of other destinations than other resorts (mean 2.83, $p <$ .005), and the resort was also ranked significantly lower for its physiography and climate (mean = 3.33, $p <$ .05). The ski areas of Banff score significantly lower for the destination policy, planning and development components. This could be explained by the fact that the survey asked respondents to group the three ski areas in Banff National Park as one. But, between them, Lake Louise, Sunshine and Mount Norquay obviously do not possess a clear positioning strategy, a shared vision or a system for monitoring and evaluation. In particular, the Banff score for system definition is significantly lower than that for any other resort (mean = 2.54, $p <$ .005), which should be of concern to policy-makers in the region.

The ranking of Sun Peaks, Silver Star and Big White below the top three Intrawest resorts perhaps reflects the heavy investments all these resorts have made in recent years. Sun Peaks is located 40 minutes north east of Kamloops, and aims to be second to Whistler for ski-able terrain in the next few years, with the recent addition of Mt Morrisey, the area's third ski-in, ski-out mountain. Sun Peaks was ranked higher than other resorts for its resource stewardship (mean = 5.13) and financial management (mean = 5.50). The resort also received high ratings for quality of service (mean = 5.38) and hospitality (mean = 5.63). Silver Star came under the ownership of neighboring Big White in 2001 and a recent CDN$74 million upgrade is described as the largest single season resort expansion ever undertaken in the BC interior. The development budget includes new and repositioned ski lifts, new on-hill condominiums, several high-end subdivisions, a youth hostel and a new Summit restaurant. At complete build-out, the plan would see a doubling of Silver Star's existing bed base from the current 4,200 beds to approximately 8,000 beds. Silver Star was ranked relatively highly for its marketing (mean = 5.36), hospitality (mean = 5.33) and accessibility (5.16). This accessibility has recently improved with the introduction of a daily non-stop service between Toronto and Kelowna airport, which serves the ski resorts of Silver Star and Big White. The new flights will mean easier access to these resorts for British skiers, who account for roughly 40 per cent of overseas ski travel expenditures in Canada.

Big White, ranked sixth in overall competitiveness with a score of 228, is only 50 minutes from Kelowna airport, and is currently the second largest resort in BC with over 100 runs. In the spring of 2000, the resort announced it would invest $35 million into an expansion called 'Happy Valley', a new village cut into the mountain below Big White's existing development. Later in the year, another $10 million was added to the budget for Trapper's Crossing, 42 town homes in the heart of the old village. These new developments will increase Big White's bed base to 11,000. It is pertinent that the only component on which Big White, recognized for its 'smart marketing overseas' (Knowles, 2000, p. 3), scored significantly higher in the survey than many other resorts was marketing (mean = 5.56, $p < .005$). According to respondents, the ski area could improve considerably on the entertainment that is offered in the resort (mean = 2.88, $p < .005$).

Other important findings include the fact that Jasper, ranked twelfth overall, is perceived as significantly less safe and secure than many other resorts (mean = 2.92, $p < .005$), less accessible (mean = 3.14, $p < .005$), and its image too is seen as significantly weaker than its competitors (mean 3.28, $p < .005$). This may explain why Jasper has just undergone a re-imaging strategy. Kicking Horse, in Golden, despite receiving a significantly higher score for physiography and climate (mean = 5.29, $p < .05$), scored significantly lower than other resorts for interdependencies (mean = 2.43, $p < .005$). Stakeholders obviously felt that the resort was too dependent on the success of other destinations, as many skiers visit the resort en route to or from other ski areas. A proposed extended runway at Cranbrook airport may improve this situation, as it will allow the arrival of international charters. At the moment, overseas skiers have to travel over four hours from the Calgary airport. Improved accessibility would also improve the competitiveness of Panorama, which received the lowest score for location (mean = 3.37). The Intrawest-owned resort, ranked seventh overall in the survey, also had low scores for entertainment (mean = 3.25) and facilitating resources (mean = 3.75), but received relatively high scores for its clear vision (mean = 5.00) and its effective marketing (mean = 5.18).

Conclusions

As mentioned previously, due to time and cost limitations, the focus of the research was limited to just 13 ski areas, mainly in Western Canada. Therefore, the results do not reveal the relative competitiveness of all ski areas in Canada. In addition, the input from a larger sample of stakeholders would have been desirable, but finding 'resort experts' proved to be problematic. Ski resorts in Western Canada are relatively small, and thus do not have a large number of managers. In addition, many others were hesitant to consider themselves as experts. However, it should be emphasized that this was an exploratory study carried out to illustrate the potential utility of the model, and the methodology employed, and can be expected to provide only an indicative picture of the market situation.

Another limitation lies in the fact that consumer inputs were not used to measure competitiveness. It could be argued that certain components of the model, like quality of service, accessibility, entertainment and hospitality, should be measured by direct consumer surveys, rather than indirect measures. Future studies could therefore incorporate a consumer survey for various components of the model. Satisfaction ratings could be obtained for factors previously identified as important for skiers (Carmichael, 1996; Hudson and Shephard, 1998).

Despite the limitations, the results do show that the opinions of a relatively small sample of key 'stakeholders' are nevertheless useful for indicative purposes. Stakeholder responses seem to reflect the true market situation, as emphasized when applying the five core dimensions of the model to Whistler. The competitiveness model used in this survey clearly offers winter sports destinations a mechanism for analyzing, diagnosing, planning and communicating its competitive strategies. It has provided valuable information to the resorts surveyed in finding an optimal match between the resources and capabilities available within the destination (strengths and weaknesses) and the environmental changes (opportunities and threats).

From a planning perspective, the application of this model of destination competitiveness has highlighted the importance of policy, planning and development for destinations. An attractive, well-functioning and highly competitive destination does not exist by chance. It requires a well-planned environment within which the appropriate forms of tourism development are encouraged and facilitated. It is no coincidence that the three resorts ranked most highly in this study are owned by Intrawest, a company that takes planning extremely seriously. Intrawest creates a master plan through the envisioning process, involving stakeholders at the community level in the planning and decision process, hiring local experts where possible. The result is a collection of real estate, recreational opportunities, retail spaces and entertainment venues that blend in with the overall master plan. Although the act of planning provides no guarantee that a destination will succeed, it does improve its chances, and Kotler *et al.* (1993) have suggested that the strategic planning process, which has been used by business organizations for many years, provides several advantages to tourism destinations. The conceptual model used in this study is likely to undergo further refinement and adaptation as destination competitiveness research continues. It is hoped that this particular study will contribute to this process In future research, the model need not be applied just to winter sports destinations. It could be applied to any resort or, indeed, any destination, be it a country, region, city or island. For a number of years, the competitiveness of national economies has been measured and reported in a World Competitiveness Report (IMD, 2003). Perhaps it is time to rank tourist destinations in a similar fashion.

References

Anon. (2002) Utah's bad news and good news, *Ski Area Management*, available from: http://www.saminfo.com/news.htm (accessed 25 March).

Bordas, E. (1994) Competitiveness of tourist destinations in long distance markets. *Revue de Tourisme*, 3(3), pp. 3–9.

Canadian Ski Council (2003) *Canadian Ski & Snowboard Industry Pacts & Stats*, October.

Carmichael, B. (1996) Conjoint analysis of downhill skiers used to improve data collection for market segmentation. *Journal of Travel and Tourism Marketing*, 5(3), pp. 187–206.

Chon, K.S. and Mayer, K.J. (1995) Destination competitiveness models in tourism and their application to Las Vegas. *Journal of Tourism Systems and Quality Management*, 1(2–4), pp. 227–46.

Crouch, G.I. and Ritchie, B.J.R. (1999) Tourism, competitiveness, and societal prosperity. *Journal of Business Research*, 44(3), pp. 137–52.

d'Hauteserre, A. (2000) Lessons in managed destination competitiveness: the case of Foxwoods Casino Resort. *Tourism Management*, 21(1), pp. 23–32.

Evans, M.R., Fox, J.B. and Johnson, R.B. (1995) Identifying competitive strategies for successful tourism destination development. *Journal of Hospitality & Leisure Marketing*, 3(1), pp. 37–45.

Faulkner, B., Opperman, M. and Fredline, E. (1999) Destination competitiveness: An exploratory examination of South Australia's core attractions. *Journal of Vacation Marketing*, 5(2), pp. 125–39.

Flagestad, A. and Hope, C.A. (2001) Strategic success in winter sports destination: A sustainable value creation perspective. *Tourism Management*, 22(5), pp. 445–61.

Goeldner, C.R. and Ritchie, J.R.B. (2003) *Tourism: Principles, Practices, Philosophies* (New York: Wiley).

Go, F. and Pine, R. (1995) *Globalization Strategy in the Hotel Industry* (London: Routledge).

Hassan, S.S. (2000) Determinants of market competitiveness in an environmentally sustainable tourism industry. *Journal of Travel Research*, 38(3), pp. 239–45.

Hudson, S. (2000) *Snow Business: A Study of the International Ski Industry* (London: The Continuum International Publishing Group).

Hudson, S. (2003) Winter sport tourism, in: S. Hudson (Ed.) *Sport and Adventure Tourism*, pp. 89–123 (Binghampton, NY: The Haworth Press).

Hudson, S. and Shephard, G.W. (1998) Measuring service quality at tourist destinations: An application of importance-performance analysis to an Alpine ski resort. *Journal of Travel & Tourism Marketing*, 7(3), pp. 61–77.

IMD (1994) *The World Competitiveness Yearbook: Executive Summary* (Lausanne: International Institute for Management Development).

IMD (2003) *The World Competitiveness Yearbook* (Lausanne: International Institute for Management Development).

Knowles, L. (2000) Best of times, worst of times for the ski industry. *Communique*, 4(19), pp. 1–3.

Kotler, P., Haider, D.H. and Rein, I. (1993) *Marketing Places: Attracting Investment, Industry, and Tourism to Cities, States, and Nations* (New York: The Free Press).

Kozak, M. and Rimmington, M. (1999) Measuring tourist destination competitiveness: Conceptual considerations and empirical findings. *Hospitality Management*, 18(3), pp. 273–83.

Mintzberg, H. and Quinn, J.B. (1991) *The Strategy Process: Concepts, Contexts, Cases*, 2nd edn (Englewood Cliffs, NJ: Prentice Hall).

Montanari, J.R., Morgan, C.P. and Bracket, J.S. (1990) *Strategic Management: A Choice Approach* (Chicago, IL: The Dryden Press).

National Ski Areas Association (2001) *Media Center*, available at: http://www.nsaa.org/media (accessed 31 October).

Olsen, M., West, J. and Tse, E.C. (1998) *Strategic Management in the Hospitality Industry* (New York: Wiley).

Pearce, D.G. (1997) Competitive destination analysis in Southeast Asia. *Journal of Travel Research*, 35(4), pp. 16–24.

Pitts, R.A. and Lei, D. (1996) *Strategic Management: Building and Sustaining Competitive Advantage* (New York: West Publishing).

Porter, M.E. (1980) *Competitive Strategy: Techniques for Analyzing Industries and Competitors* (New York: The Free Press).

Porter, M.E. (1990) *The Competitive Advantage of Nations* (New York: The Free Press).

Quinn, J.B., Mintzberg, H. and James, R.M. (1988) *The Strategy Process: Concepts, Contexts and Cases* (Englewood Cliffs, NJ: Prentice Hall).

Ritchie, J.R.B. and Crouch, G.I. (2000) The competitive destination: A sustainability perspective. *Tourism Management*, 21(1), pp. 1–7.

Ritchie, J.R.B. and Crouch, G.I. (2003) *The Competitive Destination: A Sustainable Tourism Perspective* (Wallingford: CAB International).

Ritchie, J.R.B., Crouch, G.I. and Hudson, S. (2000) Assessing the role of consumers in the measurement of destination competitiveness and sustainability. *Tourism Analysis*, 5(2–4), pp. 69–76.

Ski Magazine (2000) The top 60. *Ski Magazine*, October, p. 198.

Stueck, W. (2001) Intrawest seen on the upslope. *Globe and Mail*, Toronto, November, p. B22.

Chapter 29

Peter Williams and Paul R. Fidgeon

ADDRESSING PARTICIPATION CONSTRAINT
A case study of potential skiers

1   Introduction

CANADA'S SKI INDUSTRY has been facing flattening market demand and declining revenues and profitability since the early 1990s. In order to arrest this decline it will be necessary for the industry to develop new markets and establish a range of product development strategies in order to attract new people into the sport. Here a fundamental requirement will be to tap the potential of the non-skier.

Although skiing has many positive dimensions for non-skiers, perceived and real problems are significant enough to keep many potential skiers off the slopes and trails. These barriers must be identified and addressed by the ski industry and its partners before many non-participatory groups will pursue skiing.

This paper takes the premise that understanding constraints on the demand for skiing is vital to the tourism industry. By understanding and building demand, everyone in the tourism industry benefits – travel agents, wholesalers, carriers and resort operators. This paper, based on Canadian research, seeks not only to examine constraints on ski partici-pation, but offers an industry based perspective identifying which non-participatory target markets might be the focus for any marketing strategy. It will advocate a range of selective marketing activities that might be directed at specific non-skier market segments and advance various priorities for action. Programmes that could (and should) be established by the Canadian ski tourism industry to arrest problems of demand and declining tourist revenues will be highlighted.

2   The relationship between sport, tourism and skiing

Traditionally the two literatures, viz. sport and tourism, have tended to be quite distinct. Each has claimed its own ideas, concepts and abstract theories. The result has been that integration between the two subject disciplines has remained the exception rather than the rule – witness separate tourism and recreation departments in many British and North American universities.

To deny that there is no link between sport and tourism is untenable. Sport can be a powerful motivator for leisure travel, whether to participate in an activity or to watch an event (Yiannakis, 1986; Gibson, 1998; Glyptis, 1991, Standeven, 1996; Kurtzman & Zaukar, 1999). Sports participation can also provide meaning and purpose to the 'travel experience' (Coltman, 1989, McPherson, 1989; Gibson, 1988). Many tour wholesalers report using levels of interest in sports related inclusive tours (James, 1995; Wilson, 1997) the latter linked to demands for more active leisure lifestyles (Long, 1998). Sport can act as a stimulus for resort development (Ahn, 1987; Ferris, 1992; Barkholz, 1997, Spivack, 1997) resort investment (Swarbrooke, 1995; Seghers, 1995) and resort regeneration (Castle, 1995, 1996). Elsewhere the physical legacies of major sporting events can act as major tourist attractions as illustrated by Munich's Olympic Village and Canada Olympic Park, Calgary, Alberta (Ritchie, 1991).

Against this backdrop has come sport tourism as a recognised subset of tourism as an academic field of study (Delphy, 1998; Standeven, 1996; Gibson 1998).

Hall (1992) defines sport tourism as:

> Travel for non commercial reasons, to participate or observe sporting activities away from the home range.
>
> (p.147)

Growing reference to sport tourism within academic circles has accompanied forecasts of a trend towards more active holidays (Smith & Jenner, 1990). Standeven (1996) notes that rapid growth in this sector of the holiday industry is evident in three related components of sports tourism, namely participants, sports and destinations.

In the case of the former, the English Tourist Board suggested that holidays mainly for the purpose of activity accounted for around 12 per cent of all holiday trips in 1991 (English Tourist Board, 1992). More recently, research by Mintel identified the sports sector was responsible for 22 per cent of total UK domestic holidays (Mintel, 1995). Similar percentages emerge from elsewhere in Europe (Usher, 1996) and North America (Standeven, 1996). Research suggests the number of sports featured in tourist related activities is also increasing. The 1997 Sports Market Place Directory published in the USA lists over 130 different sports that can be experienced in tourist settings (*Sports Market Place Directory*, 1997). As participants and sports activities increase, so do the destinations in which to experience them. Here improvements in transportation and accessibility, reductions in the cost of travel; and heightened market awareness of tourism opportunities can all be cited (amongst others) to account for this relationship. Signs of increasing collaboration between sport and tourist destinations is given further credence by the identification of 200 city or regional sports commissions in the United States housed within local Convention and Visitor Bureaux (Standeven 1996).

It is, nevertheless, important to get the significance of sports tourism into context. Sports tourism, while a growing sector of the vacation market, remains a minority interest. However, in realising the potential of sports tourism, of which skiing is an integral part, the tourism industry is going some way to fulfil a wider variety of human wants and needs than ever before (Delphy, 1998).

Downhill skiing, as a sports activity, has consistently illustrated its ability to be an important travel motivator. In Great Britain, for example, over seven million people report having participated in the fun, excitement, challenge and exhilaration of a skiing holiday sometime in their lives (Richards, 1996). In North America the sociability of the sport and the opportunity it affords to explore 'the great outdoors' are cited as being some of the most important reasons why 10.6 million Americans generated about 53.5 million visits to skiing destinations during the 1997–1998 winter season (Rowan, 1998).

Research into skiing as a sport has concentrated on training methods (Gohner, 1996; Giar, 1996); proposals for developing elite athletes (Bennett et al., 1997) and the development of goals and organisational structures of national ski federations (National Ski Areas Association, 1997).

In contrast, tourism research has focused on:

- The historical origins of winter sports tourism in individual countries (Sarlin, 1995).
- The demographics (Edmonson, 1996; National Demographics and Lifestyles Inc, 1996; Snow Sports Industries America, 1996); travel patterns (National Sporting Goods Association, 1995); economic expenditure and trip planning of ski tourists (Leisure Trends Group, 1993).
- Ski resort development (Quirk & Hartmann, 1995; Castle 1996); planning (Berbin, 1995; Gachelin-Ribault, 1996); financing (Heck, 1997; Audet & Archambault 1997); and dimensions of resort attractiveness (Cairmichael, 1996).
- Ski resort management, broaching the development of competitive market strategies (Dorward & Moreau, 1997); resort marketing (Spring, 1995; Dillman 1995), establishing service quality (Pech & Vuhn, 1997); resort profitability (Audet & Archambault, 1997) and legal controls on the management of ski resorts (Servoin, 1997).
- Trends in ski resort development incorporating resort regeneration, investment in retailing and the product service mix (Castle, 1995; Best, 1997).
- Ski resorts as a tool or instrument for regional economic investment and development (Barbuer, 1978; Knafon, 1979; Guérin. 1984, Christopoulou & Papastavrou, 1997).
- Ski tourism and product development (Williams, Dossa & Fulton, 1994).
- International skier demand (Quirk & Hartrnann, 1995).
- Analyses of the environmental issues posed by ski tourism, including proposals governing the implementation of environmental management systems in ski areas. (Karameris, 1995; Morrison et al., 1995; Reis 1996; Williams & Todd, 1997; Goodspeed, 1997).

Despite extensive, albeit disparate, research in ski tourism research has tended to ignore the emotional and perceptual biases that inhibit the desire to participate in this particular aspect of tourism. Literature on non-participation is limited and somewhat dated; rooted in other areas of sports tourism and geographically specific to the United States (viz. Boothby, Tungatt & Townsend, 1981; Bialeschki & Henderson, 1998; Backman & Crompton, 1990, Dunn, 1990). Published research associated with commencing, maintaining and increasing involvement in skiing has been similarly legion (Stynes, Mahoney & Sports, 1990; Searle & Jackson, 1985, Jackson & Dunn, 1988; Ruston, Tomany and Associates, 1990).

3   The Canadian ski industry – an industry in transition

Canada's alpine skiers have represented a significant growth market for almost four decades. This has been made possible through the continual infusion of improvements to ski equipment, hill grooming, clothing, instruction, on-site food and beverage services and accommodation facilities. As a result more than a fifth of the population reportedly skied in the decade 1981–91 (Williams & Dossa, 1994) rising to a third in some local areas (Print Measurement Bureau, 1992).

Compared to the United States, where less than 6 per cent of the population ski, Canada is a nation of skiers. About 20 per cent of Canadian households owned alpine skis in 1992; the market accommodated about 1,943,000 skiers and was growing at about 1.3 per cent/annum (Williams & Dossa, 1994). Further enhancing Canada's potential as a ski nation is the fact that most Canadians live in close proximity to existing ski areas, making it feasible for them to experience skiing without much pre-planning.

Despite past levels of success, ski demand has failed to grow in the previous five years at a pace comparable with other time periods. This trend was originally noted (during the 1992/1993 ski season when a 21.9 million domestic skier visits represented a marginal 31,000 increase over levels attained in 1991/1992. Subsequent drops in skier attendance at ski areas, diminishing levels of growth in the household ownership of skis, decreased retail sales associated with ski clothing and declines in ski equipment import levels all suggest a concern for the ski industry's ability to retain existing and increase future ski markets in Canada (Williams et al., 1994). Reductions in consumer spending associated with a 'slowing down' of the Canadian economy rising levels of unemployment, especially in Western Canada; and a falling Canadian dollar inflating the price of imported equipment, further add to the problems of addressing the issue of nonparticipation in the Canadian ski industry.

4   The industry response

In response to a perceived flattening in demand, ski industry organisations have recognised the need for new product development and creative marketing initiatives. These activities are required to increase visitation levels among existing skiers and encourage non-skiers to participate (Canadian Ski Council, 1988).

Past research to support such marketing and product development programmes has focused primarily on gaining a better understanding of the socio-economic, attitudinal and behaviour characteristics of existing skiers (Ruston/Tomany and Associates, 1990). In most cases, this research has emphasised the identification of distinct market segments. These market sub groups have been based on such differentiating factors as visitor skiing capability expenditure, skiing frequency, location and ski experience satisfaction levels (Williams & Dossa, 1994). The underlying research objective typically has been to provide relevant information for marketing and product program decisions. Actions emanating from these decisions have been aimed at retaining existing skiers at current or increased levels of activity.

Parallel research concerning skiing's latest demand markets has been less evident. However as concerns for a flattened ski market demand have surfaced, so has interest in identifying potential markets that may be predisposed to skiing (Williams & Basford, 1992). Research that has been conducted has centred on lapsed skiers (i.e. those that have skied in the past but currently do not participate) and population groups who have never skied but express an interest in trying the activity in the future (Stynes & Mahoney, 1980). These studies have provided valuable insights concerning skiing's unique physical, social, economic and psychological constraints (Ruston/Tomany and Associates, 1990). However, for the most part they have failed to address the constraints associated with distinct subgroups of the non skier population or the relative significance of the impediments to these segments. As with other recreationalists it is often the relative strength of these barriers that triggers decisions concerning the eventual degree of participation (Kay & Jackson, 1991). In a Canadian ski context, managers require a more thorough understanding of the obstacles to be surmounted by non-skiers before they can effectively remove these constraints to participation.

5   Understanding constraint

Several theoretical frameworks exist for guiding research concerning those impediments confronting various population groups wishing to pursue leisure and tourism activities (McGuire, Dottavio & O'Leary, 1986). These constraint frameworks have primarily focused on two thematic areas of investigation: activity specific participation barriers, and the impediments facing particular segments of the population.

Activity research has centred on identifying the constraints associated with commencing, maintaining and increasing involvement in particular pursuits (Backman, 1991). It has also examined the reasons for dropping out of certain activities (Boothby et al., 1981). Specific activities examined in this regard include hiking (Bialeschki & Henderson, 1998); golfing (Backman & Crompton, 1990); cardplaying (Scott, 1991); camping (Backman & Crompton, 1990); tennis (Dunn, 1990); and skiing (Stynes, Mahoney & Spotts, 1980).

Research concerning participation constraints confronting specific population groups has focused on a wide variety of leisure market segments. These target groups include females (Henderson & Bialeschki, 1991); adolescents (Hultsman, 1990); disabled persons (Farber & Ellis, 1986); and the elderly (McGuire, 1982).

The many common findings emanating from these past initiatives has compelled some investigators to push research initiatives into more generic categories based on constraints facing participants as compared to non-participants. In this regard, research has been conducted on the barriers to more frequent participation facing current participants (e.g. Shaw, Bonen & McCabe, 1991). Similarly, other studies have examined the constraints facing non-participants based on their expressed predisposition toward future participation in skiing (Searle & Jackson, 1985) and previous experience with a specific activity (Jackson & Dunn, 1988). The findings suggest that the extent of previous involvement in an activity and the presence or absence of interest in participation provide useful constraint research foci (Wright & Goodale, 1991). The findings presented in this paper identify many of the constraints challenging the ski industry's interested non-participants. It not only details their overriding constraints but also clarifies the ways in which non-participants feel these impediments might be overcome.

6   Research method

To gain a fuller appreciation of skiing's latent demand, the research programme involved four complementary and sequential phases. Initially, a review of existing leisure constraint and skiing behaviour research literature provided the foundation for the overall study design and survey instrument content.

In the second phase, refinements to the issues to be examined in the survey instrument were facilitated through six focus group sessions that were held with 'interested' non-skiers. Selection of the members for these focus groups was based on their socio-demographic status and extent of previous involvement with skiing. Essentially, they were individuals who did not ski currently, but who matched typical skier profiles as reported in previous market studies. A pool of potential participants for the focus groups were identified by ski industry personnel in Canada's largest ski markets. From this pool, six groups of interviewees were selected. Each group session involved seven participants who represented distinct sub-groups of the "non-skiing" but "interested" population. For instance, younger female non-skiers who had never skied before formed one focus group, while older male non-skiers who had skied in the past attended another of these sessions. The focus group sessions were conducted in Montreal (1 session), Toronto (2 sessions), Calgary (1 session) and Vancouver (2 sessions). The insights provided by these focus group participants were invaluable to focusing the quantitative research that followed.

The third phase of the research involved conducting a household telephone survey of qualified non-skiers from Alberta. This province was chosen as the study area for two pragmatic reasons. Firstly, the Alberta government was particularly interested in enhancing its tourism performance through the retention and expansion of its ski markets. Secondly, the province's ski industry was prepared to partner with the government in financing the research needed to enhance its ability to reach domestic latent demand skiers. Eligible respondents were designated as being those persons over 17 yr of age who had never skied or who had not skied in the 2 yr preceding the study. These selection criteria closely paralleled guidelines identified by previous researchers concerned with leisure constraint in general (Wright & Goodale, 1991), and skiing in particular (Stynes *et al.*, 1980). The telephone survey sample was randomly generated with quotas designed to reflect the population proportions across the province of Alberta (Marktrend, 1990). In total, 1,400 completed interviews were conducted with qualified respondents during March of 1990.

Data analysis involved two distinct phases. Initially non-skiers were segmented according to more traditional skier socio-demographic, behavioural, and attitudinal characteristics (Mills, Couturier & Snepenger, 1986). This phase provided generic item-by-item insights into the key impediments to ski participation by non-skiers. However, in order to gain more specific insights into the constraints confronting more specific sub segments of the non-skier population, a cluster analysis was employed (Green, Tull & Albaum 1988) it followed analytical procedures suggested by Mazenec (1984). This approach was used to identify groups of respondents who were relatively homogeneous with respect to their socio-economic behavioural and attitudinal traits, and as hetero-geneous as possible from other clusters of respondents (Witt & Moutinho, 1994). This form of cluster analysis had also been used effectively in previous research concerning active skiers (Stynes & Mahoney, 1980). Non-skier responses concerning skiing's perceived cost, difficulty, dangers, rewards, and social benefits formed the basis for the cluster analysis. The analysis generated six non-skier clusters with varying degrees of interest in pursuing skiing in the future. Based on their relative affinity for skiing, those two cluster groups expressing the greatest interest in pursuing skiing were selected for further investigation (Table 29.3).

The final phase of the research entailed conducting four follow-up focus group sessions with panels of nonskiers (7 per group) who mirrored the traits of the two preceding non-skier clusters. These four group sessions were conducted with members randomly selected from each of these two clusters. Two sessions were conducted for each of the clusters. These focus groups were conducted in Alberta's largest skier market – Calgary. Facilitated by a moderator who was familiar with the findings derived from the preceding Alberta telephone survey, the purpose of these sessions was to solicit ways of overcoming the previously identified constraints to skiing. Excessive cost and time constraints prohibited the researchers from conducting further focus group or survey-based research in other Canadian market areas. However, the responses received in the focus groups highlighted many useful approaches to converting latent demand skiers into active participants.

7   Images and perceptions of skiing

Historically, skiing in Canada has been presented to the public as a 'fun' physical activity. The 'fun' aspect of skiing is thought to be derived from sharing the experience with family and friends, reliving embarrassing mistakes with companions; participating in after-ski activity, achieving improvement in skiing technique and the exhilaration of being outside in a mountain environment (Marktrend Marketing Research Inc., 1990). However, other positive imagery components are also involved. For some, skiing is an opportunity to show off their ski skill. For others skiing provides an entrée to a somewhat elite successful group of individuals. Perhaps for the majority, skiing provides a getaway – a chance to forget city life – their jobs, problems and other mundane concerns and enjoy a fast, exciting, pleasurable and perhaps somewhat romantic break from their normal routine (Fidgeon, 1995).

Among non-skiers such positive imagery components are often replaced by negative perceptions of skiing being a costly and dangerous activity, in both the qualitative and quantitative phases of this study, skiing conjured up images of injury, pain, accidents and risk. Respondents were afraid that if they were to ski, personal injury would probably result. Their fear related to several dimensions of the ski experience including its location (e.g. on steep and high mountain slopes), learning to ski (e.g. poor instruction leading to injury), manoeuvring on the slopes (e.g. going too fast, out of control) and using the lift facilities (e.g. mounting and dismounting from the lifts, falling off ski lifts of great heights). Such perceptions of skiing's dangers were derived from the experiences of friends, relatives, associates and media communications. For many non-skiers, their overall impression was that skiing was perceived as a treacherous activity not to be attempted without considerable preparation and thought (see Table 29.1).

Skiing was also perceived as an expensive and trend-conscious pursuit among many non-skiers. Cost barriers were associated with the acquisition of the necessary clothing and equipment as well as participation elements, such as lift tickets, transportation and accommodation. The perceived fashion requirements of skiing were regarded as stimulants

Table 29.1 Non-skier perceptions of skiing

	Mean level of agreement[a]
Skiing is very physically demanding	4.68
A very fast sport	3.52
Afraid of being out of control	3.59
Ski hills are very steep	4.68
Chances of serious injury are much less than five years ago	3.41
Skiers take more risks than non-skiers	3.30
Harder to learn than other ports	3.27
Ski lifts are scary	3.08

a Rated on a six-point scale: 1 = strong disagree, 6 = strongly agree.

to on-going, and prohibitive, expenditures on clothing and equipment. Other respondents claimed that other non-fiscal costs such as the perceived time, organisation and effort required to participate, kept them from making skiing a priority in their leisure life styles (Table 29.2).

In addition to skiing being perceived as an expensive physically demanding and a hard sport to learn, non-skiers also commented on the logistics of arranging a ski trip: the need for ski trips to be more effectively 'packaged' and mediocre oil-site facilities.

Even if the non-skier had previously participated in the sport (albeit briefly) making the arrangements for a trip can prove problematic. Uncertainty over equipment rental (source and cost), the choice quality and cost of accommodation (where necessary) enrolling in ski school and travelling to, from and around the mountain can breed discomfort and unease (Mean Level of Agreement 2.6). Taken to an extreme, even the most simple of ski trips can be perceived as an expedition.

A major conclusion drawn from the study of Canada's non-skier population was that the barriers to participation in skiing are both real and perceived. To entice skiers these barriers must be removed or at least lowered. In no case is this more apparent than in the need for the packaging of ski services. A perceived need for packages to include transportation, accommodation, lift tickets, equipment rental, ski instruction and after

Table 29.2 Skiing's perceived cost constraints

	Mean level of agreement[a]
Proper equipment and clothing are necessary for a more enjoyable experience	5.04
Equipment is too expensive	4.73
Need easy inexpensive transportation	4.56
Skiing would take up too much time	3.21
Low cost, all inclusive beginners, packages are needed	3.00
Many take up skiing because it is glamorous, trendy	2.90

a Rated on a six-point scale: 1 = strong disagree, 6 = strongly agree.

ski activities on the hill could serve to remove most non-skiers fears regarding preparation and safety, equipment, costs, trip organisation and embarrassment. As the level of comfort rises to an acceptable point, the major decisions regarding participating are reduced to one overall criterion: price.

The repulsion effects on the non-skier of short runs, marginal conditions and utilitarian ski facilities cannot be underestimated. Few non-skiers reported their local ski hills in vibrant aggressive terms seeing them as hang-outs for younger teenagers and ski "diehards". When combined with some of the more negative aspects of mountain skiing imagery (previously discussed) it is not surprising that respondent's perceptions of skiing as a recreational activity were passive and mediocre, at best.

8   Addressing the problem of non-participation

Addressing the problem of non participation does not require significant increases in the resources allocated to ski marketing, rather it calls for selective marketing activities targeted at specific non-skier market segments. Priorities for action and specific programmes associated with these priorities should be established by the ski industry and its partners. The Canadian Ski Council in general, and individual ski area operators, in particular. have significant roles to play in this regard.

Six distinctive non-participant groups emerged from the cluster analysis conducted in this research (Table 29.3). Two of these groups – the Young Family and Social Adventurer – exhibited considerable potential for conversion to skiing. About 68 and 47 per cent of these groups, respectively, indicated that they would be interested in pursuing skiing sometime in the 5 yr following their interviews. They were the only segments which had skiing interest levels above the 31 percent standard expressed by the entire sample of respondents (Table 29.3). Consequently, these two groups became the focus for further investigation.

The young family cluster (293 respondents) was largely made up of individuals between 18–34 yr of age. A sizeable number (63 per cent) had skied previously and/or knew of others who had skied. They currently did not ski because of familial responsibilities, skiing's costs and travel barriers. They represented about 21 per cent of the non-skier market surveyed.

When compared with other non-skier groups those labelled as Social Adventurers (204 respondents) were also favourably disposed toward skiing participation. They represented approximately 15 per cent of the non-skier market studied. As a group their incomes and representation in professional/managerial occupations were lower than that associated with other non-skier clusters. Only a third had previous downhill skiing experience.

For the most part, both young family and social adventurer clusters exhibited similar positive images concerning skiing (Table 29.4). Skiing was described as fun but a little frightening. Their image of skiing was built around the notions that skiing was an outdoor escape in the mountains; a sociable activity; something that could be shared and relived with friends and family; an escape from urban, work and mundane environments; and associated with a somewhat elite and successful group.

These positive images were not sufficiently dominant to overcome the perceived personal commitments of time, money and personal readiness required for skiing. Indeed

Table 29.3 Socio-economic distribution of non-skier clusters

	Overall (%)	Social adventurer (%)	Young family (%)	Rural sedentary (%)	Upwardly mobile (%)	Fearful elder (%)	Disinterested (%)
Market share	100	15	21	12	18	17	17
Previous skiing experience	44	13	63	17	54	14	47
Skiing likelihood							
Next year	8	13	18	1	5	1	6
Next 2 yr	9	16	22	1	4	0	8
Next 3–5 yr	14	18	28	2	9	4	13
Overall likelihood	31	47	68	4	18	5	27
Gender							
Male	50	50	52	27	73	33	59
Female	50	50	48	73	27	27	41
Age (in yr)							
Under 35	37	40	56	18	39	24	36
Over 35	63	60	44	82	61	76	64
Education							
Secondary or less	45	55	43	59	35	48	40
Post-secondary	55	45	57	41	65	52	60
Occupation							
Professional/managerial	22	16	17	10	29	17	30
Skilled technical	34	39	38	21	37	30	38
Income (annually)							
Under $35,000	42	53	44	50	43	51	43
Over $35,000	58	32	46	50	57	49	57
Marital status							
Married	73	65	70	72	75	79	74
Other	27	35	30	28	25	21	26
Base n	1,391	204	293	171	246	236	241

Table 29.4 Perceived skiing constraints and images amongst overall social adventurer and young family clusters

	Overall average scored[a]	Social adventurer average score	Young family average score
Danger/fear			
Skiing seems like a very fast sport	4.5	5.0	4.3
For someone who knows how, skiing is not dangerous	4.1	4.0	4.7
Afraid of being out of control	3.6	4.8	2.3
Ski hills are very steep	3.5	4.2	3.0
Skiers take more risks than non-skiers	3.3	4.3	2.9
Chances of serious injury are much less than 5 yr ago	3.4	3.7	3.6
Ski lifts are scary	3.1	3.7	2.3
Cost constraints			
Cost of equipment	4.7	5.1	4.8
Important to have easy inexpensive transport to ski area	4 6	5.0	4.8
Skiing would take up too much time	3.2	3.4	2.6
Low-cost, all-inclusive beginner's package would entice me to ski	3.0	5.0	5.2
Many take up skiing because it is glamorous/trendy	2.9	3.6	2.5
Difficulty			
Skiing is physically demanding	4.7	5.0	4.5
Skiing is harder to learn than other sports	3.3	4.3	2.5
Skiing is for younger people	2.8	3.1	2.0
Not sure how to learn to ski	2.7	4.1	2.0
Not enough information how to ski	2.6	3.9	2.4
Beginners look silly, I would feel embarrassed in front of friends	2.2	3.4	1.5

a 1.0 = strongly disagree, 6.0 = strongly agree.

for both groups, an all-inclusive 'hassle free' low-cost ski experience package was deemed necessary to entice them to ski. Necessary elements of this package were thought to include transportation, accommodation, equipment, ski lift and lesson services. Opportunities for socialising and togetherness were also deemed important.

Clearly any marketing strategy aimed at attracting new or 'lapsed' skiers into the sport should be designed to accentuate the positive dimensions of skiing, diffuse the negative images that are perceived to be associated with the product; and increase awareness of the diversity and number of accessible and user friendly ski aims particularly for current non-skier young family and social adventurer ski markets.

The Canadian ski industry currently does not sufficiently aggressively market a ski product particularly targeted at the high potential non-skier market. The ambitious ski development programme launched by the Canadian Ski Council in 1991 designed to attract 500,000 new and lapsed skiers to the sport of skiing by 1996 and encourage infrequent skiers to ski more often has singularly failed to meet its participation goals (Canadian Ski Council, 1991, 1996). This has been caused by a failure to recognise that first-time skiers do not focus their purchase decisions on the physical aspects of skiing, but rather on a mixture of benefits that the activity can provide. It is a particular mix of on and off slope ski facilities and services that the high potential non-skier is looking to purchase. That product is essentially 'fun' as defined in terms of sharing the experience with friends and/or family; achieving competence in skiing technique; reliving skiing events with companions; getting away from it all in a scenic mountain environment and being hassle free (Mark trend Marketing Research, 1990). It is crucial that the ski industry provides beginners with ski products which reinforce opportunities for fun experiences and dispel negative ideas of skiing.

While the existing ski product clearly has some positive dimensions for non-skiers, perceived and real problems associated with the current ski product are significant enough to keep non-skiers off the ski hills. These 'rough edges' must be tuned before non skiers will consider participating in skiing. Central to such a strategy is overcoming time constraints, cost safety and competency limitations, and breaking down the perceived barriers of elitism and an 'expedition mentality'.

Canada's high potential non-skiers claim to have significant commitments linked to a wide range of job, family and other home-related duties – witnessed by the fact that participation in skiing was thought to take up too much time (see Table 29.4). From a market development point of view, the authors' Albertan research consequently concluded that it is important that the ski industry provides a ski product which includes:

- conveniently scheduled and accessible transportation to and from the ski areas;
- on and off-site ticket purchase outlets, preferably with credit card transaction capabilities;
- high capacity lift systems;
- all-inclusive beginner ski packages which minimise transaction and preparation time;
- reliable information concerning highway traffic and snow conditions;
- on-site service orientated personnel available to guide them through the ski experience in a time efficient manner;
- fast, clean, high-quality food service facilities; and
- streamlined, hassle-free equipment purchase and rental facilities.

Overcoming cost constraints will remain a critical factor in attracting non skiers into the sport. Many high potential non-skiers are convinced that skiing is too expensive. This perception is associated not so much with the cost of the lift ticket, as it is with all the additional 'trappings' that go with the ski experience, for example, the cost of equipment (overall mean level of agreement 4.7) and transportation to the ski hills (mean level of agreement 4.6).

Non-skiers perceive the ski experience to be too expensive without knowing exactly how expensive. The ski industry needs to adjust market perceptions by communicating what actual costs are involved; how these costs can be reduced without negatively influencing the experience; and convincing the potential skier that the value they get for their money is worthwhile. Marketing messages to employ in this regard need to stress how skiing's costs on a daily or hourly basis are very competitive with several leisure time alternatives. The cost of ski equipment acquisition when amortised over its expected lifetime can also be shown to be competitive with other leisure pursuits (ESPN, 1997). Faced with a similar cost structure in the United Kingdom, ski clothing manufacturers have stressed the durability and multi purpose nature of their products, while retailers have noted how top quality rental facilities can provide the opportunity to ski without making a major capital investment (Frost, 1998). When overcoming cost constraints the ski industry has to show that skiing is more than just going up and down a hill or along a trail. Skiing is a complete experience including the trip to and from the area, on-mountain hospitality and exciting and fun events. Until such a time that the industry can show that the sport provides relatively inexpensive group access to some of Canada's most scenic environments and reduce the cost of going skiing, it is always destined to struggle to attract new participants.

If potential skiers are concerned about personal safety – witnessed by the perceived danger of the sport (overall mean level of agreement 4.1), its speed (mean level of agreement 4.5) and the fear of being out of control (mean level of agreement 3.5) – overcoming the fear of injury must be a priority and linked to new ski promotions highlighting the ways in which the ski industry has dramatically reduced the dangers of skiing. Ideally such promotions should emphasise the skills of well-trained instructors familiar with the latest in ski teaching techniques who are capable of teaching new skiers to ski under control very quickly; the friendliness and knowledgeability of ski patrollers; on-site equipment safety testing and maintenance programmes; on-hill signage indicating appropriate skiing capability requirements; snow conditions and hazard locations; and on-going safety conscious hill grooming activities. Such measures should be set alongside communicable technological improvements in ski equipment designed to minimise potential ski injuries, the development of state of the art lift equipment and well trained lift attendants capable of getting new skiers on and off the ski lifts in a relatively easy fashion.

The provision of comprehensive, accurate and cost effective communication is the key. As the Canadian Ski Council was quick to point out (Canadian Ski Council, 1988) skiing is a relatively safe physical activity and on-site skier safety awareness programmes should reflect this fact. It is certainly not all about physical challenge and 'doing battle with the mountain'. The future calls for the de-mystification of skiing and the creation of skiing opportunities which do not just emphasise the 'steep and deep' nature of the sport.

An analysis of skiing constrains revealed that many potential skiers believed that they would be embarrassed if they did not 'ski the right way' (social adventurer average score 3.4). Such individuals were, however, often unaware of what opportunities to learn existed (average score 4.1) or what the actual experience would be like (average score 3.9). These factors necessitate the need for non-skiers to know that instruction in skiing is available to them in ways that are readily accessible from cost, time and location perspectives. Non-skiers need to know that learning to ski programmes are not designed to be embarrassing, but are rather fun-filled and exciting, where everyone finds opportunities to laugh at themselves and lessons are led by well trained and hospitable ski instructors who help to keep beginners out of awkward situations.

The message needs to be communicated that skiing is a sport in which it is not difficult to succeed due to modern energy saving and time efficient techniques. Learning can take place in group situations; its hassle-free being available in packages; and is helpful to beginners who wish to learn to ski better and more safely, sooner than would normally be the case.

Potential skiers are unlikely to venture into the sport of skiing on their own (Williams & Dossa, 1994). In many cases they perceive a significant gap existing between themselves and the lifestyles of their skiing counterparts (overall mean level of agreement 2.9). They need to be guided into skiing by an experienced and committed person, either a friend or a professional who can help introduce them to a formalised and targeted program designed to make skiing a fun and exciting experience to which they can relate. The challenge to the ski industry is to provide that personal link.

Linkage can be through other skiers, ski area staff, retail sales personnel, ski instructors and other knowledgeable people in the ski industry. It is because non-skiers are not going to seek out the information or find that personal link on their own, that the ski industry has to come to the non-skier to make the connection.

Specific opportunities in this regard include encouraging retailers in conjunction with ski areas to hold low-key, informational clinics, extolling the friendliness and fun dimensions of skiing and paying less emphasis on expensive equipment and fashion. In Calgary, Alberta, current initiatives include encouraging the ski press to place more emphasis on beginner and novice ski stories which focus on the socialising and beneficial dimensions of the activity; and encouraging ski area employees through targeted seminars in community halls to focus on polite friendly factual advice for beginner skiers (Fidgeon, 1997).

8.1   Priorities for action

The perceived logistical complexities associated with skiing make it a daunting and anxiety-filled leisure pursuit for many non-skiers (overall mean level of agreement 3.2). In combination these perceptions portray the ski experience as a series of expedition related manoeuvres that are not worth the hassle of pursuing. In order to attract non- and lapsed-skiers into the sport it is critical that the ski industry reduce the reality of these perceived impediments wherever possible.

Here three possible management strategies might go some way to addressing the reservations expressed by Canadian non-skiers in this study.

8.1.1   Off-site hassle reduction

- Providing centralised off-site outlets for day, week and vacation ski packages suited to Young Family and Social Adventurer skiers;
- Assuring that transportation and parking services meet high standards of hospitality and efficiency;
- Providing timely and reliable information to target markets concerning snow conditions and optimum skiing periods.

8.1.2   On-site hassle reduction

- Providing clean, well-maintained, attractive and accessible lodges, bathrooms, parking lots, rental shops;
- Pre-selling lift tickets, ski rental packages, ski lessons wherever possible so as to reduce queuing requirements;
- Facilitating traffic flow in lodges, lift lines, parking lots, rental shops, and food and beverage areas;

- Providing hill hosts/ambassadors to greet beginner skiers, offer directions and answer questions;
- Installing high-quality and well-placed signs and displays to inform beginners of recommended trails;
- Distributing via 'advance mailing' or on-site brochure, words of advice concerning 'the world of skiing for the beginner and how to enjoy it'.

8.1.3. On-slope hassle reduction

- Minimise traffic by non-beginners in areas where beginners frequent;
- Optimise scenic viewing opportunities, snow conditions and grooming for beginner ski groups;
- Assign the most qualified and most friendly instructors to beginners;
- Provide short, low-cost clinics to people who do not want to invest lots of time and money;
- Provide well-marked trails and route guides for beginner skiers at strategic locations on the hill;
- Provide a friendly, social and fun atmosphere for learning.

8.2. Packaging

A report on the potential of the non-skier market in Alberta (Marktrend Marketing Research, 1990) revealed that packaging the beginner ski experience would go a long way towards enticing skiers to local ski hills. Indeed in this research, interviews with nonparticipating target groups that might form the focus of any marketing strategy confirmed that low cost, all-inclusive beginner's packages would go a long way towards motivating these individuals to ski. This was confirmed by the authors' subsequent research (overall mean level of agreement 3.0). Packages of interests to skiers might include ski lift tickets, transportation, accommodation, food and beverage, lessons and equipment rental.

The expected effect of this type of ski packaging is to remove many non-skier fears regarding preparation, safety, equipment cots, trip organisation and learning embarrass-ments. Examples of ski experience packaging options for non-skier markets drawn from Europe include equipment options (covering the rental of all ski equipment) transportation options (including transportation to and from the ski hills) and special interest group packaging (including all inclusive tours for clubs, societies, business organisations, etc.) (Coker, 1998).

8.3 Programming and product development

Non-skiers, when they look at Canada's ski product, see it in terms of 'what's in it for them' or 'what use they can make of it'. The actual activity and its associated facilities are usually only a backdrop of secondary importance to their more primary motivations (Fidgeon, 1995). Ski product programming can help to shape the ski experience in ways to which the non-skier can specifically relate (Gohner, 1996). In a non-participatory context, ski programs might focus on activities which clearly show the non-skier 'what's in it for them'.

Examples of beginner ski product enhancement programs could include: 'Bring a friend for less Program', 'see yourself on skis video program', 'Après-ski social Programs', 'Day care/Ski Camp Programs' (particularly successful in the resorts of the Austrian Tyrol), 'celebrity association programmes' and 'recognition of achievement programmes' (the latter comparable to the French Ski School's gold, silver and bronze medallion awards).

8.4   Pricing

Addressing the problem of price and the effect that pricing constraints have on non-skier participation is more problematic. Monetary expense is one of the foremost reasons for non-skiing in Canada (overall mean level of agreement 5.04). However, it has different dimensions in different ski markets. For young family non-skiers, discretionary income for skiing exists as long as it is accompanied with good value (mean level of agreement 4.8). For a sizeable proportion of social adventurers, the issue is more bottom line (mean level of agreement 5.05). Due to limited discretionary income, the concern for costs is based on the actual capability to pay.

Among both groups cost expectations seem to be associated with the skiing experience: a trip/expedition to the mountains, rather than an adventure to a local ski area. Marketing strategies related to the pricing issue would do well to focus on creating an awareness amongst non-skiers of the range of facilities, services and benefits received for their discretionary dollars and providing price structures for ski packages which reflect the beginners' needs and budget.

In combination these strategies involve designing a beginner ski product which is in line with (or better still, is lower than) the price that they are able to pay. It also involves conveying to non-skiers a sense that they will receive good value for their money. A problem confronting the Canadian ski industry is that its beginner ski product(s) are not clearly positioned in the minds of non-skiers. In an effort to overcome this handicap two-level positioning can be suggested. An introductory or 'feeder' position associated with day-use ski areas might stress their fun, social and value packed introduction to skiing. A second-level statement associated with existing destination/resort ski areas providing a beginner ski product might go on to note the rewards of skiing the scenic experience and the added value' such resorts provide for new skiers.

8.5   Product distribution

Attracting non-skiers into the sport will require the ski industry to question how it distributes its product. Based upon the authors' research in Western Canada it was apparent that non-participatory target markets felt that there was not enough information on how to participate in ski tourism (overall level of agreement 2.6). This was particularly noticeable among members of the Social Adventurer cluster where a score of 3.9 was recorded.

It is therefore possible to conclude that conventional channels of ski production distribution will, in most likelihood, not bring non-skiers to the slopes. Non skiers tend not to frequent ski shows, ski shops, ski facilities or ski events (Williams *et al.*, 1994). It is therefore imperative that the ski industry complements traditional approaches with a strong focus on using the travel trade to get the message out.

In this context, travel trade organisations provide an extra edge in terms of knowing non-skier markets; assembling packages designed for specific travel groups; and arranging additional services and products complementary to the beginner. Ski hills, tour operators, travel clubs, transportation companies and regional tourist organisations can all play a role in distributing the beginner ski product.

8.6 Promotion

To heighten non-skiers awareness of beginner-specific ski products and stimulate purchase decisions, the ski industry might consider mounting a non-skier promotional campaign. This was tried in 1991/1992 by the Canadian Ski Council with a limited degree of success (C.S.C 'Ski it to Believe it' Campaign). A follow-up initiative could possibly focus on a promotional mix of advertising, personal selling, sales promotion, publicity and public relations activities.

Non-skiers could be exposed to advertising which focuses on promoting the positive features of the beginner ski product, viz.: ease of participation safety and control and friendly qualified instructors, in this respect it was clear that the majority of non-participants associated these features with pain (skiing is a physically demanding sport – overall mean level of agreement 4.7), accidents (skiing is a very fast sport 4.5) and risk (skiing takes place on steep hills – 3.5, it is hard to learn – 3.3. and ski lifts are scary – 3.1). All of these factors were particularly apparent among social adventurers where scores of 5.0, 5.0, 4.2, 4.3 and 3.7 were recorded, respectively.

Clearly, any advertising programme needs to build on non-skier attitudes, interests and wants. Here it has been seen that non-skiers want opportunities for socialising with family and friends; they want to escape from everyday life, and they want challenge, safety, fun and exhilaration. Promoting the beginner ski products' distinctive and exciting personality is also vital (Spring, 1995; Dorward, 1997). Images are required that capture the vision of a fresh clean natural mountain environment; powder soft snow and accessible value-packed experiences. Building on the beginner ski product's unique marketing image an advertising campaign might stress people of varying genders, ages and athletic abilities learning to ski and having fun at a reasonable cost. Personal selling of the beginner ski product could be confined to groups, corporations associations, clubs and sectors of the travel trade that might be interested in incorporating skiing into their activities. Many non-skiers have friends and acquaintances who have skied before or who are active skiers. Because most non-skiers like the socialising dimension of skiing, it could be worthwhile to contact current skiers to determine those local organisations and groups with whom they currently associate in order to identify candidates for personal selling.

Given the unique character of the beginner ski product and its current level of unfamiliarity with most travel and tourism influences, the ski industry would be required to undertake a sales promotion campaign to highlight this new ski product. Targeted at high potential intermediary groups, such as high school club executives or Chamber of Commerce officials, sales promotions could be designed to stimulate interest in the beginner ski product and reinforce the image of skiing, as a fun, exhilarating and value-packed activity suited to people of all ages.

Typical promotional activities might include the use of brochures featuring beginner ski package components; discount or free-trial coupons for beginner skiers; gifts, novelties and premiums for bringing new skiers to ski areas; exhibits and displays featuring beginners for use in public locations, and special events, training programmes and seminars at the ski hill or at recreation centres for interested local groups.

8.7 Market image

A common concern among non participants was that ski hills were merely haunts for the young and expert skiers (overall mean level of agreement 2.8). This was a view particularly prevalent with Social Adventurers (level of agreement 3.0). While research (National Sporting Goods Association, 1995; Edmonson, 1996) has indicated that this is a misconception, it does however illustrate how the ski tourism industry has portrayed a contradictory image of itself in its promotional literature (Sager, 1997; Calgary Convention and Visitor Bureau, 1998).

At its most simple, the ski industry must develop and improve its image as a business by being concerned with *all* types of people. This includes maintaining a proper and friendly attitude with all potential user groups – even those marginally interested in skiing.

If the Canadian ski industry is going to attract new people into the sport it will be required to seek publicity for publicity serves to keep the ski industry in the public eye. Here the need to carefully manage publicity opportunities associated with the beginner ski product is vital. Publicity strategies might include staging news events involving genuine interest stories concerning beginner skiers. Alberta's oldest new skier in the province and the annual 'celebrity learning to ski week' at Sunshine Village are illustrative of how some Canadian ski resorts are exploring new ways of attracting publicity. Other strategies might however, focus on the issuing of beginner orientated press releases; the offer of ski facilities for charitable events especially catering to non-traditional potential skier groups; and providing volunteer guest speakers at meetings addressing beginner ski issues such as money saving techniques for making skiing affordable.

8.8 The importance of service and service marketing

So much of the breaking down of the barriers to skiing evolves around treating new skiers in friendly and hospitable ways. Indeed, discomfort and unease linked to uncertainty over equipment rental; the choice, quality and cost of accommodation, and enrolling in ski school were all highlighted as potential harriers to participating in ski tourism (overall mean level of agreement 2.6). Making skiers feel comfortable in a new and challenging pursuit is largely a function of customer service marketing. Canadian research merely emphasised the fact that the ski industry should take responsibility to ensure that staff make every effort to encourage new skiers to enjoy themselves, so that they will return more often and recommend skiing to then friends. The implementation of performance report cards designed to assess customer satisfaction levels with staff and the ski product at Panorama, British Columbia is one measure already adopted by a Canadian resort operator designed to recognise the importance of customer service and service quality. The development of employee customer service training programs to acquaint staff with the peculiar interests and requirements of beginner skiers (at Whistler and Blackcomb, B.C.); and the development of employee hiring practices targeted at attracting and retaining hospitable service orientated employees (at Ski Lake Louise, Alberta) are similar attempts by ski field operators to recognise the importance of customer service markcting.

9   Conclusion

Although skiing has many positive dimensions for non-skiers, perceived and real problems are significant enough to keep many potential skiers off of the slopes and trails. These barriers must be identified and addressed by ski industry organisations before many non-participatory groups will pursue skiing. This paper has shown that two significant constraints to be surmounted are fear and the costs associated with skiing.

While the study has outlined, in part, a methodological framework for identifying the constraints confronting non-skiers in particular and non-participants in general, greater emphasis has been placed upon identifying which non-participatory target markets might be the focus for any marketing strategy; what selective marketing activities might be directed at specific non-skier market segments; and what various priorities for action and programs should be established by the ski industry and its partners in order to address flattening market demand, declining revenues and bring new people into the sport.

Research conducted in Western Canada identified two specific sub-segments of non-skiers as having the greatest potential for conversion to skiing – social adventurers and young family groups. The former were characterised by specific demographics, viz. 18–44 yr old, blue collar occupations, low levels of education and income; while the latter were distinguished by higher levels of education, white collar occupations and their marital status (i.e. all were married with young children). Both groups while identifying with the fun, excitement and exhilaration of skiing highlighted a range of specific constraints associated with commencing, maintaining and increasing involvement in the sport. In the case of the social adventurer group these were linked to 'fear' and risk'. In contrast, young families were concerned about skiing's associated costs.

It has been shown the non-skiers' perception of skiing can be dominated by negative images of the mountain ski experience. These extend beyond cost and fear into the realms of commitments of time for pre-ski training and transportation, organisation and staging and ski trip management. Taken together they help to create an image of skiing and ski holidays as being something of an expedition requiring an 'expedition mentality'.

A major conclusion of this paper is that the promotion of skiing and individual mountain ski facilities have targeted the present skier. A review of major communication efforts (Calgary Convention and Visitor Bureau, 1998; Sager, 1997) illustrates a concentration on the young athletic, upscale market and not on the two most potent segments for a generation of new participants.

To attract the non-skier population, skiing needs to be repositioned as a leisure activity. The key to attracting non-skiers is the removal of the major barriers, both perceived and real, that convince a person to reject this form of leisure activity. Here a genetic campaign focusing on 'fun', the sharing of experiences, health, accessibility, rewards and challenges, that offers good value for money and can be enjoyed by all social groups is required.

To this end this paper has offered a range of market-orientated strategies designed to attract new participants into this form of leisure tourism. These concentrated on the need for packaging of ski lift tickets, transportation, accommodation and equipment rental; developing beginner's instruction programmes, looking at new ways the ski tourism industry distributes its product and promotes itself; and how it might address specific aspects of customer service marketing.

Throughout this discussion the overall premise has been that concerted industry-wide action is needed to address the problem of flattening market demand and declining revenues. However, it has been shown that by building demand everyone in the tourism industry benefits travel agents, wholesalers, carriers and resort operators. The preceding discussion has provided an insight into how the potential of the non-skier market might be tapped. It, nevertheless, remains up to the ski tourism industry itself to meet the challenges and opportunities of the next decade.

References

Ahn, J. (1987). The role and impact of mega events and attractions on tourism development in Asia, *AEIST*, pp. 133–185. St Gall: AEIST.

Audet, S., & Archambault, M. (1997). In search of alpine skiers: The situation in the cantons de l'est. *Revue de Recherche en Tourisme*, *16*(1), 28–31.

Backman, S.J. (1991). An investigation of the relationship between activity loyalty and perceived constraints. *Journal of Leisure Research*, *23*(4), 332–344.

Backman, S.J., & Crompton, J.L. (1990). Differentiating between active and passive discontinuers of two leisure activities. *Journal of Leisure Research*, *23*, 154–161.

Barbier, B. (1978). Ski et stations de sports d'hiver dans le monde. *Weiner Geographische Schriften*, *51*(52), 130–146.

Barkholz, D. (1997). State hopes tourists will hear call of the wild. *Crain's Detroit Business*, *13*(8), 8.

Bennett, D. *et al.* (1997). Snow business. *Australian Leisure Management*, *2*(3) 10–11.

Berbin, J. (1995). Mass tourism and problems of tourism planning in the French mountains. In G. Ashworth, *Tourism and spatial transformation*. CAB International.

Best, A. (1997). That's entertainment. *Ski Area Management 36*(3) 66–67, 89–91.

Bialeschki, M.D., & Henderson, K. (1998). Constraints to trail use. *Journal of Park and Recreation Management*, *6*, 20–28.

Boothby, J., Tungatt, M.F., & Townsend A.R. (1981). Ceasing participation in sports activity. *Journal of Leisure Research*, *13*, 1–14.

Cairmichael, B. (1996). Conjoint analysis of downhill skiers used to improve data collection for market segmentation. *Journal of Travel and Tourism Marketing*, *5*(3), 187–206.

Calgary Convention and Visitor Bureau (1998). Travel Track Planner, CCVB.

Canadian Ski Council (1988). Building Canada's future skier market: A handbook for promoting downhill and cross country skiing to the beginner and non-skier markets. Toronto, Canada.

Canadian Ski Council (1991). Ski it to believe it, Skier Development Program 1991/92. Toronto, Canada.

Canadian Ski Council (1996). Assessing the success of the past five years. Toronto, Canada.

Castle, K. (1995). What have we done for you? *Ski Area Management*, *34*(5), 54–55.

Castle, K. (1996). Kirkwood – the turnaround kid. *Ski Area Management*, *35*(3), 72–73.

Christopoulou, O., & Papastavrou, A. (1997). Evaluation of the behaviour of visitors to ski stations – the case of the Petra region. *Medit*, *8*(1), 37–40.

Coker, T. (1998). Intermediate promotion. *Ski and Board*, November issue, 73–103.

Coltman, M. (1989). *Introduction to travel and tourism. An international approach*. New York: Van Nostrand-Reinhold.

Delphy, L. (1998). An overview of sports tourism: Building towards a dimensional framework. *Journal of Vacation Marketing*, *4*(1), 23–38.

Dillman, K. (1995). Investing in ski shows. *Ski Area Management*, *34*(4), 42–43, 63–65.

Dorward, S., & Moreau, P. (1997). French ski resorts and North American competition. *Cahiers Espace*, *51*, 48–51.

Dunn, E. (1990). Temporary and permanent constraints on participation in camping. In B.J.A. Smale, *Leisure challenges. Bringing people, resources and policy into play. Proceedings of sixth Canadian congress on leisure research* (pp. 360–363). Toronto: Ontario Research Council on Leisure.

Edmonson, B. (1996). Skiing's demographic future. *Ski Area Management*, *35*(1), 62–63.

English Tourist Board (1992). *Activity holidays in 1993*. London: ETB.

ESPN (1997). Ski World, 23 January.

Farber, A.H., & Ellis, W.K. (1986). Outdoor recreation accessibility for persons with disabilities. In *A literature review – The President's commission on Americans outdoors* (Special Populations, pp. 83–89). Washington, DC: US Government Printing Office.

Ferris, A. (1992). Sports and resorts. A winning meeting combination. *Convention South*, *13*(10) 1–20.

Fidgeon, P.R. (1995). Explaining the motivational characteristics of the European ski market. *Ski Survey*, *13*(2), 15–17.

Fidgeon, P.R. (1997). Calling all beginners. *Calgary Ski Club Monthly Newsletter*, November issue, 14.

Frost, M. (1998). Millennium countdown. *Ski and Board*, November issue, 124–125.

Gachelin-Ribault, C. (1996). Skiing, culture and the environment. *Ecodecision*, *20*, 49–51.

Giar, F. (1996). Ski training with children. *Sportunterricht*, *44*(12), 509–514.

Gibson, H. (1988). *Tourist role preference and need satisfaction: Some continuities and discontinuities over the life course*. A paper presented at the Leisure Studies Association Conference, Brighton, England, 29 June–3 July.

Gibson, H. (1988). The fitness and tourism connection – who participates? In K. Volkwein, *Fitness as a cultural phenomenon*, vol. 4, *German American studies in sport series*, Muenster: Waxman-Verlag.

Glyptis, S.A. (1991). Sport and tourism. In C. Cooper, *Progress in tourism, recreation and hospitality management*, vol. 3. London: Belhaven Press.

Gohner, U. (1996). Skiing with a new curriculum. *Sportunterricht*, *44*(12), 503–508.

Goodspeed, L. (1997). Publicising good deeds. *Ski Area Management*, *16*(34), 54–25.

Green, P.E., Tull, D.S., & Albaurn, G. (1988). *Research for marketing decisions* (5th edn). Englewood Cliffs, New Jersey: Prentice-Hall.

Guérin, J.P. (1984). *L'Aménagement de la Montagne en France*. Paris: Ophyrs.

Hall, C.M. (1992). Review, adventure, sport and health tourism. In B. Weiler, & C.M. Hall, *Special interest tourism*. London: Belhaven Press.

Heck, T. (1997). On the road to new profits. *Ski Area Management*, *36*(2), 54–55.

Henderson, K.A., & Bialeschki M.D. (1991). A sense of entitlement to leisure as constraint and empowerment for women. *Leisure Sciences*, *13*, 51–65.

Hultsman, W.Z. (1990). Barriers to activity participation: A focus on youth. Unpublished paper presented at the National Recreation and Park Association symposium on leisure research. October. Phoenix, Arizona.

Jackson, E.L., & Dunn, P. (1988). Integrating ceasing participation with other aspects of leisure behaviour. *Journal of Leisure Research*, *20*, 31–45.

James, C. (1995). Survey of Barbados sporting holidays. *Financial Times*, 26 April, 39.

Karameries, A. (1995). Approaches for recording and assessing land use and overlaps in land use in relation to tourism development in the mountains. Farstwissenschaftliche Beitrage, ETU, Zurich, No. 15.

Kay, T., & Jackson G. (1991). Leisure constraint: The impact of leisure constraints on leisure participation. *Journal of Leisure Research*, *23*(4), 301–313.

Knafau, R. (1979). L'aménagement de territoire en économic libérale: l'exemple des stations intégrées de sports d'hiver des Alpes Françaises. *L'Espace Géographique*, *83*, 173–180.

Kurtzman, J., & Zauhar, J. (1997). A wave in time – the sports tourism phenomena. *Journal of Sports Tourism*, *4*(2), 5–20.

Leisure Trends Group (1993). *Ski trip planning survey*. Colorado: Boulder.

Long, J. (1998). *Leisure health and well-being*. Conference papers no. 44, Leisure Studies Association, Eastbourne, England.

Marktrend Inc. (1990). A report on the Alberta non-skier market. Edmonton: Alberta Tourism and Canada West Ski Areas Association.

Mazenec, J.A. (1984). How to detect travel market segments. A clustering approach. *Journal of Travel Research*, 18–19.

McGuire, F.A. (1982). Constraints on leisure involvement in the later years. *Activities Adaptation and Ageing*, *3*, 17–24.

McGuire, F.A., Dottavio, F.D., & O'Leary J.T. (1986). Constraints to participation in outdoor recreation over the life span: A nation-wide study of limiters and prohibiters. *Gerontologist*, *26*, 538–544.

McPherson, B. (1989). *The social significance of sport*. Champaign, IL: Human Kinetics.

Mills, A.S. *et al.* (1986). Segmenting Texas snow skiers. *Journal of Travel Research*, *25*, 19–73.

Mintel (1995). *Activity holidays in the UK*. London: Mintel.

Morrison, J. *et al.* (1995). The effects of ski area expansion on Elk. *Wildlife Society Bulletin*, *23*(3), 481–489.

National Demographics and Lifestyles Inc. (1996). *The lifestyle monitor*. Colorado: Denver.

National Ski Areas Association (1997). The shaping of industry marketing in ski area management. *Ski Area Management*, *36*(2) 80–81.

National Sporting Goods Association (1995). Sports participation survey. Chicago, IL.

Pech, Y., & Vuhn, P. (1997). From quality hospitality to the certification of ski lifts: The experience of Orcieres-Merlette. In C. Chaspoulc, *Certification: Each to his own method*, pp. 38–42. Paris: Espaces.

Print Measurement Bureau (1992). Unpublished Survey Reports. Toronto.

Quirk, D., & Hartmann, G. (1995). Examining the dynamics of the US ski industry. *Hotel Valuation Journal*, 7–11.

Reis, J.B. (1996). Landscape damage by skiing at the Schauinsland in the Black Forest, Germany. *Mountain Research and Development*, *16*(1), 27–40.

Richards, G. (1996). Skilled consumption and UK ski holidays. *Tourism Management*, *17*(1), 25–34.

Ritchie, J.R.B. (1991). The impact of a mega-event on a host region. *Journal of Travel Research*, *30*, 3–10.

Rowan, D. (1998). New study: More skiers, skiing less. *Ski Area Management*, *37*(4), 41–79.

Ruston/Tomany and Associates (1990). The 1990 Ontario ski study – household survey, Toronto: Ontario Ski Resorts Association.

Sager, P. (1997). Whistler resort: Up where you belong. Whistler Resort Association.

Sarlin, S. (1995). Nature, skiing and Swedish nationalism. *International Journal of the History of Sport*, *12*(2), 147–163.

Scott, D. (1991). The problematic nature of participation in contract bridge: A qualitative study of group related constraints. *Leisure Sciences*, *13*(4) 321–336.

Scarle, M.S., & Jackson, E.L. (1985). Socioeconomic variations in perceived barriers to recreation participation among would-be participants. *Leisure Sciences*, *7*, 227–249.

542   PETER WILLIAMS AND PAUL R. FIDGEON

Seghers, M. (1995). Mississippi coast tourist officials to lure out of state fisherman. *Sun Herald*, 3 September, p. 11.

Servoin, F. (1997). A new approach to the concept of the ski slope. *Espaces*, *144*, 52–56.

Shaw, S.M., Bonen, A., & McCabe, J.F. (1991). Do more constraints mean less leisure? Examining the relationship between constraints and participation. *Journal of Leisure Research*, *23*(4), 286–300.

Smith, C., & Jenner, P. (1990). Activity holidays in Europe. *EIU Travel and Tourism Analyst*, 5, 58–78.

Snow Sports Industries America (1996).

Spivack, S. (1997). Health spa development in the USA: A burgeoning component of sports to tourism. *Journal of Vacation Marketing*, *4*(1), 64–85.

Sports Market Place Directory (1997). Franklin Quest Sports Division, USA.

Spring, J. (1995). More days more fun, but not shrinking numbers. *Ski Area Management*, *35*(4), 44–45.

Standeven, J. (1996). *Sport and tourism – how symbiotic is their relationship?* A paper given at the International Society for Comparative Physical Education and Sport Conference, Hachi-ohji, Japan, 27 August.

Stynes, D.J., & Mahoney, E.M. (1980). *Michigan downhill ski marketing study: Segmenting active skiers* (Research Rep 391). East Lansing: Michigan State University, Agricultural Experiment Station.

Swarbrooke, J. (1995). *The development and management of visitor attractions*. Oxford: Butterworth-Heinemann.

Usher, R. (1996). Some don't like it hot. *Time*, 2 September, 46–49.

Williams, P.W., & Basford, R. (1992). Segmenting downhill skiing's latest demand markets. *American Behavioural Scientist*, *36*(2), 222–235.

Williams, P.W., & Dossa, K. (1994). Where do the trails lead? Perspectives on the Canadian ski industry 1994. Tourism Canada, The Canadian Ski Council, The Centre for Tourism Policy and Research Simon Fraser University.

Williams, P.W., Dossa, K., & Fulton, A. (1994). Tension on the slopes: Managing conflict between skiers and snowboarders. *Journal of Applied Recreation Research*, *19*(3), 191–213.

Williams, P.W., & Todd, S.E. (1997). Towards an environmental management system for ski areas. *Mountain Research and Development*, *37*(1), 75–90.

Wilson, S. (1997). Owner Sports Four Inc. Quoted in Delphy, L. (1998). An overview of sports tourism: Building towards a dimensional framework. *Journal of Vacation Marketing*, *4*(1) 23–38.

Witt, S.F., & Moutinho, L. (1994). *Tourism marketing and management handbook*. (2nd edn). London: Prentice Hall.

Wright, B.A. & Goodale, T.I. (1991). Beyond non-participation: Validation of interest and frequency of participation categories in constraint research. *Journal of Leisure Research*, *23*(4), 314–331.

Yiannakis, A. (1986). *The ephemeral role of the tourist. Some correlates of tourist role preference*. A paper presented at the North American Society for the Sociology of Sport Conference, Las Vegas, Nevada, October.

Chapter 30

Laurence Chalip and Anna Leyns

LOCAL BUSINESS LEVERAGING
OF A SPORT EVENT
Managing an event for economic benefit

IN RECENT YEARS, an array of cities throughout the world have incorporated sport events into their economic development mix. Van den Berg, Braun, and Otgaar (2000) describe the use of sport events in the marketing of Barcelona, Helsinki, Manchester, Rotterdam, and Turin. Bramwell (1997, 1998) outlines the use of sport events in the tourism strategy of Sheffield, England. Ghanem and Ashkenazy (1993) note the incorporation of sport events into the economic development strategy of Scarborough, Ontario.

The growing use of sport events as an economic development tool is paralleled by the growth of the events industry. Recent estimates indicate that event tourism is the fastest growing element of the leisure travel market, and that consequent roomnight demand has now surpassed that for business conventions (Shifflet & Bhatia, 1999). Although this figure includes cultural events along with sport events, other data suggest that sport events are, perhaps, the largest component of event tourism (Getz, 1998). Sport events are also one of the most widely studied elements of sport tourism (Chalip, 2001; Gibson, 1998).

One result of the use of sport for economic development purposes has been that public subsidies are often provided to enable sport events to take place. Subsidies take the form of direct cash infusion and/or provision of public services and facilities with little or no remuneration. Mules and Faulkner (1996) reviewed studies of the economic impact of large events, and found that the estimated economic impact typically exceeded the amount of public subsidy. Nevertheless, as they noted, the estimation of economic impact is an inexact science. Crompton (1995) concurs, pointing out that economic impact estimates are vulnerable to a number of methodological shortcomings. Indeed, when governments seek to justify sport event investments through studies of economic impact that they commission, there is some incentive to adopt procedures that yield favorable estimates. When all is said and done, estimates of economic impact are political numbers (cf. Sack & Johnson, 1996). In fact, independent estimates often question the economic value of public sport investments (e.g. Coates & Humphries, 1999; Rosentraub, Swindell, Przybylski & Mullins, 1994).

Findings like these have accentuated the political character of claims about economic benefits from sport events. Boyle (1997) argued that public investments in sport events are really a form of civic boosterism designed to promote local identity. He suggested that claims about contributions to economic development are really a form of political propaganda. Whitson and Macintoch (1996) agree, contending that claims of economic benefits from sport events mask a deeper purpose—namely, to legitimize public subsidy of sport events for the purpose of promoting the status of local elites. The public policymaking that enabled the Volvo International Tennis Tournament in New Haven, Connecticut (Sack & Johnson, 1996) is consistent with these claims.

The finding that elites may obtain particular benefit from sport events highlights the fact that the impact of any event may be unevenly distributed. This has the potential to erode public support for events. Consequently, several recent studies have departed from calculation of aggregate economic impact, and have chosen instead to examine the reasons that particular events have or have not lived up to expectations for their economic impact. Bramwell (1997) pointed to gaps in strategic planning throughout Sheffield as it prepared to host the 1991 World Student Games. Spilling (1996) described entrepreneurial activity stimulated by Lillehammer's organization of the 1994 Olympic Winter Games. He found that a great deal of business activity was stimulated. Although some ventures were successful, others were not. Thus, the impact of the Games on local businesses was unevenly distributed. Putsis (1998) modeled the economic impact of the 1995 Special Olympics World Games in New Haven, Connecticut, and found that the construction and business service sectors benefited from the Games, but local merchants in the downtown business district were worse off. The reason was that local residents stayed away from the downtown area during the Games, while athletes and visitors made their purchases at the event site, rather than in local shops and restaurants. Aversion effects played a comparable role in the case of Ranfurly Shield Rugby in New Plymouth, New Zealand (Garnham, 1997).

These findings suggest that some businesses are better able to capitalize on a sport event than are others. The fact that local merchants may be among those who are at a disadvantage is particularly telling because the economic impact of an event depends substantially on visitor spending (Dwyer, Mellor, Mistilis, & Mules, 2000). It would normally be expected that local merchants would be the ones to capture visitor spending. In fact, one of the reasons that sport events have been thought to be useful for economic development is that the stimulation and playful environment associated with them are conducive to impulse purchasing (cf. Godbey & Graefe, 1991; Irwin & Sandler, 1998; Hausman, 2000; Rook & Fisher, 1995). Nevertheless, other work has suggested that small local enterprises may be the least willing (Malone & Jenster, 1991) or the least able (Davis, 1997; Glen & Weerawaradena 1996; Robinson & Pearce, 1984) to leverage the kind of opportunity that a sport event represents.

The concern, then, is to locate means by which local businesses can cultivate spending by event visitors—particularly impulse spending by event visitors (Chalip, 2001). This is a form of leveraging (cf. Boulton, Libert & Samek, 2000; Slywotzky & Shapiro, 1993). In order to leverage, the opportunities that derive from event communications and the presence of event visitors must be exploited through tactics designed to generate visitor spending and foster future visitation. A related concern may be to maintain levels of spending by local residents during the event. Businesses with the greatest potential to leverage are those that provide services to visitors: restaurants, retailers, and hoteliers (cf. Getz, 1997; Inskeep, 1991).

Several questions emerge from the literature reviewed so far. To what degree do local businesses seek to leverage a sport event in their community? When leveraging is attempted, what tactics are applied? To what effect? What special opportunities or needs for small business leveraging can be identified? What are the views of small business leaders about those opportunities and needs?

These questions are addressed in the studies that follow. Following a brief description of the Gold Coast Honda Indy, four studies are reported that explore leveraging of the event by local merchants. The first study locates instances of leveraging, and identifies the reasons that most local merchants fail to leverage. The second study examines specific instances of leveraging in more detail. The third study convenes an expert task force to consider means by which to cultivate leveraging of the event by local businesses. The final study tests the degree to which the task force's recommendations are acceptable to local business leaders. The concluding discussion considers management implications for enhancing the quantity and distribution of the economic benefits of sport events for local business.

Setting

The Gold Coast Honda Indy is the penultimate race of the FedEx Cart Championship Series. It is an annual event that has been held since 1991 on a 4.5 kilometer temporary street course through the streets of Surfers Paradise on the Gold Coast of Queensland, Australia. In addition to the Indy race itself, there are a number of support races that take place over the four days of the motor racing (October 14–17, 1999, the dates around which this study revolves). These races occur as part of the lead-up to the Indy race. In 1999 these included: V8 Supercars, HQ Holdens, GT Production cars, the Porsche Cup, and drag racing. In terms of attendance and media coverage, the Indy race is Queensland's largest annual event. Surrounding this four-day event area a number of other events which are associated with the four days of racing. These are not limited to the area of the track, as they take place throughout the Gold Coast. In 1999, these included the Indy Ball, a "Meet the Drivers" breakfast, the "Miss Indy" contest, Tropicarnival (a series of local arts and music entertainments), and an array of social events organized by local clubs and sponsors. These events are terms "off-track events." They continue until the last day of racing, and make up a substantial part of the atmosphere that surrounds the Gold Coast while it is hosting the race. Taken as a whole, these are commonly referred to as "the Indy Carnival."

The race is a joint venture involving both the Queensland state government and International Management Group (IMG). The Queensland govern contributes AUS$8 million in funding to the organization staging the event. The Gold Coast City Council assists in the circuit set-up and provides some security and clean-up services. Government subsidies of the event have been legitimized on the grounds that the event's estimated economic impact exceeds the government subsidy (King, 1994; Smith, 1996; Stoltz, 1996). However, critics have noted that the costs are not fully borne by those who obtain the benefits (Mules, 1998), and that the opportunity costs associated with government subsidy of the event may render an unfavourable benefit to cost ratio (Black & Pape, 1995).

Over its four days, the event attracts approximately a quarter of a million spectators. In 1998, estimates commissioned by the state of Quensland concluded that 245,553 people attended the race. Those same estimates concluded that 27.1% were from the Gold Coast, 34.1% from other areas within Queensland, 34.7% were from other states in Australia, and 4.1% were from overseas. Estimates were also commissioned for the 1999 race, but were not released by the Queensland government. In 1999, television coverage of the final Indy race (lasting approximately 2 hours) was broadcast in 195 countries, with commentaries in 19 different languages. The event organizers claim an international audience of 61 million viewers.

The phrase "Indy precinct" is used by local officials and race administrators, and is also featured in this study. The Indy precinct stretches from the edge of the track in Main Beach (on the north) to one block south of the track in Surfers Paradise—a distance of 2 kilometers. The race precinct extends from the beach (on the east) to the Gold Coast highway—a width of only 250 meters at its narrowest point, and 625 meters at its widest point. It is necessary to have an accreditation pass, a media pass, or an event ticket in order to enter this area during the four days of the event. Accreditation passes are issued to people who reside in the precinct (either permanently or as a visitor). Since the Indy precinct encompasses an area with substantial high-rise accommodation (serving permanent residents and visitors), several thousand passes are issued.

A series of four qualitative studies was designed to explore the leveraging of the Indy by local small business. Research questions, participants, methods, data collected, and key findings from each of the studies are highlighted in Table 30.1. Each study builds on the study that precedes it. An examination and discussion of findings from each study are presented independently, followed by a synthesis and analysis of the research as a whole. Implications for enhancing the economic benefits of sport events through leveraging are discussed in the final section of the paper.

Study 1

Study 1 consisted of 22 semi-structured interviews with manager of local small businesses. Each interviewee was asked to describe how the Indy affected their business. Probes were used to explore effects on each business's volume of sales and profile of clients, as well as to identify special advantages or problems. Interviewees were then asked to describe what efforts they made to promote their businesses during the Indy. Probes were used to explore any tactics identified or to determine reasons for not implementing any special activities during the Indy. Finally, interviewees were asked about the potentials they could envision for building business from the Indy.

The data were coded for presence or absence of any leveraging strategies. For those interviewees not using any strategy, reasons they gave were listed. For those interviewees using strategies, the strategies were listed, and the manager's rationale for the strategy was identified. Strauss's (1987) open coding technique was used to generate themes and sub-themes from the strategies and rationales identified in the interview data. Themes, sub-themes, and representative quotes are presented in Table 30.2.

Results

Only 8 of the 22 businesses employed any tactic to leverage the Indy. With only three exceptions, none of the managers felt that their leveraging efforts had been (or would be) effective. (The three exceptions were subsequently studied in greater detail. These are described in Study 2.) Results are summarized below for each of the three types of business.

Accommodation.   Only one of the seven businesses offering accommodation did anything special to use the Indy. That business—which is outside the Indy precinct—merely included a picture of the Indy in its brochure. None of the other six businesses offering accommodation made any use of the Indy. Those inside or directly adjacent to the precinct felt that it was unnecessary to promote for or through the Indy. Since accommodation inside the precinct is in high demand from Indy visitors, none of the managers felt any need to develop special marketing tactics for the event. Those outside the precinct felt that since they are not within the track area itself, they are not an appealing choice for Indy visitors. Therefore, they could see no point in attempting to leverage the event.

In summary, accommodation businesses inside the track area felt that they were in sufficient demand that there was no need to employ any leveraging strategy. Those outside the track area felt that they were too far away to be attractive to Indy visitors, so there was no value in any leveraging strategy. Consequently, with the exception of a picture on one accommodation business's brochure, nothing was done to leverage the Indy.

Retail.   Two retailers directly adjacent to the Indy precinct put posters in their shop windows to advertise their merchandise. These posters were comparable to posters used at other times of the year. The one difference was simply that the posters referenced the Indy. Neither retailer claimed that the posters had increased their business. Rather, the posters were used as a means to create atmosphere in this store. One retailer adjacent to the precinct put a table of sale merchandise in front of her store and also extended trading hours over the four days of the event (adding four additional hours of trade). This retailer felt the promotion was effective. The example is described in more detail in Study 2. The two other retailers adjacent to the precinct did nothing to promote their businesses during the Indy. Each felt that Indy patrons were not interested in shopping, so they were not considered a viable market segment.

Neither of the retailers further from the precinct who were interviewed did anything to promote their business during the Indy. Both interviewees felt that the Indy pulled people away from their locations. Although they were located not far from the precinct, they felt that the overall effect of the Indy had been to reduce local patronage as people gravitated toward to Indy. These two retailers also felt that traffic congestion caused by the Indy deterred visits to local shops.

Given their expectations that the Indy would depress local retail shopping, these retailers saw no value in any special promotions or tactics to leverage the Indy for their businesses. The attitude seems to have been shared. Our perusal of media and our visits to areas around the Indy precinct during the event found no use of Indy-related signs, advertising, or promotions by any retailer adjacent to the Indy precinct. Further, we observed little special effort to leverage the event by retailers directly adjacent to the precinct.

Table 30.1 Summary of the studies' methods and results

	Study 1	Study 2	Study 3	Study 4
Key question(s)	Do local small businesses leverage events? Why or why not?	What were the key tactics used by local business to successfully leverage the event?	How can the leveraging effort of local businesses be enhanced?	How realistic are the leveraging recommendations for local business?

Participants	22 managers:
	• 8 restaurants
	• 7 retail shops
	• 7 hotels
	For each industry, businesses were chosen that were:
	• Inside the event precinct
	• Adjacent to the event precinct (1 km or less)
	• Away from the event precinct (1–3 kms)
		3 businesses identified as having successfully leveraged the event:
		(1) retail shop
		  • adjacent to precinct
		(2) restaurant
		  • adjacent to precinct
		(3) restaurant
		  • further from the precinct
			9-member Task Force with expertise in the following areas:
			• 2 tourism
			• 1 events
			• 4 marketing
			• 1 hotel management
			• 1 entrepreneurship
				8 local business leaders (not interviewed in the previous 3 studies):
				• 1 business consultant
				• 1 economic development officer
				• 1 Executive Officer from the local tourism operators association
				• 1 hotel management consultant
				• 1 restauranteur
				• 2 executives from local business associations

Method	Semi-structured interviews: • 11 prior to event • 11 after event	Semi-structured interviews: document collection	Dialectical decision making process	Semi-structured interviews

Data and analysis	Content analysis of interview transcripts (viz. Strauss, 1987)	Content analysis of interview transcript, brochures, planning documents, and local media	Task Force summaries: • Strategies from small group sessions • Notes from full group discussions • Recommendations generated	Content analysis of interview transcripts
Key findings	Only 8/22 leveraged the event in any way. Only 3 felt leveraging was successful: • 1 retailer adjacent to precinct • 1 restaurateur adjacent and 1 further away Most felt that: • Effects depend on proximity to the precinct • Market not interested in retail, and • Event disrupts regular business Dominant leveraging strategy was the creation of atmosphere by theming	Retail • Extended hours • Outdoor sale table Restaurants • Advertising with tie-in promotions • Themed areas • Entertainment	• Small businesses need assistance to leverage events • Need for alliances among core business • A central coordinating body should be put into place to assist • Marketing data relative to key market segments should be collected • Aversion markets should be targeted • Importance of promotions as a tactical element – particularly alliance-based	8/8 interviewees favored the ends recommended by the Task Force • Support for each task force recommendation *except* central coordinating body 8/8 interviewees disagreed with the means identified by the Task Force: • Avoid government involvement • No new organization – use existing business associations and/or chamber of commerce • Need for local businesses to coordinate

Table 30.2 Themes, sub-themes and representative quotes for study 1

1A Indy's effects on local business

1   Effects depend upon proximity to event precinct.

"Indy doesn't really have an effect. When the other [accommodation venues] inside the track are full, we get the overflow. We're too far away." (accommodation)

"We have a large sign and we have a very good location [close to precinct]. With so many people in town, we can't help but have an increase in business." (restaurant)

2   Event goers are not a relevant market.

"They [Indy patrons] spend their money on hotels and eating, not so much on retail." (retail)

"They're just interested in the car racing, not for shopping." (retail)

3   Indy disrupts regular business.

"It's just the way that people see the traffic flow, and they think it's an obstacle. A lot of people, I think, would stay away from the immediate shopping area." (retail)

"Indy does nothing for us. A lot of local people who might otherwise come out and eat stay away because it is a major hassle to get around." (restaurant)

1B Efforts to promote business during Indy

1   No need to do anything during Indy if in or near precinct.

"It sells itself, basically. We get a lot of repeat business. That's about how it works." (accommodation)

"We don't actually do any promotions for the Indy. Indy tends to promote itself." (accommodation)

2   No point if business is not close to the event precinct.

"We find that we are a little too far away from the actual event. . . . So, for us to go and spend money to advertise for the Indy, it's probably not worth it." (accommodation)

3   The creation of atmosphere for its own sake.

"It is just a display to create an atmosphere [so] we do it. But it doesn't increase business." (retail)

"We dress up the restaurant. . . . We put bunting all over the restaurant. . . . That's all really. We don't do any form of extra advertising." (restaurant)

4   Atmosphere as a leveraging tool.

"What we are hoping to achieve [by theming the area] is that the profile . . . and . . . awareness of [our area as an exciting one] is increased dramatically the length and breadth of the Gold Coast." (restaurant)

In summary, the use of leveraging strategies by retailers during the Indy was haphazard, and was limited to retailers directly adjacent to the Indy precinct. Further, those strategies that were employed were minimal—consisting of a few posters or a sale table with extended trading hours.

Restaurants.   Four of the eight restaurant managers interviewed reported use of leveraging strategies. One restaurant adjacent to the race precinct and one restaurant further outside the race precinct used bunting to decorate their restaurant during the event. The restaurant adjacent to the precinct used materials provided by beer suppliers to create its decorations. They used black and white checks to tie-in with the checkered flag used in auto racing. The manager did not feel this had much promotional impact. He suggested that it simply added to the atmosphere of the precinct at the time of the event.

Restaurants outside the precinct were also reticent to develop any special leveraging strategy. In order to foster some promotional activity, one nearby precinct had a "Best Dressed Restaurant" competition during the Indy period. The manager of a restaurant in that area had used bunting to decorate in order to enter the competition.

Another restaurant outside the Indy precinct participated in a coordinated theming strategy that was implemented jointly by all licensed businesses and traders in the neighborhood. An auto racing theme was designed for the entire area in order to attract customers during the day. By linking to the Indy through the auto racing theme, local businesses sought to establish the area as an exciting one that was worth visiting. This is the only example we found of a leveraging strategy that was coordinated cooperatively among a local group of businesses. The strategy became somewhat controversial. We examine it further in Study 2.

Directly adjacent to the race precinct, one restaurant implemented a coordinated series of strategies to leverage the Indy. Initially, the restaurant's management had planned to become a sponsor of the Indy. However, quality control (regarding food from the restaurant that might be served at track-side) became an issue, so the management decided against a sponsorship agreement. The Promotions Manager was then assigned the task of leveraging the Indy. Seven tactics were coordinated to make up an overall strategy. This was the only multi-faceted strategy we identified. Consequently, we examined it in more detail. That examination is described in Study 2.

The four remaining interviewees did not see any value in special promotions. Their rationales were similar to those of accommodation managers. Those close to the precinct felt that they were well enough located to obtain business. However, further outside the precinct, restaurant managers who made no special effort to leverage the Indy felt that their location was a disadvantage.

In summary, two restaurant managers articulated more leveraging strategies than did any of the other businesses. However, the only other leveraging reported by the restaurant managers we interviewed was minimal use of decoration designed to tie into auto racing, and that decoration had to be prompted from outside the business (by beer suppliers, in one instance, and by a local competition, in another). Otherwise, restaurant managers whose businesses were adjacent to the precinct did not see any need to leverage the event, and those further outside the precinct felt it would be a wasted effort.

Discussion

The majority (64%) of small business managers interviewed within and around the Indy precinct did little or nothing to leverage the event. If their business was directly adjacent t the precinct, then managers seemed to feel that increased trade would come to them simply as a function of their favourable location. If their business was further outside the precinct, most managers felt that because they were away from the main action of the event, they were therefore unattractive to Indy patrons.

In five of the eight instances where some leverage was attempted, the leveraging efforts were minimal. They were limited to a photo in a brochure (for one accommodation), a few posters (for two retailers), or some decorations (for two restaurants). Further, in the case of the restaurants, the use of decorations to tie-in with the event occurred only because outside organizations prompted those decorations. The managers did not feel that the decorations had any promotional value.

These findings are consistent with other work suggesting that many small business managers lack the inclination (Malone & Jenster, 1991), the information (Davis, 1997), or the skills (Glen & Weerawaradena, 1996; Robinson & Pearce, 1984) to engage in strategic planning or promotional leveraging. Nevertheless, it could be argued that the managers in this study who chose to do little or nothing to leverage the Indy had appropriately assessed their situation. However, the three examples we found of a more aggressive leveraging effort are instructive. The retailer and the two restaurant managers who made stronger efforts felt that their efforts paid substantial dividends. Other work has suggested that a minority of small businesses do engage in strategic planning and promotional leveraging, and that those businesses are, as a consequence, more successful (Bracker & Pearson, 1986; Mazzarol & Ramasehan, 1996). The claim by all-but-one retailer that event visitors are not interested in shopping is particularly surprising since research suggests that event visitors do shop (Godbey & Graefe, 1991; Irwin & Sandler, 1998), and that shopping plays a vital role in determining tourists' satisfaction with their visit to a destination (Turner & Reisinger, 2001). In fact, visitors to an event will vary. Some will be avidly focused on the event itself, while others may take a more casual interest in the event, perhaps because they are merely accompanying friends or family who are attending (cf. Hunt, Bristol, & Bashaw, 1999). Those with a casual focus on the event may be particularly disposed to spend time shopping while at the destination. In order to obtain further insight into the potentials for event leveraging, we examined in greater detail each of the three examples in which managers made a particular effort to leverage. The three cases are described in Study 2.

Study 2

One retailer and two restaurateurs interviewed in the initial study had made strong efforts to leverage the Indy. The retailer had extended her store's trading hours, and had placed a sale table in front of her store to lure customers. One restaurateur (in a neighborhood to the north of the Indy precinct) had joined with his local business association in an effort to attract customers by theming three blocks along the main business corridor of the neighborhood. Another restaurateur (two blocks south of the Indy precinct) put together a package of promotions and advertising to attract business from Indy patrons.

In order to learn more about what was done and the managers' satisfaction with their efforts, each of the three businesses that endeavoured to leverage the Indy was studied in greater detail. Further interviews were conducted with the three managers (one from each business). Each manager had previously been interviewed for Study 1. Managers were asked how and why they had chosen their particular strategy, and how well they felt it had worked for them. Probes were used to explore their thinking about the effort.

In addition, documents regarding the leveraging efforts were obtained where available. These included examples of brochures or media, as well as planning documents. The retailer could provide no documents; planning documents for the theming effort in which one restaurant participated were obtained (consisting of the original proposal as well as a detailed implementation plan); brochures and media were collected for both restaurants.

The interview material and the documents were analyzed to obtain a full picture of the leveraging effort, including the manager's sense of its effectiveness. No business was willing to provide financial data that would give a concrete specification of the impact on sales revenues. Consequently, we were compelled to rely on each manager's global evaluation.

Results

Retailer.   The retail shop that endeavoured to leverage the event was not merely the only one among those we interviewed that made a concerted leveraging effort, it was the only one we saw while walking adjacent to the precinct that had made such an effort. The shop was a small (48 square meters) sole proprietorship selling men's and women's clothing. It was at the southern end of the Indy precinct, surrounded by other shops, many of which also sold clothing. Since this is a tourist area throughout the year, the shop was typically open seven days per week from 9 a.m. to 5 p.m.

The owner-manager recognized that there would be added foot traffic around her store during the event. The challenge would be to get those walking past the store to stop and browse. As she put it, "For us in menswear, there are men here [for the Indy]. There's more testosterone out there than a girl would need." So, in order to attract attention, she placed a trestle table in front of her store. She scattered a mixture of clothing on the table (shirts, shorts, belts, underwear), and placed a sale sign on it. The tactic was designed to get Indy patrons to stop and look at the store's merchandise.

On Thursday, Saturday, and Sunday, the Indy ended at 5.30 p.m. This was a time the store would normally be closed, but it was a time of high foot traffic as Indy patrons left the track and wandered the area. Further, it was the one period when Indy patrons would not be focused primarily on the event itself. In other words, it was a good time to make sales. So the shop hours were extended until 9 p.m. The owner-manager said, "By going the extra mile, putting a bit more effort, and opening longer hours, we do very very well."

Although the store's owner-manager was unable (or unwilling) to give us a dollar estimate of the increase in sales, she was articulate about the value of leveraging. In the previous year, she had followed the pattern of other retailers in the area, and had not endeavored to leverage the event. It was a mistake she planned not to repeat. She summarized the value of her efforts this way:

This was our second Indy, but 100% better than last year. And I believe that is because we put in more effort. We didn't just wait for it to happen; we got in there and did it.

Restaurant (adjacent to the precinct).   The restaurant adjacent to the precinct that made the strongest attempt to build business from Indy patrons had initially planned to be one of the official event sponsors. However, when sponsorship plans proved unworkable, the restaurant's Promotions Manager was assigned the task of finding means to leverage the event. The Promotions Manager was given a budget she described as "miniscule," and was instructed to formulate a strategy.

The restaurant includes indoor and outdoor eating areas, as well as a bar. It can seat 210 patrons indoors and another 140 outdoors. It is located two blocks south of the Indy precinct.

The Promotions Manager designed a multi-faceted communications strategy that integrated promotions and advertising. The campaign was informed by efforts from the previous year, when the restaurant had attempted to build patronage during the event by redecorating its signs, hiring a high-profile band to play, and purchasing advertising to be distributed with Indy tickets. That effort had been expensive, and was deemed counter-productive because the band had taken up space that would otherwise have been available for patrons. Consequently, in 1999, the Promotions Manager concentrated on tactics designed to raise the awareness of potential patrons, and then to convert that awareness into patronage.

To generate awareness, three forms of advertising were used. Radio spots on a local station using the station announcers were purchased for morning broadcast during the two weeks leading up to the event. At the event itself, pull-through announcements (short promotional messages that are pulled through the bottom of the screen) were placed on Indy FMTV, which was broadcast into the corporate boxes and onto the large screens around the track. In addition, an Elvis impersonator and two dancing girls were hired to entertain patrons at the track and give out fliers. Meal vouchers were provided to track-side announcers, who then provided occasional drop-in announcements promoting the restaurant.

These strategies were designed to raise visitors' and locals' awareness of the restaurant. The associated challenge was to convert that awareness into business. Promotions were implemented to generate the necessary conversions. During the two-week radio campaign prior to the event, double passes to the Indy race and meal vouchers were used as a give-away prizes for listeners who phoned in. At the event itself, the Elvis impersonator and the dancing girls promoted the restaurant by handing out fliers and discount coupons.

Finally, the strategy called for a closer link to the race. In order to attract race personalities to the restaurant, meal vouchers and a letter detailing why they should visit were sent to every team in the event. The objective was to position the restaurant as "the place to be" for event enthusiasts.

The restaurant could not (or would not) provide an estimate of the numbers of meal vouchers or discount coupons that were redeemed. Nor could it (or would it) specify the effect on sales revenues. However, the restaurant was filled throughout the event. The Promotions Manager felt that her strategy had been effective, particularly when compared with efforts the previous year. She described the impact of her leveraging efforts this way:

As a result of this [the leveraging strategy], the [restaurant] had a boomer of a time over the Indy period. What it calls for is common-sense and effort. There is no need for a big budget. The amount of money spent on this year's promotion wouldn't have bought one promotional sign on the Indy track. . . . It wasn't about flag raising or anything but consumption—to get people into the restaurant.

Restaurant alliance (outside the precinct).   The Licensed Businesses and Traders Association for one of the areas bordering the Indy precinct commissioned a private company specializing in conference and event organizing to develop a proposal for means to leverage the Indy. In previous years, the Indy organizers had used the area for entertainment and some sponsor displays. Since that would not be the case in 1999, the Association felt the need to take up the initiative.

The company's proposal was presented nine weeks prior to the Indy. It called for the three blocks on which neighborhood businesses reside to be themed using an auto racing format. The theming would then be complemented with entertainment on Friday and Saturday evenings. The proposal was adopted by the Association.

The strategy had six elements:

1   The entire area was decorated using black and white to tie into auto racing's use of a black and white checkered flag. In addition, Indy posters and car paraphernalia decorated some of the businesses. Two bridges were constructed crossing the main street, and advertising space on the bridges was given to sponsors of the area's theming and entertainment.
2   Street entertainers, including "Indy girls" (dancers), traversed the area during the day entertaining those who were there or who were walking through on their way to the Indy track. They also performed on Friday and Saturday night.
3   Televisions were placed throughout local restaurants and tuned to the Indy.
4   A Friday night "multicultural experience" was designed to tie into the multi-ethnic range of cuisines offered by the area's restaurants. The entertainment hub was a calypso band playing on two moveable stages.
5   Saturday night entertainment consisted of The Ten Tenors (a popular singing group) on the two moveable stages.
6   Advertisements promoting the area as an alternative Indy and entertainment venue were placed on local television and radio stations.

The strategy was designed to counteract aversion effects caused by Indy traffic, and to increase awareness about the area among locals as well as Indy patrons. The restaurant owner-manager we interviewed described it aptly:

The Indy Carnival [has been] rather detrimental, actually. . . . People are under the somewhat misunderstanding that they can't come [to this area]. . . . [The strategy is] shotgun marketing, really, where we're simply telling all and sundry that there is something exciting happening in [this area] this year. Of course, what we are hoping to achieve in that is that the profile of [our area] and the awareness [about the area] is increased dramatically the length and breadth of the Gold Coast and also, of course, through interstate visitors that hopefully come here.

The strategy was described as "expensive" by the restaurant owner, but "worth it." Once again, we were not provided specific financial data. However, local media accounts and our own observations are consistent with the restaurateur's assessment. The area was well patronised throughout the Indy period, and restaurants throughout the area were filled on Friday and Saturday nights.

Nevertheless, the strategy was deemed counter-productive by the Indy event organizers and by local government. As an event (or series of events) in its own right, the strategy provided a substantial ambushing opportunity. Bartercard (a trade dollar card) was an official sponsor of the Indy. Ibex, a direct competitor of Bartercard, sponsored the theming strategy, effectively ambushing Bartercard in the event's back yard. This became sufficiently controversial that it was taken to court. Bartercard lost, but the Indy organizers and the city council agreed to explore means to prevent a recurrence.

Discussion

Although most businesses in the vicinity of the race did little or nothing to promote themselves through the event, those that did felt strongly that they benefited. By contemporary marketing standards, none of the three leveraging efforts that we identified for study was particularly inventive. They made use of such standard techniques as having a sale, extending trading hours, doing some advertising with tie-in promotions, theming an area, and providing entertainment. These were relatively straightforward to implement, yet they were effective—as they have been shown to be in other contexts (Gottdiener, 1997; Hardy & Magrath, 1990; Pine & Gilmore, 1999; Sternberg, 1997; Tanguary, Vallée, & Lanoie, 1995).

The theming strategy required an alliance to implement. Other researchers have suggested that the formation and leveraging of alliances among businesses can generate competitive advantages for those firms in the alliance (Jelinek & Litterer, 1995; Lorenzoni & Lipparini, 1999) and for tourist destination (Gregory & Koithan-Louderback, 1997; Murphy, 1992). However, in the context of event leveraging, an alliance-based strategy outside the control of event organizer is not without drawbacks. In this case, the fact that the theming strategy was coordinated independently of the Indy organizers established an ideal opportunity for ambush of the event sponsors. While this may benefit local businesses in the short-term, without sponsor support the Indy could cease to exist. This is a possibility if event managers are not able to provide sponsors with appropriate protection from ambushing.

The finding that most businesses do not endeavor to leverage the event, but that they might benefit if they do, suggests the value of assisting them to leverage (Chrisman & Leslie, 1989; Tendler & Amorim, 1996). If local businesses can stimulate spending from patrons, then the economic impact of the event would be enhanced. However, the fact that sponsors could be ambushed in the process poses a concern for event organizers and the host city (McAuley & Sutton, 1999). Further, if different areas develop incompatible themes or promotions, the host city could appear chaotic to event patrons (cf. Bramwell, 1998; Crouch & Ritchie, 1999).

In order to explore the challenges and potentials for facilitating (and perhaps coordinating) event leveraging, we called together a small task force of experts to consider the problem. Their deliberations are reported as Study 3.

Study 3

A task force of nine experts was formed to consider the challenges and prospects for leveraging the Indy. The purpose was to consider further the potentials and barriers to leveraging that had been identified in the first two studies. Each task force member's area of expertise is noted in Table 30.1. Each member was briefed on the problem when recruited by phone. The group then came together for an afternoon of discussion. The afternoon began with a 20-minute presentation of findings from Study 1. All those present were already familiar with the Indy as an event. (The case studies from Study 2 were not presented so that the task force's deliberations would not anchor on tactics used by any particular business.) The task force was then asked to consider ways that small businesses on the Gold Coast might leverage the Indy. They were also asked to consider the best means to help them to do so.

A dialectical decision making strategy was employed in order to explore underlying assumptions and to optimize the range of alternatives generated. Standard protocols for dialectical decision making were employed (see Mason & Emshoff, 1979). For its initial work, the task force was divided into three working groups. Each group consisted of one person from industry and two academic specialists. One group was assigned to consider retailers directly adjacent to the Indy precinct; one was assigned to consider retailers further outside the precinct; one was assigned to consider restaurant outside the precinct. These three business types were chosen as the initial point of focus because data from the first two studies suggested that they were the ones most likely to benefit from leveraging assistance.

The groups worked independently for one hour to formulate their initial ideas. Each group then presented its work to the task force as a whole. Each group's presentation was discussed by all task force members. Following this, the ideas were collated and considered together to identify missing pieces and to determine how the ideas fit together.

The two authors served as facilitators for the task force discussions, but not for the small group work at the beginning. In order to allow the task force to develop and explore ideas freely, the authors did not impose their own ideas or suggestions on the task force's deliberations. A recorder kept notes of the discussions, but did not participate in those discussions. The day after the task force's work, the authors and the recorder met to go over the outcomes and to summarize the task force recommendations.

Results

The task force concluded that small businesses need some assistance to formulate and implement strategies and tactics to leverage the Indy. The task force also felt that a great deal of the development and implementation would need to be done through alliances among core businesses. For example, retail and restaurant outlets in similar precincts would need to work together to develop common theming strategies or to implement joint promotions. Consequently, it was felt that a central coordinating body should be put into place (with personnel provided adequate time and funding) to assist. This was felt to have twelve advantages. It would:

1   provide the necessary expertise for small businesses to build effective strategies and tactics;

2   foster coordination among local businesses, the Gold Coast City Council, and the Indy organizers;
3   permit differentiation of strategies across precincts, while nonetheless making certain that they contribute to the overall "feel" of the Gold Coast during the event;
4   capitalize optimally on the Indy brand for the Gold Coast during the event, particularly if leveraging strategies were coordinated with the official off-track events;
5   provide an institutional memory so that there could be learning from year-to-year, and strategies and tactics could be freshened each year;
6   serve as a central organization to build relationships with company reps in order to foster event-appropriate stocking by local businesses;
7   further the quality of relationships with event sponsors in order to add value to sponsorships and to bring more of that value back to local businesses;
8   provide a bulwark against ambushing of event sponsors;
9   facilitate appropriate tracking, auditing, and evaluation of expenditures for the broader Indy Carnival;
10 allow the Indy leveraging to be coordinated with leveraging of other events throughout the year (particularly the Gold Coast Marathon);
11 make the Indy a Gold Coast (rather than merely a surfers Paradise) event;
12 serve as the organization to collect and analyze marketing data in order to hone leveraging strategies.

The task force concluded that in order for the leveraging to be effective, marketing data, particularly relative to key market segments, would need to be collected. It was concluded that demographic and psychographic details about visitors to the Indy should be collected for (a) locals who come to the Indy precinct during the event, (b) locals who stay in the Indy precinct, (c) visitors (from Australia and overseas) who are staying outside the precinct, and (d) visitors who are staying in the precinct.

It was expected that visitors and locals staying in the precinct would be the primary market for retailers directly adjacent to the precinct during the event. Given the fact that local retailers stock heavily for Asian tourists during most of the year, the research would identify what visitors staying in (or close to) the precinct would like to buy. These data would be used to help retailers plan appropriate stocking and/or display strategies for the period of the event. The research would also identify food and restaurant interests for purposes of restaurant promotions and bundling into activity packages for visitors.

The task force felt that research should also seek to identify (a) accompanying markets—such as spouses or children—who might be interested in activities or shopping other than (even away from) the event, (b) corporate markets (e.g., sponsors, teams, incentive visitors) and their particular needs and expectations, and (c) aversion markets of locals that might be capitalized upon by local businesses (including accommodation) outside the race area, perhaps in the mountains to the west of the Gold Coast.

The latter markets—aversion markets—were deemed to be as important as event patrons. It was recognized that keeping them within the local region would help to retain expenditures that might otherwise be lost. This was particularly important because domestic airlines offer discounted fares during the Indy to entice locals to travel away from the area.

The task force felt that promotions would be a particularly important tactical element. It was felt that promotions should be differentiated for different segments (e.g., locals, families), and that the promotions should be carried out wherever possible on an alliance basis so that small businesses would obtain some return to scale. The task force generated the following examples: (a) "passports" offering discounted shopping and activity information for accompanying visitors, (b) activities and off-track events in areas adjacent to the precinct (Southport, Broadbeach, Chevron Island) that are themed with Indy, (c) Indy-free zones elsewhere on the Gold Coast with activities and events for the aversion markets, and (d) linkages of retailers, restaurants, and accommodation within the overall supply chain for Indy so that economic activity generated by the Indy takes place within the Gold Coast wherever possible.

For all this to occur, the task force recognized that an organization or organizations should be responsible for the coordination of planning, implementation, and research. The task force concluded that five issues needed to be considered when determining the coordination:

1   whether the coordination should be assigned to an existing body or a new one;
2   how the coordinating body would be made responsive to business and accountable for results;
3   how the various stakeholders (including stakeholder organizations) would be coordinated;
4   whether the organization would be responsible for similar activities with other Gold Coast events;
5   whether staff were permanent or seconded.

Discussion

The task force was generally optimistic about the value of event leveraging, but was concerned that most small businesses lack the skills or the resources to leverage effectively. They were also concerned that without planned coordination, the results could be chaotic, and not in the best interests of the destination or the event. In contrast, coordination could provide a well-integrated look-and-feel to the Gold Coast during the event. In so doing, it could enhance the quality of experience that visitors to the event would obtain. This would be consistent with the view that events like the Indy can have promotional value for the destination (Getz, 1997).

The task force's suggestion that leveraging should be centrally planned and coordinated would represent a new level of intervention into local business practice—one that is not consistent with classic injunctions calling for markets to operate freely and without interference (cf. North, 1981; Williamson, 1985). On the other hand, interventions designed to foster cooperative effort among local businesses have been shown to enhance the local economy by engendering new efficiencies and returns to scale (Plosila, 1989; Rosenfeld, 1995). Nevertheless, interventions of that kind are often resisted by managers—either because cooperation seems antithetical to normal business practice (Herrigel, 1993) or because the businesses that must cooperate have an established tradition of competing against one another (Levin, 1993).

Consequently, it was of some interest to consider how local business leaders would react to the task force's recommendation of centralized planning and coordination. That matter was addressed in our final study.

Study 4

Eight local business leaders were identified for interview. Each individual was chosen for his or her position and profile in the local business community (see Table 30.1). In order to obtain fresh insight, each business leader was an individual who had not been included in any of the previous three studies. The findings from Studies 1 and 2 were briefly described to each interviewee. Then, the results from Study 3, which were printed onto two sides of an A4 sheet, were given to each interviewee to read. Each interviewee was then asked to state his or her reactions to the recommendations from Study 3. They were asked what they saw as the strengths and weaknesses of the recommendations, and if anything important was missing. Each was asked how the recommendations should be implemented (if at all), and through what organizations. Finally, they were asked what they saw as potential sources of contention. Probes were used to explore each interviewee's responses.

Results

All eight interviewees agreed that leveraging would be worthwhile, and all felt that the objectives identified by the task force were appropriate. As the local business consultant put it, "Anybody who's smart about business leverages [and] this would make a big difference." However, all eight interviewees were sceptical about the creation of a central body to coordinate event leveraging. The common source of concern was that new bureaucracy would not be something that would be congenial for business, particularly if the bureaucracy were based in government. As the state-based tourism consultant put it, "Businesses don't want another government department to deal with."

Respondents also worried that a central coordinating body might not represent the array of interests that need to be represented. This is because the agendas of each stakeholder organization differ. The executive director of the association for local tourism operators said, "Unless an organization has an holistic approach, the agendas will be different depending on which area [of the Gold Coast] is represented." This might seem to suggest that the city council should do the job. However, none of the interviewees felt that the city council should coordinate strategies for leveraging for Indy. Surprisingly, the economic development officer from the city council agreed, saying, "Small businesses—especially retailers—are an incredibly hard group to help."

The costs of a coordinating body were a further concern for all interviewees. Every interviewee felt that there was not an appropriate avenue for funding. It was felt that government funding would exacerbate the negative impact of politics, but that cooperative funding from businesses themselves could not be agreed among them.

Nevertheless, all eight interviewees felt that the twelve goals identified by the task force were worthwhile. They also felt that coordinated promotions strategies and market research, as recommended by the task force, would be useful. The interviewees favored finding a way to attain the desired outcomes, but through an existing organization or business network.

During the interviews, each interviewee was asked how they thought the goals of a coordinated leveraging strategy (with which they agreed) could be attained without a central coordinating body (to which they objected). The interviewees identified three possible solutions.

The first was simply to allow the free market to operate without intervention. Although this might not generate the desired outcomes in the short-term, it was thought to have potential long-term advantages insomuch as the businesses that leveraged effectively would also be the ones most likely to survive. The executive director of the association for local tourism operators commented, "The smart people will win. If businesses are interested in their investment, then they have to be smart."

Yet, he went on to suggest the second possibility: that existing organizations—such as local business associations or chambers of commerce—would be appropriate vehicles to achieve the desired ends. He said, "Opportunities exist for them to work with events. They should look after their members." The restaurateur agreed, saying:

> All the areas [of the Gold Coast] have a management association. They're already funded by businesses. They should be the ones to do this. But they'll have to coordinate with [the city] council for things like police and security.

The two executives from a local business association also felt that local business associations should work with local businesses to develop and coordinate leveraging opportunities. But, like the economic development officer, they noted that small businesses are hard to work with, even when they are members of an associated founded for mutual benefit, such as the one for which these executives worked. Consequently, they felt that some added impetus, such as success stories or incentives provided by suppliers or the Indy organizers, might facilitate the necessary coordination.

This was consistent with the suggestion by the restaurateur and the hotel management consultant that there should be some coordination by the Indy organizers. As the restaurateur noted, "They have an interest in what happens. And if it goes really well, then the sponsors are more interested [in the Indy]." The local business consultant agreed, suggesting that the Indy organizers would need to coordinate with any other body that was working on leveraging. On the other hand, the executive director of the local association for tourism operators worried that the event organizers might not recognize the potential value to themselves. As he put it, "All Indy is doing is putting on a race. The rest isn't their concern."

In summary, all eight interviewees favored the ends recommended by the task force, but disagreed with the means that the task force identified. They felt that existing organizations should be persuaded to take up the challenge. They felt that the necessary catalyst would have to be outside information about the advantages of leveraging or, perhaps, the Indy organizers.

Discussion

Despite the fact that the interviewees came from different industries, there was considerable unanimity among them. The fundamental tension, they felt, was between means and ends. They felt the ends identified by the task force were laudable, but they felt that central coordination was antithetical to the ways that small businesses function. The challenge, they felt, would be to get the businesses to coordinate among themselves, rather than to empower a new organization to impose that coordination. This would be a task of persuasion, rather than coercion. It would be a process of education, rather than one of exhortation.

This suggestion has some empirical support. Tactics designed to build a sense of common interest and an appreciation of new possibilities have been shown to foster business linkages and cooperation (Indergaard, 1996, 1997). The business leaders we interviewed felt that the requisite infrastructure was already in place in the form of local business associations and the chamber of commerce. The fundamental challenge, they suggested, would be to get the initiative going in a manner that would eventually become part of local business associations' standard agenda. The key to success, they felt, would be to identify an appropriate vehicle to help local businesses to help themselves to leverage.

General discussion

Taken together, these four studies tell a consistent story. In Study 1, it was found that most local business managers failed to recognize the Indy as an event that could be leveraged. In Study 2, it was discovered that those who did leverage obtained some benefit. Further, leveraging was not particularly complicated; it used standard marketing tactics. The expert task force brought together for Study 3 identified means to enhance leveraging efforts, and suggested that some coordination of local business's leveraging efforts would be advantageous. The business leaders interviewed in Study 4 felt that it would be most appropriate to have local business associations cultivate leveraging. As a whole, the studies suggest that the potentials for leveraging are largely unrealized, and that some degree of inertia would need to be overcome to realize those potentials. This may explain why the benefits from sport events are frequently below the level anticipated (Bramwell, 1997; Rosentraub, Swindell, Pryzybylski & Mullins, 1994) and are inequitably distributed (Mule, 1998; Putsis, 1998).

From the standpoint of both economic benefit and event marketing, there are clear short-term and long-term benefits to event leveraging. In the short-term, if event visitors can be encouraged to spend more, then the total economic gain may be increased. This, of course, assumes that event visitors can, in fact, be encouraged to spend more (and locals can be encouraged to stay and to spend). The findings of Study 2 demonstrate that it is possible for individual businesses to foster consumer spending during an event through leveraging strategies. What is less clear is whether strategies like those identified can, in fact, increase the total amount of visitor spending during an event. It might be argued that leveraging merely directs a fixed amount of visitor spending to those businesses that leverage, yielding advantages for some business, but no net gain to the local economy. So, the emergent question is: can leveraging foster greater aggregate spending during an event? Although the data of this study do not speak directly to that question, there is other research that does. It is well demonstrated that consumers do make impulse purchases, and are more likely to do so when impulse purchasing is normatively appropriate (Rook & Fisher, 1995), as it is at an event (Godbey & Graefe, 1991; Irwin & Sandler, 1998) where purchases can amplify the hedonic rewards of the visit (Hausman, 2000; Turner & Reisinger, 2001). Direct study of spending by event patrons demonstrates that they typically do spend more at an event for entertainment, shopping, and food beverages than they expect or recall (Faulkner & Raybould, 1995). This suggests that event patrons are making impulse purchases. Given these findings, it is reasonable to expect that a coordinated leveraging strategy can increase the total level of visitor spending.

The experts in Study 3 identified a potential long-term economic advantage of leveraging. They felt that a coordinated leveraging strategy would enhance the atmosphere of the event, thus enhancing the overall quality of experience that visitors obtain. This, they felt, would help to build event patronage by enhancing the event's reputation and by fostering repeat visitation. Other work in entertainment (De Vany & Lee, 2001) and destination (Keane, 1996; Mazursky, 1989) marketing supports that expectation.

If coordinated leveraging does represent a potential gain to the destination, the challenge remains to generate the necessary action. The fact that one neighborhood business association was able to implement a coordinated theming strategy demonstrates that it is possible to generate the necessary cooperation within an existing business network. Further, the presence of successful leveraging examples provides the necessary success stories to give legitimacy to a leveraging effort (cf. Human & Provan, 2000). What remains to be done is to identify an appropriate organization to foster and coordinate the necessary leveraging.

Seven key stakeholder groups are evident: state government, local government, the local tourism industry, the event organizer, even sponsors, small businesses (particularly retail, restaurant, and accommodation) in and around the event precinct, and suppliers of those small businesses (cf. Erickson & Kushner, 1999; Sautter & Leisen, 1999). Each of these could play a role in establishing the requisite leveraging activity, as each would gain. The state government seeks the largest economic impact possible in order to justify its subsidy of the event. The local government also seeks an optional economic impact in order to justify its contributions to the event. The local tourism industry wants the event to enhance the Gold Coast's appeal to tourists in order to grow the local tourism industry. Event organizers want an appealing atmosphere and good relations with the community in order to grow the event. Event sponsors want an appealing atmosphere that is free from ambush in order to protect their investment. Small businesses around the event want to obtain more revenue. Suppliers to those businesses want to move more product. Thus, there is clearly a latent basis for collaborative effort (cf. James & Getz, 1994). Given the shared interest, the creation of a special coordinating authority may not be necessary.

It could be argued that the event organizer is the stakeholder with the most to gain if leveraging is fostered, and the most to lose if leveraging remain haphazard. Other stakeholders have resources committed to agendas that extend well beyond the event, whereas the event organizer's concerns are focused directly on the event. If event leveraging builds the economic impact of the event, then the event organizer's claim to public subsidy remains credible (cf. Sheehan & Ritchie, 1997). If event leveraging enhances the look-and-feel of the community during the event, then the market for the event can be expected to grow. Further, by linking the event more closely to the host destination, event sponsors can be provided added opportunities for advertising and publicity, as well as an enhanced experience for their guests at the event (Brown, 2000). On the other hand, if leveraging is uncoordinated, then event sponsors may find themselves ambushed much as they were in the neighborhood theming example described in Study 2. Further, if leveraging remains haphazard, then some local enterprises (those that leverage) will continue to do very well during the event, but others (those that do not leverage) may do poorly. Thus, by not cultivating local leverage, the event organizer risks both sponsor and local business dissatisfaction. These are unnecessary risks, particularly given the potential benefits if leveraging is fostered and coordinated.

Sack and Johnson (1996) demonstrated that government use of sport for economic development can embroil sport managers in debates over urban policy. They recommended that sport managers learn to work more closely with local government and with local businesses in order to function effectively in the context of development policy. Analysis of the case presented here is consistent with that recommendation. The claim that sport managers make for public subsidy or government service is legitimized, at least in part, on the grounds that sport can render benefits that exceed the value of the subsidy and the services. By working with local government and local businesses to plan and implement coordinated leveraging of a sport event, event organizers could design and produce events that are consistent with that legitimation.

References

Black, T., & Pape, A. (1995). The IndyCar Grand Prix: Costs & benefits, *Australian Accountant*, 65(8), 25–28.

Boulton, R.E.S., Libert, B.D., & Samek, S.M. (2000). A business model for the new economy, *Journal of Business Strategy*, 21(4), 29–35.

Boyle, M. (1997). Civic boosterism in the politics of local economic development – "institutional positions" and "strategic orientations" in the consumption of hallmark events, *Environment and Planning A*, 29, 1975–1997.

Bracker, J., & Pearson, J. (1986). Planning and financial performance of small, mature firms, *Strategic Management Journal*, 7, 503–522.

Bramwell, B. (1997). Strategic planning before and after a mega-event, *Tourism Management*, 18, 167–176.

Bramwell, B. (1998). User satisfaction and product development in urban tourism, *Tourism Management*, 19, 35–47.

Brown, G. (2000). Emerging issues in Olympic sponsorship: Implications for host cities, *Sport Management Review*, 3, 71–92.

Chalip, L. (2001). Sport and tourism: Capitalising on the linkage. In D. Kluka & G. Schilling (Eds), *The business of sport* (pp. 78–89), Oxford, UK: Meyer & Meyer.

Chrisman, J.J., & Leslie, J. (1989). Strategic, administrative, and operating problems: The impact of outsiders on small firm performance, *Entrepreneurship: Theory and Practice*, 13(3), 37–51.

Coates, D., & Humphreys, B.R. (1999). The growth effects of sport franchises, stadia, and arenas, *Journal of Policy Analysis and Management*, 18, 601–624.

Crompton, J.L. (1995). Economic impact analysis of sports facilities and events, *Journal of Sport Management*, 9, 14–35.

Crouch, G.I., & Ritchie, J.R.B. (1999). Tourism, competitiveness, and societal prosperity, *Journal of Business Research*, 44, 137–152.

Davis, J.F. (1997). Determining promotional effectiveness in small retail firms: An empirical analysis, *Mid-American Journal of Business*, 12(2), 21–28.

De Vany, A., & Lee, C. (2001). Quality signals in information cascades and the dynamics of the distribution of motion picture box office revenues, *Journal of Economic Dynamics & Control*, 25, 593–614.

Dwyer, L., Mellor, R., Mistilis, N., & Mules, T. (2000). A framework for assessing "tangible" and "intangible" impacts of events and conventions, *Event Management*, 6, 175–189.

Erickson, G.S., & Kushner, R.J. (1999). Public event networks: An application of marketing theory to sporting events, *European Journal of Marketing*, 33, 348–364.

Faulkner, B., & Raybould, N. (1995). Monitoring event expenditure associated with attendance at sporting events: An experimental assessment of the diary and recall methods, *Festival Management and Event Tourism*, 3, 73–81.

Garnham, B. (1997). Ranfurly Shield Rugby: An investigation into the impacts of a sporting event on a provincial city, the case of New Plymouth, Taranaki, New Zealand, *Festival Management and Event Tourism*, 4, 145–149.

Getz, D. (1997). *Event management and event tourism*, Elmsford, NY: Cognizant Communication.

Getz, D. (1998). Trends, strategies, and issues in sport-event tourism, *Sport Marketing Quarterly*, 7(2), 8–13.

Ghanem, S., & Ashkenazy, A. (1993). Positioning the city of Scarborough, Ontario for the nineties, *Economic Development Review*, 1, 45–76.

Glen, W., & Weerawaradena, J. (1996). Strategic planning practices in small enterprises in Queensland, *Small Enterprise Research*, 4(3), 5–16.

Godbey, G., & Graefe, A. (1991). Repeat tourism, play, and monetary spending, *Annals of Tourism Research*, 18, 213–225.

Gottdiener, M. (1997). *The theming of America: Visions, and commercial spaces*, Boulder, CO: Westview Press.

Gregory, S., & Koithan-Louderback, K. (1997). Marketing a resort community, *Cornell Hotel & Restaurant Administration Quarterly*, 38(6), 52–59.

Hardy, K.G., & Magrath, A.J. (1990). Leveraging strategies for sales promotions, *Business Quarterly*, 54(3), 59–61.

Hausman, A. (2000). A multi-method investigation of consumer motivations in impulse buying behavior, *Journal of Consumer Marketing*, 17, 403–419.

Herrigel, G. (1993). Power and the redefinition of industrial districts: The case of Baden-Wurttemberg. In G. Grabner (Ed.), *The embedded firm: On the socioeconomics of industrial networks* (pp. 227–251), London: Routledge.

Human, S.E., & Provan, K.G. (2000). Legitimacy building in the evolution of small-firm multilateral networks: A comparative study of success and demise, *Administrative Science Quarterly*, 45, 327–365.

Hunt, K.A., Bristol, T., & Bashaw, R.E. (1999). A conceptual approach to classifying sport fans, *Journal of Services Marketing*, 13, 439–452.

Indergaard, M. (1996). Managing networks, remaking the city, *Economic Development Quarterly*, 10, 172–187.

Indergaard, M. (1997). Community-based restructuring? Institution building in the industrial Midwest, *Urban Affairs Review*, 32, 662–682.

Inskeep, E. (1991). *Tourism planning: An integrated and sustainable development approach*, New York: Van Norstrand Reinhold.

Irwin, R.L., & Sandler, M.A. (1998). An analysis of travel behaviour and event-induced expenditures among American collegiate championship patron groups, *Journal of Vacation Marketing*, 4, 78–90.

Jamal, T.B., & Getz, D. (1994). Collaboration theory and community tourism planning, *Annals of Tourism Research*, 22, 186–204.

Jelinek, M., & Litterer, J.A. (1995). Toward entrepreneurial organizations: Meeting ambiguity with engagement, *Entrepreneurship: Theory and Practice*, 19(3), 137–168.

Keane, M.J. (1996). Sustaining quality in tourism destinations: An economic model with an application, *Applied Economics*, 28, 1545–1553.

King, M. (1994, May 16). Indy Grand Prix "brings State $23m in benefits", *The Australian*, p. 6.

Levin, M. (1993). Creating networks for rural economic development in Norway, *Human Relations*, 46, 193–218.

Lorenzoni, G., & Lipparini, A. (1999). The leveraging of interfirm relationships as a distinctive organizational capability: A longitudinal study, *Strategic Management Journal*, 20, 317–338.

Malone, S., & Jenster, P. (1991). Resting on your laurels. The plateauing of the owner-manager, *European Management Journal*, 9, 412–418.

Mazursky, D. (1989). Past experience and future tourism decisions, *Annals of Tourism Research*, 16, 333–344.

Mazzarol, S., & Ramasehan, R. (1996). Small business marketing: A comparative study of high and low success firms, *Small Enterprise Research*, 4(3), 50–64.

McAuley, A.C., & Sutton, W.A. (1999). In search of a new defender: The threat of ambush marketing in the global arena, *International Journal of Sports Marketing and Sponsorship*, 1, 64–85.

Mitroff, I.L., & Emshoff, J.R. (1979). On strategic assumption making: A dialectical approach to policy and planning, *Academy of Management Review*, 4, 1–12.

Mules, T. (1998). Taxpayer subsidies for major sporting events, *Sport Management Review*, 1, 25–43.

Mules, T., & Faulkner, B. (1996). An economic perspective on special events, *Tourism Economics*, 2, 314–329.

Murphy, P.E. (1992). Urban tourism and visitor behavior, *American Behavioral Scientist*, 36, 200–211.

North, D.C. (1981). *Structure and change in economic history*, New York: Norton.

Pine, B.J., & Gilmore, J.H. (1999). *The experience economy: Work is theatre & every business a stage*, Boston: Harvard Business School Press.

Plosila, W. (1989). *Developing network relationships: The experiences of Denmark, Germany, Italy, and Sweden*, Rockville, MD: High Technology Council.

Putsis, W.P. (1998). Winners and losers: Redistribution and the use of economic impact analysis in marketing, *Journal of Macromarketing*, 18, 24–33.

Robinson, R., & Pearce, J. (1984). Research thrusts in small firm strategic planning, *Academy of Management Review*, 9, 128–137.

Rook, D.W., & Fisher, R.J. (1995). Normative influences on impulsive buying behavior, *Journal of Consumer Research*, 22, 305–313.

Rosenfeld, S. (1995). *Industrial-strength strategies: Regional business clusters and public policy*, Washington, DC: Aspen Institute.

Rosentraub, M.S., Swindell, D., Przybylski, M., & Mullins, D.R. (1994). Sport and downtown development strategy: If you build it, will jobs come? *Journal of Urban Affairs*, 16, 221–239.

Sack, A.L., & Johnson, A.T. (1996). Politics, economic development and the Volvo International Tennis Tournament, *Journal of Sport Management*, 10, 1–14.

Sautter, E.T., & Leisen, B. (1999). Managing stakeholders: A tourism planning model, *Annals of Tourism Research*, 26, 312–328.

Sheehan, L.R., & Ritchie, J.R.B. (1997). Financial management in tourism: A destination perspective, *Tourism Economics*, 3, 93–18.

Shifflet, D.K., & Bhatia, P. (1999, September 6). Event tourism market emerging, *Hotel and Motel Management*, p. 26.

Slywotzky, A.J., & Shapiro, B.P. (1993). Leveraging to beat the odds: The new marketing mind-set, *Harvard Business Review*, 71(5), 97–107.

Smith, D. (1996, April 23). Indy boasts $2.2m profit, *Gold Coast Bulletin*, p. 1.

Spilling, O.R. (1996). The entrepreneurial system: On entrepreneurship in the context of a mega-event, *Journal of Business Research*, 36, 91–103.

Sternberg, E. (1997). The iconography of the tourism experience, *Annals of Tourism Research*, 24, 951–969.

Stolz, G. (1996, April 25). IndyCar future on track—Premier, *Gold Coast Bulletin*, p. 6.

Strauss, A.L. (1987). *Qualitative analysis for social scientist*, Cambridge: Cambridge University Press.

Tanguay, G.A., Vallée, L., & Lanoie, P. (1995). Shopping hours and price levels in the retailing industry: A theoretical and empirical analysis, *Economic Inquiry*, 33, 516–524.

Tendler, J., & Amorim, M.A. (1996). Small firms and their helpers: Lessons on demand, *World Development*, 24, 407–426.

Turner, L.W., & Reisinger, Y. (2001). Shopping satisfaction for domestic tourists, *Journal of Retailing and Consumer Services*, 8, 15–27.

Van den Berg, L., Braun, E., & Otgaar, A.H.J. (2000). *Sports and city marketing in European cities*, Rotterdam, The Netherlands: Euricur.

Whitson, D., & Macintosh, D. (1996). The global circus: International sport, tourism, and the marketing of cities, *Journal of Sport and Social Issues*, 20, 278–297.

Williamson, O.E. (1985). *Economic institutions of capitalism*, New York: Free Press.

Endpiece

■   Mike Weed

THE THIRTY PAPERS FEATURED IN THIS READER were selected to showcase the best contemporary research into the relationship between sport and tourism and to highlight key themes and directions in sports tourism research. As such, a number of interesting themes emerge from these papers as a collected whole, and it is perhaps useful to attempt to draw these out in this endpiece.

The General Introduction to the Reader discussed Gartner's (1996) comment that research into the relationship between sport and tourism would develop a 'cadre' of specialist researchers, and in fact many of the key figures in sport and tourism research are contained within this collection. A further implication of Gartner's comment is that sports tourism as a phenomenon is more than the sum of the parts. As such, research that investigates the role sport might play in tourism, or the impact tourism might have on sport, paints only a partial picture of sports tourism: it subordinates sport to tourism or vice-versa, rather than considering sports tourism as a phenomenon in its own right. In this respect, the need for greater integration across academic disciplines and subjects and in terms of policy remains as salient now as when Glyptis first highlighted it in 1982. Certainly, researchers seeking to understand sports tourism need a grasp of concepts from both the disciplines of sport and of tourism; and also from broader areas of leisure research such as recreation conflict and adventure activities. The days of tourism researchers casually considering the ways in which sport might be useful in marketing destinations should become a thing of the past as the study of sports tourism seeks a more synergised understanding of behaviours.

That many researchers in this Reader recognise that sports tourism is *related to but more than the sum of* sport and tourism is an indication that sports tourism is a sub-field of academic study that is approaching a phase of maturity in which it is no longer struggling to establish itself. However, this is no reason for complacency and, as a number of authors have noted in a number of ways – see Weed (Chapter 1), Gibson (Chapter 2), Higham and Hinch (Chapter 5) and Downward (Chapter 23) – the need now is for sports tourism research to move beyond description and into an explanatory phase of research. Failure to take this step forward is likely to result in sports tourism being regarded, as it has been in the past, as an 'academic triviality' (Gammon and Kurtzman, 2002: v), and its inevitable fate will be that it is subsumed again within the subjects of sport and/or tourism, where its study is likely to be limited to the impact one area may have on the other.

A key feature of the maturing nature of sports tourism as a legitimate sub-field is an increasing focus on the academic disciplines that underpin its study. For example, the study of golf tourists has benefited from insights from social psychology in utilising role theory (Gibson and Pennington-Gray, Chapter 9) and from marketing in studying the nature of satisfaction (Petrick and Backman, Chapter 10). Undoubtedly, sports tourism is a multidisciplinary area of study, and as research matures further it may be that particular specialisms develop. Preuss, for example (see Chapter 16), is noted for his specialism in understanding event economies, whilst Chalip (see Chapters 8 and 30) is a recognised authority in leveraging approaches. However, such specialisation should not preclude the use of interdisciplinary insights nor should it be an excuse for researchers to fail to locate their work within the broader body of sports tourism knowledge. In this latter respect, a coherent and identifiable body of knowledge that builds on previous research over time and, in particular, shows a clear growth from descriptive to explanatory research, will be a clear marker of sports tourism's maturing status.

I have noted above that sports tourism is *related to but more than the sum of* sport and tourism. On one hand it is important to recognise the insights that can be drawn from the fields of sport and of tourism (for example, the concept of serious leisure as discussed by Kane and Zink in Chapter 12, or the issue of seasonality as discussed by Higham and Hinch in Chapter 27). However, on the other hand, it is important to recognise the specific sports tourism context and the nature of the sports tourism experience. Consequently, as noted in the General Introduction, I have, with others (e.g. Downward, Chapter 23; Weed and Bull, 2004), argued for a conceptualisation rather than a definition of sports tourism that seeks to understand the genre as derived from the interaction of activity, people and place. This conceptualisation, while drawing on the features of sport and of tourism, does not directly derive from definitions of sport and of tourism and, consequently, helps to establish sports tourism as a phenomenon in its own right, meriting a specific programme of study.

An implication of the conceptualisation of sports tourism as derived from the interaction of activity, people and place is that, because activities, people and places vary throughout any particular trip, sports tourism might be best understood as trip behaviour rather than as trip purpose. This allows for the interaction of a range of tourist and sports tourist roles during any particular trip (see Gibson and Pennington-Gray, Chapter 9), rather than defining a trip as being primarily about sport or primarily about tourism. Furthermore, it allows a trip to be understood in terms of the way in which a range of sports tourist behaviours (e.g. event attendance, nostalgia, active participation) might interact with more general tourist behaviours (e.g. shopping, eating, drinking) and functional behaviours (e.g. ironing, cleaning) to comprise an overall trip experience.

Fairley's paper (Chapter 15) is a very useful illustration of the benefits of understanding the interaction of a range of behaviours within the context of the trip experience, and this is an area which is ripe for further research.

Throughout this Reader, the fundamental nature of research on behaviours – both in understanding impacts and, in turn, the policy and provision requirements of such impacts, and in contributing directly to the development of policy and management approaches – has been highlighted. Undoubtedly, there is a clear link between behaviours, impacts and policy and management in sports tourism, and it is perhaps the consideration of leveraging approaches that highlights this link most clearly. Papers on leveraging have featured in Part Two of this Reader on understanding the sports tourist (Costa and Chalip, Chapter 8), in Part Three on impacts (Green, Chapter 20), and in Part Four on policy and management (Chalip and Leyns, Chapter 30), further reinforcing the 'bridging' nature of the concept. A leveraging approach assumes that policies and management strategies can be introduced, having been derived from an understanding of behaviours in order to maximise positive impacts. As such, behavioural, impacts and policy and management research in sports tourism can all contribute to leveraging the benefits of sports tourism, and for this reason it seems that such leveraging approaches will play a central part in future sports tourism research.

Of course, the investigation of the areas mentioned above, and the resulting maturing of research from description to explanation is predicated on robust, appropriate and transparent methods and methodology. To take events as an example, Part Three of this Reader contains three papers that address aspects of method and methodology in the understanding of event impacts. Preuss (Chapter 16) highlights the importance of fully understanding behaviours of event-affected people (not just visitors) in assessing event impacts, while both Kasimati (Chapter 17) and Hudson (Chapter 18) highlight the differing assumptions, and methodological failings, in such research. However, Kasimati also notes that as long as the methodologies used are clear and transparent, then studies with varying assumptions can be useful, particularly if procedures such as the meta-analysis conducted by Hudson are used to 'equalise' the findings.

The chapters on event impact methodology highlight the need for an understanding of methodology in reading sports tourism, and indeed any, research. Considerations such as combating potential bias, methodological appropriateness, and adequate care in method and analysis are issues that readers should be aware of, and authors should take steps to demonstrate. Again, an indication of a maturing sub-field will be the extent to which sports tourism research is seen as methodologically robust and theoretically informed, with a healthy level of methodological diversity across the sub-field as a whole as befits a multidisciplinary area of study. In this respect, it is mildly encouraging to note that the five-year systematic review (2000–4) I presented in Chapter 6 indicated a slight growth in interpretive qualitative research in comparison to the preliminary four-year review (2000–3) I referred to in Chapter 1. However, there remains a lack of methodological diversity and the sub-field is still dominated by quantitative research underpinned by positivist epistemologies (71 per cent of research in the 2000–4 review presented in Chapter 6). In this respect, researchers might consider whether they are applying particular methods or approaches on the basis of being the most appropriate method to answer their research questions or whether they are simply being employed on the basis of convention. At a broader level, researchers might consider the extent to which the research questions they are seeking to answer contribute to the body of sports tourism knowledge. In this respect, it is worth re-emphasising here the standard for publication that the *Journal of Sport & Tourism* (*JS&T*) has applied since its relaunch in 2006, namely that research should 'make a clear contribution substantively, theoretically, or methodologically to the body of knowledge relating to the relationship between sport and tourism'. It is an adherence to this standard by all those researching the relationship between sport and tourism that will make the most significant contribution to ensuring that sports tourism moves towards full maturity as an academic sub-field.

REFERENCES

Gammon, S. and Kurtzman, J. (2002) 'Editors' Introduction', in S. Gammon and J. Kurtzman (eds), *Sport Tourism: Principles and Practice*. Eastbourne: LSA.

Gartner, W. (1996) *Tourism Development: Principles, Processes and Policies*. New York: Van Nostrand Reinhold.

Glyptis, S.A. (1982) *Sport and Tourism in Western Europe*. London: British Travel Education Trust.

Weed, M. and Bull, C.J. (2004) *Sports Tourism: Participants, Policy and Providers*. Oxford: Elsevier.

Index